AFRO-AMERICAN RELIGIOUS HISTORY

AFRO-AMERICAN RELIGIOUS HISTORY

A Documentary Witness

EDITED BY MILTON C. SERNETT

DUKE UNIVERSITY PRESS DURHAM 1985

Permissions to reprint selections appear
at the end of this book.
© 1985 Duke University Press
All rights reserved
Printed in the United States of America
on acid-free paper ∞
Sixth paperback printing, 1992
Library of Congress Cataloging-in-Publication Data
Afro-American religious history.
Includes bibliographies and index.
1. Afro-Americans—Religion—Addresses, essays,
lectures. I. Sernett, Milton C., 1942–.
BR563.N4A37 1985 200'.8996073 84-24686
ISBN 0-8223-0591-7
ISBN 0-8223-0594-1 (pbk.)

To the memory of
Bishop Daniel Alexander Payne
[1811–1893]

Contents

Preface

My interest in primary sources relating to the religious pilgrimage of Afro-Americans began fortuitously enough. Some sixteen years ago I happened to be browsing in the bookstore of a Lutheran college from which I had recently graduated. A reprint edition of Daniel Alexander Payne's *Recollections of Seventy Years* literally fell into my hands. Here was an Afro-American graduate of Lutheran Theological Seminary, Gettysburg, Pennsylvania, and historian of a black Methodist denomination of which not a word had been said in my many courses on church history. Somewhat humbled by the all too obvious lacuna in my seminary education, I began remedial work with Bishop Payne's narrative and in the years that followed pursued a dissertation topic that once again precipitated a search for documentary sources.

Eventually opportunities arose to teach survey courses concerning Afro-American religious history at the seminary and university level. I wanted to enable students to experience the excitement of having a variety of original sources in front of them, documents that collectively might illuminate the grand sweep of Afro-American religious history from the shores of Africa to the immediate past. I compiled and tested a reader of primary and secondary sources at Syracuse University, found it useful, but yearned for an opportunity to compile a new anthology composed exclusively of primary, mostly rare or out-of-print, documents that would be useful to a variety of publics—students, historians, scholars in allied fields, church members, and an interested general readership.

The present book of more than fifty documents is the result of a winnowing process that, because of limitations on size and cost, entailed an inherent frustration. Apart from the sins of omission that are unavoidable, especially in light of the scholarly awakening of interest in and discovery of historical sources during the past decade or so, this particular compiler wishes for the proverbial catbird's seat from which to offer more historical background and commentary than could be done in the brief headnotes. Readers, and especially classroom instructors, will want to consult the bibliographies appended to each selection. I have tried to include suggestions for further reading that enhance an under-

standing of the specific historic context in which the documents originated as well as those that provide a more general historical backdrop.
Additionally, readers will want to consult the acknowledgement of
sources for the originals from which, by necessity, excerpts were taken.

In acknowledging my own indebtedness, I must begin, of course,
with the authors of the documents that follow. Though many of their
voices have been stilled by the passing of time, these men and women
give eloquent testimony to the richly textured religious heritage of Afro-
Americans. To the living witnesses and the various copyright holders
who granted permission to include documents, I am also grateful and
apologize for this all-too-brief acknowledgement of their generosity. I
have tried to be faithful to all authors by republishing their works without changes in grammar, spelling, or style.

Numerous friends and colleagues have offered suggestions and words
of encouragement along the way. The members of the Northeast Seminar on Black Religion, notably Randall Burkett, Richard Newman, Albert Raboteau, David Swift, David Wills, James M. Washington, and
Preston Williams, gave generously of their impressive knowledge of
Afro-Americana and inspired me with their own research and writing
when the magnitude and difficulty of this project overwhelmed personal
abilities and fortitude. Will Gravely, whose Colorado base makes it impossible for him to participate in the quarterly meetings of the Northeast Seminar, raised my spirits, sharing the table of contents from a
classroom reader he assembled some years ago.

Roxanne Raicht of the staff in the Department of Afro-American
Studies at Syracuse University assisted in the daunting task of obtaining
permissions, retyping nearly illegible older documents, and assembling
the nearly 800-page manuscript. Joanne Ferguson, editor-in-chief at Duke
University Press, and her colleagues, proved unfailingly helpful and enthusiastic as the anthology moved from manuscript to printed text.
Finally, none will rejoice in the appearance of this anthology more
than my wife Janet and children, Rebecca and Matthew. They have
been inordinately patient, tolerating my absences out of town and dis-
appearances into the study. The dedication of this volume honors the
memory of the scholar and clergyman who initially inspired my interest
in Afro-American religious history and who demonstrated a passion for
historical documentation to which we are all indebted.

Milton C. Sernett
Syracuse, New York
August 1984

AFRO-AMERICAN RELIGIOUS HISTORY

Introduction

The study of Afro-American religious history needs no special warrant. The story is self-authenticating, bearing its own witness to the travail and triumph of the human spirit. Carter G. Woodson wrote in 1939: "A definitive history of the Negro Church . . . would leave practically no phase of the history of the Negro in America untouched."[1] No one has yet attempted a synoptic, not to mention definitive, history of Afro-American religion. Woodson's pioneering *History of the Negro Church*, published in 1921, is a celebration of firsts on the order of a family scrapbook.[2] At the beginning of his own mammoth rendition, Sydney Ahlstrom acknowledged that historical surveys of American religion have "virtually closed out" the black religious experience. Ahlstrom predicted that serious consideration of the religious history of Americans of African descent would become "the basic paradigm for a renovation of church history."[3] In the 1960s historians began to concern themselves with the factors of race and ethnicity in the makeup of religious America.[4] Merely splicing references to black religion into a main strand that told someone else's story produced only a rope of sand.[5] From time to time, scholars from outside the field of church history suggested alterna-

1 Carter G. Woodson, "The Negro Church, an All-Comprehending Institution," *The Negro History Bulletin* 3, no. 1 (October 1939) : 7.
2 Carter G. Woodson, *The History of the Negro Church* (Washington, D.C.: The Associated Publishers, 1921).
3 Sydney E. Ahlstrom, *A Religious History of the American People* (New Haven: Yale University Press, 1972), pp. 12–13.
4 See, for example, Martin E. Marty, "Ethnicity: The Skeleton of Religion in America," *Church History* 41, no. 1 (March 1972) : 5–21; and Robert T. Handy, "Negro Christianity and American Church Historiography," in *Reinterpretations in American Church History*, edited by Jerald C. Brauer (Chicago: University of Chicago Press, 1968), pp. 91–112.
5 Roger D. Hatch, "Integrating the Issue of Race into the History of Christianity in America: An Essay-Review of Sydney E. Ahlstrom," *A Religious History of the American People*; Martin E. Marty, *Righteous Empire: The Protestant Experience in America*; Robert T. Handy, "A Christian America: Protestant Hopes and Historical Realities," *Journal of the American Academy of Religion* 46, no. 4 (1978) : 545–69.

tive perspectives and methodologies for dealing with the "invisibility" in the standard surveys of the religious reality of non-Europeans, though none has gone further than general diagnosis of the malady.[6]

This anthology is offered as one effort to dispel the myth that the "invisibility" question is primarily one of an inadequacy of resources. Though the search for primary sources necessitates persistence and a modicum of bibliographical talent, these sources do exist. Thanks to such indispensable tools as *The Howard University Bibliography of African and Afro-American Religious Studies*,[7] students of Afro-American religious history occupy the proverbial catbird seat in comparison to those of a generation ago. The research and archival skills of a thousand Carter G. Woodsons will be necessary before any "definitive" history of Afro-American religion can be written, for without adequate histories of local churches, regional jurisdictions, and national denominations, no general synthesis and interpretation are possible. We await, for example, something on the order of Albert J. Raboteau's *Slave Religion*[8] for other periods and issues. It is something of a scholarly embarrassment that detailed studies exist on minor traditions popularly known as the Black Jews and Black Muslims, but no contemporary historian has published a comprehensive history of the National Baptist Convention, Inc., with its millions of members.

The academic study of Afro-American religious history has only recently taken on recognizable definition and content within the fields of history and religious studies. In that fiery crucible of emotions, politics, and academics, out of which programs and departments of Afro-American studies originated, there was a rather puzzling lack of concern for courses on religious culture.

In 1970 James H. Cone attended the first annual convention of the Congress of African People in Atlanta. At the invitation of Imamu Amiri Baraka, Cone presided over a religion workshop. He encountered, he recalls, a barrage of "insulting and uninformed denunciations of black Christianity" by the nationalist participants, mostly young college students. Cone had a year earlier published *Black Theology and Black Power*, in which he sought to link the black power and nationalist per-

6 See two contributions by Charles H. Long, "Perspectives for a Study of Afro-American Religion in the United States," *History of Religions* 2, no. 1 (August 1971): 54–66; and "Civil Rights–Civil Religion: Visible People and Invisible Religion," in *American Civil Religion*, edited by Russell E. Richer and Donald G. Jones (New York: Harper & Row, 1974), pp. 211–21.
7 Ethel L. Williams and Clifton F. Brown, compilers, *The Howard University Bibliography of African and Afro-American Religious Studies with Locations in American Libraries* (Wilmington, Del.: Scholarly Resources, Inc., 1977).
8 Albert J. Raboteau, *Slave Religion* (New York: Oxford University Press, 1978).

spectives to the black religious experience. Cone had been raised in an African Methodist Episcopal congregation in Arkansas and had entered the ministry when sixteen. "Therefore," he wrote, "when these young Blacks, who appeared to know very little about the past and present reality of the black church, began to denounce the God of my parents and grandparents, I wanted to challenge the authenticity of their arrogant denunciations."[9] Alienation from the black church on ideological grounds, the generally secular spirit of the black power movement, and, perhaps, the rather common tendency for the young and radical to question the faith of their parents and grandparents contributed to the lack of interest in religion and church history as black studies programs took shape. A peculiar irony persisted here, for, as Cone noted, "the same religion which these young Blacks were denouncing has been the source of black people's hope that trouble won't last always."[10]

Religious belonging is an elemental bond of group identity. Communities define themselves around a set of religious beliefs, symbols, and rituals. Except for those comparatively few who rejected Christianity for an Islamic or Jewish identity, most Afro-Americans have adopted and adapted Christian, chiefly Protestant, traditions to mark their place on the pluralistic American landscape. Exact statistics are difficult to gather, but perhaps as many as 17 million members belong to the seven largest U.S. black denominations, representing the Methodist, Baptist, and Pentecostal-Holiness connections.[11] Thousands more are associated with the predominantly white denominations. No demographer is willing even to estimate the number who may be marginal members of local churches, who belong to the countless house and storefront churches that have no organization beyond the local community, or who comprise the many small black sects and cults. But whatever the total adherence figure, the institutional church clearly is still a significant part of Afro-American life and culture.

At the beginning of this century, W. E. B. Du Bois wrote, "The Negro church of today is the social center of Negro life in the United States, and the most characteristic expression of African character."[12] In 1909 Booker T. Washington echoed: "The Negro Church represents the masses of the Negro people. It was the first institution to develope out of the life of the Negro masses and it still retains the strongest hold

9 James H. Cone, "Black Theology and the Black College Student," *Journal of Afro-American Issues* 4, nos. 3 and 4 (Summer/Fall 1976): 421.
10 *Ibid.*
11 Cited in "Jesse Takes Up the Collection," *Time* (February 6, 1984), p. 57.
12 W. E. B. Du Bois, *The Souls of Black Folk* (1903; reprint, New York: Fawcett World Library, 1961), p. 142.

upon them."[13] Both statements reflected primarily on the religious culture of rural southern blacks. There the comprehensive nature or multi-
functional role of the black church was most apparent. In *Born to Rebel*,
Benjamin Elijah Mays sketched a portrait of the church of his youth in
rural South Carolina:

> Old Mount Zion was an important institution in my community.
> Negroes had nowhere to go but to church. They went there to wor-
> ship, to hear the choir sing, to listen to the preacher, and to hear
> and see the people shout. The young people went to Mount Zion
> to socialize, or simply to stand around and talk. It was a place of
> worship and a social center as well. There was no other place to go.[14]

These social conditions placed a special burden on black churches; they
had to be social centers, political forums, schoolhouses, mutual aid societies, refuges from racism and violence, and places of worship. But as
blacks moved to the cities and as other institutions, such as fraternal
groups, civil rights organizations, and social clubs, developed within the
black community, the black church and the black preacher had to adjust
to a less pivotal role.

Though the church became less of a central institution, it continued
to influence Afro-American culture. Those scholars who took black music
and literature seriously—from the gospel songs of Mahalia Jackson to
James Baldwin's portrayal of black Pentecostalism in *Go Tell It On the
Mountain*—could not escape the cultural carryover. What might appear
to be a secular form, such as the evolution of the blues and jazz, turned
out to have intimate connections with the folk traditions of black religion. Watching fellow blues singers at their craft, B. B. King once testified, "I feel like I'm in church and even want to shout."[15] With a wide-
angle lens, therefore, a view of the religious experience of Afro-Americans
encompasses more than the story of ecclesiastical institutions, preachers,
and the people in the pews. The folk traditions of the street corner and
the cotton fields, of those who belonged to no church, existed in dynamic
tension with the institutional expressions of black religion. This anthology of primary sources witnesses to the more formal and institutional
tradition.

A collection of documents such as this does not constitute a history

13 Booker T. Washington, *The Story of the Negro* (New York: Doubleday, Page,
1909), I: 278.
14 Benjamin E. Mays, *Born to Rebel—An Autobiography* (New York: Charles
Scribner's Sons, 1971), p. 13.
15 Quoted in Lawrence W. Levine, *Black Culture and Black Consciousness* (New
York: Oxford University Press, 1977), p. 236.

of Afro-American religion. Apart from the problem of selectivity, the editor is frustrated by the inability of the documents to speak for themselves. The best that can be hoped is that by arranging the documents within a historical framework, choosing a variety of sources, and briefly introducing them, the editor has enabled readers to *think* about Afro-American religious history. The passive reader who skips lightly from one document to another, ignoring the historical context in which they were created, or who reads them as mere flat words on paper, will not be instructed by them. Only in the interaction between original author and contemporary reader can there be any historical witnessing to the development and meaning of Afro-American religion. The editor, semaphore-like, can only signal attention to important issues and themes. I shall suggest six.

Preston Williams has noted that "Americans have at every point attempted to create one image, one picture, one mirror in which all black men might be seen."[16] This points to the problem of the one and the many. Generalizations about black religion, whether made out of ignorance or ideological blindness, frequently fail upon close attention to particular examples. The diversity revealed in even this anthology suggests that monolithic constructs such as "the Black Church" are suspect. When measured against sociological realities, they must give way. The contours of ethno-religious identity of any group appear more homogeneous when compared to another, but aggregate patterns break up when individual stories are accounted for. Contextual factors such as economic status, educational level, rural or urban life-style, family history, and personal experience make generalizations difficult. "One of the continuing paradoxes of the Black Church as the custodian of a great portion of Black culture and religion," Gayraud S. Wilmore reminds us, "is that it is at once the most reactionary and the most radical of Black institutions, the most imbued with the mythology and values of white America, and yet the most proud, the most independent and indigenous collectivity in the Black community."[17]

The problem of the one and the many suggests a second interpretative issue. Simply put, it is the question, "How black is black religion?" Despite the diversity, or perhaps because of it, cases have been made for an "authentic black religion" or an "authentic black worship," usually during times of heightened race consciousness. To the cultural nationalists, "authentic" means closest to their understanding of traditional Af-

16 Preston Williams, "The Black Experience and Black Religion," *Theology Today* 26 (October 1969): 246.
17 Gayraud S. Wilmore, *Black Religion and Black Radicalism* (Garden City, N.Y.: Doubleday Anchor Books, 1973), p. xiii.

rica. To them the protracted academic debate over African religious survivals has been no idle pastime. Proponents of the tenacity of African
cultures in the New World have found Africanisms in everything from
the slaves' predilection for baptism by immersion to grave decorations.
Opponents have stressed the loss of African cultural forms over time, except in isolated areas such as the Carolina Sea Islands. This debate was renewed in the 1960s during a revival of cultural nationalism, leading to
sometimes dubious claims about parallels between contemporary Afro-
American religious practices and those of traditional Africa. Today
scholars generally recognize that in comparison to certain Afro-Carib-
bean and Afro-Brazilian societies, where evidence of Africanisms is much
stronger, some explanation must be given for the "death of the gods" in
North America. One looks to differing cultural contexts, slave systems,
population demographies, and contrasts between Protestantism and Roman Catholicism.[18] To acknowledge that the African traditions weakened with each succeeding generation is not to imply that Afro-Americans
merely copied European culture. Afro-Americans, even in slavery,
created new cultures, making bricks from whatever figurative clay and
straw there was.

To hold to Christianity while receiving blows from its professed
practitioners, to avoid wishing evil upon those who prayed with them
on Sunday but beat them on Monday, tried the souls of black Christians. Black slaves knew full well the meaning of the spiritual that says,
"Old Satan's church is here below; Up to God's free church I hope to
go." Black Christians found hope in the good news that God had delivered the children of Israel from bondage and would do the same for
them. One day slave and master would stand before the throne of divine
justice where God would balance the scales. The clandestine religious
meetings in the slave quarters and "hush harbors" were staging grounds
for black freedom. They put the lie to the slaveholding ethic by discovering in Christianity a message of hope and victory that escaped even the
most pious slaveholders. As Donald Mathews has written, "By becoming
more Christian than whites, blacks were confirmed in the knowledge of
their own moral superiority and further strengthened in their claim to
ultimate vindication."[19]

Frederick Douglass felt uneasy about the emergence of independent
black denominations in the early nineteenth century. An ardent abolitionist and integrationist, Douglass viewed the northern black religious

18 A useful summary of the debate concerning African religious retentions can be
found in Raboteau, *Slave Religion*, pp. 44–92.
19 Donald G. Mathews, *Religion in the Old South* (Chicago: University of Chicago Press, 1977), p. 226.

connections, such as the African Methodist Episcopal Church led by Richard Allen, as *"negro pews on a higher and larger scale."*[20] Though the African Methodists retained the doctrines and disciplines of the Wesleyan tradition and defended themselves against charges of separatism, they have been described as coming "as close to a black nation within the United States as any black organization in the country's history."[21] These contrasting viewpoints suggest the third interpretative concern, namely, the dynamic tension between assimilation and nationalism. Readers will doubtless have varying definitions of both ideologies and differing views as to the merits of each. The historian can only caution against letting the search for a usable past, that is, a reading of history in terms of the demands of the present, override careful consideration of the documents on their own terms and in their own contexts. Broadening the concept of "black nationalism" to include Marcus Garvey's "back to Africa" movement and Richard Allen's African Methodists sacrifices the distinctiveness of each.

Perhaps the assimilationist or integrationist goal should not be seen as the opposite of black cultural pride or ethnic consciousness. Preston N. Williams argues that assimilation is not the goal or the opposite of ethnicity, but is rather the very process by which ethnicity lives in America. What is being questioned when one examines ethnicity is not the process of assimilation but the nature of the new communities that will result from assimilation and their continuity with previous communities of their own kind.[22] This suggests that the very struggle for integration, the end result of assimilation, produces a consciousness of ethnicity. Ethnicity emerges as a form of assimilation. In this context, the emergence of the independent black churches and the debates about cultural assimilation and nationalism become clearer, less distorted by inclinations to force the religious history of Afro-Americans into artificial categories. Such an operational perspective also might lessen the need for heroic history in which one selectively chooses the story that best fits a predetermined ideological need.

The relation of black religiosity to black political activism or militancy, our fourth issue, cannot be approached simplistically. In the 1960s the names of Nat Turner, Denmark Vesey, and David Walker were celebrated. Their militant use of religion served to inspire; their radical-

---

20 Quoted in Leon F. Litwack, *North of Slavery* (Chicago: University of Chicago Press, 1961), p. 212.
21 Alain Rogers, "The African Methodist Episcopal Church: A Study of Black Nationalism," *The Black Church* 1, no. 1 (1972): 17.
22 Preston N. Williams, "Religion and the Making of Community in America," *Journal of the American Academy of Religion* 44, no. 4 (1976): 603.

ism squared with the mood of the times and helped to correct the notion that the black churches had been altogether passive in the face of oppression. Some, however, failed the heroic criteria. The post-Civil War black churches, especially those of the South, were said to be too infected with "Uncle Tomism," too concerned with providing an emotional safety valve in ecstatic worship, and too preoccupied with chicken suppers and debates over who the next bishop might be.[23]

Interpreting all Afro-American religion as political radicalism is as much a distortion of the whole as is dismissing the black churches as universally escapist, otherworldly, and politically dysfunctional. "Very few peoples," Martin E. Marty reminds us, "have used their spiritual sustenance only in order to organize themselves for eventual revolution. They use religion to situate themselves in a universe which demands interpretation, where they must be as Sartre called them, 'stalkers of meaning.' "[24] Why is it so surprising that converted slaves were "struck dead" by the Spirit of the Lord and raised up to a new sense of self and an ability to "keep on keeping on" in the face of dehumanizing forces? The testimonies of thousands of ex-slaves reveal that few heard the call to arms when they went to the mountaintop, but many came down with "attitudes which enabled the weak and powerless to make the oppressor and his instruments psychologically irrelevant."[25] Those who dismissed Martin Luther King, Jr.'s philosophy of nonviolent civil disobedience as an ineffective "turn the other cheek" tactic had not reckoned with the moral force within the black church worldview.

As black protest became more intense in the 1960s and cries of "black power" were heard in the streets of many cities, a number of theologians turned to crafting a distinctively black theology. The fifth issue presented by the documents concerns the origin, definition, and impact of "black theology," both in its contemporary form and as it relates to previous eras in Afro-American religious history. The leadership of the largest black denomination feared that a radical black theology would circumscribe the Christian gospel, be counterproductive to the civil rights struggle, and lead to further racial polarization.[26] Others

23 See James H. Cone's portrayal of the apostasy of the post-Civil War black church in *Black Theology and Black Power* (New York: Seabury Press, 1969), pp. 91–115.

24 Martin E. Marty, "Foreword" to Milton C. Sernett, *Black Religion and American Evangelicalism: White Protestants, Plantation Missions, and the Independent Negro Church, 1787–1865* (Metuchen, N.J.: Scarecrow Press, 1975), p. xv.

25 Mathews, *Religion in the Old South*, p. 229.

26 J[oseph] H. Jackson, "An Appraisal of 'A Black Theology of Liberation' in the Light of the Basic Theological Position of the National Baptist Convention,

were less critical, but considerable ambivalence existed about simply baptizing the secular nationalism that came out of the urban riots. This ambivalence, as Rosemary Radford Reuther observed in 1972, reflected "a sense that the character of black ideologies at the present time goes against the grain of the deep commitment of the black church to a black liberation in the context of full human liberation."[27]

Proponents of black theology emphasized its roots in the historical black church and in the religious history of the slaves. The story of the long struggle for black freedom turns to those who have worn the shoe, fought the battle, and hoped. If nothing else, the documentary witness that follows compels us to rethink American religious history. It is not satisfactory simply to doctor up the standard texts by adding a paragraph or two about slave religion, Richard Allen, or Father Divine. The problem is more than one of inclusion as opposed to exclusion. If the Afro-American religious experience is allowed to stand on its own merit, not as a footnote to someone else's story, then we will discover a great deal about American culture that is opaque unless seen from the vantage point of those who, according to a nineteenth-century black spiritual, have "been in the storm so long." This sixth and final issue translates into a historical moral lesson. Lawrence N. Jones stated it well during his inaugural address on the occasion of becoming the first professor of Afro-American church history at Union Theological Seminary, New York City:

> By its very existence, Black church history is a vigorous assertion that that with which we have to deal in America is a vital pluralism, a national culture to which all races and creeds have contributed. In this sense it introduces a reality principle into the self-concept of the Christian Community and of the nation.[28]

U.S.A., INC.," in Appendix A of Peter J. Paris, *Black Leaders in Conflict* (Philadelphia: Pilgrim Press, 1978), pp. 227–31.
27 Rosemary Radford Reuther, *Liberation Theology* (Ramsey, N.J.: Paulist Press, 1972), p. 127.
28 Lawrence N. Jones, "They Sought a City: The Black Church and Churchmen in the Nineteenth Century," *Union Seminary Quarterly Review* 26, no. 3 (Spring 1971): 265.

ONE

*From Africa through
Early America*

1

OLAUDAH EQUIANO

Traditional Ibo Religion and Culture

The lineage tree of Afro-American religion is rooted in the cultures of traditional Africa. Africans were a religious people long before encountering European slavers and Christian missionaries. Olaudah Equiano's memoirs, published in 1789 in England and two years later in America, depict the integral relationship of religion to traditional culture. Kidnapped when eleven from his home in what is now eastern Nigeria, Olaudah Equiano (1745–1801) passed through several hands before being sold to the captain of an English trading vessel in Virginia. After many maritime adventures and experiences as a slave in Barbados, Philadelphia, and England, he purchased his freedom in 1766.

When first able to read the Bible, Equiano expressed amazement at seeing "the laws and rules of my own country written almost exactly." Baptized as Gustavus Vassa, after the Swedish Protestant monarch, Olaudah identified himself with the Christian abolitionists in England and wrote his autobiography to chronicle the evils of the slave trade. Some of the details are suspect in light of ethnographic research, but important aspects of Ibo religion, such as its diffused monotheism, intricate ritual, beliefs about ancestors, or the "living dead," and the influence of diviners and sorcerers, can be gleaned from the narrative. In 1786 English authorities appointed Equiano commissary of provisions and stores for the "Black Poor going to Sierra Leone." Dismissed from his post, he returned to vindicate his character, write his narrative, and speak throughout England against the barbarous slave traffic.

As TO RELIGION, the natives believe that there is one Creator of all things, and that he lives in the sun, and is girded round with a belt, that he may never eat or drink; but according to some, he smokes a pipe, which is our own favorite luxury. They believe he governs events, especially our deaths or captivity; but, as for the doctrine of eternity, I do not remember to have ever heard of it: some however believe in the transmigration of souls in a certain degree. Those spirits, which are not trans-

Source: *The Interesting Narrative of the Life of Olaudah Equiano, or Gustavus Vassa, The African, Written by Himself.* Vol. I. First American edition. New York: W. Durell, 1791, pp. 19–31.

migrated, such as their dear friends or relations, they believe always attend them, and guard them from the bad spirits of their foes. For this reason, they always, before eating, as I have observed, put some small portion of the meat, and pour some of their drink, on the ground for them; and they often make oblations of the blood of beasts or fowls at their graves. I was very fond of my mother, and almost constantly with her. When she went to make these oblations at her mother's tomb, which was a kind of small solitary thatched house, I sometimes attended her. There she made her libations, and spent most of the night in cries and lamentation. I have been often extremely terrified on these occasions. The loneliness of the place, the darkness of the night, and the ceremony of libation, naturally awful and gloomy, were heightened by my mother's lamentations; and these concurring with the doleful cries of birds, by which these places were frequented, gave an inexpressible terror to the scene.

We compute the year from the day on which the sun crosses the line; and, on its setting that evening, there is a general shout throughout the land; at least, I can speak from my own knowledge, throughout our vicinity. The people at the same time made a great noise with rattles not unlike the basket rattles used by children here, though much larger, and hold up their hands to heaven for a blessing. It is then the greatest offerings are made; and those children whom our wise men foretell will be fortunate are then presented to different people. I remember many used to come to see me, and I was carried about to others for that purpose. They have many offerings, particularly at full moons, generally two at harvest, before the fruits are taken out of the ground; and, when any young animals are killed, sometimes they offer up part of them as a sacrifice. These offerings, when made by one of the heads of a family, serve for the whole. I remember we often had them at my father's and my uncle's, and their families have been present. Some of our offerings are eaten with bitter herbs. We had a saying among us to any one of a cross temper, "That if they were to be eaten, they should be eaten with bitter herbs."

We practised circumcision like the Jews, and made offerings and feasts on that occasion in the same manner as they did. Like them also our children were named from some event, some circumstance, or fancied foreboding, at the time of their birth. I was named Olaudah, which, in our language, signifies vicissitude, or fortune also; one favoured, and having a loud voice, and well spoken. I remember we never polluted the name of the object of our adoration; on the contrary, it was always mentioned with the greatest reverence; and we were totally unacquainted with swearing, and all those terms of abuse and reproach which find their way so readily and copiously into the language of more civilized people. The only expressions of that kind I remember were "May you rot, or may you swell, or may a beast take you."

I have before remarked, that the natives of this part of Africa are extremely cleanly. This necessary habit of decency was with us a part of religion, and therefore we had many purifications and washings; indeed almost as many, and used on the same occasions, if my recollection does not fail me, as the Jews. Those that touched the dead at any time were obliged to wash and purify themselves before they could enter a dwelling-house. Every woman too, at certain times, was forbidden to come into a dwelling-house, or touch any person, or anything we eat. I was so fond of my mother I could not keep from her, or avoid touching her at some of those periods, in consequence of which I was obliged to be kept out with her in a little house made for that purpose, till offering was made, and then we were purified.

Though we had no places of public worship, we had priests and magicians, or wise men. I do not remember whether they had different offices, or whether they were united in the same persons, but they were held in great reverence by the people. They calculated our time and fore-told events, as their name imported, for we called them Ah-affoe-way-cah, which signifies calculators or yearly men, our year being called Ah-affoe. They wore their beards; and, when they died, they were succeeded by their sons. Most of their implements and things of value were interred along with them. Pipes and tobacco were also put into the grave with the corpse, which was always perfumed and ornamented; and animals were offered in sacrifice to them. None accompanied their funerals, but those of the same profession or tribe. These buried them after sunset, and always returned from the grave by a different way from that which they went.

These magicians were also our doctors or physicians. They practised bleeding by cupping; and were very successful in healing wounds and expelling poisons. They had likewise some extraordinary method of discovering jealousy, theft, and poisoning; the success of which no doubt they derived from the unbounded influence over the credulity and superstition of the people. I do not remember what those methods were, except that as to poisoning. I recollect an instance or two, which I hope it will not be deemed impertinent here to insert, as it may serve as a kind of specimen of the rest, and is still used by the negroes in the West Indies. A young woman had been poisoned, but it was not known by whom: the doctors ordered the corpse to be taken up by some persons, and carried to the grave. As soon as the bearers had raised it on their shoulders, they seemed seized with some sudden impulse, and ran to and fro, unable to stop themselves. At last, after having passed through a number of thorns and prickly bushes unhurt, the corpse fell from them close to a house, and defaced it in the fall; and the owner being taken up, he immediately confessed the poisoning.[1]

The natives are extremely cautious about poison. When they buy any eatable, the seller kisses it all round before the buyer, to show him it is not poisoned; and the same is done when any meat or drink is presented, particularly to a stranger. We have serpents of different kinds, some of which are esteemed ominous when they appear in our houses, and these we never molest. I remember two of those ominous snakes, each of which was as thick as the calf of a man's leg, and in colour resembling a dolphin in the water, crept at different times into my mother's night-house, where I always lay with her, and coiled themselves into folds, and each time they crowed like a cock. I was desired by some of our wise men to touch these, that I might be interested in the good omens, which I did, for they are quite harmless, and would tamely suffer themselves to be handled; and then they were put into a large open earthen pan, and set on one side of the high-way. Some of our snakes, however, were poisonous. One of them crossed the road one day as I was standing on it, and passed between my feet, without offering to touch me, to the great surprise of many who saw it; and these incidents were accounted, by the wise men, and likewise by my mother and the rest of the people, as remarkable omens in my favour.

Such is the imperfect sketch my memory has furnished me with of the manners and customs of a people among whom I first drew my breath. And here I cannot forbear suggesting what has long struck me very forcibly, namely, the strong analogy which even by this sketch, imperfect as it is, appears to prevail in the manners and customs of my countrymen, and those of the Jews, before they reached the Land of

---

1 An instance of this kind happened at Montserrat in the West Indies in the year 1763. I then belonged to the *Charming Sally*, Capt. Doran. The chief mate, Mr. Mansfield, and some of the crew being one day on shore, were present at the burying of a poisoned negro girl. Though they had often heard of the circumstance of the running in such cases, and had even seen it, they imagined it to be a trick of the corpse bearers. The mate therefore desired two of the sailors to take up the coffin, and carry it to the grave. The sailors, who were all of the same opinion, readily obeyed; but they scarcely raised it to their shoulders before they began to run furiously about, quite unable to direct themselves, till at last, without intention, they came to the hut of him who had poisoned the girl. The coffin then immediately fell from their shoulders against the hut, and damaged part of the wall. The owner of the hut was taken into custody on this and confessed the poisoning—I give this story as it was related by the mate and crew on their return to the ship. The credit which is due to it I leave with the reader.

Promise, and particularly the patriarchs, while they were yet in that pastoral state which is described in Genesis—an analogy which alone would induce me to think that the one people had sprung from the other.[2] Indeed this is the opinion of Dr. Gill, who, in his *Commentary on Genesis*, very ably deduces the pedigree of the Africans from Afer and Afra, the descendants of Abraham by Keturah his wife and concubine (for both these titles are applied to her). It is also conformable to the sentiments of Dr. John Clarke, formerly Dean of Sarum, in his *Truth of the Christian Religion:* Both these authors concur in ascribing to us this original. The reasonings of those gentlemen are still further confirmed by the *Scripture Chronology* of the Rev. Arthur Bedford; and, if any further corroboration were required, this resemblance in so many respects, is a strong evidence in support of the opinion. Like the Israelites in their primitive state, our government was conducted by our chiefs, our judges, our wise men, and elders; and the head of a family with us enjoyed a similar authority over his household with that which is ascribed to Abraham and the other patriarchs. The law of retaliation obtained almost universally with us as with them: and even their religion appeared to have shed upon us a ray of its glory, though broken and spent in its passage, or eclipsed by the cloud with which time, tradition, and ignorance, might have enveloped it: for we had our circumcision (a rule I believe peculiar to that people): we had also our sacrifices and burnt-offerings, our washings and purifications, on the same occasions as they had.

As to the difference of colour between the Eboan Africans and the modern Jews, I shall not presume to account for it. It is a subject which has engaged the pens of men of both genius and learning, and is far above my strength. The most able and Reverend Mr. T. Clarkson, however, in his much admired *Essay on the Slavery and Commerce of the Human Species*, has ascertained the cause in a manner that at once solves every objection on that account, and, on my mind at least, has produced the fullest conviction. I shall therefore refer to that performance for the theory,[3] contenting myself with extracting a fact as related by Dr. Mitchel.[4] "The Spaniards who have inhabited America, under the torrid zone, for any time, are become as dark coloured as our native Indians of Virginia, of which I myself have been a witness." There is also another instance[5] of a Portuguese settlement at Mitomba, a river in Sierra Leona, where the inhabitants are bred from a mixture

2 See I Chron. 1:33. Also John Brown's *Dictionary of the Bible* on the same verse.
3 Pp. 178–216.
4 *Philos. Trans.* No. 476. Sect. 4, cited by the Reverend Mr. Clarkson, p. 205.
5 Same page.

of the first Portuguese discoverers with the natives, and are now become, in their complexion, and in the wooly quality of their hair, perfect
negroes, retaining, however, a smattering of the Portuguese language.

These instances, and a great many more which might be adduced,
while they show how the complexions of the same persons vary in different climates, it is hoped may tend also to remove the prejudice that
some conceive against the natives of Africa on account of their colour.
Surely the minds of the Spaniards did not change with their complexions! Are there not causes enough to which the apparent inferiority
of an African may be ascribed, without limiting the goodness of God,
and supposing he forebore to stamp understanding on certainly his own
image, because "carved in ebony"? Might it not naturally be ascribed
to their situation? When they come among Europeans, they are ignorant of their language, religion, manners, and customs. Are any pains
taken to teach them these? Are they treated as men? Does not slavery
itself depress the mind, and extinguish all its fire, and every noble
sentiment? But, above all, what advantages do not a refined people
possess over those who are rude and uncultivated? Let the polished and
haughty European recollect, that his ancestors were once, like the
Africans, uncivilized, and even barbarous. Did Nature make them inferior to their sons, and should they too have been made slaves? Every
rational mind answers, No. Let such reflections as these melt the pride
of their superiority into sympathy for the wants and miseries of their
sable brethren, and compel them to acknowledge, that understanding is
not confined to feature or colour. If, when they look round the world,
they feel exultation, let it be tempered with benevolence to others, and
gratitude to God, "who hath made of one blood all nations of men for
to dwell on all the face of the earth;[6] and whose wisdom is not our
wisdom, neither are our ways his ways."

SUPPLEMENTARY READINGS

Edwards, Paul, ed. *Equiano's Travels*. New York: Frederick A. Praeger, 1967.

Francis, Elman V. "Olaudah Equiano: A Profile." *Negro History Bulletin* 44, no. 2
(April–May–June 1981): 31, 43–44.

Mbiti, John S. *Introduction to African Religion*. New York: Praeger Publishers,
1975.

Ray, Benjamin C. *African Religions*. Englewood Cliffs, N.J.: Prentice-Hall, 1976.

Zahan, Dominique. *The Religion, Spirituality, and Thought of Traditional Africa*.
Chicago: University of Chicago Press, 1979.

6   Acts xvii, 26.

2

BRYAN EDWARDS

African Religions in Colonial Jamaica

Evidence of the cultural tenacity of religious Africanisms was much stronger in the slave cultures of the Caribbean and South America than on the plantations of the American South. Though this eighteenth-century English planter's interpretations of African religious survivals in colonial Jamaica betray his own cultural biases, Edwards accurately records how strongly Jamaican slaves clung to traditional beliefs and practices associated with witchcraft and sorcery. Obeah and myalism had roots among those West African traditions that stressed the dual potential of magico-religious powers for help or harm. The obeahman or sorcerer practiced negative spiritual medicine. The myalman counteracted with positive spiritual medicine, which came through dancing and possession trances, sometimes referred to as Jamaican Cumina, an ancestral cult. Though the African gods did not survive by name in Jamaica, as they did in Haitian vaudou, enslaved Africans clung to beliefs in family spirits and "ancestral zombies," sometimes in support of rebellion. The colonial planters and their representatives guarded against the influence of obeahmen, whose charms were said to protect insurgents from the weapons of whites.

WHEN AT ANY TIME sudden or untimely death overtakes any of their companions, they impute it to the malicious arts of some practitioners in Obeah, which is a term of African origin, and signifies sorcery or witchcraft. The practice of this art has a very powerful effect on the negroes; for, in a considerable degree, it gives a bias to their general conduct, dispositions, and manners. The following very curious account, therefore, of this art, which was transmitted by the agent of Jamaica to the lords of the committee of privy council, and by them subjoined to their report on the slave trade, cannot fail of being acceptable to the reader.

The term *Obeah, Obiah,* or *Obia* (for it is variously written), we

Source: *An Abridgment of Mr. Edwards's Civil and Commercial History of the British West Indies in Two Volumes.* London: J. Parsons and J. Bell, 1794. Vol. II. Pp. 390–96.

conceive to be the adjective, and *Obe* or *Obi* the noun substantive; and
that by the words *Obia*-men or women, are meant those who practise
Obi. The origin of the term we should consider as of no importance in
our answer to the questions proposed, if, in search of it, we were not
led to disquisitions that are highly gratifying to curiosity. From the
learned Mr. Bryant's commentary upon the word *Oph*, we obtain a very
probable etymology of the term—"A serpent, in the Egyptian language,
was called *Ob* or *Aub*. *Obion* is still the Egyptian name for a serpent;
and *Oubaios* according to Horus Apollo, was the name of the Basilisk
or royal serpent, emblem of the sun, and an ancient oracular deity of
Africa." This derivation, which applies to one particular sect, the remnant probably of a very celebrated religious order in remote ages, is now
become in Jamaica the general term to denote those Africans who in
that island practise witchcraft or sorcery, comprehending also the class
of what are called Myal-men, or those who, by means of a narcotic po-
tion, made with the juice of an herb (said to be the branched *Calalue*
or species of *Solanum*) which occasions a trance or profound sleep of a
certain duration, endeavour to convince the spectators of their power to
re-animate dead bodies.

As far as we are able to decide from our own experience and information when we lived in the island, and from the current testimony of
all the negroes we have ever conversed with on the subject, the professors of Obi are, and always were, natives of Africa, and none other;
and they have brought the science with them from thence to Jamaica,
where it is so universally practised, that we believe there are few of the
larger estates possessing native Africans, which have not one or more
of them. The oldest and most crafty are those who usually attract the
greatest devotion and confidence; those whose hoary heads, and a somewhat peculiarly harsh and forbidding in their aspect, together with a
skill in plants of the medicinal and poisonous species, have qualified
them for the exercise of this art. The negroes in general, whether Africans or Creoles, revere, consult, and fear them; to these oracles they
resort, and with the most implicit faith, upon all occasions, whether for
the cure of disorders, the obtaining revenge for injuries or insults, the
conciliating of favor, the discovery and punishment of the thief or the
adulterer, and the prediction of future events. Their incantations, to
which the midnight hours are allotted, are studiously veiled in mystery;
and as the negroes thoroughly believe in their supernatural power, the
stoutest among them tremble at the very sight of the ragged bundle, the
bottle, or the egg-shells, which are stuck in the thatch, or hung over
the door of a hut, or upon the branch of a plantain tree, to deter maraud-
ers. With minds so firmly prepossessed, they no sooner find *Obi is set for*

them near the door of their house, or in the path which leads to it, than they give themselves up for lost. When a negro is robbed of a fowl or a hog, he applies directly to the Obeah man or women; it is then made known among his fellow blacks, that *Obi is set* for the thief; and as soon as the latter hears the dreadful news, his terrified imagination begins to work; no resource is left but in the superior skill of some more eminent *Obeah-man* of the neighborhood who may conteract the magical operations of the other; but if no one can be found of higher rank and ability, or if after gaining such an ally he should still fancy himself affected, he presently falls into a decline, under the incessant horror of impending calamities. The slightest painful sensation in the head, the bowels, or any other part, any casual loss or hurt, confirms his apprehensions, and he believes himself the devoted victim of an invisible and irresistible agency. Sleep, appetite, and cheerfulness, forsake him, his strength decays, his disturbed imagination is haunted without respite, his features wear the settled gloom of despondency: dirt, or any other unwholesome substance, becomes his only food, he contracts a morbid habit of body, and gradually sinks into the grave. A negro, who is taken ill, enquires of the *Obeah-man* the cause of his sickness, whether it will prove mortal or not, and within what time he shall die or recover. The oracle generally ascribes the distemper to the malice of some particular person by name, and advises to set *Obi* for that person; but if no hopes are given of recovery, immediate despair takes place, which no medicine can remove, and death is the certain consequence. These anomalous symptoms are found to baffle the skill of the ablest physician.

Considering the multitude of occasions which may provoke the negroes to exercise the powers of *Obi* against each other, and the astonishing influence of this art upon their minds, we cannot but attribute a very considerable portion of the annual mortality among the negroes of Jamaica to this fascinating mischief.

The *Obi* is usually composed of various materials, most of which are enumerated in the Jamaica law, viz. Blood, feathers, parrots' beaks, dogs' teeth, alligators' teeth, broken bottles, grave-dirt, rum, and eggshells.

With a view to illustrate the description we have given of this practice, and its common effects, we have subjoined a few examples out of the very great number which have occurred in Jamaica; not that they are peculiar to that island only, for we believe similar examples may be found in other West India colonies. *Pere Labat,* in his history of Martinico, has mentioned some which are very remarkable.

It may seem extraordinary, that a practice, alleged to be so frequent in Jamaica, should not have received an earlier check from the legislature. The truth is, that the skill of some negroes in the art of poisoning has been noticed ever since the colonists became much acquainted with them. Sloane and Barham, who practised physic in Jamaica in the last century, have mentioned particular instances of it. The secret and insidious manner, in which this crime is generally perpetrated, makes the legal proof of it extremely difficult. Suspicions therefore have been frequent, but detections rare: these murderers have sometimes been brought to justice, but it is reasonable to believe that a far greater number have escaped with impunity. In regard to the other and more common arts of *Obi*, such as hanging up feathers, bottles, egg-shells, &c. &c. in order to intimidate negroes of a thievish disposition from plundering huts, hog-sties, or provision-grounds, these were laughed at by the white inhabitants as harmless strategems, contrived by the more sagacious, for deterring the more simple and superstitious blacks, and serving for much the same purpose as the scare-crows which are in general used among our English farmers and gardeners. But in the year 1760, when a very formidable insurrection of the Koromantyn or Gold-Coast negroes broke out in the parish of St. Mary, and spread through almost every other district of the island, an old Koromantyn negro, the chief instigator and oracle of the insurgents in that parish, who had administered the Fetish or solemn oath to the conspirators, and furnished them with a magical preparation which was to render them invulnerable, was fortunately apprehended, convicted, and hung up with all his feathers and magical implements about him; and his execution struck the insurgents with a general panic, from which they never afterwards recovered. The examinations which were taken at that period first opened the eyes of the public to the very dangerous tendency of the *Obeah* practices, and gave birth to the law which was then enacted for their suppression and punishment. But neither the terror of this law, the strict investigation which has ever since been made after the professors of *Obi*, nor the many examples of those who from time to time have been hanged or transported, have hitherto produced the desired effect. We conclude therefore, that either this sect, like others in the world, has flourished under persecution; or that fresh supplies are annually introduced from the African seminaries.

SUPPLEMENTARY READINGS

Barrett, Leonard. "African Religion in the Americas: The 'Islands in Between.'" In *African Religions*, edited by Newell S. Booth, Jr. New York: NOK Publishers International, 1977.

Blassingame, John W. *The Slave Community*. Rev. ed. New York: Oxford University Press, 1979. Chaps. 1 and 2.

Raboteau, Albert. *Slave Religion*. New York: Oxford University Press, 1978. Chaps. 1 and 2.

Schuler, Monica. "Myalism and the African Religious Tradition in Jamaica." In *Africa and the Caribbean*, edited by Margaret E. Crahan and Franklin W. Knight. Baltimore: Johns Hopkins University Press, 1979. Pp. 65–79.

Simpson, George. *Black Religions in the New World*. New York: Columbia University Press, 1978.

3

FRANCIS LE JAU

Slave Conversion on the Carolina Frontier

Most surveys of American religious history begin with the establishment of Puritanism in New England. Rethinking the American experience with full attention to the children of Africa in this land could redefine the outlines of our collective religious story. Imagine it beginning along the early eighteenth-century southern seacoast. The letters of the Reverend Francis Le Jau, stationed at the Goose Creek parish near Charleston, to the secretary of the Society for the Propagation of the Gospel are a major source for the religious history of colonial South Carolina. His reports of the difficulties of an Anglican minister in an outpost of the British empire often touch upon efforts to convert the Native American and African populations. A few slaves did become Christians, often against the wishes or will of planters who feared that baptism would lead to social revolution.

In his efforts to encourage more humane treatment for them, Dr. Le Jau confronted both suspicion from the slaves and opposition from the planters. Though Afro-American converts to Anglicanism hardly entered pew and pulpit on an equal footing with whites, they provided the nucleus of a black Christian community that would increase in number through the American Revolution. It is estimated that the black population of South Carolina in 1715 outnumbered the white by 10,500 to 6,250. Le Jau's converts therefore represented only a small fraction of the Carolinians of African descent. The historian is left with the problem of writing the history of religion for this period not in terms of transplanted European beliefs but according to the legacy of the African diaspora. The Christianization and acculturation of the slaves was an intergenerational process.

[October 20, 1709] As for the Spiritual State of my Parish this is the Account I can give of it for the present.

The extent of it is 20 Miles in length, and from 7 to 14 in breadth. Number of families 80, of the Church of England. Dissenting families 7, if so many, I find but 4 very strict. Baptised this half year past a

Source: *The Carolina Chronicle of Dr. Francis Le Jau, 1706–1717*. Edited by Frank W. Klingberg. Berkeley: University of California Press, 1956. Pp. 60–61, 69–70, 76–77, 124–25, 128–30, and 136–37.

Marryed Woman and 17 Children. Actual Communicants in all about 50: Constant Communicants every two Months near 30, among whom are two Negroes.

Since I came I baptised in all 2 Adults & 47 Children. Our Congregation is generally of about 100 Persons, sometimes more, several that were inclinable to some of the dissenting partys shew themselves pritty constant among us, and I do what possible to edify them and give them satisfaction in their doubts. On Sunday next I design God willing to baptise two very sensible and honest Negro Men whom I have kept upon tryal these two Years. Several others have spoken to me also; I do nothing too hastily in that respect. I instruct them and must have the consent of their Masters with a good Testimony and proof of their honest life and sober Conversation: Some Masters in my parish are very well satisfyed with my Proceedings in that respect: others do not seem to be so; yet they have given over opposing my design openly; it is to be hoped the good Example of the one will have an influence over the others. I must do the Justice to my Parishioners that tho' many Young Gentlemen are Masters of Great Estates, they and almost all the heads of all our Neighbouring families are an Example of Sobriety, honest & Zeal for the Service of the Church to all the province.

To remove all pretence from the Adult Slaves I shall baptise of their being free upon that Account, I have thought fit to require first their consent to this following declaration *You declare in the Presence of God and before this Congregation that you do not ask for the holy baptism out of any design to ffree yourself from the Duty and Obedience you owe to your Master while you live, but meerly for the good of Your Soul and to partake of the Graces and Blessings promised to the Members of the Church of Jesus Christ.* One of the most Scandalous and common Crimes of our Slaves is their perpetual Changing of Wives and husbands, which occasions great disorders: I also tell them whom I baptise, *The Christian Religion dos not allow plurality of Wives, nor any changing of them: You promise truly to keep to the Wife you now have till Death dos part you.* I[t] has been Customary among them to have their ffeasts, dances, and merry Meetings upon the Lord's day, that practice is pretty well over in this Parish, but not absolutely: I tell them that present themselves to be admitted to Baptism, they must promise they'l spend no more the Lord's day in idleness, and if they do I'l cut them off from the Comunion.

These I most humbly Submit to the judgment of my Superiors whose Commands and instructions I will follow while I live: I see with an incredible joy the fervor of several of those poor Slaves. Our free Indians our Neighbours come to see me, I admire the sense they have

of Justice, and their patience; they have no Ambition; as for their sense
of God, their Notions are obscure indeed, but when we take pains to
Converse with them, in a jargon they are able to understand: We perceive their Souls are fit Materials which may be easily polish't, they
agree with me about the duty of praying, & doing the good & eschewing
the evil. The late Colonel Moore and our present Governor have in a
great measure put a Stop to their perpetual murdering one another
which some of them cannot to this day cannot conceive to be evil. Some
of them to whom the Devil has formerly appeared, as they coldly declared to myself, say that evil Spirit never incites them to any thing
more than hatred, revenge, and Murder of those that offend them.

I am told still that if anything opposes the publishing of the Gospel
among the Indians it shall be the manner how our Indian Trade is
carried on, chiefly the fomenting of War among them for our people
to get Slaves. I am so told in general but know no particulars; but it is
too true interest has a great power here and dos occasion injustices too
visibly to my great sorrow, and thro' misfortune I see no remedy but to
be patient and pray and labour as much as I am able in the place I
am sent to. . . .

[February 1, 1710] The Spiral State of my Parish is much the Same;
I have baptised two sensible and honest Negroe Slaves as I had the
Honour to tell you in my last; several come constantly to Church and
are instructed and I hope in time will do well. I have in this parish a few
Negroe Slaves and were born and baptised among the Portuguese, but
speak very good English, they come to Church and are well instructed so
as to express a great desire to receive the H. Communion amongst us, I
proposed to them to declare openly their Abjuring the Errors of the
Romish Church without which Declaration I cou'd not receive them I
bid them consider of it against Easter. On the first Sunday in Lent next
we design and prepare to Communicate, our Constant Number is near
30 at a time and about 50 in all; At Easter some who never did receive
intend to prepare themselves for that Sacred duty after which time I
will give a regular full Account of all. I earnestly labour to bring that
holy performance to a Monthly one or oftner if I cou'd, but our houses
are so scatter'd and remote, that it is not without great difficulties that
we meet so many as we do: I am sensible that for this present, it were
not convenient to require more; let me begg of You that I may not be
Ordered to urge it till we are a little better settled; I must say the like as
to the Associating our Selves for a Reformation of Manners; such a thing
wou'd be of great use in Town, but I apprehend it shall be warmly op-

posed when it is mention'd, and I cannot foresee any good effect till our Chief Men stand for us; and I don't see any tendency towards it to my great Sorrow. To inform you of the State of my Parish in respect to manners. Our Gentry in General is sober and Modest; there is but one single publick house upon the high way in all this vast Tract of Land about me where I sometimes call as I ride along & exhort the best I can generally things are orderly enough, a few Men of the meanest sort wou'd sometimes take too much Liquor, but it is pretty well over and I seldom hear of it. I hear of no Scandalous Cohabitations but of a Couple who are brought to the Necessity either of Marrying or going out of the Parish. I keep a constant Correspondence of visiting & friendship with our Justices of the Peace that are Worthy Psons and of very edifying life, and we all endeavour to keep our Neighbours at peace without the trouble of going to Law but to the last extremity; but when people will be Stubborn and unreasonable, we cannot hinder them. I shou'd say something of Propagating the Xtian Knowledge: We want a Schoolmaster in my parish for our White peoples Children but as for the Negroes or Indians with all submission I wou'd desire that such a thing shou'd be taken into Consideration as the importance of the matter and the Consequences wch. may follow do deserve. The best Scholar of all the Negroes in my Parish and a very sober and honest Liver, thro' his Learning was like to Create some Confusion among all the Negroes in this Country; he had a Book wherein he read some description of the several judgmts. that Chastise Men because of their Sins in these latter days, that description made an Impression upon his Spirit, and he told his Master abruptly there wou'd be a dismal time and the Moon wou'd be turned into Blood, and there wou'd be dearth of darkness and went away: When I heard of that I sent for the Negroe who ingeniously told me he had read so in a Book; I advised him and Charged him not to speak so, which he promised to me but yet wou'd never shew me the Book; but when he spoke those few Words to his Master, some Negroe overheard a part, and it was publickly blazed abroad that an Angel came and spake to the Man, he had seen a hand that gave him a Book, he had heard Voices, seen fires &c. As I had opportunities I took care to undeceive those who asked me about it; now it is over. I fear that those Men have not judgment enough to make good use of their Learning; and I have thought most convenient not to urge too far that Indians and Negroes shou'd be indifferently admitted to learn to read, but I leave it to the discretion of their Masters whom I exhort to examine well their Inclinations. I have often observed and lately hear that it had been better if persons of a Melancholy Constitution or those that run into the Search after Curious matter had never seen a Book: pardon me if I disclose my thoughts wth too much freedome. . . .

[June 13, 1710] Permit me to assure My Lord President his Grace, My Lord of London and the Members of the Religious Society of my Obedience, respect & perfect gratitude. The Number of Our families the same 87. Since the 20th Octr. 1709. I baptised 19. among whom 3 Negroe Men; the Constant Number of Communicants 30. or 36, among whom 4 Negroe Men; all the Communicants together are still about 50. because some went to live in other places; Marriages 3; Buryals 2 Children; the Number of Our Negroe Slaves may be near 500. but above ⅓ part of 'em are Children.

Since it has pleased Almighty God to bless me with health I have upon Sundays, after our Divine Service invited the Negroes & Indian Slaves to stay for half an hour, the Invitation to my great Comfort has been joyfully reced by about 50 of 'em; We begin and end Our particular Assembly with the Collect *prevent us O Lord* &c. I teach 'em the Creed, the Lords Prayer, and the Commandments; I explain some portion of the Catechism, I give them an entire Liberty to ask questions, I endeavour to proportion my answers and all my Instructions to their want and Capacity: I must acknowledge that the hand of God dos visibly appear on this particular occasion. I had often attempted and proposed a time, a Method and means easy, as I thought, for the Instruction of those poor Souls, but all in vain, till this last was put in my mind by special mercy, the Most Pious among their Masters stay also and hear; others not so zealous wou'd find fault, if possible, their Murmerings sometimes reach my Ears, but I am not discouraged: The Caution I have taken & which the Society is pleased to approve of, vizt. to do nothing without the Masters good testimony and consent, is a sufficient answer to them that oppose most the happyness of their Slaves; but the good example of some truely Religious Masters is a Check upon the others, the Alteration is so considerable of late that in general very few Masters excepted, the Slaves shall be fed and provided for by the Masters, and the whole time of the Slaves shall be their Masters; this is what I have continually urged; knowing how idly and criminally the Slaves spent the time given to them to Work for themselves. I bless God for having at last rendred the Masters sensible of their own Advantage in that respect. Four or 6 shall be soon baptised by the Consent of their Masters, and the others with the Children in time, except in danger of death, those Slaves behave themselves very well, and do better for their Masters profit than formerly, for they are taught to serve out of Christian Love & Duty; they tell me openly that they will ever bless God for their knowing good things which they knew not before. The Lord's day is no more profaned by their dancings at least about me: I asked once a pretty ancient and very fine Slave whether he cou'd read, his answer was he wou'd rather choose hereafter to practice the good he could remember. As I had the honour to represent in one of my last Letters the inconveniences which I perceive . . . I forbear urging too far the exercise of reading among them leaving to the discretion of their Masters to choose the fitest persons to learn till I receive further Instructions about that point. There are 3. or 4. Portuguese Slaves in this parish very desirous to receive the Communion amongst us; I framed a short Modell of Submission grounded upon some Popish Tenets which they told me of their own Accord, without troubling them with things they know not; I require of them their renouncing of those particular points, the Chief of which is praying to the Saints and that they must not return to the Popish Worship in case they shou'd be sent to Medera again. I gave them that fform of Submission in Writing and left it to their Consideration, they come constantly to Church and are very sensible. I have proposed to some Masters a thing that seems to me very easy to be done and will prevent horrid Crimes and Confusions amongst Negroes and Indian Slaves for the future, that none of those that are not yet married presume to do it without his Masters consent, and likewise those that are now Marryed do not part without the like Consent (I know some will transgress) but I hope 'twill do good to many, especially in time to come; This thought of mine I most humbly Submit to the Judgment of the Society to which I will ever yield with the utmost respect. . . .

[December 11, 1712] I thought to have baptized some more Negro Slaves this Advent they are well Instructed and I hear no complaint concerning them. Their Masters Seem very much Averse to my Design, Some of them will not give them Leave to come to Church to learn how to Pray to God & to Serve him, I cannot find any reason for this New Opposition but the Old pretext that Baptism makes the Slaves proud and Undutifull: I endeavour to convince them of the Contrary From the Example of those I have baptized, and Chiefly those who are Admitted to our holy Comunion who behave themselves very well, I humbly ask that if the Society Orders any Thing to be Publisht to Induce the Masters to shrew more Charity towards their Slaves I may have some Copies to distribute. . . .

[February 23, 1713] What Afflicts and Discourages me beyond Expression is to see the pious Designes of the Honrble Society very much Obstructed by the rash Conduct of Some of our Inhabitants. I humbly

Apprehend That it is Expected the Missionaries should Endeavour to Promote the knowledge of Christ among the Ignorant Heathens begining with the Poor Negroe & Indian Slaves that live in our ffamilies, and Seeking all Opportunities to do good to the free Indians Scattered in the Province till God Gives us meanes to Instruct those Indian Nations that are our Neighbours, Which I firmly hope shall be Accomplished in his own time, But indeed few Masters appear Zealous or even pleased with what the Missionaries try to do for the Good of their Slaves, they are more Cruel Some of them of late Dayes than before, They hamstring main & unlimb those poor Creatures for Small faults, A man within this Month had a very fine Negroe batized, Sensible Carefull & good in all Respects who being wearyed with Labour & fallen asleep had the Mischance to loose a parcell of Rice wch by the Oversetting of a Periogua fell into a River. The man tho Intreated by the Minister of the Parish, who is Brother Maule and some Persons of the best Consideration among us to forgive the Negroe, who had Offended only through Neglect without Malice, thought fit to keep him for several Dayes in Chains, & I am told muffled up that he might not Eat, & Scourge him twice a Day, and at Night to put him into a hellish Machine contrived by him into the Shape of a Coffin where could not Stirr, The punishmt having continued Several Dayes & Nights and there being no Appearance when it should End, the poor Negroe through Despair Ask't one of his Children for a knife & manacled as he was Stabb'd himself with it; I am told this is the 5th Slave that Same man has destroyed by his Cruelty within 2 or 3 Yeares, but he is onely an hired Overseer the Owner of the Slaves lives out of this Province, I own I See everybody almost angry at So much Barbarity, Yet he pretends to go to Church, and they look upon the Man as Guilty of Murder, and So do great many of my Acquaintance who tho not So Barbarous take no Care at all of the Souls of their Slaves, and as little as the[y] can of their bodies I am at a loss when I see them in a praying posture knowing that at the same time they do not love their Neighbour, and what is most Amazeing I cannot make them Comprehend that their Neglect is an habitual state of Sin, I have Seen very Severe Judgemts. . . .

[January 22, 1714] The Spiritual state of my Parish from July 1st 1713 to the 1st of this instant is as follows, baptized 11 among whom three Adult Negro's, one burial, three Marriages at Christmas last. I had 5 new communicants. 31 Actual Communicants among whome 5 Negroe men & 2 women in my Parish about 65 Communicants.

Being uncertain whether my last Letter came to your hands I take this Liberty to insert in this that the number of the Baptized in this Parish from Janry to July 1713 was 11 among whom a Gentleman and Gentlewoman & four Negroe Women, 2 Marriages no Burial, 3 new Communicants, actual Communicants on whitesunday 32 Communicants in all 60.

Since the first of this month I baptized an old Sensible Negroe Man upon his death bed, and three Negroe children, and all of them with their masters consent some more come to me. Shewing an Earnest desire to receive that holy Sacrament. I Encourage them and instruct them the best I can by Divine Grace.

It is a singular comfort to me to see that while so many professed Christians appear but Lukewarm, it pleases God to raise to himself faithfull and devout Servts from among the heathens, who are very zealous in the Practice of our Christian dutyes. I hear no Complaining of our Proselytes, their masters commend them for their faithfullness, and from what I am going to relate, the Honble Society shall have a satisfactory Instance that their Pious designs are not fruitless, as Irreligious men would insinuate, when they pretend That the knowledge of the true God and Jesus his Son renders our Slaves worse.

About Christmas last past there was a rumour spread of an Intended Conspiracy of the Negro's against us all like that of New York. I was told that the Plot had been form'd in Goose Creek where there is a good number of fine Negro's. This News made me Inquire and observe being resolved to find out how true the thing might be. The matter has been examined very diligently by our Government this very week. 12 or 15 Negroes living on the North side of Cooper River, having been apprehended under suspicion it has appeared upon good evidence that a Negroe fellow brought hither some years ago from Martineco, and of a very stubborn temper, had Inticed some Slaves to joyn with him that they might get their liberty by force. the thing being proved against him he has been put to death for it, two more Slaves have been very severely chastis'd for hearkening to him, but there was not any sufficient proof to take their life and all denied the Crime, the other prisoners have been acquited but what I consider as a singular Providence there has not been so much as one of our Goose Creek Negroes accused of having knowledge of the Plot, far from having consented to so great a Crime. The most sensible of our Slaves whom I have admitted to the holy Sacrament have solemnly protested to me that if ever they hear of any Ill design of the Slaves I shall know it from them that it may be prevented, and I can't but depend upon the truth of their words, knowing them to be Exemplarily Pious and Honest. . . .

SUPPLEMENTARY READINGS

Jernegan, Marcus W. "Slavery and Conversion in the American Colonies." *The American Historical Review* 21, no. 33 (April 1916): 505–27.

Jordan, Winthrop D. *White Over Black: American Attitudes Toward the Negro, 1550–1812.* Chapel Hill: University of North Carolina Press, 1968.

Vibert, Faith. "The Society for the Propagation of the Gospel in Foreign Parts: Its Work for the Negroes in North America before 1783." *The Journal of Negro History* 18, no. 2 (April 1933): 171–212.

Wood, Peter H. *Black Majority: Negroes in Colonial South Carolina from 1670 through the Stono Rebellion.* New York: W. W. Norton, 1974.

Wood, Peter H. " 'Jesus Christ Has Got Thee at Last': Afro-American Conversion as a Forgotten Chapter in Eighteenth-Century Southern Intellectual History." *The Bulletin of the Center for the Study of Southern Culture and Religion* 3, no. 3 (November 1979): 1–7.

4

JUPITER HAMMON

"Address to the Negroes in the State of New York"

Jupiter Hammon (1720–1806?) was the first Afro-American to write and publish poetry, antedating his more famous contemporary, Phillis Wheatley of Boston. Like her, he exhibited a deeply religious and conservative temperament. A favored slave to three generations of the Lloyd family of Long Island, Hammon came under the influence of the Wesleyan evangelical revival and devoted himself to the study of the Bible and, according to some sources, preaching among fellow slaves. The following address was originally presented to members of the African Society in the city of New York in 1786. The Pennsylvania Society for Promoting the Abolition of Slavery ordered it reprinted, though Hammon's views regarding slavery were decidedly more conservative than those of such contemporaries as Richard Allen and Prince Hall. Perhaps because of his age and personal situation, Hammon felt it his duty to bear slavery with patience. Yet he hoped for the gradual emancipation of the younger slaves and acknowledged that "liberty is a great thing and worth seeking for." The sublimation of spiritual freedom for physical freedom, the reinforcement of the biblical model of the master-slave relationship, and doubts about the capacity of blacks to handle freedom—echoed by others such as John Chavis, the famous black Presbyterian minister in North Carolina—placed Hammon in a distinct minority in the Afro-American community. Only in death did Hammon find freedom.

WHEN I AM WRITING TO YOU with a design to say something to you for your good, and with a view to promote your happiness, I can with truth and sincerity join with the apostle Paul, when speaking of his own nation the Jews, and say: *"That I have great heaviness and continual sorrow in my heart for my brethren, my kinsmen according to the flesh."* Yes my dear brethren, when I think of you, which is very often, and of the poor, despised and miserable state you are in, as to the things of this

Source: *An Address to the Negroes in the State of New York, by Jupiter Hammon, Servant of John Lloyd, jun, Esq of the Manor of Queen's Village, Long Island.* New York: Carroll and Patterson, 1786.

world, and when I think of your ignorance and stupidity, and the great wickedness of the most of you, I am pained to the heart. It is at times, almost too much for human nature to bear, and I am obliged to turn my thoughts from the subject or endeavour to still my mind, by considering that it is permitted thus to be, by that God who governs all things, who setteth up one and pulleth down another. While I have been thinking on this subject, I have frequently had great struggles in my own mind, and have been at a loss to know what to do. I have wanted exceedingly to say something to you, to call upon you with the tenderness of a father and friend, and to give you the last, and I may say dying advice, of an old man, who wishes your best good in this world, and in the world to come. But while I have had such desires, a sense of my own ignorance, and unfitness to teach others, has frequently discouraged me from attempting to say any thing to you; yet when I thought of your situation, I could not rest easy.

When I was at Hartford in Connecticut, where I lived during the war, I published several pieces which were well received, not only by those of my own colour, but by a number of the white people, who thought they might do good among their servants. This is one consideration, among others, that emboldens me now to publish what I have written to you. Another is, I think you will be more likely to listen to what is said, when you know it comes from a negro, one of your own nation and colour, and therefore can have no interest in deceiving you, or in saying any thing to you, but what he really thinks is your interest, and duty to comply with. My age, I think, gives me some right to speak to you, and reason to expect you will hearken to my advice. I am now upwards of seventy years old, and cannot expect, though I am well, and able to do almost any kind of business, to live much longer. I have passed the common bounds set for man, and must soon go the way of all the earth. I have had more experience in the world than most of you, and I have seen a great deal of the vanity and wickedness of it, I have great reason to be thankful that my lot has been so much better than most slaves have had. I suppose I have had more advantages and privileges than most of you, who are slaves, have ever known, and I believe more than many white people have enjoyed, for which I desire to bless God, and pray that he may bless those who have given them to me. I do not, my dear friends, say these things about myself, to make you think that I am wiser or better than others; but that you might hearken, without prejudice, to what I have to say to you on the following particulars.

1st. *Respecting obedience to masters.* Now whether it is right, and lawful, in the sight of God, for them to make slaves of us or not. I am certain that while we are slaves, it is our duty to obey our masters, in all their lawful commands, and mind them unless we are bid to do that which we know to be sin, or forbidden in God's word. The apostle Paul says. "Servants be obedient to them that are your masters according to the flesh, with fear and trembling in singleness in your heart as unto Christ: Not with eye service, as men pleasers, but as the servants of Christ doing the will of God from the heart: With good will doing service to the Lord, and not to men: Knowing that whatever thing a man doeth the same shall he receive of the Lord, whether he be bond or free."—Here is a plain command of God for us to obey our masters. It may seem hard for us, if we think our masters wrong in holding us slaves, to obey in all things, but who of us dare dispute with God! He has commanded us to obey, and we ought to do it cheerfully, and freely. This should be done by us, not only because God commands, but because our own peace and comfort depend upon it. As we depend upon our masters, for what we eat and drink and wear, and for all our comfortable things in this world, we cannot be happy, unless we please them. This we cannot do without obeying them freely, without muttering or finding fault. If a servant strives to please his master and studies and takes pains to do it, I believe there are but few masters who would use such a servant cruelly. Good servants frequently make good masters. If your master is really hard, unreasonable and cruel, there is no way so likely for you to convince him of it, as always to obey his commands, and try to serve him, and take care of his interest, and try to promote it all in your power. If you are proud and stubborn and always finding fault, your master will think the fault lies wholly on your side; but if you are humble, and meek, and bear all things patiently, your master may think he is wrong; if he does not, his neighbours will be apt to see it, and will befriend you, and try to alter his conduct. If this does not do, you must cry to him, who has the hearts of all men in his hands, and turneth them as the rivers of waters are turned.

2nd. The particular I would mention, is honesty and faithfulness.

You must suffer me now to deal plainly with you, my dear brethren, for I do not mean to flatter or omit speaking the truth, whether it is for you, or against you. How many of you are there, who allow yourselves in stealing from your masters. It is very wicked for you not to take care of your masters' goods; but how much worse is it to pilfer and steal from them, whenever you think you shall not be found out. This you must know is very wicked and provoking to God. There are none of you so ignorant but that you must know that this is wrong. Though you may try to excuse yourselves by saying that your masters are unjust to you, and though you may try to quiet your consciences in this way, yet if you are honest in owning the truth, you must think it is as wicked, and on some accounts more wicked to steal from your masters, than from others.

We cannot certainly have any excuse, either for taking any thing that belongs to our masters, without their leave, or for being unfaithful in their business. It is our duty to be faithful, *not with eye service as men pleasers.* We have no right to stay, when we are sent on errands, any longer than to do the business we were sent upon. All the time spent idly is spent wickedly, and is unfaithfulness to our masters. In these things I must say, that I think many of you are guilty. I know that many of you endeavour to excuse yourselves, and say that you have nothing that you can call your own, and that you are under great temptations to be unfaithful and take from your masters. But this will not do; God will certainly punish you for stealing, and for being unfaithful. All that we have to mind, is our own duty. If God has put us in bad circumstances, that is not our fault, and he will not punish us for it. If any are wicked in keeping us so, we cannot help it; they must answer to God for it. Nothing will serve as an excuse to us for not doing our duty. The same God will judge both them and us. Pray then, my dear friends, fear to offend in this way, but be faithful to God, to your masters, and to your own souls.

The next thing I would mention and warn you against, is profaneness. This you know is forbidden by God. Christ tells us, "Swear not at all," and again it is said, "Thou shalt not take the name of the Lord thy God in vain, for the Lord will not hold him guiltless that taketh his name in vain." Now, though the great God has forbidden it, yet how dreadfully profane are many, and I don't know but I may say the most of you! How common is it to hear you take the terrible and awful name of the great God in vain!—To swear by it, and by Jesus Christ, his Son.— How common is it to hear you wish damnation to your companions, and to your own souls—and to sport with, in the name of Heaven and Hell, as if there were no such places for you to hope for or to fear. Oh my friends, be warned to forsake this dreadful sin of profaneness. Pray, my dear friends, believe and realize that there is a God—that he is great and terrible beyond what you can think—that he keeps you in life every moment—and that he can send you to that awful Hell that you laugh at, in an instant, and confine you there for ever; and that he will certainly do it, if you do not repent. You certainly do not believe that there is a God, or that there is a Heaven or Hell, or you would never trifle with them. It would make you shudder, if you hear others do it, if you believe them as much as you believe any thing you see with your bodily eyes.

I have heard some learned and good men say that the heathen, and all that worshipped false gods, never spoke lightly or irreverently of their gods; they never took their names in vain, or jested with those things which they held sacred. Now, why should the true God, who made all things, be treated worse in this respect than those false gods that were made of wood and stone? I believe it is because Satan tempts men to do it. He tried to make them love their false gods, and to speak well of them; but he wishes to have men think lightly of the true God, to take his holy name in vain, and to scoff at and make a jest of all things that are really good. You may think that Satan has not power to do so much, and have so great influence on the minds of men: But the Scripture says, "*He goeth about like a roaring Lion, seeking whom he may devour—That he is the prince of the power of the air—and that he rules in the hearts of the children of disobedience,—and that wicked men are led captive by him, to do his will.*" All those of you who are profane, are serving the Devil. You are doing what he tempts and desires you to do. If you could see him with your bodily eyes, would you like to make an agreement with him to serve him, and do as he bid you? I believe most of you would be shocked at this; but you may be certain that all of you who allow yourselves in this sin, are as really serving him, and to just as good purpose, as if you met him and promised to dishonor God, and serve him with all your might. Do you believe this? It is true whether you believe it or not. Some of you to excuse yourselves, may plead the example of others, and say that you hear a great many white people, who know more than such poor ignorant Negroes as you are, and some who are rich and great gentlemen, swear, and talk profanely; and some of you may say this of your masters, and say no more than is true. But all this is not a sufficient excuse for you. You know that murder is wicked. If you saw your master kill a man, do you suppose this would be any excuse for you, if you should commit the same crime? You must know it would not; nor will your hearing him curse and swear, and take the name of God in vain, or any other man, be he ever so great or rich, excuse you. God is greater than all other beings, and him we are bound to obey. To him we must give an account for every *idle* word that we speak. He will bring us all, rich and poor, white and black, to his judgment seat. If we are found among those who *feared his name*, and *trembled at his word*, we shall be called good and faithful servants. Our slavery will be at an end, and though ever so mean, low and despised in this world, we shall sit with God in his kingdom, as Kings and Priests, and rejoice for ever and ever. Do not then, my dear friends, take God's holy name in vain, or speak profanely in any way. Let not the example of others lead you into the sin, but reverence and fear that great *and fearful name, the Lord our God.*

    I might now caution you against other sins to which you are exposed; but as I meant only to mention those you were exposed to, more than others, by your being slaves, I will conclude what I have to say to you, by advising you to become religious, and to make religion the great business of your lives.

Now I acknowledge that liberty is a great thing, and worth seeking for, if we can get it honestly; and by our good conduct prevail on our masters to set us free: though for my own part I do not wish to be free, yet I should be glad if others, especially the young Negroes, were to be free; for many of us who are grown up slaves, and have always had masters to take care of us, should hardly know how to take care of ourselves; and it may be more for our own comfort to remain as we are. That liberty is a great thing we may know from our own feelings, and we may likewise judge so from the conduct of the white people in the late war. How much money has been spent, and how many lives have been lost to defend their liberty! I must say that I have hoped that God would open their eyes, when they were so much engaged for liberty, to think of the state of the poor blacks, and to pity us. He has done it in some measure, and has raised us up many friends; for which we have reason to be thankful, and to hope in his mercy. What may be done further, he only knows, for *known unto God are all his ways from the beginning.* But this, my dear brethren, is by no means the greatest thing we have to be concerned about. Getting our liberty in this world is nothing to our having the liberty of the children of God. Now the Bible tells us that we are all, by nature, sinners; that we are slaves to sin and Satan, and that unless we are converted, or born again, we must be miserable for ever. Christ says, except a man be born again, he cannot see the kingdom of God; and all that do not see the kingdom of God, must be in the kingdom of darkness. There are but two places where all go after death, white and black, rich and poor; those places are Heaven and Hell. Heaven is a place made for those who are born again, and who love God; and it is a place where they will be happy for ever. Hell is a place made for those who hate God, and are his enemies, and where they will be miserable to all eternity. Now you may think you are not enemies to God, and do not hate him: but if your heart has not been changed, and you have not become true Christians, you certainly are enemies to God, and have been opposed to him ever since you were born. Many of you, I suppose, never think of this, and are almost as ignorant as the beasts that perish. Those of you who can read, I must beg you to read the Bible; and whenever you can get time, study the Bible; and if you can get no other time, spare some of your time from sleep, and learn what the mind and will of God is. But what shall I say to them who cannot read? This lay with great weight on my mind, when I thought of writing to my poor brethren; but I hope that those who can read will take pity on them, and read what I have to say to them. In hopes of this, I will beg of you to spare no pains in trying to learn to read. If you are once engaged, you may learn. Let all the time you can get be spent in trying to learn to read. Get those who can read, to learn you; but remember, that what you learn for, is to read the Bible. If there was no Bible, it would be no matter whether you could read or not. Reading other books would do you no good. But the Bible is the word of God, and tells you what you must do to please God; it tells you how you may escape misery, and be happy for ever. If you see most people neglect the Bible, and many that can read never look into it, let it not harden you, and make you think lightly of it, and that it is a book of no worth. All those who are really good love the Bible, and meditate on it day and night. In the Bible God has told us every thing it is necessary we should know, in order to be happy here and hereafter. The Bible is a revelation of the mind and will of God to men. Therein we may learn what God is. That he made all things by the power of his word; and that he made all things for his own glory, and not for our glory. That he is over all, and above all his creatures, and more above them than we can think or conceive—that they can do nothing without him—that he upholds them all, and will overrule all things for his own glory. In the Bible likewise we are told what man is. That he was at first made holy, in the image of God; that he fell from that state of holiness, and became an enemy to God; and that since the fall, *all the imaginations of the thoughts of his heart are evil, and only evil, and that continually. That the carnal mind is not subject to the law of God, neither indeed can be.* And that all mankind were under the wrath and curse of God, and must have been for ever miserable, if they had been left to suffer what their sins deserved. It tells us that God, to save some of mankind, sent his Son into this world to die, in the room and stead of sinners; and that now God can save from eternal misery all that believe in his Son, and take him for their Saviour; and that all are called upon to repent, and believe in Jesus Christ. It tells us that those who do repent and believe, and are friends to Christ, shall have many trials and sufferings in this world, but that they shall be happy for ever, after death, and reign with Christ to all eternity. The Bible tells us that this world is a place of trial, and that there is no other time or place for us to alter, but in this life. If we are Christians when we die, we shall awake to the resurrection of life; if not, we shall awake to the resurrection of damnation. It tells us we must all live in Heaven or Hell, be happy or miserable, and that without end. The Bible does not tell us of but two places, for all to go to. There is no place for innocent folks, that are not Christians. There is no place for ignorant folks, that did not know how to be Christians. What I mean is, that there is no place besides

Heaven and Hell. These two places will receive all mankind, for Christ says, there are but two sorts, *he that is not with me is against me; and he that gathereth not with me, scattereth abroad.*—The Bible likewise tells us that this world, and all things in it, shall be burnt up—and that "God has appointed a day in which he will judge the world; and that he will bring every secret thing, whether it be good or bad, into judgment—that which is done in secret shall be declared on the house top." I do not know, nor do I think any can tell, but that the day of judgment may last a thousand years. God could tell the state of all his creatures in a moment, but then every thing that every one has done, through his whole life, is to be told before the whole world of angels and men. Oh how solemn is the thought! You and I must stand, and hear every thing we have thought or done, however secret, however wicked and vile, told before all the men and women that ever have been, or ever will be, and before all the angels, good and bad.

Now, my dear friends, seeing the Bible is the word of God, and every thing in it is true, and it reveals such awful and glorious things, what can be more important than that you should learn to read it; and when you have learned to read, that you should study it day and night. There are some things very encouraging in God's word for such ignorant creatures as we are; for God hath not chosen the rich of this world. Not many rich, not many noble are called, but God hath chosen the weak things of this world, and things which are not, to confound the things that are. And when the great and the rich refused coming to the gospel feast, the servant was told to go into the highways and hedges, and compel those poor creatures that he found there, to come in. Now, my brethren, it seems to me that there are no people that ought to attend to the hope of happiness in another world so much as we. Most of us are cut off from comfort and happiness here in this world, and can expect nothing from it. Now seeing this is the case, why should we not take care to be happy after death? Why should we spend our whole lives in sinning against God; and be miserable in this world, and in the world to come? If we do thus, we shall certainly be the greatest fools. We shall be slaves here, and slaves for ever. We cannot plead so great temptations to neglect religion as others. Riches and honours which drown the greater part of mankind, who have the gospel, in perdition, can be little or no temptations to us.

We have so little time in this world that it is no matter how wretched and miserable we are, if it prepares us for Heaven. What is forty, fifty, or sixty years, when compared to eternity? When thousands and millions of years have rolled away, this eternity will be no nigher coming to an end. Oh how glorious is an eternal life of happiness! And how dreadful an eternity of misery! Those of us who have had religious matters, and have been taught to read the Bible, and have been brought by their example and teaching to a sense of divine things, how happy shall we be to meet them in Heaven, where we shall join them in praising God for ever. But if any of us have had such masters, and yet have lived and died wicked, how will it add to our misery to think of our folly. If any of us, who have wicked and profane masters, should become religious, how will our estates be changed in another world. Oh, my friends, let me intreat of you to think on these things, and to live as if you believed them to be true. If you become Christians, you will have reason to bless God for ever, that you have been brought into a land where you have heard the gospel, though you have been slaves. If we should ever get to Heaven, we shall find nobody to reproach us for being black, or for being slaves. Let me beg of you, my dear African brethren, to think very little of your bondage in this life; for your thinking of it will do you no good. If God designs to set us free, he will do it in his own time and way; but think of your bondage to sin and Satan, and do not rest until you are delivered from it.

We cannot be happy, if we are ever so free or ever so rich, while we are servants of sin, and slaves to Satan. We must be miserable here, and to all eternity.

I will conclude what I have to say with a few words to those Negroes who have their liberty. The most of what I have said to those who are slaves, may be of use to you; but you have more advantages, on some accounts, if you will improve your freedom, as you may do, than they. You have more time to read God's holy word, and to take care of the salvation of your souls. Let me beg of you to spend your time in this way, or it will be better for you if you had always been slaves. If you think seriously of the matter, you must conclude that if you do not use your freedom to promote the salvation of your souls, it will not be of any lasting good to you. Besides all this, if you are idle, and take to bad courses, you will hurt those of your brethren who are slaves, and do all in your power to prevent their being free. One great reason that is given by some for not freeing us, I understand, is, that we should not know how to take care of ourselves, and should take to bad courses; that we should be lazy and idle, and get drunk and steal. Now all those of you who follow any bad courses, and who do not take care to get an honest living by your labour and industry, are doing more to prevent our being free than any body else. Let me beg of you then, for the sake of your own good and happiness, in time, and for eternity, and for the sake of your poor brethren, who are still in bondage, *"to lead quiet and peaceable lives in all Godliness and honesty,"* and may God bless you, and bring you to his kingdom, for Christ's sake, Amen.

SUPPLEMENTARY READINGS

Greene, Lorenzo J. *The Negro in Colonial New England.* New York: Atheneum, 1968.

Ransom, Stanley Austin, Jr., ed. *America's First Negro Poet: The Complete Works of Jupiter Hammon of Long Island.* Port Washington, N.Y.: Kennikat Press, 1970.

Robinson, William M., ed. *Early Black American Prose.* Dubuque, Ia.: Wm. C. Brown, 1971.

Scherer, Lester B. *Slavery and the Churches in Early America, 1619–1819.* Grand Rapids, Mich.: William B. Eerdmans, 1975.

Wegelin, Oscar. *Jupiter Hammon—American Negro Poet; Selections from His Writings and a Bibliography.* New York: Heartman, 1915.

5

GEORGE LIELE AND ANDREW BRYAN

Letters from Pioneer Black Baptists

Independent black congregations arose in the South during the Revolutionary era in the wake of a general religious awakening and under the egalitarian spirituality espoused by dissenting white Baptists. The following letters report on the activities of pioneering Afro-American Baptist clergy who were anxious to share with fellow blacks "God's precious dealings" with their souls. George Liele, baptized around 1774, preached in the area of Silver Bluff, South Carolina, in company with David George, another slave. Liele founded a black congregation in 1777 at Yama Craw, outside Savannah. Freed by his Baptist deacon owner, Liele left Georgia in 1782 for Jamaica, where he established several Afro-Baptist churches. David George emigrated first to Nova Scotia and then in 1792 to Sierra Leone. One of Liele's Yama Craw converts, Andrew Bryan (1737–1812), reorganized the work in Savannah and established the First African Church in 1788. In 1802 the congregation claimed 850 members and belonged to the racially mixed Savannah River Association. Whipped, imprisoned twice, but able to purchase his freedom in 1802, Bryan successfully pastored First African until 1812 and witnessed the founding of several daughter congregations. The separate Afro-Baptist churches of the late 1700s are notable in that they predated the rise of independent black denominations in the North.

An Account of Several Baptist Churches, Consisting Chiefly of Negro Slaves: Particularly of one at Kingston, in Jamaica: and Another at Savannah in Georgia

A LETTER from the late Rev. Mr. Joseph Cook of the Euhaw, upper Indian Land, South Carolina, bearing date Sept. 15, 1790, "A poor negro, commonly called, among his own friends, Brother George, has been so highly favoured of God, as to plant the first Baptist Church in Savan-

Source: John Rippon, *The Baptist Annual Register, for 1790, 1791, 1792, and Part of 1793.* London: Dilly, Button, and Thomas, 1793. Pp. 332–37. *The Baptist Annual Register, for 1798, 1799, 1800, and Part of 1801.* London: Button and Conder, 1801. Pp. 366–67.

nah, and another in Jamaica." This account produced an earnest desire
to know the circumstances of both these societies. Hence letters were
written to the Rev. Mr. Cook at the Euhaw; to Mr. Jonathan Clarke, at
Savannah; to Mr. Wesley's people at Kingston; with a view to obtain
information, in which particular regard was had to the *character* of this
poor but successful minister of Christ. Satisfactory accounts have been
received from each of these quarters, and a letter from brother George
himself, containing an answer to more than fifty questions proposed in a
letter to him: We presume to give an epitome of the whole to our
friends, hoping that they will have the goodness to let a plain unlettered
people convey their ideas in their own simple way.

Brother George's words are distinguished by inverted commas, and
what is not so marked, is either matter compressed or information received from such persons to whom application has been made of it.

George Liele, called also George *Sharp* because his owner's name
was Sharp, in a letter dated Kingston, Dec. 18, 1791, says, "I was born
in Virginia, my father's name was Liele, and my mother's name Nancy;
I can not ascertain much of them, as I went to several parts of America
when young, and at length resided in New Georgia; but was informed
both by white and black people, that my father was the only black person who knew the Lord in a spiritual way in that country: I always had
a natural fear of God from my youth, and was often checked in conscience with thoughts of death, which barred me from many sins and
bad company. I knew no other way at that time to hope for salvation
but only in the performance of my good works." *About two years before
the late war,* "the Rev. Mr. Matthew Moore, one Sabbath afternoon, as
I stood with curiosity to hear him, he unfolded all my dark views, opened
my best behaviour and good works to me which I thought I was to be
saved by, and I was convinced that I was not in the way to heaven, but
in the way to hell. This state I laboured under for the space of five or six
months. The more I heard or read, the more I" saw that I "was condemned as a sinner before God; till at length I was brought to perceive
that my life hung by a slender thread, and if it was the will of God to
cut me off at that time, I was sure I should be found in hell, as sure as
God was in Heaven. I saw my condemnation in my own heart, and I
found no way wherein I could escape the damnation of hell, only
through the merits of my dying Lord and Saviour Jesus Christ; which
caused me to make intercession with Christ, for the salvation of my poor
immortal soul; and I full well recollect, I requested of my Lord and Master to give me a work, I did not care how mean it was, only to try and see
how good I would do it." When he became acquainted with the method
of salvation by our Lord Jesus Christ, he soon found relief, particularly

at a time when he was earnestly engaged in prayer; yea, he says, "I felt such love and joy as my tongue was not able to express. After this I declared before the congregation of believers the work which God had done for my soul, and the same minister, the Rev. Matthew Moore, baptized me, and I continued in this church about four years, till the vacuation" of Savannah by the British. When Mr. Liele was called by grace himself, he was desirous of promoting the felicity of others. One who was an eyewitness of it, says, *That he began to discover his love to other negroes, on the same plantation with himself, by reading hymns among them, encouraging them to sing, and sometimes by explaining the most striking parts of them.* His own account is this, "Desiring to prove the sense I had of my obligations to God, I endeavoured to instruct" the people of "my own color in the word of God: the white brethren seeing my endeavours, and that the word of the Lord seemed to be blessed, gave me a call at a quarterly meeting to preach before the congregation." Afterwards Mr. Moore took the sense of the church concerning brother Liele's abilities, when it appeared to be their unanimous opinion, "that he was possessed of ministerial gifts," and according to the custom which obtains in some of the American churches, he was licensed as a probationer. He now exercised at different plantations, especially on those Lord's Day evenings when there was no service performed in the church to which he belonged; and preached "about three years at Brunton land, and at Yamacraw," which last place is about half a mile from Savannah. Mr. Henry Sharp, his master, being a deacon of the church which called George Liele to the work of the ministry, some years before his death gave him his freedom, only he continued in the family till his master's exit. Mr. Sharp in the time of the war was an officer, and was at last killed in the king's service, by a ball which shot off his hand. The author of this account handled the bloody glove, which he wore when he received the fatal wound. Some persons were at this time dissatisfied with George's liberation, and threw him into prison, but by producing the proper papers he was released; his particular friend in this business was colonel Kirkland. "At the vacuation of the country I was partly obliged to come to Jamaica, as an indented servant, for money I owed him, he promising to be my friend in this country. I was landed at Kingston, and by the colonel's recommendation to general Campbell, the governor of the Island, I was employed by him two years, and on leaving the island, he gave me a written certificate from under his own hand of my good behaviour. As soon as I had settled Col. Kirkland's demands on me, I had a certificate of my freedom from the vestry and governor, according to the act of this Island, both for myself and family. Governor Campbell left the Island. I began, about September 1784, to

preach in Kingston, in a small private house, to a good smart congregation, and I formed the church with four brethren from America besides
myself, and the preaching took very good effect with the poorer sort,
especially the slaves. The people at first persecuted us both at meetings
and baptisms, but, God be praised, they seldom interrupt us now. We
have applied to the Honourable House of Assembly, with a petition of
our distresses, being poor people, desiring to worship Almighty God according to the tenets of the Bible, and they have granted us liberty, and
given us their sanction. Thanks be to God we have liberty to worship
him as we please in the Kingdom. You ask about those who," in a judgment of charity, "have been converted to Christ. I think they are about
four hundred and fifty. I have baptized four hundred in Jamaica. At
Kingston I baptize in the sea, at Spanish Town in the river, and at convenient places in the country. We have nigh *three hundred and fifty
members;* a few white people among them, one white brother of the first
battalion of royals, from England, baptized by Rev. Thomas Davis. Several members have been dismissed to other churches, and twelve have
died. I have sent enclosed" an account of "the conversion and death of
some. A few of Mr. Wesley's people, after immersion, join us and continue with us. We have, together with well wishers and followers, in
different parts of the country, about fifteen hundred people. We receive
none into the church without a few lines from their owners of their good
behaviour towards them and religion. The creoles of the country, after
they are converted and baptized, as God enables them, prove very faithful. I have deacons and elders, a few; and teachers of small congregations
in the town and country, where convenience suits them to come together; and I am pastor. I preach twice on the Lord's Day, in the forenoon and afternoon, and twice in the week, and have not been absent six
Sabbath Days since I formed the church in this country. I receive nothing for my services; I preach, baptize, administer the Lord's Supper, and
travel from one place to another to publish the gospel, and to settle
church affairs, all freely. I have one of the chosen men, whom I baptized,
a deacon of the church, and a native of this country, who keeps the regulations of church matters; and I promoted a *free school* for the instruction of the children, both free and slaves, and he is the schoolmaster.

"I cannot justly tell what is my age, as I have no account of the
time of my birth, but I suppose I am about forty years old. I have a wife
and four children. My wife was baptized by me in Savannah, at Brunton
land, and I have every satisfaction in life from her. She is much the same
age as myself. My eldest son is nineteen years, my next son seventeen,
the third fourteen, and the last child, a girl of eleven years; they are all
members of the church. My occupation is a farmer, but as the seasons

in this part of the country, are uncertain, I also keep a team of horses, and waggons for the carrying goods from one place to another, which I attend to myself, with the assistance of my sons; and by this way of life have gained the good will of the public, who recommend me to business, and to some very principal work for government.

"I have a few books, some good old authors and sermons, and one large bible that was given to me by a gentleman; a good many of our members can read, and are all desirous to learn; they will be very thankful for a few books to read on Sundays and other days.

"The last accounts I had from Savannah were, that the Gospel had taken very great effect both there and in South Carolina. Brother Andrew Bryan, a black minister at Savannah, has TWO HUNDRED MEMBERS, in full fellowship and had certificates from their owners of ONE HUNDRED MORE, who had given in their experiences and were ready to be baptized. Also I received accounts from Nova Scotia of a black Baptist preacher, Brother David George, who was a member of the church at Savannah; he had the permission of the Governor to preach in three provinces; his members in full communion were then *sixty*, white and black, the Gospel spreading. Brother Amos is at Providence, he writes me that the Gospel has taken good effect, and is spreading greatly; he has about THREE HUNDRED MEMBERS. Brother Jessy Gaulsing, another black minister, preaches near Augusta, in South Carolina, at a place where I used to preach; he was a member of the church at Savannah, and has *sixty members*; and a great work is going on there.

"I agree to election, redemption, the fall of Adam, regeneration, and perseverance, knowing the promise is to all who endure, in grace, faith, and good works, to the end, shall be saved.

"There is no Baptist church in this country but ours. We have purchased a piece of land, at the east end of Kingston, containing three acres for the sum of 155 l. currency, and on it have begun a meeting-house fifty-seven feet in length by thirty-seven in breadth. We have raised the brick wall eight feet high from the foundation, and intend to have a gallery. Several gentlemen, members of the house of assembly, and other gentlemen, have subscribed towards the building about 40 l. The chief part of our congregation are SLAVES, and their owners allow them, in common, but three or four bits per week for allowance to feed themselves; and out of so small a sum we cannot expect any thing that can be of service from them; if we did it would soon bring a scandal upon religion; and the FREE PEOPLE in our society are but poor, but they are all willing, both free and slaves, to do what they can. As for my part, I am too much entangled with the affairs of the world to go on," as I would, "with my design, in supporting the cause: this has, I acknowledge, been a great hindrance to the Gospel in one way; but as I have endeavored to set a good example" of industry "before the inhabitants of the land, it has given general satisfaction another way. . . . And, Rev. Sir, we think the Lord has put it in the power of the Baptist societies in England to help and assist us in completing this building, which we look upon will be the greatest undertaking ever was in this country for the bringing of souls from darkness into the light of the Gospel. . . . And as the Lord has put it into your heart to enquire after us, we place all our confidence in you, to make our circumstances known to the several Baptist churches in England; and we look upon you as our father, friend, and brother.

"Within the brick wall we have a shelter, in which we worship, until our building can be accomplished.

"Your . . . letter was read to the church two or three times, and did create a great deal of love and warmness throughout the whole congregation, who shouted for joy and comfort, to think that the Lord had been so gracious as to satisfy us in this country with the very same religion with . . . our beloved brethren in the old country, according to the scriptures; and that such a worthy . . . of London, should write in so loving a manner to such poor worms as we are. And I beg leave to say, That the whole congregation sang out that they would, through the assistance of God, remember you in their prayers. They altogether give their Christian love to you, and all the worthy professors of Jesus Christ in your church at London, and beg the prayers of your congregation, and the prayers of the churches in general, wherever it pleases you to make known our circumstances. I remain with the utmost love . . . Rev. Sir, your unworthy fellow-labourer, servant, and brother in Christ."

(Signed) George Liele.

A Letter from the Negro Baptist Church in Savannah, Addressed to the Reverend Doctor Rippon

Savannah-Georgia, U.S.A., Dec. 23, 1800.

My Dear and Reverend Brother,

After a long silence occasioned by various hindrances, I sit down to answer your inestimable favour by the late dear Mr. White, who I hope is rejoicing, far above the troubles and trials of this frail sinful state. All the books mentioned in your truly condescending and affectionate letter, came safe, and were distributed according to your humane directions. You can scarcely conceive, much less than I describe, the gratitude excited by so seasonably and precious a supply of the means of knowledge and grace, accompanied with benevolent proposals of further assistance.

Deign, dear sir, to accept our united and sincere thanks for your great kindness to us, who have been so little accustomed to such attentions. Be assured that our prayers have ascended, and I trust will continue to ascend to God, for your health and happiness, and that you may be rendered a lasting ornament to our holy Religion, and a successful Minister of the Gospel.

With much pleasure, I inform you, dear sir, that I enjoy good health, and am strong in body, tho' sixty-three years old, and am blessed with a pious wife, whose freedom I have obtained, and an only daughter and child who is married to a free man, tho' she, and consequently, under our laws, her seven children, five sons and two daughters, are slaves. By a kind Providence I am well provided for, as to worldly comforts, (tho' I have had very little given me as a minister) having a house and lot in this city, besides the land on which several buildings stand, for which I receive a small rent, and a fifty-six acre tract of land, with all necessary buildings, four miles in the country, and eight slaves; for whose education and happiness, I am enabled thro' mercy to provide.

But what will be infinitely more interesting to my friend, and is so much more prized by myself, we enjoy the rights of conscience to a valuable extent, worshiping in our families and preaching three times every Lord's-day, baptizing frequently from ten to thirty at a time in the Savannah, and administering the sacred supper, not only without molestation, but in the presence, and with the approbation and encouragement of many of the white people. We are now about seven hundred in number, and the work of the Lord goes on prosperously.

An event which has had a happy influence on our affairs was the coming of Mr. Holcombe, late pastor of Euhaw Church, to this place at the call of the heads of the city, of all denominations, who have remained for the thirteen months he has been here among his constant hearers and his liberal supporters. His salary is 2000 a year. He has just had a baptistery, with convenient appendages, built in his place of worship, and has commenced baptizing.

Another dispensation of Providence has much strengthened our hands, and increased our means of information; Henry Francis, lately a slave to the widow of the late Colonel Leroy Hammond, of Augusta, has been purchased by a few humane gentlemen of this place, and liberated to exercise the handsome ministerial gifts he possesses amongst us, and teach our youth to read and write. He is a strong man about forty-nine years of age, whose mother was white and whose father was an Indian. His wife and only son are slaves.

Brother Francis has been in the ministry fifteen years, and will soon receive ordination, and will probably become the pastor of a branch of my large church, which is getting too unwieldy for one body. Should this event take place, and his charge receive constitution, it will take the rank and title of the 3rd Baptist Church in Savannah.

With the most sincere and ardent prayers to God for your temporal and eternal welfare, and with the most unfeigned gratitude, I remain, reverend and dear sir, your obliged servant in the gospel.

(Signed) Andrew Bryan.

P.S. I should be glad that my African friends could hear the above account of my affairs.

SUPPLEMENTARY READINGS

Brooks, Walter H. "The Priority of the Silver Bluff Church and Its Promoters." *The Journal of Negro History* 7, no. 2 (April 1922): 172–96.

Holmes, Edward A. "George Liele: Negro Slavery's Prophet of Deliverance." *Foundations* 9, no. 4 (October–December 1966): 333–45.

Simms, James M. *The First Colored Baptist Church in North America, Constituted at Savannah, Georgia, January 20, A.D. 1788.* Philadelphia: J. B. Lippincott, 1888.

Sobel, Mechal. *Trabelin' On: The Slave Journey to an Afro-Baptist Faith.* Westport, Conn.: Greenwood Press, 1979.

Thomas, Edgar G. *The First African Baptist Church of North America.* Savannah, Ga.: By the Author, 1925.

6

LEMUEL HAYNES

A Black Puritan's Farewell

Born at West Hartford, Connecticut, in 1753, of a white mother and black father, Lemuel Haynes lived his entire eighty years in Congregationalist New England. He completed his indenture in time to serve in the Continental Army. Privately tutored, he became in 1785 the first Afro-American to be ordained by any religious denomination. He served white congregations for more than thirty years. Haynes achieved remarkable notoriety for a sermon entitled Universal Salvation that defended orthodox Calvinism against the threat of Universalism. Middlebury College awarded him the master's degree, honoris causa, in 1804, another first for Afro-Americans.

When he was sixty-five, Haynes left his Rutland, Vermont, parish under circumstances that suggest both racial and political friction. His farewell sermon of 1818 rehearses the trials and tribulations of a black minister to a white congregation, yet it dwells not so much on the matter of color as on the necessity for spiritual renewal and discipline. Haynes felt the burden of increasing age and was weary of trying to stem the growing impiety of his flock. He expresses the urgency of one hastening toward the divine bar of justice. He left Rutland in May, 1818, served briefly at Manchester, Vermont, and spent his declining years at Granville, New York, a stone's throw across the Vermont border. He died in 1833, having composed a fitting epitaph: "Here lies the dust of a poor hell-deserving sinner, who ventured into eternity trusting wholly on the merits of Christ for salvation. In the full belief of the great doctrines he preached while on earth, he invites his children and all who read this, to trust their eternal interest on the same foundation."

My Brethren and Friends,

The church of Christ in this place was organized forty-two years ago the 20th day of October last, by the assistance of the Rev. Benajah Roots, my worthy predecessor.

It was thirty years ago, the 28th day of March last, since I took the

Source: *The Sufferings, Support, and Reward of Faithful Ministers, Illustrated. Being the Substance of Two Valedictory Discourses. Delivered at Rutland, West Parish, May 24th, A.D. 1818.* Bennington, Vt.: Darius Clark, 1820. Pp. 20–27.

pastoral care of this church and people; the church then consisted of
forty-two members; since which time, there has been about three hundred and twelve added to it, about sixty have been removed by death,
and about four hundred have died in this society, including those above
mentioned.—There are only ten of the church now living in this place
who were here when I first came among you; the greater part sleep in
death. I have preached about five thousand five hundred discourses, four
hundred of them have been funeral sermons. I have solemnized more
than an hundred marriages.—During this period we have had two remarkable seasons of the out-pourings of the spirit, as well as some re-
freshings at other times, which many of us who are yet alive recognize
with emotions of joy. Twice I have been brought, in my own apprehensions, to the borders of the grave; but God has spared me to see this day
of trial, which I desire to meet with resignation to His will.

The flower of my life has been devoted to your service:—and while
I lament a thousand imperfections which have attended my ministry;
yet if I am not deceived, it has been my hearty desire to do something
for the salvation of your souls. He that provided the motto of our discourse could say on his farewell, I have coveted no man's silver or gold,
or apparel.—Yea, ye yourselves know, that these hands have ministered
unto my necessity. The appropriation of such language is in a degree
congenial with the testimony that many present could give, and might
be admitted were it not for the danger of comparison. I have sometimes
thought that, perhaps God designed that I should spend the few of my
remaining days among you, and with a degree of satisfaction I have
looked into the repository of the dead, adjoining this house, intending to
sleep with them, claiming a sort of kindred dust, intending to rise with
them; but the ways of God are mysterious, who often destroys the hope
of man. In my solitary reflections, I cast a look towards this house, to
bid it a final adieu; but in spite of all that fortitude, dictated by reason
and religion, the sympathetic tear will betray the imbecility of human
nature. Can we suppose that even a Paul was unmoved, when they all
wept sore, and fell on his neck, sorrowing most of all that they should see
his face no more, Acts, xx, 37, 38.

A three years ministry had excited such reciprocal endearments, that
made the parting like tearing soul and body asunder. More than one
thousand five hundred Sabbaths have I spent with you, the most of them
in this house. More than one hundred and thirty seasons of communion
have we enjoyed around the table of the Lord. Oh! how many sweet and
comfortable days have I spent in this house with you that are alive, and
those who are dead! We have taken sweet counsel together; I trust I have

at times felt the powerful presence of Christ, while speaking from this desk; cannot we adopt the language of the Psalmist,

> " 'Tis with a mournful pleasure now,
> "I think on ancient days:
> "When to thy house did numbers go,
> "And all our work was praise."

It appears in the course of Divine Providence that my labours among you have come to an end. We have done meeting in this house; I am called to give you the parting hand; but let us all remember that a very solemn meeting awaits us at that day suggested in my text, when we shall all have finished our course.

Our meeting at that day will greatly differ from what it has been in this house: I have often been here and found but few within these walls, some trifling excuse has detained you; but at that day, it will not be optional with people whether they attend or not, all will be there: the congregation will be full, not one in a town, state, or in the world, but what will appear. Some times you have manifested great stupidity, and I have witnessed drowsiness and carelessness while I have been speaking; but at that day you will be awake, and be all attention. You will believe, realize, and feel interested in the things exhibited. Often through the depravity of the human heart, and the prejudice that sinners have to the truth, and to the servants of Christ, they will turn their backs on divine worship, and leave the house of God: But when ministers and people meet before the tribunal of Christ, there will be no deserting or quitting the assembly, there they must hear, however disagreeable their preaching will be, and tormenting to their consciences. In this house our meeting has been promiscuous, or indiscriminate; saints and sinners sit on the same seat; around the same table, we cannot certainly say who has, and who has not on the wedding garment; but at the day of judgment there will be an exact separation, Christ will separate the sheep from the goats.

In this house we have *often* met, not less than four thousand times; we go and we come: Although we see no fruit of our labour, we do not wholly despair, we hope God may yet bless his word; but when ministers and people meet before the bar of God, it will be the last interview, none to follow it: The case of sinners will then be forever hopeless, and helpless.

One great design of our meeting together in this world is to offer salvation to sinners, to entreat and to beseech them to be reconciled to

God; but at the day of judgment an irreversible sentence will be pronounced on the righteous and on the wicked; the saints will be rewarded, and sinners condemned, and sent to endless perdition.

When the ambassadors of Christ have finished their course, and meet their people a critical examination will take place; I must give an account concerning the motives which influenced me to come among you, and how I have conducted during my thirty years residence in this place: the doctrines I have inculcated: whether I have designedly kept back any thing that might be profitable to you, or have, through fear of man, or any other criminal cause, shunned to declare the whole counsel of God. Also, as to the *manner* of my preaching, whether I have delivered my discourses in a cold, formal manner, and of my external deportment. You, who have been the people of my charge, must give an account, what improvement you have made of my ministry: Whether you have attended as you ought: whether your excuses for withdrawing from public worship at any time, were sufficient. God will attend to them, and they will be weighted in a just balance: not a single neglect will escape divine notice. We have a thousand excuses, when put in the scale of the sanctuary, will be lighter than a feather.

You must give a strict account as to the *manner* of your attending in this house: whether you have received the word with joy, and obeyed its precepts. Parents must render an account, whether they have taught their children, by precept and example, to reverence the word of God, and respect the servants of Christ. Whether they have endeavoured to maintain or support the influence of their minister among the youth of rising generation, and so been workers together with him. Whether the servants of Christ do not fall into contempt in a measure through their instrumentality. People will be examined whether they have contributed to the temporal support of the ministers of Christ; it will not be left with men how much they ought to impart; but God will be the judge how much was suitable, and whether it was agreeable to the word of God, and the exigencies of the preacher.

On the separation of a minister from his people there are often very criminal causes existing, either on the part of the minister, or people, or both. There may be *pretended* reasons while the truth may be kept out of sight, to escape censure.—Ecclesiastical councils may think it inexpedient to make any inquiry into the matter; but they will have a plain, candid and thorough investigation before the tribunal of Christ. No deception, no hypocrisy will be concealed under religious pretences; but it will all be detected and exposed before the assembled universe, and the hearts of all men be revealed.

"Nothing but truth before his throne,
"With honour can appear:
"The painted hypocrites are known
"Through the disguise they wear."

The accusations brought against the ministers of Christ will be examined. Ministers will fare no better for the name they sustain; their wickedness will be exposed; they condemned, or exonerated, not according to popular noise and clamour, but coincident to truth and equity. These are scenes, my brethren, that are just opening before us, and to which we are hastening with the utmost rapidity. These are things that should move us, and call up our attention. It is a small, very small thing to be judged of man's judgment. Oh! let us labour to be found of God in peace. This day to me in some respects is very solemn and interesting, on which I am called to give you the parting hand: but its importance is eclipsed when contrasted with that awful period when we are to meet before him, who is to judge the quick and the dead.

There you and I must shortly appear. Much has been said on the subject of my dismission: that it has been in consequence of my request. I think I have been sufficiently explicit on the matter; but I am willing to repeat it in this public manner, that had the people been united, wholesome discipline properly exercised, a firm and unshaken attachment to the cause of God manifested among all the professors of religion, I should have chosen to have continued with you, at the expense of temporal emolument; but considering the divisions existing, and the uncommon stupidity prevalent, I have been fully satisfied that it was my duty to be dismissed, and have requested my friends not to oppose it. I am persuaded that it will appear another day, that unfaithfulness in the minister did not originate the event, to the exclusion of criminal causes in this society; but this matter is laid over to the day of final decision. I trust I feel in a degree reconciled: knowing that God's way is in the sea, and in the deep waters, and his footsteps are unknown.

I find my strength in a degree inadequate to itinerant labours, and that I am shortly to put off this my tabernacle; but I purpose, so long as life and health continues, to preach the same gospel that I have been publishing to you for more than thirty years, and on which, I humbly hope, I have ventured my eternal salvation. O that I may be enabled to discharge the duty with greater zeal and fidelity! And now I am called to go, not to Jerusalem, but from place to place, not knowing the things that shall befall me, saving what the Holy Ghost, and the providence of God witnesseth in every city, that trials await me; but I hope I can in some small degree say, But none of these things move me, neither count I my life dear unto myself, so that I might finish my course with joy, and the ministry which I have received of the Lord Jesus, to testify the gospel of the grace of God.

My dear brethren and friends, I did not realize my attachment to you before the parting time came. Many disagreeable things have taken place; but still I feel my heart going out toward this people. How many pleasant days have I spent with you in this house? How many hours under your roofs, and delightful visits in your families? I will not except a single door that has not been hospitably opened for my reception. Many kindnesses have I received from you, both in sickness and in health. You will accept my warmest gratitude for the many instances of kindness shown me. I hope, my dear brethren and sisters in the Lord, that you will still remember me at the throne of grace; that God would support me under every trial, and that he would render the evening of my life useful to the church of God: that utterance may be given unto me, that I may open my mouth boldly to make known the mystery of the gospel.

May the great head of the church send you a pastor after his own heart, vastly superior in gifts and grace to him who is giving you his farewell address. 'Tis a distressing thought to think that I am about to leave any of you in an unconverted state: that my labour among you will prove to your heavier condemnation. Particularly let me call on you that are young: this house, and your own consciences, are witnesses that I have repeatedly called on you to attend to the important concerns of your never, never dying souls, and I fear too many of you in vain. Have you not turned a deaf ear to the calls and invitations of the gospel? and to the solemn warnings of God in his providence? I fear you are going down to eternal destruction under the intolerable weight of aggravated sins. I will now, perhaps for the last time, invite you to Jesus, the God-man Mediator. Some of your parents on a death bed have charged me with their dying breath, to be faithful to you; should it appear at our meeting at the day of judgment, that I have in any good measure answered their request, must I re-echo to the tremendous sentence of the judge, depart, Amen! Amen! Oh! how dreadful! how heart-rending the anticipation! Must this be the case? Nothing but a speedy and thorough repentance and turning unto God can prevent it.—Dear youth, your souls were once committed to me, I would now commit them to him, who is able to keep you from falling, and present you faultless before the presence of his glory, with exceeding joy.

In general you have treated me with respect; I do not remember of ever receiving an insult from a single youth.—Many of your parents sleep in dust, where I must shortly be; should I be so happy as to sit down with them in the kingdom of heaven, and should you arrive to those blissful regions, Oh! what a blessed interview! With what ecstatic joy and congratulation should we present the offering before the throne of God, with the humble, grateful, and astonishing exclamation, Here Lord we are, and the natural and spiritual children thou hast graciously given us!

You will shortly hear of the death of the speaker: whether his grave will be here or elsewhere, is to us uncertain; O remember that those icy fingers were once employed in writing sermons for you, those lips, that are now chained in gloomy silence, were once speaking to you, in accents that were sounding from Sabbath to Sabbath, and from year to year within the walls of this house: that his soul has taken its flight to yonder tribunal, where a rehearsal of those discourses, that you have heard from him, will be made in your ears, and before the assembled universe. Ministers, who have finished their course, may be useful to people after they are dead: this is an idea suggested by a dying apostle, 2 Pet. i. 15. Moreover, I will endeavour that you may be able after my decease to have these things always in remembrance. How far, consistent with truth, and christian modesty, I may adopt the language of the holy apostle, ver. 26. will be better known hereafter. Wherefore I take you to record this day, that I am pure from the blood of all men: for I have not shunned to declare unto you the whole counsel of God.

It was for your sake principally that your fathers called me here, they sat under my ministry but a short time, their memory is still precious, and though dead still speak. O! for their sake, and for your souls sake, and above all for the sake of him that created you, hearken to the things that concern your eternal interest. Could you consider your former minister worthy of any respect, I beseech you to manifest it by preparing to meet him, and be a crown of his rejoicing in the day of the Lord Jesus. You that are young will be those who will compose this society within a short time: we who are advanced in life must soon leave you.

Let me warn you against Sabbath breaking, against neglecting the public worship of God. Willingly and promptly contribute to the support of the gospel ministry, as you would prosper in this world, and meet your judge in peace. Beware of carnal dissipation, a sin which I have often warned you against. Beware of slander and detraction, those banes of society; the influence of which, even among us, you cannot be strangers to. According to scripture testimony, they have their origin in hell, James iii, 6. and are incorporated with characters not very ornamental to human nature, nor do they stand fair candidates for the kingdom of heaven, 1 Cor. vi. 9, 10. Know ye not that the unrighteous shall not inherit the kingdom of God? be not deceived; neither fornicators, nor idolaters, nor aduterers, nor effeminate, nor abusers of themselves with mankind; nor thieves, nor covetous, nor drunkards, nor REVILERS, nor extortioners, shall inherit the kingdom of God.

Suffer me to warn you against false doctrines, such as are pleasing to the carnal heart. The inventions of men are skilful in exciting prejudices to the plain truths of the gospel:—hence it is, that faithful ministers are accused with being too pointed and unpolite in their discourses. Beware of false teachers, and of being led astray by the errors of the present day. Remember there are damnable *heresies* as well as damnable *practices*. Paul predicted this danger, ver. 29: For I know this that after my departing shall grievous wolves enter in among you, not sparing the flock. But, beloved, I would hope better things of you, things that accompany salvation, though I thus speak. Dear children, and lambs of the flock, you have in a sense for a time been committed to my care; with the tenderest affection I would, in the arms of faith, bear you to that divine Saviour, who has said, suffer little children to come unto me, and forbid them not: for of such is the kingdom of God. May your cheerful hosannahs fill this house, when your fathers and mothers, shall sleep in dust.

My friends in general,

Whatever we have seen amiss in each other, it becomes us to exercise forgiveness, as we hope God, for Christ's sake hath forgiven us, and as we would find mercy in that day. How often have our united prayers ascended up in this house; may we not forget each other for time to come. Live in peace, and may the God of peace be with you. May my family have a care in your affections, and intercessions, who have been brought up among you; they will doubtless soon be left without parents. May the wife of my youth, who has been my companion in tribulation, whose health and strength, and domestic ease have been sacrificed and devoted to your service; should she survive me, not be forgotten. As I still continue to reside among you, should you at any time be destitute of a minister on a sick bed, be ready to send for me; it will be the rejoicing of my heart to do all I can to comfort you in the hour of distress, and to facilitate the groans and terrors of a dying moment; I request the same from you, as there is opportunity.

And now brethren, I commend you to God, and to the word of his grace, which is able to build you up, and to give you an inheritance among all them which are sanctified. Amen.

SUPPLEMENTARY READINGS

Cooley, Timothy M. *Sketches of the Life and Character of the Rev. Lemuel Haynes.* New York: Harper and Bros., 1837; reprint, Westport, Conn.: Negro Universities Press, 1969.

Douglass, Paul. *Black Apostle to Yankeeland: Egalitarian Catchcolt Who Overlived His Caste.* Brandon, Vt.: The Sullivans, 1972.

Greene, Lorenzo J. *The Negro in Colonial New England.* New York: Atheneum, 1968.

MacLam, Helen M. "Black Puritan on the Northern Frontier: The Vermont Ministry of Lemuel Haynes." In *Black Apostles at Home and Abroad,* edited by David W. Wills and Richard Newman. Boston: G. K. Hall, 1982. Pp. 3–20.

Newman, Richard. *Lemuel Haynes: A Bio-bibliography.* New York: Lambeth Press, 1984.

TWO

Slave Religion in the Antebellum South

PETER RANDOLPH

Plantation Churches: Visible and Invisible

Peter Randolph's pious slave mother told him to "look to Jesus," but when he scrutinized the words and deeds of the white preachers of Prince George County, Virginia, he saw hypocrisy in the seat of holy instruction. The slaves yearned for greater spiritual refreshing in their communal meetings and often stole away to Jesus by assembling in the quarters, swamps, and "hush harbors." There they could hold meetings with preachers of their own. There they consoled one another, prayed, sang, and, as Randolph remembered, joined in ritual movement patterned after the African "ring-shout." They lifted up the name of Jesus as their liberator and held forth the vision of a better day when there would be no more cowskin lashes. Such secretive meetings were always prey to disruption by the white authorities. Slave preachers risked much in daring to defy laws that prohibited blacks gathering for religious purposes without the supervision of whites. Randolph endured until 1847 when he was emancipated upon the death of his owner. Licensed a Baptist minister, he served as an antislavery agent, ministered in the North and among fugitive slaves in Canada, and ran a small newspaper business. After the Civil War this redoubtable man took charge of the pulpit of the Ryland or Old African Baptist Church in Richmond, Virginia. Here he witnessed the merging of what has been called the "invisible institution" of the slaves with the black churches of the freedom generation.

MANY SAY the Negroes receive religious education—that Sabbath worship is instituted for them as for others, and were it not for slavery, they would die in their sins—that really, the institution of slavery is a benevolent missionary enterprise. Yes, they are preached to, and I will give my readers some faint glimpses of these preachers, and their doctrines and practices.

In Prince George County there were two meeting-houses intended for public worship. Both were occupied by the Baptist denomination.

Source: *Slave Cabin to the Pulpit, The Autobiography of Reverend Peter Randolph: The Southern Question Illustrated and Sketches of Slave Life.* Boston: James H. Earle, 1893. Pp. 196–204.

These houses were built by William and George Harrison, brothers. Mr. G. Harrison's was built on the line of his brother's farm, that their slaves might go there on the Sabbath and receive instruction, such as slave-holding ministers would give. The prominent preaching to the slaves was, " 'Servants, obey your masters'. Do not *steal* or *lie*, for this is very wrong. Such conduct is sinning against the Holy Ghost, *and is base ingratitude to your kind masters, who feed, clothe and protect you.*" All Gospel, my readers! It was great policy to build a church for the *"dear slave"*, and allow him the wondrous privilege of such holy instruction! Edloe's slaves sometimes obtained the consent of Harrison to listen to the Sabbath teachings so generously dealt out to his servants. Shame! shame! to take upon yourselves the name of Christ, with all that blackness of heart. I should think, when making such statements, the slaveholders would feel the rebuke of the Apostle, and fall down and be carried out from the face of day, as were Ananias and Sapphira, when they betrayed the trust committed to them, or refused to bear true testimony in regard to that trust.

There was another church, about fourteen miles from the one just mentioned. It was called "Brandon's church", and there the white Baptists worshiped. Edloe's slaves sometimes went there. The colored people had a very small place allotted them to sit in, so they used to get as near the window as they could to hear the preacher talk to his congregation. But sometimes, while the preacher was exhorting to obedience, some of those outside would be selling refreshments, cake, candy and rum, and others would be horse-racing. This was the way, my readers, the Word of God was delivered and received in Prince George County. The Gospel was so mixed with slavery, that the people could see no beauty in it, and feel no reverence for it.

There was one Brother Shell who used to preach. One Sabbath, while exhorting the poor, impenitent, hard-hearted, ungrateful slaves, so much beloved by their masters, to repentance and prayerfulness, while entreating them to lead good lives, that they might escape the wrath (of the lash) to come, some of his crocodile tears overflowed his cheek, which so affected his hearers, that they shouted and gave thanks to God, that Brother Shell had at length felt the spirit of the Lord in his heart; and many went away rejoicing that a heart of stone had become softened. But, my readers, Monday morning, Brother Shell was afflicted with his old malady, hardness of heart, so that he was obliged to catch one of the sisters by the throat, and give her a terrible flogging.

The like of this is the preaching, and these are the men that spread the Gospel among the slaves. Ah! such a Gospel had better be buried in oblivion, for it makes more heathens than Christians. Such preachers ought to be forbidden by the laws of the land ever to mock again at the blessed religion of Jesus, which was sent as a light to the world.

Another Sunday, when Shell was expounding (very much engaged was he in his own attempts to enlighten his hearers), there was one Jem Fulcrum became so enlightened that he fell from his seat quite a distance to the floor. Brother Shell thought he had preached unusually well so to affect Jem; so he stopped in the midst of his sermon, and asked, "Is that poor Jemmy? poor fellow!" But, my readers, he did not know the secret—*brother Jem had fallen asleep.* Poor Shell did not do so much good as he thought he had, so Monday morning he gave Jem enough of his raw-hide spirit to last him all the week; at least, till the next Sabbath, when he could have an opportunity to preach to him.

I could only think, when Shell took so much glory to himself for the effect of his preaching upon the slaves, of the man who owned colored Pompey. This slave-holder was a great fighter (as most of them are), and had prepared himself for the contest with great care, and wished to know how he looked; so he said, "Pompey, how do I look?" "Oh, massa, *mighty!*" "What do you mean by 'mighty', Pompey?" "Why, massa, you look noble." "What do you mean by 'noble'?" "Why, sar, you look just like one *lion.*" "Why, Pompey, where have you ever seen a lion?" "I seen one down in yonder field the other day, massa." "Pompey, you foolish fellow, that was a *jackass.*" "Was it, massa? Well, you look just like him."

This may seem very simple to my readers, but surely, nothing more noble than a jackass, without his simplicity and innocence, can that man be, who will rise up as an advocate of this system of wrong. He who trains his dogs to hunt foxes, and enjoys the hunt or the horse-race on the Sabbath, who teaches his blood-hounds to follow upon the track of the freedom-loving Negro, is not more guilty or immoral than he who stands in a northern pulpit, and hunts down the flying fugitive, or urges his hearers to bind the yoke again upon the neck of the escaped bondman. He who will lisp one word in favor of a system which will send blood-hounds through the forests of Virginia, the Carolinas, Georgia, Kentucky, and all the South, chasing human beings (who are seeking the inalienable rights of all men, "life, liberty, and the pursuit of happiness,") possesses no heart; and that minister of religion who will do it is unworthy his trust, knows not what the Gospel teaches, and had better turn to the heathen for a religion to guide him nearer the right; for the heathen in their blindness have some regard for the rights of others, and seldom will they invade the honor and virtue of their neighbors, or cause them to be torn in pieces by infuriated beasts.

Mr. James L. Goltney was a Baptist preacher, and was employed by

Mr. M. B. Harrison to give religious instruction to his slaves. He often used the common text: "Servants, obey your masters." He would try to make it appear that he knew what the slaves were thinking of—telling them they thought they had a right to be free, but he could tell them better—referring them to some passages of Scripture. "It is the devil," he would say, "who tells you to try and be free." And again he bid them be patient at work, warning them that it would be his duty to whip them, if they appeared dissatisfied—all which would be pleasing to God! "If you run away, you will be turned out of God's church, until you repent, return, and ask God and your master's pardon." In this way he would continue to preach his slave-holding gospel.

This same Goltney used to administer the Lord's Supper to the slaves. After such preaching, let no one say that the slaves have the Gospel of Jesus preached to them.

One of the Baptist ministers was named B. Harrison. He owned slaves, and was very cruel to them. He came to an untimely end. While he was riding out one afternoon, the report of a gun was heard, and he was found dead—his brains being blown out. It could never be found who killed him, and so he went to judgment, with all his sins on his head.

Mr. L. Hanner was a Christian preacher, selecting texts like the following: "The Spirit of the Lord is upon me, because he hath anointed me to preach deliverance to the captives, he hath sent me to bind up the broken-hearted." But Hanner was soon mobbed out of Prince George County, and had to flee for his life, and all for preaching a true Gospel to colored people.

I did not know of any other denomination where I lived in Virginia, than the Baptists and Presbyterians. Most of the colored people, and many of the poorer class of whites, were Baptists.

On the Sabbath, after doing their morning work, and breakfast over (such as it was), that portion of the slaves who belong to the church ask of the overseer permission to attend meeting. If he is in the mood to grant their request, he writes them a pass, as follows:—

"Permit the bearer to pass and repass to ———, *this evening, unmolested."*

Should a pass not be granted, the slave lies down, and sleeps for the day—the only way to drown his sorrow and disappointment.

Others of the slaves, who do not belong to the church, spend their Sabbath in playing with marbles, and other games, for each other's food, etc.

Some occupy the time in dancing to the music of a banjo, made out of a large gourd. This is continued till the after part of the day, when they separate, and gather wood for their log-cabin fires the ensuing week.

Not being allowed to hold meetings on the plantation, the slaves assemble in the swamps, out of reach of the patrols. They have an understanding among themselves as to the time and place of getting together. This is often done by the first one arriving breaking boughs from the trees, and bending them in the direction of the selected spot. Arrangements are then made for conducting the exercises. They first ask each other how they feel, the state of their minds, etc. The male members then select a certain space, in separate groups, for their division of the meeting. Preaching in order, by the brethren; then praying and singing all round, until they generally feel quite happy. The speaker usually commences by calling himself unworthy, and talks very slowly, until, feeling the spirit, he grows excited, and in a short time, there fall to the ground twenty or thirty men and women under its influence. Enlightened people call it excitement; but I wish the same was felt by everybody, so far as they are sincere.

The slave forgets all his sufferings, except to remind others of the trials during the past week, exclaiming: "Thank God, I shall not live here always!" Then they pass from one to another, shaking hands, and bidding each other farewell, promising, should they meet no more on earth, to strive and meet in heaven, where all is joy, happiness and liberty. As they separate, they sing a parting hymn of praise.

Sometimes the slaves meet in an old log-cabin, when they find it necessary to keep a watch. If discovered, they escape, if possible; but those who are caught often get whipped. Some are willing to be punished thus for Jesus' sake. Most of the songs used in worship are composed by the slaves themselves, and describe their own sufferings. Thus:

> "Oh, that I had a bosom friend,
>   To tell my secrets to,
> One always to depend upon
>   In everything I do!"

> "How I do wander, up and down!
> I seem a stranger, quite undone;
> None to lend an ear to my complaint,
> No one to cheer me, though I faint."

Some of the slaves sing—

> "No more rain, no more snow,
> No more cowskin on my back!"

Then they change it by singing—

"Glory be to God that rules on high."

In some places, if the slaves are caught praying to God, they are whipped more than if they had committed a great crime. The slave-holders will allow the slaves to dance, but do not want them to pray to God. Sometimes, when a slave, on being whipped, calls upon God, he is forbidden to do so, under threat of having his throat cut, or brains blown out. Oh, reader! this seems very hard—that slaves cannot call on their Maker, when the case most needs it. Sometimes the poor slave takes courage to ask his master to let him pray, and is driven away, with the answer, that if discovered praying, his back will pay the bill.

SUPPLEMENTARY READINGS

Blassingame, John W. *The Slave Community*. Rev. ed. New York: Oxford University Press, 1979. Chap. 3.

Genovese, Eugene D. *Roll, Jordan, Roll: The World the Slaves Made*. New York: Pantheon Books, 1974. Bk. 2, pt. 1.

Levine, Lawrence E. *Black Culture and Black Consciousness*. New York: Oxford University Press, 1977. Chaps. 1 and 2.

Raboteau, Albert J. *Slave Religion*. New York: Oxford University Press, 1978. Chaps. 3–5.

Sernett, Milton C. *Black Religion and American Evangelicalism: White Protestants, Plantation Missions, and the Flowering of Negro Christianity, 1787–1865*. Metuchen, N.J.: Scarecrow Press, 1975. Chap. 4.

8

SISTER KELLY

"Proud of That 'Ole Time' Religion"

Those who wore the shoe of slavery have left a legacy of oral witness testifying to the power of the conversion experience. Thousands of interviews with aged ex-slaves are now on record. Ophelia Settle Egypt, while a member of the research staff of the Social Science Institute at Fisk University, conducted interviews with former slaves in Tennessee and Kentucky during 1929 and 1930. One of her respondents, Sister Kelly, a washerwoman in Nashville after the Civil War, described in vivid detail the classic conversion or "God struck me dead" experience. Sister Kelly had participated in the gatherings of slaves for singing and praying around a turned-over pot, one ordinarily used for boiling clothes but employed in the secretive meetings to "keep the white folks from meddling." This widely reported practice suggests at least symbolic continuity with traditional West African sacrificial vessels. At the age of twelve Sister Kelly got religion. The verb is important, for her conversion did not follow upon a period of mystic seclusion or intellectual contemplation of the truth claims of the various Christian denominations. As with most of the ex-slave conversion accounts, she testifies to an existential experience credited to the "holy uplifting spirit" of God. This transformation of self gave Sister Kelly confidence to deal with whatever life had in store for one of God's "little ones."

WELL, CHILE, I tell you, my mind ain't on old times today but I'll tell you what I kin. When the War broke out I had three little children. You know when I come along we didn't know our ages nor nothing. They stealed just like they stealed now, times ain't changed much, and people ain't changed none, you kin take that from ole sister Kelly. The white folks throwed the book what had our ages in it in the fire to keep us from having it, and none of us never knowed just how old we was.

When I was about 12 years old, just look like one day the stars was falling, and it got just as dark as it could be. If you wants me to tell you what a hard time the po' ole slave had working and gitting whupped,

Source: *Unwritten History of Slavery: Autobiographical Accounts of Negro Ex-slaves.* Nashville: Fisk University, 1945; reprint ed., Washington, D.C.: Microcard Editions, 1968. Pp. 81–84.

and sech like a that, I knows about that, yessir, and I ain't forgot neither. I never will forget none of that this side of the grave. I have plowed many a field, honey. Sometime, we was in the field time it was daylight, and sometime even before day broke; we would work there all day, then we had to shell corn at night when it was too dark to bend yo' back any longer in the field. Everybody had to shell a bushel of corn most every night, after we had come in from the field.

Well, my old marster was dead when I got old enough to know things. He died and left a widow, and she had all us slaves under a overseer and some guardians. Well, she was good as most any old white woman. She was the best white woman that ever broke bread, but you know, honey, that wasn't much, 'cause they all hated the po' nigger. When she died she said the only reason she hated to die was on account of her children; didn't say a word 'bout her po' slaves what had done wuked theyselves to death for her. Her name was Mary Booker, and they had a big farm here near Columbia, Tennessee, just 'bout one mile from the courthouse.

Well, we lived and wuked there till she died, then I was hired out; I was 'bout 13 years old then. Yes, you know white folks is always after the money. I tell you, honey, I wuked and lived with good ones and bad ones, too. You got to know something 'bout the Lord to git along anywhere. You don't know nothing 'bout him? Well, you better know him; better learn 'bout him, that's what'll help you. When the War came I married a man by the name of Jim Kelly, and then he died and I come home and lived on the white folks' place. When Christmas come, we would come home; all the white folks would come from New York and places, and there was sho' nuf fine times, I tell you. Them ole red-headed yaps would bid us off to the highest bidder and we couldn't do nothin' but pray. Yes, fine times for them, but awful for us po' niggers. Yes'm, they would cry you off to the highest bidder for the next year. One by one, we had to get up on that block, and he bid us off.

Well, we used to have little singing and praying like good ole time revival; and we would take pots and put them right in the middle of the floor to keep the sound in the room; yeah, keep the white folks from meddling. Yes'm, the sound will stay right in the room after you do that. Well, we allus used these old house wash pots like you boil clothes in, you know. Just turn one down in the middle of the floor, that was sufficient.

Let me tell you how I got it. And I sho' got a good one, too; my 'ligion will stand for all time, I'm a-telling you. One Sunday morning I got up. I was just 12 years old. That morning, I commenced to crying and I just couldn't stop; seem like my heart was full of water. Well, I cried all that morning, and when we got dinner done, I went in and asked the old white woman to let me go home. That was when I was at the Brook place. I never said nothin' 'bout why I wanted to go, I just asked her to let me go. She wouldn't let me leave, o'course, 'cause I was hired out to her. You see, honey, that wasn't the Brook place; that was 'bout four miles from there where I was hired out. Well, then, seem like my heart would bust sho' 'nuf. By and by something just said to me, you go but don't stay long. I went on home and cried most all the way. I couldn't help it to save my life. Well, Ole Miss Mary Brook ask me what was the matter, and I said I didn't know. You know in them times folks had little chairs sitting back in the chimney corner; and I went and set back in there and cried some more. 'Pear like to me I couldn't keep from it, and so by and by she says to me, "Honey, time you was goin' home." I don't know what was the matter with me, but I took and got over the fence and started on down the road. Well, I walked along, and by and by I got down into a little flat place right near a pond, and 'pear like to me something said, "You never shall die a sinner." Well, I jest trembled and shook like a leaf. I know what was the matter with me, then. Well, I heard that voice three times, and every time it said, "You never shall die a sinner." It seem like it was inside of me, somehow or other. I said, "What is that talking to me?" Well, chile, I got happy and I jest went up and down, jest shouting and praying and crying for dear life. I said, "Lord what was that talking to me that way?" I jest asked him like that; ooh yes, good God, I 'members it jest like it was yesterday. Something said like I'm speaking to you right now, "You better gwan, might come back and talk to you again." I stopped right still and started thinking, and seem like a clear loud voice said, "You is jest in God's hands, and you must praise and bless God all the time." Well, honey, you know I was young, and I knowed no more about it than this here rock, but I sho' felt something and I heard something, too.

Well, by and by I kinda got composed and went on up to the house. I didn't know nothin' 'bout it, cept'n I felt funny and sorta light, and I went on in the house and told ole Aunt July. She said, "Chile, jest hold yo' peace, you done been left in God's hands." Well, you know I didn't know what that meant, now you know I was ignorant, jest young, you know. Aunt July told me to pray, pray. Well, I didn't know no more 'bout praying than this here rock. I just cried, 'cause I had nobody to tell me nothing, and nobody what could 'splain the grace of God to me then.

Well, I went on like that for a long time, didn't know nothing 'bout nothin', bless yo' heart, but I jest felt something, didn't know what. I went on my way by myself, and one day I went behind the house and sat down to cry. Well, I got back there and went to sit down, and I tell you the gospel's truth, I kin go and put my hand on the spot right now, where I jest fell face foremost—something just struck me. "Ooh Lord!" I cried, "have mercy on me, a poor hell-deserving sinner." You heard me, I said I didn't know how to pray, but them words jest come to me from nowheres; chile, I fell to crying, jest like I was crazy; I felt right crazy, too, praise God, but I wasn't; it was jest the grace of God I had done been looking for, lo them many weeks. Oooh, merciful Jesus, honey, you ain't never been through all that has you? Why, I went three days and nights without eating and drinking; didn't want nothin', jest was uplifted and free from sin. Somehow or other that morning, I was jest as light as a feather. I got up and I had to go to the foot of the bed to git my clothes, and I stooped down to get 'em, and seem like something jest stopped me, just struck me still, ooh, Jesus, chile, I got right stiff; finally I got my clothes off the floor and wrapped my arms around them right tight, and then, great God, I got upon my knees and prayed the Lord with a prayer that tumbled from my lips, that the Lord had give me to pray hisself—ooh chile, I tell you it's a wonderful feeling when you feel the spirit of the Lord God Almighty in the tips of your fingers, and the bottom of yo' heart. I didn't know then what was the matter with me. I knows now when I feel that spirit arising in my body, yessiree.

Well, I tell you chile, when I got up from prayer, I felt like I was brand new—I had done been washed in Jesus' blood, ooh my great and holy Father! Sometimes I gits to thinking 'bout it and I git happy. Yessirree, chile, if you wants ole sister Kelly to tell you 'bout her 'ligious 'sperience, I sho' kin tell you that, 'cause I sho' been through a great fight with the devil, I tell you, oooh praise God. I didn't know no more 'bout nothin' than this rock, but honey you asks me now, I kin tell you with the very words what God put in my mouth.

That morning, seem like Jesus said to me, "My little one, what makes you so hard to believe, when you know I am the one and only God?"—oooh blessed Jesus, there ain't but one God, honey, and that is the one I am telling you 'bout right now. Yessir, I heard him all on the inside, saying "Come unto me, oh my little one, what makes you so hard to believe when you know I am the one and only God, and there ain't but one God but me?" Seems jest like yesterday 'stid of years and years ago, and I still feels the blessed spirit jest like brand new, ain't like this here rock now, I tell you, oooh praise His holy name.

Well, I still didn't know nothin' 'bout praying, but I says "Oooh, my good and holy Father, what can I say to Thee for Thy blessings," and he said in a voice that shook me like a storm, "Open your mouth and I will fill it with all the elements from on high." Lord, bless his holy name, I never will forget that morning when I was saved by his blood, and changed to the woman you see today. I'm sho' Sister Kelly now.

I tell you, honey, you got to be touched from the inside, and be struck by his hand like I was 'fore you feel that holy uplifting spirit.

Well, the last time the Lord spoke to me, he said, "My little one, I have carried you out of this world, and you is no more of this world, but of another world, the holy world, and they will hate you for my sake." That's the truth, ain't it. I don't fear no man but Jesus. He is my God, do you hear me?

Well, next thing happened to me was when my husband died, and I said, "Lord, why didn't you tell me, why did you take him away from me?" Poor me, I said, "Lord you took him away from me." Well, he spoke to me agin, and he said, "I will forever open the way and provide for you down here on this earth," and he sho' has done it, too, I tell you. The devil tried to cheat me, but I jest held on to His blessed hand. What is written of trouble on the heart is written in His blood, and nobody can take the glory of His name away from you. He sho' guides my trembling feet, I tell you, bless His holy name; He sho' is my heavenly Father, ooh merciful God.

Yes, honey, you jest remember this what Sister Kelly's telling you. This ole world is mighty happy to some of you young folks, but when you is running around having yo' good time, jest remember that you got to stand before the most holy of all, God a'mighty, every deed you done, you gotta give strict account of, you got to know yourself, too, don't never fergit that. When I'm dead and gone on to take my seat beside his blessed throne, you'll 'member what ole Sister Kelly told you.

Honey, right now, you young folks is blind, deaf and dumb to the knowledge of God's name; that can't last, you gonna change, do you hear me? We can't do no good unless we got God in our heart, and our heads, too. Bless God, he holds you in the hollow of his hand, and when he changes yo' soul, you gonna make the world know it, do you hear me? You young folks can't carry on yo' wicked ways without some kinda terrible fall, do you hear me. I ain't caring nothin' 'bout nothing else but God now. He's got me in the hollow of his most holy hand. You youngsters don't understand that, but you mark my word, you will 'fore it's done with. You young folks don't want to humble yourself to the Lord and ask him for these things, but I'm going home to Jesus, yessir, oooh praise His holy name.

After I found Jesus I didn't fool with all these youngsters' pranks. I tell you I'm sorry for you, and you young folks what don't know nothin'. You think this world is all of it, but I tell you it ain't; there's sho' a better world 'n this waiting for all those who trust the Lord, do you hear

me? I'm a-telling you, you better get that ole time religion, that's what
yo'all better do. You got to stand 'fore God for yo'self, jest like me and
anybody else.

Well, you young folks wants to know all 'bout everything but the
Lord; now you wants to know 'bout cures for rheumatism. Well people
used to get polk root, and sasaparilla for rheumatism. Horehound and
catnip and mullin, if you git them and make a syrup, it'll sho' cure a
cold. I've tried it lots a times, and it's good.

Another thing, when a dog bite you, if you git some hair from out
the middle of his back it will draw the poison out. When you stick a
nail in yo' foot, if you git some yarn rag and make a fire, and hold yo'
foot over it while the rag smokes, it'll take the soreness out. Hurts something awful, though.

Now what you want to know that for? Lord, you youngsters is awful, I tell you. If you dream something and see it in yo' dream, it's sho'
to come to pass. If you dream 'bout a man dying, it's going to be a
woman what dies in yo' family, that's the way it go, I believe. Been so
long since I heared tell of them kinda things, I done kinda forgot.

There's one thing sho', when you stump yo' foot going to somebody
else's house to visit, you kin jest be sure that they don't want you, so you
jest turn 'round and go right on back. I 'member 'fore I got sick I started
cross the street one day to see one of the neighbors, and they was laughing and talking loud, and jest 'bout time I started in the yard I stumped
my foot something awful. I jest says to myself, "I know these here niggers don' want me here, and I'm going right back where I come from."

I seen the last fight they had in the War up here in Nashville. Now,
children, I'se tired, and I ain't gonna fool with yo'all no longer, yo'all go
on home now. I tell you one thing, I done forgot more'n you young folks
will ever know; you mind ain't settled enough to know nothing in these
days.

Well, children, old Sister Kelly is getting tired a talking; you see I'se
gitting old; yo'all come back agin' and I'll tell you some more 'bout the
Grace of God. I kin read you many a line in the Bible by rote and I
ain't never read a line or writ a line in my life.

SUPPLEMENTARY READINGS

Blassingame, John W. "Using the Testimony of Ex-Slaves; Approaches and Problems." *The Journal of Southern History* 41, no. 4 (November 1975): 473–92.

Johnson, Clifton H., ed. *God Struck Me Dead: Religious Conversion Experiences
and Autobiographies of Ex-slaves.* Philadelphia: Pilgrim Press, 1969.

Nichols, Charles H. *Many Thousand Gone: The Ex-slaves' Account of Their Bondage and Freedom*. Bloomington: Indiana University Press, 1969.

Rawick, George, ed. *The American Slave: A Composite Autobiography*. 31 vols. Westport, Conn.: Greenwood Press, 1972–78.

Yetman, Norman P. *Life Under the "Peculiar Institution": Selections from the Slave Narrative Collection*. New York: Holt, Rinehart & Winston, 1970.

9

Conjuration and Witchcraft

Henry Bibb (1815–54) asserted that he had been "educated in the school of adversity, whips and chains." His narrative belongs to the fugitive slave genre, for he wrote while traveling and laboring for the emancipation of every hereditary bondsman. Born to a white father and slave mother in Shelby County, Kentucky, he escaped to Detroit and Canada West [this was the correct designation then] about 1840 and founded the Voice of the Fugitive. A Methodist by declaration, Bibb vowed to expose the evils of slavery, especially its distortion of Christianity. Many slaves put their confidence not in pro-slavery preaching but in an alternative system of belief variously known as conjure, hoodooing, or root doctoring. The practitioners used various charms and concoctions to inflict misfortune, tell the future, protect their clients, and, as in Bibb's case, aid in affairs of the heart. Some Christian slaves viewed conjuration as trafficking with the devil, but others paid their fee and tried their luck. Bibb employed roots and powders to prevent floggings and paid a conjurer for assistance in romance, with predictable results. The practices of herbalism, divination, and conjuration survived alongside Christianity in the folk culture of southern blacks, and rural whites for that matter, long after the Civil War. Conjuration served as a countercultural protest to the worldview of the dominant society and met needs in the slave quarters that Christianity did not.

IN 1833, I had some very serious religious impressions, and there was quite a number of slaves in that neighborhood, who felt very desirous to be taught to read the Bible. There was a Miss Davis, a poor white girl, who offered to teach a Sabbath School for the slaves, notwithstanding public opinion and the law was opposed to it. Books were furnished and she commenced the school; but the news soon got to our owners that she was teaching us to read. This caused quite an excitement in the neighborhood. Patrols were appointed to go and break it up the next Sabbath. They were determined that we should not have a Sabbath

Source: *Narrative of the Life and Adventures of Henry Bibb, An American Slave.* New York: Published by the Author, 1849. Pp. 25–32, passim.

School in operation. For slaves this was called an incendiary movement.

The Sabbath is not regarded by a large number of the slaves as a day of rest. They have no schools to go to; no moral nor religious instruction at all in many localities where there are hundreds of slaves. Hence they resort to some kind of amusement. Those who make no profession of religion, resort to the woods in large numbers on that day to gamble, fight, get drunk, and break the Sabbath. This is often encouraged by slaveholders. When they wish to have a little sport of that kind, they go among the slaves and give them whiskey, to see them dance, "pat juber," sing and play on the banjo. Then get them to wrestling, fighting, jumping, running foot races, and butting each other like sheep. This is urged on by giving them whiskey; making bets on them; laying chips on one slave's head, and daring another to tip it off with his hand; and if he tipped it off, it would be called an insult, and cause a fight. Before fighting, the parties choose their seconds to stand by them while fighting; a ring or a circle is formed to fight in, and no one is allowed to enter the ring while they are fighting, but their seconds, and the white gentlemen. They are not allowed to fight a duel, nor to use weapons of any kind. The blows are made by kicking, knocking, and butting with their heads; they grab each other by their ears, and jam their heads together like sheep. If they are likely to hurt each other very bad, their masters would rap them with their walking canes, and make them stop. After fighting, they make friends, shake hands, and take a dram together, and there is no more of it.

But this is all principally for want of moral instruction. This is where they have no Sabbath Schools; no one to read the Bible to them; no one to preach the gospel who is competent to expound the Scriptures, except slaveholders. And the slaves, with but few exceptions, have no confidence at all in their preaching, because they preach a pro-slavery doctrine. They say, "Servants be obedient to your masters;—and he that knoweth his master's will and doeth it not, shall be beaten with many stripes;—" means that God will send them to hell, if they disobey their masters. This kind of preaching has driven thousands into infidelity. They view themselves as suffering unjustly under the lash, without friends, without protection of law or gospel, and the green-eyed monster tyranny staring them in the face. They know that they are destined to die in that wretched condition, unless they are delivered by the arm of Omnipotence. And they cannot believe or trust in such a religion, as above named. . . .

There is much superstition among the slaves. Many of them believe in what they call "conjuration," tricking, and witchcraft; and some of them pretend to understand the art, and say that by it they can prevent their masters from exercising their will over their slaves. Such are often applied to by others, to give them power to prevent their masters from flogging them. The remedy is most generally some kind of bitter root; they are directed to chew it and spit towards their masters when they are angry with their slaves. At other times they prepare certain kinds of powders, to sprinkle about their masters dwellings. This is all done for the purpose of defending themselves in some peaceable manner, although I am satisfied that there is no virtue at all in it. I have tried it to perfection when I was a slave at the South. I was then a young man, full of life and vigor, and was very fond of visiting our neighbors' slaves, but had no time to visit only Sundays, when I could get a permit to go, or after night, when I could slip off without being seen. If it was found out, the next morning I was called up to give an account of myself for going off without permission; and would very often get a flogging for it.

I got myself into a scrape at a certain time, by going off in this way, and I expected to be severely punished for it. I had a strong notion of running off, to escape being flogged, but was advised by a friend to go to one of those conjurers, who could prevent me from being flogged. I went and informed him of the difficulty. He said if I would pay him a small sum, he would prevent my being flogged. After I had paid him, he mixed up some alum, salt and other stuff into a powder, and said I must sprinkle it about my master, if he should offer to strike me; this would prevent him. He also gave me some kind of bitter root to chew, and spit towards him, which would certainly prevent my being flogged. According to order I used his remedy, and for some cause I was let pass without being flogged that time.

I had then great faith in conjuration and witchcraft. I was led to believe that I could do almost as I pleased, without being flogged. So on the next Sabbath my conjuration was fully tested by my going off, and staying away until Monday morning, without permission. When I returned home, my master declared that he would punish me for going off; but I did not believe that he could do it, while I had this root and dust; and as he approached me, I commenced talking saucy to him. But he soon convinced me that there was no virtue in them. He became so enraged at me for saucing him, that he grasped a handful of switches and punished me severely, in spite of all my roots and powders.

But there was another old slave in that neighborhood, who professed to understand all about conjuration, and I thought I would try his skill. He told me that the first one was only a quack, and if I would only pay him a certain amount in cash, that he would tell me how to prevent any person from striking me. After I had paid him his charge, he told me to go to the cow-pen after night, and get some fresh cow manure, and mix it with red pepper and white people's hair, all to be put into a pot over the fire, and scorched until it could be ground into snuff. I was then to sprinkle it about my master's bedroom, in his hat and boots, and it would prevent him from ever abusing me in any way. After I got it all ready prepared, the smallest pinch of it scattered over a room, was enough to make a horse sneeze from the strength of it; but it did no good. I tried it to my satisfaction. It was my business to make fires in my master's chamber, night and morning. Whenever I could get a chance, I sprinkled a little of this dust about the linen of the bed, where they would breathe it on retiring. This was to act upon them as what is called a kind of love powder, to change their sentiments of anger, to those of love, towards me, but this all proved to be vain imagination. The old man had my money, and I was treated no better for it.

One night when I went in to make a fire, I availed myself of the opportunity of sprinkling a very heavy charge of this powder about my master's bed. Soon after their going to bed, they began to cough and sneeze. Being close around the house, watching and listening, to know what the effect would be, I heard them ask each other what in the world it could be, that made them cough and sneeze so. All the while, I was trembling with fear, expecting every moment I should be called and asked if I knew any thing about it. After this, for fear they might find me out in my dangerous experiments upon them, I had to give them up, for the time being. I was then convinced that running away was the most effectual way by which a slave could escape cruel punishment. . . .

But my attention was gradually turned in a measure from this subject, by being introduced into the society of young women. This for the time being took my attention from running away, as waiting on the girls appeared to be perfectly congenial to my nature. I wanted to be well thought of by them, and would go to great lengths to gain their affection. I had been taught by the old superstitious slaves, to believe in conjuration, and it was hard for me to give up the notion, for all I had been deceived by them. One of these conjurers, for a small sum agreed to teach me to make any girl love me that I wished. After I had paid him, he told me to get a bull frog, and take a certain bone out of the frog, dry it, and when I got a chance I must step up to any girl whom I wished to make love me, and scratch her somewhere on her naked skin with this bone, and she would be certain to love me, and would follow me in spite of herself; no matter who she might be engaged to, nor who she might be walking with.

So I got me a bone for a certain girl, whom I knew to be under the influence of another young man. I happened to meet her in the company of her lover, one Sunday evening, walking out; so when I got a chance, I fetched her a tremendous rasp across her neck with this bone, which made her jump. But in place of making her love me, it only made her angry with me. She felt more like running after me to retaliate on me for thus abusing her, than she felt like loving me. After I found there was no virtue in the bone of a frog, I thought I would try some other way to carry out my object. I then sought another counsellor among the old superstitious influential slaves; one who professed to be a great friend of mine, told me to get a lock of hair from the head of any girl, and wear it in my shoes: this would cause her to love me above all other persons. As there was another girl whose affections I was anxious to gain, but could not succeed, I thought, without trying the experiment of this hair. I slipped off one night to see the girl, and asked her for a lock of her hair; but she refused to give it. Believing that my success depended greatly upon this bunch of hair, I was bent on having a lock before I left that night let it cost what it might. As it was time for me to start home in order to get any sleep that night, I grasped hold of a lock of her hair, which caused her to screech, but I never let go until I had pulled it out. This of course made the girl mad with me, and I accomplished nothing but gained her displeasure.

Such are the superstitious notions of the great masses of southern slaves. It is given to them by tradition, and can never be erased, while the doors of education are bolted and barred against them. . . .

SUPPLEMENTARY READINGS

Georgia Writers' Project, Works Progress Administration. *Drums and Shadows.* Garden City, N.Y.: Doubleday/Anchor Books, 1972.

Haskins, James. *Voodoo & Hoodoo.* New York: Stein and Day, 1978.

Hurston, Zora Neale. *Mules & Men.* Bloomington: Indiana University Press, 1963.

Puckett, Newbell Niles. *Folk Beliefs of the Southern Negro.* Chapel Hill: University of North Carolina Press, 1926.

Tallant, Robert. *Voodoo in New Orleans.* London: Collier-Macmillan, 1961.

10

JAMES W. C. PENNINGTON

"Great Moral Dilemma"

James W. C. Pennington (1808–70), better known as the "fugitive black-smith," tried to attend classes at Yale in 1845 but had to stand outside its lecture rooms. One wonders if he caught any presentations on moral theology, for he could have taught Yale's faculty something of the practice of day-to-day moral reasoning. Born in Maryland, Pennington spent his first twenty-one years as a slave before finally escaping. Self-taught, he conducted a school on Long Island, pastored Congregational churches in Connecticut, and visited Europe under antislavery auspices. He lectured before the theology faculty of the University of Heidelberg in Germany and received the honorary doctor of divinity degree. He returned to the pulpit of New York's Shiloh Congregational Church and eventually went to the Fourth Street Abyssinian Church in Portland, Maine.

Pennington's interests were scholarly—theology, logic, and history. In 1841 he published the first Afro-American history, entitled A Textbook of the Origin and History of the Colored People. *His autobiography began as lecture notes made during his stay in England. The following excerpt concerns the dilemma of a Christian slave who cannot serve two masters. Pennington felt responsible to a higher law, the law of self-preservation, and fashioned a contextual ethic that many fugitive slaves honored. Here is an example of what contemporary moralists term "situation ethics." The slaves knew it as a higher morality than that of the master.*

A FEW MOMENTS after I was taken into the bar-room, the news having gone as by electricity, the house and yard were crowded with gossippers, who had left their business to come and see "the runaway nigger." This hastily assembled congregation consisted of men, women, and children, each one had a look to give at, and a word to say about, the "nigger."

But among the whole, there stood one whose name I have never known, but who evidently wore the garb of a man whose profession

Source: *The Fugitive Blacksmith, or Events in the History of James W. C. Pennington, Pastor of a Presbyterian Church, New York, Formerly a Slave in the State of Maryland, United States.* Second edition. London: Charles Gilpin, 1849. Pp. 21–30.

bound him to speak for the dumb, but he, standing head and shoulders above all that were round about, spoke the first hard sentence against me. Said he, "That fellow is a runaway I know; put him in jail a few days, and you will soon hear where he came from." And then fixing a fiend-like gaze upon me, he continued, "if I lived on this road, *you* fellows would not find such clear running as you do, I'd trap more of you."

But now comes the pinch of the case, the case of conscience to me even at this moment. Emboldened by the cruel speech just recited, my captors enclosed me, and said, "Come now, this matter may easily be settled without you going to jail; who do you belong to, and where did you come from?"

The facts here demanded were in my breast. I knew according to the law of slavery, who I belonged to and where I came from, and I must now do one of three things—I must refuse to speak at all, or I must communicate the fact, or I must tell an untruth. How would an untutored slave, who had never heard of such a writer as Archdeacon Paley, be likely to act in such a dilemma? The first point decided, was, the facts in this case are my private property. These men have no more right to them than a highway robber has to my purse. What will be the consequence if I put them in possession of the facts. In forty-eight hours, I shall have received perhaps one hundred lashes, and be on my way to the Louisiana cotton fields. Of what service will it be to them. They will get a paltry sum of two hundred dollars. Is not my liberty worth more to me than two hundred dollars are to them?

I resolved therefore, to insist that I was free. This not being satisfactory without other evidence, they tied my hands and set out, and went to a magistrate who lived about half a mile distant. It so happened, that when we arrived at his house he was not at home. This was to them a disappointment, but to me it was a relief; but I soon learned by their conversation, that there was still another magistrate in the neighbourhood, and that they would go to him. In about twenty minutes, and after climbing fences and jumping ditches, we, captors and captive, stood before his door, but it was after the same manner as before—he was not at home. By this time the day had worn away to one or two o'clock, and my captors evidently began to feel somewhat impatient of the loss of time. We were about a mile and a quarter from the tavern. As we set out on our return, they began to parley. Finding it was difficult for me to get over fences with my hands tied, they untied me, and said, "Now John," that being the name they had given me, "if you have run away from any one, it would be much better for you to tell us!" but I continued to affirm that I was free. I knew, however, that my situation was very critical, owing to the shortness of the distance I must be from home: my advertisement might overtake me at any moment.

On our way back to the tavern, we passed through a small skirt of wood, where I resolved to make an effort to escape again. One of my captors was walking on either side of me; I made a sudden turn, with my left arm sweeping the legs of one of my captors from under him; I left him nearly standing on his head, and took to my heels. As soon as they could recover they both took after me. We had to mount a fence. This I did most successfully, and making across an open field towards another wood; one of my captors being a long-legged man, was in advance of the other, and consequently nearing me. We had a hill to rise, and during the ascent he gained on me. Once more I thought of self-defence. I am trying to escape peaceably, but this man is determined that I shall not.

My case was now desperate; and I took this desperate thought: "I will run him a little farther from his coadjutor; I will then suddenly catch a stone, and wound him in the breast." This was my fixed purpose, and I had arrived near the point on the top of the hill, where I expected to do the act, when to my surprise and dismay, I saw the other side of the hill was not only all ploughed up, but we came suddenly upon a man ploughing, who as suddenly left his plough and cut off my flight, by seizing me by the collar, when at the same moment my pursuer seized my arms behind. Here I was again in a sad fix. By this time the other pursuer had come up; I was most savagely thrown down on the ploughed ground with my face downward, the ploughman placed his knee upon my shoulders, one of my captors put his upon my legs, while the other tied my arms behind me. I was then dragged up, and marched off with kicks, punches and imprecations.

We got to the tavern at three o'clock. Here they again cooled down, and made an appeal to me to make a disclosure. I saw that my attempt to escape strengthened their belief that I was a fugitive. I said to them, "If you will not put me in jail, I will now tell you where I am from." They promised. "Well," said I, "a few weeks ago, I was sold from the eastern shore to a slave-trader, who had a large gang, and set out for Georgia, but when he got to a town in Virginia, he was taken sick, and died with the small-pox. Several of his gang also died with it, so that the people in the town became alarmed, and did not wish the gang to remain among them. No one claimed us, or wished to have anything to do with us; I left the rest, and thought I would go somewhere and get work."

When I said this, it was evidently believed by those who were present, and notwithstanding the unkind feeling that had existed, there was a murmur of approbation. At the same time I perceived that a panic began to seize some, at the idea that I was one of a small-pox gang. Several who had clustered near me, moved off to a respectful distance. One or two left the bar-room, and murmured, "better let the small-pox nigger go."

I was then asked what was the name of the slave-trader. Without premeditation, I said, "John Henderson."

"John Henderson!" said one of my captors, "I knew him; I took up a yaller boy for him about two years ago, and got fifty dollars. He passed out with a gang about that time, and the boy ran away from him at Frederickstown. What kind of a man was he?"

At a venture, I gave a description of him. "Yes," said he, "that is the man." By this time, all the gossippers had cleared the coast; our friend, "Jake Shouster," had also gone back to his bench to finish his custom work, after having "lost nearly the whole day, trotting about with a nigger tied," as I heard his wife say as she called him home to his dinner. I was now left alone with the man who first called to me in the morning. In a sober manner, he made this proposal to me: "John, I have a brother living in Risterstown, four miles off, who keeps a tavern; I think you had better go and live with him, till we see what will turn up. He wants an ostler." I at once assented to this. "Well," said he, "take something to eat, and I will go with you."

Although I had so completely frustrated their designs for the moment, I knew that it would by no means answer for me to go into that town, where there were prisons, handbills, newspapers, and travellers. My intention was, to start with him, but not to enter the town alive.

I sat down to eat; it was Wednesday, four o'clock, and this was the first regular meal I had since Sunday morning. This over, we set out, and to my surprise, he proposed to walk. We had gone about a mile and a-half, and were approaching a wood through which the road passed with a bend. I fixed upon that as the spot where I would either free myself from this man, or die in his arms. I had resolved upon a plan of operation—it was this: to stop short, face about, and commence action; and neither ask or give quarters, until I was free or dead!

We had got within six rods of the spot, when a gentleman turned the corner, meeting us on horseback. He came up, and entered into conversation with my captor, both of them speaking in Dutch, so that I knew not what they said. After a few moments, this gentleman addressed himself to me in English, and I then learned that he was one of the magistrates on whom we had called in the morning; I felt that another crisis was at hand. Using his saddle as his bench, he put on an extremely stern and magisterial-like face, holding up his horse not unlike a field-marshal in the act of reviewing troops, and carried me through a most rigid examination in reference to the statement I had made. I repeated carefully all I had said; at the close, he said, "Well, you had better stay among us a few months, until we see what is to be done with you." It was then agreed that we should go back to the tavern, and there settle upon some further plan. When we arrived at the tavern, the magistrate alighted from his horse, and went into the bar-room. He took another close glance at me, and went over some points of the former examination. He seemed quite satisfied of the correctness of my statement, and made the following proposition: that I should go and live with him for a short time, stating that he had a few acres of corn and potatoes to get in, and that he would give me twenty-five cents per day. I most cheerfully assented to this proposal. It was also agreed that I should remain at the tavern with my captor that night, and that he would accompany me in the morning. This part of the arrangement I did not like, but of course I could not say so. Things being thus arranged, the magistrate mounted his horse, and went on his way home.

It had been cloudy and rainy during the afternoon, but the western sky having partially cleared at this moment, I perceived that it was near the setting of the sun.

My captor had left his hired man most of the day to dig potatoes alone; but the waggon being now loaded, it being time to convey the potatoes into the barn, and the horses being all ready for that purpose, he was obliged to go into the potatoe field and give assistance.

I should say here, that his wife had been driven away by the small-pox panic about three o'clock, and had not yet returned; this left no one in the house, but a boy, about nine years of age.

As he went out, he spoke to the boy in Dutch, which I supposed, from the little fellow's conduct, to be instructions to watch me closely, which he certainly did.

The potatoe lot was across the public road, directly in front of the house; at the back of the house, and about 300 yards distant, there was a thick wood. The circumstances of the case would not allow me to think for one moment of remaining there for the night—the time had come for another effort—but there were two serious difficulties. One was, that I must either deceive or dispatch this boy who is watching me with intense vigilance. I am glad to say, that the latter did not for a moment seriously enter my mind. To deceive him effectually, I left my coat and went to the back door, from which my course would be direct to the wood. When I got to the door, I found that the barn, to which the waggon must soon come, lay just to the right, and overlooking the path I must take to the wood. In front of me lay a garden surrounded by a

picket fence, to the left of me was a small gate, and that by passing
through that gate would throw me into an open field, and give me clear
running to the wood; but on looking through the gate, I saw that my
captor, being with the team, would see me if I attempted to start before
he moved from the position he then occupied. To add to my difficulty
the horses had baulked; while waiting for the decisive moment, the boy
came to the door and asked me why I did not come in. I told him, I felt
unwell, and wished him to be so kind as to hand me a glass of water; expecting while he was gone to get it, the team would clear, so that I
could start. While he was gone, another attempt was made to start the
team but failed; he came with the water and I quickly used it up by
gargling my throat and by drinking a part. I asked him to serve me by
giving me another glass: he gave me a look of close scrutiny, but went
in for the water. I heard him fill the glass, and start to return with it;
when the hind end of the waggon cleared the corner of the house, which
stood in a range with the fence along which I was to pass in getting to
the wood. As I passed out the gate, I "squared my main yard," and laid
my course up the line of fence, I cast a last glance over my right shoulder,
and saw the boy just perch his head above the garden picket to look
after me; I heard at the same time great confusion with the team, the
rain having made the ground slippery, and the horses having to cross the
road with a slant and rise to get into the barn, it required great effort
after they started to prevent their baulking. I felt some assurance that
although the boy might give the alarm, my captor could not leave the
team until it was in the barn. I heard the horses' feet on the barn-floor,
just as I leaped the fence, and darted into the wood.

The sun was now quite down behind the western horizon, and just
at this time a heavy dark curtain of clouds was let down, which seemed
to usher in haste the night shade. I have never before or since seen anything which seemed to me to compare in sublimity with the spreading of
the night shades at the close of that day. My reflections upon the events
of that day, and upon the close of it, since I became acquainted with
the Bible, have frequently brought to my mind that beautiful passage in
the Book of Job, "He holdeth back the face of His throne, and spreadeth
a cloud before it."

Before I proceed to the critical events and final deliverance of the
next chapter, I cannot forbear to pause a moment here for reflection.
The reader may well imagine how the events of the past day affected my
mind. You have seen what was done to me; you have heard what was
said to me—you have also seen what I have done, and heard what I have
said. If you ask me whether I had expected before I left home, to gain
my liberty by shedding men's blood, or breaking their limbs? I answer,

no! and as evidence of this, I had provided no weapon whatever; not so much as a penknife—it never once entered my mind. I cannot say that I expected to have the ill fortune of meeting with any human being who would attempt to impede my flight.

If you ask me if I expected when I left home to gain my liberty by fabrications and untruths? I answer, no! my parents, slaves as they were, had always taught me, when they could, that "truth may be blamed but cannot be shamed"; so far as their example was concerned, I had no habits of untruth. I was arrested, and the demand made upon me, "Who do you belong to?" knowing the fatal use these men would make of *my* truth, I at once concluded that they had no more right to it than a highwayman has to a traveller's purse.

If you ask me whether I now really believe that I gained my liberty by those lies? I answer, no! I now believe that I should be free, had I told the truth; but, at that moment, I could not see any other way to baffle my enemies, and escape their clutches.

The history of that day has never ceased to inspire me with a deeper hatred of slavery; I never recur to it but with the most intense horror at a system which can put a man not only in peril of liberty, limb, and life itself, but which may even send him in haste to the bar of God with a lie upon his lips.

Whatever my readers may think, therefore, of the history of events of the day, do not admire in it the fabrications; but *see* in it the impediments that often fall into the pathway of the flying bondman. *See* how human bloodhounds gratuitously chase, catch, and tempt him to shed blood and lie; how, when he would do good, evil is thrust upon him.

SUPPLEMENTARY READINGS

Bontemps, Arna, ed. *Great Slave Narratives.* Boston: Beacon Press, 1969.

Hudson, Gossie Harold. "John Chavis, 1763–1838: A Social-Psychological Study." *The Journal of Negro History* 64, no. 2 (Spring 1979): 142–56.

Murray, Andrew E. *Presbyterians and the Negro—A History.* Philadelphia: Presbyterian Historical Society, 1966. Chap. 2.

Swift, David E. "Black Presbyterian Attacks on Racism: Samuel Cornish, Theodore Wright and Their Contemporaries." In *Black Apostles at Home and Abroad,* edited by David W. Wills and Richard Newman. Boston: G. K. Hall, 1982. Pp. 43–84.

Ward, Samuel R. *Autobiography of a Fugitive Negro.* London: John Snow, 1855; reprint ed., New York: Arno Press, 1968.

Religion and Slave Insurrection

Like Gabriel in Richmond in 1800 and Denmark Vesey in Charleston in 1822, Nat Turner of Southampton County, Virginia, heard a call to arms. Depicted both as a "gloomy fanatic" and as a "bold emancipator," he inspired what was perhaps the most widely discussed insurrection in the antebellum South. It began on August 21, 1831, and resulted in the deaths of some fifty-five whites and two hundred blacks, though perhaps only twenty or thirty slaves were involved in killing whites. Turner eluded capture, thereby adding to the hysteria that spread throughout the South. On October 31, 1831, he was placed in jail at Jerusalem, the county seat. Thomas R. Gray, a white court-appointed attorney, interviewed him and subsequently published this narrative.

Though Turner does not speak to us directly in Gray's account and the lawyer seems intent on portraying the rebel as a religious fanatic whose deeds did not really represent a widespread slave restlessness, something of the prophetic vision of Nat Turner does come through here. He was a student of the Bible whose mind turned toward visions of righteous vengeance. When he took up the sword in the fall of 1831, he moved onto that fateful field where the Bible prophesied that the hosts of good would meet the armies of evil. Turner went to the gallows on November 11, 1831, unrepentant. The publication of The Confessions of Nat Turner did little to stem the reactionary tide of white fear. South Carolina passed a law aimed at preventing blacks from gathering "for the purpose of mental instruction or religious worship" between sunset and sunrise.

SIR.—You have asked me to give a history of the motives which induced me to undertake the late insurrection, as you call it—To do so I must go back to the days of my infancy, and even before I was born. I was thirty-one years of age the 2nd of October last, and born the property of Benj. Turner, of this county. In my childhood a circumstance occurred which made an indelible impression on my mind, and laid the ground work of

Source: *The Confessions of Nat Turner, the Leader of the late Insurrection in Southampton, Va. as fully and voluntarily made to Thomas R. Gray* . . . . Baltimore: Thomas R. Gray, Lucas and Deaver, 1831. Pp. 1–21.

that enthusiasm, which has terminated so fatally to many, both white and black, and for which I am about to atone at the gallows. It is here necessary to relate this circumstance—trifling as it may seem, it was the commencement of that belief which has grown with time, and even now, sir, in this dungeon, helpless and forsaken as I am, I cannot divest myself of. Being at play with other children, when three or four years old, I was telling them something, which my mother overhearing, said it had happened before I was born—I stuck to my story, however, and related somethings which went, in her opinion, to confirm it—others being called on were greatly astonished, knowing that these things had happened, and caused them to say in my hearing, I surely would be a prophet, as the Lord had shewn me things that had happened before my birth. And my father and mother strengthened me in this my first impression, saying in my presence, I was intended for some great purpose, which they had always thought from certain marks on my head and breast—[a parcel of excrescences which I believe are not at all uncommon, particularly among negroes, as I have seen several with the same. In this case he has either cut them off or they have nearly disappeared]— My grandmother, who was very religious, and to whom I was much attached—my master, who belonged to the church, and other religious persons who visited the house, and whom I often saw at prayers, noticing the singularity of my manners, I suppose, and my uncommon intelligence for a child, remarked I had too much sense to be raised, and if I was, I would never be of any service to any one as a slave—To a mind like mine, restless, inquisitive and observant of every thing that was passing, it is easy to suppose that religion was the subject to which it would be directed, and although this subject principally occupied my thoughts— there was nothing that I saw or heard of to which my attention was not directed—The manner in which I learned to read and write, not only had great influence on my own mind, as I acquired it with the most perfect ease, so much so, that I have no recollection whatever of learning the alphabet—but to the astonishment of the family, one day, when a book was shewn to me to keep me from crying, I began spelling the names of different objects—this was a source of wonder to all in the neighborhood, particularly the blacks—and this learning was constantly improved at all opportunities—when I got large enough to go to work, while employed, I was reflecting on many things that would present themselves to my imagination, and whenever an opportunity occurred of looking at a book, when the school children were getting their lessons, I would find many things that the fertility of my own imagination had depicted to me before; all my time, not devoted to my master's service, was spent either in prayer, or in making experiments in casting different things in moulds made of earth, in attempting to make paper, gunpowder, and many other experiments, that although I could not perfect, yet convinced me of its practicability if I had the means. I was not addicted to stealing in my youth, nor have ever been—Yet such was the confidence of the negroes in the neighborhood, even at this early period of my life, in my superior judgment, that they would often carry me with them when they were going on any roguery, to plan for them. Growing up among them, with this confidence in my superior judgment, and when this, in their opinions, was perfected by Divine inspiration, from the circumstances already alluded to in my infancy, and which belief was ever afterwards zealously inculcated by the austerity of my life and manners, which became the subject of remark by white and black.— Having soon discovered to be great, I must appear so, and therefore studiously avoided mixing in society, and wrapped myself in mystery, devoting my time to fasting and prayer—by this time, having arrived to man's estate, and hearing the scriptures commented on at meetings, I was struck with that particular passage which says: "Seek ye the kingdom of Heaven and all things shall be added unto you." I reflected much on this passage, and prayed daily for light on this subject—As I was praying one day at my plough, the spirit spoke to me, saying "Seek ye the kingdom of Heaven and all things shall be added unto you." *Question*— what do you mean by the Spirit. *Ans.* The Spirit that spoke to the prophets in former days—and I was greatly astonished, and for two years prayed continually, whenever my duty would permit—and then again I had the same revelation, which fully confirmed me in the impression that I was ordained for some great purpose in the hands of the Almighty. Several years rolled round, in which many events occurred to strengthen me in this my belief. At this time I reverted in my mind to the remarks made of me in my childhood, and the things that had been shewn me— and as it had been said of me in my childhood by those by whom I had been taught to pray, both white and black, and in whom I had the greatest confidence, that I had too much sense to be raised, and if I was, I would never be of any use to any one as a slave. Now finding I had arrived to man's estate, and was a slave, and these revelations being made known to me, I began to direct my attention to this great object, to fulfill the purpose for which, by this time, I felt assured I was intended. Knowing the influence I had obtained over the minds of my fellow servants, (not by the means of conjuring and such like tricks—for to them I always spoke of such things with contempt) but by the communion of the Spirit whose revelations I often communicated to them, and they believed and said my wisdom came from God. I now began to prepare them for my purpose, by telling them something was about to happen that would terminate in fulfilling the great promise that had been made to me—About this time I was placed under an overseer, from whom I ran away—and after remaining in the woods thirty days, I returned, to the astonishment of the negroes on the plantation, who thought I had made my escape to some other part of the country, as my father had done before. But the reason of my return was, that the Spirit appeared to me and said I had my wishes directed to the things of this world, and not to the kingdom of Heaven, and that I should return to the service of my earthly master—"For he who knoweth his Master's will, and doeth it not, shall be beaten with many stripes, and thus have I chastened you." And the negroes found fault, and murmured against me, saying that if they had my sense they would not serve any master in the world. And about this time I had a vision—and I saw white spirits and black spirits engaged in battle, and the sun was darkened—the thunder rolled in the Heavens, and blood flowed in streams—and I heard a voice saying, "Such is your luck, such you are called to see, and let it come rough or smooth, you must surely bare it." I now withdrew myself as much as my situation would permit, from the intercourse of my fellow servants, for the avowed purpose of serving the Spirit more fully—and it appeared to me, and reminded me of the things it had already shown me, and that it would then reveal to me the knowledge of the elements, the revolution of the planets, the operation of tides, and changes of the seasons. After this revelation in the year of 1825, and the knowledge of the elements being made known to me, I sought more than ever to obtain true holiness before the great day of judgment should appear, and then I began to receive the true knowledge of faith. And from the first steps of righteousness until the last, was I made perfect, and the Holy Ghost was with me, and said, "Behold me as I stand in the Heavens"—and I looked and saw the forms of men in different attitudes—and there were lights in the sky to which the children of darkness gave other names than what they really were—for they were the lights of the Savior's hands, stretched forth from east to west, even as they were extended on the cross on Calvary for the redemption of sinners. And I wondered greatly at these miracles, and prayed to be informed of a certainty of the meaning thereof—and shortly afterwards, while laboring in the field, I discovered drops of blood on the corn as though it were dew from heaven—and I communicated it to many, both white and black, in the neighborhood—and I then found on the leaves in the woods hieroglyphic characters, and numbers, with the forms of men in different attitudes, portrayed in blood, and representing the figures I had seen before in the heavens. And now the Holy Ghost had revealed itself to me, and made plain the miracles it had shown me—For as the blood of Christ had been shed on this earth, and

had ascended to heaven for the salvation of sinners, and was now returning to earth again in the form of dew—and as the leaves on the trees
bore the impression of the figures I had seen in the heavens, it was plain
to me that the Savior was about to lay down the yoke he had borne for
the sins of men, and the great day of judgment was at hand. About this
time I told these things to a white man, (Etheldred T. Brantley) on
whom it had a wonderful effect—and he ceased from his wickedness, and
was attacked immediately with a cutaneous eruption, and blood oozed
from the pores of his skin, and after praying and fasting nine days, he
was healed, and the Spirit appeared to me again, and said, as the Savior
had been baptised so should we be also—and when the white people
would not let us be baptised by the church, we went down into the water together, in the sight of many who reviled us, and were baptised by
the Spirit—After this I rejoiced greatly, and gave thanks to God. And
on the 12th of May, 1828, I heard a loud noise in the heavens, and the
Spirit instantly appeared to me and said the Serpent was loosened, and
Christ had laid down the yoke he had borne for the sins of men, and
that I should take it on and fight against the Serpent, for the time was
fast approaching when the first should be last and the last should be
first. _Ques._ Do you not find yourself mistaken now? _Ans._ Was not Christ
crucified? And by signs in the heavens that it would make known to me
when I should commence the great work—and until the first sign appeared, I should conceal it from the knowledge of men—And on the appearance of the sign, (the eclipse of the sun last February) I should arise
and prepare myself, and slay my enemies with their own weapons. And
immediately on the sign appearing in the heavens, the seal was removed
from my lips, and I communicated the great work laid out for me to do,
to four in whom I had the greatest confidence, (Henry, Hark, Nelson,
and Sam)—It was intended by us to have begun the work of death on
the 4th July last—Many were the plans formed and rejected by us, and
it affected my mind to such a degree, that I fell sick, and the time passed
without our coming to any determination how to commence—Still forming new schemes and rejecting them, when the sign appeared again,
which determined me not to wait longer.

Since the commencement of 1830, I had been living with Mr. Joseph Travis, who was to me a kind master, and placed the greatest confidence in me; in fact, I had no cause to complain of his treatment to
me. On Saturday evening, the 20th of August, it was agreed between
Henry, Hank and myself, to prepare a dinner the next day for the men
we expected, and then to concert a plan, as we had not yet determined
on any. Hank, on the following morning, brought a pig, and Henry

brandy, and being joined by Sam, Nelson, Will and Jack, they prepared in the woods a dinner, where, about three o'clock, I joined them.

Q. Why were you so backward in joining them?

A. The same reason that had caused me not to mix with them for years before.

I saluted them on coming up, and asked Will how came he there, he answered, his life was worth no more than others, and his liberty as dear to him. I asked him if he thought to obtain it? He said he would, or lose his life. This was enough to put him in full confidence. Jack, I knew, was only a tool in the hands of Hark, it was quickly agreed we should commence at home (Mr. J. Travis') on that night, and until we had armed and equipped ourselves, and gathered sufficient force, neither age nor sex was to be spared, (which was invariably adhered to). We remained at the feast, until about two hours in the night, when we went to the house and found Austin; they all went to the cider press and drank, except myself. On returning to the house, Hark went to the door with an axe, for the purpose of breaking it open, as we knew we were strong enough to murder the family, if they were awakened by the noise; but reflecting that it might create an alarm in the neighborhood, we determined to enter the house secretly, and murder them whilst sleeping. Hark got a ladder and set it against the chimney, on which I ascended, and hoisting a window, entered and came down stairs, unbarred the door, and removed the guns from their places. It was then observed that I must spill the first blood. On which, armed with a hatchet, and accompanied by Will, I entered my master's chamber, it being dark, I could not give a death blow, the hatchet glanced from his head, he sprang from the bed and called his wife, it was his last word, Will laid him dead, with a blow of his axe, and Mrs. Travis shared the same fate, as she lay in bed. The murder of this family, five in number, was the work of a moment, not one of them awoke; there was a little infant sleeping in a cradle, that was forgotten, until we had left the house and gone some distance, when Henry and Will returned and killed it; we got here, four guns that would shoot, and several old muskets, with a pound or two of powder. We remained some time at the barn, where we paraded; I formed them in a line as soldiers, and after carrying them through all the manoeuvres I was master of marched them off to Mr. Salathul Francis', about six hundred yards distant. Sam and Will went to the door and knocked. Mr. Francis asked who was there, Sam replied it was him, and he had a letter for him on which he got up and came to the door; they immediately seized him, and dragging him out a little from the door, he was dispatched by repeated blows on the head; there was no other white person in the family. We started from there for Mrs. Reese's, maintaining the most perfect silence on our march, where finding the door unlocked, we entered, and murdered Mrs. Reese in her bed, while sleeping; her son awoke, but it was only to sleep the sleep of death, he had only time to say who is that, and he was no more. From Mrs. Reese's we went to Mrs. Turner's, a mile distant, which we reached about sunrise, on Monday morning. Henry, Austin, and Sam, went to the still, where, finding Mr. Peebles, Austin shot him, and the rest of us went to the house; as we approached, the family discovered us, and shut the door. Vain hope! Will, with one stroke of his axe, opened it, and we entered and found Mrs. Turner and Mrs. Newsome in the middle of a room, almost frightened to death. Will immediately killed Mrs. Turner, with one blow of his axe. I took Mrs. Newsome by the hand, and with the sword I had when I was apprehended, I struck her several blows over the head, but not being able to kill her, as the sword was dull. Will turning around and discovering it, despatched her also. A general destruction of property and search for money and ammunition, always succeeded the murders. By this time my company amounted to fifteen, and nine men mounted, who started for Mrs. Whitehead's, (the other six were to go through a by way to Mr. Bryant's, and rejoin us at Mrs. Whitehead's,) as we approached the house we discovered Mr. Richard Whitehead standing in the cotton patch, near the lane fence; we called him over into the lane, and Will, the executioner, was near at hand, with his fatal axe, to send him to an untimely grave. As we pushed on to the house, I discovered some one run round the garden, and thinking it was some of the white family, I pursued them, but finding it was a servant girl belonging to the house, I returned to commence the work of death, but they whom I left, had not been idle; all the family were already murdered, but Mrs. Whitehead and her daughter Margaret. As I came round to the door I saw Will pulling Mrs. Whitehead out of the house, and at the step he nearly severed her head from her body, with his broad axe. Miss Margaret, when I discovered her, had concealed herself in the corner, formed by the projection of cellar cap from the house; on my approach she fled, but was soon overtaken, and after repeated blows with a sword, I killed her by a blow on the head, with a fence rail. By this time, the six who had gone by Mr. Bryant's, rejoined us, and informed me they had done the work of death assigned them. We again divided, part going to Mr. Richard Porter's, and from thence to Nathaniel Francis', the others to Mr. Howell Harris', and Mr. T. Doyles. On my reaching Mr. Porter's, he had escaped with his family. I understood there, that the alarm had already spread, and I immediately returned to bring up those sent to Mr. Doyles, and Mr. Howell Harris'; the party I left going

on to Mr. Francis', having told them I would join them in that neighborhood. I met these sent to Mr. Doyles' and Mr. Harris' returning, having met Mr. Doyle on the road and killed him; and learning from some
who joined them, that Mr. Harris was from home, I immediately pursued
the course taken by the party gone on before; but knowing they would
complete the work of death and pillage, at Mr. Francis' before I could
get there, I went to Mr. Peter Edwards', expecting to find them there,
but they had been here also. I then went to Mr. John T. Barrow's, they
had been here and murdered him. I pursued on their track to Capt.
Newit Harris', where I found the greater part mounted, and ready to
start; the men now amounting to about forty, shouted and hurraed as I
rode up, some were in the yard, loading their guns, others drinking. They
said Captain Harris and his family had escaped, the property in the
house they destroyed, robbing him of money and other valuables. I ordered them to mount and march instantly, this was about nine or ten
o'clock, Monday morning. I proceeded to Mr. Levi Waller's, two or
three miles distant. I took my station in the rear, and as it was my object
to carry terror and devastation wherever we went, I placed fifteen or
twenty of the best armed and most relied on, in front, who generally
approached the houses as fast as their horses could run; this was for
two purposes, to prevent escape and strike terror to the inhabitants—on
this account I never got to the houses, after leaving Mrs. Whitehead's,
until the murders were committed, except in one case. I sometimes got
in sight in time to see the work of death completed, viewed the mangled
bodies as they lay, in silent satisfaction, and immediately started in quest
of other victims—Having murdered Mrs. Waller and ten children, we
started for Mr. William Williams'—having killed him and two little boys
that were there; while engaged in this, Mrs. Williams fled and got some
distance from the house, but she was pursued, overtaken, and compelled
to get up behind one of the company, who brought her back, and after
showing her the mangled body of her lifeless husband, she was told to
get down and lay by his side, where she was shot dead. I then started for
Mr. Jacob Williams, where the family were murdered—Here he found
a young man named Drury, who had come on business with Mr. Williams—he was pursued, overtaken and shot. Mrs. Vaughan was the next
place we visited—and after murdering the family here, I determined on
starting for Jerusalem—Our number amounted now to fifty or sixty, all
mounted and armed with guns, axes, swords and clubs—On reaching
Mr. James W. Parker's gate, immediately on the road leading to Jerusalem, and about three miles distant, it was proposed to me to call there,
but I objected, as I knew he was gone to Jerusalem, and my object was
to reach there as soon as possible; but some of the men having relations

at Mr. Parker's it was agreed that they might call and get his people. I remained at the gate on the road, with seven or eight; the others going across the field to the house, about half a mile off. After waiting some time for them, I became impatient, and started to the house for them, and on our return we were met by a party of white men, who had pursued our blood-stained track, and who had fired on those at the gate, and dispersed them, which I knew nothing of, not having been at that time rejoined by any of them—Immediately on discovering the whites, I ordered my men to halt and form, as they appeared to be alarmed— The white men, eighteen in number, approached us in about one hundred yards, when one of them fired, (this was against the positive orders of Captain Alexander P. Peete, who commanded, and who had directed the men to reserve their fire until within thirty paces)—And I discovered about half of them retreating, I then ordered my men to fire and rush on them; the few remaining stood their ground until we approached within fifty yards, when they fired and retreated. We pursued and overtook some of them who we thought we left dead; (they were not killed) after pursuing them about two hundred yards, and rising a little hill, I discovered they were met by another party, and had halted, and were reloading their guns, (this was a small party from Jerusalem who knew the negroes were in the field, and had just tied their horses to await their return to the road, knowing that Mr. Parker and family were in Jerusalem, but knew nothing of the party that had gone in with Captain Peete; on hearing the firing they immediately rushed to the spot and arrived just in time to arrest the progress of these barbarous villains, and save the lives of their friends and fellow citizens). Thinking that those who retreated first, and the party who fired on us at fifty or sixty yards distant, had all fallen back to meet others with ammunition. As I saw them reloading their guns, and more coming up than I saw at first, and several of my bravest men being wounded, the others became panick struck and squandered over the field; the white men pursued and fired on us several times. Hark had his horse shot under him, and I caught another for him as it was running by me; five or six of my men were wounded, but none left on the field; finding myself defeated here I instantly determined to go through a private way, and cross the Nottoway river at the Cypress Bridge, three miles below Jerusalem, and attack that place in the rear, as I expected they would look for me on the other road, and I had a great desire to get there to procure arms and ammunition. After going a short distance in this private way, accompanied by about twenty men, I overtook two or three who told me the others were dispersed in every direction. After trying in vain to collect a sufficient force to proceed to Jerusalem, I determined to return, as I was sure they would make back to their old neighborhood, where they would rejoin me, make new recruits, and come down again. On my way back, I called at Mrs. Thomas's, Mrs. Spencer's, and several other places, the white families having fled, we found no more victims to gratify our thirst for blood, we stopped at Maj. Ridley's quarter for the night, and being joined by four of his men, with the recruits made since my defeat, we mustered now about forty strong. After placing out sentinels, I laid down to sleep, but was quickly roused by a great racket; starting up, I found some mounted, and others in great confusion; one of the sentinels having given the alarm that we were about to be attacked, I ordered some to ride round and reconnoitre, and on their return the others being more alarmed, not knowing who they were, fled in different ways, so that I was reduced to about twenty again; with this I determined to attempt to recruit, and proceed on to rally in the neighborhood, I had left. Dr. Blunt's was the nearest house, which we reached just before day; on riding up the yard, Hark fired a gun. We expected Dr. Blunt and his family were at Maj. Ridley's, as I knew there was a company of men there; the gun was fired to ascertain if any of the family were at home; we were immediately fired upon and retreated, leaving several of my men. I do not know what became of them, as I never saw them afterwards. Pursuing our course back and coming in sight of Captain Harris', where we had been the day before, we discovered a party of white men at the house, on which all deserted me but two, (Jacob and Nat), we concealed ourselves in the woods until near night, when I sent them in search of Henry, Sam, Nelson, and Hark, and directed them to rally all they could, at the place we had had our dinner the Sunday before, where they would find me, and I accordingly returned there as soon as it was dark and remained until Wednesday evening, when discovering white men riding around the place as though they were looking for some one, and none of my men joining me, I concluded Jacob and Nat had been taken, and compelled to betray me. On this I gave up all hope for the present, and on Thursday night after having supplied myself with provisions from Mr. Travis's, I scratched a hole under a pile of fence rails in a field, where I concealed myself for six weeks, never leaving my hiding place but for a few minutes in the dead of night to get water which was very near; thinking by this time I could venture out, I began to go about in the night and eaves drop the houses in the neighborhood; pursuing this course for about a fortnight and gathering little or no intelligence, afraid of speaking to any human being, and returning every morning to my cave before the dawn of day. I know not how long I might have led this life, if accident had not betrayed me, a dog in the neighborhood passing by my hiding place one night while I was out, was attracted by some meat I had in my cave, and crawled in and stole it, and was coming out just as I returned. A few nights after, two negroes having started to go hunting with the same dog, and passed that way, the dog came again to the place, and having just gone out to walk about, discovered me and barked, on which thinking myself discovered, I spoke to them to beg concealment. On making myself known they fled from me. Knowing then they would betray me, I immediately left my hiding place, and was pursued almost incessantly until I was taken a fortnight afterwards by Mr. Benjamin Phipps, in a little hole I had dug out with my sword, for the purpose of concealment, under the top of a fallen tree. On Mr. Phipps' discovering the place of my concealment, he cocked his gun and aimed at me. I requested him not to shoot and I would give up, upon which he demanded my sword. I delivered it to him, and he brought me to prison. During the time I was pursued, I had many hair breadth escapes, which your time will not permit you to relate. I am here loaded with chains, and willing to suffer the fate that awaits me.

I here proceeded to make some inquiries of him, after assuring him of the certain death that awaited him, and that concealment would only bring destruction on the innocent as well as guilty, of his own color, if he knew of any extensive or concerted plan. His answer was, I do not. When I questioned him as to the insurrection in North Carolina happening about the same time, he denied any knowledge of it; and when I looked him in the face as though I would search his inmost thoughts, he replied, "I see sir, you doubt my word; but can you not think the same ideas, and strange appearances about this time in the heaven's might prompt others, as well as myself, to this undertaking." I now had much conversation with and asked him many questions, having forborne to do so previously, except in the cases noted in parenthesis; but during his statement, I had, unnoticed by him, taken notes as to some particular circumstances, and having the advantage of his statement before me in writing, on the evening of the third day that I had been with him, I began a cross examination, and found his statement corroborated by every circumstance coming within my own knowledge or the confessions of others who had been either killed or executed, and whom he had not seen nor had any knowledge since 22nd of August last, he expressed himself fully satisfied as to the impracticability of his attempt. It has been said he was ignorant and cowardly, and that his object was to murder and rob for the purpose of obtaining money to make his escape. It is notorious, that he was never known to have a dollar in his life; to swear an oath, or drink a drop of spirits. As to his ignorance, he certainly never had the advantages of education, but he can read and write, (it was taught him by his parents,) and for natural intelligence and quickness of apprehension, is surpassed by few men I have ever seen. As to his being a coward, his reason as given for not resisting Mr. Phipps, shews the decision of his character. When he saw Mr. Phipps present his gun, he said he knew it was impossible for him to escape as the woods were full of men; he therefore thought it was better to surrender, and trust to fortune for his escape. He is a complete fanatic, or plays his part most admirably. On other subjects he possesses an uncommon share of intelligence, with a mind capable of attaining any thing; but warped and perverted by the influence of early impressions. He is below the ordinary stature, though strong and active, having the true negro face, every feature of which is strongly marked. I shall not attempt to describe the effect of his narrative, as told and commented on by himself, in the condemned hole of the prison. The calm, deliberate composure with which he spoke of his late deeds and intentions, the expression of his fiend-like face when excited by enthusiasm, still bearing the stains of the blood of helpless innocence about him; clothed with rags and covered with chains; yet daring to raise his manacled hands to heaven, with a spirit soaring above the attributes of man; I looked on him and my blood curdled in my veins. . . .

SUPPLEMENTARY READINGS

Bontemps, Arna. *Black Thunder.* Boston: Beacon Press, 1936, 1963. (Gabriel's revolt, Virginia, 1800.)

Duff, John B., and Peter M. Mitchell, eds. *The Nat Turner Rebellion: The Historical Event and the Modern Controversy.* New York: Harper & Row, 1971.

Gross, Seymour L., and Eileen Bender. "History, Politics and Literature: The Myth of Nat Turner." *American Quarterly* 23, no. 4 (October 1971): 487–518.

Killens, John Oliver, ed. *The Trial Record of Denmark Vesey.* Boston: Beacon Press, 1970.

Raboteau, Albert J. *Slave Religion.* New York: Oxford University Press, 1978. Chap. 6.

12

FREDERICK DOUGLASS

Slaveholding Religion and the Christianity of Christ

Why did so many Afro-Americans emerge from slavery's dark veil as self-declared Christians? Baptism and bondage were inherently in conflict. Christianity and slavery, despite the protestations of southern theocrats, were fundamentally at odds. The noted abolitionist, orator, and writer, Frederick Douglass (1818–95) wrote forcefully of this paradox. The first of his three autobiographies, published in 1845, relates Douglass's life from slavery in Maryland to his escape in 1838. Those masters who covered their crimes with a veneer of piety draw his strongest rebuke. By force of logic and personal agony, some slaves became practical atheists, scoffing at the religion of masters who prayed with them on Sunday but beat them on Monday, while others sought to distinguish between slaveholding religion and Christianity proper. Douglass described slaveholding piety as bad, corrupt, and wicked, and true Christianity as good, pure, and holy. In an appendix to his narrative he sought to dispel the impression that his stinging attack on slaveholding Christianity was directed at true Christianity. To those who would dismiss the slaves' religion as escapist fantasy, Douglass's words speak eloquently of the capacity of Afro-Americans to construct houses of faith even from loose straw gleaned from fields they worked but did not own. In the Afro-American Christian worldview, God moved within human history to carry the slaves to freedom, just as in the time of Moses and the Egyptian slaves.

ON THE FIRST of January, 1834, I left Mr. Covey, and went to live with Mr. William Freeland, who lived about three miles from St. Michael's. I soon found Mr. Freeland a very different man from Mr. Covey. Though not rich, he was what would be called an educated southern gentleman. Mr. Covey, as I have shown, was a well-trained negro-breaker and slave-driver. The former (slaveholder though he was) seemed to possess some regard for honor, some reverence for justice, and some respect for hu-

Source: *Narrative of the Life of Frederick Douglass, An American Slave.* Boston: Anti-Slavery Office, 1845. Pp. 77–82 and [118]–25.

manity. The latter seemed totally insensible to all such sentiments. Mr. Freeland had many of the faults peculiar to slaveholders, such as being very passionate and fretful; but I must do him the justice to say, that he was exceedingly free from those degrading vices to which Mr. Covey was constantly addicted. The one was open and frank, and we always knew where to find him. The other was a most artful deceiver, and could be understood only by such as were skilful enough to detect his cunningly-devised frauds. Another advantage I gained in my new master was, he made no pretensions to, or profession of, religion; and this, in my opinion, was truly a great advantage. I assert most unhesitatingly, that the religion of the south is a mere covering for the most horrid crimes,—a justifier of the most appalling barbarity,—a sanctifier of the most hateful frauds,—and a dark shelter under, which the darkest, foulest, grossest, and most infernal deeds of slaveholders find the strongest protection. Were I to be again reduced to the chains of slavery, next to that enslavement, I should regard being the slave of a religious master the greatest calamity that could befall me. For of all slaveholders with whom I have ever met, religious slaveholders are the worst. I have ever found them the meanest and basest, the most cruel and cowardly, of all others. It was my unhappy lot not only to belong to a religious slaveholder, but to live in a community of such religionists. Very near Mr. Freeland lived the Rev. Daniel Weeden, and in the same neighborhood lived the Rev. Rigby Hopkins. These were members and ministers in the Reformed Methodist Church. Mr. Weeden owned, among others, a woman slave, whose name I have forgotten. This woman's back, for weeks, was kept literally raw, made so by the lash of this merciless, *religious* wretch. He used to hire hands. His maxim was, Behave well or behave ill, it is the duty of a master occasionally to whip a slave, to remind him of his master's authority. Such was his theory, and such his practice.

Mr. Hopkins was even worse than Mr. Weeden. His chief boast was his ability to manage slaves. The peculiar feature of his government was that of whipping slaves in advance of deserving it. He always managed to have one or more of his slaves to whip every Monday morning. He did this to alarm their fears, and strike terror into those who escaped. His plan was to whip for the smallest offences, to prevent the commission of large ones. Mr. Hopkins could always find some excuse for whipping a slave. It would astonish one, unaccustomed to a slaveholding life, to see with what wonderful ease a slaveholder can find things, of which to make occasion to whip a slave. A mere look, word, or motion,—a mistake, accident, or want of power,—are all matters for which a slave may be whipped at any time. Does a slave look dissatisfied? It is said, he has the devil in him, and it must be whipped out. Does he speak loudly when spoken to by his master? Then he is getting high-minded, and should be taken down a button-hole lower. Does he forget to pull off his hat at the approach of a white person? Then he is wanting in reverence, and should be whipped for it. Does he ever venture to vindicate his conduct, when censured for it? Then he is guilty of impudence,—one of the greatest crimes of which a slave can be guilty. Does he ever venture to suggest a different mode of doing things from that pointed out by his master? He is indeed presumptuous, and getting above himself; and nothing less than a flogging will do for him. Does he, while ploughing, break a plough,—or, while hoeing, break a hoe? It is owing to his carelessness, and for it a slave must always be whipped. Mr. Hopkins could always find something of this sort to justify the use of the lash, and he seldom failed to embrace such opportunities. There was not a man in the whole county, with whom the slaves who had the getting their own home, would not prefer to live, rather than with this Rev. Mr. Hopkins. And yet there was not a man any where round, who made higher professions of religion, or was more active in revivals,—more attentive to the class, love-feast, prayer and preaching meetings, or more devotional in his family,—that prayed earlier, later, louder, and longer,—than this same reverend slave-driver, Rigby Hopkins.

But to return to Mr. Freeland, and to my experience while in his employment. He, like Mr. Covey, gave us enough to eat; but, unlike Mr. Covey, he also gave us sufficient time to take our meals. He worked us hard, but always between sunrise and sunset. He required a good deal of work to be done, but gave us good tools with which to work. His farm was large, but he employed hands enough to work it, and with ease, compared with many of his neighbors. My treatment, while in his employment, was heavenly, compared with what I experienced at the hands of Mr. Edward Covey.

Mr. Freeland was himself the owner of but two slaves. Their names were Henry Harris and John Harris. The rest of his hands he hired. These consisted of myself, Sandy Jenkins, and Handy Caldwell. Henry and John were quite intelligent, and in a very little while after I went there, I succeeded in creating in them a strong desire to learn how to read. This desire soon sprang up in the others also. They very soon mustered up some old spelling-books, and nothing would do but that I must keep a Sabbath school. I agreed to do so, and accordingly devoted my Sundays to teaching these my loved fellow-slaves how to read. Neither of them knew his letters when I went there. Some of the slaves of the neighboring farms found what was going on, and also availed themselves of this little opportunity to learn to read. It was understood, among all who came, that there must be as little display about it as possible. It was necessary to keep our religious masters at St. Michael's unacquainted with the fact, that, instead of spending the Sabbath in wrestling, boxing, and drinking whisky, we were trying to learn how to read the will of God; for they had much rather see us engaged in those degrading sports, than to see us behaving like intellectual, moral, and accountable beings. My blood boils as I think of the bloody manner in which Messrs. Wright Fairbanks and Garrison West, both class-leaders, in connection with many others, rushed in upon us with sticks and stones, and broke up our virtuous little Sabbath school, at St. Michael's—all calling themselves Christians! humble followers of the Lord Jesus Christ! But I am again digressing.

I held my Sabbath school at the house of a free colored man, whose name I deem it imprudent to mention; for should it be known, it might embarrass him greatly, though the crime of holding the school was committed ten years ago. I had at one time over forty scholars, and those of the right sort, ardently desiring to learn. They were of all ages, though mostly men and women. I look back to those Sundays with an amount of pleasure not to be expressed. They were great days to my soul. The work of instructing my dear fellow-slaves was the sweetest engagement with which I was ever blessed. We loved each other, and to leave them at the close of the Sabbath was a severe cross indeed. When I think that these precious souls are to-day shut up in the prison-house of slavery, my feelings overcome me, and I am almost ready to ask, "Does a righteous God govern the universe? and for what does he hold the thunders in his right hand, if not to smite the oppressor, and deliver the spoiled out of the hand of the spoiler?" These dear souls came not to Sabbath school because it was popular to do so, nor did I teach them because it was reputable to be thus engaged. Every moment they spent in that school, they were liable to be taken up, and given thirty-nine lashes. They came because they wished to learn. Their minds had been starved by their cruel masters. They had been shut up in mental darkness. I taught them, because it was the delight of my soul to be doing something that looked like bettering the condition of my race. I kept up my school nearly the whole year I lived with Mr. Freeland; and, beside my Sabbath school, I devoted three evenings in the week, during the winter, to teaching the slaves at home. And I have the happiness to know, that several of those who came to Sabbath school learned how to read; and that one, at least, is now free through my agency. . . .

Appendix

I find, since reading over the foregoing Narrative that I have, in several instances, spoken in such a tone and manner, respecting religion, as may possibly lead those unacquainted with my religious views to suppose me an opponent of all religion. To remove the liability of such misapprehension, I deem it proper to append the following brief explanation. What I have said respecting and against religion, I mean strictly to apply to the *slaveholding religion* of this land, and with no possible reference to Christianity proper; for, between the Christianity of this land, and the Christianity of Christ, I recognize the widest possible difference—so wide, that to receive the one as good, pure, and holy, is of necessity to reject the other as bad, corrupt, and wicked. To be the friend of the one, is of necessity to be the enemy of the other. I love the pure, peaceable, and impartial Christianity of Christ: I therefore hate the corrupt, slaveholding, women-whipping, cradle-plundering, partial and hypocritical Christianity of this land. Indeed, I can see no reason, but the most deceitful one, for calling the religion of this land Christianity. I look upon it as the climax of all misnomers, the boldest of all frauds, and the grossest of all libels. Never was there a clearer case of "stealing the livery of the court of heaven to serve the devil in." I am filled with unutterable loathing when I contemplate the religious pomp and show, together with the horrible inconsistencies, which every where surround me. We have men-stealers for ministers, women-whippers for missionaries, and cradle-plunderers for church members. The man who wields the blood-clotted cowskin during the week fills the pulpit on Sunday, and claims to be a minister of the meek and lowly Jesus. The man who robs me of my earnings at the end of each week meets me as a class-leader on Sunday morning, to show me the way of life, and the path of salvation. He who sells my sister, for purposes of prostitution, stands forth as the pious advocate of purity. He who proclaims it a religious duty to read the Bible denies me the right of learning to read the name of the God who made me. He who is the religious advocate of marriage robs whole millions of its sacred influence, and leaves them to the ravages of wholesale pollution. The warm defender of the sacredness of the family relation is the same that scatters whole families,—sundering husbands and wives, parents and children, sisters and brothers,—leaving the hut vacant, and the hearth desolate. We see the thief preaching against theft, and the adulterer against adultery. We have men sold to build churches, women sold to support the gospel, and babes sold to purchase Bibles for the *poor heathen! all for the glory of God and the good of souls!* The slave auctioneer's bell and the church-going bell chime in with each other, and the bitter cries of the heart-broken slave are drowned in the religious shouts of his pious master. Revivals of religion and revivals in the slave-trade go hand in hand together. The slave prison and the church stand near each other. The clanking of fetters and the rattling of chains in the prison, and the pious psalm and solemn prayer in the church, may be heard at the same time. The dealers in the bodies and souls of men erect their stand in the presence of the pulpit, and they mutually help each other. The dealer gives his blood-stained gold to support the pulpit, and the pulpit, in return, covers his infernal business with the garb of Christianity. Here we have religion and robbery the allies of each other—devils dressed in angels' robes, and hell presenting the semblance of paradise.

> "Just God! and these are they,
>   Who minister at thine altar, God of right!
> Men who their hands, with prayer and blessing, lay
>   On Israel's ark of light.
>
> "What! preach, and kidnap men?
>   Give thanks, and rob thy own afflicted poor?
> Talk of thy glorious liberty, and then
>   Bolt hard the captive's door?
>
> "What! servants of thy own
>   Merciful Son, who came to seek and save
> The homeless and the outcast, fettering down
>   The tasked and plundered slave!
>
> "Pilate and Herod friends!
>   Chief priests and rulers, as of old, combine!
> Just God and holy! is that church which lends
>   Strength to the spoiler thine?"

The Christianity of America is a Christianity, of whose votaries it may be as truly said, as it was of the ancient scribes and Pharisees, "They bind heavy burdens, and grievous to be borne, and lay them on men's shoulders, but they themselves will not move them with one of their fingers. All their works they do for to be seen of men.——They love the uppermost rooms at feasts, and the chief seats in the synagogues, . . . and to be called of men, Rabbi, Rabbi.——But woe unto you, scribes and Pharisees, hypocrites! for ye shut up the kingdom of heaven against men; for ye neither go in yourselves, neither suffer ye them that are entering to go in. Ye devour widows' houses, and for a pretence make long prayers; therefore ye shall receive the greater damnation. Ye compass sea and land to make one proselyte, and when he is made, ye make him twofold more the child of hell than yourselves.————Woe unto you, scribes and Pharisees, hypocrites! for ye pay tithe of mint, and anise, and cumin, and have omitted the weightier matters of the law, judgment, mercy, and faith; these ought ye to have done, and not to leave the other undone. Ye blind guides! which strain at a gnat, and swallow a camel. Woe unto you, scribes and Pharisees, hypocrites! for ye make clean the outside of the cup and of the platter; but within, they are full of extortion and excess.————Woe unto you, scribes and Pharisees, hypocrites! for ye are like unto whited sepulchres, which indeed appear beautiful outward, but are within full of dead men's bones, and of all uncleanness. Even so ye also outwardly appear righteous unto men, but within ye are full of hypocrisy and iniquity."

Dark and terrible as is this picture, I hold it to be strictly true of the overwhelming mass of professed Christians in America. They strain at a gnat, and swallow a camel. Could any thing be more true of our churches? They would be shocked at the proposition of fellowshipping a *sheep*-stealer; and at the same time they hug to their communion a *man*-stealer, and brand me with being an infidel, if I find fault with them for it. They attend with Pharisaical strictness to the outward forms of religion, and at the same time neglect the weightier matters of the law, judgment, mercy, and faith. They are always ready to sacrifice, but seldom to show mercy. They are they who are represented as professing to love God whom they have not seen, whilst they hate their brother whom they have seen. They love the heathen on the other side of the globe. They can pray for him, pay money to have the Bible put into his hand, and missionaries to instruct him; while they despise and totally neglect the heathen at their own doors.

Such is, very briefly, my view of the religion of this land; and to avoid any misunderstanding, growing out of the use of general terms, I mean, by the religion of this land, that which is revealed in the words, deeds, and actions, of those bodies, north and south, calling themselves Christian churches, and yet in union with slave-holders. It is against religion, as presented by these bodies, that I have felt it my duty to testify.

I conclude these remarks by copying the following portrait of the religion of the south, (which is, by communion and fellowship, the religion of the north,) which I soberly affirm is "true to the life," and without caricature or the slightest exaggeration. It is said to have been drawn, several years before the present anti-slavery agitation began, by a northern Methodist preacher, who, while residing at the south, had an opportunity to see slaveholding morals, manners, and piety, with his own eyes. "Shall I not visit for these things? saith the Lord. Shall not my soul be avenged on such a nation as this?"

"A Parody.

"Come, saints and sinners, hear me tell
How pious priests whip Jack and Nell,
And women buy and children sell,
And preach all sinners down to hell,
   And sing of heavenly union.

"They'll bleat and baa, dona like goats,
Gorge down black sheep, and strain at motes,
Array their backs in fine black coats,
Then seize their negroes by their throats,
   And choke, for heavenly union.

"They'll church you if you sip a dram,
And damn you if you steal a lamb;
Yet rob old Tony, Doll, and Sam,
Of human rights, and bread and ham;
   Kidnapper's heavenly union.

"They'll loudly talk of Christ's reward,
And bind his image with a cord,
And scold, and swing the lash abhorred,
And sell their brother in the Lord
   To handcuffed heavenly union.

"They'll read and sing a sacred song,
And make a prayer both loud and long,
And teach the right and do the wrong,
Hailing the brother, sister throng,
   With words of heavenly union.

"We wonder how such saints can sing,
Or praise the Lord upon the wing,
Who roar, and scold, and whip, and sting,
And to their slaves and mammon cling,
   In guilty conscience union.

"They'll raise tobacco, corn, and rye,
And drive, and thieve, and cheat, and lie,
And lay up treasures in the sky,
By making switch and cowskin fly,
   In hope of heavenly union.

"They'll crack old Tony on the skull,
And preach and roar like Bashan bull,
Or braying ass, of mischief full,
Then seize old Jacob by the wool,
    And pull for heavenly union.

"A roaring, ranting sleek man-thief,
Who lived on mutton, veal, and beef,
Yet never would afford relief
To needy, sable sons of grief,
    Was big with heavenly union.

" 'Love not the world,' the preacher said,
And winked his eye, and shook his head;
He seized on Tom, and Dick, and Ned,
Cut short their meat, and clothes, and bread,
    Yet still loved heavenly union.

"Another preacher whining spoke
Of One whose heart for sinners broke:
He tied old Nanny to an oak,
And drew the blood at every stroke,
    And prayed for heavenly union.

"Two others oped their iron jaws,
And waved their children-stealing paws;
There sat their children in gewgaws;
By stinting negroes' backs and maws,
    They kept up heavenly union.

"All good from Jack another takes,
And entertains their flirts and rakes,
Who dress as sleek as glossy snakes,
And cram their mouths with sweetened cakes;
    And this goes down for union."

Sincerely and earnestly hoping that this little book may do something toward throwing light on the American slave system, and hastening the glad day of deliverance to the millions of my brethren in bonds—faithfully relying upon the power of truth, love, and justice, for success in my humble efforts—and solemnly pledging myself anew to the sacred cause,—I subscribe myself,

                                    Frederick Douglass.
                                    Lynn, *Mass., April* 28, 1845.

SUPPLEMENTARY READINGS

Douglass, Frederick. *Life and Times of Frederick Douglass* [1892]. New York: Collier Books, 1969.

Mathews, Donald G. *Religion in the Old South.* Chicago: University of Chicago Press, 1977. Chaps. 5 and 6.

Meyer, Michael, ed. *Frederick Douglass: The Narrative and Selected Writings.* New York: Modern Library, 1984.

Smith, H. Shelton. *In His Image, But . . . Racism in Southern Religion, 1780–1910.* Durham, N.C.: Duke University Press, 1972. Chap. 3.

Smith, Timothy. "Slavery and Theology: The Emergence of Black Christian Consciousness in Nineteenth Century America." *Church History* 41, no. 4 (December 1972): 497–512.

13

THOMAS WENTWORTH HIGGINSON

Slave Songs and Spirituals

In "O Black and Unknown Bards" the poet James Weldon Johnson asked, "Heart of what slave poured out such melody as 'Steal away to Jesus?'" Folklorists, musicologists, and historians have also pondered the question of the origin of the slave spirituals. Some credited white camp meetings and revivals; others pointed to similarities with traditional African chants and praise songs. The militant New England abolitionist, Thomas W. Higginson (1823–1911), commanded the first freed slave regiment to fight against the Confederacy. He heard "the choked voice of a race at last unloosed" and diligently took down the songs sung by the 1st South Carolina Volunteers around evening campfires. Higginson failed to recognize the African musical components of the slave songs, but he did catch something of the communal process by which this rich musical heritage evolved. Drawing from stories in the Bible, evangelical sermons and hymns, African musical styles, and their own experiences in the slave quarters and "hush harbors," the slaves fashioned a unique means to "keep on keeping on" under the physical and psychological pressures of daily life. As Frederick Douglass also observed, some slave songs bore coded protest messages, but the "spirituals" or "sorrow songs" are sacred not secular music. Afro-American Christians believed that the supernatural interacted with the natural; the whole world rested in the hands of God.

THE WAR BROUGHT to some of us, besides its direct experiences, many a strange fulfilment of dreams of other days. For instance, the present writer had been a faithful student of the Scottish ballads, and had always envied Sir Walter the delight of tracing them out amid their own heather, and of writing them down piecemeal from the lips of aged crones. It was a strange enjoyment, therefore, to be suddenly brought into the midst of a kindred world of unwritten songs, as simple and indigenous as the Border Minstrelsy, more uniformly plaintive, almost always more quaint, and often as essentially poetic.

This interest was rather increased by the fact that I had for many

Source: "Negro Spirituals." *Atlantic Monthly* 19, no. 116 (June 1867): 685–94.

years heard of this class of songs under the name of "Negro Spirituals," and had even heard some of them sung by friends from South Carolina. I could now gather on their own soil these strange plants, which I had before seen as in museums alone. True, the individual songs rarely coincided; there was a line here, a chorus there,—just enough to fix the class, but this was unmistakable. It was not strange that they differed, for the range seemed almost endless, and South Carolina, Georgia, and Florida seemed to have nothing but the generic character in common, until all were mingled in the united stock of camp-melodies.

Often in the starlit evening I have returned from some lonely ride by the swift river, or on the plover-haunted barrens, and, entering the camp, have silently approached some glimmering fire, round which the dusky figures moved in the rhythmical barbaric dance the negroes call a "shout," chanting, often harshly, but always in the most perfect time, some monotonous refrain. Writing down in the darkness, as I best could,—perhaps with my hand in the safe covert of my pocket,—the words of the song, I have afterwards carried it to my tent, like some captured bird or insect, and then, after examination, put it by. Or, summoning one of the men at some period of leisure,—Corporal Robert Sutton, for instance, whose iron memory held all the details of a song as if it were a ford or a forest,—I have completed the new specimen by supplying the absent parts. The music I could only retain by ear, and though the more common strains were repeated often enough to fix their impression, there were others that occurred only once or twice.

The words will be here given, as nearly as possible, in the original dialect, and if the spelling seems sometimes inconsistent, or the misspelling insufficient, it is because I could get no nearer. I wished to avoid what seems to me the only error of Lowell's "Biglow Papers" in respect to dialect,—the occasional use of an extreme misspelling, which merely confuses the eye, without taking us any closer to the peculiarity of sound.

The favorite song in camp was the following,—sung with no accompaniment but the measured clapping of hands and the clatter of many feet. It was sung perhaps twice as often as any other. This was partly due to the fact that it properly consisted of a chorus alone, with which the verses of other songs might be combined at random.

i. Hold Your Light.

"Hold your light, Brudder Robert,—
   Hold your light,
Hold your light on Canaan's shore.

"What make ole Satan for follow me so?
Satan ain't got notin' for do wid me.
  Hold your light,
  Hold your light,
  Hold your light on Canaan's shore."

This would be sung for half an hour at a time, perhaps, each person present being named in turn. It seemed the simplest primitive type of "spiritual." The next in popularity was almost as elementary, and, like this, named successively each one of the circle. It was, however, much more resounding and convivial in its music.

ii. Bound to Go.

"Jordan River, I'm bound to go,
  Bound to go, bound to go,—
Jordan River, I'm bound to go,
  And bid 'em fare ye well.

"My Brudder Robert, I'm bound to go,
  Bound to go, &c.

"My Sister Lucy, I'm bound to go,
  Bound to go," &c.

Sometimes it was "tink 'em" (think them) "fare ye well." The *ye* was so detached, that I thought at first it was "very" or "vary well."

Another picturesque song, which seemed immensely popular, was at first very bewildering to me. I could not make out the first words of the chorus, and called it the "Romandàr," being reminded of some Romaic song which I had formerly heard. That association quite fell in with the Orientalism of the new tent-life.

iii. Room in There.

"O, my mudder is gone! my mudder is gone!
My mudder is gone into heaven, my Lord!
  I can't stay behind!
Dere's room in dar, room in dar,
Room in dar, in de heaven, my Lord!
  I can't stay behind,

Can't stay behind, my dear,
  I can't stay behind!

"O, my fader is gone!" &c.

"O, de angels are gone!" &c.

"O, I'se been on de road! I'se been on de road!
I'se been on de road into heaven, my Lord!
   I can't stay behind!
O, room in dar, room in dar,
Room in dar, in de heaven, my Lord!
   I can't stay behind!"

By this time every man within hearing, from oldest to youngest, would be wriggling and shuffling, as if through some magic piper's bewitchment; for even those who at first affected contemptuous indifference would be drawn into the vortex erelong.

Next to these in popularity ranked a class of songs belonging emphatically to the Church Militant, and available for camp purposes with very little strain upon their symbolism. This, for instance, had a true companion-in-arms heartiness about it, not impaired by the feminine invocation at the end.

iv. Hail Mary.

"One more valiant soldier here,
   One more valiant soldier here,
One more valiant soldier here,
   To help me bear de cross.
O hail, Mary, hail!
   Hail, Mary, hail!
Hail, Mary, hail!
   To help me bear de cross."

I fancied that the original reading might have been "soul," instead of "soldier,"—with some other syllable inserted, to fill out the metre,—and that the "Hail, Mary," might denote a Roman Catholic origin, as I had several men from St. Augustine who held in a dim way to that faith. It was a very ringing song, though not so grandly jubilant as the next, which was really impressive as the singers pealed it out, when marching or rowing or embarking.

v. My Army Cross Over.

"My army cross over,
My army cross over.
O, Pharaoh's army drownded!
My army cross over.

"We'll cross de mighty river,
   My army cross over;

> We'll cross de river Jordan,
>   My army cross over;
> We'll cross de danger water,
>   My army cross over;
> We'll cross de mighty Myo,
>   My army cross over. (*Thrice.*)
> O, Pharaoh's army drownded!
>   My army cross over."

I could get no explanation of the "mighty Myo," except that one of the old men thought it meant the river of death. Perhaps it is an African word. In the Cameroon dialect, "Mawa" signifies "to die."

The next also has a military ring about it, and the first line is well matched by the music. The rest is conglomerate, and one or two lines show a more Northern origin. "Done" is a Virginia shibboleth, quite distinct from the "been" which replaces it in South Carolina. Yet one of their best choruses, without any fixed words, was, "De bell done ringing," for which, in proper South Carolina dialect, would have been substituted, "De bell been a-ring." This refrain may have gone South with our army.

vi. Ride In, Kind Saviour.

> "Ride in, kind Saviour!
>   No man can hinder me.
> O, Jesus is a mighty man!
>   No man, &c.
> We're marching through Virginny fields.
>   No man, &c.
> O, Satan is a busy man,
>   No man, &c.
> And he has his sword and shield,
>   No man, &c.
> O, old Secesh done come and gone!
>   No man can hinder me."

Sometimes they substituted "hinder *we*," which was more spicy to the ear, and more in keeping with the usual head-over-heels arrangement of their pronouns.

Almost all their songs were thoroughly religious in their tone, however quaint their expression, and were in a minor key, both as to words and music. The attitude is always the same, and as a commentary on the life of the race, is infinitely pathetic. Nothing but patience for this life,—nothing but triumph in the next. Sometimes the present predominates, sometimes the future; but the combination is always implied. In the following, for instance, we hear simply the patience.

vii. This World Almost Done.

"Brudder, keep your lamp trimmin' and a-burnin',
Keep your lamp trimmin' and a-burnin',
Keep your lamp trimmin' and a-burnin',
 For dis world most done.
So keep your lamp, &c.
 Dis world most done."

But in the next, the final reward of patience is proclaimed as plaintively.

viii. I Want To Go Home.

"Dere's no rain to wet you,
 O, yes, I want to go home.
Dere's no sun to burn you,
 O, yes, I want to go home;
O, push along, believers,
 O, yes, &c.
Dere's no hard trials,
 O, yes, &c.
Dere's no whips-a-crackin',
 O, yes, &c.
My brudder on de wayside,
 O, yes, &c.
O, push along, my brudder,
 O, yes, &c.
Where dere's no stormy weather,
 O, yes, &c.
Dere's no tribulation,
 O, yes, &c."

This next was a boat-song, and timed well with the tug of the oar.

ix. The Coming Day.

"I want to go to Canaan,
I want to go to Canaan,
I want to go to Canaan,
 To meet 'em at de comin' day.
O, remember, let me go to Canaan,
 (*Thrice.*)

To meet 'em, &c.
O brudder, let me go to Canaan,
   (*Thrice.*)
To meet 'em, &c.
My brudder, you—of!—remember
   (*Thrice.*)
To meet 'em at de comin' day."

The following begins with a startling affirmation, yet the last line quite outdoes the first. This, too, was a capital boat-song.

x. One More River.

"O, Jordan bank was a great old bank!
   Dere ain't but one more river to cross.
We have some valiant soldier here,
   Dere ain't, &c.
O, Jordan stream will never run dry,
   Dere ain't, &c.
Dere's a hill on my leff, and he catch on my right,
Dere ain't but one more river to cross."

I could get no explanation of this last riddle, except, "Dat mean, if you go on de leff go to 'struction, and if you go on de right, go to God, for sure."

In others, more of spiritual conflict is implied, as in this next.

xi. O the Dying Lamb!

"I wants to go where Moses trod,
   O de dying Lamb!
For Moses gone to de promised land,
   O de dying Lamb!
To drink from springs dat never run dry,
   O, &c.
Cry O my Lord!
   O, &c.
Before I'll stay in hell one day,
   O, &c.
I'm in hopes to pray my sins away,
   O, &c.
Cry O my Lord!
   O, &c.
Brudder Moses promised for be dar too,
   O, &c.

To drink from streams dat never run dry,
O de dying Lamb!"

In the next, the conflict is at its height, and the lurid imagery of the Apocalypse is brought to bear. This book, with the books of Moses, constituted their Bible; all that lay between, even the narratives of the life of Jesus, they hardly cared to read or to hear.

XII. Down in the Valley.

"We'll run and never tire,
We'll run and never tire,
We'll run and never tire,
     Jesus set poor sinners free.
Way down in de valley,
     Who will rise and go with me?
You've heern talk of Jesus,
     Who set poor sinners free.

"De lightnin' and de flashin',
De lightnin' and de flashin',
De lightnin' and de flashin',
     Jesus set poor sinners free.
I can't stand de fire. (*Thrice.*)
     Jesus set poor sinners free,
De green trees a-flamin'. (*Thrice.*)
     Jesus set poor sinners free,
          Way down in de valley,
               Who will rise and go with me?
     You've heern talk of Jesus
          Who set poor sinners free."

"De valley" and "de lonesome valley" were familiar words in their religious experience. To descend into that region implied the same process with the "anxious-seat" of the camp-meeting. When a young girl was supposed to enter it, she bound a handkerchief by a peculiar knot over her head, and made it a point of honor not to change a single garment till the day of her baptism, so that she was sure of being in physical readiness for the cleansing rite, whatever her spiritual mood might be. More than once, in noticing a damsel thus mystically kerchiefed, I have asked some dusky attendant its meaning, and have received the unfailing answer,—framed with their usual indifference to the genders of pronouns,—"He in de lonesome valley, sa."

The next gives the same dramatic conflict, while its detached and impersonal refrain gives it strikingly the character of the Scotch and Scandinavian ballads.

xiii. Cry Holy.

"Cry holy, holy!
　　Look at de people dat is born of God.
And I run down de valley, and I run down to pray,
　　Says, look at de people dat is born of God.
When I get dar, Cappen Satan was dar
　　Says, look at, &c.
Says, young man, young man, dere's no use for pray,
　　Says, look at, &c.
For Jesus is dead, and God gone away,
　　Says, look at, &c.
And I made him out a liar and I went my way,
　　Says, look at, &c.
　　Sing holy, holy!

"O, Mary was a woman, and he had a one Son,
　　Says, look at, &c.
And de Jews and de Romans had him hung,
　　Says, look at, &c.
　　Cry holy, holy!

"And I tell you, sinner, you had better had pray,
　　Says, look at, &c.
For hell is a dark and dismal place,
　　Says, look at, &c.
And I tell you, sinner, and I wouldn't go dar!
　　Says, look at, &c.
　　Cry holy, holy!"

Here is an infinitely quaint description of the length of the heavenly road:—

xiv. O'er the Crossing.

"Yonder's my old mudder,
　　Been a-waggin' at de hill so long.
It's about time she'll cross over;
　　Get home bimeby.
Keep prayin', I do believe
　　We're a long time waggin' o'er de crossin'.
Keep prayin', I do believe
　　We'll get home to heaven bimeby.

> "Hear dat mournful thunder
>   Roll from door to door,
> Calling home God's children;
>   Get home bimeby.
> Little chil'en, I do believe
>   We'll get home, &c.
> Little chil'en, I do believe
>   We'll get home, &c.
>
> "See dat forked lightnin'
>   Flash from tree to tree,
> Callin' home God's chil'en;
>   Get home bimeby.
> True believer, I do believe
>   We're a long time, &c.
> O brudders, I do believe,
>   We'll get home to heaven bimeby."

One of the most singular pictures of future joys, and with a fine flavor of hospitality about it, was this:—

xv. Walk 'em Easy.

> "O, walk 'em easy round de heaven,
> Walk 'em easy round de heaven,
> Walk 'em easy round de heaven,
>   Dat all de people may join de band.
> Walk 'em easy round de heaven.
>   (*Thrice.*)
> O, shout glory till 'em join dat band!"

The chorus was usually the greater part of the song, and often came in paradoxically, thus:—

xvi. O Yes, Lord.

> "O, must I be like de foolish mans?
>   O yes, Lord!
> Will build de house on de sandy hill.
>   O yes, Lord!
> I'll build my house on Zion hill,
>   O yes, Lord!
> No wind nor rain can blow me down
>   O yes, Lord!"

The next is very graceful and lyrical, and with more variety of rhythm than usual:—

xvii. Bow Low, Mary.

"Bow low, Mary, bow low, Martha,
    For Jesus come and lock de door,
    And carry de keys away.
Sail, sail, over yonder,
    And view de promised land.
    For Jesus come, &c.
Weep, O Mary, bow low, Martha,
    For Jesus come, &c.
Sail, sail, my true believer;
Sail, sail, over yonder;
Mary, bow low, Martha, bow low,
    For Jesus come and lock de door
    And carry de keys away."

But of all the "spirituals" that which surprised me the most, I think,—perhaps because it was that in which external nature furnished the images most directly,—was this. With all my experience of their ideal ways of speech, I was startled when first I came on such a flower of poetry in that dark soil.

xviii. I Know Moon-Rise.

"I know moon-rise, I know star-rise,
    Lay dis body down.
I walk in de moonlight, I walk in de starlight,
    To lay dis body down.
I'll walk in de graveyard, I'll walk through de graveyard,
    To lay dis body down.
I'll lie in de grave and stretch out my arms;
    Lay dis body down.
I go to de judgment in de evenin' of de day,
    When I lay dis body down;
And my soul and your soul will meet in de day
    When I lay dis body down."

"I'll lie in de grave and stretch out my arms." Never, it seems to me, since man first lived and suffered, was his infinite longing for peace uttered more plaintively than in that line.

The next is one of the wildest and most striking of the whole series:

there is a mystical effect and a passionate striving throughout the whole. The Scriptural struggle between Jacob and the angel, which is only dimly expressed in the words, seems all uttered in the music. I think it impressed by imagination more powerfully than any other of these songs.

xix. Wrestling Jacob.

"O wrestlin' Jacob, Jacob, day's a-breakin';
    I will not let thee go!
O wrestlin' Jacob, Jacob, day's a-breakin';
    He will not let me go!
O, I hold my brudder wid a tremblin' hand;
    I would not let him go!
I hold my sister wid a tremblin' hand;
    I would not let her go!

"O, Jacob do hang from a tremblin' limb,
    He would not let him go!
O, Jacob do hang from a tremblin' limb;
    De Lord will bless my soul.
O wrestlin' Jacob, Jacob," &c.

Of "occasional hymns," properly so called, I noticed but one, a funeral hymn for an infant, which is sung plaintively over and over, without variety of words.

xx. The Baby Gone Home.

"De little baby gone home,
De little baby gone home,
De little baby gone along,
    For to climb up Jacob's ladder.
And I wish I'd been dar,
I wish I'd been dar,
I wish I'd been dar, my Lord,
    For to climb up Jacob's ladder."

Still simpler is this, which is yet quite sweet and touching.

xxi. Jesus With Us.

"He have been wid us, Jesus,
    He still wid us, Jesus,
He will be wid us, Jesus,
    Be wid us to the end."

The next seemed to be a favorite about Christmas time, when meditations on "de rollin' year" were frequent among them.

xxii. Lord, Remember Me!

"O do, Lord, remember me!
  O do, Lord, remember me!
O, do remember me, until de year roll round!
  Do, Lord, remember me!

"If you want to die like Jesus died,
  Lay in de grave.
You would fold your arms and close your eyes
  And die wid a free good will.

"For Death is a simple ting,
  And he go from door to door,
And he knock down some, and he cripple up some,
  And he leave some here to pray.

"O do, Lord, remember me!
  O do, Lord, remember me!
My old fader's gone till de year roll round;
  Do, Lord, remember me!"

The next was sung in such an operatic and rollicking way that it
was quite hard to fancy it a religious performance, which, however, it
was. I heard it but once.

xxiii. Early in the Morning.

"I meet little Rosa early in de mornin',
  O Jerusalem! early in de mornin';
And I ax her, How you do, my darter?
  O Jerusalem! early in de mornin'.

"I meet my mudder early in de mornin',
  O Jerusalem! &c.
And I ax her, How you do, my mudder?
  O Jerusalem! &c.

"I meet Budder Robert early in de mornin',
  O Jerusalem! &c.

And I ax him, How you do, my sonny?
  O Jerusalem! &c.

"I meet Tittawisa early in de mornin',
   O Jerusalem! &c.
And I ax her, How you do, my darter?
   O Jerusalem!" &c.

"Tittawisa" means "Sister Louisa." In songs of this class the name
of every person present successively appears.

Their best marching song, and one which was invaluable to lift
their feet along, as they expressed it, was the following. There was a
kind of spring and *lilt* to it, quite indescribable by words.

xxiv. Go in the Wilderness.

"Jesus call you. Go in de wilderness,
   Go in de wilderness, go in de wilderness,
Jesus call you. Go in de wilderness
   To wait upon de Lord.
Go wait upon de Lord,
Go wait upon de Lord,
Go wait upon de Lord, my God,
   He take away de sins of de world.

"Jesus a-waitin'. Go in de wilderness,
   Go, &c.
All dem chil'en go in de wilderness
   To wait upon de Lord."

The next was one of those which I had heard in boyish days,
brought North from Charleston. But the chorus alone was identical; the
words were mainly different, and those here given are quaint enough.

xxv. Blow Your Trumpet, Gabriel.

"O, blow your trumpet, Gabriel,
   Blow your trumpet louder;
   And I want dat trumpet to blow me home
   To my new Jerusalem.

"De prettiest ting dat ever I done
Was to serve de Lord when I was young.
   So blow your trumpet, Gabriel, &c.

"O, Satan is a liar, and he conjure too,
And if you don't mind, he'll conjure you.
   So blow your trumpet, Gabriel, &c.

"O, I was lost in de wilderness,
King Jesus hand me de candle down.
    So blow your trumpet, Gabriel," &c.

The following contains one of those odd transformations of proper names with which their Scriptural citations were often enriched. It rivals their text, "Paul may plant, and may polish wid water," which I have elsewhere quoted, and in which the sainted Apollos would hardly have recognized himself.

xxvi. In the Morning.

"In de mornin',
In de mornin',
Chil'en? Yes, my Lord!
    Don't you hear de trumpet sound?
If I had a-died when I was young,
I never would had de race for run.
    Don't you hear de trumpet sound?

"O Sam and Peter was fishin' in de sea,
And dey drop de net and follow my Lord.
    Don't you hear de trumpet sound?

"Dere's a silver spade for to dig my grave
And a golden chain for to let me down.
    Don't you hear de trumpet sound?
In de mornin',
In de mornin',
Chil'en? Yes, my Lord!
    Don't you hear de trumpet sound?"

These golden and silver fancies remind one of the King of Spain's daughter in "Mother Goose," and the golden apple, and the silver pear, which are doubtless themselves but the vestiges of some simple early composition like this. The next has a humbler and more domestic style of fancy.

xxvii. Fare Ye Well.

"My true believers, fare ye well,
Fare ye well, fare ye well,
Fare ye well, by de grace of God,
    For I'm going home.

Massa Jesus give me a little broom
For to sweep my heart clean,

And I will try, by de grace of God,
To win my way home."

Among the songs not available for marching, but requiring the concentrated enthusiasm of the camp, was "The Ship of Zion," of which they had three wholly distinct versions, all quite exuberant and tumultuous.

xxviii. The Ship of Zion.

"Come along, come along,
And let us go home,
O, glory, hallelujah!
Dis de old ship o' Zion,
Halleloo! Halleloo!
Dis de ole ship o' Zion,
Hallelujah!

"She has landed many a tousand,
She can land as many more.
O, glory, hallelujah! &c.

"Do you tink she will be able
For to take us all home?
O, glory, hallelujah! &c.

"You can tell 'em I'm a comin',
Halleloo! Halleloo!
You can tell 'em I'm a comin',
Hallelujah!
Come along, come along," &c.

xxix. The Ship of Zion.
(*Second version.*)

"Dis de good ole ship o' Zion,
Dis de good ole ship o' Zion,
Dis de good ole ship o' Zion,
    And she's makin' for de Promise Land.
She hab angels for de sailors. (*Thrice.*)
    And she's, &c.
And how you know dey's angels? (*Thrice.*)
    And she's, &c.
Good Lord, shall I be de one? (*Thrice.*)
    And she's, &c.

"Dat ship is out a-sailin', sailin', sailin',
    And she's, &c.
She's a-sailin' mighty steady, steady, steady,
    And she's, &c.
She'll neither reel nor totter, totter, totter,
    And she's, &c.
She's a-sailin' away cold Jordan, Jordan, Jordan,
    And she's, &c.
King Jesus is de captain, captain, captain,
    And she's makin' for de Promise Land."

xxx. The Ship of Zion.
(*Third version.*)

"De Gospel ship is sailin',
    Hosann—sann.
O, Jesus is de captain,
    Hosann—sann.
De angels are de sailors,
    Hosann—sann.
O, is your bundle ready?
    Hosann—sann.
O, have you got your ticket?
    Hosann—sann."

This abbreviated chorus is given with unspeakable unction.

The three just given are modifications of an old camp-meeting melody; and the same may be true of the three following, although I cannot find them in the Methodist hymn-books. Each, however, has its characteristic modifications, which make it well worth giving. In the second verse of this next, for instance, "Saviour" evidently has become "soldier."

xxxi. Sweet Music.

"Sweet music in heaven,
    Just beginning for to roll.
Don't you love God?
    Glory, hallelujah!

"Yes, late I heard my soldier say,
Come, heavy soul, I am de way.
    Don't you love God?
    Glory, hallelujah!

"I'll go and tell to sinners round
What a kind Saviour I have found.
   Don't you love God?
   Glory, hallelujah!

"My grief my burden long has been,
Because I was not cease from sin.
   Don't you love God?
   Glory, hallelujah!"

xxxii. Good News.

"O, good news! O, good news!
De angels brought de tidings down,
   Just comin' from de trone.
"As grief from out my soul shall fly,
   Just comin' from de trone;
I'll shout salvation when I die,
   Good news, O, good news!
   Just comin' from de trone.

"Lord, I want to go to heaven when I die,
Good news, O, good news! &c.

"De white folks call us a noisy crew,
   Good news, O, good news!
But dis I know, we are happy too,
   Just comin' from de trone."

xxxiii. The Heavenly Road.

"You may talk of my name as much as you please,
   And carry my name abroad,
But I really do believe I'm a child of God
   As I walk in de heavenly road.
O, won't you go wid me? (*Thrice.*)
   For to keep our garments clean.

"O, Satan is a mighty busy ole man,
   And roll rocks in my way;
But Jesus is my bosom friend,
   And roll 'em out of de way.
O, won't you go wid me? (*Thrice.*)
   For to keep our garments clean.

"Come, my brudder, if you never did pray,
   I hope you may pray to-night;

> For I really believe I'm a child of God
> As I walk in de heavenly road.
> O, won't you," &c.

Some of the songs had played an historic part during the war. For singing the next, for instance, the negroes had been put in jail in Georgetown, S.C., at the outbreak of the Rebellion. "We'll soon be free," was too dangerous an assertion; and though the chant was an old one, it was no doubt sung with redoubled emphasis during the new events. "De Lord will call us home," was evidently thought to be a symbolical verse; for, as a little drummer-boy explained to me, showing all his white teeth as he sat in the moonlight by the door of my tent, "Dey tink *de Lord* mean for say *de Yankees*."

xxxiv. We'll Soon Be Free.

> "We'll soon be free,
> We'll soon be free,
> We'll soon be free,
>   When de Lord will call us home.
> My brudder, how long,
> My brudder, how long,
> My brudder, how long,
>   'Fore we done sufferin' here?
> It won't be long (*Thrice.*)
>   'Fore de Lord will call us home.
> We'll walk de miry road (*Thrice.*)
>   Where pleasure never dies.
> We'll walk de golden street (*Thrice.*)
>   Where pleasure never dies.
> My brudder, how long (*Thrice.*)
>   'Fore we done sufferin' here?
> We'll soon be free (*Thrice.*)
>   When Jesus sets me free.
> We'll fight for liberty (*Thrice.*)
>   When de Lord will call us home."

The suspicion in this case was unfounded, but they had another song to which the Rebellion had actually given rise. This was composed by nobody knew whom,—though it was the most recent, doubtless, of all these "spirituals,"—and had been sung in secret to avoid detection. It is certainly plaintive enough. The peck of corn and pint of salt were slavery's rations.

xxxv. Many Thousand Go.

"No more peck o' corn for me,
No more, no more,—
No more peck o' corn for me,
Many tousand go.

"No more driver's lash for me, (*Twice.*)
No more, &c.

"No more pint o' salt for me, (*Twice.*)
No more, &c.

"No more hundred lash for me, (*Twice.*)
No more, &c.

"No more mistress' call for me,
No more, no more,—
No more mistress' call for me,
Many tousand go."

Even of this last composition, however, we have only the approximate date, and know nothing of the mode of composition. Allan Ramsay says of the Scotch songs, that, no matter who made them, they were soon attributed to the minister of the parish whence they sprang. And I always wondered, about these, whether they had always a conscious and definite origin in some leading mind, or whether they grew by gradual accretion, in an almost unconscious way. On this point I could get no information, though I asked many questions, until at last, one day when I was being rowed across from Beaufort to Ladies' Island, I found myself, with delight, on the actual trail of a song. One of the oarsmen, a brisk young fellow, not a soldier, on being asked for his theory of the matter, dropped out a coy confession. "Some good speri-tuals," he said, "are start jess out o' curiosity. I been a-raise a sing, my-self, once."

My dream was fulfilled, and I had traced out, not the poem alone, but the poet. I implored him to proceed.

"Once we boys," he said, "went for tote some rice, and de nigger-driver, he keep a-callin' on us; and I say, 'O, de ole nigger-driver!' Den anudder said, 'Fust ting my mammy tole me was, notin' so bad as nigger-driver.' Den I made a sing, just puttin' a word, and den anudder word."

Then he began singing, and the men, after listening a moment, joined in the chorus as if it were an old acquaintance, though they evidently had never heard it before. I saw how easily a new "sing" took root among them.

xxxvi. The Driver.

"O, de ole nigger-driver!
O, gwine away!
Fust ting my mammy tell me,
O, gwine away!
Tell me 'bout de nigger-driver,
O, gwine away!
Nigger-driver second devil,
O, gwine away!
Best ting for do he driver,
O, gwine away!
Knock he down and spoil he labor,
O, gwine away!"

It will be observed that, although this song is quite secular in its character, its author yet called it a "spiritual." I heard but two songs among them, at any time, to which they would not, perhaps, have given this generic name. One of these consisted simply in the endless repetition—after the manner of certain college songs—of the mysterious line,

"Rain fall and wet Becky Martin."

But who Becky Martin was, and why she should or should not be wet, and whether the dryness was a reward or a penalty, none could say. I got the impression that, in either case, the event was posthumous, and that there was some tradition of grass not growing over the grave of a sinner; but even this was vague, and all else vaguer.

The other song I heard but once, on a morning when a squad of men came in from picket duty, and chanted it in the most rousing way. It had been a stormy and comfortless night, and the picket station was very exposed. It still rained in the morning when I strolled to the edge of the camp, looking out for the men, and wondering how they had stood it. Presently they came striding along the road, at a great pace, with their shining rubber blankets worn as cloaks around them, the rain streaming from these and from their equally shining faces, which were almost all upon the broad grin, as they pealed out this remarkable ditty:—

xxxvii. Hangman Johnny.

"O, dey call me Hangman Johnny!
 O, ho! O, ho!
But I never hang nobody,
 O, hang, boys, hang!

"O, dey call me Hangman Johnny!
 O, ho! O, ho!
But we'll all hang togedder,
 O, hang, boys, hang!"

My presence apparently checked the performance of another verse, beginning, "De buckra 'list for money," apparently in reference to the controversy about the pay-question, then just beginning, and to the more mercenary aims they attributed to the white soldiers. But "Hangman Johnny" remained always a myth as inscrutable as "Becky Martin."

As they learned all their songs by ear, they often strayed into wholly new versions, which sometimes became popular, and entirely banished the others. This was amusingly the case, for instance, with one phrase in the popular camp-song of "Marching Along," which was entirely new to them until our quartermaster taught it to them, at my request. The words, "Gird on the armor," were to them a stumbling-block, and no wonder, until some ingenious ear substituted, "Guide on de army," which was at once accepted, and became universal.

"We'll guide on de army,
and be marching along,"

is now the established version on the Sea Islands.

These quaint religious songs were to the men more than a source of relaxation, they were a stimulus to courage and a tie to heaven. I never overheard in camp a profane or vulgar song. With the trifling exceptions given, all had a religious motive, while the most secular melody could not have been more exciting. A few youths from Savannah, who were comparatively men of the world, had learned some of the "Ethiopian Minstrel" ditties, imported from the North. These took no hold upon the mass; and, on the other hand, they sang reluctantly, even on Sunday, the long and short metres of the hymn-books, always gladly yielding to the more potent excitement of their own "spirituals." By these they could sing themselves, as had their fathers before them, out of the contemplation of their own low estate, into the sublime scenery of the Apocalypse. I remember that this minor-keyed pathos used to seem to me almost too sad to dwell upon, while slavery seemed destined to last for generations; but now that their patience has had its perfect work, history cannot afford to lose this portion of its record. There is no parallel instance of an oppressed race thus sustained by the religious sentiment alone. These songs are but the vocal expression of the simplicity of their faith and the sublimity of their long resignation.

SUPPLEMENTARY READINGS

Epstein, Dena J. *Sinful Tunes and Spirituals: Black Folk Music to the Civil War.* Urbana: University of Illinois Press, 1977.

Katz, Bernard, ed. *The Social Implications of Early Negro Music in the United States.* New York: Arno Press, and the New York Times, 1969.

Levine, Lawrence W. *Black Culture and Black Consciousness.* New York: Oxford University Press, 1977. Chaps. 1 and 2.

Lovell, John, Jr. *The Forge and the Flame: The Story of How the Afro-American Spiritual Was Hammered Out.* New York: Macmillan, 1972.

White, John. "Veiled Testimony: Negro Spirituals and the Slave Experience." *Journal of American Studies* 17, no. 2 (August 1983): 251–63.

THREE

Black Churches
North of Slavery and the
Freedom Struggle

RICHARD ALLEN

"Life Experience and Gospel Labors"

Richard Allen's autobiography, discovered in a trunk after his death in 1831, stands as a classic in Afro-American religious history. Born in 1760 in Philadelphia, the slave of a Quaker master, Allen passed into the hands of a Methodist near Dover, Delaware. When seventeen he converted to Methodism and soon purchased his freedom. Allen travelled as a Methodist exhorter and returned to Philadelphia in 1786. When the Free African Society drifted toward Quakerism, he sought to establish a black Methodist congregation that would be free of the discrimination experienced in historic St. George's Methodist Church. Bethel Chapel was dedicated in 1794, and Allen was ordained by Bishop Francis Asbury in 1799.

Though convinced that Methodism best suited the religious needs of Afro-Americans and dedicated to preserving the unity of the body of Christ, Allen led the African Methodists into a separate denomination in 1816 after many years of struggle against white control. In addition to serving as the A.M.E.'s first bishop, Allen took an active part in promoting the welfare of blacks in Philadelphia. He worked as a shoemaker, teamster, and labor contractor, opened his home to fugitive slaves, assisted fellow citizens during a yellow fever epidemic, and earned the esteem of prominent whites in both religious and political circles.

Though his memoirs telescope the chronology of the early Philadelphia years, they are an invaluable record of the beginnings of the black freedom movement in the North and its intimate connections with the black church. The preface to the 1833 edition of Allen's memoirs reads: "A great part of this work having been written many years after events actually took place; and as my memory could not exactly point out the exact time of many occurrences; they are, however, (as many as I can recollect) pointed out; some without day or date, which I presume, will be of no material consequence, so that they are confined to the truth."

Source: *The Life Experience and Gospel Labors of the Rt. Rev. Richard Allen*. Philadelphia: Martin & Boston, 1833.

I WAS BORN in the year of our Lord 1760, on February 14th, a slave to Benjamin Chew, of Philadelphia. My mother and father and four children of us were sold into Delaware state, near Dover; and I was a child and lived with him until I was upwards of twenty years of age, during which time I was awakened and brought to see myself, poor, wretched and undone, and without the mercy of God must be lost. Shortly after, I obtained mercy through the blood of Christ, and was constrained to exhort my old companions to seek the Lord. I went rejoicing for several days and was happy in the Lord, in conversing with many old, experienced Christians. I was brought under doubts, and was tempted to believe I was deceived, and was constrained to seek the Lord afresh. I went with my head bowed down for many days. My sins were a heavy burden. I was tempted to believe there was no mercy for me. I cried to the Lord both night and day. One night I thought hell would be my portion. I cried unto Him who delighteth to hear the prayers of a poor sinner, and all of a sudden my dungeon shook, my chains flew off, and, glory to God, I cried. My soul was filled. I cried, enough for me—the Saviour died. Now my confidence was strengthened that the Lord, for Christ's sake, had heard my prayers and pardoned all my sins. I was constrained to go from house to house, exhorting my old companions, and telling to all around what a dear Saviour I had found. I joined the Methodist Society and met in class at Benjamin Wells's, in the forest, Delaware state. John Gray was the class leader. I met in his class for several years.

My master was an unconverted man, and all the family, but he was what the world called a good master. He was more like a father to his slaves than anything else. He was a very tender, humane man. My mother and father lived with him for many years. He was brought into difficulty, not being able to pay for us, and mother having several children after he had bought us, he sold my mother and three children. My mother sought the Lord and found favor with him, and became a very pious woman. There were three children of us remained with our old master. My oldest brother embraced religion and my sister. Our neighbors, seeing that our master indulged us with the privilege of attending meeting once in two weeks, said that Stokeley's Negroes would soon ruin him; and so my brother and myself held a council together, that we would attend more faithfully to our master's business, so that it should not be said that religion made us worse servants; we would work night and day to get our crops forward, so that they should be disappointed. We frequently went to meeting on every other Thursday; but if we were likely to be backward with our crops we would refrain from going to meeting. When our master found we were making no provision to go to meeting, he would frequently ask us if it was not our meeting day, and if we were not going. We would frequently tell him: "No sir, we would rather stay at home and get our work done." He would tell us: "Boys, I would rather you would go to your meeting; if I am not good myself, I like to see you striving yourselves to be good." Our reply would be: "Thank you, sir, but we would rather stay and get our crops forward." So we always continued to keep our crops more forward than our neighbors, and we would attend public preaching once in two weeks, and class meeting once a week. At length, our master said he was convinced that religion made slaves better and not worse, and often boasted of his slaves for their honesty and industry. Some time after, I asked him if I might ask the preachers to come and preach at his house. He being old and infirm, my master and mistress cheerfully agreed for me to ask some of the Methodist preachers to come and preach at his house. I asked him for a note. He replied, if my word was not sufficient, he should send no note. I accordingly asked the preacher. He seemed somewhat backward at first, as my master did not send a written request; but the class leader (John Gray) observed that my word was sufficient; so he preached at my old master's house on the next Wednesday. Preaching continued for some months; at length, Freeborn Garrettson preached from these words, "Thou art weighed in the balance, and art found wanting." In pointing out and weighing the different characters, and among the rest weighed the slaveholders, my master believed himself to be one of that number, and after that he could not be satisfied to hold slaves, believing it to be wrong. And after that he proposed to me and my brother buying our times, to pay him 60£. gold and silver, or $2000, Continental money, which we complied with in the year 17——.

We left our master's house, and I may truly say it was like leaving our father's house; for he was a kind, affectionate and tender-hearted master, and told us to make his house our home when we were out of a place or sick. While living with him we had family prayer in the kitchen, to which he frequently would come out himself at time of prayer, and my mistress with him. At length he invited us from the kitchen to the parlor to hold family prayer, which we attended to. We had our stated times to hold our prayer meetings and give exhortations at in the neighborhood.

I had it often impressed upon my mind that I should one day enjoy my freedom; for slavery is a bitter pill, notwithstanding we had a good master. But when we would think that our day's work was never done, we often thought that after our master's death we were liable to be sold to the highest bidder, as he was much in debt; and thus my troubles were increased, and I was often brought to weep between the porch and the altar. But I have had reason to bless my dear Lord that a door was opened unexpectedly for me to buy my time and enjoy my liberty. When I left my master's house I knew not what to do, not being used to hard work, what business I should follow to pay my master and get my living. I went to cutting of cord wood. The first day my hands were so blistered and sore, that it was with difficulty I could open or shut them. I kneeled down upon my knees and prayed that the Lord would open some way for me to get my living. In a few days, my hands recovered and became accustomed to cutting of wood and other hardships; so I soon became able to cut my cord and a half and two cords a day. After I was done cutting I was employed in a brickyard by one Robert Register, at $50 a month, Continental money. After I was done with the brickyard I went to days' work, but did not forget to serve my dear Lord. I used ofttimes to pray, sitting, standing or lying; and while my hands were employed to earn my bread, my heart was devoted to my dear Redeemer. Sometimes I would awake from my sleep, preaching and praying. I was after this employed in driving of wagon in time of the Continental war, in drawing salt from Rehoboth, Sussex County, in Delaware. I had my regular stops and preaching places on the road. I enjoyed many happy seasons in meditation and prayer while in this employment.

After peace was proclaimed, I then travelled extensively, striving to preach the Gospel. My lot was cast in Wilmington. Shortly after, I was taken sick with the fall fever and then the pleurisy. September the 3rd 1783, I left my native place. After leaving Wilmington, I went into New Jersey, and there traveled and strove to preach the Gospel until the spring of 1784. I then became acquainted with Benjamin Abbott, that great and good apostle. He was one of the greatest men that ever I was acquainted with. He seldom preached but what there were souls added to his labor. He was a man of as great faith as any that ever I saw. The Lord was with him, and blessed his labors abundantly. He was a friend and father to me. I was sorry when I had to leave West Jersey, knowing I had to leave a father. I was employed in cutting of wood for Captain Cruenkleton, although I preached the Gospel at nights and on Sundays. My dear Lord was with me, and blessed my labors—Glory to God—and gave me souls for my hire. I then visited East Jersey, and labored for my dear Lord, and became acquainted with Joseph Budd, and made my home with him, near the mills—a family, I trust, who loved and served the Lord. I labored some time there, but being much afflicted in body with the inflammatory rheumatism, was not so successful as in some other places. I went from there to Jonathan Bunn's near Bennington, East New Jersey. There I labored in that neighborhood for some time. I found him and his family kind and affectionate, and he and his dear wife were a father and mother of Israel. In the year 1784, I left East Jersey and labored in Pennsylvania. I walked until my feet became so sore and blistered the first day, that I scarcely could bear them to the ground. I found the people very humane and kind in Pennsylvania. I having but little money, I stopped at Caesar Waters's, at Radnor township, twelve miles from Philadelphia. I found him and his wife very kind and affectionate to me. In the evening they asked me if I would come and take tea with them; but after sitting awhile, my feet became so sore and painful that I could scarcely be able to put them to the floor. I told them that I would accept their kind invitation, but my feet pained me so that I could not come to the table. They brought the table to me. Never was I more kindly received by strangers that I had never before seen, than by them. She bathed my feet with warm water and bran; the next morning my feet were better and free from pain. They asked me if I would preach for them. I preached for them the next evening. We had a glorious meeting. They invited me to stay till Sabbath day, and preach for them. I agreed to do so, and preached on Sabbath day to a large congregation of different persuasions, and my dear Lord was with me, and I believe there were many souls cut to the heart, and were added to the ministry. They insisted on me to stay longer with them. I stayed and labored in Radnor several weeks. Many souls were awakened and cried aloud to the Lord to have mercy upon them. I was frequently called upon by many inquiring what they should do to be saved. I appointed them to prayer and supplication at the throne of grace, and to make use of all manner of prayer, and pointed them to the invitation of our Lord and Saviour, Jesus Christ, who has said: "Come unto me, all ye that are weary and heavy laden, and I will give you rest." Glory be to God! and now I know he was a God at hand and not afar off. I preached my farewell sermon, and left these dear people. It was a time of visitation from above, many were the slain of the Lord. Seldom did I ever experience such a time of mourning and lamentation among a people. There were but few colored people in the neighborhood—the most of my congregation was white. Some said, "this man must be a man of God, I never heard such preaching before." We spent a greater part of the night in singing and prayer with the mourners. I expected I should have had to walk, as I had done before; but Mr. Davis had a creature that he made a present to me; but I intended to pay him for his horse if ever I got able. My dear Lord was kind and gracious to me. Some years after I got into business and thought myself able to pay for the horse. The horse was too light and small for me to travel on far. I traded it away with George Huftman for a blind horse but larger. I found my friend Huftman very kind and affectionate to me, and his family also. I preached several times at Huftman's meeting-house to a large and numerous congregation.

I proceeded on to Lancaster, Pennsylvania. I found the people in general dead to religion and scarcely a form of godliness. I went on to Little York, and put up at George Tess's, a sadler, and I believed him to be a man that loved and served the Lord. I had comfortable meetings with the Germans. I left Little York and proceeded on to the state of Maryland, and stopped at Mr. Benjamin Grover's; and I believed him to be a man that loved and served the Lord. I had many happy seasons with my dear friends. His wife was a very pious woman; but their dear children were strangers to vital religion. I preached in the neighborhood for some time, and travelled Hartford circuit with Mr. Porters, who travelled that circuit. I found him very useful to me. I also travelled with Jonathan Forest and Leari Coal.

December 1784, General Conference sat in Baltimore, the first General Conference ever held in America. The English preachers just arrived from Europe were, Rev. Dr. Coke, Richard Whatcoat and Thomas Vassey. This was the beginning of the Episcopal Church amongst the Methodists. Many of the ministers were set apart in holy orders at this conference, and were said to be entitled to the gown; and I have thought religion has been declining in the church ever since. There was a pamphlet published by some person, which stated, that when the Methodists were no people, then they were a people; and now they have become a people they were no people; which had often serious weight upon my mind.

In 1785 the Rev. Richard Whatcoat was appointed on Baltimore circuit. He was, I believe, a man of God. I found great strength in travelling with him—a father in Israel. In his advice he was fatherly and friendly. He was of a mild and serene disposition. My lot was cast in Baltimore, in a small meeting-house called Methodist Alley. I stopped at Richard Mould's, and was sent to my lodgings, and lodged at Mr. McCannon's. I had some happy meetings in Baltimore. I was introduced to Richard Russell, who was very kind and affectionate to me, and attended several meetings. Rev. Bishop Asbury sent for me to meet him at Henry Gaff's. I did so. He told me he wished me to travel with him. He told me that in the slave countries, Carolina and other places, I must not intermix with the slaves, and I would frequently have to sleep in his carriage, and he would allow me my victuals and clothes. I told him I would not travel with him on these conditions. He asked me my reason. I told him if I was taken sick, who was to support me? and that I thought people ought to lay up something while they were able, to support themselves in time of sickness or old age. He said that was as much as he got, his victuals and clothes. I told him he would be taken care of, let his afflictions be as they were, or let him be taken sick where he would, he would be taken care of; but I doubted whether it would be the case with myself. He smiled, and told me he would give me from then until he returned from the eastward to make up my mind, which would be about three months. But I made up my mind that I would not accept of his proposals. Shortly after I left Hartford Circuit, and came to Pennsylvania, on Lancaster circuit. I travelled several months on Lancaster circuit with the Rev. Peter Morratte and Irie Ellis. They were very kind and affectionate to me in building me up; for I had many trials to pass through, and I received nothing from the Methodist connection. My usual method was, when I would get bare of clothes, to stop travelling and go to work, so that no man could say I was chargeable to the connection. My hands administered to my necessities. The autumn of 1785 I returned again to Radnor. I stopped at George Giger's, a man of God, and went to work. His family were all kind and affectionate to me. I killed seven beeves, and supplied the neighbors with meat; got myself pretty well clad through my own industry—thank God—and preached occasionally. The elder in charge in Philadelphia frequently sent for me to come to the city. February, 1786, I came to Philadelphia. Preaching was given out for me at five o'clock in the morning at St. George church. I strove to preach as well as I could, but it was a great cross to me; but the Lord was with me. We had a good time, and several souls were awakened, and were earnestly seeking redemption in the blood of Christ. I thought I would stop in Philadelphia a week or two. I preached at different places in the city. My labor was much blessed. I soon saw a large field open in seeking and instructing my African brethren, who had been a long forgotten people and few of them attended public worship. I preached in the commons, in Southwark, Northern Liberties, and wherever I could find an opening. I frequently preached twice a day, at 5 o'clock in the morning and in the evening, and it was not uncommon for me to preach from four to five times a day. I established prayer meetings; I raised a society in 1786 for forty-two members. I saw the necessity of erecting a place of worship for the colored people. I proposed it to the most respectable people of color in this city; but here I met with opposition. I had but three colored brethren that united with me in erecting a place of worship—the Rev. Absalom Jones, William White and Dorus Ginnings. These united with me as soon as it became public and known by the elder who was stationed in the city. The Rev. C——B—— opposed the plan, and would not submit to any argument we could raise; but he was shortly removed from the charge. The Rev. Mr. W—— took the charge,

and the Rev. L——G——. Mr. W—— was much opposed to an African church, and used very degrading and insulting language to us, to
try and prevent us from going on. We all belonged to St. George's
church—Rev. Absalom Jones, William White and Dorus Ginnings. We
felt ourselves much cramped; but my dear Lord was with us, and we
believed, if it was his will, the work would go on, and that we would
be able to succeed in building the house of the Lord. We established
prayer meetings and meetings of exhortation, and the Lord blessed our
endeavors, and many souls were awakened; but the elder soon forbid
us holding any such meetings; but we viewed the forlorn state of our
colored brethren, and that they were destitute of a place of worship.
They were considered as a nuisance.

A number of us usually attended St. George's church in Fourth
street; and when the colored people began to get numerous in attending
the church, they moved us from the seats we usually sat on, and placed
us around the wall, and on Sabbath morning we went to church and
the sexton stood at the door, and told us to go in the gallery. He told
us to go, and we would see where to sit. We expected to take the seats
over the ones we formerly occupied below, not knowing any better. We
took those seats. Meeting had begun, and they were nearly done singing, and just as we got to the seats, the elder said, "Let us pray." We
had not been long upon our knees before I heard considerable scuffling
and low talking. I raised my head up and saw one of the trustees, H——
M——, having hold of the Rev. Absalom Jones, pulling him up off of
his knees, and saying, "You must get up—you must not kneel here."
Mr. Jones replied, "Wait until prayer is over." Mr. H—— M—— said
"No, you must get up now, or I will call for aid and force you away."
Mr. Jones said, "Wait until prayer is over, and I will get up and trouble
you no more." With that he beckoned to one of the other trustees, Mr.
L—— S—— to come to his assistance. He came, and went to William
White to pull him up. By this time prayer was over, and we all went
out of the church in a body, and they were no more plagued with us
in the church. This raised a great excitement and inquiry among the
citizens, in so much that I believe they were ashamed of their conduct.
But my dear Lord was with us, and we were filled with fresh vigor to
get a house erected to worship God in. Seeing our forlorn and distressed
situation, many of the hearts of our citizens were moved to urge us
forward; notwithstanding we had subscribed largely towards finishing
St. George's church, in building the gallery and laying new floors, and
just as the house was made comfortable, we were turned out from enjoying the comforts of worshipping therein. We then hired a store-room,
and held worship by ourselves. Here we were pursued with threats of

being disowned, and read publicly out of meeting if we did continue worship in the place we had hired; but we believed the Lord would be our friend. We got subscription papers out to raise money to build the house of the Lord. By this time we had waited on Dr. Rush and Mr. Robert Ralston, and told them of our distressing situation. We considered it a blessing that the Lord had put it into our hearts to wait upon those gentlemen. They pitied our situation, and subscribed largely towards the church, and were very friendly towards us, and advised us how to go on. We appointed Mr. Ralston our treasurer. Dr. Rush did much for us in public by his influence. I hope the name of Dr. Benjamin Rush and Robert Ralston will never be forgotten among us. They were the first two gentlemen who espoused the cause of the oppressed, and aided us in building the house of the Lord for the poor Africans to worship in. Here was the beginning and rise of the first African church in America. But the elder of the Methodist Church still pursued us. Mr. John McClaskey called upon us and told us if we did not erase our names from the subscription paper, and give up the paper, we would be publicly turned out of meeting. We asked him if we had violated any rules of discipline by so doing. He replied, "I have the charge given to me by the Conference, and unless you submit I will read you publicly out of meeting." We told him we were willing to abide by the discipline of the Methodist Church, "And if you will show us where we have violated any law of discipline of the Methodist Church, we will submit; and if there is no rule violated in the discipline we will proceed on." He replied, "We will read you all out." We told him if he turned us out contrary to rule of discipline, we should seek further redress. We told him we were dragged off of our knees in St. George's church, and treated worse than heathens; and we were determined to seek out for ourselves, the Lord being our helper. He told us we were not Methodists, and left us. Finding we would go on in raising money to build the church, he called upon us again, and wished to see us all together. We met him. He told us that he wished us well, that he was a friend to us, and used many arguments to convince us that we were wrong in building a church. We told him we had no place of worship; and we did not mean to go to St. George's church any more, as we were so scandalously treated in the presence of all the congregation present; "and if you deny us your name, you cannot seal up the scriptures from us, and deny us a name in heaven. We believe heaven is free for all who worship in spirit and truth." And he said, "So you are determined to go on." We told him "Yes, God being our helper." He then replied, "We will disown you all from the Methodist connection." We believed if we put our trust in the Lord, he would stand by us. This was a trial that I never had to pass through before. I was confident that the great head of the church would support us. My dear Lord was with us. We went out with our subscription paper, and met with great success. We had no reason to complain of the liberality of the citizens. The first day the Rev. Absalom Jones and myself went out we collected three hundred and sixty dollars. This was the greatest day's collection that we met with. We appointed a committee to look out for a lot—the Rev. Absalom Jones, William Gray, William Wilcher and myself. We pitched upon a lot at the corner of Lombard and Sixth streets. They authorized me to go and agree for it. I did accordingly. The lot belonged to Mr. Mark Wilcox. We entered into articles of agreement for the lot. Afterwards the committee found a lot in Fifth street, in a more commodious part of the city, which we bought; and the first lot they threw upon my hands, and wished me to give it up. I told them they had authorized me to agree for the lot, and they were all well satisfied with the agreement I had made, and I thought it was hard that they would throw it upon my hands. I told them I would sooner keep it myself than to forfeit the agreement I had made. And so I did.

We bore much persecution from many of the Methodist connection; but we have reason to be thankful to Almighty God, who was our deliverer. The day was appointed to go and dig the cellar. I arose early in the morning and addressed the throne of grace, praying that the Lord would bless our endeavors. Having by this time two or three teams of my own—as I was the first proposer of the African church, I put the first spade in the ground to dig a cellar for the same. This was the first African Church or meetinghouse that was erected in the United States of America. We intended it for the African preaching-house or church; but finding that the elder stationed in this city was such an opposer to our proceedings of erecting a place of worship, though the principal part of the directors of this church belonged to the Methodist connection, the elder stationed here would neither preach for us, nor have anything to do with us. We then held an election, to know what religious denomination we should unite with. At the election it was determined— there were two in favor of the Methodist, the Rev. Absalom Jones and myself, and a large majority in favor of the Church of England. The majority carried. Notwithstanding we had been so violently persecuted by the elder, we were in favor of being attached to the Methodist connection; for I was confident that there was no religious sect or denomination would suit the capacity of the colored people as well as the Methodist; for the plain and simple gospel suits best for any people; for the unlearned can understand, and the learned are sure to understand;

and the reason that the Methodist is so successful in the awakening and conversion of the colored people, the plain doctrine and having a good discipline. But in many cases the preachers would act to please their own fancy, without discipline, till some of them became such tyrants, and more especially to the colored people. They would turn them out of society, giving them no trial, for the smallest offense, perhaps only hearsay. They would frequently, in meeting the class, impeach some of the members of whom they had heard an ill report, and turn them out, saying, "I have heard thus and thus of you, and you are no more a member of society"—without witnesses on either side. This has been frequently done, notwithstanding in the first rise and progress in Delaware state, and elsewhere, the colored people were their greatest support; for there were but few of us free; but the slaves would toil in their little patches many a night until midnight to raise their little truck and sell to get something to support them more than what their masters gave them, but we used often to divide our little support among the white preachers of the Gospel. This was once a quarter. It was in the time of the old Revolutionary War between Great Britain and the United States. The Methodists were the first people that brought glad tidings to the colored people. I feel thankful that ever I heard a Methodist preach. We are beholden to the Methodists, under God, for the light of the Gospel we enjoy; for all other denominations preached so high-flown that we were not able to comprehend their doctrine. Sure am I that reading sermons will never prove so beneficial to the colored people as spiritual or extempore preaching. I am well convinced that the Methodist has proved beneficial to thousands and ten times thousands. It is to be awfully feared that the simplicity of the Gospel that was among them fifty years ago, and that they conform more to the world and the fashions thereof, they would fare very little better than the people of the world. The discipline is altered considerably from what it was. We would ask for the good old way, and desire to walk therein.

In 1793 a committee was appointed from the African Church to solicit me to be their minister, for there was no colored preacher in Philadelphia but myself. I told them I could not accept of their offer, as I was a Methodist. I was indebted to the Methodists, under God, for what little religion I had; being convinced that they were the people of God, I informed them that I could not be anything else but a Methodist, as I was born and awakened under them, and I could go no further with them, for I was a Methodist, and would leave you in peace and love. I would do nothing to retard them in building a church as it was an extensive building, neither would I go out with a subscription paper until they were done going out with their subscription. I bought an old frame that had been formerly occupied as a blacksmith shop, from Mr. Sims, and hauled it on the lot in Sixth near Lombard street, that had formerly been taken for the Church of England. I employed carpenters to repair the old frame, and fit it for a place of worship. In July 1794, Bishop Asbury being in town I solicited him to open the church[1] for us which he accepted. The Rev. John Dickins sung and prayed, and Bishop Asbury preached. The house was called Bethel, agreeable to the prayer that was made. Mr. Dickins prayed that it might be a bethel[2] to the gathering in of thousands of souls. My dear Lord was with us, so that there were many hearty "amen's" echoed through the house. This house of worship has been favored with the awakening of many souls, and I trust they are in the Kingdom, both white and colored. Our warfare and troubles now began afresh. Mr. C. proposed that we should make over the church to the Conference. This we objected to, he asserted that we could not be Methodists unless we did; we told him he might deny us their name, but they could not deny us a seat in Heaven. Finding that he could not prevail with us so to do, he observed that we had better be incorporated, then we could get any legacies that were left for us, if not, we could not. We agreed to be incorporated. He offered to draw the incorporation himself, that it would save us the trouble of paying for to get it drawn. We cheerfully submitted to his proposed plan. He drew the incorporation, but incorporated our church under the Conference, our property was then all consigned to the Conference for the present bishops, elders, ministers, etc., that belonged to the white Conference, and our property was gone. Being ignorant of incorporations we cheerfully agreed thereto. We labored about ten years under this incorporation, until James Smith was appointed to take the charge in Philadelphia; he soon waked us up by demanding the keys and books of the church, and forbid us holding any meetings except by orders from him; these propositions we told him we could not agree to. He observed he was elder, appointed to the charge, and unless we submitted to him, he would read us all out of meeting. We told him the house was ours, we had bought it, and paid for it. He said he would let us know it was not ours, it belonged to the Conference; we took counsel on it; counsel informed us we had been taken in; according to the incorporation it belonged to the white connection. We asked him if it couldn't be altered; he told us if two-thirds of the society agreed to have it altered, it could be altered. He gave me a transcript to lay before them; I called the society together and laid it

1   This church will at present [c. 1830] accommodate between 3,000 and 4,000 persons.
2   See Genesis Chapter 28.

before them. My dear Lord was with us. It was unanimously agreed to, by both male and female. We had another incorporation drawn that took the church from Conference, and got it passed, before the elder knew anything about it. This raised a considerable rumpus, for the elder contended that it would not be good unless he had signed it. The elder, with the trustees of St. George's, called us together, and said we must pay six hundred dollars a year for their services, or they could not serve us. We told them we were not able so to do. The trustees of St. George's insisted that we should or should not be supplied by their preachers. At last they made a move that they would take four hundred; we told them that our house was considerably in debt, and we were poor people, and we could not agree to pay four hundred, but we agreed to give them two hundred. It was moved by one of the trustees of St. George's that the money should be paid into their treasury; we refused paying it into their treasury, but we would pay it to the preacher that served; they made a move that the preacher should not receive the money from us. The Bethel trustees made a move that their funds should be shut and they would pay none; this caused a considerable contention. At length they withdrew their motion. The elder supplied us preaching five times in a year for two hundred dollars. Finding that they supplied us so seldom, the trustees of Bethel church passed a resolution that they would pay but one hundred dollars a year, as the elder only preached five times in a year for us; they called for the money, we paid him twenty-five dollars a quarter, but he being dissatisfied, returned the money back again, and would not have it unless we paid him fifty dollars. The trustees concluded it was enough for five sermons, and said they would pay no more; the elder of St. George's was determined to preach for us no more, unless we gave him two hundred dollars, and we were left alone for upwards of one year.

Mr. Samuel Royal being appointed to the charge of Philadelphia, declared unless we should repeal the Supplement, neither he nor any white preacher, travelling or local, should preach any more for us; so we were left to ourselves. At length the preachers and stewards belonging to the Academy, proposed serving us on the same terms that we had offered to the St. George's preachers, and they preached for us better than twelve months, and then demanded $150 per year; this not being complied with, they declined preaching for us, and we were once more left to ourselves, as an edict was passed by the elder, that if any local preacher should serve us, he should be expelled from the connection. John Emory, then elder of the Academy, published a circular letter, in which we were disowned by the Methodists. A house was also hired and fitted up for worship, not far from Bethel, and an invitation given to all who desired to be Methodists to resort thither. But being disappointed in this plan, Robert R. Roberts, the resident elder, came to Bethel, insisted on preaching to us and taking the spiritual charge of the congregation, for we were Methodists he was told he should come on some terms with the trustees; his answer was, that "He did not come to consult with Richard Allen or other trustees, but to inform the congregation, that on next Sunday afternoon, he would come and take the spiritual charge." We told him he could not preach for us under existing circumstances. However, at the appointed time he came, but having taken previous advice we had our preacher in the pulpit when he came, and the house was so fixed that he could not get but more than half way to the pulpit. Finding himself disappointed he appealed to those who came with him as witnesses, that "That man (meaning the preacher), had taken his appointment." Several respectable white citizens who knew the colored people had been ill-used, were present, and told us not to fear, for they would see us righted, and not suffer Roberts to preach in a forcible manner, after which Roberts went away.

The next elder stationed in Philadelphia was Robert Birch, who, following the example of his predecessor, came and published a meeting for himself. But the method just mentioned was adopted and he had to go away disappointed. In consequence of this, he applied to the Supreme Court for a writ of mandamus, to know why the pulpit was denied him. Being elder, this brought on a lawsuit, which ended in our favor. Thus by the Providence of God we were delivered from a long, distressing and expensive suit, which could not be resumed, being determined by the Supreme Court. For this mercy we desire to be unfeignedly thankful.

About this time, our colored friends in Baltimore were treated in a similar manner by the white preachers and trustees, and many of them driven away who were disposed to seek a place of worship, rather than go to law.

Many of the colored people in other places were in a situation nearly like those of Philadelphia and Baltimore, which induced us, in April 1816, to call a general meeting, by way of Conference. Delegates from Baltimore and other places which met those of Philadelphia, and taking into consideration their grievances, and in order to secure the privileges, promote union and harmony among themselves, it was resolved: "That the people of Philadelphia, Baltimore, etc., etc., should become one body, under the name of the African Methodist Episcopal Church." We deemed it expedient to have a form of discipline, whereby we may guide our people in the fear of God, in the unity of the Spirit, and in the bonds of peace, and preserve us from that spiritual despotism which we have so recently experienced—remembering that we are not to lord it over God's heritage, as greedy dogs that can never have enough. But with long suffering and bowels of compassion, to bear each other's burdens, and so fulfill the Law of Christ, praying that our mutual striving together for the promulgation of the Gospel may be crowned with abundant success.

The God of Bethel heard her cries,
He let his power be seen;
He stopp'd the proud oppressor's frown,
And proved himself a King.

Thou sav'd them in the trying hour,
Ministers and councils joined,
And all stood ready to retain
That helpless church of Thine.

Bethel surrounded by her foes,
But not yet in despair,
Christ heard her supplicating cries;
The God of Bethel heard.

SUPPLEMENTARY READINGS

George, Carol V. R. *Segregated Sabbaths: Richard Allen and the Emergence of Independent Black Churches, 1760–1840*. New York: Oxford University Press, 1973.

Gregg, Howard D. *History of the African Methodist Episcopal Church*. Nashville: A.M.E. Sunday School Union, 1980.

Richardson, Harry V. *Dark Salvation: The Story of Methodism as It Developed Among Blacks in America*. Garden City, N.Y.: Doubleday/Anchor Books, 1976.

Sernett, Milton C. *Black Religion and American Evangelicalism: White Protestants, Plantation Missions, and the Flowering of Negro Christianity, 1787–1865*. Metuchen, N.J.: Scarecrow Press, 1975. Chaps. 5 and 6.

Wesley, Charles H. *Richard Allen: Apostle of Freedom*. Washington, D.C.: Associated Publishers, 1935.

15

CHRISTOPHER RUSH

Rise of the African Methodist
Episcopal Zion Church

In New York City, black Methodists moved toward independence without
the dramatic confrontations Allen and associates experienced in Philadelphia.
Blacks worshiped at the John Street Methodist Church. Bishop Francis Asbury gave his blessing to additional services for them at an "African chapel"
called Zion in 1796. When a split within the John Street congregation forced
the blacks to choose between two white factions, they decided for the one led
by Samuel Stillwell because it promised them the greatest freedom in man-
aging their own affairs and ordaining their own elders. Bishop Allen met with
the elders of Zion Chapel, but Zionites elected not to join with his connection for fear of losing their independence. The resulting division among
African Methodists has yet to be healed. In 1821 the Zionites organized the
second African Methodist denomination and a year later celebrated the ordination of three black elders at the hands of Stillwell supporters. James Varick
became the first bishop of the New York-based African Methodist Episcopal
Church. The name "Zion" was added at a later date.

Christopher Rush, from whose history the following selection is taken,
succeeded Varick in 1828. Rush relates how the white Methodists of the
New York Conference resisted the move toward independence, but those of
the Philadelphia Conference, in Richard Allen's territory, gave a conditional
blessing, an irony that must have galled the Bethelites (as Allen's group was
popularly known). Of the two black denominations, the Bethelites enjoyed
greater growth and more stable leadership in the pre-Civil War decades.

To the Bishops and Preachers of the Philadelphia
and New-York Conferences, assembled:

Respected Brethren,

We, the official members of the African Methodist Zion and Asbury Churches, in the city of New-York, and of the Wesleyan Church,

Source: A Short Account of the Rise and Progress of the African Methodist Episcopal Church in America. New York: Published by the Author, 1843. Pp. 60–73.

in the city of Philadelphia, on behalf of our brethren, members of the aforesaid Churches; likewise of a small society at New-Haven, and some of our coloured brethren on Long Island, beg the favour of addressing you on a subject, to us of great importance, and we presume not a matter of indifference to you.

In the first place, suffer us to beg you will accept of our humble and sincere thanks for your kind services to us when in our infant state, trusting that the Great Head of the Church, the all-wise and gracious God, has, and will continue to reward you for your labours among us, having made you the instruments of bringing us from darkness to light, and from the power of sin and Satan, to Him, the true and living God.

In the next place we proceed to say—When the Methodist Society in the United States was small, the Africans enjoyed comfortable privileges among their white brethren in the same meeting-house; but as the whites increased very fast the Africans were pressed back; therefore, it was thought essentially necessary for them to have meeting-houses of their own, in those places where they could obtain them, in order to have more room to invite their coloured brethren yet out of the ark of safety to come in; and it is well known that the Lord has greatly enlarged their number since that memorable time, by owning their endeavours in the conversion of many hundreds. Many Preachers have been raised up among them, who have been very useful in a located state; but they have hitherto been confined; they have had no opportunities to travel, being generally poor men, and having no provision made for them to go forth and dispense the Word of Life to their brethren, their usefulness has been greatly hindered, and their coloured brethren have been deprived of those blessings which Almighty God might have designed to grant through their instrumentality. And now, it seems, the time is come when something must be done for the prosperity of the ministry amongst our coloured brethren; and how shall this be accomplished? for we have not the least expectation that African or coloured Preachers will be admitted to a seat and vote in the Conferences of their white brethren, let them be how much soever qualified for the work of the ministry; nor do we desire to unite with our brother Richard Allen's connexion, being dissatisfied with their general manner of proceedings; (for our brethren, the members of the Wesleyan Church, in Philadelphia, withdrew from them to build their present house of worship named as above,) therefore, our brethren in the city of New-York, after due consideration, have been led to conclude that to form an itinerant plan and establish a Conference for African Methodist Preachers, under the patronage of the white Methodist Bishops and Conference, would be the means of accomplishing the desired end; believing that such an establishment would tend greatly to the prosperity of the spiritual concerns of our coloured brethren in general, and would be the means of great encouragement to our Preachers, who are now in regular standing in connexion with the white Methodist Episcopal Church in the United States, and also to such as may be hereafter raised up among us, who may be disposed to join the said Conference and enter on the travelling plan. And in order to commence this great work, the two Societies in the city of New-York united and agreed that the title of the connexion shall be "The African Methodist Episcopal Church in America," and have selected a form of Discipline from that of the mother (white) church, which, with a little alteration, we have adopted for the government of the said connexion, and to which we beg to refer you.

After the perusal of our selection and consideration of our case, should our proceedings meet your approbation and you should be disposed to patronise the same, we will stand ready and shall be glad to receive such advice and instruction as you may think proper to give us, through our father in the Lord, Bishop McKendree, or any other person the Conference may be pleased to appoint. On the subject of ordination to Eldership, (a privilege which our Preachers have been long deprived of,) permit us to say we might have obtained it from other sources, but we preferred and determined to follow the advice of Bishop McKendree, given to our brethren in New-York the last time he was with them, and wait until the meeting of your annual Conference in this and the District of New-York, in order to understand what encouragement we may look for from the mother church. But in consequence of some uneasiness in the minds of some of our members in New-York, occasioned by our brother Richard Allen's determination to establish a society of his connexion in that city, our brethren there have been under the necessity of solemnly electing three of their Deacons to the office of Elders, and some of their Preachers to the office of Deacons, to act only in cases of necessity, and to show to our people that our Preachers can be authorized to administer the sacrament of the Lord's Supper, as well as those of brother Allen's connexion, that thereby they might keep the body together; and we believe it has had the desired effect, for very few have left the Societies there, notwithstanding the efforts made to induce them to leave us. We expect that our first yearly Conference will be held in the city of New-York, on the 14th day of June next, at which we hope to have the happiness of hearing that our father in the Lord,

Bishop McKendree, presided, and commenced his fatherly instructions in an African Methodist Conference, formed under the patronage of the Methodist Episcopal Church in the United States of America. With this hope we shall rest, waiting your answer; meanwhile praying that the great Shepherd and Bishop of souls and our most merciful Father, will be pleased to bless and guide you in your deliberations on our case, so that your conclusions may be such as shall be pleasing in his sight, and tend most to the prosperity of his kingdom amongst the Africans, and consequently prove an everlasting blessing to many precious souls.

N. B. Should the above address be sanctioned by your respected body, and you should be pleased to act upon it, we will thank you to transmit the same to the New-York Annual Conference, for their consideration; and should the time appointed for the sitting of the African Conference be inconvenient for the person who may be appointed to organize the same, we are willing that it should be altered to a few days sooner or later, provided you would be pleased to give us timely notice of said alteration. But should you be disposed not to favour the said address in any respect, you will please have the goodness to return it to the bearer.

Signed in behalf of the official members of both Societies, at a meeting called specially for that purpose, March 23d, 1821, in the city of New-York.

James Varick, *President.*
George Collins, *Secretary.*

The foregoing being prepared and all ready, the brethren appointed Abraham Thompson and Leven Smith to take it to Philadelphia. It was presented to the official brethren of the Wesleyan Church, who approved the same and also signed it by the President and Secretary of their meeting, and was taken by Abraham Thompson to their Conference, which was held at Milford, in the state of Delaware. The Conference at Milford accepted the address, and having acted upon it, they transmitted the same to the New-York Conference, according to our request. We will insert a copy of their proceedings, which reads as follows:

The committee, to whom was referred the memorial of the official members of the African Methodist Zion and Asbury Churches, in the city of New-York, and the Wesley Church, in the city of Philadelphia, in behalf of themselves and others of their coloured brethren, proposing and requesting the organization of a Conference for the African Methodist Preachers, under the patronage of the Bishops and Conferences of the white Methodist Episcopal Church, having had the subject under serious and close consideration, in its various bearings and relations, ask leave now to report:

1. We view it as a subject of great importance to the coloured people, demanding from us our friendly patronage and pastoral attention, so far as circumstances will admit of it. We have always acted upon the principle toward the people of colour, of doing them all the good that was in our power, in promoting and improving their moral and religious instruction and character, and in protecting and defending them in all their just rights and privileges, and more particularly we have, as instruments under God, laboured much for the conversion and salvation of their souls. They know, and it is generally known and acknowledged, that our labours of good will and christian love toward them for many years past, have been crowned with gracious success and much good effect among them, as it respects both their moral and religious character, and also to the improvement to some considerable degree, of their condition and circumstances in life.

2. There are at this time various societies and congregations of coloured people, in different places, who have been collected and raised under our ministerial labours, and who have erected and built themselves houses for the public worship of God, wherein they assemble separate from the white people for their religious devotions; and also, there are a considerable number of pious coloured men, whom we have reason to believe are qualified to preach the word of life and salvation, and to be useful in their labours among the people of their own colour; but upon our present plan, under existing circumstances and regulations, their privileges as ministers are very much circumscribed, and their opportunities for improvement and usefulness are very limited. There exists no expectation or prospect, that the coloured Preachers will be admitted to a vote or seat in our Conferences, or participate in sundry other privileges among the white Preachers, in their labours and pastoral care of the churches and societies generally; neither is it understood that they wish or desire it. They request a Conference themselves in unity and friendship with, and under the patronage of the Bishops and Conferences of the white Preachers, and that our Bishops should preside among them and ordain their Preachers, and extend to them their superintending protection, counsel and direction in their itinerant regulations and ministerial operations. It appears that they could obtain orders from another quarter, and become a connexion distinct from, and indepen-

dent of the white Bishops and Conferences, but they prefer and desire patronage from, and a certain degree of union with us. They have refused to unite with Richard Allen and his African connexion, being dissatisfied with their general manner of proceedings.

3. From every view of the subject we have been able to take, we are of opinion the time is come when something must be done, more than yet has been done, for our coloured people, especially for such as are situated and circumstanced as the memorialists are, in order to enlarge their sphere of labours, and to extend their privileges and opportunities of usefulness among themselves, under our protection and direction, otherwise we shall lose their confidence in us and our influence over them, and they will become separate from, and independent of us, and then our usefulness among them will in a great measure be lost. And it appears in the present case under consideration, that they are fixed and resolved to have a Conference among themselves, whether patronized by us or not, and they have appointed the time for holding it, but that they wish us to take them under our patronage: Therefore, your committee proposes the following resolutions to the Conference for adoption, viz.

First, *Resolved*, that the Philadelphia Conference do advise and recommend that one of our Bishops do attend and preside in the African Conference, appointed to sit in New-York, and to superintend their organization as an African Methodist Conference, under the patronage of our Bishops and Conferences, agreeably to the proper plan, viz. (if the New-York Conference concur with us.)

1. One of the Bishops always to preside in the said Conference, or in case no Bishop be present, then, such white Elder as the Bishop shall appoint is to preside.

2. Our Bishops to ordain all their Deacons and Elders, such as shall be elected by their own Conference and approved of by the Bishop as qualified for the office.

3. The Bishop, or the Elder appointed by him, to preside in the Conference, with an advisory committee of three, chosen by the Conference, to make out the stations and appointments of the Preachers.

4. All the other proceedings of the Conference to be as conformable to the rules and regulations generally followed in our Conferences, as circumstances will admit of.

5. Their Discipline, doctrines, government, and rules of order in all things, to be as conformable to ours as possible, so as to secure to themselves their own peculiar rights and privileges.

6. The Bishop, or such Elder as shall be appointed by him, with his proper instructions, together with the said African Conference, to agree upon the several points, terms and considerations of unity and amity mutually to exist, as reciprocal duties and obligations between them and us. This agreement to take place and be entered into at the time of organizing the said Conference.

Secondly, *Resolved*, that a copy of this report be forwarded with the African Memorial to the New-York Conference, and that the said New-York Conference be recommended and requested to concur with us in the proposed plan of organizing the said African Conference under our patronage, with such additions to, or alterations of the above items, as to them may appear best.

> Ezekiel Cooper,
> Thomas Ware,
> Alward White,
> *Committee*

The above report was adopted by the Philadelphia Conference, and the Secretary was instructed to communicate a copy of it to the New-York Conference.

> Samuel Cox, *Secretary*
> *Milford, April* 19, 1821.

The foregoing report was approved of by the official brethren, and they were encouraged to hope that their request would be granted, but they found their hope to be of short duration when they heard from the New-York Annual Conference, for that body, in their report, gave them to understand that they could do nothing for them, except they renounce the form of discipline which they had selected and adopted, and be willing to be governed by the old Discipline. We will also give a copy of their report, which reads as follows: viz.

The committee, to whom was referred the Memorial of the Africans in the city of New-York and other places, together with the accompanying documents, after due consideration, report as follows:

1. The committee conceive that humanity and religion combine to influence us to do all in our power for the instruction and salvation of

coloured people. To have the pure word of life preached among them, and the discipline and ordinances of the Gospel faithfully administered, is of indispensable necessity, and requisite to their happiness and prosperity. It is believed that in these respects we have cause to charge ourselves with too little attention to their spiritual interest, and as though they were an inferior class of beings, they have too often been treated with unwarrantable neglect. It is to be feared that their loss of confidence in us, and the consequent measures which many of them have pursued, may, in a considerable degree, be traced to our neglect as the cause. But painful as this consideration is, we cannot approve of the course which our coloured brethren have taken in separating themselves from us, and forming themselves under a distinct title, as an independent body. This course is the more to be regretted, because it places them in a position which the constitution of our church cannot cover. Your committee conceive that the primary object contemplated in the memorial and accompanying documents, lies beyond the limits of the constitutional powers of an annual Conference. To organize a Conference *subject to the order* and discipline of the Methodist Episcopal Church, is the prerogative of the General Conference alone. An annual Conference, or Conferences, therefore, cannot organize even *such* a Conference, much less one acting under a distinct discipline and independent authority. In this view of the subject your committee are of opinion, that the African Conference, specified in the memorial, cannot be constitutionally organized or adopted; that it would not be advisable for our Bishops, or any one appointed by them, officially to preside at said Conference, or to ordain any Deacon or Elder elected by them. But, although we judge it inexpedient to prostrate the constitution and government of the church to accommodate any case whatever, firmly believing the evil would ultimately over-balance any good which might be supposed to result from it, we consider the condition of the Africans such as to demand every prudent exertion within our power to recover them from their wandering, and preserve them in the confidence and communion of the church. Your committee, therefore, recommend the adoption of the following Resolutions:

Resolved 1st, That if the African brethren, who have addressed the Conference by memorial, will agree to be subject to the government of the Methodist Episcopal Church, in common with their white brethren, in such case, under the present existing circumstances, it is expedient and advisable that such coloured Preachers as are regularly constituted, be appointed to labour among them and take the pastoral charge of them until the next General Conference.

Resolved 2nd, That the coloured brethren submitting themselves to the order and discipline of the church, are entitled to the same rights and privileges with respect to the election and ordination of Local Deacons and Elders, as the white societies, the same form of order and discipline applying to both.

Resolved 3rd, That the organization of an African annual Conference, on the same principles, and subject to the same order and government as other Conferences, may be effected by the General Conference, but cannot be by one or more annual Conferences.

Resolved 4th, That it is advisable a member or members of this Conference, be appointed by the Bishop, to present the above Resolutions to the African brethren in New-York, together with any explanations and instructions which may be thought proper, and to receive their answer. Joshua Souls was appointed to present the foregoing report, and Thomas Mason accompanied him.

On the 12th of June, 1821, our official brethren met together, for the purpose of considering the report of the New-York Annual Conference; which, being so contrary to that of the Philadelphia Conference, caused much dissatisfaction, and after deliberately considering the case, they resolved to proceed according to the ideas advanced by the Philadelphia Conference, viz., that one of the white Bishops preside at all our yearly Conferences, ordain all our Ministers and appoint them to their stations, according to our Discipline, and that we be willing to come on terms of unity and amity to that effect, if the next General Conference of the whites will receive us under their patronage; and George Collins and Charles Anderson were appointed to inform Joshua Souls of the above resolution. Our official brethren had an interview with Bishop Enoch George, and had some conversation relative to our intended yearly Conference; at which time he informed them that the other two Bishops were sick, and his engagements were such as to put it out of his power to attend the African Conference, and therefore he advised them to endeavour to do as well as they could in holding the aforesaid meeting.

SUPPLEMENTARY READINGS

Bradley, David H. *History of the A.M.E. Zion Church.* Two vols. Nashville: Parthenon Press, 1956 and 1970.

Hood, James Walker. *One Hundred Years of the African Methodist Episcopal Zion Church; or, The Centennial of African Methodism.* New York: A.M.E. Zion Book Concern, 1895.

Richardson, Harry V. *Dark Salvation: The Story of Methodism as It Developed Among Blacks in America.* Garden City, N.Y.: Doubleday/Anchor Books, 1976. Chap. 7.

Shaw, James Beverly Ford. *The Negro in the History of Methodism.* Nashville: Parthenon Press, 1954. Chap. 5.

Walls, William J. *The African Methodist Episcopal Zion Church: Reality of the Black Church.* Charlotte, N.C.: A.M.E.Z. Publishing House, 1974.

16

JARENA LEE

A Female Preacher among the African Methodists

Upon hearing Bishop Richard Allen preach one afternoon in 1804, Jarena Lee (b. 1783) embraced the opportunity to unite with the African Methodists of Philadelphia. Some five years later she felt the call to preach and entered upon a charismatic ministry that would carry her to many parts of the African Methodist connection. Though allowed by Allen to preach at Mother Bethel in Philadelphia, Lee found other pulpits closed to her. Neither the black nor the white churches ordained women; the very idea of women addressing mixed assemblies ran counter to prevailing attitudes regarding woman's proper sphere. Jarena Lee claimed the authority of an inner spiritual experience and preached "by inspiration" as an itinerant revivalist. Women have historically outnumbered men in the black denominations and been more supportive of local ministries, but rarely have they occupied positions of leadership. Even today, some churches ordain women while others still think it "unseemly" that a woman should preach or have authority over men in religious matters. Like Amanda Smith some fifty years later, as well as other female evangelists, healers, and preachers, particularly in the pentecostal tradition, Jarena Lee had to make her own way, design her own ministry, and rely on spiritual inspiration and authority.

And it shall come to pass . . . that I will pour out my Spirit upon all flesh; and your sons, and your *daughters* shall prophecy.

Joel ii. 28.

I WAS BORN FEBRUARY 11TH, 1783, at Cape May, state of New Jersey. At the age of seven years I was parted from my parents, and went to live as a servant maid, with a Mr. Sharp, at the distance of about sixty miles from the place of my birth.

Source: *The Life and Religious Experience of Jarena Lee, A Coloured Lady, Giving an Account of Her Call to Preach the Gospel. Revised and Corrected from the Original Manuscript, Written by Herself.* Philadelphia: Printed and Published for the Author, 1836.

My parents being wholly ignorant of the knowledge of God, had not therefore instructed me in any degree in this great matter. Not long after the commencement of my attendance on this lady, she had bid me do something respecting my work, which in a little while after, she asked me if I had done, when I replied, yes—but this was not true.

At this awful point, in my early history, the spirit of God moved in power through my conscience, and told me I was a wretched sinner. On this account so great was the impression, and so strong were the feelings of guilt, that I promised in my heart that I would not tell another lie.

But notwithstanding this promise my heart grew harder after a while; yet the spirit of the Lord never entirely forsook me, but continued mercifully striving with me, until his gracious power converted my soul.

The manner of this great accomplishment was as follows: In the year 1804, it so happened that I went with others to hear a missionary of the Presbyterian order preach. It was an afternoon meeting, but few were there, the place was a school room; but the preacher was solemn, and in his countenance the earnestness of his master's business appeared equally strong, as though he were about to speak to a multitude.

At the reading of the Psalms, a ray of renewed conviction darted into my soul. These were the words, composing the first verse of the Psalms for the service:

> Lord, I am vile, conceived in sin,
> Born unholy and unclean.
> Sprung from man, whose guilty fall
> Corrupts the race, and taints us all.

This description of my condition struck me to the heart, and made me to feel in some measure, the weight of my sins, and sinful nature. But not knowing how to run immediately to the Lord for help, I was driven of Satan, in the course of a few days, and tempted to destroy myself.

There was a brook about a quarter of a mile from the house, in which there was a deep hole, where the water whirled about among the rocks; to this place it was suggested, I must go and drown myself.

At the time I had a book in my hand; it was on a Sabbath morning, about ten o'clock; to this place I resorted, where on coming to the water I sat down on the bank, and on my looking into it; it was suggested, that drowning would be an easy death. It seemed as if some one was speaking to me, saying put your head under, it will not distress you. But by some means, of which I can give no account, my thoughts were taken entirely from this purpose, when I went from the place to the house again. It was the unseen arm of God which saved me from self murder.

But notwithstanding this escape from death, my mind was not at rest—but so great was the labour of my spirit and the fearful oppressions of a judgment to come, that I was reduced as one extremely ill. On which account a physician was called to attend me, from which illness I recovered in about three months.

But as yet I had not found him of whom Moses and the prophets did write, being extremely ignorant: there being no one to instruct me in the way of life and salvation as yet. After my recovery, I left the lady, who during my sickness, was exceedingly kind, and went to Philadelphia. From this place I soon went a few miles into the country, where I resided in the family of a Roman Catholic. But my anxiety still continued respecting my poor soul, on which account I used to watch my opportunity to read in the Bible; and this lady observing this, took the Bible from me and hid it, giving me a novel in its stead—which when I perceived, I refused to read.

Soon after this I again went to the city of Philadelphia; and commenced going to the English Church, the pastor of which was an Englishman, by the name of Pilmore, one of the number, who at first preached Methodism in America, in the city of New York.

But while sitting under the ministration of this man, which was about three months, and at the last time, it appeared that there was a wall between me and a communion with that people, which was higher than I could possibly see over, and seemed to make this impression upon my mind, *this is not the people for you.*

But on returning home at noon I inquired of the head cook of the house respecting the rules of the Methodists,—as I knew she belonged to that society—who told me what they were; on which account I replied that I should not be able to abide by such strict rules not even one year. However, I told her that I would go with her and hear what they had to say.

The man who was to speak in the afternoon of that day, was the Rev. Richard Allen, since Bishop of the African Episcopal Methodists in America. During the labors of this man that afternoon, I had come to the conclusion, that this is the people to which my heart unites, and it so happened, that as soon as the service closed he invited such as felt a desire to flee the wrath to come, to unite on trial with them—I embraced the opportunity. Three weeks from that day, my soul was gloriously converted to God, under preaching, at the very outset of the sermon. The text was barely pronounced, which was: "I perceive thy heart is not right in the sight of God," when there appeared to *my* view, in the centre of the heart *one* sin; and this was *malice*, against one particular individual, who had strove deeply to injure me, which I resented. At this discovery

I said, *Lord* I forgive *every* creature. That instant it appeared to me as if a garment, which had entirely enveloped my whole person, even to my fingers' ends, split at the crown of my head, and was stripped away from me, passing like a shadow from my sight; when the glory of God seemed to cover me in its stead.

That moment, though hundreds were present, I did leap to my feet, and declare that God, for Christ's sake, had pardoned the sins of my soul. Great was the ecstasy of my mind, for I felt that not only the sin of *malice* was pardoned, but all other sins were swept away together. That day was the first when my heart had believed, and my tongue had made confession unto salvation. The first words uttered, a part of that song, which shall fill eternity with its sound, was *glory to God*. For a few moments I had power to exhort sinners, and to tell of the wonders and of the goodness of him who had clothed me with *his* salvation. During this, the minister was silent, until my soul felt its duty had been performed, when he declared another witness of the power of Christ to forgive sins on earth was manifest in my conversion.

From the day on which I first went to the Methodist church, until the hour of my deliverance, I was strangely buffeted by that enemy of all righteousness—the devil.

I was naturally of a lively turn of disposition; and during the space of time from my first awakening until I knew my peace was made with God, I rejoiced in the vanities of this life, and then again sunk back into sorrow.

For four years I had continued in this way, frequently labouring under the awful apprehension that I could never be happy in this life. This persuasion was greatly strengthened, during the three weeks which was the last of Satan's power over me, in this peculiar manner: on which account, I had come to the conclusion that I had better be dead than alive. Here I was again tempted to destroy my life by drowning; but suddenly this mode was changed, and while in the dusk of the evening, as I was walking to and fro in the yard of the house, I was beset to hang myself with a cord suspended from the wall enclosing the secluded spot.

But no sooner was the intention resolved on in my mind than an awful dread came over me, when I ran into the house; still the tempter pursued me. There was standing a vessel of water; into this I was strongly impressed to plunge my head, so as to extinguish the life which God had given me. Had I have done this, I have been always of the opinion that I should have been unable to have released myself; although the vessel was scarcely large enough to hold a gallon of water. Of me may it not be said, as written by Isaiah, (chap. 65, verses 1, 2.) "I am sought of

them that asked not for me; I am found of them that sought me not."
Glory be to God for his redeeming power, which saved me from the violence of my own hands, from the malice of Satan, and from eternal
death; for had I have killed myself, a great ransom could not have delivered me; for it is written, "No murderer hath eternal life abiding in him."
How appropriately can I sing

> Jesus sought me, when a stranger,
> Wandering from the fold of God:
> He to rescue me from danger,
> Interposed his precious blood.

But notwithstanding the terror which seized upon me, when about to
end my life, I had no view of the precipice on the edge of which I was
tottering, until it was over, and my eyes were opened. Then the awful
gulf of hell seemed to be open beneath me, covered only, as it were, by
a spider's web, on which I stood. I seemed to hear the howling of the
damned, to see the smoke of the bottomless pit, and to hear the rattling
of those chains which hold the impenitent under clouds of darkness to
the judgment of the great day.

I trembled like Belshazzar, and cried out in the horror of my spirit,
"God be merciful to me a sinner." That night I formed a resolution to
pray; which, when resolved upon, there appeared, sitting in one corner
of the room, Satan, in the form of a monstrous dog, and in a rage, as if
in pursuit, his tongue protruding from his mouth to a great length, and
his eyes looked like two balls of fire; it soon, however, vanished out of
my sight. From this state of terror and dismay I was happily delivered
under the preaching of the Gospel as before related.

This view which I was permitted to have of Satan in the form of a
dog is evidence, which corroborates in my estimation, the Bible account
of a hell of fire, which burneth with brimstone, called in Scripture the
bottomless pit, the place where all liars, who repent not, shall have their
portion; as also the Sabbath breaker, the adulterer, the fornicator, with
the fearful, the abominable, and the unbelieving, this shall be the portion of their cup.

This language is too strong and expressive to be applied to any state
of suffering in *time*. Were it to be thus applied, the reality could nowhere be found in human life; the consequence would be, that *this*
scripture would be found a false testimony. But when made to apply to
an endless state of perdition, in eternity, beyond the bounds of human
life, then this language is found not to exceed our views of a state of
eternal damnation.

During the latter part of my state of conviction, I can now apply to my case, as it then was, the beautiful words of the poet:

> The more I strove against its power,
> I felt its weight and guilt the more;
> Till late I hear'd my Saviour say,
> Come hither soul, I am the way.

This I found to be true, to the joy of my disconsolate and despairing heart, in the hour of my conversion to God.

During this state of mind, while sitting near the fire one evening, after I had heard Rev. Richard Allen, as before related, a view of my distressed condition so affected my heart, that I could not refrain from weeping and crying aloud; which caused the lady with whom I then lived to inquire with surprise, what ailed me; to which I answered that I knew not what ailed me. She replied that I ought to pray. I arose from where I was sitting, being in an agony, and weeping convulsively, requested her to pray for me; but at the very moment when she would have done so, some person rapped heavily at the door for admittance; it was but a person of the house, but this occurrence was sufficient to interrupt us in our intentions; and I believe to this day, I should then have found salvation to my soul. This interruption was doubtless also the work of Satan.

Although at this time, when my conviction was so great, yet I knew not that Jesus Christ was the Son of God, the second person in the adorable trinity. I knew him not in the pardon of my sins, yet I felt a consciousness that if I died without pardon, that my lot must inevitably be damnation. If I would pray—I knew not how. I could form no connexion of ideas into words; but I knew the Lord's prayer; this I uttered with a loud voice, and with all my might and strength. I was the most ignorant creature in the world; I did not even know that Christ had died for the sins of the world, and to save sinners. Every circumstance, however, was so directed as still to continue and increase the sorrows of my heart, which I now know to have been a godly sorrow which wrought repentance, which is not to be repented of. Even the falling of the dead leaves from the forests, and the dried spires of the mown grass, showed me that I too must die in like manner. But my case was awfully different from that of the grass of the field, or the widespread decay of a thousand forests, as I felt within me a living principle, an immortal spirit, which cannot die, and must forever either enjoy the smiles of its Creator, or feel the pangs of ceaseless damnation.

But the Lord led me on. Being gracious, he took pity on my ignorance; he heard my wailings, which had entered into the ear of the Lord of Sabaoth. Circumstances so transpired that I soon came to a knowledge of the being and character of the Son of God, of whom I knew nothing.

My strength had left me. I had become feverish and sickly through the violence of my feelings, on which account I left my place of service to spend a week with a coloured physician, who was a member of the Methodist society, and also to spend this week in going to places where prayer and supplication was statedly [regularly] made for such as me.

Through this means I had learned much, so as to be able in some degree to comprehend the spiritual meaning of the text which the minister took on the Sabbath morning, as before related, which was, "I perceive thy heart is not right in the sight of God." Acts, chap. 8, verse 21.

This text, as already related, became the power of God unto salvation to me, because I believed. I was baptized according to the direction of our Lord, who said, as he was about to ascend from the mount, to his disciples, "Go ye into all the world and preach my gospel to every creature, he that believeth and is baptized shall be saved."

I have now passed through the account of my conviction, and also of my conversion to God; and shall next speak of the blessing of sanctification.

A time after I had received forgiveness flowed sweetly on; day and night my joy was full, no temptation was permitted to molest me. I could say continually with the psalmist, that "God had separated my sins from me, as far as the east is from the west." I was ready continually to cry

> Come all the world, come sinner thou,
> All things in Christ are ready now.

I continued in this happy state of mind for almost three months, when a certain coloured man, by name William Scott, came to pay me a religious visit. He had been for many years a faithful follower of the Lamb; and he had also taken much time in visiting the sick and distressed of our colour, and understood well the great things belonging to a man of full stature in Christ Jesus.

In the course of our conversation, he inquired if the Lord had justified my soul. I answered, yes. He then asked me if he had sanctified me. I answered, no; and that I did not know what that was. He then undertook to instruct me further in the knowledge of the Lord respecting this blessing.

He told me the progress of the soul from a state of darkness, or of nature, was threefold; or consisted in three degrees, as follows: First,

conviction for sin. Second, justification from sin. Third, the entire sanctification of the soul to God. I thought this description was beautiful, and
immediately believed in it. He then inquired if I would promise to pray
for this in my secret devotions. I told him, yes. Very soon I began to
call upon the Lord to show me all that was in my heart, which was not
according to his will. Now there appeared to be a new struggle commencing in my soul, not accompanied with fear, guilt, and bitter distress, as while under my first conviction for sin; but a labouring of the
mind to know more of the right way of the Lord. I began now to feel
that my heart was not clean in his sight; that there yet remained the
roots of bitterness, which if not destroyed, would ere long sprout up
from these roots, and overwhelm me in a new growth of the brambles
and brushwood of sin.

By the increasing light of the Spirit, I had found there yet remained
the root of pride, anger, self-will, with many evils, the result of fallen
nature. I now became alarmed at this discovery, and began to fear that
I had been deceived in my experience. I was now greatly alarmed, lest I
should fall away from what I knew I had enjoyed; and to guard against
this I prayed almost incessantly, without acting faith on the power and
promises of God to keep me from falling. I had not yet learned how to
war against temptation of this kind. Satan well knew that if he could
succeed in making me disbelieve my conversion, that he would catch
me either on the ground of complete despair, or on the ground of infidelity. For if all I had passed through was to go for nothing, and was
but a fiction, the mere ravings of a disordered mind, then I would naturally be led to believe that there is nothing in religion at all.

From this snare I was mercifully preserved, and led to believe that
there was yet a greater work than that of pardon to be wrought in me.
I retired to a secret place (after having sought this blessing, as well as I
could, for nearly three months, from the time brother Scott had instructed me respecting it) for prayer, about four o'clock in the afternoon. I had struggled long and hard, but found not the desire of my
heart. When I rose from my knees, there seemed a voice speaking to me,
as I yet stood in a leaning posture—"Ask for sanctification." When to
my surprise, I recollected that I had not even thought of it in my whole
prayer. It would seem Satan had hidden the very object from my mind,
for which I had purposely kneeled to pray. But when this voice whis-
pered in my heart, saying, "Pray for sanctification," I again bowed in
the same place, at the same time, and said, "Lord *sanctify* my soul for
Christ's sake?" That very instant, as if lightning had darted through me,
I sprang to my feet, and cried, "The Lord has sanctified my soul!" There
was none to hear this but the angels who stood around to witness my

joy—and Satan, whose malice raged the more. That Satan was there, I knew, for no sooner had I cried out "The Lord has sanctified my soul," than there seemed another voice behind me, saying, "No, it is too great a work to be done." But another spirit said, "Bow down for the witness—I received it—*thou art sanctified!*" The first I knew of myself after that, I was standing in the yard with my hands spread out, and looking with my face toward heaven.

I now ran into the house and told them what had happened to me, when, as it were, a new rush of the same ecstasy came upon me, and caused me to feel as if I were in an ocean of light and bliss.

During this, I stood perfectly still, the tears rolling in a flood from my eyes. So great was the joy that it is past description. There is no language that can describe it, except that which was heard by St. Paul, when he was caught up to the third heaven, and heard words which it was not lawful to utter.

My Call to Preach the Gospel

Between four and five years after my sanctification, on a certain time, an impressive silence fell upon me, and I stood as if some one was about to speak to me, yet I had no such thought in my heart. But to my utter surprise there seemed to sound a voice which I thought I distinctly heard, and most certainly understood, which said to me, "Go preach the Gospel!" I immediately replied aloud, "No one will believe me." Again I listened, and again the same voice seemed to say, "Preach the Gospel; I will put words in your mouth, and will turn your enemies to become your friends."

At first I supposed that Satan had spoken to me, for I had read that he could transform himself into an angel of light, for the purpose of deception. Immediately I went into a secret place, and called upon the Lord to know if he had called me to preach, and whether I was deceived or not; when there appeared to my view the form and figure of a pulpit, with a Bible lying thereon, the back of which was presented to me as plainly as if it had been a literal fact.

In consequence of this, my mind became so exercised that during the night following, I took a text and preached in my sleep. I thought there stood before me a great multitude, while I expounded to them the things of religion. So violent were my exertions, and so loud were my exclamations, that I awoke from the sound of my own voice, which also awoke the family of the house where I resided. Two days after, I went to see the preacher in charge of the African Society, who was the Rev. Richard Allen (the same before named in these pages) to tell him that

I felt it my duty to preach the gospel. But as I drew near the street in which his house was, which was in the city of Philadelphia, my courage began to fail me; so terrible did the cross appear, it seemed that I should not be able to bear it. Previous to my setting out to go to see him, so agitated was my mind that my appetite for my daily food failed me entirely. Several times on my way there, I turned back again; but as often I felt my strength again renewed, and I soon found that the nearer I approached to the house of the minister, the less was my fear. Accordingly, as soon as I came to the door, my fears subsided, the cross was removed, all things appeared pleasant—I was tranquil.

I now told him that the Lord had revealed it to me that I must preach the gospel. He replied by asking, in what sphere I wished to move in? I said, among the Methodists. He then replied, that a Mrs. Cook, a Methodist lady, had also some time before requested the same privilege; who it was believed, had done much good in the way of exhortation, and holding prayer meetings; and who had been permitted to do so by the verbal license of the preacher in charge at the time. But as to women preaching, he said that our Discipline knew nothing at all about it—that it did not call for women preachers. This I was glad to hear, because it removed the fear of the cross—but no sooner did this feeling cross my mind, than I found that a love of souls had in a measure departed from me; that holy energy which burned within me as a fire, began to be smothered. This I soon perceived.

O how careful ought we to be, lest through our bylaws of church government and discipline, we bring into disrepute even the word of life. For as unseemly as it may appear nowadays for a woman to preach, it should be remembered that nothing is impossible with God. And why should it be thought impossible, heterodox, or improper for a woman to preach, seeing the Saviour died for the woman as well as the man?

If the man may preach, because the Saviour died for him, why not the woman, seeing he died for her also? Is he not a whole Saviour, instead of a half one, as those who hold it wrong for a woman to preach, would seem to make it appear?

Did not Mary *first* preach the risen Saviour, and is not the doctrine of the resurrection the very climax of Christianity—hangs not all our hope on this, as argued by St. Paul? Then did not Mary, a woman, preach the gospel? For she preached the resurrection of the crucified Son of God.

But some will say that Mary did not expound the Scripture, therefore she did not preach, in the proper sense of the term. To this I reply, it may be that the term *preach*, in those primitive times, did not mean exactly what it is now *made* to mean; perhaps it was a great deal more simple then, than it is now; if it were not, the unlearned fishermen could not have preached the gospel at all, as they had no learning.

To this it may be replied by those who are determined not to believe that it is right for a woman to preach, that the disciples, though they were fishermen, and ignorant of letters too, were inspired so to do. To which I would reply, that though they were inspired, yet that inspiration did not save them from showing their ignorance of letters, and of man's wisdom; this the multitude soon found out, by listening to the remarks of the envious Jewish priests. If then, to preach the gospel, by the gift of heaven, comes by inspiration solely, is God straitened; must he take the man exclusively? May he not, did he not, and can he not inspire a female to preach the simple story of the birth, life, death, and resurrection of our Lord, and accompany it too, with power to the sinner's heart. As for me, I am fully persuaded that the Lord called me to labour according to what I have received, in his vineyard. If he has not, how could he consistently bear testimony in favour of my poor labours, in awakening and converting sinners?

In my wanderings up and down among men, preaching according to my ability, I have frequently found families who told me that they had not for several years been to a meeting, and yet, while listening to hear what God would say by his poor coloured female instrument, have believed with trembling, tears rolling down their cheeks—the signs of contrition and repentance towards God. I firmly believe that I have sown seed in the name of the Lord, which shall appear with its increase at the great day of accounts, when Christ shall come to make up his jewels.

At a certain time I was beset with the idea that soon or late I should fall from grace, and lose my soul at last. I was frequently called to the throne of grace about this matter, but found no relief; the temptation pursued me still. Being more and more afflicted with it, till at a certain time when the spirit strongly impressed it on my mind to enter into my closet, and carry my case once more to the Lord; the Lord enabled me to draw nigh to him, and to his mercy seat, at this time, in an extraordinary manner; for while I wrestled with him for the victory over this disposition to doubt whether I should persevere, there appeared a form of fire, about the size of a man's hand, as I was on my knees; at the same moment, there appeared to the eye of faith a man robed in a white garment, from the shoulders down to the feet; from him a voice proceeded, saying: "Thou shalt never return from the cross." Since that time I have never doubted, but believe that God will keep me until the day of redemption. Now I could adopt the very language of St. Paul, and say that nothing could have separated my soul from the love of God, which is in

Christ Jesus. From that time, 1807, until the present, 1833, I have not yet doubted the power and goodness of God to keep me from falling, through sanctification of the spirit and belief of the truth.

My Marriage

In the year 1811, I changed my situation in life, having married Mr. Joseph Lee, Pastor of a Coloured Society at Snow Hill, about six miles from the city of Philadelphia. It became necessary therefore for me to remove. This was a great trial at first, as I knew no person at Snow Hill, except my husband; and to leave my associates in the society, and especially those who composed the band of which I was one. Not but those who have been in sweet fellowship with such as really love God, and have together drank bliss and happiness from the same fountain, can tell how dear such company is, and how hard it is to part from them.

At Snow Hill, as was feared, I never found that agreement and closeness in communion and fellowship, that I had in Philadelphia among my young companions, nor ought I to have expected it. The manners and customs at this place were somewhat different, on which account I became discontented in the course of a year, and began to importune my husband to remove to the city. But this plan did not suit him, as he was the Pastor of the Society; he could not bring his mind to leave them. This afflicted me a little. But the Lord soon showed me in a dream what his will was concerning this matter.

I dreamed that as I was walking on the summit of a beautiful hill, that I saw near me a flock of sheep, fair and white, as if but newly washed; when there came walking toward me a man of a grave and dignified countenance, dressed entirely in white, as it were in a robe, and looking at me, said emphatically, "Joseph Lee must take care of these sheep, or the wolf will come and devour them." When I awoke, I was convinced of my error, and immediately, with a glad heart, yielded to the right way of the Lord. This also greatly strengthened my husband in his care over them, for fear the wolf should by some means take any of them away. The following verse was beautifully suited to our condition, as well as to all the little flocks of God scattered up and down this land:

> Us into Thy protection take,
> And gather with Thine arm;
> Unless the fold we first forsake,
> The wolf can never harm.

After this, I fell into a state of general debility and in an ill state of health; so much so, that I could not sit up; but a desire to warn sinners to flee the wrath to come burned vehemently in my heart, when the Lord would send sinners into the house to see me. Such opportunities I embraced to press home on their consciences the things of eternity, and so effectual was the word of exhortation made through the Spirit, that I have seen them fall to the floor crying aloud for mercy.

From this sickness I did not expect to recover; and there was but one thing which bound me to earth, and this was, that I had not as yet preached the gospel to the fallen sons and daughters of Adam's race, to the satisfaction of my mind. I wished to go from one end of the earth to the other, crying, Behold, behold the Lamb! To this end I earnestly prayed the Lord to raise me up, if consistent with his will. He condescended to hear my prayer, and to give me a token in a dream, that in due time I should recover my health. The dream was as follows: I thought I saw the sun rise in the morning, and ascend to an altitude of about half an hour high, and then become obscured by a dense black cloud, which continued to hide its rays for about one-third part of the day, and then it burst forth again with renewed splendour.

This dream I interpreted to signify my early life, my conversion to God, and this sickness, which was a great affliction, as it hindered me, and I feared would forever hinder me from preaching the gospel, was signified by the cloud; and the bursting forth of the sun, again, was the recovery of my health, and being permitted to preach.

I went to the throne of grace on this subject, where the Lord made this impressive reply in my heart, while on my knees: "Ye shall be restored to thy health again, and worship God in full purpose of heart."

This manifestation was so impressive that I could but hide my face, as if someone was gazing upon me, to think of the great goodness of the Almighty God to my poor soul and body. From that very time I began to gain strength of body and mind, glory to God in the highest, until my health was fully recovered.

For six years from this time I continued to receive from above such baptisms of the Spirit as mortality could scarcely bear. About that time I was called to suffer in my family by death—five, in the course of about six years, fell by his hand; my husband being one of the number, which was the greatest affliction of all.

I was now left alone in the world, with two infant children, one of the age of about two years, the other six months, with no other dependence than the promise of Him who hath said, "I will be the widow's God, and a father to the fatherless." Accordingly, he raised me up friends, whose liberality comforted and solaced me in my state of widowhood and sorrows. I could sing with the greatest propriety the words of the poet.

> He helps the stranger in distress,
> The widow and the fatherless,
> And grants the prisoner sweet release.

I can say even now, with the Psalmist, "Once I was young, but now I am old, yet I have never seen the righteous forsaken, nor his seed begging bread." I have ever been fed by his bounty, clothed by his mercy, comforted and healed when sick, succoured when tempted, and every where upheld by his hand.

The Subject of My Call to Preach Renewed

It was now eight years since I had made application to be permitted to preach the gospel, during which time I had only been allowed to exhort, and even this privilege but seldom. This subject now was renewed afresh in my mind; it was as a fire shut up in my bones. About thirteen months passed on, while under this renewed impression. During this time, I had solicited of the Rev. Bishop Richard Allen, who at this time had become Bishop of the African Episcopal Methodists in America, to be permitted the liberty of holding prayer meetings in my own hired house, and of exhorting as I found liberty, which was granted me. By this means, my mind was relieved, as the house was soon filled when the hour appointed for prayer had arrived.

I cannot but relate in this place, before I proceed further with the above subject, the singular conversion of a very wicked young man. He was a coloured man, who had generally attended our meetings, but not for any good purpose; but rather to disturb and to ridicule our denomination. He openly and uniformly declared that he neither believed in religion, nor wanted anything to do with it. He was of a Gallio disposition, and took the lead among the young people of colour. But after a while he fell sick, and lay about three months in a state of ill health; his disease was a consumption. Toward the close of his days, his sister who was a member of the society, came and desired me to go and see her brother, as she had no hopes of his recovery; perhaps the Lord might break into his mind. I went alone, and found him very low. I soon commenced to inquire respecting his state of feeling, and how he found his mind. His answer was, "O tolerable well," with an air of great indifference. I asked him if I should pray for him. He answered in a sluggish and careless manner, "O yes, if you have time." I then sung a hymn, kneeled down and prayed for him, and then went my way.

Three days after this, I went again to visit the young man. At this time there went with me two of the sisters in Christ. We found the Rev.

Mr. Cornish, of our denomination, labouring with him. But he said he received but little satisfaction from him. Pretty soon, however, brother Cornish took his leave; when myself, with the other two sisters, one of which was an elderly woman named Jane Hutt, the other was younger, both coloured, commenced conversing with him, respecting his eternal interest, and of his hopes of a happy eternity, if any he had. He said but little; we then kneeled down together and besought the Lord in his behalf, praying that if mercy were not clear gone forever, to shed a ray of softening grace upon the hardness of his heart. He appeared now to be somewhat more tender, and we thought we could perceive some tokens of conviction, as he wished us to visit him again, in a tone of voice not quite as indifferent as he had hitherto manifested.

But two days had elapsed after this visit, when his sister came for me in haste, saying, that she believed her brother was then dying, and that he had sent for me. I immediately called on Jane Hutt, who was still among us as a mother in Israel, to go with me. When we arrived there, we found him sitting up in his bed, very restless and uneasy, but he soon laid down again. He now wished me to come to him, by the side of his bed. I asked him how he was. He said, "Very ill", and added, "Pray for me, quick?" We now perceived his time in this world to be short. I took up the hymnbook and opened to a hymn suitable to his case, and commenced to sing. But there seemed to be a horror in the room—a darkness of a mental kind, which was felt by us all; there being five persons, except the sick young man and his nurse. We had sung but one verse, when they all gave over singing, on account of this unearthly sensation, but myself. I continued to sing on alone, but in a dull and heavy manner, though looking up to God all the while for help. Suddenly, I felt a spring of energy awake in my heart, when darkness gave way in some degree. It was but a glimmer from above. When the hymn was finished, we all kneeled down to pray for him. While calling on the name of the Lord, to have mercy on his soul, and to grant him repentance unto life, it came suddenly into my mind never to rise from my knees until God should hear prayer in his behalf, until he should convert and save his soul.

Now, while I thus continued importuning heaven, as I felt I was led, a ray of light, more abundant, broke forth among us. There appeared to my view (though my eyes were closed) the Saviour in full stature, nailed to the cross, just over the head of the young man, against the ceiling of the room. I cried out, brother look up, the Saviour is come, he will pardon you, your sins he will forgive. My sorrow for the soul of the young man was gone; I could no longer pray—joy and rapture made it impossible. We rose up from our knees, when lo, his eyes were gazing with ecstasy upward; over his face there was an expression of joy; his lips were clothed in a sweet and holy smile; but no sound came from his tongue; it was heard in its stillness of bliss, full of hope and immortality. Thus, as I held him by the hand his happy and purified soul soared away, without a sigh or a groan, to its eternal rest.

I now closed his eyes, straightened out his limbs, and left him to be dressed for the grave. But as for me, I was filled with the power of the Holy Ghost—the very room seemed filled with glory. His sister and all that were in the room rejoiced, nothing doubting but he had entered into Paradise; and I believe I shall see him at the last and great day, safe on the shores of salvation.

But to return to the subject of my call to preach. Soon after this, as above related, the Rev. Richard Williams was to preach at Bethel Church, where I with others were assembled. He entered the pulpit, gave out the hymn, which was sung, and then addressed the throne of grace; took his text, passed through the exordium, and commenced to expound it. The text he took is in Jonah, 2d chap. 9th verse,—"Salvation is of the Lord." But as he proceeded to explain, he seemed to have lost the spirit; when in the same instant, I sprang, as by an altogether supernatural impulse, to my feet, when I was aided from above to give an exhortation on the very text which my brother Williams had taken.

I told them that I was like Jonah; for it had been then nearly eight years since the Lord had called me to preach his gospel to the fallen sons and daughters of Adam's race, but that I had lingered like him, and delayed to go at the bidding of the Lord, and warn those who are as deeply guilty as were the people of Ninevah.

During the exhortation, God made manifest his power in a manner sufficient to show the world that I was called to labour according to my ability, and the grace given unto me, in the vineyard of the good husbandman.

I now sat down, scarcely knowing what I had done, being frightened. I imagined, that for this indecorum, as I feared it might be called, I should be expelled from the church. But instead of this, the Bishop rose up in the assembly, and related that I had called upon him eight years before, asking to be permitted to preach, and that he had put me off, but that he now as much believed that I was called to that work, as any of the preachers present. These remarks greatly strengthened me, so that my fears of having given an offence and made myself liable as an offender subsided, giving place to a sweet serenity, a holy joy of a peculiar kind, untasted in my bosom until then.

The next Sabbath day while sitting under the word of the gospel, I felt moved to attempt to speak to the people in a public manner, but I could not bring my mind to attempt it in the church. I said, Lord, any-where but here. Accordingly, there was a house not far off which was pointed out to me; to this I went. It was the house of a sister belonging to the same society with myself. Her name was Anderson. I told her I had come to hold a meeting in her house, if she would call in her neigh-bours. With this request she immediately complied. My congregation consisted of but five persons. I commenced by reading and singing a hymn, when I dropped to my knees by the side of a table to pray. When I arose I found my hand resting on the Bible, which I had not noticed till that moment. It now occurred to me to take a text. I opened the Scripture, as it happened, at the 141st Psalm, fixing my eye on the 3d verse, which reads: "Set a watch, O Lord, before my mouth, keep the door of my lips." My sermon, such as it was, I applied wholly to myself, and added an exhortation. Two of my congregation wept much, as the fruit of my labour this time. In closing I said to the few, that if any one would open a door, I would hold a meeting the next sixth-day evening; when one answered that her house was at my service. Accordingly I went, and God made manifest his power among the people. Some wept, while others shouted for joy. One whole seat of females, by the power of God, as the rushing of a wind, were all bowed to the floor at once, and screamed out. Also a sick man and woman in one house, the Lord con-victed them both; one lived, and the other died. God wrought a judg-ment—some were well at night, and died in the morning. At this place I continued to hold meetings about six months. During that time I kept house with my little son, who was very sickly. About this time I had a call to preach at a place about thirty miles distant, among the Method-ists, with whom I remained one week, and during the whole time not a thought of my little son came into my mind; it was hid from me, lest I should have been diverted from the work I had to do, to look after my son. Here by the instrumentality of a poor coloured woman, the Lord poured forth his spirit among the people. Though, as I was told, there were lawyers, doctors, and magistrates present to hear me speak, yet there was mourning and crying among sinners, for the Lord scattered fire among them of his own kindling. The Lord gave his handmaiden power to speak for his great name, for he arrested the hearts of the peo-ple, and caused a shaking amongst the multitude, for God was in the midst.

I now returned home, found all well; no harm had come to my child, although I left it very sick. Friends had taken care of it which was of the Lord. I now began to think seriously of breaking up house-keeping, and forsaking all to preach the everlasting Gospel. I felt a strong desire to return to the place of my nativity, at Cape May, after an absence of about fourteen years. To this place, where the heaviest cross was to be met with, the Lord sent me, as Saul of Tarsus was sent to Jerusalem, to preach the same gospel which he had neglected and despised before his conversion. I went by water, and on my passage was much distressed by sea sickness, so much so that I expected to have died, but such was not the will of the Lord respecting me. After I had disembarked, I proceeded on as opportunities offered, toward where my mother lived. When within ten miles of that place, I appointed an evening meeting. There were a goodly number came out to hear. The Lord was pleased to give me light and liberty among the people. After meeting, there came an elderly lady to me and said she believed the Lord had sent me among them; she then appointed me another meeting there two weeks from that night. The next day I hastened forward to the place of my mother, who was happy to see me, and the happiness was mutual between us. With her I left my poor sickly boy, while I departed to do my Master's will. In this neighborhood I had an uncle who was a Methodist, and who gladly threw open his door for meetings to be held there. At the first meeting which I held at my uncle's house, there was, with others who had come from curiosity to hear the coloured woman preacher, an old man, who was a deist, and who said he did not believe the coloured people had any souls—he was sure they had none. He took a seat very near where I was standing, and boldly tried to look me out of countenance. But as I laboured on in the best manner I was able, looking to God all the while, though it seemed to me I had but little liberty, yet there went an arrow from the bent bow of the gospel, and fastened in his till then obdurate heart. After I had done speaking, he went out, and called the people around him, said that my preaching might seem a small thing, yet he believed I had the worth of souls at heart. This language was different from what it was a little time before, as he now seemed to admit that coloured people had souls, as it was to these I was chiefly speaking; and unless they had souls, whose good I had in view, his remark must have been without meaning. He now came into the house, and in the most friendly manner shook hands with me, saying he hoped God had spared him to some good purpose. This man was a great slave holder, and had been very cruel, thinking nothing of knocking down a slave with a fence stake, or whatever might come to hand. From this time it was said of him that he became greatly altered in his ways for the better. At that time he was about seventy years old, his head as white as snow; but whether he became a converted man or not, I never heard.

The week following, I had an invitation to hold a meeting at the Court House of the County, when I spoke from the 53d chap of Isaiah,

3d verse. It was a solemn time, and the Lord attended the word; I had
life and liberty, though there were people there of various denominations. Here again I saw the aged slaveholder, who notwithstanding his
age, walked about three miles to hear me. This day I spoke twice, and
walked six miles to the place appointed. There was a magistrate present,
who showed his friendship by saying in a friendly manner that he had
heard of me: he handed me a hymn-book, pointing to a hymn which he
had selected. When the meeting was over, he invited me to preach in a
schoolhouse in his neighbourhood, about three miles distant from where
I then was. During this meeting one backslider was reclaimed. This day
I walked six miles, and preached twice to large congregations, both in
the morning and evening. The Lord was with me, glory be to his holy
name. I next went six miles and held a meeting in a coloured friend's
house, at eleven o'clock in the morning, and preached to a well behaved
congregation of both coloured and white. After service I again walked
back, which was in all twelve miles in the same day. This was on Sabbath, or as I sometimes call it, seventh-day; for after my conversion I
preferred the plain language of the Quakers: On fourth day, after this,
in compliance with an invitation received by note, from the same magistrate who had heard me at the above place, I preached to a large congregation, where we had a precious time: much weeping was heard
among the people. The same gentleman, now at the close of the meeting, gave out another appointment at the same place, that day week.
Here again I had liberty, there was a move among the people. Ten years
from that time, in the neighbourhood of Cape May, I held a prayer
meeting in a school house, which was then the regular place of preaching for the Episcopal Methodists; after service, there came a white lady
of the first distinction, a member of the Methodist Society, and told me
that at the same schoolhouse ten years before, under my preaching, the
Lord first awakened her. She rejoiced much to see me, and invited me
home with her, where I staid till the next day. This was bread cast on
the waters, seen after many days.

From this place I next went to Dennis Creek meeting house, where
at the invitation of an elder, I spoke to a large congregation of various
and conflicting sentiments, when a wonderful shock of God's power
was felt, shown everywhere by groans, by sighs, and loud and happy
amens. I felt as if aided from above. My tongue was cut loose, the stam-
merer spoke freely; the love of God, and of his service, burned with a
vehement flame within me; his name was glorified among the people.

But here I feel myself constrained to give over, as from the small-
ness of this pamphlet I cannot go through with the whole of my journal,
as it would probably make a volume of two hundred pages; which, if the

Lord be willing, may at some future day be published. But for the satisfaction of such as may follow after me, when I am no more, I have recorded how the Lord called me to his work, and how he has kept me from falling from grace, as I feared I should. In all things he has proved himself a God of truth to me; and in his service I am now as much determined to spend and be spent, as at the very first. My ardour for the progress of his cause abates not a whit, so far as I am able to judge, though I am now something more than fifty years of age.

As to the nature of uncommon impressions, which the reader cannot but have noticed, and possibly sneered at in the course of these pages, they may be accounted for in this way: It is known that the blind have the sense of hearing in a manner much more acute than those who can see: also their sense of feeling is exceedingly fine, and is found to detect any roughness on the smoothest surface, where those who can see can find none. So it may be with such as I am, who has never had more than three months schooling; and wishing to know much of the way and law of God, have therefore watched the more closely the operations of the Spirit, and have in consequence been led thereby. But let it be remarked that I have never found that Spirit to lead me contrary to the Scriptures of truth, as I understand them. "For as many as are led by the *Spirit* of God are the sons of God."—Rom. viii. 14.

I have now only to say, May the blessing of the Father, and of the Son, and of the Holy Ghost, accompany the reading of this poor effort to speak well of his name, wherever it may be read. AMEN.

SUPPLEMENTARY READINGS

Cott, Nancy F. *The Bonds of Womanhood: "Woman's Sphere" in New England, 1780–1835.* New Haven: Yale University Press, 1977.

Humez, Jean McMahon, ed. *Gifts of Power: The Writings of Rebecca Jackson, Black Visionary, Shaker Eldress.* Amherst: University of Massachusetts Press, 1981.

Richardson, Marilyn. *Black Women and Religion, a Bibliography.* Boston: G.K. Hall, 1980.

Smith, Amanda Berry. *An Autobiography: The Story of the Lord's Dealings with Mrs. Amanda Smith, the Colored Evangelist.* Chicago: Meyer & Brother, 1893.

Wills, David W. "Womanhood and Domesticity in the A.M.E. Tradition: The Influence of Daniel Alexander Payne." In *Black Apostles at Home and Abroad,* edited by David W. Wills and Richard Newman. Boston: G.K. Hall, 1982. Pp. 133–46.

17

NATHANIEL PAUL

African Baptists Celebrate Emancipation in New York State

The Fourth of July 1827 is Emancipation Day in the state of New York. New York passed a gradual emancipation act in 1799, which freed no slaves but provided that children born after July 4, 1799, would become free at twenty-eight years of age if male and twenty-five if female. An 1817 statute went further, declaring that all slaves born before July 4, 1799, were to be free after July 3, 1827. Blacks throughout the state celebrated when the law of 1817 became effective on July 4, 1827. The Reverend Nathaniel Paul (1775?–1839), pastor of the Hamilton Street Baptist Church in Albany, notes the historic import of the day in the following address. Born in New Hampshire, pastor in Albany since 1820, and on record as opposing the African colonization scheme, Paul expresses here his confidence that the progress of emancipation is certain in the hands of God. He delivered a similar commemorative address in 1829 but departed Albany two years later for the fugitive slave colony at Wilberforce in Canada West. This agrarian settlement sent him to England to gather funds. After four years Paul had little to show for his efforts and encountered considerable criticism from others at Wilberforce who alleged that he had squandered what had been given him. He returned to Albany where he died a pauper in 1839.

THROUGH THE LONG LAPSE of ages, it has been common for nations to record whatever was peculiar or interesting in the course of their history. Thus when Heaven, provoked by the iniquities of man, has visited the earth with the pestilence which moves in darkness or destruction, that wasteth at noonday, and has swept from existence, by thousands, its numerous inhabitants; or when the milder terms of mercy have been dispensed in rich abundance, and the goodness of God has crowned the efforts of any people with peace and prosperity; they have been placed upon their annals, and handed down to future ages, both for their

Source: *An Address, Delivered on the Celebration of the Abolition of Slavery, in the State of New York, July 5, 1827.* Albany, N.Y.: John B. Van Steenbergh, 1827.

amusement and profit. And as the nations which have already passed away, have been careful to select the most important events, peculiar to themselves, and have recorded them for the good of the people that should succeed them, so will we place it upon our history; and we will tell the good story to our children and to our children's children, down to the latest posterity, that on the *fourth day of July,* in the year of our Lord 1827, slavery was abolished in the state of New-York.

Seldom, if ever, was there an occasion which required a public acknowledgment, or that deserved to be retained with gratitude of heart to the all-wise disposer of events, more than the present on which we have assembled.

It is not the mere gratification of the pride of the heart, or any vain ambitious notion, that has influenced us to make our appearance in the public streets of our city, or to assemble in the sanctuary of the Most High this morning; but we have met to offer our tribute of thanksgiving and praise to almighty God for his goodness; to retrace the acts and express our gratitude to our public benefactors, and to stimulate each other to the performance of every good and virtuous act, which now does, or hereafter may devolve as a duty upon us, as freemen and citizens, in common with the rest of community.

And if ever it were necessary for me to offer an apology to an audience for my absolute inability to perform a task assigned me, I feel that the present is the period. However, relying, for support on the hand of Him who has said, "I will never leave nor forsake"; and confiding in your charity for every necessary allowance, I venture to engage in the arduous undertaking.

In contemplating the subject before us, in connection with the means by which so glorious an event has been accomplished, we find much which requires our deep humiliation and our most exalted praises. We are permitted to behold one of the most pernicious and abominable of all enterprises, in which the depravity of human nature ever led man to engage, entirely eradicated. The power of the tyrant is subdued, the heart of the oppressed is cheered, liberty is proclaimed to the captive, and the opening of the prison to those who were bound, and he who had long been the miserable victim of cruelty and degradation, is elevated to the common rank in which our benevolent Creator first designed, that man should move—all of which have been effected by means the most simple, yet perfectly efficient: Not by those fearful judgments of the almighty, which have so often fell upon the different parts of the earth; which have overturned nations and kingdoms; scattered thrones and sceptres; nor is the glory of the achievement, tarnished with the horrors of the field of battle. We hear not the cries of the widow and the fatherless; nor are our hearts affected with the sight of garments rolled in blood; but all has been done by the diffusion and influence of the pure, yet powerful principles of benevolence, before which the pitiful impotency of tyranny and oppression, is scattered and dispersed, like the chaff before the rage of the whirlwind.

I will not, on this occasion, attempt fully to detail the abominations of the traffic to which we have already alluded. Slavery, with its concomitants and consequences, in the best attire in which it can possibly be presented, is but a hateful monster, the very demon of avarice and oppression, from its first introduction to the present time; it has been among all nations the scourge of heaven, and the curse of the earth. It is so contrary to the laws which the God of nature has laid down as the rule of action by which the conduct of man is to be regulated towards his fellow man, which binds him to love his neighbour as himself, that it ever has, and ever will meet the decided disapprobation of heaven.

In whatever form we behold it, its visage is satanic, its origin the very offspring of hell, and in all cases its effects are grievous.

On the shores of Africa, the horror of the scene commences; here, the merciless tyrant, divested of every thing human, except the form, begins the action. The laws of God and the tears of the oppressed are alike disregarded; and with more than savage barbarity, husbands and wives, parents and children, are parted to meet no more: and, if not doomed to an untimely death, while on the passage, yet are they for life consigned to a captivity still more terrible; a captivity, at the very thought of which, every heart, not already biassed with unhallowed prejudices, or callous to every tender impression, pauses and revolts; exposed to the caprice of those whose tender mercies are cruel; unprotected by the laws of the land, and doomed to drag out miserable existence, without the remotest shadow of a hope of deliverence, until the king of terrors shall have executed his office, and consigned them to the kinder slumbers of death. But its pernicious tendency may be traced still farther: not only are its effects of the most disastrous character, in relation to the slave, but it extends its influence to the slave holder; and in many instances it is hard to say which is most wretched, the slave or the master.

After the fall of man, it would seem that God, foreseeing that pride and arrogance would be the necessary consequences of the apostacy, and that man would seek to usurp undue authority over his fellow, wisely ordained that he should obtain his bread by the sweat of his brow; but contrary to this sacred mandate of heaven, slavery has been introduced, supporting the one in all the absurd luxuries of life, at the expense of the liberty and independence of the other. Point me to any section of the earth where slavery, to any considerable extent exists, and I will point you to a people whose morals are corrupted; and when pride, vanity and profusion are permitted to range unrestrained in all their desolating effects, and thereby idleness and luxury are promoted, under the influence of which, man, becoming insensible of his duty to his God and his fellow creature; and indulging in all the pride and vanity of his own heart, says to his soul, thou hast much goods laid up for many years. But while thus sporting, can it be done with impunity? Has conscience ceased to be active? Are there no forebodings of a future day of punishment, and of meeting the merited avenger? Can he retire after the business of the day and repose in safety? Let the guards around his mansion, the barred doors of his sleeping room, and the loaded instruments of death beneath his pillow, answer the question.—And if this were all, it would become us, perhaps, to cease to murmur, and bow in silent submission to that providence which had ordained this present state of existence, to be but a life of degradation and suffering.

Since affliction is but the common lot of men, this life, at best, is but a vapor that ariseth and soon passeth away. Man, said the inspired sage, that is born of a woman, is of few days and full of trouble; and in a certain sense, it is not material what our present situation may be, for short is the period that humbles all to the dust, and places the monarch and the beggar, the slave and the master, upon equal thrones. But although this life is short, and attended with one entire scene of anxious perplexity, and few and evil are the days of our pilgrimage; yet man is advancing to another state of existence, bounded only by the vast duration of eternity! in which happiness or misery await us all. The great author of our existence has marked out the way that leads to the glories of the upper world, and through the redemption which is in Christ Jesus, salvation is offered to all. But slavery forbids even the approach of mercy; it stands as a barrier in the way to ward off the influence of divine grace; it shuts up the avenues of the soul, and prevents its receiving divine instruction; and scarce does it permit its miserable captives to know that there is a God, a Heaven or a Hell!

Its more than detestable picture has been attempted to be portrayed by the learned, and the wise, but all have fallen short, and acknowledged their inadequacy to the task, and have been compelled to submit, by merely giving an imperfect shadow of its reality. Even the immortal Wilberforce, a name that can never die while Africa lives, after exerting his ingenuity, and exhausting the strength of his masterly mind, resigns the effort, and calmly submits by saying, "never was there, indeed, a system so replete with wickedness and cruelty to whatever part of it we turn our eyes; we could find no comfort, no satisfaction, no relief. It was the gracious ordinance of providence, both in the natural and moral world, that good should often arise out of evil. Hurricanes clear the air; and the propagation of truth was promoted by persecution, pride, vanity, and profusion contributed often, in their remoter consequences, to the happiness of mankind. In common, what was in itself evil and vicious, was permitted to carry along with it some circumstances of palliation. The Arab was hospitable, the robber brave; we did not necessarily find cruelty associated with fraud or meanness with injustice. But here the case was far otherwise. It was the prerogative of this detestable traffic, to separate from evil its concomitant good, and to reconcile discordant mischief. It robbed war of its generosity, it deprived peace of its security. We saw in it the vices of polished society, without its knowledge or its comforts, and the evils of barbarism without its simplicity; no age, no sex, no rank, no condition, was exempt from the fatal influence of this wide wasting calamity. Thus it attained to the fullest measure of its pure, unmixed, unsophisticated wickedness; and scorning all competition or comparison, it stood without a rival in the secure and undisputed possession of its detestable pre-eminence.

Such were the views which this truly great and good man, together with his fellow philanthropists, took of this subject, and such are the strong terms in which he has seen fit to express his utter abhorrence of its origin and effects. Thus have we hinted at some of the miseries connected with slavery. And while I turn my thoughts back and survey what is past, I see our forefathers seized by the hand of the rude ruffian, and torn from their native homes and all that they held dear or sacred. I follow them down the lonesome way, until I see each safely placed on board the gloomy slave ship; I hear the passive groan, and the clanking of the chains which bind them. I see the tears which follow each other in quick succession adown the dusky cheek.

I view them casting the last and longing look towards the land which gave them birth, until at length the ponderous anchor is weighed, and the canvass spread to catch the favored breeze; I view them wafted onward until they arrive at the destined port; I behold those who have been so unfortunate as to survive the passage, emerging from their loathsome prison, and landing amidst the noisy rattling of the massy fetters which confine them; I see the crowd of trafficers in human flesh gathering, each anxious to seize the favored opportunity of enriching himself with their toils, their tears and their blood. I view them doomed to the most abject state of degraded misery, and exposed to suffer all that unrestrained tyranny can inflict, or that human nature is capable of sustaining.

Tell me, ye mighty waters, why did ye sustain the ponderous load of misery? or speak, ye winds, and say why it was that ye executed your office to waft them onward to the still more dismal state; and ye proud waves, why did you refuse to lend your aid and to have overwhelmed them with your billows? Then should they have slept sweetly in the bosom of the great deep, and so have been hid from sorrow. And, oh thou immaculate God, be not angry with us, while we come into this thy sanctuary, and make the bold inquiry in this thy holy temple, why it was that thou didst look on with the calm indifference of an unconcerned spectator, when thy holy law was violated, thy divine authority despised and a portion of thine own creatures reduced to a state of mere vassalage and misery? Hark! while he answers from on high: hear him proclaiming from the skies—Be still, and know that I am God! Clouds and darkness are round about me; yet righteousness and judgment are the habitation of my throne. I do my will and pleasure in the heavens above, and in the earth beneath; it is my sovereign prerogative to bring good out of evil, and cause the wrath of man to praise me, and the remainder of that wrath I will restrain.

Strange, indeed, is the idea, that such a system, fraught with such consummate wickedness, should ever have found a place in this the otherwise happiest of all countries,—a country, the very soil of which is said to be consecrated to liberty, and its fruits the equal rights of man. But strange as the idea may seem, or paradoxical as it may appear to those acquainted with the constitution of the government, or who have read the bold declaration of this nation's independence; yet it is a fact that can neither be denied or controverted, that in the United States of America, at the expiration of fifty years after its becoming a free and independent nation, there are no less than fifteen hundred thousand human beings still in a state of unconditional vassalage.

Yet America is first in the profession of the love of liberty, and loudest in proclaiming liberal sentiments towards all other nations, and feels herself insulted, to be branded with any thing bearing the appearance of tyranny or oppression. Such are the palpable inconsistencies that abound among us and such is the medley of contradictions which stain the national character, and renders the American republic a by-word, even among despotic nations. But while we pause and wonder at the contradictory sentiments held forth by the nation, and contrast its profession and practice, we are happy to have it in our power to render an apology for the existence of the evil, and to offer an excuse for the framers of the constitution. It was before the sons of Columbia felt the yoke of their oppressors, and rose in their strength to put it off that this land become contaminated with slavery. Had this not been the case,

led by the spirit of pure republicanism, that then possessed the souls of
those patriots who were struggling for liberty, this soil would have been
sufficiently guarded against its intrusion, and the people of these United
States to this day, would have been strangers to so great a curse. It was
by the permission of the British parliament, that the human species first
became an article of merchandize among them, and as they were acces-
sary to its introduction, it well becomes them to be first, as a nation, in
arresting its progress and effecting its expulsion. It was the immortal
Clarkson, a name that will be associated with all that is sublime in
mercy, until the final consummation of all things, who first looking
abroad, beheld the sufferings of Africa, and looking at home, he saw his
country stained with her blood. He threw aside the vestments of the
priesthood, and consecrated himself to the holy purpose of rescuing a
continent from rapine and murder, and of erasing this one sin from the
book of his nation's iniquities. Many were the difficulties to be encountered, many were the hardships to be endured, many were the persecu-
tions to be met with; formidable, indeed, was the opposing party. The
sensibility of the slave merchants and planters was raised to the highest
pitch of resentment. Influenced by the love of money, every scheme was
devised, every measure was adopted, every plan was executed, that might
throw the least barrier in the way of the holy cause of the abolition of
this traffic. The consequences of such a measure were placed in the most
appalling light that ingenious falsehood could invent; the destruction of
commerce, the ruin of the merchants, the rebellion of the slaves, the
massacre of the planters, were all artfully and fancifully pictured, and
reduced to a certainty in the minds of many of the members of parliament, and a large proportion of the community. But the cause of justice
and humanity were not to be deserted by him and his fellow philanthropists, on account of difficulties. We have seen them for twenty years
persevering against all opposition, and surmounting every obstacle they
found in their way. Nor did they relax aught of their exertions, until the
cries of the oppressed having roused the sensibility of the nation, the
island empress rose in her strength, and said to this foul traffic, "thus far
hast thou gone, but thou shalt go no farther." Happy for us, my brethren, that the principles of benevolence were not exclusively confined to
the isle of Great Britain. There have lived, and there still do live, men
in this country, who are patriots and philanthropists, not merely in
name, but in heart and practice; men whose compassions have long
since led them to pity the poor and despised sons of Africa. They have
heard their groans, and have seen their blood, and have looked with an
holy indignation upon the oppressor: nor was there any thing wanting
except the power to have crushed the tyrant and liberated the captive.

Through their instrumentality, the blessings of freedom have long since been enjoyed by all classes of people throughout New-England, and through their influence, under the Almighty, we are enabled to recognize the fourth day of the present month, as the day in which the cause of justice and humanity have triumphed over tyranny and oppression, and slavery is forever banished from the state of New York. . . .

SUPPLEMENTARY READINGS

Litwack, Leon F. *North of Slavery: The Negro in the Free States, 1790–1860*. Chicago: University of Chicago Press, 1961.

McManus, Edgar J. *A History of Negro Slavery in New York*. Syracuse, N.Y.: Syracuse University Press, 1966.

Pease, William H., and Jane Pease. *Black Utopia: Negro Communal Experiments in America*. Madison: The State Historical Society of Wisconsin, 1963. Chap. 3.

Young, Henry J. *Major Black Religious Leaders*. Nashville: Abingdon Press, 1977. Chap. 1.

Zilversmit, Arthur. *The First Emancipation: The Abolition of Slavery in the North*. Chicago: University of Chicago Press, 1967.

18

DAVID WALKER

"Our Wretchedness in Consequence of the Preachers of Religion"

The black abolitionist Henry Highland Garnet, no stranger to fiery attacks upon slavery, wrote of David Walker's Appeal: "It was merely a smooth stone which this David took up, yet it terrified a host of Goliaths." Walker's pamphlet struck the South as so incendiary that any black person found with it in his or her possession suffered immediate recrimination. Though his father was a slave, Walker was born free to a free black mother in Wilmington, North Carolina, in 1785. He eventually settled in Boston where he maintained a used clothing store and involved himself in black Baptist church life and abolitionism, opening his home to fugitive slaves and serving as an agent for Freedom's Journal.

Walker's Appeal in Four Articles appeared in 1829, to the consternation of even such dedicated abolitionists as William Lloyd Garrison, who called for immediate universal emancipation but read Walker as advocating armed slave insurrection. Though Walker, as is evident in "Article III" that is reprinted here, veiled his call to arms in millennialist language, the pamphlet was sufficiently inflammatory to cause divisions within the Afro-American Baptist community in Boston. Garnet reported that Walker "had many enemies and not a few were his brethren whose cause he espoused." The South put a price on Walker's head. Upon his death in 1830 stories abounded that he had been poisoned or kidnapped. Neither Garnet in the 1830s nor contemporary researchers have been able to confirm or deny the allegations, except to note that Walker died at home in Boston.

RELIGION, MY BRETHREN, is a substance of deep consideration among all nations of the earth. The Pagans have a kind, as well as the Mahometans, the Jews and the Christians. But pure and undefiled religion, such as was preached by Jesus Christ and his apostles, is hard to be found

Source: *Walker's Appeal, in Four Articles; Together with a Preamble, to the Coloured Citizens of the World, But in Particular, and Very Expressly, to Those of the United States of America. Written in Boston, State of Massachusetts, September 28, 1829.* Third edition. Boston: D. Walker, 1830. Pp. 39–49.

in all the earth. God, through his instrument, Moses, handed a dispensation of his divine will to the children of Israel after they had left Egypt for the land of Canaan, or of Promise, who through hypocrisy, oppression, and unbelief, departed from the faith. He then, by his apostles handed a dispensation of his, together with the will of Jesus Christ, to the Europeans in Europe, who, in open violation of which, have made *merchandize* of us, and it does appear as though they take this very dispensation to aid them in their infernal depredations upon us. Indeed, the way in which religion was and is conducted by the Europeans and their descendants, one might believe it was a plan fabricated by themselves and the *devils* to oppress us. But hark! my master has taught me better than to believe it—he has taught me that his gospel as it was preached by himself and his apostles remains the same, notwithstanding Europe has tried to mingle blood and oppression with it.

It is well known to the Christian world that Bartholomew Las Casas, that very notoriously avaricious Catholic priest or preacher, and adventurer with Columbus in his second voyage, proposed to his countrymen, the Spaniards in Hispaniola, to import the Africans from the Portuguese settlement in Africa, to dig up gold and silver, and work their plantations for them, to effect which, he made a voyage thence to Spain, and opened the subject to his master, Ferdinand, then in declining health, who listened to the plan; but who died soon after, and left it in the hands of his successor, Charles V.[1]—This wretch, ("Las Cassas, the Preacher,") succeeded so well in his plans of oppression, that in 1503, the first blacks had been imported into the new world. Elated with this success, and stimulated by sordid avarice only, he importuned Charles V. in 1511, to grant permission to a Flemish merchant to import 4000 blacks at one time.[2] Thus we see, through the instrumentality of a pretended preacher of the gospel of Jesus Christ our common master, our wretchedness first commenced in America—where

1 See *Butler's History of the United States,* vol. 1, p. 24. See also p. 25.

2 "It is not unworthy of remark, that the Portuese and Spaniards, were among, if not the very first Nations upon Earth, about three hundred and fifty or sixty years ago—But see what those *Christians* have come to now in consequence of afflicting our fathers and us, who have never molested, or disturbed them or any other of the white *Christians* but have they received one quarter of what the Lord will yet bring upon them, for the murders they have inflicted upon us?—They have had, and in some degree have now, sweet times on our blood and groans, the time however, of bitterness have sometime since commenced with them.—There is a God the Maker and preserver of all things, who will as sure as the world exists, give all his creatures their just recompense of reward in this and in the world to come,—we may fool or deceive, and keep each other out of what is our lawful rights, or the rights of man, yet it is impossible for us to deceive or escape the Lord Almighty."

it has been continued from 1503 to this day, 1829. A period of three hundred and twenty-six years. But two hundred and nine, from 1620— when twenty of our fathers were brought into Jamestown, Virginia, by a Dutch man-of-war, and sold off like brutes to the highest bidders; and there is not a doubt in my mind, but that tyrants are in hopes to perpetuate our miseries under them and their children until the final consummation of all things. But if they do not get dreadfully deceived, it will be because God has forgotten them.

The Pagans, Jews and Mahometans try to make proselytes to their religions, and whatever human beings adopt their religions, they extend to them their protection. But Christian Americans not only hinder their fellow creatures, the Africans, but thousands of them will *absolutely beat a coloured person nearly to death, if they catch him on his knees, supplicating the throne of grace.* This barbarous cruelty was by all the heathen nations of antiquity, and is by the Pagans, Jews and Mahometans of the present day, left entirely to Christian Americans to inflict on the Africans and their descendants that their cup which is nearly full may be completed. I have known tyrants or usurpers of human liberty in different parts of this country take their fellow creatures, the colored people, and beat them until they would scarcely leave life in them; what for? Why they say, "The black devils had the audacity to be found *making prayers and supplications to the God who made them!!!*" Yes, I have known small collections of coloured people to have convened together, for no other purpose than to worship God Almighty, in spirit and in truth, to the best of their knowledge; when tyrants, calling themselves *patrols*, would also convene and wait almost in breathless silence for the poor coloured people to commence singing and praying to the Lord our God, and as soon as they had commenced the wretches would burst in upon them and drag them out and commence beating them as they would rattle-snakes—many of whom, they would beat so unmercifully, that they would hardly be able to crawl for weeks and sometimes for months.—Yet the American ministers send out missionaries to convert the heathen, while they keep us and our children sunk at their feet in the most abject ignorance and wretchedness that ever a people was afflicted with since the world began. Will the Lord suffer this people to proceed much longer? Will he not stop them in their career? Does he regard the heathens abroad, more than the heathens among the Americans? Surely the Americans must believe that God is partial, notwithstanding his Apostle Peter, declared before Cornelius and others that he has no respect to persons, but in every nation he that feareth God and worketh righteousness is accepted with him.— "The word," said he, "which God sent unto the children of Israel, preaching peace, by Jesus Christ, (he is the Lord of all.")[3] Have not the Americans the Bible in their hands? Do they believe it? Surely they do not. See how they treat us in open violation of the Bible!! They no doubt will be greatly offended with me, but if God does not awaken them, it will be, because they are superior to other men, as they have represented themselves to be. Our divine Lord and Master said "all things whatsoever ye would that men should do unto you, do ye even so unto them." But an American minister, with the Bible in his hand, holds us and our children in the most abject slavery and wretchedness. Now I ask them, would they like for us to hold them and their children in abject slavery and wretchedness? No says one, that never can be done—you are too abject and ignorant to do it—you are not men—you were made to be slaves to us, to dig up gold and silver for us and our children. Know this, my dear sirs, that although you treat us and our children now, as you do your domestic beasts—yet the final result of all future events are known but to God Almighty alone, who rules in the armies of heaven and among the inhabitants of the earth, and who de-thrones one earthly king and sits up another, as it seemeth good in his holy sight. We may attribute these vicissitudes to what we please, but the God of armies and of justice rules in heaven and in earth, and the whole American people shall see and know it yet, to their satisfaction. I have known pretended preachers of the gospel of my Master, who not only held us as their natural inheritance, but treated us with as much rigor as any Infidel or Deist in the world—just as though they were intent only on taking our blood and groans to glorify the Lord Jesus Christ. The wicked and ungodly, seeing their preachers treat us with so much cruelty, they say: our preachers, who must be right, if any body are, treat them like brutes, and why cannot we?—They think it is no harm to keep them in slavery and put the whip to them, and why can-not we do the same!—They being preachers of the gospel of Jesus Christ, if it were any harm, they would surely preach against their oppression and do their utmost to erase it from the country; not only in one or two cities, but one continual cry would be raised in all parts of this con-federacy, and would cease only with the complete overthrow of the sys-tem of slavery, in every part of the country. But how far the American preachers are from preaching against slavery and oppression, which have carried their country to the brink of a precipice; to save them from plunging down the side of which, will hardly be effected, will appear in the sequel of this paragraph, which I shall narrate just as it transpired. I remember a Camp Meeting in South Carolina, for which I embarked

3   See Acts of the Apostles, 10:36.

in a Steam Boat at Charleston, and having been five or six hours on the water, we at last arrived at the place of hearing, where was a very great concourse of people, who were no doubt, collected together to hear the word of God, (that some had collected barely as spectators to the scene, I will not here pretend to doubt, however, that is left to themselves and their God.) Myself and boat companions, having been there a little while, we were all called up to hear; I among the rest, went up and took my seat—being seated, I fixed myself in a complete position to hear the word of my Saviour and to receive such as I thought was authenticated by the Holy Scriptures; but to my no ordinary astonishment, our Reverend gentleman got up and told us (colored people) that slaves must be obedient to their masters—must do their duty to their masters or be whipped—the whip was made for the backs of fools, &c. Here I pause for a moment, to give the world time to consider what was my surprise, to hear such preaching from a minister of my Master, whose very gospel is that of peace and not of blood and whips, as this pretended preacher tried to make us believe. What the American preachers can think of us, I aver this day before my God, I have never been able to define. They have newspapers and monthly periodicals, which they receive in continual succession, but on the pages of which, you will scarcely ever find a paragraph respecting slavery, which is ten thousand times more injurious to this country than all the other evils put together; and which will be the final overthrow of its government, unless something is very speedily done; for their cup is nearly full.— Perhaps they will laugh at, or make light of this; but I tell you Americans! that unless you speedily alter your course, *you* and your *Country are gone!!!!!!* For God Almighty will tear up the very face of the earth!!!! Will not that very remarkable passage of Scripture be fulfilled on Christian Americans? Hear it Americans!! "He that is unjust, let him be unjust still:—and he which is filthy, let him be filthy still; and he that is righteous, let him be righteous still; and he that is holy, let him be holy still."[4] I hope that the Americans may hear, but I am afraid that they have done us so much injury, and are so firm in the belief that our Creator made us to be an inheritance to them forever, that their hearts will be hardened, so that their destruction may be sure.—This language, perhaps is too harsh for the American's delicate ears. But Oh Americans! Americans!! I warn you in the name of the Lord, (whether you will hear, or forbear,) to repent and reform, or you are ruined!!!!!! Do you think that our blood is hidden from the Lord, because you can hide it from the rest of the world by sending out

4 See Revelation, chap. xxii. 11.

missionaries, and by your charitable deeds to the Greeks, Irish, &c.? Will he not publish your secret crimes on the house top? Even here in Boston, pride and prejudice have got to such a pitch, that in the very houses erected to the Lord, they have built little places for the reception of colored people, where they must sit during meeting, or keep away from the house of God; and the preachers say nothing about it—much less, go into the hedges and highways seeking the lost sheep of the house of Israel, and try to bring them in, to their Lord and Master. There are hardly a more wretched, ignorant, miserable, and abject set of beings in all the world, than the blacks in the Southern and Western sections of this country, under tyrants and devils. The preachers of America cannot see them, but they can send out missionaries to convert the heathens, notwithstanding. Americans! unless you speedily alter your course of proceeding, if God Almighty does not stop you, I say it in his name, that you may go on and do as you please for ever, both in time and eternity—never fear any evil at all!!!!!!!!!

[☞ ADDITION.—The preachers and people of the United States form societies against Free Masonry and Intemperance, and write against Sabbath breaking, Sabbath mails, Infidelity, &c. &c. But the fountain head,[5] compared with which all those other evils are comparatively nothing, and from the bloody and murderous head of which, they receive no trifling support, is hardly noticed by the Americans. This is a fair illustration of the state of society in this country—it shows what a bearing *avarice* has upon a people, when they are nearly given up by the Lord to a hard heart and a reprobate mind, in consequence of afflicting their fellow creatures. God suffers some to go on until they are ruined for ever!! Will it be the case with our brethren the whites of the United States of America? We hope not—we would not wish to see them destroyed, notwithstanding they have and do now treat us more cruel than any people have treated another, on this earth since it came from the hands of its creator (with the exception of the French and the Dutch, they treat us nearly as bad as the Americans of the United States.) The will of God must however, in spite of us, *be done.*

The English are the best friends the colored people have upon earth. Tho' they have oppressed us a little, and have colonies now in the West Indies, which oppress us *sorely*,—Yet notwithstanding they (the English) have done one hundred times more for the melioration of our condition, than all the other nations of the earth put together. The blacks cannot but respect the English as a nation, notwithstanding they have treated us a little cruel.

5 Slavery and oppression.

There is no intelligent *black man* who knows any thing, but esteems a real English man, let him see him in what part of the world he will—for they are the greatest benefactors we have upon earth. We have here and there, in other nations, good friends. But as a nation, the English are our friends. ⬛]

How can the preachers and people of America believe the Bible? Does it teach them any distinction on account of a man's color? Hearken, Americans! to the injunctions of our Lord and Master, to his humble followers.

"And Jesus came and spake unto them saying, "all power is given unto me in heaven and in earth.

"Go ye, therefore, and teach all nations, baptizing them in the name of the Father, and of the Son, and of the Holy Ghost,

"Teaching them to observe all things whatsoever I have commanded you; and lo, I am with you alway, even unto the end of the world. Amen."[6]

I declare, that the very face of these injunctions appears to be of God and not of man. They do not show the slightest degree of distinction. "Go ye, therefore," (says my divine Master) and teach all "nations," (or in other words, all people) "baptizing them in the name of the Father, and of the Son, and of the Holy Ghost." Do you understand the above, Americans? We are a people, notwithstanding many of you doubt it. You have the Bible in your hands, with this very injunction. Have you been to Africa, teaching the inhabitants thereof the words of the Lord Jesus? "Baptizing them in the name of the Father, and of the Son, and of the Holy Ghost." Have you not, on the contrary, entered among us, and learnt us the art of throat-cutting, by setting us to fight, one against another, to take each other as prisoners of war, and sell to you for small bits of calicoes, old swords, knives, &c. to make slaves for you and your children? This being done, have you not brought us among you, in chains and handcuffs, like brutes, and treated us with all the cruelties and rigour your ingenuity could invent, consistent with the laws of your country, which (for the blacks) are tyrannical enough? Can the American preachers appeal unto God, the Maker and Searcher of hearts, and tell him, with the Bible in their hands, that they make no distinction on account of men's colour? Can they say, O God! thou knowest all things—thou knowest that we make no distinction between thy creatures to whom we have to preach thy Word? Let them answer the Lord; and if they cannot do it in the affirmative, have

---

6 See St. Matthew's Gospel, chap. xxviii. 18, 19, 20. After Jesus was risen from the dead.

they not departed from the Lord Jesus Christ, their master? But some may say, that they never had or were in possession of a religion, which makes no distinction, and of course they could not have departed from it. I ask you then, in the name of the Lord, of what kind can your religion be? Can it be that which was preached by our Lord Jesus Christ from Heaven? I believe you cannot be so wicked as to tell him that his Gospel was that of *distinction*. What can the American preachers and people take God to be?—Do they believe his words? If they do, do they believe that he will be mocked? Or do they believe because they are whites and we blacks, that God will have respect to them? Did not God make us as it seemed best to himself? What right, then, has one of us, to despise another and to treat him cruel, on account of his colour, which none but the God who made it can alter? Can there be a greater absurdity in nature, and particularly in a free republican country? But the Americans, having introduced slavery among them, their hearts have become almost seared, as with an hot iron, and God has nearly given them up to believe a lie in preference to the truth!!! and I am awfully afraid that pride, prejudice, avarice and blood, will, before long, prove the final ruin of this happy republic, or land of liberty!!! Can any thing be a greater mockery of religion than the way in which it is conducted by the Americans? It appears as though they are bent only on daring God Almighty to do his best—they chain and handcuff us and our children and drive us around the country like brutes, and go into the house of the God of justice to return Him thanks for having aided him in their infernal cruelties inflicted upon us. Will the Lord suffer this people to go on much longer, taking his holy name in vain? Will he not stop them, PREACHERS and all? O Americans! Americans!! I call God—I call angels—I call men, to witness, that your DESTRUCTION *is at hand*, and will be speedily consummated unless you REPENT.

SUPPLEMENTARY READINGS

Aptheker, Herbert, ed. *One Continual Cry: David Walker's Appeal to the Colored Citizens of the World*. New York: Humanities Press, 1965.

Jacobs, Donald M. "David Walker: Boston Race Leader, 1825–1830." *Essex Institute Historical Collections* 107 (January 1971): 94–107.

Harding, Vincent. *There Is a River: The Black Freedom Struggle in America*. New York: Vintage Books, 1983. Chap. 4.

Levesque, George A. "Inherent Reformers—Inherited Orthodoxy: Black Baptists in Boston, 1800–1873." *The Journal of Negro History* 60, no. 4 (October 1975): 491–525.

Pease, Jane H., and William H. Pease. *They Who Would Be Free: Blacks' Search for Freedom, 1830–1861*. New York: Atheneum, 1974. Chap. 6.

"To the Citizens of New York"

Peter Williams, Jr., born about 1780, affiliated with the Episcopalians, received ordination in 1820, and was appointed rector of St. Philip's Episcopal Church, one of New York City's prominent black institutions. At the constituting convention of the American Anti-Slavery Society at Philadelphia in December 1833, Williams was one of three blacks appointed to the board of managers, and later sat on the executive committee. Bishop Benjamin T. Onderdonk, Williams's ecclesiastical superior, urged him to resign. Onderdonk, like many prominent whites, preferred the conservative policies of the American Society for Colonizing the Free People of Colour of the United States, organized in 1816 to send free blacks to Liberia. The abolitionists viewed this organization as just another prop for slavery and called instead for the immediate, unconditional, and uncompensated freeing of the slaves. Because of its rector's connections with the American Anti-Slavery Society, St. Philip's Church was subject to white attack. Bishop Onderdonk wrote the Reverend Mr. Williams on July 12, 1834, advising him to be "prudent" and to resign "for the peace of the community." Williams's response, published with Onderdonk's letter on July 15th in the New York Spectator, *embodies the struggle of a preacher forced to choose between conscience and duty.*

Copy of a Letter from Bishop Onderdonk to Rev. Peter Williams.

College Place, July 12, 1834

Rev. and Dear Sir:—

    I am sure I need not assure you of the sincere sympathy which I feel for you and your people. The inclosed* was prepared by me to be read to them to-morrow, if they had been assembled. Perhaps, however, you have pursued the most prudent course in closing your church.

---

* A Pastoral Letter from the Bishop to the parish of St. Philip's Church, which owing to the congregation not assembling on Sunday, has not yet been communicated to them.

Source: "Address of Rev. Peter Williams." *New York Spectator.* July 15, 1834.

Let me advise you to resign, at once, your connexion, in every department, with the Anti-Slavery Society, and to make public your resignation. I cannot now give you all my reasons. Let me see you as soon as you can. I can better say than write all I think. Make the within known in any way, and as extensively as you can. "The raging of the sea, and *the madness of the people*," you know are connected in Holy Writ, and the one might as well be attempted to be stopped as the other. My advice, therefore is, give up at once. Let it be seen that on whichsoever side right may be, St. Philip's Church will be found on the Christian side of meekness, order, and self-sacrifice to common good and the peace of the community. You will be no losers by it, for the God of peace will be to you also a God of all consolation.

Let me hear from you or see you soon. And believe me to be with faithful prayer for you and yours, your affectionate brother in Christ.

Benj. T. Onderdonk.

Rev. Mr. Williams:

To the Citizens of New York:—

It has always been painful to me to appear before the public. It is especially painful to me to appear before them in the columns of a newspaper, at a time of great public excitement like the present: but when I received Holy orders, I promised "reverently to obey my Bishop, to follow with a glad mind his godly admonitions, and to submit myself to his godly judgment."

My Bishop, without giving his opinions on the subject of Abolitions has now advised me, in order that the Church under my care "may be found on the Christian side of meekness, order, and self-sacrifice to the community," to resign connexion with the Anti-Slavery Society, and to make public my resignation. There has been no instance hitherto, in which I have not sought his advice in matters of importance to the Church, and endeavored to follow it when given; and I have no wish that the present should be an exception.

But in doing this, I hope I shall not be considered as thrusting myself too much upon public attention, by adverting to some facts in relation to myself and the subject of the present excitement, in the hope that when they are calmly considered, a generous public will not censure me for the course I have pursued.

My father was born in Beekman street in this city, and was never, in all his life, further from it than Albany; nor have I ever been absent from it longer than three months, when I went to Hayti for the benefit of my brethren who had migrated there from this country. In the revolutionary war, my father was a decided advocate for American Independence, and his life was repeatedly jeopardized in its cause. Permit me to relate one instance, which shows that neither the British sword, nor British gold, could make him a traitor to his country. He was living in the state of Jersey, and Parson Chapman, a champion of American liberty, of great influence throughout that part of the country, was sought after by the British troops. My father immediately mounted a horse and rode round among his parishioners, to notify them of his danger, and to call them to help in removing him and his goods to a place of safety. He then carried him to a private place, and as he was returning a British officer rode up to him, and demanded in the most peremptory manner, "where is Parson Chapman?" "I cannot tell," was the reply. On that he drew his sword, and raising it over his head, said, "Tell me where he is, or I will instantly cut you down." Again he replied, "I cannot tell." Finding threats useless, the officer put up his sword and drew out a purse of gold, saying, "If you will tell me where he is, I will give you this." The reply still was, "I cannot tell." The officer cursed him and rode off.

This attachment to the country of his birth was strengthened and confirmed by the circumstance that the very day on which the British evacuated this city, was the day on which he obtained his freedom by purchase through the help of some republican friends of the Methodist Church, who loaned him money for that purpose, and to the last year of his life he always spoke of that day as one which gave double joy to his heart, by freeing him from domestic bondage and his native city from foreign enemies.

The hearing him talk of these and similar matters, when I was a child, filled my soul with an ardent love for the American government, and made me feel, as I said in my first public discourse, that it was my greatest glory to be an American.

A lively and growing interest for the prosperity of my country pervaded my whole soul and led to the belief, notwithstanding the peculiarly unhappy condition of my brethren in the United States, that by striving to become intelligent, useful and virtuous members of the community, the time would come when they would all have abundant reason to rejoice in the glorious Declaration of American Independence.

Reared with these feelings, though fond of retirement I felt a burning desire to be useful to my brethren and to my country; and when the last war between this country and Great Britain broke out, I felt happy to render the humble services of my pen, my tongue, and my hands, towards rearing fortifications to defend our shores against invasion. I entreated my brethren to help in the defense of the country, and went with them to the work; and no sacrifice has been considered too great by me, for the benefit of it or them.

These were among the feelings that led me into the ministry, and induced me to sacrifice all my worldly prospects, and live upon the scanty pittance which a colored minister must expect to receive for his labors, and to endure the numerous severe trials peculiar to his situation.

My friends who assisted me in entering into the ministry, know that if the Church with which I am connected as Pastor, could have been established without my becoming its minister, I should have been this day enjoying the sweets of private life, and there has not been a day since I have entered upon the duties of my office, that I would not have cheerfully retired to earn my living in some humbler occupation, could I have done so consistently with my sense of duty.

By the transaction of last Friday evening, my church is now closed, and I have been compelled to leave my people. Whether I shall be permitted to return to them again, I cannot say, but whether or not, I have the satisfaction of feeling that I have laboured earnestly and sincerely for their temporal and spiritual benefit, and the promotion of the public good.

In regard to my opposition to the Colonization Society it has extended no farther than that Society has held out the idea, that a colored man, however he may strive to make himself intelligent, virtuous and useful, can never enjoy the privileges of a citizen of the United States, but must ever remain a degraded and oppressed being. I could not, and do not believe that the principles of the Declaration of Independence, and of the Gospel of Christ, have not power sufficient to raise him, at some future day, to that rank. I believe that such doctrines tend very much to discourage the efforts which are making for his improvement at home. But whenever any man of color, after having carefully considered the subject, has thought it best to emigrate to Africa, I have not opposed him, but have felt it my duty to aid him, in all my power, on his way, and I have the satisfaction of being able to prove that the most prominent and most useful men in the Colony have been helped there by me.

I helped John B. Russwurm to go to Liberia, and as a token of gratitude for my aid in the case, he sent me his thermometer, which I have now hanging up in my house. I helped James M. Thompson, whom all speak of as a most excellent man, and good scholar, to go there. He was a member of my church; and when he went there, I gave him letters of recommendation, and procured a number of books, to enable him to introduce the Episcopal Service; and I offered lately to contribute my mite towards establishing the Episcopal Church there. I was the first person who advised James R. Daily (Russwurm's partner) to go and establish himself in Liberia as a merchant. When Washington Davis was sent to this city, by Governor Ashmun, to study medicine, as a physician for the colony, I received him in my house, and boarded him a week, without charging the Society for it, though they offered to bear the expense.

When I found that strong prejudices were forming against me, because of my disapprobation of some of the Society's measures, and that my usefulness was thereby affected, I ceased to speak on the subject, except in the private circle of my friends, or when my opinions were asked privately by others; and in my short address to the Phenix Society, last spring, I carefully avoided the subject; and the only sentiment I uttered, referring to it, was this: "Who that witnesses an assembly like this, composed of persons of all colors, can doubt that people of all colors can live in the same country, without doing each other harm?"

It was my anxiety to promote the object of the Phenix Society, which is the improvement of the people of color in this city, in morals, literature, and the mechanic arts, that brought me to an acquaintance with the members of the Anti-Slavery Society. For several years, I had given considerable attention to the education of our people, and was much interested about our Public Schools.

I was anxious that some of our youth should have the opportunity of acquiring a liberal education, and felt that it was my duty to strive to rear up some well qualified colored ministers. I selected two lads of great promise, and made every possible effort to get them a collegiate education. But the Colleges were all closed against them. Anti-Slavery men generously offered to aid us in establishing a Manual Labor College, or High School, for ourselves, and to aid us in all the objects of the Phenix Society. I joined with them in this work heartily, and wished them all success, as I still do in their endeavors, by all means sanctioned by law, humanity and religion, to obtain freedom for my brethren, and to elevate them to the enjoyment of equal rights with the other citizens of the community; but I insisted that while they were laboring to restore us to our rights, it was exclusively our duty to labor to qualify our people for the enjoyment of those rights.

Hence when the Anti-Slavery Convention was held in Philadelphia, though strongly solicited, I refused to attend, and though I was then appointed a member of the Board of Managers, I never met with that Board but for a few moments at the close of their session, and then without uttering a word. I was also appointed, at the anniversary in May, a member of the executive Committee. But when asked if I would serve, I replied that I could not attend to it, and have never attended but on one occasion, when I went for the sole purpose of advising the Board to be careful not to take any measures that would have a tendency to encourage in our people a spirit of vanity, and I urged this advice by saying that by so doing, our people, and the cause of emancipation, would both be injured. This opinion I have, on all proper occasions expressed, and have endeavored to enforce by example; for, in all the Anti-Slavery Meetings held in the Chapel, I have always taken my seat in the gallery, excepting that on the day of the Anniversary I felt it to speak to one of the committee in the orchestra, or stage, and did not return. My brethren have rebuked me for this course, but I have not censured them for theirs. They did as they thought best, and I did as I thought best; but I have learned that it is a most difficult matter to avoid extremes on subjects of great public excitement, without being more censured than those who go to all lengths with either party.

Having given this simple and faithful statement of facts; I now, in conformity to the advice of my Bishop, publicly resign my station as a member of the Board of Managers of the Anti-Slavery Society, and of its executive committee, without, however, passing any opinion respecting the principles on which that society is founded.

I would have offered my resignation long before this, had I not thought that there might be occasions, when by having the privilege of addressing the Board, I might exercise a restraining influence upon measures calculated to advance our people faster than they were prepared to be advanced, and the public feeling would bear. But I am not disposed to blame the members of the Anti-Slavery Society for their measures. I consider them as good men, and good Christians, and true lovers of their country, and of all mankind. I thought they had not an opportunity of knowing my brethren, nor the state of public prejudice against them, as well as myself, and all I supposed that I could do was to aid them in this particular.

I hope that both they and the public generally will judge charitably of this hastily drawn communication.

Peter Williams,
Rector of St. Philip's Church, Centre st.
New York, July 14, 1834.

SUPPLEMENTARY READINGS

Bennett, Robert A. "Black Episcopalians: A History from the Colonial Period to the Present." *Historical Magazine of the Protestant Episcopal Church* 43, no. 3 (September 1974): 231–45

Bishop, Shelton H. "A History of St. Philip's Church New York City." *Historical Magazine of the Protestant Episcopal Church* 15, no. 4 (December 1946): 298–317.

Bragg, George F. *History of the Afro-American Group of the Episcopal Church.* Baltimore: Church Advocate Press, 1922.

Fitts, Leroy. *Lott Carey: First Black Missionary to Africa.* Valley Forge, Pa.: Judson Press, 1978.

Staudenraus, P. J. *The African Colonization Movement, 1816–1865.* New York: Columbia University Press, 1961.

20

CHARLES B. RAY

Black Churches in New York City, 1840

Charles B. Ray was born in Falmouth, Massachusetts, in 1807 and attended local schools and academies. In the early 1830s he attempted to enroll at Wesleyan University in Middletown, Connecticut, but failed owing to the spirit of caste. He moved to New York City in 1832 and opened a boot and shoe store. In 1833 he joined the American Anti-Slavery Society. Ray assisted fugitive slaves and served on New York City's vigilance committee. Ordained in 1834 as a Methodist, he pastored various congregations for more than thirty years, including twenty-two at Bethesda Congregational Church in New York City. He was also the last editor of the Colored American, *which ran from 1836 to 1841. Ray attempted to promote black institutional life as well as abolitionism. He believed that white prejudice was based upon ignorance of what was "meritorious, and virtuous, and consistent" within the Afro-American community. The following is his survey of black churches in New York City as of 1840.*

Colored Churches in This City

THE CAPTION of this article, taken in its broadest sense, may subject it to criticism on the one hand, and to certain objection on the other; in reference to the latter we would say, we take things as we find them, and make the best use of them—to reform what is wrong.

In presenting to the public the different churches in this city, in which our people worship, and under their control, the different denominations to which they stand related, their several pastors, and appending a few remarks thereto, we have more than one object to accomplish.

Mankind generally act towards a people, as they feel towards them, and feel in accordance with their views of them, and the views they entertain are measured by what they know or do not know of their character, their virtues or their vices. We are convinced that the greatest

Source: "Colored Churches in This City." *The Colored American.* March 28, 1840.

amount of the prejudice in our country, which exists against our people, has its foundation in wrong views of them, and that such views are predicated upon ignorance, or upon what the people do not know of what is meritorious, and virtuous, and consistent amongst them, and that contact by our people, in every possible way, will be a very efficient method to change the views and the feelings of the public, and the course they pursue towards us; because, it will develope the whole people, and the whole character of the people. We know of no better way to effect this, than to develope through the press, the mind of the people, and those institutions existing among them, which of themselves are an index to the moral character and condition of any people. In refering to the different churches, we begin with those farthest up, in the suburbs of the city.

Union Church is a frame building, owned by the congregation, and having been built about three years, located in Fifteenth street, a growing part of the city, and near to which, most of the members and congregation reside. The exact number of communicants attached to it we do not know; we presume they number more than a hundred, and they are a plain and exemplary people. A branch of this church is also located in Yorkville, three miles distant, where they have a small frame building, and both are under the pastoral care of the worthy and benevolent Rev. James Barney, as Elder. They are an *independent sect of Methodists*, the main body of which is located in the State of Delaware, in the city of Wilmington, and vicinity. Rev. Peter Spencer of the latter place, is general superintendent of the sect.

Bethel Church—a commodious brick building, owned by the congregation, four years old, located in Second street, near the East River, a very favorable location, it being contiguous to a large number of our people residing in that part of the city, and who need to be brought under the influence of the Church and of the Sabbath School, and who live quite removed from any place in which our people worship. It has some hundred communicants, and a respectable congregation, and is now under the pastoral charge of the Rev. Mr. Robinson, with whom we are not acquainted, though we hear him spoken of as a very worthy man. This church stands connected with another sect of Methodists, denominated the first African Methodist E. Church in the United States. They were the first of our people, who seceded from the Methodist E. Church in Philadelphia, with the Rev. Richard Allen as their leader, who was afterwards bishop of the connection until his death. This denomination embraces four conferences, over which the Rev. Morris Brown, of Philadelphia, presides as bishop.

St. Matthew's Free Church, Protestant Episcopal, is a commodious brick building, capable of holding more than fifteen hundred people, and is located in the upper part of Mott street. Its relative location to other churches is good, it being sufficiently distant to make it a desirable spot for a place of worship for our people. The building is not owned by the congregation, but leased; the church is in its infancy, having been organized but a few years. A few of the communicants were formerly members of another church, but, to extend the Redeemer's kingdom, withdrew to build up another branch of the Church in this city. The congregation is respectable; the number of communicants we do not know. It is now under the pastoral charge of our talented and learned brother, the Rev. I. G. DeGrasse, whose ministrations are of high order.

St. Philip's Church, also Protestant Episcopal—is a neat brick building, owned by the congregation, and capable of holding two thousand people; and is located about midway in Centre street, which since having been improved, is one of the most pleasant streets in the city. The location is a good one, it being contiguous to our people, in all directions. It has a plain exterior appearance, but the interior, though not having all the modern improvements, is exceedingly neat and comfortable. It has a large congregation, and about 350 communicants, to whom the *liturgy* is read most pathetically, and responded to most orderly and harmoniously. It is under the pastoral charge of the meek Rev. Peter Williams, all of whose ministrations are inviting and affecting.

Abyssinian Baptist Church, of the Calvinistic close communion order, is a frame building, and located in Anthony street, west of Broadway, formerly owned by the congregation, now having passed into other hands, in consequence of a mortgage and heavy assessment. It is now leased, an effort will probably be made to buy it back.—The location of this church is not so pleasant as many others, yet it is very convenient to a large body of our people. It is capable of holding fifteen hundred persons, and has in its communion about three hundred members, and attached to it a large congregation. It has now no settled minister; the pulpit is supplied by a licentiate, a white gentleman.

Zion Baptist Church is of the same order. This is a frame building, sufficiently large to hold at least twelve hundred people, and formerly belonged to the Sweedenborgians sect; it is now leased by this congregation. It is located in Pearl street, near Chatham, not so desirable a location for the church and congregation as though it were in another part of the city. This is a branch originally from the Abyssinian Church, which withdrew a few years since. It now has about one hundred and fifty communicants, who with a respectable congregation, do more to sustain the temporalities of their church, than any other congregation of our people in the city, and probably as much as any congregation, of any

people, of the same number, and with similar means. It was until recently under the pastoral charge of our worthy brother the Rev. J. T.
Raymond; now it has no settled minister.

First Colored Presbyterian Church. This is a substantial and commodious stone building, owned by the congregation, and capable of accommodating at least fifteen hundred persons. It is located in Frank-
fort street, corner of William. The exterior of this church has nothing
about it very inviting. The interior is plain and neat, and in the evening,
when lighted up, is probably the most pleasant of any of the churches.
The location of this church is not so good now as formerly, it being too
far down town for the congregation. The rush of all classes of the people
up town, for a few years past, has carried with it many of the people belonging to, and worshipping in this church, so that the congregation is
not on all the services of the day so large as formerly. It is however well
attended, and numbers about four hundred communicants. It is now,
as it ever has been, under the pastoral charge of the pious and devoted
Rev. Theodore S. Wright, whose ministrations are plain, pointed and
faithful. There is another Presbyterian congregation of our people, but
we believe no organized church, who worship in a convenient hall in
Spring street, near Hudson, a very desirable location for a congregation
of our people, being some distance, in another direction, from any of
the other churches. It is under the spiritual direction of the Rev. William Mansfield Lively.

Asbury Church—a respectable frame building, capable of holding
from twelve to fifteen hundred people, and located in Elizabeth street,
in a healthy and desirable part of the city. The building is owned by
the congregation—the lot, we believe, by a former member of the
church, now a respectable minister of the denomination. It has now
about three hundred communicants, and a respectable congregation,
and is under the pastoral charge of the amiable and faithful Rev. Jacob
D. Richardson, whose ministrations are of the latter trait in his character. It is of the Methodist order, of which we shall have occasion to
speak more fully, in connection with another church.

Zion Church. This though last, is by no means least; it may be said
to be the mother church of all the rest. There is perhaps no one, of
all the churches, though of other sects, in which may not be found some
one or more, who has been either a member of this church or of the
congregation. Upon the site where the present one now building stands,
we believe was erected the first building dedicated to religious service,
and opened as a place of worship exclusively for our people in this city.

Whether the first building was burned down or not, we are not now able to say; we know it was displaced by a large stone building which seated more people than any of the above mentioned churches. This was destroyed by a fire in August last. They now have upon the same site, quite in progress, a still larger brick building, nearly finished, to be opened in a few weeks, with nearly all the modern improvements in church building. It is nearly three stories high, the first story being divided into class rooms, school rooms for Sabbath schools, and a commodious lecture room. The main body of the church is above this, and the spacious galleries, of course, still above.—The exterior of the building does not strike the eye so favorably, but the interior, spacious as it is, is being fitted up in excellent plain taste, blending with it all that is modern in the interior arrangements of churches. We doubt not the services to be performed there will as much improve from formerly, as the present church is more "glorious" than the former.

The location of this church is in Church street, corner of Leonard, a pleasant part of the city, and very central to the main body of our people. It numbers about eight hundred or more communicants, with a congregation ordinarily of from twelve hundred to two thousand people, and is now under the pastoral charge of the zealous Rev. Timothy Eato, whose administrations are like this trait in his character.

This church is the head of another denomination of Methodists in this country, denominated the African Methodist E. Zion Church, standing independent of every other sect of Methodists, embracing two conferences, presided over by our worthy and venerable father, Rev. Christopher Rush, of this city, in the character of Superintendent. They seceded some years since, from the Methodist E. Church of this city. Asbury church above mentioned, holds its relation to this ecclesiastical body.

The above are the ten places of religious worship of our people in this city, and they are more spacious, more costly, and more tasteful than the churches belonging to our people in any other city, or any other place, at least in the free States, we have had ample opportunity to know. We have appended more remarks in enumerating the different churches, than we at first anticipated, but perhaps we could not better occupy our columns, for once, than by doing so; they will be before the public, and our people in this city will be represented by them, to be judged of for good or for evil, as they may appear, either favorably or unfavorably, in the view of the public. They will also furnish the public with an index to our *heathenism*, or to our religious character, and moral condition, and they will be *stereotyped*, as a matter of *history*, though imperfect.

SUPPLEMENTARY READINGS

Litwack, Leon. *North of Slavery*. Chicago: University of Chicago Press, 1961. Chap. 6.

Ottley, Roi, and William J. Weatherby, eds. *The Negro in New York*. New York: Praeger Publishers, 1969. Bk. 2.

Quarles, Benjamin. *Black Abolitionists*. New York: Oxford University Press, 1969. Chap. 4.

Ray, Florence T., and Henrietta Ray. *Sketch of the Life of Rev. Charles B. Ray*. N.Y.: Press of J. J. Little & Co., 1887.

Swift, David E. "'O! This Heartless Prejudice,'" Wesleyan 67, no. 2 (Spring 1984): 13–17.

21

JEREMIAH ASHER

Protesting the "Negro Pew"

Northern blacks, though spared the lash and the whip, confronted the color line in most institutions north of slavery. Segregation in public conveyances, schools, and the churches, for example, was the rule. Even those whites who up the abolitionist flag, often at the risk of social ostracism in their own families and communities, rarely conceived of a reconstruction of the North along lines of perfect racial and social equality. The "negro pew" was an especially onerous symbol of white racism. Frederick Douglass encountered it in New Bedford, Massachusetts, as did Jeremiah Asher in Hartford, Connecticut. The latter's reactions are here excerpted from an autobiography published in 1850. Asher withdrew from the white church in Hartford for the more Christian fellowship of the Afro-American Baptist churches. He helped organize one in Providence, Rhode Island, served it as pastor for nine years, and then went to the Shiloh congregation in Philadelphia. He died in 1865.

SOON AFTER my return to Hartford, a singular and rather novel circumstance occurred in the church of which I was a member. In that, as in most of the Baptist, as well as other chapels, they have, as a matter of course, the negro pew. This was the most objectionable one I had ever seen, though I had been accustomed to sit there with a degree of comfort up to this time. I will give a description of it:—In the first place, it was unlike every thing else in the house except its fellow; for there is usually two, one in each extreme corner of the gallery. The rest of the seats in the house are much like the seats in the chapels in England. These, however, were about six feet square, with the sides so high it was almost impossible to see the minister or the rest of the congregation, and calculated to accommodate about fifteen or twenty persons. There was one seat in this pew which had, I suppose by general consent been con-

Source: *Incidents in the Life of the Rev. J. Asher, Pastor of Shiloh (Coloured) Baptist Church, Philadelphia, and a Concluding Chapter of Facts Illustrating the Unrighteous Prejudice Existing in the Minds of American Citizens Toward Their Coloured Brethren.* London: Charles Gilpin, 1850. Pp. 43–48.

ceded to me ever since my connexion with the church. However, one sabbath morning it so happened, contrary to my usual practice, I was late, and the seat I was accustomed to occupy was taken; I was obliged to take one of the most objectionable; and that morning I was so tried, (for it is always difficult for me to hear when I cannot see), I resolved I would never go into that place again, and I was as good as my word, for I think I never went in after.

In that city there was, as I have already stated, a place where coloured persons of all denominations were in the habit of meeting for worship, so I resolved hereafter to meet there, the place where the Lord on a former occasion passed by me in the way of mercy; a place (however much there was in doctrine or practice which I deemed to be wrong,) yet dear to me, so I took my seat there for a time. Very soon, enquiries were made for me, and a reason demanded, for this strange conduct. At first I was reluctant about giving an answer, but being somewhat pressed I gave the reason, stating at the same time my determination to stand to my resolution.

I was advised to give up my determination, for such a course could not fail to bring me under the discipline of the church. However, I was immoveable; but the enquiry still was among the members of the church, why I had left. I refused to give any information on the subject to any one except the deacons, and finally they communicated my reasons to some of the members, and the subject came up at a subsequent meeting for consideration, and instead of disciplining me they disciplined the negro pews, for they were arraigned, and proved guilty of the charge of making distinction between the members of the body of Christ, condemned and excluded, never more to be admitted. This I regarded as a great triumph in behalf of my coloured brethren and sisters. But to my surprise, I was requested to meet a committee of the church to inform them what would satisfy the coloured members, for they were getting quite out of their place.

I informed these brethren in behalf of my coloured brethren and sisters, that the charge was not true—we were not at all difficult or hard to please—they asked nothing more than what had been already done; there were plenty of unoccupied seats in the gallery (I did not of course presume that black christians had a right to sit below in their Father's house) on either side; all we asked, was to sit in the seats just as they were, without one penny expense by way of alteration. I contended, that those seats which were made for whites were good enough for blacks; if they did not wish us to mix together, they could give us a certain number of seats expressly for coloured persons. But they were aware that, without some visible distinction, whites coming in would often be sitting in the negro seat, and their devotions would be frequently disturbed by the pew-opener, who would be obliged to remove them, and regulate all such irregularities. Hence they contended for the necessity of making considerable alterations, said it would be so much better and more respectable, to make some nice seats on purpose for the coloured people. I said they were quite respectable and nice enough; we were quite willing to take sittings in them at the rate of those rented in the gallery; but if they were to be altered, I must decline having anything to do with it—I should neither hire nor occupy one of them, even if they made them the best seats in the house; I would not pay for *proscription* any where, much less in the house of God, and especially in a Baptist church, after having been welcomed to all of the privileges of God's house in that place.

If men will disfranchise and separate me from the rest of my Father's children, they shall do it at their own expense, not mine. I cannot prevent it, but I will not help them to do it. I will lift up my voice against it. However, my counsel was set aside, and it was decided to make some nice seats on purpose for the coloured members; so they proceeded forthwith to carry this plan into execution. When finished, and an expense was incurred of about forty pounds, then it was noticed that these seats would be rented to the coloured people at one dollar a sitting per year. The time came, and I think there was not more than two or three present, and they did not take sittings. Now I was charged with preventing them, which certainly I did not. Matters came to such a crisis, I really thought I should be excluded. I was quite willing to be. At this time I did not attend any of the meetings for business. However, I received a very polite invitation to attend a meeting which was to be held in one of the coloured member's houses, in F. Street, when the pastor and deacons and all the coloured members would be present, and then this troublesome matter must be settled. So I complied with this request, and when the time came attended. I was called upon to open the meeting by prayer, which I at first declined; but as they urged it, I tried to pray, and I have never been sorry since, for the Lord heard my prayer, and I learnt a lesson that day which I have not forgotten since, that is, to call upon God in the day of trouble. After prayer, the pastor presiding, began a kind of inquiry with the members, as to their objections to the nice little seats they had made them. All were inquired of before they interrogated me. I think there was not an objection raised. Then they inquired what I had to say; when I rose up from my seat and addressed them for about twenty or thirty minutes, and if ever I felt the presence of God, it was that day. I was not replied to either by the chair or any one of the assembly. It was agreed to report to the church favourably. The committee were satisfied; the coloured members might sit where they pleased in the galleries, and that was the end of this revolution. A short time after this, I was told by one of the deacons, my friend B., the church had a desire to hear me preach before them some evening—I might choose my own time and subject. It was then that the whole of my conduct and disappointment was explained to me. The whole transaction came up before me. I saw most clearly what God had done for me—how unfaithful I had been; and there was a woe to me if I preach not the gospel. At a convenient time I signified my intention to accept the invitation, and appointed the time. When the evening came we had a large gathering of the church. I endeavoured to speak from these words,—"Seek ye first the kingdom of God and his righteousness, and all these things shall be added unto you,"—Matthew vi. 33; after which it was resolved that I have the approbation of this church to preach wherever an opportunity presents. The following is a copy:—

"This may certify that the bearer, Jeremiah Asher, is a member in full standing and fellowship with us, and we believe that he has gifts, which, if improved, will render him useful in the ministry. We therefore cordially recommend him to improve his talents whenever God in his providence shall open a door.

"Done by order and in behalf of the first Baptist Church, Hartford, Connecticut. March, 1839."

J. B. GILBERT,   ⎫
JEREMIAH BROWN,⎬ *Deacons.*
                                 ⎭
JOSEPH W. DIMOCK, *Ch. Clk.*
J. S. EATON, *Pastor.*

SUPPLEMENTARY READINGS

Asher, Jeremiah. *An Autobiography with Details of a Visit to England and Some Account of the History of the Meeting Street Baptist Church, Providence, Rhode Island, and of the Shiloh Baptist Church, Philadelphia.* Philadelphia: By the Author, 1862.

Fordham, Monroe. *Major Themes in Northern Black Religious Thought, 1800–1860.* Hicksville, N.Y.: Exposition Press, 1975.

Newcomb, Harvey. *The "Negro Pew" Being an Inquiry Concerning the Propriety of Distinctions in the House of God on Account of Color.* Boston: Isaac Knapp, 1837.

Ofari, Earl. *"Let Your Motto Be Resistance:" The Life and Thought of Henry Highland Garnet.* Boston: Beacon Press, 1972.

Warner, Robert A. "Amos Gerry Beman—1812–1874, A Memoir on a Forgotten Leader." *The Journal of Negro History* 22, no. 1 (January 1937): 200–226.

22

JERMAIN W. LOGUEN

"I Will Not Live a Slave"

People crowded into Syracuse, New York, on October 1, 1851, some to attend an agricultural fair and others to participate in a Liberty party convention. Shortly after noon the church bells tolled and the Liberty party convention broke up at the news that a fugitive slave from Missouri, one William or Jerry McHenry, had been taken from the cooperage shop where he worked and placed in shackles by the deputy United States marshal. Syracuse's racially mixed vigilance committee, organized to prevent enforcement of the Fugitive Slave Law of 1850, went into action. Members stormed the office of the police justice, liberated Jerry, and spirited him to Canada.

Jermain Wesley Loguen was one of those who participated in the "Jerry Rescue." Loguen (1809–72) was reputed to be the superintendent of the Underground Railroad in Syracuse. After escaping around 1834 from Tennessee, Loguen farmed in Canada, worked as a hotel porter in Rochester, taught "colored school" in Utica, and attended Beriah Green's radically abolitionist Oneida Institute at Whitesboro, New York. Loguen settled in Syracuse in 1841 and became a preacher of the African Methodist Episcopal Zion Church. He attained the rank of bishop in 1868, but his early ministry was devoted more to abolitionism than to routine church work. On October 4, 1850, three days after the Fugitive Slave Law went into effect, Loguen addressed a protest meeting in Syracuse to denounce publicly the obnoxious statute. Following his appeal, the participants voted to make Syracuse an "open city" for fugitive slaves, and the stage was set for the "Jerry Rescue" a year later.

I WAS A SLAVE; I knew the dangers I was exposed to. I had made up my mind as to the course I was to take. On that score I needed no counsel, nor did the colored citizens generally. They had taken their stand—they would not be taken back to slavery. If to shoot down their assailants should forfeit their lives, such result was the least of the evil. They will have their liberties or die in their defence. What is life to me if I am

Source: *The Rev. J. W. Loguen, As a Slave and As a Freeman: A Narrative of Real Life.* Syracuse, N.Y.: Rev. J. W. Loguen, 1859. Pp. 391–94.

to be a slave in Tennessee? My neighbors! I have lived with you many years, and you know me. My home is here, and my children were born here. I am bound to Syracuse by pecuniary interests, and social and family bonds. And do you think I can be taken away from you and from my wife and children, and be a slave in Tennessee? Has the President and his Secretary sent this enactment up here, to you, Mr. Chairman, to enforce on me in Syracuse?—and will you obey him? Did I think so meanly of you—did I suppose the people of Syracuse, strong as they are in numbers and love of liberty—or did I believe their love of liberty was so selfish, unmanly and unchristian—did I believe them so sunken and servile and degraded as to remain at their homes and labors, or, with none of that spirit which smites a tyrant down, to surround a United States Marshal to see me torn from my home and family, and hurled back to bondage—I say did I think so meanly of you, I could never come to live with you. Nor should I have stopped, on my return from Troy, twenty-four hours since, but to take my family and moveables to a neighborhood which would take fire, and arms, too, to resist the least attempt to execute this diobolical law among them. Some kind and good friends advise me to quit my country, and stay in Canada, until this tempest is passed. I doubt not the sincerity of such counsellors. But my conviction is strong, that their advice comes from a lack of knowledge of themselves and the case in hand. I believe that their own bosoms are charged to the brim with qualities that will smite to the earth the villains who may interfere to enslave any man in Syracuse. I apprehend the advice is suggested by the perturbation of the moment, and not by the tranquil spirit that rules above the storm, in the eternal home of truth and wisdom. Therefore have I hesitated to adopt this advice, at least until I have the opinion of this meeting. Those friends have not canvassed this subject. I have. They are called suddenly to look at it. I have looked at it steadily, calmly, resolutely, and at length defiantly, for a long time. I tell you the people of Syracuse and of the whole North must meet this tyranny and crush it by force, or be crushed by it. This hellish enactment has precipitated the conclusion that white men must live in dishonorable submission, and colored men be slaves, or they must give their physical as well as intellectual powers to the defence of human rights. The time has come to change the tones of submission into tones of defiance,—and to tell Mr. Fillmore and Mr. Webster, if they propose to execute this measure upon us, to send on their blood-hounds. Mr. President, long ago I was beset by over prudent and good men and women to purchase my freedom. Nay, I was frequently importuned to consent that they purchase it, and present it as an evidence of their partiality to my person and character. Generous and kind as those friends were, my heart recoiled from the proposal. I owe my freedom to the God who made me, and who stirred me to claim it against all other beings in God's universe. I will not, nor will I consent, that any body else shall countenance the claims of a vulgar despot to my soul and body. Were I in chains, and did these kind people come to buy me out of prison, I would acknowledge the boon with inexpressible thankfulness. But I feel no chains, and am in no prison. I received my freedom from Heaven, and with it came the command to defend my title to it. I have long since resolved to do nothing and suffer nothing that can, in any way, imply that I am indebted to any power but the Almighty for my manhood and personality.

Now, you are assembled here, the strength of this city is here to express their sense of this fugitive act, and to proclaim to the despots at Washington whether it shall be enforced here—whether you will permit the government to return me and other fugitives who have sought an asylum among you, to the Hell of slavery. The question is with you. If you will give us up, say so, and we will shake the dust from our feet and leave you. But we believe better things. We know you are taken by surprize. The immensity of this meeting testifies to the general consternation that has brought it together, necessarily, precipitately, to decide the most stirring question that can be presented, to wit, whether, the government having transgressed constitutional and natural limits, you will bravely resist its aggressions, and tell its soulless agents that no slave-holder shall make your city and county a hunting field for slaves.

"Whatever may be your decision, my ground is taken. I have declared it everywhere. It is known over the State and out of the State— over the line in the North, and over the line in the South. I don't respect this law—I don't fear it—I won't obey it! It outlaws me, and I outlaw it, and the men who attempt to enforce it on me. I place the governmental officials on the ground that they place me. I will not live a slave, and if force is employed to re-enslave me, I shall make preparations to meet the crisis as becomes a man. If you will stand by me—and I believe you will do it, for your freedom and honor are involved as well as mine—it requires no microscope to see that—I say if you will stand with us in resistance to this measure, you will be the saviours of your country. Your decision to-night in favor of resistance will give vent to the spirit of liberty, and it will break the bands of party, and shout for joy all over the North. Your example only is needed to be the type of popular action in Auburn, and Rochester, and Utica, and Buffalo, and all the West, and eventually in the Atlantic cities. Heaven knows that this act of noble daring will break out somewhere—and may God grant that Syracuse be the honored spot, whence it shall send an earthquake voice through the land!

SUPPLEMENTARY READINGS

Galpin, W. Freeman. "The Jerry Rescue." *New York History* 26, no. 1 (January 1945): 19–34.

George, Carol V. R. "Widening the Circle: The Black Church and the Abolitionist Crusade, 1830–1860." In *Antislavery Reconsidered*, edited by Lewis Perry and Michael Fellman. Baton Rouge: Louisiana State University Press, 1979. Pp. 75–95.

May, Samuel J. *Some Recollections of Our Anti-Slavery Conflict*. Boston: Fields, Osgood & Co., 1869; reprint, Miami, Fla.: Mnemosyne, 1969.

Sokolow, Jayme A. "The Jerry McHenry Rescue and the Growth of Northern Antislavery Sentiment during the 1850s." *Journal of American Studies* 16, no. 3 (December 1982): 427–45.

Ward, Samuel R. *Autobiography of a Fugitive Negro*. London: John Snow, 1855; reprint, New York: Arno Press, 1968.

23

DANIEL ALEXANDER PAYNE

"Welcome to the Ransomed"

On April 11, 1862, Congress passed a bill abolishing slavery in the District of Columbia. Shortly thereafter President Abraham Lincoln received a visit from the Reverend Daniel Alexander Payne (1811–93), then presiding bishop of the Second Episcopal District of the African Methodist Episcopal Church, with headquarters in the District of Columbia. Payne urged Lincoln to sign the bill, was impressed with his "real greatness and of his fitness to rule a nation composed of almost all the races on the face of the globe," but left without any assurances. After Lincoln signed the bill on April 16, Bishop Payne penned a welcoming address to those who could now enjoy "the boon of holy freedom."

An orphan at ten, school instructor at nineteen, licensed preacher at twenty-six, and bishop at forty-one, Payne was born of free parents in Charleston, South Carolina. He left the South in 1834 and attended the Lutheran Theological Seminary at Gettysburg, Pennsylvania. Though ordained by the Franckean Lutheran Synod, an abolitionist connection in New York state, Payne joined the church of Richard Allen in 1841. He became the official historian of the African Methodists, their greatest educator, and perhaps the most influential bishop of the nineteenth-century black denominations. Payne spoke for the institutional side of Afro-American Christianity, constantly urging personal morality, domestic stability, thrift, industry, and education, virtues that he believed would help to shore up the free black community.

St. Paul addressed the Epistles to Timothy, the young Bishop of Ephesus, for the purpose of giving him instructions touching the false doctrines inculcated by certain false teachers, as well as instructions respecting the qualifications of the Christian ministry, their duties to themselves, to God, and the flock committed by the Holy Spirit to their special guidance.

But foremost of all the duties which he enjoined upon the Ephe-

Source: Welcome to the Ransomed; or Duties of the Colored Inhabitants of the District of Columbia. Baltimore: Bull and Tuttle, 1862.

sian ministry and laity were those of making "Supplications, prayers, intercessions, and giving of thanks for all men." For men in general, embracing the whole family of Adam, in all their *varieties* as nations, tribes, communities, peoples.

This is God-like, because the Eternal loves all, and manifests the infinity of his nature, by his universal care for all mankind. In this, He also demonstrates His universal Fatherhood, and thereby establishes the brotherhood of man.

But guided by the benevolence of unerring wisdom, the Apostle descends from a general to a particular statement of the case, and *commands* us to single out from among the nations of the earth their chieftains—*Kings* and *authorities*—for whom we are to make special "Supplications, prayers, intercessions, and giving of thanks."

To the cheerful and fervent performance of this gracious work, he presses several motives upon us—"that we may live a quiet and peaceable life in all godliness and honesty"—because "it is good and acceptable in the sight of God our Saviour"—because God "will have all men to be saved and to come unto the knowledge of the truth." Let us briefly trace out this line of thought.

To supplicate, is to *implore* God *submissively*. To pray to God, is to adore Him for His glorious perfection, to confess our sins to Him, and to beseech Him for mercy and pardon. To intercede with God is to entreat Him by the fervent, effectual prayer of faith, to be reconciled to offending man. This we may do as well for our enemies as for our friends.

We are gathered to celebrate the emancipation, yea, rather, the *Redemption* of the enslaved people of the District of Columbia, the exact number of whom we have no means of ascertaining, because, since the benevolent intention of Congress became manifest, many have been removed by their owners beyond the reach of this beneficent act.

Our pleasing task then, is to welcome to the Churches, the homesteads, and circles of free colored Americans, those who remain to enjoy *the boon of holy Freedom.*

Brethren, sisters, friends, we say welcome to our Churches, welcome to our homesteads, welcome to our social circles.

Enter the great family of Holy Freedom; not to *lounge in sinful indolence,* not to *degrade yourselves by vice,* nor to *corrupt society by licentiousness,* neither to *offend the laws by crime,* but to the *enjoyment of a well regulated liberty,* the offspring of generous laws; of law as just as generous, as righteous as just—a liberty to be *perpetuated* by equitable law, and sanctioned by the divine; for law is never equitable, righteous, just, until it harmonizes with the will of Him, who is "*King* of kings, and *Lord* of lords," and who commanded Israel to *have but one law for the home-born* and the *stranger*.

We repeat ourselves, welcome then *ye ransomed ones*; welcome *not* to indolence, to vice, licentiousness, and crime, but to a well-regulated liberty, sanctioned by the Divine, maintained by the Human law.

Welcome to habits of industry and thrift—to duties of religion and piety—to obligations of law, order, government—of government divine, of government human: these two, though not one, are inseparable. The man who refuses to obey divine law, will never obey human laws. *The divine first*, the *human next*. The latter is the consequence of the former, and follows it as light does the rising sun.

We invite you to our Churches, because we desire you to be religious; to be more than religious; we urge you *to be godly*. We entreat you to never be content until you are emancipated from sin, from sin without, and from sin within you. But this kind of freedom is attained only through the faith of Jesus, love for Jesus, obedience to Jesus. As certain as the American Congress has *ransomed* you, so certain, yea, more certainly has Jesus redeemed you from the guilt and power of sin by his own precious blood.

As you are now free in body, so now seek to be free in soul and spirit, from sin and Satan. The *noblest freeman is he whom Christ makes free*.

We invite you to our homesteads, in order that we may aid you as well by the power of good examples as by the beauty of holy precept, in raising up intelligent, virtuous, pious, happy families. We invite you to our social circles, in order that you may have none of those inducements which grow out of a mere love of society, to frequent the *gambling hells*, and groggeries, which gradually lead their votaries to infamy and the pit that is bottomless.

Permit us, also, to advise you to seek every opportunity for the cultivation of your minds. To the adults we say, enter the Sunday Schools and the Night Schools, so opportunely opened by Dr. Pierson, in behalf of the American Tract Society. In these latter you can very soon learn to read the precious word of God, even before you shall have a familiar knowledge of the letters which constitute the alphabet.

Rest not till you have learned to read the Bible. 'Tis the greatest, the best of books. In it is contained the Divine law. O! meditate therein by day and by night, for "the law of the Lord is perfect, converting the soul; the testimony of the Lord is sure, making wise the simple; the statutes of the Lord are right, rejoicing the heart; the commandment of the Lord is pure, enlightening the eyes;—more to be desired are they than gold, yea, than much fine gold; sweeter also than honey and the honeycomb." *"In keeping of them there is great reward."* Yield uniform, implicit obedience to their teachings. They will purify your hearts and make them the abodes of the Ever-Blessed Trinity.

When you shall have reached this point, you will be morally prepared to recognize and respond to all the relations of civilized and christianized life.

But of the children take *special care.* Heaven has entrusted them to you for a *special purpose.* What is that purpose? Not merely to eat and to drink, still less to *gormandize.* Not merely to dress finely in broadcloths, silks, satins, jewelry, nor to dance to the sound of the tamborine and fiddle; but *to learn them how to live and how to die—to train them for great usefulness on earth—to prepare them for greater glory in heaven.*

Keep your children in the schools, even if you have to eat less, drink less and wear coarser raiments; though you eat but two meals a day, purchase but one change of garment during the year, and relinquish all the luxuries of which we are so fond, but which are as injurious to health and long life as they are pleasing to the taste.

Let the education of your children penetrate the heart.—That education which forgets, or purposely omits, the culture of the heart, *is better adapted to devilism than manhood.* But the education which reaches the heart, moulds it, humbles it before the Cross, is rather the work of the homestead than the common school or the college. It is given by the *parents* rather than the schoolmaster—by the *mother* rather than the father.

How important, then, that the mothers be *right-minded;* that our young women, of whom our mothers come, be brought up with a high sense of personal character—be taught to prefer virtue to gold, and death itself rather than a violated chastity. The women make the men; therefore the women should be greater than the men, in order that they be the mothers of great men. I mean good men, *for none are great who are not good.*

But this requires the transforming grace of God; requires that our mothers be women of strong faith and fervent daily prayers; requires that they live beneath the wings of the Cherubim—at the foot of the Cross—loving the God-man "whose favor is life, and whose loving kindness is better than life."

Such mothers will care for the heart education of their children, and will consequently lay continuous siege to the Throne of God in behalf of their sons and daughters, even as the Syrophœnician mother importuned the compassionate Jesus in behalf of her afflicted daughter, or as Queen Esther did Ahasuerus in behalf of her menaced kinsmen.

Such mothers will carefully train their children, as Moses was trained by his mother, preserving him pure from *the vices of a Court* and the baneful examples of lordly superiors; or, like Susanna Wesley, will educate their sons, as she did John and Charles, in the atmosphere of such spiritual excellence, and with such a moral power, as will make them ministering angels of good to man and glory to God Most High.

Lastly—Let us advise you respecting money. Some people value it too much, others too little. Of these extremes take the medium; for money has its proper value. That value *lies in its adaptedness to promote the ends of Christian enlightenment*; to purchase the best medical aid and other comforts in the days of affliction; to administer to the wants of old age, and to enable us to assist in making mankind wiser and better.

But how are we to get money? Get it by diligent labor. Work, work, work! Shun no work that will bring you an honest penny. 'Tis honorable to labor with our own hands. God works, and shall man be greater than God? Fools only think labor dishonorable. Wise men feel themselves honored in following the example of God, whose works adorn and bless both heaven and earth.

But when you get the pennies save them. Then you will soon have dollars. The dollars will enable you to buy comfortable homes for yourselves and your children.

You can save your pennies—yea, dollars—if you will *run away* from whiskey, rum and tobacco. A few years ago an intelligent minister said that the colored people of the District of Columbia spent ten thousand dollars a year for tobacco.—What a sum for poison! Better take that money to build churches and school houses; better take it to obtain and pay thoroughly educated teachers for your pulpits and your school houses—*the schoolmasters* as well as the preachers.

Work for money; work every day, work diligently, and *save your money when you get it.*

Be *obliging* and *faithful* to your employers, and you will be sure to keep your places. Never be above your business.—Many a man has ruined himself and his family by this foolish pride.

Ever since the first stone in the foundations of the Universe was laid by God's own hand till now, he has been working, and will continue working through endless ages. Follow his glorious example. Work, work, work, for an honest penny; but when you get it, pause and think three times before you spend it; but when you spend it, be sure it will yield a permanent benefit.

That the hearty welcome which we have given you, our *ransomed* kinsmen, may be rendered a blessing, and that the advices which we have tendered may be as good seed sown in good ground, we shall continue to make supplications, prayers, intercessions and thanksgivings to Him whose care reaches all, because His love embraces all.

To Him we commend you, O ye who are now as sheep without a shepherd—as *exiles in the land of your nativity.*

May He who led Abraham, Isaac and Jacob, as they wandered over Canaan and Egypt, guide, protect and bless you; raise up kind, influential friends to do you good; and when the purposes of his grace shall have been accomplished in you, may you be able, like Jacob, to say: "With my staff I passed over this Jordan, and now I am become two bands."

Now, if we ask, who has sent us this great deliverance? The answer shall be, the Lord; the Lord God Almighty, the God of Abraham and Isaac and Jacob.

But as He blessed the chosen seed, by the ministry of men and angels, so in our case, the angels of mercy, justice and liberty, hovering over the towering Capitol, inspired the heads and hearts of the noble men who have plead the cause of the poor, the needy and enslaved, in the Senate and House of Representatives.

For the oppressed and enslaved of all peoples, God has raised up, and will continue to raise up, his Moses and Aaron. Sometimes the hand of the Lord is so signally displayed that Moses and Aaron are not recognized. Seldom do they recognize themselves.

There was neither bow, spear, nor shield, in the hand of Israel, when the Lord led him forth from Egypt, so also, there was no weapon of offence nor defence in your hands when this *ransom* was brought you.

"Great and marvelous are thy works, Lord God Almighty, just and true are thy ways, thou King of Saints. Who shall not fear thee, O Lord, and glorify thy name? We praise thee, we bless thee, we worship thee, we glorify thee, we give thanks to thee for thy great glory. O Lord God, Heavenly King, God the Father Almighty."

Thou, O Lord, and thou alone couldst have moved the heart of this Nation to have done so great a deed for this weak, despised and needy people!

We will, therefore, make supplications, prayers, intercessions, and thanksgivings, for "All that are in authority."

The duty of supplications in behalf of the Government is rendered more binding upon us, when we consider the circumstances under which it was written. St. Paul lived under the reign of Nero, the bloody emperor, who having set Rome on fire, amused himself with drinking and music while the city was in flames; and afterwards, accused the

Christians of the crime which he himself had committed, thereby causing many of them to be put to death in the most cruel manner.

Now, if it was the duty of the ancient Christians to pray for such monsters of wickedness, by how much more is it our duty to pray for a Christian Government.

Congress need our supplications, they shall have them. The President and his Cabinet need our prayers, they shall possess them. The Supreme Court, that awful emblem of impartial justice, need our intercessions, it shall not be forgotten.

Upon all these departments of law, authority and power, we shall beseech the God of Nations to send the spirit of wisdom, justice, liberty—of wisdom seeing the end from the beginning—of justice incorruptible—of liberty governed by righteous law.

To make supplications, prayers, intercessions, and thanksgiving for these authorities, is the peculiar privilege of the Colored People in the United States.

They are not permitted, as in the days of the Revolution and the war of 1812, to take up arms in defence of the Government. Some, both among Anglo-Saxons and Anglo-Africans, complain of this prohibition. For my part, I am glad of it, because I think I see the hand of God in it.

The present war is a kind of family quarrel. Therefore, let a stranger take heed how he meddles, lest both parties unite to drive him out of the house. "Why shouldst thou meddle to thy hurt?"

But we can wield a power in behalf of the Government which neither rifled cannon, nor mortar, nor rocket-battery can assail, nor bomb-proof walls resist.

That power is the right arm of God—of God, who lifts up and casts down nations according as they obey, or disregard the principles of truth, justice, liberty.

The service of prayer which is required from us, contemplates the most difficult as well as the noblest objects. It contemplates the end of the war. It contemplates legislation before and after the end.

Now, to manage this war, so as to bring permanent good to all concerned, requires more than human wisdom—more than human power. To legislate so as to make the masses see and feel that the laws are just, wise, beneficial, demand more than human learning or skill in government. To determine the sense and just application of these laws as Judges—to execute them faithfully and impartially as a Chief Magistrate, O how much of the spirit of God is needful! How much in the President! how much in his Cabinet!

Then there is the army. Let us not forget the brave men who constitute it—who have left their comfortable homes, beloved families, fond parents, affectionate sisters and brothers, for the hardships, dangers and painful deaths of the battle field.

Let us pray that, as *some of them are*, so *all may become*, soldiers of the Cross; so that such as are doomed to fall in the fight, may rise from their gory beds to obtain a crown of life; and those who may return to the peaceful pursuits of civil life, may be wiser and better men.

Now, then, although weak, few, despised and persecuted, we can aid all these departments of government by our daily supplications, prayers and intercessions.

In doing this service, we can accomplish what we could not if we were leading the van of battle; for conquering armies are preceded and succeeded by anguish, misery and death, but our service brings down nothing but blessings upon all.

They are also weapons, "not carnal, but mighty through God, to the pulling down of strongholds;" even the casting down of principalities and powers—the moving of heaven and earth.

Take two examples: When Israel fought against the five kings of the Amorites, Joshua prayed and the sun stood still upon Gibeon, while the moon hung over the valley of Ajalon, till Israel had conquered.

"John Knox was a man famous for his power in prayer, so that Queen Mary used to say she feared his prayers more than all the armies of Europe. And events showed she had reason to do it. He used to be in such an agony for the deliverance of his country that he could not sleep. He had a place in his garden, where he used to go to pray. One night he and several friends were praying together, and as they prayed Knox spoke and said that deliverance had come. He could not tell what had happened, but he felt that something had taken place, for God had heard their prayers. What was it? Why the next news they heard was: 'Queen Mary is dead!' "

But the motives for all this work of mercy, faith, and love as furnished by the text are as weighty as they are numerous. 1st. "That we may lead a quiet and peaceable life." Peace and quietude are some of the conditions of happiness. Dr. Adam Bluche says: "If the State be not in safety, the individual cannot be secure; self preservation, therefore, should lead men to pray for the government under which they live. Rebellions and insurrections seldom terminate even in political good— and even where the government is radically bad, revolutions are most precarious and hazardous. They who wish such commotions would not be quiet under the most mild and benevolent government." This is true of communities and nations, as well as of individuals. We all desire it, and therefore it is our duty to labor for it by every instrument which Infinite wisdom has ordained and man can employ. And lo! how excellent the instruments! *Prayers, supplications, intercessions*—thanksgiving. As Aaron approached the Mercy Seat, with the smoking censor, and was accepted, so do we approach the throne of the Eternal with the burning incense of heaven's own making, and will be accepted. O, let us supplicate God for the peace and quietude of the whole nation!

2d. The other motive which Inspiration presents is, that we may live "*in all godliness* and *honesty.*" Godliness first, honesty afterwards. The latter is the fruit of the former. The godly man, is he who fears God and keeps his commandments. Such a man will be honest in words as well as in deeds; in matters of truth as well as in matters of property. *Honesty is the only policy of godliness.* Colored men, write this sentiment upon your hearts, engrave it in your memory. Let all your thoughts, words, actions, be controled by this principle, *it is always safe to be honest, as it is always safe to be godly*. One has said, that "An honest man is the noblest work of God." But whence comes the honest man? Does he not spring out of the godly? Most assuredly. For no man is truly honest, uniformly honest, and universally honest, but he who is godly. Therefore be godly, and you will be honest in all things, at all times, in all places.

3d. The third motive for this heavenly duty, this intercession in behalf of the Government is, that "It is good and acceptable in the sight of God our Saviour." Whatever God accepts and pronounces good, *must be good:* good in itself; good in its effects, always good; good for man, because ordained of God.

4th. The last motive we present for this godlike work is, that God "*Will have all men to be saved, and to come unto the knowledge of the truth.*"

Hence, we must pray for these Authorities not as public men only, but as private individuals also,—not as Chieftains of the Nation only, but as heads of families also,—as husbands, fathers, Christians. So that, while they think, write, speak, act for the public weal, their own souls may be brought under the saving power of the Gospel, and with all the members of their respective families be made the heirs of the grace of life.

O, that God may bring them all to the knowledge of the truth as it is in Christ Jesus! O, that every one of these Authorities may become a holy, wise, and just man! Then will the laws be enacted in righteousness and executed in the fear of the Lord.

These motives are enforced upon our considerations by the glorious example of the Lord Jesus Christ, who is the Mediator between God and Man, who ever liveth to make intercession for his foes as well as his friends, and with whom there is no respect of persons. Black men, red men, white men, are all alike before Him, and rise or fall, live or die as they please or offend Him.

To make prayers, intercessions, supplications, thanksgivings for national authorities you now clearly see *is a command from heaven.* Obey it, and you shall be blessed—always do it, and you shall be made a blessing to others. Whom God has blessed no man can curse. If God has blessed this nation, neither internal foes, nor foreign enemies can crush it.

But God will bless it if it will do right, administering justice to each and to all, protecting the weak as well as the strong, and throwing the broad wings of its power equally over men of every color. This is God-like, and God will bless his own image, be it in a nation or in a man. Then, O my country, "shall thy light break forth as the morning— thy health shall spring forth speedily—thy righteousness shall go before thee," and "the glory of the Lord shall be thy reward."

Then shall justice be engraven on our arms, and righteousness on our star-spangled banners; our armies shall then be led to battle by the Lord, and victory secured by the right arm of our God.

SUPPLEMENTARY READINGS

Killian, Charles, ed. *Daniel Alexander Payne: Sermons and Addresses, 1853–1891.* New York: Arno Press, 1972.

McPherson, James H. *The Negro's Civil War.* Urbana: University of Illinois Press, 1982.

Payne, Daniel A. *The Semi-Centenary and Retrospection of the African Methodist Episcopal Church.* Baltimore: Sherwood & Co., 1866.

Walker, Clarence E. *A Rock in a Weary Land: The African Methodist Episcopal Church During the Civil War and Reconstruction.* Baton Rouge: Louisiana State University Press, 1982.

Wiley, Bell Irvin. *Southern Negroes, 1861–1865.* New Haven: Yale University Press, 1965. Chap. 6.

FOUR

Freedom's Time of Trial:
1865–World War I

24

ISAAC LANE

From Slave to Preacher
among the Freedmen

Freedom offered cultural and institutional alternatives and necessitated choices not possible under the laws of slavery. Now blacks could set up churches for themselves or decide to join up with a host of competing agencies and denominations, white and black, northern and southern, each of which claimed the freedmen as a kind of religious contraband. The autobiography of Isaac Lane tells of the ecclesiastical struggles that followed the military conflict. Born in 1834 near Jackson, Tennessee, Lane worked during slavery as a licensed preacher or exhorter for fellow slaves under the auspices of the Methodist Episcopal Church, South. After the war he participated in the conferences of black Methodists that the white bishops organized in 1867 to keep any more blacks from exiting, as had nearly two-thirds of the slave membership during the Civil War. The remaining seventy thousand or so were "set aside" in 1870 as the Colored Methodist Episcopal Church, now known as the Christian Methodist Episcopal Church. Lane became a C.M.E. bishop in 1873, convinced that it was the "most fitted religious power to meet the peculiar conditions that exist[ed] in the Southern states" after the Civil War. He carried the Colored Methodist banner into Louisiana and Texas and stood behind the founding of Lane College in Jackson, Tennessee.

My Early Life in the Ministry

SHORTLY AFTER MY CONVERSION I was overcome with a feeling that I ought to preach. I strove for months to get rid of it, but without success. I went to a man in whose piety and Christian virtue I had much confidence and made known to him my struggle and the feeling that was then strong upon me. He gave me his sympathy and directed me to a certain preacher for counsel and aid; but this man did not believe in

Source: *Autobiography of Bishop Isaac Lane, LL.D. with a Short History of the C.M.E. Church in America and of Methodism.* Nashville: Publishing House of the M.E. Church, South, 1916. Pp. 52–59.

Negroes preaching, and he gave me no encouragement. I next sought the advice of a colored man whom the Methodists had helped. He was a pure Christian man, and he told me that if God had really called me to preach he surely knew his own business better than man and advised me not to trouble myself, but trust God. I did trust him; and soon thereafter the inspiration came, and I firmly decided to enter upon the work of a minister.

I sent in my petition to a Quarterly Conference of the Methodist Episcopal Church, South, for license to preach. The Conference did not grant my request, but gave me license to exhort instead. The committee explained that the Church did not believe it proper to grant license to Negroes to preach. Rev. George Harris was the presiding elder, and Rev. A. R. Wilson was the preacher in charge of the local Church. Rev. Wilson was my personal friend up to the time of his death, and he took a lively interest in my career and my work. In the early days of my ministry I regarded him as a great and good man, and during all the years of our acquaintance thereafter the esteem in which I held him when I was a young man did not suffer in any way.

During the Civil War the attitude of the Southern Methodist Church toward granting license to Negroes to preach had undergone some changes and so I appeared again for license to preach. This time I was sent before the Quarterly Conference presided over by Elder William H. Lee. After asking many questions bearing upon almost every phase of the doctrines of Christ and the Church, I was granted license to preach. I recall many of the questions that were asked and the answers that I gave. I shall never forget the occasion and the keen interest every one seemed to feel in the examination I was called upon to take. I give below a few of the questions and the answers that provoked considerable interest and discussion—viz.:

Question. Are all men sinners?
Answer. Yes.
Q. What Scriptural proof or reference have you to offer?
A. "For as in Adam all die, even so in Christ shall all be made alive."
Q. Is conviction a voluntary act or an involuntary one?
A. Involuntary.
Q. Can you give a Scriptural reference?
A. "The grace that brings salvation has appeared unto all men, teaching them godliness."
Q. What is the difference between justification and repentance?

A. Justification is the work done for me, while regeneration is the work done in me. The former takes place in the courts of heaven, while the latter takes place in the human heart.

These questions, together with others somewhat similar, being satisfactorily answered, I was granted license to preach, and I felt a freedom that I had not enjoyed before.

I have already spoken of the prayer meetings and the splendid opportunity they afforded in exercising the gifts that God had given me and the deepening of the work of grace in our hearts. These meetings proved to be a great preparation for the work that I was called upon to do after I had entered fully into the work of the Christian ministry. Being licensed to preach, I was frequently called upon to preach and exhort, especially on Sunday afternoons, not only to my people, but the white people also would come out in large numbers to hear me. At first I was very much embarrassed to preach before such large crowds, because I realized fully that I was without education and had but little opportunity of learning anything. But God helped me wonderfully and blessed my work.

From the time I was licensed to exhort up to 1865 I held meetings for our people. We had glorious times, and many converts would rise and "tell of Jesus and his love." These meetings made our country famous for Methodism during the war. At some places we had stormy times. The old days of the beginning of the Wesleyan Movement in England, in Ireland, and in Wales had their reflex in these. Many times my life was in great danger, and the white people were constantly being reviled and reprimanded because they had encouraged me in preaching. The persecutors went so far as to burn down the church houses in which I had preached to my people. But I had gone too far in the work to be stopped by such methods. Too many people, both white and colored, believed in me to be sidetracked by any such methods; for at this time not only Methodists, but Christian people of all denominations, upheld me and sought to give encouragement. One good old Presbyterian brother said to me after I had preached in his church: "Brother Lane, keep on preaching the gospel, and we will keep on building church houses until the trumpet blows. Let them burn down. We will build, and you shall preach."

The Early Days of Freedom

The Emancipation Proclamation that had been prepared by President Abraham Lincoln in the month of July, of the year 1862, was not issued until January 1 of the year 1863. It did not go into effect at this time, as we all know, but its influence was felt at once the country over. A studious effort was made on the part of a good many people to keep the issuance of this proclamation a profound secret to the Negroes. But it could not be done. There was too much excitement for such a clever piece of work to be done with any degree of success, and there were too many Negroes who were able to read and understand the trend of affairs to be misled by any subterfuge that might be resorted to by the sympathizers of the Lost Cause. The Confederacy was doomed, and this proclamation was the death knell to slavery on the American continent. The moral effect was wonderful. Strong men who had put all their faith in the supremacy of the Confederate army now began to weaken and became despaired of success. The slaves saw it, and it required great effort on their part to suppress their feelings of rejoicing.

After Lee had surrendered and the Confederacy had gone to pieces and Jefferson Davis had become a refugee, our owners called us together and told us we were free and had to take care of ourselves. There I was with a large, dependent family to support. I had no money, no education, no mother nor father to whom to look for help in any form. Our former owners prophesied that half of us would starve, but not so. It must be admitted, however, that we had a hard time, and it seemed at times that the prophecy would come true; but the harder the time, the harder we worked and the more we endured. For six months we lived on nothing but bread, milk, and water. We had a time to keep alive; but by praying all the time, with faith in God, and believing that he would provide for his own, we saved enough to get the next year not only bread, milk, and water, but meat also.

The next year my family fared much better, and I was able to devote more time to the work of the ministry. I took an active part in the Church and soon gained the confidence and respect of both white and colored people. At our own request, our Church was organized as an independent society, and we took the name of the Colored Methodist Episcopal Church in America. In 1866 we had a Conference of our own in Jackson, Tenn., known as the Tennessee, North Alabama, and North Mississippi Annual Conference. I was elected and ordained deacon one day, and on the next day I was elected and ordained elder. At the close of this Conference I was appointed the presiding elder of the Jackson District of the above-named Annual Conference, which position I held for four years. Meanwhile we found that the territory and membership embraced by this Annual Conference were entirely too large; and so later on out of this Conference we organized the Tennessee, North Alabama, North Mississippi, and West Tennessee Annual Conferences.

As I won the confidence and respect of the people I grew into prominence in the Church. At the session of the Tennessee Annual Conference that convened in Brownsville, Tenn., I was elected the leader of the Tennessee delegation to the first General Conference of the Colored Methodist Episcopal Church in America. Bishop David S. Doggett, D.D., of the Methodist Episcopal Church, South, presided over the deliberations of this Conference and gave service that was highly satisfactory to all the brethren. It is difficult for any one who was not present to understand and appreciate the attitude of the Southern Methodist Church, as exemplified through its bishops and other leaders, toward the colored work. It is far more difficult to explain it. There was a fraternal sympathy, a mutual good will, a kindly interest that made the relation cordial and highly helpful.

The Jackson District was a prominent appointment. As the elder I was given an assessment in the way of a salary of four hundred dollars per year. As a matter of fact, I was paid all the way from one hundred and fifty to two hundred dollars a year during the four years I served in this capacity. Having served the time limit, I was afterwards assigned to the work as pastor of Liberty Colored Methodist Episcopal Church at Jackson, Tenn., and served that congregation for a little more than a year for the handsome salary of one hundred and seventy-five dollars! My family was large and growing, and I had to do much work on the farm in order to support my family properly. Nevertheless, during my pastorate I was successful in increasing the membership of this Church from seventy to three hundred members. These were great days for me in the ministry. I preached with much freedom and great power. My conversion and conduct showed to the people that I was sincere in my purpose and earnest in my efforts, and men seemed to realize that I was called of God. All of these things gave me the confidence and respect of the people, and I gradually grew into prominence and general favor.

SUPPLEMENTARY READINGS

Du Bois, W. E. B. *Black Reconstruction in America, 1860–1880.* New York: Atheneum, 1969.

Heard, William H. *From Slavery to the Bishopric in the A.M.E. Church.* Philadelphia: The A.M.E. Book Concern, 1924; reprint, New York: Arno Press and *The New York Times,* 1969.

Levine, Lawrence W. *Black Culture and Black Consciousness.* New York: Oxford University Press, 1977. Chap. 3.

Litwack, Leon F. *Been in the Storm So Long.* New York: Vintage Books, 1979. Chap. 9.

Savage, Horace C. *Life and Times of Bishop Isaac Lane.* Nashville: National Publication Co., 1958.

25

LUCIUS H. HOLSEY

"The Colored Methodist Episcopal Church"

*Lucius H. Holsey boasted: "From 1856–1914, the movement to establish
the Colored Methodist Episcopal Church in America was almost absolutely
under my direction." Such claims derived from Holsey's fierce commitment
to a black Methodist connection composed and led primarily by ex-slaves.
He resented accusations that theirs was a "bootlick" operation and "the little
slave church." Born near Columbia, Georgia, Holsey (1842–1920) farmed,
taught school, and obtained a license from the Methodist Episcopal Church,
South, to preach after the Civil War. He participated in the formation of
the C.M.E. Church in 1870 and took charge of a church in Savannah.
Gifted with natural leadership qualities and a forceful personality, he quickly
advanced to the office of bishop in 1873. During the next two decades he
fought long and hard to strengthen the Colored Methodists, but tried to
steer clear of entanglements in Reconstruction and post-Reconstruction politics. "As ministers of the gospel," he wrote, "we make no stump-speeches
and fight no battles of the politicians." This stance precipitated severe criticism from others such as Henry M. Turner, the African Methodist Episcopal
leader and political activist in Georgia. But Holsey persisted in building up
the C.M.E. in the way he thought best, was active in the founding of Paine
College in Augusta, Georgia, and represented his church at the first Ecumenical Council in London in 1881. His brief history of the Colored Methodists appeared in the* Independent *in March, 1891.*

THIS, THE YOUNGEST BRANCH of American Methodism, was organized under the auspices and authority of the Methodist Episcopal Church,
South, in the city of Jackson, Tenn., December 15th and 23d, 1870. As
far back as 1866, its organization was contemplated and desired by both
classes of those who composed the membership of the Methodist Episcopal Church, South. In this year (1866) the General Conference of
the Mother Church requested their bishops to ordain colored men to the
ministry, form them into conferences, preside over and superintend

Source: *Autobiography, Sermons, Addresses and Essays of Bishop L. H. Holsey, D.D.*
Atlanta: The Franklin Publishing Co., 1898. Pp. 214–19.

the colored work in assemblies, separate and distinct from those of the whites. It was also provided "that when three or more annual conferences of colored ministers were organized and presided over by the bishops" of the Methodist Episcopal Church, South; and that also when thought befitting and agreeable to both classes of members, "a separate and independent ecclesiastical jurisdiction should be established for the colored people," with all the regularities and outfits of established Methodism.

These initiatory provisions, being agreeable to both classes of persons concerned, and being consistent with what was conceived to be the harmony and best interests of both and all, the separation was authorized—legal, formal, and productive of the best feelings and results.

It is simply justice to state that the Methodist Episcopal Church, South, at the beginning of the late war, had over two hundred thousand members of color within her pales, having churches of their own, and ministers sent to them regularly from the conferences. Often one pastor served both the white and the colored members, preaching to the whites in the forenoon and to the colored in the afternoon. Of this two hundred thousand, the great majority informally dissolved their relationship with the Methodist Episcopal Church, South, and went into other branches of Methodism, the African Methodist Episcopal Church receiving the largest share of them. However, there still remained about forty thousand who adhered to the Methodist Episcopal Church, South, and who could not be induced to disband their church relation and enter others which came upon the ground immediately after the emancipation. For some years after the war the reduced number of members of color who still remained adherents of the Methodist Episcopal Church, South, was looked after and cared for as was the case during the years of slavery. As the General Conference of the Methodist Episcopal Church, South, which met in New Orleans, May, 1866, had authorized the bishops to organize conferences of colored ministers, so, four years after, the same body held its quadrennial session in Memphis, Tenn.; and upon the petition of some of the leading colored ministers, the General Conference of the Mother Church delegated their bishops, with other distinguished ministers and laymen, to organize the colored members into a separate and distinct body, which was satisfactorily consummated in December of the same year (1870).

The organization of this branch of our common Methodism seemed necessary for several reasons.

Among them we may note the following: As a result, the war had changed the ancient relation of master and servant. The former, though divested of his slaves, yet carried with him all the notions, feelings and elements in his religious and social life that characterized his former years. On the other hand, the emancipated slave had but little in common with the former master. In fact, he had nothing but his religion, poverty and ignorance. With social elements so distinct and dissimilar, the best results of a common church relation could not be expected. Harmony, friendship and peaceful co-operation between the two peoples in the propagation of a divine and vital Christianity, were among the essential elements of a successful evangelization of the people of color. Social religious equality, as well as any other kind of social equality, was utterly impracticable and undesirable, and coveted by neither class of persons composing a churchship.

With this state of things steadily in view, we had but one horn of the dilemma left us, and that was a free, friendly and authorized separation from the mother body. Although we are become two bands, yet it is, and was understood that this does not, in any sense, release the Methodist Episcopal Church, South, from those duties and obligations that Providence seems to have imposed upon her, in aiding the American African in his Christian development.

The Colored Methodist Episcopal Church in America has had a remarkable career. As a branch or product of the Methodist Episcopal Church, South, it has been opposed by strong hands and accomplished leaders among the colored people, from its birthday to the present; though, happily for us, these oppositions are now subsiding and the young organization is taking on a firm and expanding aspect that is most interesting and extraordinary. To sustain and propagate such an institution amid so many opposing forces as those that have presented themselves for the last twenty years, seemed, at first, to be a forlorn and hopeless undertaking. Green from the fields of slavery, raw in the experiences of church tactics, in membership and ministry, without houses of worship or literature, with many of its organizing feats being performed out of doors and under trees, it overcame difficulties that make it more than a mere experiment. Being in the dews of its youth, it has not yet attained its destined dignity and power for good among the colored race. But it is advancing in every department.

Its aim is the evangelization of the colored race. First, by preaching the pure and simple gospel of Christ to the masses, in the simplest form of speech. Second, to do this in the best and most effective manner, we aim, as far as possible, to establish and maintain schools for the impartation of Christian education among our people, and especially among the ministry, and that part of the race who are expecting to be teachers. As we cannot expect to do a great deal at present, by way of educating the masses, we begin with preachers and teachers, carefully and patiently training and indoctrinating them in those great moral and religious principles that lie at the base of an elevated and sound moral manhood. It is said that man is naturally a religious being. The sense of a Supreme Power intrudes itself upon all his spiritual and moral functions, and if men in general are thus religionists, the colored man is particularly so. He seems especially susceptible of religious culture and of reaching those spiritual climaxes and benedictions that have characterized the most pious of men. While these seem apparent facts, it is also apparent that all these safeguards of the gospel, and those that have grown out of the experiences of men, should be thrown around him, lest his Christian or religious zeal should subvert, cover or hide the weightier matters of the moral law, and those principles and practices that constitute the vital flame of the reformatory moral power of Christianity. Christianity pure and simple is what he needs. As a church, we come upon the stage of being to propagate the gospel along these lines and no others. To sustain this position we have always stood aloof from politics, not as individuals, but as officials representing an organization for a certain and specific purpose.

While our ministry and members represent all political parties and creeds, yet, as ministers of the gospel, we make no stump-speeches and fight no battles of the politicians. We think it better to "let the dead bury the dead," while we follow Christ. Of course we have no control over any man's vote; whether he be minister or member, he is free to vote as he pleases. We regard Christianity not only as reformatory and redeeming, but as a moral power of civilization. At present, it must be acknowledged that Negro civilization is yet in its infancy and crude evolutions. He is now laying the foundations upon which future generations are to build those institutions that are to make him and his progeny solid Christians and valued citizens. We regard him as a part of the people, a permanent fixture in the United States of America. It is true, we hope, that many of the race will, some day, go to Africa—their native land—but the masses will fight the battle of life here, and live and die on the American continent. We also recognize the fact that he is, and will be, singularly and collectively, a separate and distinct race from the others.

Friction in church or state cannot be productive of good to him and his children, and we think it is a legitimate part of Christianity to ameliorate and soften those cruder conditions under which he finds himself as an element in society; hence, we seek the friendship of all, and especially and particularly the fatherly directorship of the Methodist Episcopal Church, South. Beyond and behind the immediate work of the christianization of the colored race, there lie a faith, a principle, and a practice, that seem peculiar and interesting; and as these factors have done much to unite the races in harmonious co-operation and exile any hostile feelings that may have existed in the South between the two. Their aim is to bring about peace, and perpetuate the era of mutual brotherhood and concert of action.

We claim that the spirit, nature and practice of the Colored Methodist Episcopal Church in America have done, and are doing much in this direction. Some have thought that Providence has placed it where it is for this purpose. Already it has enlisted the special attention of the Methodist Episcopal Church, South, which by legislative action has appointed a Commissioner of Education for the purpose of establishing and maintaining schools for "the education of preachers and teachers," for the Colored Methodist Episcopal Church in America. This educational interest is controlled by the two churches jointly for the benefit of the Colored Church. It is the aim of this church to prosecute the work along these lines in the fear of God and in the love of a common humanity.

SUPPLEMENTARY READINGS

Bailey, Kenneth. "The Post-Civil War Racial Separations in Southern Protestantism." *Church History* 46, no. 4 (December 1977): 453–73.

Cade, John Brother. *Holsey . . . The Incomparable.* New York: Pageant Press, 1963.

Gravely, William B. "The Social, Political and Religious Significance of the Foundation of the Colored Methodist Episcopal Church (1870)." *Methodist History* 18 (October 1979): 3–25.

Lakey, Othal Hawthorne. *The Rise of "Colored Methodism": A Study of the Background and the Beginnings of the Christian Methodist Episcopal Church.* Dallas: Crescendo Book Publications, 1972.

Pettigrew, M. C. *From Miles to Johnson: One Hundred Years of Progress, 1870–1970.* Memphis: C.M.E. Church Publishing House, 1970.

26

WILLIAM WELLS BROWN

Black Religion
in the Post-Reconstruction South

William Wells Brown, often called America's first black man of letters, escaped from slavery in 1834 and joined in the abolitionist movement. Noted for his novel Clotel *and for his plays and historical essays, Brown (1816–84) also wrote a book of travel—*My Southern Home: or The South and Its People, *comprised of impressions gathered during a trip through the South in 1879–80. The Boston author and reformer did not like what he saw. Resurgent white racism, the withdrawal of most northern liberals from the numerous freedman's agencies, and the return to power of the traditional white elite had contributed to black regression in economics, politics, education, and health. "Jim Crow" ruled the day. When Brown visited black churches in Tennessee he voiced disapproval of their styles of worship and religious folkways. He believed that the black itinerant revivalists were a plague all over the South and that the only remedy was to induce the masses to demand an educated Christian ministry. Brown's feelings reflected those of northern black religious leaders who had worked among the ex-slaves. As the latter began to swell the rosters of the northern-based denominations, struggles for institutional power developed. During the last decades of the nineteenth century, according to one interpretation, southern blacks retreated into a folk religiosity that lacked the social protest emphasis of the antebellum black denominations.*

AFTER SETTLING the question with his bacon and cabbage, the next dearest thing to a colored man, in the South, is his religion. I call it a "thing," because they always speak of getting religion as if they were going to market for it.

"You better go an' get religion, dat's what you better do, fer de devil will be arter you one of dees days, and den whar will yer be?" said an elderly Sister, who was on her way to the "Revival," at St. Paul's, in

Source: *My Southern Home: or, The South and Its People.* Boston: A. G. Brown and Co., 1880. Pp. 190–97.

Nashville, last winter. The man to whom she addressed these words of advice stopped, raised his hat, and replied:

"Anty, I ain't quite ready to-night, but I em gwine to get it before the meetins close, kase when that getting-up day comes, I want to have the witness; that I do."

"Yes, yer better, fer ef yer don't, dar'll be a mighty stir 'mong de brimstone down dar, dat dey will, fer yer's bin bad nuff; I knows yer fum A to izzard," returned the old lady.

The church was already well filled, and the minister had taken his text. As the speaker warmed up in his subject, the Sisters began to swing their heads and reel to and fro, and eventually began a shout. Soon, five or six were fairly at it, which threw the house into a buzz. Seats were soon vacated near the shouters, to give them more room, because the women did not wish to have their hats smashed in by the frenzied Sisters. As a woman sprung up in her seat, throwing up her long arms, with a loud scream the lady on the adjoining seat quickly left, and did not stop till she got to a safe distance.

"Ah, ha!" exclaimed a woman near by, " 'fraid of your new bonnet! Ain't got much religion, I reckon. Specks you'll have to come out of that if you want to save your soul."

"She thinks more of that hat now, than she does of a seat in heaven," said another.

"Never mind," said a third, "when she gets de witness, she'll drap dat hat an' shout herself out of breath."

The shouting now became general; a dozen or more entering into it most heartily. These demonstrations increased or abated, according to movements of the leaders, who were in and about the pulpit; for the minister had closed his discourse, and first one, and then another would engage in prayer. The meeting was kept up till a late hour, during which, four or five sisters becoming exhausted, had fallen upon the floor and lay there, or had been removed by their friends.

St. Paul is a fine structure, with its spire bathed in the clouds, and standing on the rising land in South Cherry Street, it is a building that the citizens may well be proud of.

In the evening I went to the First Baptist Church, in Spruce Street. This house is equal in size and finish to St. Paul. A large assembly was in attendance, and a young man from Cincinnati was introduced by the pastor as the preacher for the time being. He evidently felt that to set a congregation to shouting, was the highest point to be attained, and he was equal to the occasion. Failing to raise a good shout by a reasonable amount of exertion, he took from his pocket a letter, opened it, held it up and began, "When you reach the other world you'll be hunting for your mother, and the angel will read from this paper. Yes, the angel will read from this paper."

For fully ten minutes the preacher walked the pulpit, repeating in a loud, incoherent manner, "And the angel will read from this letter." This created the wildest excitement, and not less than ten or fifteen were shouting in different parts of the house, while four or five were going from seat to seat shaking hands with the occupants of the pews. "Let dat angel come right down now an' read dat letter," shouted a Sister, at the top of her voice. This was the signal for loud exclamations from various parts of the house. "Yes, yes, I want's to hear the letter." "Come, Jesus, come, or send an angel to read the letter." "Lord, send us the power." And other remarks filled the house. The pastor highly complimented the effort, as one of "great power," which the audience most cordially endorsed. At the close of the service the strange minister had hearty shakes of the hand from a large number of leading men and women of the church. And this was one of the most refined congregations in Nashville.

It will be difficult to erase from the mind of the negro of the South, the prevailing idea that outward demonstrations, such as, shouting, the loud "amen," and the most boisterous noise in prayer, are not necessary adjuncts to piety.

A young lady of good education and refinement, residing in East Tennessee, told me that she had joined the church about a year previous, and not until she had one shouting spell, did most of her Sisters believe that she had "the Witness."

"And did you really shout?" I inquired.

"Yes. I did it to stop their mouths, for at nearly every meeting, one or more would say, 'Sister Smith, I hope to live to see you show that you've got the Witness, for where the grace of God is, there will be shouting, and the sooner you comes to that point the better it will be for you in the world to come.' "

To get religion, join a benevolent society that will pay them "sick dues" when they are ill, and to bury them when they die, appears to be the beginning, the aim, and the end of the desires of the colored people of the South. In Petersburg I was informed that there were thirty-two different secret societies in that city, and I met persons who held membership in four at the same time. While such associations are of great benefit to the improvident, they are, upon the whole, very injurious. They take away all stimulus to secure homes and to provide for the future.

As a man observed to me, "I b'longs ter four s'ieties, de 'Samaritans,' de 'Gallalean Fisherman,' de 'Sons of Moses,' an' de 'Wise Men of de East.' All of dees pays me two dollars a week when I is sick, an' twenty-five dollars ter bury me when I dies. Now ain't dat good?"

I replied that I thought it would be far better, if he put his money in a home and educated himself."

"Well," said he, "I is satisfied, kas, ef I put de money in a house, maybe when I got sick some udder man might be hangin' roun' wantin' me ter die, an' maybe de ole 'oman might want me gone too, an' not take good kere of me, an' let me die an' let de town bury me. But, now, yer see, de s'iety takes kere of me and burries me. So, now, I am all right fer dis worl' an' I is got de Witness, an' dat fixes me fer hebben."

This was all said in an earnest manner, showing that the brother had an eye to business.

The determination of late years to ape the whites in the erection of costly structures to worship in, is very injurious to our people. In Petersburg, Va., a Baptist society pulled down a noble building, which was of ample size, to give place to a more fashionable and expensive one, simply because a sister Church had surpassed them in putting up a house of worship. It is more consistent with piety and Godly sincerity to say that we don't believe there is any soul-saving and God-honoring element in such expensive and useless ornaments to houses in which to meet and humbly worship in simplicity and sincerity the true and living God, according to his revealed will. Poor, laboring people who are without homes of their own, and without (in many instances) steady remunerative employment, can ill afford to pay high for useless and showy things that neither instruct nor edify them. The manner, too, in which the money is raised, is none of the best, to say the least of it. For most of the money, both to build the churches and to pay the ministers, is the hard earnings of men in the fields, at service, or by our women over the wash-tub. When our people met and worshipped in less costly and ornamental houses, their piety and sincerity was equally as good as now, if not better. With more polish within and less ornament without, we would be more spiritually and less worldly-minded.

Revival meetings, and the lateness of the hours at which they close, are injurious to both health and morals. Many of the churches begin in October, and continue till the holidays; and commencing again the middle of January, they close in April. They often keep the meetings in till eleven o'clock; sometimes till twelve; and in some country places, they have gone on later. I was informed of a young woman who lost her situation—a very good one—because the family could not sit up till twelve o'clock every night to let her in, and she would not leave her meeting so as to return earlier. Another source of moral degradation lies in the fact that a very large number of men, calling themselves "missionaries," travel the length and breadth of the country, stopping longest where they are best treated. The "missionary" is usually armed with a recommendation from some minister in charge, or has a forged one, it makes but little difference which. He may be able to read enough to line a hymn, but that is about all.

His paper that he carries speaks of him as a man "gifted in revival efforts," and he at once sets about getting up a revival meeting. This tramp, for he cannot be called anything else, has with him generally a hymn-book, and an old faded, worn-out carpet-bag, with little or nothing in it. He remains in a place just as long as the people will keep him, which usually depends upon his ability to keep up an excitement. I met a swarm of these lazy fellows all over the South, the greatest number, however, in West Virginia.

The only remedy for this great evil lies in an educated ministry, which is being supplied to a limited extent. It is very difficult, however, to induce the uneducated, superstitious masses to receive and support an intelligent Christian clergyman. . . .

SUPPLEMENTARY READINGS

Cable, George W. *The Negro Question.* Edited by Arlin Turner. Garden City, N.Y.: Doubleday, 1958.

Farrison, William Edward. *William Wells Brown, Author & Reformer.* Chicago: University of Chicago Press, 1969.

Rabinowitz, Howard N. *Race Relations in the Urban South, 1865–1900.* New York: Oxford University Press, 1978. Chap. 9.

Spain, Rufus B. *At Ease in Zion: A Social History of Southern Baptists, 1865–1900.* Nashville: Vanderbilt University Press, 1967. Chaps. 2–4.

Woodward, C. Vann. *The Strange Career of Jim Crow.* Second rev. ed. New York: Oxford University Press, 1966.

27

DANIEL ALEXANDER PAYNE

"Education in the A.M.E. Church"

Young Daniel Alexander Payne decided that the only difference between the master and the slave was superior knowledge. Education was the key to black liberation: "In my nineteenth year I forsook the carpenter's trade for the life of an educator." Payne never wavered from this vocational call. As one of the most influential bishops of the A.M.E. Church, he fought for higher educational standards and the establishment of ministerial reading courses and schools. The African Methodists failed in 1847 to establish a permanent manual labor and literary institute at Wilberforce, Ohio. In 1863 the Cincinnati Conference of the Methodist Episcopal Church offered a school for sale, which it had founded in 1856 to train "colored" teachers and missionaries. Payne led in purchasing it and became the president of the first Afro-American institution of higher education in the country—Wilberforce University, Xenia, Ohio, incorporated in 1866. In addition to the normal and industrial education departments, Payne inaugurated theological studies. He retired from the presidency in 1876, but his influence left its mark, especially because of his dedication to academic excellence, personal morality, and a self-disciplined, almost ascetic, Christian life-style. The African Methodist Episcopal Zion Church founded Livingstone College at Salisbury, North Carolina, in 1885, and by 1923–24 fifty-two black schools in the United States advertised theological studies.

IN VIEW OF THE FACT that my whole public life has been spent in close connection with the school-room and the cause of education in general, and that for thirteen years I was closely connected with the principal institution of learning of our Church, I turn aside here to speak briefly of the progress of the Church in education and in other things pertaining to its culture and intellectual development, and of its best-equipped school in particular, as I consider the years spent as its President the most interesting of my later years.

Source: *Recollections of Seventy Years.* Nashville: A.M.E. Sunday School Union, 1888. Pp. 220–32.

English Methodism and American Methodism began their career with planning and executing in behalf of education. Not so with African Methodism in America, because Bishop Allen and his coadjutors were illiterate men. They founded no institution of learning, nor is there a trace of a thought in their minds about a school of learning. The reason of the difference between the beginning of these three bodies is seen in the fact that the founding of schools of learning is a result of education. It does not precede, but follows in the wake of education. What is not in a man cannot be evolved out of him. As I have said before, Daniel Coker was the most intelligent of the men connected with the ministry of the A. M. E. Church at the beginning of its career. In 1818 there was found no one in the Baltimore Annual Conference competent to act as secretary, and the youthful son of Bishop Allen, a lad about fourteen years of age, was constituted secretary, and filled this office for two consecutive years. This circumstance is a proof of the statement that the ministry of the A. M. E. Church was at the beginning of its career unlearned. Therefore, it was not until 1833 that we hear the first voice speaking out on the subject of education. It was in the Ohio Annual Conference of that date—then the youngest of the Conferences—which passed two resolutions recognizing the high importance of schools and temperance societies especially to our people, and pledging the members to do all possible to establish such among us. Ten years later (1843) the Baltimore Annual Conference passed resolutions looking to an increase of learning. Out of this grew a course of studies to be pursued, which was laid down by the Philadelphia Conference the same year, which Conference took another step in the right direction in resolving to present this recommendation to the next General Conference. My epistles on "The Education of the Ministry" were written between June, 1843, and May, 1844, and the opponents of an educated ministry became alarmed; but, as we have seen elsewhere, the General Conference of 1844 adopted a scheme of studies and placed it in the Discipline. My series of essays on "The Education of the Ministry," written in 1845, softened down the general opposition until the General Conference of 1848, when there was another heated discussion. In 1845 the first educational convention was called. It was held in Philadelphia and called at the instance of the Baltimore Conference. In this various plans were considered for promoting the work of education among the colored people of the United States generally, but chiefly in our own Connection. This convention indulged in heated and violent arguments for an educational association by one faction, and for founding a collegiate institution by another. It was argued against the latter proposition that

there were at least three educational institutions accessible to us,[1] and
that it was possible for us, by combining our efforts, to support a half-
dozen young men every year, but that all our efforts and means combined were inadequate to the founding and support of a single college.
The opposition maintained our ability to do so, and finally both plans
were adopted—the institution to be in the West. Then arose another
faction contending for one in the East also, and finally all three propositions were adopted. The association was organized on the spot. But for
lack of unity in purpose and oneness in action we did nothing in the
form of an educational association; and because we were all too poor to
assume individual responsibility we founded no college. O ignorance!
O disunion! Ye did curse and destroy Carthage! Ye can also curse and
destroy the A. M. E. Church! Not the Christian Church! No; never!
because that is for humanity; but the A. M. E. Church, because that is
for a race. The races perish sometimes, or they become scattered to the
four corners of the earth; but humanity can never perish nor be thus
scattered, because every spot of the earth is hers and shall be in her possession till the new heaven and the new earth be brought into being.
This educational convention met in October, and represented the Baltimore, Philadelphia, and New York Conferences; but, as has been said in
a previous chapter, the Ohio Annual Conference met in September and
heard the report of its committee, which had been appointed the year
before to select land for a seminary on the manual labor plan.

From these two historical facts it can be seen that the influence of
the action of the General Conference of 1844 on the subject of education took immediate effect, and that in the effort for the founding of an
institution of learning Ohio led the van. Some schools had been instituted previous to this, but it must be recorded as a matter of fact that
not one of these was established by any organized effort on the part of
the denomination. They were the results of individual effort. These individuals were moved by the Spirit of God to do what they could to
impart knowledge to the rising generations. The first of these secular
schools was commenced by the Rev. Daniel Coker in the basement of

1   These were Gettysburg, Oberlin, and Oneida. At Gettysburg D. A. Payne received his theological training; at Oberlin Bishop J. M. Brown received his; and
Rev. Alexander Crummel, D.D., of the Protestant Episcopal Church, received his
academical training at Oneida, N.Y., and completed it at Oxford University, England.
It was also at Oneida that Rev. Henry Highland Garnett, of the Presbyterian
Church, was trained for his brilliant career. After graduating, Dr. Crummel spent
two or three years as a curate in one of the English rural Churches. Subsequently he
went to Liberia, Africa, where he spent the prime of his manhood. He is now pastor
of St. Luke's Protestant Episcopal Church in the city of Washington. He is the
founder of St. Luke's. Dr. Garnett died in Africa as United States Embassador [sic].

Bethel Church, Saratoga Street, Baltimore, Md., in 1810. It was a school for the instruction of children and youths in the elementary branches of an English education. He was succeeded in his useful and elevating work by a Mr. Cooly (tradition says by Misses Russell and Collins). This school, like that of Mr. Coker's, must have been primary. How long his school was in existence I know not. On my arrival in Baltimore in 1843, then only on a visit to the Baltimore Annual Conference at the request of Bishop Morris Brown, a maiden lady named Miss Mary Prout kept a school for primary instruction in Rubourgh Street. This was the third as far as I can learn. She was a prominent member of Bethel, and was considered one of its bright and shining lights. She was born in 1800, and was still living in 1882.

The fourth school was opened by myself in Philadelphia, not as a minister of the A. M. E. Church, for I was at the time (1840) in connection with the Franklin [Frankean] Synod of the Lutheran Church, but my first pupils were three children of Rev. Joseph M. Corr, who lived as one of her most gifted and godly local preachers, and who died as one of the most venerated and lamented. My school was in its character equal to what is now regarded as a grammar school. After I transferred my ministerial relations from the Lutheran to the A. M. E. Church I made annual reports to the Philadelphia Annual Conference. Rev. David Ware, a local preacher of the Philadelphia Conference, was also at the head of another school of less pretensions.

The first organized effort of a denominational character on the part of the Church was made by the Ohio Annual Conference in 1845. This Conference passed a resolution to establish an institution of a high order, and named it "Union Seminary." It was opened in the basement of our chapel in Columbus, O. Rev. J. M. Brown was its first Principal, and he was assisted by Miss Francis Watkins; but it was not a success. Much time was spent in collecting funds to buy the land—one hundred and eighty acres about fourteen miles south-west from Columbus—and to erect a comparatively small frame building upon it. A primary school was kept for some years, but better schools were at the command of the colored people in all the large towns of Ohio. It lingered on in a miserable condition until Wilberforce University became the property of the Church, when it was abolished and the property ordered to be sold for the benefit of that institution, but through mismanagement the sale was of little benefit to the latter.

The founding of Wilberforce University opened a new chapter in the history of the Church. As has been already said, it was projected and organized in a very simple and primary form, by the Cincinnati Conference of the M. E. Church in the autumn of 1856, at Tawawa Springs,

Greene County, O. about three and a half miles from the city of Xenia.
These facts, with those stated in previous chapters, clearly show that the
hand of God was leading these two branches of the Methodist family
in the same direction, at the same time, for the accomplishment of
the same great end—the Christian education of a race, a race then enslaved and ostracized by Christians in a so-called Christian land; and
that, too, in the name of Christianity. The clouds were blackening, the
darkness deepening, and yet the dawn of day was just at hand.

In the first and original form this school was managed almost entirely by white persons. There were twenty-four trustees, of whom only
four were men of color—viz.: Rev. Lewis Woodson, Mr. Alfred Anderson, Mr. Ishmael Keeth, and myself. Mr. Keeth attended but one meeting of the Board. Mr. Woodson attended but three or four. Mr. Anderson
and myself were almost always present. The only one of the trustees of
color who aided in the actual management was myself, because, first, I
was a member of the Executive Committee; second, I lived with my
family on the college campus and had two of my step-children in the
school; third, during the summer the white teachers and managers went
away to recruit, and the establishment was left in my care; and fourth,
I spent most of my time night and day watching over the interests left
in my care during these months. It passed into the hands of the A. M. E.
Church in 1863, as the reader will remember, and was re-opened in
the same year under our administration. This was our first school of
importance. On its re-opening I was elected President, but the Principal
who opened it in July was Prof. John G. Mitchell, who was succeeded
by Dr. Kent, an Englishman, and he by Prof. Fry, and then I took active charge of the work. In 1876 Rev. B. F. Lee was placed at its head,
where he remained until 1884, when he was succeeded by Prof. S. T.
Mitchel, who is still (1886) in the position. It is now to be seen that
Wilberforce has been in existence thirty-two years, twenty-three of
which have been passed under the management of our Connection; so
that it is rapidly nearing the twenty-fifth anniversary for us, and stands
to-day the oldest school in the Church. As such it has a history, and
deserves more than a passing notice. Let us glance at what it has accomplished. But first let me pay a passing tribute to the liberality and generosity of the Cincinnati Conference of the M. E. Church, which placed
this seat of learning within our reach; as it was sold to us for its indebtedness of ten thousand dollars, at a time when the agent of the
State of Ohio stood ready and anxious to buy it for an asylum at its real
value—a much larger price.

In material interests it has accomplished much for itself and the community in which it stands. The building which replaced the wooden one burned by an incendiary in 1865 is more substantial, and the school is now surrounded by colored property-owners, many of whom possess attractive and comfortable homes. It brought a number of intelligent families, who made their homes there, and there educated their children. Before that date there was not a single house owned by colored persons in connection with the school. Its first class in theology was graduated in 1871. Since then, up to 1886–7, it has sent out graduates from the different departments—theological, collegiate (scientific and classical), and normal. Hundreds of its under-graduates have become successful teachers and preachers, and others are to be found in various fields of usefulness. But the most remarkable thing is the fact that all who have been trained in its halls and on its grounds from early childhood have proved themselves most thorough and accurate in scholarship; also most laborious, industrious, and thrifty. From a school of one Principal and assistant, with only primary work, it has been developed with power to send out its graduates yearly with degrees conferred. It has now a working faculty consisting of six members. An art-room and a museum have been also added. The former is the gift of the lamented Rev. John F. W. Ware, and bears his name—"Ware Art-room."

When I had my official head-quarters at Baltimore I became acquainted with this gentleman, who was among the foremost who by personal efforts aided in raising funds to help feed and clothe the distressed and needy "contrabands of war," as General Butler in 1861 had declared the slaves coming within his lines. He was the pastor of a Unitarian Church in Baltimore at that time, but transferred his pastoral relations later to Boston. I called upon him while at his summer residence at Swamstead, near Lynn, Mass., when I was endeavoring to raise funds to furnish the university with models for an art-room. Said he: "I will give you one hundred dollars toward it." He did so, adding: "Whenever you are in need of one hundred dollars for any such purpose, you can always obtain it from me." The next year he gave me another hundred for the same, with which models were furnished. The museum was offered me by Prof. Ward for fourteen hundred dollars, and valued at two thousand. I laid the proposition before the trustees, and begged them to aid me in raising the sum; but not one volunteered, nor would any one touch it with a forty-rod pole. Finally I was allowed to put the museum in the building, with the understanding that I should raise the funds to meet the expenses, and when consummated should hand over the receipted bill in proof that it was paid for at no cost to the trustees. The cases were also put in at a cost of about three hundred dollars, which sum I also raised. These sums, with the interest, made the whole cost about eighteen hundred dollars, every cent of which I paid—about three hundred dollars coming from my own purse. It is now called Payne Museum. Both this and the art-room were obtained after I left the presidency of the institution.

In 1867–8 the Society for the Promotion of Collegiate and Theological Education at the West aided the institution in the sum of eighteen hundred dollars. After we were burned out we had erected the western wing of the new edifice of brick, but its walls were not only unpictured, its floors uncarpeted, but they were unplastered and rough. The good Secretary, Mr. Theron Baldwin, came at my request and saw the appalling obstacles. His soul was stirred, and his eloquent plea induced the society to vote this sum for our relief. In 1868–9 they again voted us a like sum, and although their funds did not enable them to make good the whole of this last amount, what we did receive was of signal good. From 1868 to 1875 the American Unitarian Association aided us in all about four thousand dollars. In 1868 Hon. Gerrit Smith sent us five hundred dollars, and the same year the equally noble Chief-justice Chase induced an English gentleman to send us three hundred dollars, and in his own last will and testament he left us ten thousand dollars. In 1869 we received through General Howard from the Freedmen's Bureau three thousand dollars, and again in 1870 from the same, by special act of Congress, twenty-five thousand dollars. We applied for fifty thousand dollars, receiving the indorsement of leading men in Xenia, and securing the influence of the State Legislature of Ohio. Our agent prepared to go to Washington, but on going to Cincinnati and finding insuperable difficulties in his way, he consulted Dr. Richard Rust, who told him he could not succeed without me, as I was not only at the head of the school, but had a greater knowledge of all its needs, a much more extensive acquaintance among the whites, and therefore a much stronger influence than any other party; that I must drop all, and go to Washington myself. This I did, the governor of Ohio giving me the documents ordered by the Legislature, and a letter of introduction to one of the supreme court judges, who gave me letters to the senators. Senator Sumner was at first opposed to granting it, as he claimed that the work of education was assigned to the States, and Congress should not make appropriations for such. I replied that the master minds of both races could be brought from the South; and, having been educated in Northern sentiments, Northern ideas, and Northern principles, would develop a nobler manhood and a broader patriotism than could be realized in the South for generations to come. This argument was used with all who made that objection, and all were overcome by it. Three times I had to meet the Committee on Education and Labor and answer all objections, the whole being a tedious affair. Every one was at last removed, but General Howard said that the funds had been so reduced and so many applications for aid had been made by other institutions that we could have but twenty-five thousand, which sum we received.

Small sums have been received from private individuals at various times, who thus testified to their confidence and exhibited their interest in us. May all be blessed abundantly. Concerning our benefactors whose earthly career has been finished we hope that they may "be rewarded at the resurrection of the just." Concerning those who are still living we pray that they and theirs may never lack a friend nor aid in the time of need or the day of adversity.

During the last decade (1876–1886) more institutions of learning have sprung into existence than in any preceding it. Among them are the Johnson Divinity School, located at Raleigh, N. C., now removed to Kittrell and called the Kittrell Industrial School; Allen University, in Columbia, S. C., founded by Bishop William F. Dickerson in 1881; Morris Brown University, but a primary school as yet, in Atlanta, Ga., opened in 1885, having one fine building chiefly through the efforts of Dr. (now Bishop) W. J. Gaines; Turner College, in Hernando, Miss., in 1881; the Scientific Normal and Divinity Institute, Jacksonville, Fla., projected under the administration of Bishop Wayman in 1883; Paul Quinn College, Waco, Tex., projected by Bishop J. M. Brown in 1872, and located at Austin, Tex., and kept in motion after he left the district by Bishop Ward, and given its present name by Bishop Cain. Several other schools have been named, some of which are only paper schools, while others have no existence even on paper. The projectors began before they were ready. Thousands of dollars have been spent in such fruitless efforts. The founding of a college requires a great deal of forethought and preparation. This is true of those who can command a deep, long, and wide purse. This is emphatically true of a poverty-stricken and illiterate people.

SUPPLEMENTARY READINGS

Coan, Josephus R. *Daniel Alexander Payne: Christian Educator.* Philadelphia: A.M.E. Book Concern, 1935.

Daniel, W. A. *The Education of Negro Ministers.* New York: George H. Doran, 1925; reprint, New York: Negro Universities Press, 1969.

Payne, Daniel Alexander. *History of the African Methodist Episcopal Church*. Nashville: n.p., 1891; reprint, New York: Johnson Reprint, 1968.

Talbert, Horace. *The Sons of Allen: Together with a Sketch of the Rise and Progress of Wilberforce University, Wilberforce, Ohio*. Xenia, Ohio: Aldine Press, 1906.

Wright, Richard R. *Bishops of the A.M.E. Church*. Nashville: A.M.E. Sunday School Union, 1963. Pp. 266–79.

28

ALEXANDER CRUMMELL

"The Regeneration of Africa"

Afro-American interest in Liberia waxed and waned according to conditions in the United States. Alexander Crummell (1819–98) went in 1853 on a civilizing mission to "redeem" Africa and remained in Liberia for two decades. Born of free parents in New York City, a graduate of Oneida Institute, and (despite being barred from General Theological Seminary) consecrated an Episcopal priest in 1844, Crummell exhibited great strength of character and intellectual gifts of a high order. More than eight thousand Afro-Americans had settled in Liberia when Crummell arrived. They differentiated themselves from the indigenous peoples by their American cultural orientation and their control of political and educational affairs. Crummell too held notions of the "crudeness" of African traditional life and the need for Christian civilizing influences. But he also championed the idea of "African Nationality" and the prospect of the "regeneration of Africa," both materially and spiritually. He eventually sided with those who sought improvement of the status of the ethnic Liberians. After a protracted struggle against the domination of the Americo-Liberian mulatto elite, Crummell returned to the United States for good. From 1873 to 1894, he served as rector of St. Luke's Episcopal Church in Washington, D.C. Upon his death in 1898, the Washington Bee hailed him as the "most educated Negro in America." The discourse, source of the following excerpt, was presented to the Pennsylvania Colonization Society in 1865.

The great principle which lies at the basis of all successful propagation of the Gospel is this, namely, the employment of all indigenous agency. Christianity never secures *thorough* entrance and complete authority in any land, save by the use of men and minds somewhat native to the soil. And from the very start of the Christian faith this idea has always been illustrated in the general facts of its conquest.

In the work of Jewish evangelization our Lord himself employed

Source: *Addresses and Discourses*. Springfield, Mass.: Wiley and Co., 1891. Pp. 438–46.

the agency of Jews. For the evangelization of Greeks, he employed, indeed, Jews, but Jews who had become *hellenized*. At an early period the Romans were to be brought under the influence of Christianity; and although the faith was introduced among them by an agency which was exotic, yet Romans themselves stamped the impress of the faith upon the Empire, and strangled nigh to death, in less than three centuries, its fierce and vulpine paganism. So, in like manner, it became rooted in the soil of Britain. So, likewise, at a later period, in Russia and Scandinavia. Hardly a generation passed away, in either of these cases, ere the zealous and adventurous pioneers of the new system resigned their work, and handed over their prerogatives to the hardy and convicted sons of the soil.

It seems clear, then, that for the evangelization of *any* country, the main instrumentality to be set to work is that of men of like sentiments, feelings, blood and ancestry, with the people whose evangelization is desired. The faith, so to speak, must needs become incorporated with a people's mental, moral, and even physical constitution—vitalize their being, and run along the channels of their blood.

Now this principle applies, in common with all other lands, to Africa. It is, under God, the condition of the success of the Cross throughout that vast continent.

All this, however, is but theory. The facts which more especially prove it, are the successful missions of the English in West Africa, both Episcopal and Wesleyan. Nothing can be more glorious than the heroic, almost god-like self-sacrifice of their missionaries, for nigh forty years, to introduce Christianity among the natives; nothing, on the other hand, more discouraging than the small results which at first followed their efforts. But by-and-by, one native and then another, and another was raised up, fitted and prepared to be preachers of the Gospel. The Christian faith had become engrafted upon the native stock. It swelled with the inspirations of their breath; it coursed along the channels of their veins. Then the truth began to spread; it had lodged itself in a new race and began to assert its authority in a new land. The new soil was genial; and the Divine principle, although transplanted, put forth all its original vitality. As when a new plant or seed is brought from some distant country to a new land, akin in soil and climate to its parent bed, it shoots up and spreads abroad with all its former vigor and luxuriance; so Christianity, so soon as it became indigenous to Africa, commenced a successful career; and now mission stations are to be found two thousand miles along the coast; catechists, by scores are employed; ministers are preaching the Gospel on the coast and in the interior. Missions conducted by native clergymen, are being carried into the strongholds of ancient, sanguinary kingdoms; and are advancing, with authority and power, up the great Niger, towards the very heart of the continent.

And in all this we see illustrated the great principle that, for the propagation of the faith, the main lever and agency must needs be indigenous. The faith, at first, is an exotic, in all new lands; but, in order to make its roots strike deep into the new soil, men, native in blood, lineage, feelings, and sentiments, must needs be raised up and put to active effort.

Now, the Almighty, in a most marvelous manner, has been providing just this agency, with almost every indigenous quality, for the propagation of the faith on the continent of Africa. Millions of the Negro race have been stolen from the land of their fathers. They have been the serfs, for centuries, on the plantations and in households, in the West Indies and the United States, of civilized and Christian people. By contact with Anglo-Saxon culture and religion, they have, themselves, been somewhat permeated and vitalized by the civilization and the Christian principles of their superiors. Numbers of them have become emigrants, settlers, denizens of a free Republic, and of thriving colonies of the British on the West Coast of Africa; and numbers more of them ever and anon emigrate from the lands of their past thraldom back, not unfrequently, to the very spots whence their parents were first stolen. And these emigrants almost invariably profess the faith of Jesus. They are *Christian* emigrants, journeying across the wide ocean, with Bibles, and Prayer Books, and Tracts, and Sermons, and family altars, seeking a new home amid the heathen population of Africa.

Now, I say, that when you send out such companies of people, you send Christianity to Africa; and I would fain emphasize this remark, and invite attention to it.

If you send a missionary to Africa, you send, indeed, a good, holy, faithful minister; but he is but an individual; he may, or he may not, plant Christianity in the field. The probability is that he will not; for the greatest of saints can only represent a partial Christianity. Hence the likelihood, the almost certainty is, that his work will have to be followed up by others. When, therefore, you send a single individual, as a missionary, you do not necessarily send Christianity to Africa; albeit you send a devoted Christian.

On the other hand, when you send out a *company of Christian emigrants*, you send a *church*. Planted on the coast of Africa, its rootlets burst forth on one side and another like the "little daughters" of the plantain in a tropical soil.

But facts are more powerful, more convincing than mere theories. I will, therefore, attempt briefly to illustrate this principle by facts:

1. The Presbyterians have a school in Pennsylvania called the "Ashmun Institute," for the training of colored men for missionary duty in Africa. A few years ago, three of these students left the United States with their families, as emigrants to Liberia. Now, when the Presbyterians sent forth this little company of Christians, they sent out organized Christianity to heathen Africa. In each of those little bands, there was "the church in the house," with the Bible and the preacher, and baptized children; the germs of a new outgrowth of Christianity in the future. Civilization, moreover, was allied to all their life, work and habits, in their new homes.

And these men, settled at Liberia, take root there; increase is given to their families there as well as here. Native heathen also come into their families, work for them in their gardens, in their work-shops, and on their farms; are touched by their civilized habits, and moved by their family prayers and Sunday teachings. As their children grow up, they, in their turn, become the centres, to other heathen, of new and wider influences, both civilizing and Christian. Native converts become incorporated with them in the household of faith. By-and-by these native converts raise up Christian children; who, in some cases, are married to persons of the emigrant stock; and thus the native and the emigrant blood, at times, *both* Christianized, flow, mingled together, through the veins of a new race, thoroughly indigenous and native.

Now, just *such* power, strength, and permanent influence cannot go forth from your foreign missionary; because he is an exotic. Beneath the burning sun of Africa he withers and pines away, and alas, too often dies, a glorious martyr for Christianity! And when he departs to paradise, his wife and children return to Europe or America, weak, enfeebled, bereaved; but they rarely have permanent influence in Africa!

The black Christian emigrant, on the other hand, is indigenous, in blood, constitution, and adaptability. Two centuries of absence from the continent of Africa, has not destroyed his physical adaptation to the land of his ancestors. There is a tropical fitness, which inheres in our constitution, whereby we are enabled, when we leave this country, to sit down under an African sun; and soon, and with comparative ease, feel ourselves at home, and move about in the land as though we had always lived there. Children, too, are born to us in our adopted country, who have as much strength and vitality as native children; and soon we find ourselves establishing families right beside those of our heathen kinsfolk.

Now you can easily see what a powerful influence that denomination of Christians—the Presbyterians—can wield by such an agency as I have described, to bless and save Africa. They send thither living, concrete, organic, indigenous Christianity in the young men and their families, trained at their Institute; send it there to abide; to be reproduced in their children; to be spread out in their families; and not to be an evanescent and fugitive thing, without root in the soil, and void of bud, and fruit, and flower; nor yet a tender exotic, needing a hot-house carefulness and nurture; but a thing of life and robustness, mindless of sun and dews, and storms and tempests, fitted to every circumstance of life and nature!

Such is the great power which the Almighty has given our Presbyterian brethren for planting Christianity in Africa.

2. But here is another illustration of the same power, which, just at this time, is given the Baptists of this country, for the same blessed work for Christianity and Africa. Only two months ago, one hundred and fifty colored Baptists in Virginia applied for passage to Liberia for themselves and children. No inducements were held out to them; no persuasions used among them. It was a spontaneous movement of their own. I may add, here, that I am told by a student in the Episcopal "Divinity School," in this city, that he had seen in Virginia colored Baptist ministers, men moved, we may believe, by the Spirit of God, who were seeking opportunities to get to Africa to preach the Gospel. These ministers, these emigrants, wish to go to Africa to *remain* there. They are seeking a home for themselves and their children in that, the land of their sires. They desire to go back to their fatherland, and to root themselves and their offspring in the ancestral soil, and to send down their blood and lineage, amid the scenes and the rights which were familiar to their unfortunate ancestors.

3. And now tell me what nobler plan could the great Baptist denomination fall upon, than just this providential movement, to effect that which is dear to their hearts, and to the hearts of all Christians—the redemption of Africa! And what a living thing would not their work be, if perchance, they could plant some half dozen compact, intelligent, enterprising villages of such Christian people, amid the heathen populations of West Africa!

4. But now, even at the risk of wearying you, I will advert briefly to one more distinct and providential illustration of this principle. There is the island of Barbadoes, a British colony; it contains a black population of 130,000 people. For years these people have had organizations among themselves, intending emigration to West Africa. Two years ago the President of Liberia extended an official invitation to the sons of Africa in the West Indies to come over to Liberia, and aid us in the great work of Christianity and civilization which God has imposed upon us. And the response from these our brethren was immediate. Just a

week before I sailed from Liberia, the brig "Corn," from Barbadoes, arrived in the "Roads of Monrovia" with 346 emigrants. The most of these persons were Episcopalians; well-trained handicraftsmen, skillful sugar-makers, intelligent, spirited, well-educated persons. Not merely hundreds, but *thousands* more of their kinsfolk and fellow-islanders, in Barbadoes, stand ready, nay, anxious, to colonize themselves in the Republic of Africa.

Whose work is this? Who has prompted this movement of Christian black men from Barbadoes, back to the land of their ancestors; laden with gifts, and talents; sanctified, as numbers of them are, by the spirit of grace? Who, but the Spirit of God is moving these Christian "remnants" of black society—this seed of civilization—from the West Indies and America, to the coast of Africa. Who but God himself has called and elected this germ of Christianity to a great work of duty in the land of their fathers? And what more facile and effectual means could the Episcopalians of this country use than this, that is to seize upon this movement to plant their own phase of Christianity in villages and towns along the coast, and in the interior of Africa?

Does any man doubt this assertion of distinctive providence? Come, then, with me for a moment to the West Coast of Africa—take your position, say at Sierra Leone; run your eye along the whole line of the coast, from Gambia to the Cameroons, and watch that steady, quiet, uninterrupted emigration of cultivated colored men, who are coming over from Jamaica, Antigua, Barbadoes, St. Kitts, St. Thomas and Demarara; many of them men who have "ate their terms" at the Inns of London; some graduates of Edinburg, St. Augustine's, Canterbury, Codrington College, and other great schools—coming over to the West Coast of Africa, and becoming merchants, planters, postmasters, government officials, lawyers, doctors, judges, and blessed be God, catechists and clergymen, at British settlements in Western Africa! Then go down two hundred miles to the Republic of Liberia, and see there 14,000 black emigrants from more than half of the States of America; and see there, too, how that God, after carrying on His work of preparation in the black race in America in dark, mysterious and distressful ways, has at length brought out a "remnant of them and placed them in a free Republic, to achieve high nationality, to advance civilization and to subserve the highest interests of the Cross and the Church!

I have rested this matter, this evening, almost, if not quite, entirely, upon the one single point, that is, THE EVANGELIZATION OF AFRICA. I can present and urge it upon no lower, no inferior consideration. I recognize the need of Trade, Agriculture, Commerce, Art, Letters and Government, as the collateral and indispensable aids to the complete restoration of my fatherland. That man must be blind who does not see *that*. But they are but *collateral* and auxiliary; not the end, and aim, and object of that divine will and providence which the Almighty has been working out by the means of institutions and governments, by afflictions and sufferings, and even oppressions, during the course of centuries. . . .

SUPPLEMENTARY READINGS

Akpan, M. B. "Alexander Crummell and His African 'Race Work': An Assessment of His Contribution in Liberia to Africa's 'Redemption.'" In *Black Apostles at Home and Abroad*, edited by David W. Wills and Richard Newman. Boston: G.K. Hall, 1982. Pp. 283–310.

Du Bois, W. E. B. *The Souls of Black Folk* [1903]. Edited by Herbert Aptheker. Milwood, N.Y.: Kraus-Thomson Organization, 1973. Chap. 12.

Moses, Wilson J. "Civilizing Missionary: A Study of Alexander Crummell." *The Journal of Negro History* 15, no. 2 (April 1975): 229–51.

Scruggs, Otey M. "We the Children of Africa in This Land: Alexander Crummell." In *Africa and the Afro-American Experience: Eight Essays*, edited by Lorraine A. Williams. Washington, D.C.: Howard University Press, 1977. Pp. 77–95.

Williams, Walter L. *Black Americans and the Evangelization of Africa, 1877–1900*. Madison: University of Wisconsin Press, 1982.

29

HENRY MCNEAL TURNER

Emigration to Africa

Henry McNeal Turner (1834–1915) began his ministerial career as an exhorter for the Methodist Episcopal Church, South. He withdrew from the white Methodists in 1858 and joined the African Methodist Episcopal Church. President Lincoln appointed him chaplain to the First Regiment of Colored Troops in 1863, and President Johnson designated him the first black chaplain in the regular army. Turner resigned to build up the A.M.E. Church in Georgia, where he was one of the founders of the Republican party. He served as bishop for the African Methodists in Georgia from 1880 to 1892 and wielded great influence among the freedmen. Their worsening plight after the end of Reconstruction caused Bishop Turner to view emigration to Africa as a positive solution to the "race problem" in America. The other bishops, however, did not support his "back to Africa" plans. Bishop Benjamin Tanner told the Pennsylvania Colonization Society, an auxiliary of the American Colonization Society, of which Turner was a vice president, that Afro-Americans had no desire to leave the United States. Turner took to the columns of the church paper, the Christian Recorder, *to defend himself and promote African colonization as a solution to the race problem. Turner's voice echoed eloquently but with little effect. The practical problems of large-scale emigration were overwhelming, and those most desperate to go had neither the resources nor the skills necessary to build up new settlements.*

JANUARY 4, 1883:

But, O Jumbo! there are a host of us who see our condition from another standpoint, and our future equally as differently, and that host believes Africa somehow is to give the relief for which our people sigh, and not the theories and speculations of Dr. Tanner, founded in moral philosophy though they be. A statesman of this country, in high repute, puts the murders and outrages perpetrated upon our people in the

Source: *Respect Black: The Writings and Speeches of Henry McNeal Turner.* Compiled and edited by Edwin S. Redkey. New York: Arno Press and *The New York Times,* 1971. Pp. 52–57.

South alone, since 1867, at two hundred thousand. Many of us think that the acclimating headaches of Africa, though sometimes possibly fatal, are not to be compared with such an orgy of blood and death.

Passing by much that might be said on the subject, I beg to say that Dr. Tanner does not represent even the ministry of his own church. I have asked at least fifty ministers of our church, before they knew my opinion, if they agreed with Dr. Tanner's African position, &c., and I am not sure that over half a dozen have answered in the affirmative, though I confess some have, but I have heard no man, minister or layman, endorse his attacks upon Dr. Blyden. I cannot speak for the North, but I know the South generally disapproves of them. . . .

There never was a time when the colored people were more concerned about Africa in every respect, than at present. In some portions of the country it is the topic of conversation, and if a line of steamers were started from New Orleans, Mobile, Savannah or Charleston, they would be crowded to density every trip they made to Africa. There is a general unrest and a wholesale dissatisfaction among our people in a number of sections of the country to my certain knowledge, and they sigh for conveniences to and from the continent of Africa. Something has to be done. Matters cannot go on as at present, and the remedy is thought by tens of thousands to be in a negro nationality. This much the history of our world establishes, that races either fossilized, oppressed or degraded must emigrate before any material change takes place in their civil, intellectual, or moral status, otherwise extinction is the sequence.

January 25, 1883:

Do you know of any instance in the world's history where a people shut out from all honorable positions, from being kings and queens, lords, dukes, presidents, governors, mayors, generals and all positions of honor and trust by reason of their race, ever amounted to anything? No sir, I will answer for you. There is no instance on record, except where preceded by revolution. People must have one like them on high to inspire them to go high. Jesus Christ had to take upon himself our very nature before his plan of redemption was a success. It required a God-man on the throne of the universe to awaken the aspiration of a world. And till we have black men in the seat of power, respected, honored, beloved, feared, hated and reverenced, our young men will never rise for the reason they will never look up. . . . Now all I contend for is this, that we must raise a symbol somewhere. We are bitten, we are poisoned, we are sick and we are dying. We need a remedy. Oh for some Moses to lift a brazen serpent, some goal for our ambition, some object to induce us to look up. Have we that object here? Is there any possibility of getting it here? I do not see it. Therefore I maintain that African colonization should be encouraged. Let the brave-hearted men, who are advanced enough to peril land and sea in search of better conditions, alone. Let them give us a respectable civil and Christian negro nation. Let them raise a banner standard that the world will respect and its glory and influence will tell upon the destinies of the race from pole to pole; our children's children can rest securely under the aegis, whether in Africa, Europe, Asia, America or upon the high seas.

February 22, 1883:

The learned Doctor [Tanner] reminds me of what the North did for our freedom, especially the Quaker City, and thinks I am not wise in pouring contempt upon the North, &c. I understand his language, conversely expressed, to say, you should thank the North, and your gratitude should be of such an overwhelming character as to blind your eyes to all her faults. I have only to reply that the North did no more than her duty. If my recollection is not at fault, Bancroft says in the first volume of his *History of the United States,* that all the slave ships that brought negroes to this country were fitted out in the North, except foreign slavers. Grant that the North did give her millions of sons and money to free the slave; grant that they died in countless numbers to furnish blood to cleanse the nation's escutcheon, it was only the visitation of the sins of the fathers upon the children. The North was as guilty in every respect as the South for the crime of slavery, both in its origin and perpetuity, and had the South been quiet and not inaugurated the rebellion, the North would have been chasing and catching slaves today for their masters. Negatively speaking, the South deserves more credit, more gratitude, more consideration in every way than the North. But I do not thank either of them. True, I am grateful for the services of a few individuals, but in the aggregate I have no thanks for either. . . .

This is the first time in my life I have found a colored man [Tanner] who had the effrontery to deny, or even attempt a partial negation of the inhuman treatment we have suffered at the hands of the nation's banditti. I employ the term "nation's" because the country could have stopped it long since had there been a disposition to do so. Dr. Tanner was evidently unaware of the force of his words. Instead of exaggeration, the half has never been told, nor will it ever be told till it shall be revealed at the great assize of all nations. And the most vexatious fact in this connection is that neither the North nor the South wants it told. Thus they close up the great dailies of the country to all communications which essay to recite the deeds of death and horror perpetrated upon our people, unless it bears the rumor of rape or some hideous crime which, nineteen times out of twenty, is a blatant-face untruth. But in the pregnant and thunder-charged words of Mr. Sumner, "Beware of the groans of wounded souls, since the inward sore will soon break out. Oppress not a single heart, for a solitary sigh has power to overthrow the world." . . . There is not a night, or a day either, the year round, that our people are not most brutally being murdered. The reign of blood and slaughter is but little less than it was ten years ago, if any. True, we do not hear so much of the Ku Klux and White Leaguers as formerly, but it is because the vampires have changed their tactics and not because there has been any material reformation in the condition of things.

The Doctor says that my only interest in Africa is to make it a city of refuge. That is not so, by any means. But suppose it were? Does not our existence depend upon providing for self? Would the Doctor ask me to crack a joke while my feet were burning in the furnace? Yes, I would make Africa the place of refuge, because I see no other shelter from the stormy blast, from the red tide of persecution, from the horrors of American prejudice. Self-interest, self-preservation, and self in all its aspects, have been the germ thoughts of all emigrations, immigrations and colonizations which have gone on since man left the foot of Babel tower, nor do I recollect an instance to the contrary, except when the old Romans used to colonize by force to impart to the aborigines a knowledge of their language. . . .

The Doctor, however, carries his assumptions too far when he says that if they will stop persecuting the negro, I will cease to plead for Africa. I am actuated by more lofty motives than any such sordid sentimentalities as he surmises. Before defining my position, however, I beg to say I recognize the fact of our American-ship as fully as he does. I know we are Americans to all intents and purposes. We were born here, raised here, fought, bled and died here, and have a thousand times more right here than hundreds of thousands of those who help to snub, proscribe and persecute us, and that is one of the reasons I almost despise the land of my birth. I have been commissioned twice as a chaplain in the United States army, and have seen colored men die by the thousands on the field of battle in defense of the country, yet their comrades in time of peace, who survived the war blast, I have also seen ignored on account of their color to such an extent that they could not procure a dinner on the public highway without going into some dirty old kitchen and sitting among the pots, while the riff-raff from the ends of the earth were treated as princes.

But why recount these evils and a thousand others that might fill forty volumes, when men of our race, high in prominence, are virtually saying your statements are not true, and if true, what matters it? Hush prattling about the ill treatment of your race and let us discuss theories, deal in technicalities, brag on some big white man. Let us see whether the term negro should be spelled with a large or small N. Stop talking about the negro doing anything by his own strength, brain and merits. Wait till the whites go over and civilize Africa, and homestead all the land and take us along to black their boots and groom their horses. Wait till the French or English find some great mines of gold, diamonds or some other precious metal or treasures, so we can raise a howl over it and charge the whites with endeavoring to take away our fathers' inheritance, and lift a wail for the sympathy of the world. So much for Dr. Tanner and his mistaken position. I will now define my African position:

1st. I do not believe any race will ever be respected, or ought to be respected, who do not show themselves capable of founding and manning a government of their own creation. This has not been done creditably yet by the civilized negro, and till it is done he will be a mere scullion in the eyes of the world. The Colonization Society proposes to aid him in accomplishing that grand result. They are our best friends and greatest benefactors, as the stern and inexorable logic of facts will soon show.

2nd. I do not believe that American slavery was a divine institution, but I do believe it was a providential institution and that God intends to make it the primal factor in the civilization and Christianization of that dark continent, and that any person whomsoever opposes the return of a sufficient number of her descendants to begin the grand work, which in the near future will be consummated, is fighting the God of the universe face to face.

3rd. The civilized world is turning its attention to Africa as never before, including all the Christian and semi-Christian nations under heaven except America, (for the Colonization Society gives the movement here no national character) and it seems to me as if the time had arrived when America, too, or the United States, at least, should awake to her share of duty in this great movement, as she owes us forty billions of dollars for actual services rendered, estimating one hundred dollars a year for two million of us for two hundred years.

4th. I am no advocate for wholesale emigration; I know we are not prepared for it, nor is Africa herself prepared for it. Such a course would be madness in the extreme and folly unpardonable. Five or ten thousand a year would be enough. I would like to take yearly those who are sent to the penitentiary, hung and lynched for nothing. With them alone I could establish a government, build a country and raise a national symbol that could give character to our people everywhere. Empty to me your jails and penitentiaries and in ten years I will give you a country before which your theories will pale and disappear.

5th. To me the nonsensical jargon that the climate of Africa is against us, we can't live there, the tropics are no place for moral and intellectual development, coming from the mouths of so-called intelligent men and would-be leaders, is simply ridiculous. If I were so ignorant, I would hold my tongue and pen and not let the people know it. Such language not only charges God with folly, but contradicts the teachings of both science and philosophy. They have not even learned that man is a cosmopolitan, that his home is everywhere upon the face of the globe. They have not read the history of this country that they pretend to love so well. They appear to be ignorant totally of the fearful mortality that visited the early settlers of his nation at Roanoke, Annapolis, Plymouth Rock, Baltimore, Philadelphia, Charleston, and there is nothing on record, possibly, that equals the fatality of Louisville, Ky. I read it with horror at this late day. Men seem to be ignorant on the philosophy of human existence, yet they plunge into the whirlpool of great questions with intoxicated impunity. God have mercy upon their little heads and smaller hearts, is my prayer.

6th. The last thing I will say at present by way of defining my position is this: I can see through the dim future a grand hereafter for the negro. I know he is increasing in the South much more rapidly than the whites, and the ration of increase, should it go on as it did from 1870 to 1880, will put the Southern States in the hands of the negro in 1900. I can see another thing, I can see that the Southern whites are apprehensive of such a contingency, and to avert it they are moving heaven and earth to procure white immigration, but with all they can get and all they can kill and starve to death in the penitentiaries, the fecundity of the negro is gaining on them rapidly. Now what is to be the end of this race? Why, the negro is going to beat, and the barriers to amalgamation are going to be widened. Thus white will continue to be white and black will continue to be black. All right; they are both God's colors and no sensible man will object. Now for the sequel: War, efforts of extermination, anarchy, horror and a wail to heaven. This is a gloomy picture, I know, but there is only one thing that will prevent its realization, and that is marriage between whites and blacks; social contact that will divide blood; blood that will unify and centralize feelings, sympathy, interest, and abrogate prejudice, race, caste, color barriers and hair textures, is the only hope of our future in this country. Now, let Dr. Tanner's learned committee come forth with a plan that will introduce intermarriage between the two races and the problem of our future is solved, the darkness is lifted and the breakers are passed. But unless that is done, there is no peaceable future here for the negro.

Lastly, I have not been in love with these self-improvised committees since 1872, when such a one waited upon the great Sumner and told him he had only to speak and the colored people of the nation would obey. Mr. Sumner, in an hour of weakness, did speak, and said, "Vote for Greeley." What followed, we too well know. I will not comment for the reason that gentlemen who were on the committee have lamented it ever since, if I am to credit their words to me. . . . I favor delegations of my race, when properly authorized, as much as anyone. I think it was a great mistake to abolish colored conventions, if it was done at the bidding of Mr. [Frederick] Douglass, that prince of negroes. A national colored convention has been greatly needed for the last seven years. If the Northern negro is satisfied with matters and things, we of the South are far from being. Indeed I have been thinking of calling one for the last twelve months; not political, but a civil and moral convention. Gov. [P.B.S.] Pinchback said to me, a few years ago, that the colored people should hold a national convention every three or four years till they ceased to have grievances and complaints. So says lawyer C. A. Ridout of Arkansas, and so say others. Such a convention is needed more, yes far more needed, than any more self-improvised committees.

SUPPLEMENTARY READINGS

Batten, J. Minton. "Henry M. Turner, Negro Bishop Extraordinary." *Church History* 7, no. 3 (September 1938): 231–46.

Redkey, Edwin S. *Black Exodus: Black Nationalist and Back-to-Africa Movements, 1890–1910.* New Haven: Yale University Press, 1969.

Redkey, Edwin S., ed. *Respect Black: The Writings and Speeches of Henry McNeal Turner.* New York: Arno Press and *The New York Times,* 1971.

Stuckey, Sterling. *The Ideological Origins of Black Nationalism.* Boston: Beacon Press, 1972.

Wilmore, Gayraud S. *Black Religion and Black Radicalism.* Second ed. Maryknoll, N.Y.: Orbis Books, 1983. Chap. 5.

30

AFRO-AMERICAN CATHOLICISM

The First Afro-American Catholic Congress, 1889

The federal census for 1890 reported approximately one hundred thousand Catholic Afro-Americans. A year earlier—in January 1889—representatives of the various black Catholic churches met for the first of three Afro-American Catholic congresses at St. Augustine's Church in Washington, D.C. In his welcoming address Cardinal Gibbons noted that this was the first time black Catholics had assembled to consider collectively their status in the church. Each "Colored Catholic" parish had been invited to send one delegate for every five hundred members or fraction thereof.

The Reverend Father Augustus Tolton, of Quincy, Illinois, attended this first congress. In 1886 he became the first American priest of pure African descent, having studied at the De Propanganda Fide in Rome. The Congress noted that significant gains in black Catholic membership had been made since the Civil War, mostly in the cities. Since Catholicism in the antebellum rural South was noteworthy for having survived at all, and since the European immigrants who swelled the ranks of urban Catholicism in the North had exhibited considerable hostility toward blacks in the cities, these gains were small comfort to the delegates asking for a more aggressive Catholic outreach to the Afro-American populace. At the conclusion of the 1889 congress the delegates addressed their Catholic fellow citizens.

ASSEMBLED IN [the] capital of our country, on the opening of the year 1889, in the presence and under the patronage of His Eminence Cardinal Gibbons, Archbishop of Baltimore, and with the approval of our Catholic hierarchy we delegates of the Colored Catholics of the United States, deem it proper, at the close of the deliberations, to address our Fellow Catholic-citizens of this country, and to put before them a summary of the work we have accomplished.

Source: "Address of the Congress to Their Catholic Fellow-Citizens of the United States." From *Three Catholic Afro-American Congresses*. Cincinnati: The American Catholic Tribune, 1893. Pp. 66–72.

Several hundred in number, gathered from the various States of the Union—from the Mississippi to the Atlantic, from the Great Lakes to the Gulf—we opened our convention with Solemn Mass, of which the celebrant was the Rev. Augustus Tolton, our trusted and worthy brother in race as in creed, in whose elevation to the priesthood we rejoice; and in the presence of Cardinal Gibbons, who graciously condescended to be with us, and who, by his words of encouragement, stimulated our efforts.

In thus meeting, even under such encouraging patronage, to consider, in a public manner and for the first time in our history the needs and claims of our race, it was natural to feel that a herculean task awaited us. But, relying on the assistance of the Holy Ghost, whose inspiration, we have no doubt prompted the call of this assembly; confiding also in the spirit of ardent patriotism, of Christian Prudence and humble forbearance actuating the hearts of each and every member of this Convention; and encouraged in our labors by the beautiful spectacle of nearly two hundred intelligent and Christian men, representing every section of this vast country, we congratulate ourselves upon the results at which we have arrived.

Although we did not, at the outset, presume to think that this Congress could be other than an humble experiment—although we do not, even still, presume to claim that its results be other than an entering wedge in the breaking of the mighty wall of difficulties lifted up for centuries against us and a mere preliminary step in the progressive march and final regeneration of our people—yet we feel that we can safely present these results to the entire world, assured that they will mark the dawn of a new and brighter era in the history of our race in every land wherein it is established.

While we may well rejoice over the progress made by our Colored fellow-citizens within the last quarter of a century, since they have been permitted to enjoy, to some extent, the inalienable rights given to every man in the very dawn of creation, we must admit—only to lament it— the fact that the sacred rights of justice and of humanity are still sadly wounded—are still immeasurably obstructed—even in a country where liberty, so long an exile, so long abused, so long a wanderer the world over has found at last a secure refuge, a permanent home, a grand and lasting temple.

Knowing too well, however, that time alone, accompanied and overshadowed by the providential shaping of an all wise God, will eventually remove such obstructions. Knowing, too that our divinely established and divinely guided Church, ever the true friend of the down trodden, will, by the innate force of her truth, gradually dispel the prejudices un-happily prevailing amongst so many of our misguided people, and therefore, anxious not to forestall in any way the time marked by God for bringing about this great work, we feel confident that this solemn expression of our convictions, of our hopes and of our resolutions, will have at least the advantage of proving that we—the Catholic representa-tives of our people—have earnestly contributed our humble share to the great work for whose final accomplishment all our brothers are ardently yearning.

The education of a people being the great and fundamental means of elevating it to the higher planes to which all Christian civilization tends, we pledge ourselves to aid in establishing, wherever we are to be found, Catholic schools, embracing the primary and higher branches of knowledge, as in them and through them alone can we expect to reach the large masses of Colored children now growing up in this country without a semblance of Christian education.

Aware of the importance and necessity of literary societies as a means of completing our young men's training and attainments, we declare that this Congress encourage all such societies as an abundant and fruitful source of social and intellectual improvement.

As manliness and sobriety go hand in hand, we strenuously exhort all our fellow citizens to practice the self-sacrificing virtue of temper-ance, either individually or in the societies already existing in connec-tion with the Church.

We appeal to all labor organizations, trade unions, etc. to admit Colored men within their ranks on the same conditions as others are admitted. We appeal, likewise, to all factory owners and operators, tele-graph and railroad companies, store and shopkeepers, to give employ-ment to Colored people, men and women, in all departments of their business, as help may be required, without discrimination, and on the merit of their individual capacity, intelligence and integrity.

Conscious that one of our greatest and most pressing needs is the establishing of industrial schools, where the hand of our youth may be trained, as well as the mind and heart, we heartily endorse every move-ment tending to promote such a good work.

Sincerely deploring the fate of so many children, so many sick and indigent persons thrown upon the mercy of the world, we should not forget the consequent need of orphanages, hospitals and asylums for the care of those unfortunates whom Divine Providence thus entrusts to the care of their stronger brothers.

We condemn in the most emphatic terms the custom of renting to our people, or constructing for the purpose of renting to them poorly lighted, poorly ventilated and roughly planned tenement houses, as they are not only dangerous to public health, but are moreover hot beds of vice and consequently a standing menace to morality.

In this connection we desire to draw attention to the discrimination practiced by real estate owners and agents against respectable Colored people in refusing to rent them desirable property because of their color, or, when renting to them, of charging a higher rate of rental than would be charged other people under similar circumstances.

Having learned in this Congress the admirable and remarkable efforts thus far accomplished for the benefit of the African race, either in this country or on the African continent, by the various religious orders of the Catholic Church, we tender these zealous and noble hearted pioneers of the Gospel the expression of our admiration and gratitude, and trust they will continue the work of devotion thus done for the regeneration of our people.

It is, too, a pleasure to us to endorse the noble stand which the AMERICAN CATHOLIC TRIBUNE, to which this Congress owes so much, has from the start taken to furnish our people with useful and entertaining reading.

In conclusion, after pledging ourselves to carry out to the full extent of our ability the solemn wishes of the Third Plenary Council of Baltimore, we express a hope that the fruits of this Convention will be far reaching and lasting and that our Catholic brethren throughout the land will generously help us by their sympathy and fellowship in the great and noble work which we have thus inaugurated for the welfare—social, moral and intellectual—of our entire people. Respectfully, Robt. L. Ruffin, Boston, Mass.; Nicholas Gaillard, St. Paul, Minn.; P. A. M'Dermott, Pittsburgh, Pa.; Washington Parker, New York; R. N. Wood, New York; Lincoln Valle, St. Louis, Mo.; John R. Rud, Cincinnati, Ohio; Jas. A. Spencer, Charleston, S.C.; D. S. Mahoney, Pittsburgh Pa.; W. H. Smith, District of Columbia; Dan A. Rudd, Ohio; Wm. S. Lofton, District of Columbia, chairman, committee. The report was unanimously adopted.

SUPPLEMENTARY READINGS

"Black Catholics and Their Church." America 142, no. 12 (March 29, 1980).

Collins, John T. "Black Conversion to Catholicism: Its Implications for the Negro Church." Journal for the Scientific Study of Religion 10, no. 3 (Fall 1971): 208–19.

Foley, Albert S. *God's Men of Color: The Colored Catholic Priests of the United States, 1854–1954*. New York: Farrar, Strauss, 1955.

Gillard, John Thomas. *Colored Catholics in the United States*. Baltimore: The Josephite Press, 1941.

Miller, Randall M. "The Failed Mission: The Catholic Church and Black Catholics in the Old South." In *The Southern Common People: Studies in Nineteenth-Century Social History*. Edited by Edward Magdol and Jon Wakelyn. Westport, Conn.: Greenwood Press, 1980. Pp. 37–54.

31

ELIAS C. MORRIS

1899 Presidential Address to the National Baptist Convention

The Reverend Joseph H. Jackson, also a perennial holder of the National Baptist presidential chair, wrote: "For 27 years the name E. C. Morris was synonymous with the National Baptist Convention." Elias C. Morris was born in 1855 near Springplace, Georgia, of slave parentage. He earned his living as a shoemaker, felt the call to the ministry, and served Baptist churches in Arkansas, where he helped organize the Arkansas Baptist State Convention. Morris was active in the Baptist Foreign Mission Convention in the 1880s, which after protracted debate united with the National Baptist Convention (1880) and the National Baptist Education Convention (1893) to form the National Baptist Convention, Inc., in 1895. As the new president of the united body, Morris weathered numerous storms, including liberal versus conservative debates, controversy over control of the publishing board, and the secession in 1897 of a group that called itself the Lott Carey Missionary Convention. The major schism of 1915, resulting in the formation of the National Baptist Convention, Unincorporated, was still in the future when President Morris addressed the parent body at its 1899 convention in Nashville. As the century drew to a close, he took inventory of the strengths and weaknesses of the largest black denomination in the United States, claiming nearly 1.7 million members.

Brethren of the Convention, Ladies, and Gentlemen:

Again, by permission of a kind Providence, I have the honor of coming before you to deliver my annual address as President of your great Convention. I congratulate you upon the wonderful record and unparalleled progress made by the Baptists since the organization of this Convention. It came into existence at the right time and for the very purposes it has so ably served—viz., to save this wing of our great and invincible denomination from disgrace; to show that in the onward

Source: *Sermons, Addresses and Reminiscences and Important Correspondence.* Nashville: National Baptist Publishing Board, 1901. Pp. 93–103.

movement of the great army of God in the world Negro Baptists are a potent factor. Until thrown into separate organization, such as this, it was not known what part those of our race in Baptist churches were bearing in the mighty conquest against the kingdom of darkness and in the upbuilding of the Master's kingdom on earth.

The wisdom which dictated such an organization was, in my opinion, divine. Had it not been divine, the strong and well-organized forces which have conspired to overthrow every enterprise put on foot by this Convention would have succeeded. But I am glad to say that instead of being overthrown, the Convention and its enterprises are stronger to-day than at any time before, and it has, by its peerless record, drawn to it many who once stood in open rebellion against its objects. It has been my opinion for some time that the leaders in this Convention have been for many years misunderstood, and, therefore, misrepresented, and that when the real objects and policy of the leaders are fully known all opposition will cease, and we will have the encouragement and coöperation of all the great Baptist societies in the country.

I wish to repeat what I have said on several occasions: that this Society entertains no ill will toward any other Christian organization in the world. It seeks to be on friendly terms with all, and the charge that this organization means to draw the color line, and thereby create prejudice in "Negro" Christians against "white" Christians, is without foundation. We admit, however, that practically, and not constitutionally, the color line has been drawn by the establishment of churches and schools for the "colored people" and the employment of missionaries, colporters, etc., to the colored people, which has resulted in the organization of associations and conventions by the Negroes in more than half of the States in the Union. And since these organizations exist, it is the duty of all to do everything in their power to build up the cause of Christ in and through these agencies.

But if these separate organizations did not exist, there is a reason for the existence of a National Baptist Convention, because, owing to the agitation of the slavery question, the white Baptists of the North and South had divided into two societies, represented respectively by Northern Baptists and Southern Baptists and when the cause of the division had been removed, the Northern Baptists went immediately to work to educate and evangelize the emancipated. The Southern white people soon fell in line and began by a system of taxation to aid the emancipated in acquiring a common school education, and many of the Southern white ministers lent their aid in church work. But their organizations remained separate and are separate to-day. Hence, it was one of the prime objects of the promoters of this Convention to obliterate all sectional lines among Baptists and have one grand national society, which would know no North, no South, no East, no West; and in this we have been successful. From Maine to California we are one, notwithstanding the efforts of designing men to disrupt the Convention by making false publications concerning it. If you will pardon the particular reference, I will say that one of our number who for three years held official position in this Convention had published in a little paper out in North Carolina the startling statement that the "Convention has departed from the New Testament standard and has turned into an ecclesiastical body; and that it exists for political purposes, the President exercising his powers the year round, attempting to dictate the policy for one million seven hundred thousand Baptists." Others of our ranks have styled us ingrates—all because we

> "Dare to be a Daniel,
> Dare to stand alone!
> Dare to have a purpose firm!
> Dare to make it known!"

But against all we have marched steadily on, and disproved all that has been said, until we have enlisted the coöperation of the most thoughtful Negro Baptists throughout the civilized world. We have endeavored to avoid any entangling alliances with other Baptist organizations, but have prayed for and sought to maintain friendly relations with all. I cannot account for the apparent disposition of some of our Baptist societies to ignore utterly the existence of the National Baptist Convention. Since the Negro Baptists in all the States of this great Union are in harmony with the work of this Convention and are contributors to its objects, there can be no good reason why any organization should attempt to form alliances with the respective States to do the very work which the Convention is endeavoring to do. In the matter of Cuban missions, notwithstanding the fact that this Convention has declared its purpose to do mission work in Cuba, other Baptist societies which had a similar purpose in view, consulted and even had correspondence with persons not officially connected with the National Convention upon the matter of coöperation. This breach of fraternal courtesy is not understood, except it be that others think that they can more easily handle our people by having them divided than by recognizing an organization with an official Board or Boards empowered by the constitution to act for the whole body. That the time will come when all the Baptist societies in America will recognize the existence of this Society, I have not the slightest doubt; but for reasons known only to themselves they have not done so yet.

A prominent minister of our denomination told me a few weeks ago at Greenville, Miss., that he had opposed the work of the National Baptist Convention because he did not think it possible to get the Negro Baptists of this country organized, and that their notions of church independence and church sovereignty were such as to preclude any such thing as a national organization. "But," says he, "I see you are about to get them together." I was a bit modest in giving a reply at that time, but I will assure you, my brethren, that the time is not far away when our organization will be so systematic that at the pressing of a button the Baptists from Maine to California and from the Canadian border to the Gulf of Mexico will spring to action as one man, and there will be a oneness of faith, a oneness of purpose in holding forth the truths of that Book which teaches that there is but one God.

I stated that the Convention had declared its purpose to do mission work in Cuba. And it did, at the meeting held in Kansas City one year ago, appoint a commission to visit the island with a view of ascertaining the moral, religious, and educational status of the Cuban people. An appeal was made to the churches to send up money to pay the expenses of the commissioners, and I am glad to say that many churches responded to the appeal and sent money to the Treasurer of our Convention. The commission, owing to the unsettled state of affairs, thought it would be a useless expenditure of money to go there at the time designated by the Convention; hence, the money sent is now in the treasury subject to the orders of the Convention. The principal points in Cuba had been entered through the agency of our Foreign Mission Board and other Baptist societies before the time had come for the committee to go out, so that we may say, Baptist missions are already under way in Cuba. Providence seems to have favored us in that Rev. Campbell and wife were secured by our Board, and that Dr. C. T. Walker and Rev. Richard Carroll were given chaplaincies in the army. Dr. Walker succeeded in gaining one hundred conversions while there, and you may surmise the rest. We are in duty bound to aid in carrying the Gospel to the Cuban people. Like the black troopers who went up El Caney and saved the lives of their white comrades from destruction, so must the Negro Baptists of this country join their white brethren in carrying the Gospel of the Son of God to that people.

The Philippine Affair

Before the Cuban question had been settled and Spain had been forced to take her barbarous hand off those people, a war broke out in the Philippine Islands, and our country is one of the principals in that conflict. The United States, having given Spain $20,000,000 for the Spanish possessions in the Archipelago, attempted to secure those rights and was met by all the force the Filipinos could command. While the scene of operation is a great way off, the situation is far more serious than is generally thought. More than 40,000 Americans are there exposed to the malarial conditions of the country and the determined spirit of a relentless foe.

The policy of our government in the prosecution of the Philippine war has been severely criticised, and even now, many are openly opposing the further prosecution of the war. Necessarily, Christians are opposed to armed conflicts and bloodshed. And we contend that all international questions can and should be settled by arbitration. The war which is now upon us has divided our country into two strong factions—viz., Expansionists and Anti-Expansionists, and the contention growing out of the points of this division makes the horizon dark with commotion, and calls to Christians everywhere to appeal to that God who holds the reins of governments, that he might intervene and establish peace among the nations.

Law and Order Versus a Race Problem

In our domestic relations to this country, many of our people feel that they have a just cause to complain of the treatment they receive at the hands of the people among whom they live. And the man is indeed blind who cannot see that the race feeling in this country has grown continually for the last two decades. But since the organic law of the land stands unimpeached, there is room left to inquire, Is it only race hatred, or is it not the out-growth of a lawless spirit which has taken possession of many of the people in this country? Perhaps it appeared when this spirit of anarchy first took hold in this country that it was directed to a particular class or race of people. But that can no longer be said. For, indeed, it is evident that those who will forget themselves so far as to take the laws into their own hands and hang, shoot down, and burn helpless Negroes, will ere long turn and slaughter one another. Indeed, such is the case now. Mob violence is not confined to any particular section of our country. The same disregard for law and order which exists in the South when a Negro is involved, exists in the North when the miners or other laborers are involved. The people have become crazed and have lost their respect for the law and the administrators of the law, and unless there is a change no man will be secure in life or property. The apologies which are being given for the mob's shameful work, by no means remove the fact that there is a growing disregard for the laws of our country. I would counsel my people everywhere to be law-abiding, no matter how much they may suffer thereby. It does not stand to reason that the whole race is a set of cowards because the inhuman treatment administered to members of our race is not resented. But one thing is true: the men who will take the laws into their own hands and thereby prevent the piercing rays of the letter and spirit of the law from shining through the courts upon the crimes committed, are themselves a set of cowards. Ministers of the Gospel and good people everywhere should lift their voices against all classes of crime which is blackening the record of our country. The man who will not lift his voice in defense of the sacredness of the home and the chastity of the women in this country, is unworthy to be called a man. It is but right that the man who breaks over the sacred precincts of the home and perpetrates a dastardly deed—it is but right that he be made to pay the penalty of the inhuman act. But let all such be done by and through the law. The wisest and most prudent men of our country foresee the evils which threaten the perpetuity of our republican institutions if the present disregard for law and order be kept up. The agitations which are going on will soon bring a reaction. Reason will again be enthroned; the laws of the country, like the laws of God will be supreme; and from the least to the greatest, the people will "submit to every ordinance of man, for the Lord's sake." Those who are inclined to the opinion that there is a great "Race Problem" confronting us, are asked to look beyond racial lines for a moment and behold the civil strife in many of the States in the Union where the State militia, United States marshals and sheriffs with strong guard, are called upon to protect life and property, to stand and guarantee the moving of the wheels of commerce, while the cries of hungry women and children force husbands, fathers, and brothers to wage open conflict with the administrators of the law, and then they will modify their opinion as to a race problem and agree that a serious law and order problem confronts the people of this country.

Local Dissension

The work of the National Baptist Convention has been somewhat hindered by local dissensions, most notably in Georgia and Virginia. The National Convention officers have endeavored to steer clear of local disturbances which have divided our brethren in several of the states, notwithstanding the fact that in one State (Virginia), the contention was made that the National Convention was responsible for the opposition to the cooperative plan as carried on by the Home Mission Society. The charge was made without reason. No men regret more than the officers of this Convention that our people should divide into factions in their state and national work; nor have the officers of the Convention at any time interfered with the coöperative plans adopted in any of the states. We have frequently expressed ourselves in favor of coöperation in all lines of Christian work, and have not changed our opinion in the matter. But when I say this, I mean to be understood as favoring that the plans to be drawn and the conditions to be met and followed should be mutually agreed upon by all the parties concerned in the work; that the plans should be such as not to lift up one and humiliate the other; but to place all upon absolute equality in Christian work, making fitness the only essential in promotion of one above the other. But recent developments go to show that this country is not yet ready for the kind of coöperation I have in mind. I insist, however, that coöperation in any of the states which will force a division of the Baptists in their organizations of long standing, should be discontinued and the plans so changed as to meet the reunited body. The National Baptist Convention does not hope to gain anything by reason of these divisions, but pleads for unity in every state, even though, for the time being, the Convention should lose all its support in those states.

District Convention

Much has been said concerning the utility of a District Convention. At first it was said that the organization was to antagonize the National Baptist Convention in Foreign Mission work. But the leaders of the movement insisted that they had no such purpose, and made the representation at the Kansas City meeting that they proposed to work in harmony with the National Baptist Convention; but recent developments go to show that the leaders of the District Convention have endeavored to induce some of our missionaries to resign work under the Foreign Mission Board and accept work under the District Convention Board. If this be true, and the issues are thus drawn, without any words of abuse or ill-feeling toward the promoters of the District Convention, the National Baptist Convention will proceed to occupy the entire field in so far as our representatives are received by the churches. There can be no doubt of the people being in favor of one grand national society among the colored Baptists, and any effort or scheme to defeat that object will be repudiated.

Foreign Missions

The all-important question of the hour is that of Foreign Missions. The Foreign Mission Society is the oldest of our national organizations and has a greater claim upon our people than any other, for it indeed represents the spirit and mission of the Master, as well as his Church. No man can be true to Christ and refuse to support the cause of missions. And, yet, I am sorry to say, that many of our churches have turned a deaf ear to the urgent appeals of the Board for means to support our missionaries, and have really joined in with our enemies to deride the Board when it failed to pay the salaries promptly.

While there has not been as much adverse criticism during the present year as the past, there has been some. Our Baptist papers have been more considerate of the Board's responsibilities, and have not permitted so many things which are intended to impede the progress of the Foreign Mission work, to find circulation through them.

It has been difficult for the Board to keep in harmony with some of the workers in South Africa. The Board deemed it wise and expedient that Rev. R. A. Jackson be dropped from the list of missionaries, and I am informed that he was paid up in full. I am of the opinion that the Board should place a ticket at the disposal of Brother Jackson in case he desires to return to this country. Brother and Sister Tule have resigned, and I am told that their salaries were paid in full. This leaves only eleven workers on the field at this time. I am of the opinion that much of the dissatisfaction arose on account of the fact that our tireless and earnest Corresponding Secretary does not give enough personal attention to the duties of his office. No man can give satisfaction in that office who attempts to traverse the country from one end to the other. If the churches of this country are to be reached and stirred up to their duty in the work of Missions, it must be done by a system different from the one followed for the last five or six years. I have not the slightest doubt that the Foreign Mission Board has done the best it could, under the circumstances. But with a little more aggressiveness on the part of the officers of that Board, many of the circumstances which hinder the work very materially will be removed. A new impetus must be given to this department of our work. We can no longer hope to retain the confidence and respect of other peoples of the world, unless we do more for the redemption of the heathen, and especially those of our fatherland. If it should appear that we are a little selfish in our missionary operations, we can offer the just apology that the heathen of Africa are by far the most neglected of any on the globe—less money is being given for

their evangelization than for any others. This Convention will not rise
to the full dignity of a great missionary organization until it has at least
fifty active workers on the field. This can and should be done. As the
Foreign Mission Board will give a full report of its work for the year, I
shall not say more on this theme just now, but will ask you to consider
some recommendations respecting the work of the Board which I will
mention later.

Home Mission Board

The Home Mission Board was constitutionally established in September, 1895. But in 1896 it brought into existence one of the most notable
heritages the Negro Baptist ever did, or ever will have, in that our Publishing House was then established. This enterprise was started with
nothing save faith in God and the justice of the cause, backed by Negro
brain and ambition. And to-day ten thousand dollars' worth of real
property, sixteen thousand dollars' worth of printing material and machinery, an average monthly distribution of nearly two thousand dollars'
worth of periodicals, sixty-eight ardent workers and writers of our own
race, causing a pay-roll amounting to one hundred dollars per day, speak
out in one tremendous voice and tell whether or not we have made
progress. The sun has forever gone down on any race of people who will
not encourage and employ their literary talent. How could the Negro
Baptists ever hope to be or do anything while they were committing literary suicide? From year to year scores of our young men and women
were graduating from school without the slightest hope or encouragement, in a land where the color of their skin debars them from a liberal
or equal chance with others. Were we to stand still and do nothing?
No. Our Home Mission Board put forth an effort to remedy this condition to some extent, and it has been successful so far.

The Baptists have read a little history, and are endeavoring to
profit by the mistakes and useful deeds of others. They find that the literary standing of the Greeks and Romans keeps them before the world
as a vivid example of ancient progress, and they are quoted with pride
the world over by many of the ripest scholars of the day. Furthermore,
we will find by reflection that although the former were the slaves of
the latter, by the excellent reputation of Grecian philosophers, teachers,
etc., the Romans at the same time were only too glad to bow at the
Grecians' feet to learn from them the secret of that higher power which
intellect wields over mere brute force. The Greeks were able to give this
knowledge, and never would have become slaves had they only watched
carefully their true literary standing, and not gone off into skepticism,

and the variegated porch of the poets would, no doubt, have still been in use had it not been that "cooks were in as great demand as philosophers." It has been well said that "no man who persists in thinking can be kept in bondage."

If we mean to improve, why should we not make an attempt at the preparation of our Sunday school literature as well as a few books and papers to which we can lay claim? In religion, the key to which comes from the Bible, we must not, as a great Christian society, be found wanting. Then, we must not agree for others to take all the advantage of studying and then writing the Bible lessons as presented to our Sunday schools. If the Negro had no chance to study and interpret the Holy Scriptures, he could only be expected to stand off and talk about what has been prepared by somebody else, and never be able to give authority for what he holds. If we are to preach and teach, we must have some personal, unbridled knowledge of our subjects, and the interest which is at the bottom of this knowledge is caused by the taking on of responsibility. If we have to go through the same test of others (and we do), why not have the same advantages?

The progressive Negro Baptists deliberated on all these things for four or five years, and have consequently given some of their business managers a chance to manage business, their bookkeepers opportunity to keep books, their printers and binders a chance to print and bind, their Bible students and writers impetus to study and write, and their thousands of anxious Sunday school students, both young and old, opportunity to get their lessons from books made by their own brothers in color.

Although the publication of Sunday school periodicals has proved to be an expedient work of Home Missions, this has not been the only work of our Home Board. It is doing no small amount of missionary work in supplying needy stations and in the support of missionary workers. In this latter work the Board hopes to enlarge its operations in the near future.

Educational Board

The progress made by this Board has been very slow, but the plans which have been laid are well laid. It has continued the publication of the magazine under very stringent circumstances. Through the efforts of the Corresponding Secretary, arrangements have been made which will insure the regular and permanent issuance of the magazine from the Publishing House at Nashville. I regret very much that the Board has not yet undertaken the formation of a federation of the schools owned

by our people, with a view to aiding them through means solicited by
the Board. It is quite evident to me that these institutions cannot become the beneficiaries of philanthropic people until a proper channel is
created through which their gifts may be conveyed.

Our B. Y. P. U

Too much cannot be said in commendation of the movement of our
Baptist young people. We have a vast army in our churches who are
yet to be developed into practical, useful Christians, and the effort to
form a national organization should meet with the encouragement of
all lovers of our grand old Church. Thousands of the best and most
highly cultivated young men and women of the race are in our churches,
and are capable of performing any and all the duties necessary to lead
our young people to success. There is no reason why all the literature
used by our B. Y. P. U.'s should not be produced by our own folks. For
the first time in the history of our Convention one session will be devoted to the young people's work.

A Look Ahead

Thirty-six years have passed since the shackles of slavery were broken
from the limbs of our people in this country. And these have been years
of trial and conflict of which the Negro Baptists have borne no little
part. In this brief period they have succeeded in building more schools
and colleges than any other denomination of Negro Christians, and
have enrolled as members of their churches more than all the rest combined. For this glorious heritage we sincerely thank God, and have a
heart full of love for all who have aided in any way to bring about such
a condition. But the fact that such a vast army has volunteered to follow the lead of those who contend for the principles enunciated at Olivet
and for which the Apostles suffered and died; for which Bunyan, Hall,
Roger Williams, Spurgeon, and an innumerable host of others battled to
uphold, it is but meet that we pause to ask: What of the future? A very
large number of the one million seven hundred thousand Negro Baptists are crude and undeveloped. They know but little of the practical
side of Christianity. The work of developing these that they may become the safe guardians of the undying principles which have distinguished our Church in all ages of the Christian era, is no small task.
But I assure you, my brethren, that we have the men and means to keep
our organization abreast of the times. And we will keep it so if we will
only be united and submit to proper leadership, I have no doubt that
the census of 1900 will show nearly two million Negro Baptists in this

country. Can you as leaders trust that host to support the present and future enterprises as you trusted them in the past to build and support churches all over this land? The charge of mutiny seldom ever comes against a Baptist; and as they have been loyal and true to their local organizations, so will they be to this Convention and every enterprise put in motion by it.

We are nearing the close of the present century, the most remarkable in many respects of all the centuries since the dawn of creation. And, without reference to the wonderful achievements in steam, printing, and electricity, and many more unparalleled discoveries and inventions, I come to say that when the light from the eternal hills announced the birth of the nineteenth century, our race—our fathers and mothers— groaned in the grasp of slavery, and held the place of goods and chattels. But by the direction of an unerring providence, when a little past the meridian of the century, a decree was handed down that the "slaves are and henceforth shall be free." Hence, I conclude that one of the marvels of the century will be that although it opened and looked for sixty-three years on a race of slaves, it closes with that same race a happy, free people, having built more churches and school houses, in proportion to their numbers, than any people dwelling beneath the sun. While the flickering light and agonizing groans of the nineteenth century are being lost in the misty and retreating past, let us look ahead. A little less than sixteen months from now that tireless steed, Time, will come forth and announce the birth of the twentieth century. Already in the distance can be heard the thunder of his neck and the fury of his nostrils, and the inhabitants of the world are preparing to greet his coming. Many of the great Christian societies are planning to make the opening year the most important and aggressive in Christian missions since the beginning of the New Dispensation. Some are asking for a million dollars, some for half a million, and some for still less. And as I see these great societies line up as if on dress parade and call for more men and means to go more strongly against the power of darkness, I am forced to ask: What is the duty of the Negro Baptists? The answer comes back that as the nineteenth century opened upon us as slaves and closed upon us as freemen, so may the Gospel, borne on the tongues of the liberated, set at liberty during the twentieth century, the millions bound in heathen darkness.

SUPPLEMENTARY READINGS

Boone, Theodore Sylvester. *A Social History of Negro Baptists*. Detroit: Historical Commission of the National Baptist Convention, U.S.A., 1952.

Brawley, Edward M., ed. *The Negro Baptist Pulpit*. Philadelphia: American Baptist Publication Society, 1890; reprint, Freeport, N.Y.: Books for Libraries Press, 1971.

Freeman, Edward A. *The Epoch of Negro Baptists and the Foreign Mission Board, National Baptist Convention, U.S.A., Inc.* Kansas City, Kansas: Central Seminary Press, 1953.

Jackson, Joseph Harrison. *A Story of Christian Activism: The History of the National Baptist Convention, U.S.A., Inc.* Nashville: Townsend Press, 1980. Chap. 2.

Jordan, Lewis G. *Negro Baptist History, U.S.A., 1780–1932*. Nashville: The Sunday School Publishing Board, National Baptist Convention, 1936.

32

ELSIE W. MASON

Bishop C. H. Mason, Church of God in Christ

In 1907, blacks and whites from all over the nation flocked to 312 Azusa Street in Los Angeles. There, under the leadership of the black preacher William J. Seymour, they witnessed a pentecostal revival, replete with tongue-speaking, which the pilgrims carried back to their homes. One of those present was Charles Harrison Mason (1866–1961), a former black Baptist who in 1894 had been "sanctified" and withdrew from the Baptists to organize a holiness denomination. Interracial in membership during the early decades, the holiness movement stressed the need to go beyond conversion to seek a "second blessing," namely, moral and spiritual perfection. Together with C. P. Jones, another former black Baptist, Mason called a holiness convention in 1897 and named a new body, the Church of God in Christ, after I Thessalonians 2:14. Its strength was initially in parts of Tennessee, Alabama, and Mississippi. After Mason returned from the Azusa Street pentecostal revival, he and Jones disagreed over the necessity of tongue-speaking, sometimes referred to as spiritual baptism or the "third work of grace." Jones and the nonpentecostal faction withdrew from the Church of God in Christ. Mason's organization grew rapidly after 1907, spreading west and north, especially into the cities. By the 1930s nearly 70 percent of the membership lived in urban areas. The following is selected from a biographical portrait of Charles "Dad" Mason by Elsie W. Mason.

Bishop C. H. Mason, Sanctified

IN THE YEAR 1894, Charles Mason was sanctified through the Word. He preached his first sermon on holiness using the text of II Timothy 3:12, "Thou therefore endure hardness as a good soldier. . . ." After his very first sermon on sanctification, Mason was away for two weeks. He returned to discover that a revival had broken out due to that first holiness sermon.

Source: *The Man, Charles Harrison Mason* (1866–1961). Memphis: Church of God in Christ, 1979. Pp. 10–20.

Although the revival had started with a tremendous surge of enthusiasm, it was rapidly declining without any souls having been saved. The pastor of that Baptist Church—in Preston, Arkansas—asked Mason to assume duties as the evangelist for the revival. Said Mason: "I felt it was my first duty to consult the Lord. I went into the woods, fell to my knees, and asked the Lord to give evidence of my call to the ministry by giving success and converting leading sinners of that community in the revival." Just as he had prayed, his ministry was confirmed—by results. Returning from the woods, he met a lady weeping and crying out for salvation. She and many others were saved—some in the church and others during baptism at the waterside.

When the revival had ended, Charles Mason travelled to Lee County, Arkansas, to see his brother, Nelson. His brother and others who had known him well found Charles Mason to be greatly changed in doctrine and in deed. Soon, they grew somewhat uncomfortable with his uncompromising teaching against the practice of sin. But young Mason continued to preach, and many repented as they heard the Word of God.

Although some fought against his new teachings, many people were 'thirsting' to hear these holiness doctrines. And, in 1894, Charles Mason was growing in popularity among the 'grass roots' people. He was pastoring the Tabernacle Baptist Church in Selma, Alabama. Said Mason:

". . . my ministry with that church and with the Alabama Baptist Ministry at large seemed to be accepted and much beloved. But as I read my Bible and observed conditions, I felt that we were not, as a brother once said to me, 'toting fair with Jesus.' I began then to seek Him with all my heart for the power that would make my life wholly His. . . . I was not satisfied with a faith that brought no fruit, or else fruit of so poor a quality, spiritually, and a religion that had none of the signs spoken of in the scriptures in Mark 16:14-18 and Hebrews 2:1-11. I wanted to be one of wisdom's true sons and, like Abraham, a friend of God. As we sought God, the Spirit promised that if we would fast three days and nights, He would sanctify us: which we did and were filled with light, with joy. . . . O, the splendid glory of that exalted state. Do not be satisfied with the attitude merely that holiness is right. Get the experience; get saved; get a knowledge of it. Have the mind of Christ. You will really know something then that you never knew before. Try it out. From then on, with more zeal, we sought renewings of power and pushed the claims of Christ on the churches. . . ."

Finally, the perfect will of God was being carried out in the life of Charles Harrison Mason. Hundreds of souls were being saved and sanctified because of hearing his sound scriptural teachings on the 'second' work of grace. The divine master plan for a new holiness church was gradually being unfolded to Charles Mason. Mason continued:

"In 1895, I accepted a unanimous call to the Mount Helm Baptist Church in Jackson, Mississippi. Here I began my deeper spiritual labors among the people. I worked in the Association (Baptist) at Byrum, Big Creek, Mt. Olive, and Charlton where—later—Elder F. S. Sherrill was pastor."

Also, in 1895, Mason met the man who was to become his very closest friend and colleague in the gospel:

"In 1895, I met C. P. Jones of Jackson, Mississippi, who was very sweet in the spirit of the Lord and prayed much. Soon I loved him with unfeigned love. In 1896, we called a meeting at Jackson, Mississippi. It was a wonderful meeting full of power and the outpour of the Spirit of the Lord in which many were converted, sanctified and healed by the power of faith. The wonderful work done in this meeting brought a more international relationship among the brotherhood, by which we were able to turn many to the Lord in this faith."

The Church of God in Christ 'pioneers' were rapidly appearing on the 'stage' of God's activities, and the moment had arrived when a separation from the Baptist Church became an inevitability:

". . . in 1896, the General Association of the Baptist Church was held at Mt. Helm Church, Jackson. At that time we came to know Elder Kelly Bucks, A. Reed, R. J. Temple, W. S. Pleasant and others who regarded our zeal with more or less apparent favor. At this Association, we sold our first booklet, a treatise on the twelfth chapter of I Corinthians, under the title: 'The Work of the Holy Spirit in the Churches.' We also began about this time to publish 'Truth.' Sometime after this Association, the Holy Spirit bade me call a Holiness Convention. Said I, 'When Lord?' 'The sixth of June,' said He. 'What day will that be Lord?' I asked. 'Sunday,' said He. Later, when the almanac for 1897 came out, I found it was Sunday. Then I, young as I was in the way, 'knew it was the Lord.'"

The combination of this decision to call a Holiness Convention and Mason's consistent teachings on the holiness doctrines caused a tremendous surge of hostility from the Baptist clergy. But this did not cause the convention or the teachings to be cancelled. Instead, Charles Mason and his colleagues intensified their efforts.

"In due time we made the call. We had already in 1896 as I said, begun to publish 'Truth.' So it became the special organ of the call. But special invitations, I think, were sent out to those men who seemed interested in their own souls and the souls of the people. We began the meeting on Sunday, June 6, 1897, and continued two weeks, studying the Bible and praying night and day. But we were persecuted by the churches . . . Associations and sects combined against us. But this persecution compelled us to build another sect, which was not our aim nor desire. We contended that Christ is all. But we were extreme in our fight. The times demanded it. But we, from the first, only wanted to exalt Jesus and put down man-made traditions. A move on the part of the Mt. Helm Church gave the enemies of the Holy Spirit a chance and they put us in court. Though we won our liberty in the lower court, the Supreme Court put us out, not on general law, but on a technicality involving Mt. Helm's holdings . . . But God was with us and year after year we have held on. . . ."

Having been totally rejected by his own denomination, Elder Mason sought the Lord carefully for a name for this new holiness church. While he was walking down the street in Little Rock, Arkansas, the Lord revealed to him the name Church of God in Christ. To confirm the name, God placed upon his heart the scripture: I Thessalonians 2:14. This scripture refers to the "churches of God which are in Christ." Hence, a new denomination—comprised of saved and sanctified saints— was born in 1897. And even though Elder Mason had not yet experienced the baptism of the Holy Ghost, the Spirit of God was certainly at work directing the development of His Church.

In that same year, the Church of God in Christ established its first church in an old gin on the bank of a little creek in Lexington, Mississippi. People were drawn there from the surrounding areas because Jesus Christ—and His doctrines of holiness—were being magnified. Eventually, Satan was motivated to action because of their large success. While the saints were praising the Lord, someone fired several rounds from a shotgun into the building. A few persons were wounded, but not one was killed. When the report of this event reached the local newspapers, the worshipping crowds were further increased. Many said: 'If the sanctified people are having meetings under such conditions, truly it must be of the Lord.'

Soon afterwards, a 40 feet by 60 feet lot was purchased from Mrs. John Ashcraft on Yazoo Street. The congregation outgrew this structure almost immediately. During many services, all of the seats were carried out-of-doors to accommodate all those who gathered and could not possibly fit inside of the church. In 1906, a large brick church was erected which cost approximately $6,000—a fairly large amount of money at the time.

Bishop C. H. Mason, Filled with the Holy Ghost

Elder Mason began to thirst for a more complete relationship with God in 1907. He hoped to retreat to some secluded place to remain there until his soul was satisfied. Meanwhile, a very exciting report arrived from Los Angeles, California. The Azusa Street Revival was in progress, and large numbers of people were being saved, sanctified, filled with the Holy Ghost, healed, along with many other miracles and spiritual demonstrations.

Elder C. P. Jones, Mason's dearest friend, offered further information and insight concerning the baptism of the Holy Ghost (over which doctrine they were later destined to part company). But as did Charles Mason, C. P. Jones contended that every saint should receive that spiritual baptism. This he believed would 'complete' the believer-in-Christ by a 'third work of grace' to empower him/her for effective service. However, Charles Mason and C. P. Jones were to finally dissolve their ministerial partnership and friendship because Jones did not agree that tongue-speaking was necessary and Mason felt that it was biblical and therefore necessary.

After studying the baptism of the Holy Ghost with C. P. Jones, Elder Charles H. Mason was directed by God to visit the Azusa Street Revival. Said Mason: "I was led by the Spirit to go to Los Angeles, California, where the great fire of the latter rain of the Holy Ghost had fallen on many." Elder Mason travelled the great distance from Mississippi—accompanied by a few friends—with great anticipation of God's blessings. When he arrived on Azusa Street, the forty-year-old Elder Mason witnessed some very unique occurrences:

> "The first day of the meeting I sat by myself, away from those who went with me. I saw and heard some things that did not seem scriptural to me, but at this I did not stumble. I began to thank God in my heart for all things for when I heard some speak in tongues I knew it was right, though I did not understand it. Nevertheless it was sweet to me."

Already, Mason's heart was being prepared to receive 'the Gift.'
And, the dynamic, Holy Ghost-filled preaching of Elder W. J. Seymour
was the instrument that the Almighty had chosen to bring Elder Mason to the point of baptism:

"I also thank God for Elder Seymour who came and preached a
wonderful sermon. His words were sweet and powerful and it seems
that I can hear them now. . . . When he closed his sermon, he
said: All of those that want to be sanctified or baptized with the
Holy Ghost, go to the upper room, and all those that want to be
healed, go to the prayer room, and all those that want to be justified, come to the altar. I said that (the altar) is the place for me,
for it may be that I am not converted, and if not, God knows it
and can convert me."

The great humility of the Church of God in Christ founder is portrayed strikingly herein as he is seen beginning again—at the very beginning—to assure himself of personal salvation and personal access to
"the gift of the Holy Ghost." The sanctification of Elder Mason was
never presented to 'the world' in a self-righteous manner, although he
was firm and unwavering in personal commitment. Elder Mason chose
the 'low road' of personal piety and humility; and thereby, he was exalted by God. The founder continued to reflect on the Azusa Street
Revival experiences:

"I stood on my feet while waiting at the altar, fearing someone would bother me. Just as I attempted to bow down someone
called me and said, 'The pastor wants you three brethren in his
room.' I obeyed and went up. He received us and seemed to be so
glad to see us there. He said, 'Brethren, the Lord will do great
things for us and bless us.' And he cautioned us not to be running
around in the city seeking worldly pleasure, but to seek the pleasure
of the Lord. The Word just suited me."

Because Elder Mason was obedient to the voice of the Lord which
summoned him to Azusa Street, the adversary mounted a tremendous
onslaught against him—desperately attempting to thwart what would
be a tremendously successful personal ministry once he had received
the spiritual baptism:

". . . a sister came into the room at the time we were bowing to
pray, one that I had a thought about that might not have been
right. I had not seen her in a number of years. I arose, took her into
a room and confessed it to her. And we prayed."

And, as if that were not enough in the way of temptation, Satan continued to present still others:

"I arose and returned to the pastor's room and began to pray again, and the enemy got into a minister, a brother, to tempt me. I said to him, 'go away, I do not want to be bothered.' And he tempted me the third time, but I refused to hear him. I told him that he did not know what he wanted, but I knew what I needed from God. I did not intend to be interfered with by anyone—so he gave up and ceased to annoy me further. . . ."

Even among Elder Mason's associates, there were basic problems and misunderstandings:

"Elder J. A. Jeter of Little Rock, Arkansas, and Elder D. J. Young of Pine Bluff, Arkansas . . . we three, went together, boarded together, and prayed for the same blessing. The enemy had put into the ear of Brother Jeter to find fault with the work, but God kept me out of it."

It was tempting for Elder Mason to try his hand at correcting the situation, but he was warned of God not to interfere:

"That night the Lord spoke to me, that Jesus saw all of this world's wrongs but did not attempt to set it right until God overshadowed Him with the Holy Ghost. And I said, 'I am no better than my Lord, and if I want Him to baptize me I will have to let the people's rights and wrongs all alone, and look to Him and not to the people. Then He will baptize me.' And I said 'yes' to God, for it was He who wanted to baptize me and not the people."

With this new insight, God began to literally 'unveil the heavens' and to speak directly to the mind and heart of Elder Mason every day:

"Glory! The second night of prayer I saw a vision. I saw myself standing alone and had a dry roll of paper in my hands. I had to chew it. When I had gotten it all in my mouth—trying to swallow it while looking up towards the heavens—a man appeared at my side. I turned my eyes at once, then I awoke and the interpretation came. God had me swallowing the whole book; and if I would not turn my eyes to anyone other than God and Him only, He would baptize me. I said 'yes' to Him, and at once, in the morning when I arose I could hear a voice in me saying, 'I see.' "

In spite of the clarity of those direct divine messages to Elder Mason—and despite his personal sincerity—Satan was yet present to tempt him to distraction from his purpose:

"I had joy but was not satisfied. A sister began to tell me about the faults that were among the saints, but stopped as she was not wanting to hinder me by telling me of them. I sat and looked at her and said, 'You may all stand on your heads, God has told me what to do. God is going to baptize me.'"

With this renewed resolve, Elder Mason was able to increase his spiritual momentum and to make the quest for the baptism somewhat easier:

"I got a place at the altar and began to thank God. After that I said, 'Lord, if I could only baptize myself I would do so.' For I wanted the baptism so badly that I did not know what to do. I said, 'Lord, you will have to do the work for me.' So I just turned it all over into His hands to do the work for me. A brother came and prayed for me. I did not feel any better or any worse. One sister came and said, 'Satan will try to make you feel sad, but that is not the way to receive Him; you must be glad and praise the Lord.' I told her that I was letting the Lord search my heart, for I did not want to receive new wine in old bottles. But I said, 'My heart does not condemn me.' Then I quoted the scripture to her which readeth thus, 'Beloved, if our hearts condemn us not, then have we confidence towards God, and whatsoever we ask we receive of him.' I John 3:21-22. Then I realized in my heart that I had confidence in God and did not have to get it, for my heart was free from condemnation. Then I began to seek for the baptism of the Holy Ghost according to Acts 2:41, which readeth thus: 'Then they that gladly received His Word were baptized.' Then I saw that I had a right to be glad and not sad. As the enemy was trying to make me believe the way to receive the Holy Ghost was to be sad, the light of the Word was putting his argument out. There came a reason in my mind which said, 'Were you sad when you were going to marry?' I said, 'No, I was glad.' The voice said that this baptism meant wedlock to Christ. Then I saw more in being glad than in being sad."

Satan was outraged at the progress that Charles Mason was making toward receiving 'the Gift.' He began to step up his attack on the mind of the Church of God in Christ founder. But his attempts were consistently vanquished by the Word of God:

"The enemy said to me, 'There may be something wrong with you.' Then a voice spoke to me and said: 'If there is anything wrong with you, Christ will find it and take away and will marry you, at any rate, and will not break the vow.' More light came and my heart rejoiced! Some said, 'Let us sing.' I arose and the first song that came to me was, 'He brought me out of the miry clay; He set my feet on the Rock to stay.' The Spirit came upon the saints and upon me! Afterwards I soon sat down and soon my hands went up and I resolved in my heart not to take them down until the Lord baptized me. The enemy tried to show me again how much pain it would cause me to endure not knowing how long it would be before the Lord would baptize me. The enemy said that I might not be able to hold out. The Spirit rebuked him and said that the Lord was able to make my stand and if not I would be a liar. And the Spirit gave me to know that I was looking to God and not to myself for anything."

The relentless attacks of Satan have not produced their intended result for Elder Mason has chosen to listen attentively to the voice of God. The Word of God, which Mason affirmed early in his ministry to be his singular guide for living, had sustained him and had brought him to the very point at which the Comforter was to come. And, Elder Charles Harrison Mason's heart quickened with anticipation:

"The sound of a mighty wind was in me and my soul cried, 'Jesus, only, one like you.' My soul cried and soon I began to die. It seemed that I heard the groaning of Christ on the cross dying for me. All of the work was in me until I died out of the old man. The sound stopped for a little while. My soul cried, 'Oh, God, finish your work in me.' Then the sound broke out in me again. Then I felt something raising me out of my seat without any effort of my own. I said, 'It may be imagination.' Then I looked down to see if it was really so. I saw that I was rising. Then I gave up for the Lord to have His way within me. So there came a wave of glory into me, and all of my being was filled with the glory of the Lord. So when I had gotten myself straight on my feet there came a light which enveloped my entire being above the brightness of the sun. When I opened my mouth to say glory, a flame touched my tongue which ran down to me. My language changed and no word could I speak in my own tongue. Oh, I was filled with the glory of my Lord. My soul was then satisfied. I rejoiced in Jesus my Savior, whom I love so dearly. And from that day until now there has been an overflowing joy of the glory of the Lord in my heart."

The Holy Ghost had come! Finally, Elder Charles Harrison Mason had received "the promise" which he had so heartily sought. And, his personal baptism had been quite reminiscent of the first Day of Pentecost when the "sound" came from heaven "like as a rushing mighty wind" and "cloven tongues like as of fire" sat upon each of the 120 waiting disciples as they spake in "other tongues as the Spirit gave them utterance." He had experienced all three operations of divine grace: regeneration, sanctification, and spiritual baptism. And as a result, Elder Mason was fully equipped to lead God's people.

Remaining at the Azusa Street Revival for a total of five weeks, Elder Mason refined his knowledge of the operations of the Holy Spirit within the Body of Christ. And, just as the scriptures had stated, the Holy Ghost began to "teach" Elder Mason and to "lead" him. He noted dynamic differences in his ministry to the saints. And he was increasingly effective in his teaching and preaching ministry. When Elder Mason had returned home, he wrote:

"After five weeks I left Los Angeles, California for Memphis, Tennessee, my home. The fire had fallen before my arrival. Brother Glenn Cook, of Los Angeles, was there telling the story and the Lord was sending the rain. I was full of the power when I reached home. The Spirit had taken full control of me and everything was new to me and to all the saints. The way that He did things was all new. At the same time I soon found that He could and was teaching me all things and showing the things of the Lord. He taught me how and what to sing, and all His songs were new. The third day after reaching Memphis I asked Him to give me the interpretation of what was spoken in tongues, for I did not fully understand the operation of the Spirit. I wanted the church to understand what the Spirit was saying through me, so that they might be edified. My prayers were not in vain. The Lord stood me up and began to speak in tongues and interpret the same. He soon gave me the gift of interpretation—that is, He would interpret sounds, groans and any kind of spiritual utterance."

Elder Charles Harrison Mason returned from California full of the Holy Ghost. Immediately, his ministry was launched into a more dynamic dimension. And the Church of God in Christ began to literally spread its 'branches' in all directions. No denomination in America has matched its rapid growth and development. And, it is all because of God's goodness and the personal dedication of one man who dared to believe wholly in the Word of God, Charles Harrison Mason.

SUPPLEMENTARY READINGS

Kroll-Smith, J. Stephen. "The Testimony As Performance: The Relationship of an Expressive Event to the Belief System of a Holiness Sect." *Journal for the Scientific Study of Religion* 19, no. 1 (1980): 16–25.

Patterson, J. O., German R. Ross, and Julia Atkinson, eds. *History and Formative Years of the Church of God in Christ with Excerpts from the Life and Works of Its Founder—Bishop C. H. Mason.* Memphis: Church of God in Christ Publishing House, 1969.

Synan, Vinson. *The Holiness-Pentecostal Movement in the United States.* Grand Rapids, Mich.: Wm. B. Eerdmans, 1971. Chap. 8.

Tinney, James S. "William J. Seymour: Father of Modern-Day Pentecostalism." In *Black Apostles*, edited by Randall K. Burkett and Richard Newman. Boston: G.K. Hall, 1978. Pp. 213–25.

Williams, Melvin D. *Community in a Black Pentecostal Church.* Pittsburgh: University of Pittsburgh Press, 1974.

33

REVERDY C. RANSOM

"The Race Problem in a Christian State, 1906"

W. E. B. Du Bois wrote in 1903 that the A.M.E. Church was "probably . . . the greatest voluntary organization of Negroes in the world." Perhaps no African Methodist preacher fit Du Bois's ideal more closely than Reverdy C. Ransom, social-activist leader in Chicago and catalyst for the Institutional Church and Settlement House, modeled after Jane Addams's Hull House. Born in 1861 at Flushing, Ohio, "Harriet Ransom's son" graduated from Wilberforce University in 1886 despite his disenchantment with its authoritarian atmosphere and conservative theology. He served an apprenticeship in churches in Ohio and Pennsylvania and then moved in 1896 to Bethel Church in Chicago.

Ransom's independent ways and his involvement in activist groups dedicated to racial advancement, such as the Afro-American Council and the Niagara Movement, created problems for him in the labyrinth of African Methodist internal politics. He left Chicago in 1905 and moved to the Charles Street A.M.E. Church in Boston. Ransom delivered the address reprinted here in April 1906 at the Park Street Church in Boston. His concern for more effective urban ministry, his involvement in black protest organizations, and his association with anti-Booker T. Washington black intellectuals and politicians continued during his assignment to the influential Bethel A.M.E. Church in New York City. In 1912 Ransom became editor of the A.M.E. Review, and in 1924 he was elected to the office of bishop. He retired in 1952 and died in 1959.

THERE SHOULD BE no Race problem in the Christian State.

When Christianity received its Pentecostal baptism and seal from heaven it is recorded that, "there were dwelling at Jerusalem Jews, devout men, out of every nation under heaven. Parthians, and Medes, and Elamites, and the dwellers in Mesopotamia, and in Judea, and Cappadocia, in Pontus and Asia. Phrygia, and Pamphylia in Egypt, and in

Source: *The Spirit of Freedom and Justice.* Nashville: A.M.E. Sunday School Union, 1926. Pp. 128–37.

parts of Lybia about Cyrene; and strangers of Rome; Jews and Proselytes, Cretes and Arabians."

St. Paul, standing in the Areopagus, declared to the Athenians that,
"God hath made of one blood all nations of men for to dwell on all the
face of the earth."

Jesus Christ founded Christianity in the midst of the most bitter
and intense antagonisms of race and class. Yet he ignored them all,
dealing alike with Jew, Samaritan, Syro-Phoenician, Greek and Roman.
It is true that the Jewish religion and the entire social and political
structure of Hebrew civilization rested upon the idea of race. "First the
blade, then the ear, after that the full corn in the ear," is as true in human society as it is in nature. God, through the Jew, was educating the
world, and laying a moral and spiritual foundation. That foundation
was the establishment of the *one God idea*. Upon this foundation Jesus
Christ built the superstructure of "the Fatherhood of God," and its
corollary, "the Brotherhood of man."

The crowning object at which Jesus Christ aimed was, to "break
down the middle wall of partition," between man and man, and to take
away all the Old Testament laws and ordinances that prevented Jew
and Gentile from approaching God on an equal plane. And this He did,
"that He might reconcile both unto God in one body by the cross,
having slain the enmity thereby, so making peace."

What is a Christian State?

A Christian State is one founded upon the teachings of Jesus; being
thus founded, its constitution and laws and all the complex social relations of its people's life will partake of the character and spirit of His
teachings. This is the ideal which the Christian State has set before it,
toward which it must ever strive. It cannot hesitate or turn back, without turning its back upon Him. From the time that St. Paul answered
the Macedonians' cry by introducing Christianity into Europe down to
the present hour, the states calling themselves Christian have had to
deal with the race problem, and they have done it with the rack, the
torch, the Spanish Inquisition, the Kishnev Massacre, political disability, social exclusion and by all other means passion and prejudice could
devise. America has this right to call itself a Christian nation, that it is
the first nation that was born with the Bible in its hands. It has had to
face problems new to the civilization of Europe, and to walk in untried
paths. The Negro Question has been with this nation from the time
that the foundations of the government were laid. James G. Blaine in
his "Twenty Years in Congress" says: "The compromises on the Slavery

Question, inserted in the Constitution, were among the essential conditions upon which the federal government was organized. If the African slave trade had not been permitted to continue for twenty years; if it had not been conceded that three-fifths of the slaves should be counted in the apportionment of representatives in Congress, if it had not been agreed that fugitives from service should be returned to their owners, the Thirteen States would not have been able in 1787 "to form a more perfect union."

In dealing with this question, the history of our past is well known. The Race Problem in this country is not only still with us an unsolved problem, but it constitutes perhaps the most serious problem in our country today. In Church and State, from the beginning, we have tried to settle it by compromise, but all compromises have ended in failure. It is only when we have faced it courageously and sought to settle it right that we have triumphed, as in the case of Lincoln's immortal "Proclamation of Emancipation." American Christianity will un-christ itself if it refuses to strive on, until this Race Problem is not only settled, but settled right; and until this is done, however much men may temporize and seek to compromise, and cry "peace! peace!" there will be no peace until this is done.

Facing the Industrial Question

Those who brought the Negro to this country had no thought of him as a human being above the mere level of brute strength and animalism. The thought of admitting him even into the outer courts of opportunity for progress, much less according him the rights of a man, had never for a moment been entertained. He was to be forever tied to the soil, enjoy no rights nor privileges, exercise no will save the will of his master. Negro slavery was for generations, the corner-stone of Southern civilization. Whatever progress or prosperity the South enjoyed for two hundred years was based upon it. All the power of her pulpits, the learning of her schools, the ability of her statesmen were employed to justify, to uphold, to maintain and to defend it. It was, in fact, constitutional and it was declared to be also in accordance with the will of heaven, which had decreed that the Negro should be a servant forever. The North partly from climatic reasons and partly from differences of its political, intellectual and moral inheritance and training, was unfriendly to slavery; more than this, there were high-souled men and women who were sufficiently acquainted with the will of God and the teachings of Jesus Christ, to know that a Christian nation founded in liberty could not long survive upon the foundation of human slavery. At last God's hour came; He spoke from heaven; men's eyes were opened, their hearts were a flame of fire, they marched to the field of battle and fought until the ground ran red with blood; both North and South gave their beauty, their chivalry, their wealth, their brain and brawn. When the thick blackness piled up by the smoke from the cannon's roar was lifted, the world beheld the fetters of four million slaves piled up like a monument to heaven. After these days passed, men felt that the Negro would be permitted to tread the pathway of industrial opportunity with perfect freedom, according to his capability and desires, but not so. The attitude of this nation today both North and South, seems to be, that the Negro should live only upon the fringes of the industrial world, that his place should be that of a menial. This idea has become so fixed, that it is thought to be a presumption amounting to impertinence, for qualified Negro men and women to seek to enter the doors of the great banking, manufacturing, mercantile and business avenues open to all others with perfect freedom. Following upon this idea, a propaganda has arisen, which has found willing assent in the North, to the extent that it is shared by clergymen, newspapers, magazines and most of the great organs of public opinion, as well as the wealthy, who willingly contribute millions in its behalf. No one can successfully prove what is claimed, that industrial education will solve the Negro Problem. How can industrial education solve the Negro Problem? The South has assented to this proposition in which northern sentiment seems to have acquiesced; but what the South undoubtedly means by this solution, is that a great peasant class, composed of ten million Negroes shall be built up and established in this land; that they shall be trained to more intelligently till the soil, ply the trades and render domestic service. This Republic, conceived in liberty, cannot stand upon its foundation by establishing here a peasant class.

Rev. Thomas Dixon, Jr. has recently complained in the public prints that Dr. Booker T. Washington's great school at Tuskegee was not turning out servants, but men, who would go out into the world to be themselves leaders of men, as contractors, master mechanics and employers or directors of labor, and because of this, he says that Tuskegee will be a failure; that it cannot survive. Here in Massachusetts and throughout all the North and West, yea even in the Southland, colored boys and girls are studying the same books and drinking from the same fountains of aspirations as are the whites. They read the same books, papers and magazines; they cherish the same ideals and ambitions. Can one think of a greater crime, almost against the very life of human spirit, than this, that these youths should go thus out into life only to find that their ability, coupled with high character, counted for very little when they sought to enter the doors of industrial opportunity?

We admit that the Negro has been a servant, and only a servant, so long has been in a place of inferiority for so many generations, that it is difficult, no doubt, to conceive of him entering a path which character and fitness would permit any other person to tread with perfect freedom. The Negro does work, and has done nothing but work since he landed upon these shores centuries ago. He should become a more skilled, and a more intelligent worker, it is true; but he should be permitted to work not only as a servant, but as a man, with all the opportunities open to him that are open to others no better qualified than he. White men may not feel it thus and some Negroes may not see it, but the great and menacing danger that surrounds the Negro and the nation at this hour, is the circumscribed limitations which this nation has put around the opportunities of the Negroes of this land, to occupy themselves freely, in any sphere, according to their ambitions, capability and desire. The government does deal justly with the Negro so far as permitting him to be employed in its various branches which may be entered through Civil Service examination, but even here, when it comes to promotion for merit, the boundary line beyond which he may not go is fixed. This nation is not rich enough in trained minds, skilled hands and cultured brains to put a discount upon the ability and aspiration of any class of its citizens, nor will it act in the spirit of Christ toward the black toilers of this land, until Negroes are as freely permitted to run locomotive engines as they are elevators; to work in a national bank, as they are a coal bank; to sell dry goods over the counters of the store as they are to wash them in the laundry; to work in a cotton mill, as they are in a cotton field; and to follow the pig-iron from the furnace, all the way to the iron and steel mills, through all the various forms of utility into which it is capable of being manufactured; this and nothing less than this, is the justice which a Christian nation should be willing to give. Willing because such giving would not impoverish, but would greatly enrich it in all lines and branches by the reenforcement of these millions of eager hands, whose fingers have been twitching in hopeful anticipation for the day when they might seize these opportunities from which they have been so long debarred. It would add to the nation's strength by making so many more millions of her citizens prosperous; by permitting them to contribute to the upbuilding of the nation along all the lines of its defense, production, development and growth.

Citizenship in the Republic

The first right of an American citizen is the right to vote, to cast a ballot which shall represent untrammelled exercise of his judgment and expression of his will. It is the highest duty of the state to protect each citizen in the free exercise of that right. The state owes this duty to the citizen, no less for his protection than for the preservation of its own life. When the franchise may be violated, corrupted or refused, a death blow is aimed at the very life of democracy and the Christian institutions founded upon it here.

Our institutions rest not upon race or class, but are founded upon the expression of the people's will. For the State to refuse the right to vote for any cause not founded upon constitutional disability, is to place the entering wedge for the overthrow of these institutions founded in hope, and perpetuated in sacrifice, suffering and patriotic devotion. As in the days of slavery it was argued that it would be a crime against the Negro to set him free, because he would lapse into barbarism and would be unable, in competition with white men, to support himself without the guiding hand of the master; so now, it is argued, that it is no injustice to the Negro citizen, to either forcibly, or by legal artifice, deprive him of the right to vote. White men must do this, we are told, in defense of Anglo-Saxon liberty, and to prevent our institutions from becoming Africanized. Whence this great apprehension? Of all Americans, there is a sense in which the Negro is the most American of them all. Excluding the Indian, he has been here almost ever since the first of the founders of this nation arrived, and he has witnessed the arrival of the many conglomerate elements of our population who have been swarming to these shores for more than one hundred years. Unlike these people who have come to us, the Negro brought with him no political ideas or traditions, no theories of government or religion, no social schemes for the organization of society which could in any way contaminate, blight, or injure the great ideas or principles upon which this nation was established. He was a seed ripe for germination, sown deep into the rich soil of the first ideas and principles upon which this nation was established, and he has been an apt student; he has grown with every moment of the nation's growth, he has developed with every phase of the development of the nation's life; he has been present at every crisis when the soul of the nation was tried, when her strength was put to the test upon the field of battle; on land and sea he has never been found wanting in a single conflict. In the development of her resources, his sweat and toil have contributed from the beginning, to the increase of the nation's wealth, and her stability and strength in all material things.

The Negro in America cherishes no ideals, holds to no other principles save those that are soundly American. Why then this fear of being Africanized? We hear no fear expressed of our country being Germanized or Jewized; we hear no cry going up from North or South against Irish political ascendancy. Is there any evidence anywhere in a single page of American history where the Negro has been less patriotic and true to our institutions than any of these elements which we have named? There are those claiming to be the Negro's best friends, who tell us that the Negro should give up politics for the time and devote himself to saving money, buying land and educating his children. We grant that he should do these things; but why do these and leave the others undone—namely, the assertion of his first right as a citizen, the right to vote. How without the ballot is he to protect his house and land, his goods and chattels, his wife, his children and his home, his life, his liberty, his rights under the constitution and the laws? Is this cry raised that it is to the Negro's best interest to give up the franchise for the time because the Negro has done anything against the interest of the state, the church, or society? We know that it is not. No man is good enough to govern another without that man's consent; no man is worthy to be trusted to hold another man in his power. From the beginning of human society until now, throughout all the centuries of history, it has meant tyranny, oppression upon the one hand, and slavery or serfdom upon the other, yet Northern timidity and indifference have yielded to this cry until now, even the government itself has become quasi acquiescent. People become impatient when an attempt is made to discuss this question; they whisper, "quiet, be still, let alone"; but we cannot let it alone, and we will not be still. A man who advises the Negro to give up his right to the franchise is not a good friend to the Negro, and he is an enemy of his country. This cry that goes up from the South for the suppression of the Negro vote is against the Negro as such, regardless of his character, intelligence or wealth. These men desire what they have always desired, to have and to hold the Negro in their power, thus obtaining for themselves a disproportionate political influence and power in the councils of the nation, in all that pertains to the enactment of legislation and the administration of law; not only this, but the Negro is thus rendered helpless and made the defenseless victim, an easy prey of any who may desire to prey upon him.

Are the lovers of righteousness so numerous, are the friends of good government so wise, are the supporters of Christian civilization so strong, that they can refuse to accept the aid and co-operation of millions of Negro citizens who are also intelligent, patriotic and virtuous, from joining with them in upholding and maintaining these ideas and principles which they cherish with as much devotion as do the white men who refuse their aid? The true supporters of the Christian State will stand unmoved amid clamor, class prejudice and race hatred. They will resist in the name of God and of human liberty all those enemies of the Republic who would put aboard the Ship of State any pilot who would attempt to guide her out of the safe waters of that constitutional liberty, founded on equality, upon which in the beginning she was launched.

The Bogy of Social Equality

Much of the persecution and brutality visited upon members of the Negro race in America is justified by the plea that it is necessary in order to protect the homes of white men and the chastity of their women. The highest ambition of the Negro, it is claimed, is to achieve social equality with the whites, therefore, he may be beaten, hung, shot and burned at the stake, in the name of the preservation of social purity.

We present to the world the spectacle of a nation sympathizing with the oppressed of all lands, and opening our gates to furnish an asylum for those who flee to us from oppression and tyranny at home. We sympathize with persecuted Irishmen in Ireland, the Jews of Russia and the Armenians who suffer at the hands of the Turks. We went to war in the name of humanity, to break forever the power of Spain in the western hemisphere and to deliver Cuba from the yoke of Spanish oppression, while within our own borders a Negro may be beaten with more brutality than one would dare treat a horse or even a dog, for an alleged crime against a white person, and in many instances for no alleged crime at all. He may be tortured and put to death with all the shocking horrors of savage ferocity. These things are done within the borders of this nation and have become so common that if the public conscience is not dead, it is at least asleep for the time. The perpetrators of mob violence have ceased to mask themselves, not even shielding themselves with the veil of darkness. They stalk abroad in the open light of day, quite frequently that Day, the holy Sabbath. It is made a gala day, the railroads run excursions to the scene of burning at the stake, children, reared in our Sunday Schools and Christian homes are witnesses to these scenes, while men contend with each other for ghastly trophies of the incinerated bodies of the victims. Against all these there is no united voice of protest from the American pulpit. The daily papers print the news which is carried to the homes of the nation, but there is rarely editorial comment in condemnation. The President of the United States in his annual message makes no recommendations; the voice of Congress is silent. Must we assume, is it too much to assume, that this nation, calling itself Christian, is acquiescent? But the attempts of the public sentiment of this nation to humiliate and to degradate the Negro stop not here; he has been rigorously segregated by being generally refused admission to places of public resort, entertainment and amusement, and upon equal terms upon the common carriers. In the South upon the railroads he is forced to ride in a separate car, with inferior accommodations, though paying first-class fare; forced to ride there no matter what his education, wealth, character or culture. He is excluded from parks, libraries, museums and even Young Men's Christian Associations. If this be the spirit of Jesus, then give us Mohammed or any other redeemer.

The white millions of this nation can never lift themselves up in Christianity and civilization by beating back and trampling under foot the simple rights and aspirations of ten million blacks. We know that men cannot be made social equals by legislation; we know also that equality cannot be based upon color any more than it can be based upon the fashion plate. The attitude of the Christian State toward this question should be to seek to lift up all men who are sinking down, and to clear the way and throw wide the gates to all peoples who are seeking to climb upward in education, in wealth, in character and in all that better growth of the human spirit which makes for manhood.

As God is above man, so man is above race. There is nothing to fear by forever demolishing every wall, religious, political, industrial, social, that separates man from his brotherman. God has given us a splendid heritage here upon these shores; he has made us the pioneers of human liberty for all mankind. He has placed the Negro and white man here for centuries, to grow together side by side. The white man's heart will grow softer, as it goes out in helpfulness, to assist his black brother up to the heights whereon he stands, and the black man will take courage and confidence, as he finds himself progressing, by slow and difficult steps upward toward the realization of all the higher and better things of human attainment; thus will these two peoples one at last become the school masters of all the world, teaching by example the doctrines of the brotherhood of man. If the new Jerusalem tarries in its descent to earth, coming down from God out of heaven, then we, not like some foolish tower-builders upon the plains of Shinar, but taught from heaven in a better way, shall build upon the teachings of Jesus, with the doctrine of human brotherhood as taught by Him, until fraternity realized, shall raise us to the skies.

SUPPLEMENTARY READINGS

Meier, August. *Negro Thought in America, 1880–1915: Racial Ideologies in the Age of Booker T. Washington.* Ann Arbor: University of Michigan Press, 1963.

Singleton, George A. *The Romance of African Methodism.* New York: Exposition Press, 1952. Chap. 12.

Weeks, Louis B., III. "Racism, World War I and the Christian Life: Francis J. Grimke in the Nation's Capital." In *Black Apostles,* edited by Randall K. Burkett and Richard Newman. Boston: G.K. Hall, 1978. Pp. 57–75.

Wills, David. "Reverdy C. Ransom: The Making of an A.M.E. Bishop." In *Black Apostles,* edited by Randall K. Burkett and Richard Newman. Boston: G.K. Hall, 1978. Pp. 181–212.

Wright, Richard R., Jr. *The Bishops of the African Methodist Episcopal Church.* Nashville: A.M.E. Sunday School Union, 1963.

FIVE

Rural and Urban Churches,
1900–World War II

W. E. B. DU BOIS

"Of the Faith of the Fathers"

William Edward Burghardt Du Bois was born at Great Barrington, Massachusetts, in 1868 and died a citizen of Ghana in 1963. Between those dates and places lies a story of such monumental significance that no adequate summary can be given. Suffice it to say that he devoted his life to scholarship, civil rights, and a wide variety of social and political causes. Du Bois disliked denominational religion, rarely attended church, and for the last two or three decades of his life was an agnostic. Yet as a young faculty professor of economics and history at Atlanta University he composed prayers and brief meditations for the chapel services and took a personal interest in the power of religion among blacks in the rural South. Du Bois the scholar recognized that black religion, in both its institutional and folk forms, was the life-soul of Afro-American communities. Of Du Bois's various writings concerning the black church and black religion, none is more powerfully evocative than the tenth chapter of his classic personal recollections and reflections entitled The Souls of Black Folk. *First published in 1900 in* New World, *this essay strikes the contemporary reader as a mystical pilgrimage by Du Bois into a world he could not have known in New England.*

IT WAS OUT in the country, far from home, far from my foster home, on a dark Sunday night. The road wandered from our rambling log-house up the stony bed of a creek, past wheat and corn, until we could hear dimly across the fields a rhythmic cadence of song,—soft, thrilling, powerful, that swelled and died sorrowfully in our ears. I was a country school-teacher then, fresh from the East, and had never seen a Southern Negro revival. To be sure, we in Berkshire were not perhaps as stiff and formal as they in Suffolk of olden time; yet we were very quiet and subdued, and I know not what would have happened those clear Sabbath mornings had some one punctuated the sermon with a wild scream, or interrupted the long prayer with a loud Amen! And so most striking to me, as I approached the village and the little plain church perched aloft,

Source: *The Souls of Black Folk.* Edited by Herbert Aptheker. Milwood, N.Y.: Kraus-Thomson Organization, 1973. Pp. 189–206.

was the air of intense excitement that possessed that mass of black folk. A sort of suppressed terror hung in the air and seemed to seize us,—a pythian madness, a demoniac possession, that lent terrible reality to song and word. The black and massive form of the preacher swayed and quivered as the words crowded to his lips and flew at us in singular eloquence. The people moaned and fluttered, and then the gaunt-cheeked brown woman beside me suddenly leaped straight into the air and shrieked like a lost soul, while round about came wail and groan and outcry, and a scene of human passion such as I had never conceived before.

Those who have not thus witnessed the frenzy of a Negro revival in the untouched backwoods of the South can but dimly realize the religious feeling of the slave; as described, such scenes appear grotesque and funny, but as seen they are awful. Three things characterized this religion of the slave,—the Preacher, the Music, and the Frenzy. The Preacher is the most unique personality developed by the Negro on American soil. A leader, a politician, an orator, a "boss," an intriguer, an idealist,—all these he is, and ever, too, the centre of a group of men, now twenty, now a thousand in number. The combination of a certain adroitness with deep-seated earnestness, of tact with consummate ability, gave him his preëminence, and helps him maintain it. The type, of course, varies according to time and place, from the West Indies in the sixteenth century to New England in the nineteenth, and from the Mississippi bottoms to cities like New Orleans or New York.

The Music of Negro religion is that plaintive rhythmic melody, with its touching minor cadences, which, despite caricature and defilement, still remains the most original and beautiful expression of human life and longing yet born on American soil. Sprung from the African forests, where its counterpart can still be heard, it was adapted, changed, and intensified by the tragic soul-life of the slave, until, under the stress of law and whip, it became the one true expression of a people's sorrow, despair, and hope.

Finally the Frenzy or "Shouting," when the Spirit of the Lord passed by, and, seizing the devotee, made him mad with supernatural joy, was the last essential of Negro religion and the one more devoutly believed in than all the rest. It varied in expression from the silent rapt countenance or the low murmur and moan to the mad abandon of physical fervor,—the stamping, shrieking, and shouting, the rushing to and fro and wild waving of arms, the weeping and laughing, the vision and the trance. All this is nothing new in the world, but old as religion, as Delphi and Endor. And so firm a hold did it have on the Negro, that many generations firmly believed that without this visible manifestation of the God there could be no true communion with the Invisible.

These were the characteristics of Negro religious life as developed up to the time of Emancipation. Since under the peculiar circumstances of the black man's environment they were the one expression of his higher life, they are of deep interest to the student of his development, both socially and psychologically. Numerous are the attractive lines of inquiry that here group themselves. What did slavery mean to the African savage? What was his attitude toward the World and Life? What seemed to him good and evil,—God and Devil? Whither went his longings and strivings, and wherefore were his heart-burnings and disappointments? Answers to such questions can come only from a study of Negro religion as a development, through its gradual changes from the heathenism of the Gold Coast to the institutional Negro church of Chicago.

Moreover, the religious growth of millions of men, even though they be slaves, cannot be without potent influence upon their contemporaries. The Methodists and Baptists of America owe much of their condition to the silent but potent influence of their millions of Negro converts. Especially is this noticeable in the South, where theology and religious philosophy are on this account a long way behind the North, and where the religion of the poor whites is a plain copy of Negro thought and methods. The mass of "gospel" hymns which has swept through American churches and well-nigh ruined our sense of song consists largely of debased imitations of Negro melodies made by ears that caught the jingle but not the music, the body but not the soul, of the Jubilee songs. It is thus clear that the study of Negro religion is not only a vital part of the history of the Negro in America, but no uninteresting part of American history.

The Negro church of to-day is the social centre of Negro life in the United States, and the most characteristic expression of African character. Take a typical church in a small Virginian town: it is the "First Baptist"—a roomy brick edifice seating five hundred or more persons, tastefully finished in Georgia pine, with a carpet, a small organ, and stained-glass windows. Underneath is a large assembly room with benches. This building is the central club-house of a community of a thousand or more Negroes. Various organizations meet here—the church proper, the Sunday-school, two or three insurance societies, women's societies, secret societies, and mass meetings of various kinds. Entertainments, suppers, and lectures are held beside the five or six regular weekly religious services. Considerable sums of money are collected and expended here, employment is found for the idle, strangers are introduced, news is disseminated and charity distributed. At the same time this social, intellectual, and economic centre is a religious centre of great power. Depravity, Sin, Redemption, Heaven, Hell, and Damnation are preached twice a Sunday with much fervor, and revivals take place every year after the crops are laid by; and few indeed of the community have the hardihood to withstand conversion. Back of this more formal religion, the Church often stands as a real conserver of morals, a strengthener of family life, and the final authority on what is Good and Right.

Thus one can see in the Negro church to-day, reproduced in microcosm, all that great world from which the Negro is cut off by color-prejudice and social condition. In the great city churches the same tendency is noticeable and in many respects emphasized. A great church like the Bethel of Philadelphia has over eleven hundred members, an edifice seating fifteen hundred persons and valued at one hundred thousand dollars, an annual budget of five thousand dollars, and a government consisting of a pastor with several assisting local preachers, an executive and legislative board, financial boards and tax collectors; general church meetings for making laws; subdivided groups led by class leaders, a company of militia, and twenty-four auxiliary societies. The activity of a church like this is immense and far-reaching, and the bishops who preside over these organizations throughout the land are among the most powerful Negro rulers in the world.

Such churches are really governments of men, and consequently a little investigation reveals the curious fact that, in the South, at least, practically every American Negro is a church member. Some, to be sure, are not regularly enrolled, and a few do not habitually attend services; but, practically, a proscribed people must have a social centre, and that centre for this people is the Negro church. The census of 1890 showed nearly twenty-four thousand Negro churches in the country, with a total enrolled membership of over two and a half millions, or ten actual church members to every twenty-eight persons, and in some Southern States one in every two persons. Besides these there is the large number who, while not enrolled as members, attend and take part in many of the activities of the church. There is an organized Negro church for every sixty black families in the nation, and in some States for every forty families, owning, on an average, a thousand dollars' worth of property each, or nearly twenty-six million dollars in all.

Such, then, is the large development of the Negro church since Emancipation. The question now is, What have been the successive steps of this social history and what are the present tendencies? First, we must realize that no such institution as the Negro church could rear itself without definite historical foundations. These foundations we can find if we remember that the social history of the Negro did not start in America. He was brought from a definite social environment,—the polygamous clan life under the headship of the chief and the potent influence of the priest. His religion was nature-worship, with profound belief in invisible surrounding influences, good and bad, and his worship was through incantation and sacrifice. The first rude change in this life was the slave ship and the West Indian sugar-fields. The plantation organization replaced the clan and tribe, and the white master replaced the chief with far greater and more despotic powers. Forced and long-continued toil became the rule of life, the old ties of blood relationship and kinship disappeared, and instead of the family appeared a new polygamy and polyandry, which, in some cases, almost reached promiscuity. It was a terrific social revolution, and yet some traces were retained of the former group life, and the chief remaining institution was the Priest or Medicine-man. He early appeared on the plantation and found his function as the healer of the sick, the interpreter of the Unknown, the comforter of the sorrowing, the supernatural avenger of wrong, and the one who rudely but picturesquely expressed the longing, disappointment, and resentment of a stolen and oppressed people. Thus, as bard, physician, judge, and priest, within the narrow limits allowed by the slave system, rose the Negro preacher, and under him the first Afro-American institution, the Negro church. This church was not at first by any means Christian nor definitely organized; rather it was an adaptation and mingling of heathen rites among the members of each plantation, and roughly designated as Voodooism. Association with the masters, missionary effort and motives of expediency gave these rites an early veneer of Christianity, and after the lapse of many generations the Negro church became Christian.

Two characteristic things must be noticed in regard to this church. First, it became almost entirely Baptist and Methodist in faith; secondly, as a social institution it antedated by many decades the monogamic Negro home. From the very circumstances of its beginning, the church was confined to the plantation, and consisted primarily of a series of disconnected units; although, later on, some freedom of movement was allowed, still this geographical limitation was always important and was one cause of the spread of the decentralized and democratic Baptist faith among the slaves. At the same time, the visible rite of baptism appealed strongly to their mystic temperament. To-day the Baptist Church is still largest in membership among Negroes, and has a million and a half communicants. Next in popularity came the churches organized in connection with the white neighboring churches, chiefly Baptist and Methodist, with a few Episcopalian and others. The Methodists still form the second greatest denomination, with nearly a million members. The faith of these two leading denominations was more suited to the slave church from the prominence they gave to religious feeling and fervor. The Negro membership in other denominations has always been small and relatively unimportant, although the Episcopalians and Presbyterians are gaining among the more intelligent classes to-day, and the Catholic Church is making headway in certain sections. After Emancipation, and still earlier in the North, the Negro churches largely severed such affiliations as they had had with the white churches, either by choice or by compulsion. The Baptist churches became independent, but the Methodists were compelled early to unite for purposes of episcopal government. This gave rise to the great African Methodist Church, the greatest Negro organization in the world, to the Zion Church and the Colored Methodist, and to the black conferences and churches in this and other denominations.

The second fact noted, namely, that the Negro church antedates the Negro home, leads to an explanation of much that is paradoxical in this communistic institution and in the morals of its members. But especially it leads us to regard this institution as peculiarly the expression of the inner ethical life of a people in a sense seldom true elsewhere. Let us turn, then, from the outer physical development of the church to the more important inner ethical life of the people who compose it. The Negro has already been pointed out many times as a religious animal,—a being of that deep emotional nature which turns instinctively toward the supernatural. Endowed with a rich tropical imagination and a keen, delicate appreciation of Nature, the transplanted African lived in a world animate with gods and devils, elves and witches; full of strange influences,—of Good to be implored, of Evil to be propitiated. Slavery, then, was to him the dark triumph of Evil over him. All the hateful powers of the Under-world were striving against him, and a spirit of revolt and revenge filled his heart. He called up all the resources of heathenism to aid,—exorcism and witchcraft, the mysterious Obi worship with its barbarous rites, spells, and blood-sacrifice even, now and then, of human victims. Weird midnight orgies and mystic conjurations were invoked, the witch-woman and the voodoo-priest became the centre of Negro group life, and that vein of vague superstition which characterizes the unlettered Negro even to-day was deepened and strengthened.

In spite, however, of such success as that of the fierce Maroons, the Danish blacks, and others, the spirit of revolt gradually died away under the untiring energy and superior strength of the slave masters. By the middle of the eighteenth century the black slave had sunk, with hushed murmurs, to his place at the bottom of a new economic system, and was unconsciously ripe for a new philosophy of life. Nothing suited his condition then better than the doctrines of passive submission embodied in the newly learned Christianity. Slave masters early realized this, and cheerfully aided religious propaganda within certain bounds. The long system of repression and degradation of the Negro tended to emphasize the elements in his character which made him a valuable chattel: courtesy became humility, moral strength degenerated into submission, and the exquisite native appreciation of the beautiful became an infinite capacity for dumb suffering. The Negro, losing the joy of this world, eagerly seized upon the offered conceptions of the next; the avenging Spirit of the Lord enjoining patience in this world, under sorrow and tribulation until the Great Day when He should lead His dark children home,—this became his comforting dream. His preacher repeated the prophecy, and his bards sang,—

> "Children, we all shall be free
> When the Lord shall appear!"

This deep religious fatalism, painted so beautifully in "Uncle Tom," came soon to breed, as all fatalistic faiths will, the sensualist side by side with the martyr. Under the lax moral life of the plantation, where marriage was a farce, laziness a virtue, and property a theft, a religion of resignation and submission degenerated easily, in less strenuous minds, into a philosophy of indulgence and crime. Many of the worst characteristics of the Negro masses of to-day had their seed in this period of the slave's ethical growth. Here it was that the Home was ruined under the very shadow of the Church, white and black; here habits of shiftlessness took root, and sullen hopelessness replaced hopeful strife.

With the beginning of the abolition movement and the gradual growth of a class of free Negroes came a change. We often neglect the influence of the freedman before the war, because of the paucity of his numbers and the small weight he had in the history of the nation. But we must not forget that his chief influence was internal,—was exerted on the black world; and that there he was the ethical and social leader. Huddled as he was in a few centres like Philadelphia, New York, and New Orleans, the masses of the freedmen sank into poverty and listlessness; but not all of them. The free Negro leader early arose and his chief characteristic was intense earnestness and deep feeling on the slavery question. Freedom became to him a real thing and not a dream. His religion became darker and more intense, and into his ethics crept a note of revenge, into his songs a day of reckoning close at hand. The "Coming of the Lord" swept this side of Death, and came to be a thing to be hoped for in this day. Through fugitive slaves and irrepressible discussion this desire for freedom seized the black millions still in bondage, and became their one ideal of life. The black bards caught new notes, and sometimes even dared to sing,—

> "O Freedom, O Freedom, O Freedom over me!
> Before I'll be a slave
> I'll be buried in my grave,
> And go home to my Lord
> And be free."

For fifty years Negro religion thus transformed itself and identified itself with the dream of Abolition, until that which was a radical fad in the white North and an anarchistic plot in the white South had become a religion to the black world. Thus, when Emancipation finally came, it seemed to the freedman a literal Coming of the Lord. His fervid imagination was stirred as never before, by the tramp of armies, the blood and dust of battle, and the wail and whirl of social upheaval. He stood dumb and motionless before the whirlwind: what had he to do with it? Was it not the Lord's doing, and marvellous in his eyes? Joyed and bewildered with what came, he stood awaiting new wonders till the inevitable Age of Reaction swept over the nation and brought the crisis of to-day.

It is difficult to explain clearly the present critical stage of Negro religion. First, we must remember that living as the blacks do in close contact with a great modern nation, and sharing, although imperfectly, the soul-life of that nation, they must necessarily be affected more or less directly by all the religious and ethical forces that are to-day moving the United States. These questions and movements are, however, overshadowed and dwarfed by the (to them) all-important question of their civil, political, and economic status. They must perpetually discuss the "Negro Problem,"—must live, move, and have their being in it, and interpret all else in its light or darkness. With this come, too, peculiar problems of their inner life,—of the status of women, the maintenance of Home, the training of children, the accumulation of wealth, and the prevention of crime. All this must mean a time of intense ethical ferment, of religious heart-searching and intellectual unrest. From the double life every American Negro must live, as a Negro and as an American, as swept on by the current of the nineteenth while yet struggling in the eddies of the fifteenth century,—from this must arise a painful self-consciousness, an almost morbid sense of personality and a moral hesitancy which is fatal to self-confidence. The worlds within and without the Veil of Color are changing, and changing rapidly, but not at the same rate, not in the same way; and this must produce a peculiar wrenching of the soul, a peculiar sense of doubt and bewilderment. Such a double life, with double thoughts, double duties, and double social classes, must give rise to double words and double ideals, and tempt the mind to pretence or to revolt, to hypocrisy or to radicalism.

In some such doubtful words and phrases can one perhaps most clearly picture the peculiar ethical paradox that faces the Negro of to-day and is tingeing and changing his religious life. Feeling that his rights and his dearest ideals are being trampled upon, that the public conscience is ever more deaf to his righteous appeal, and that all the reactionary forces of prejudice, greed, and revenge are daily gaining new strength and fresh allies, the Negro faces no enviable dilemma. Conscious of his impotence, and pessimistic, he often becomes bitter and vindictive; and his religion, instead of a worship, is a complaint and a curse, a wail rather than a hope, a sneer rather than a faith. On the other hand, another type of mind, shrewder and keener and more tortuous too, sees in the very strength of the anti-Negro movement its patent weaknesses, and with Jesuitic casuistry is deterred by no ethical considerations in the endeavor to turn this weakness to the black man's strength. Thus we have two great and hardly reconcilable streams of thought and ethical strivings; the danger of the one lies in anarchy, that of the other in hypocrisy. The one type of Negro stands almost ready to curse God and die, and the other is too often found a traitor to right and a coward before force; the one is wedded to ideals remote, whimsical, perhaps impossible of realization; the other forgets that life is more than meat and the body more than raiment. But, after all, is not this simply the writhing of the age translated into black,—the triumph of the Lie which to-day, with its false culture, faces the hideousness of the anarchist assassin?

To-day the two groups of Negroes, the one in the North, the other in the South, represent these divergent ethical tendencies, the first tending toward radicalism, the other toward hypocritical compromise. It is no idle regret with which the white South mourns the loss of the old-time Negro,—the frank, honest, simple old servant who stood for the earlier religious age of submission and humility. With all his laziness and lack of many elements of true manhood, he was at least open-hearted, faithful, and sincere. To-day he is gone, but who is to blame for his going? Is it not those very persons who mourn for him? Is it not the tendency, born of Reconstruction and Reaction, to found a society on lawlessness and deception, to tamper with the moral fibre of a naturally honest and straightforward people until the whites threaten to become ungovernable tyrants and the blacks criminals and hypocrites? Deception is the natural defence of the weak against the strong, and the South used it for many years against its conquerors; to-day it must be prepared to see its black proletariat turn that same two-edged weapon against itself. And how natural this is! The death of Denmark Vesey and Nat Turner proved long since to the Negro the present hopelessness of physical defence. Political defence is becoming less and less available, and economic defence is still only partially effective. But there is a patent defence at hand,—the defence of deception and flattery, of cajoling and lying. It is the same defence which peasants of the Middle Age used and which left its stamp on their character for centuries. To-day the young Negro of the South who would succeed cannot be frank and outspoken, honest and self-assertive, but rather he is daily tempted to be silent and wary, politic and sly; he must flatter and be pleasant, endure petty insults with a smile, shut his eyes to wrong; in too many cases he sees positive personal advantage in deception and lying. His real thoughts, his real aspirations, must be guarded in whispers; he must not criticise, he must not complain. Patience, humility, and adroitness must, in these growing black youth, replace impulse, manliness, and courage. With this sacrifice there is an economic opening, and perhaps peace and some prosperity. Without this there is riot, migration, or crime. Nor is this situation peculiar to the Southern United States,—is it not rather the only method by which undeveloped races have gained the right to share modern culture? The price of culture is a Lie.

On the other hand, in the North the tendency is to emphasize the radicalism of the Negro. Driven from his birthright in the South by a situation at which every fibre of his more outspoken and assertive nature revolts, he finds himself in a land where he can scarcely earn a decent living amid the harsh competition and the color discrimination. At the same time, through schools and periodicals, discussions and lectures, he is intellectually quickened and awakened. The soul, long pent up and dwarfed, suddenly expands in new-found freedom. What wonder that every tendency is to excess,—radical complaint, radical remedies, bitter denunciation or angry silence. Some sink, some rise. The criminal and the sensualist leave the church for the gambling-hell and the brothel, and fill the slums of Chicago and Baltimore; the better classes segregate themselves from the group-life of both white and black, and form an aristocracy, cultured but pessimistic, whose bitter criticism stings while it points out no way of escape. They despise the submission and subserviency of the Southern Negroes, but offer no other means by which a poor and oppressed minority can exist side by side with its masters. Feeling deeply and keenly the tendencies and opportunities of the age in which they live, their souls are bitter at the fate which drops the Veil between; and the very fact that this bitterness is natural and justifiable only serves to intensify it and make it more maddening.

Between the two extreme types of ethical attitude which I have thus sought to make clear wavers the mass of the millions of Negroes, North and South; and their religious life and activity partake of this social conflict within their ranks. Their churches are differentiating,— now into groups of cold, fashionable devotees, in no way distinguishable from similar white groups save in color of skin; now into large social and business institutions catering to the desire for information and amusement of their members, warily avoiding unpleasant questions both within and without the black world, and preaching in effect if not in word: *Dum vivimus, vivamus.*

But back of this still broods silently the deep religious feeling of the real Negro heart, the stirring, unguided might of powerful human souls who have lost the guiding star of the past and are seeking in the great night a new religious ideal. Some day the Awakening will come, when the pent-up vigor of ten million souls shall sweep irresistibly toward the Goal, out of the Valley of the Shadow of Death, where all that makes life worth living—Liberty, Justice, and Right—is marked "For White People Only."

SUPPLEMENTARY READINGS

Du Bois, W. E. Burghardt. *Dusk of Dawn: An Essay Toward an Autobiography of a Race Concept.* New York: Harcourt, Brace & World, 1940.

Du Bois, W. E. Burghardt. *The Negro Church.* Atlanta: Atlanta University Press, 1903.

Du Bois, W. E. Burghardt. *Prayers for Dark People.* Edited by Herbert Aptheker. Amherst: University of Massachusetts Press, 1980.

Rudwick, Elliott. *W. E. B. Du Bois: Propagandist of the Negro Protest.* New York: Atheneum, 1972.

Washington, Booker T., and W. E. Burghardt Du Bois. *The Negro in the South: His Economic Progress in Relation to His Moral and Religious Development* [1907]. New York: Citadel Press, 1970.

35

ROSA YOUNG

"What Induced Me to Build a School in the Rural District"

Rosa Young, daughter of an African Methodist preacher and a graduate of Payne University in Selma, Alabama, vowed to return to the rural areas and start a school for poor black children ignored by the white educational system and whose parents were still living in the shadow of the plantation. In 1912 she opened the Rosebud School, in Rosebud, Alabama, with seven children in a small shed previously used to shelter cattle. By 1915 there were 215 children, but a boll weevil infestation that year killed the cotton in the area, making it impossible for the parents to pay even the pittance of a tuition. Desperate for help, Rosa Young wrote Booker T. Washington for the name of some individual or association in the North. He advised her to contact the Board of Colored Missions of the Lutheran Church, which he felt was doing more for blacks in the South than any other denomination. Missionary N. J. Bakke of the German-speaking Evangelical Lutheran Synodical Conference, based in St. Louis, arrived in 1916, took over the Rosebud school, and began an aggressive program of establishing schools and churches throughout the "black belt." White Lutherans in the upper Midwest, ensconced in their German cultural enclaves, viewed the mission work in Alabama as a "foreign" field but persisted sufficiently to establish the Lutheran presence. Today there are fourth-generation black Lutherans, a reminder that a religious history of Afro-Americans should not exclude those who belong to predominantly white denominations.

For, behold, the darkness shall cover the earth and gross darkness the people—*Is.* 60, 2.

IT WAS NOT the thought of money that induced me to be willing to assume the heavy burden, the weighty responsibility, and the binding obligation to buy land, erect a building, and operate a school for the benefit of my race. There was no money appropriated or set aside in any

Source: *Light in the Dark Belt*. St. Louis: Concordia Publishing House, 1951. Pp. 46–58.

form for the support of such a difficult task or great and expensive undertaking. There was no outside source to draw on, no board, no organization, no philanthropist backing it, not even the promise of as much as one penny from a single individual. The whole situation depended on me. To start with, I was to be the board, the bank, and the organization.

Now, what did I have? Nothing. I was no wealthy woman possessing great riches, owning a number of investments producing large incomes. I had the pitiful sum of two hundred dollars, my own personal money, the sum I had saved above my personal use besides what I had to give my parents to help them along with the support of my younger brothers and sisters. What was that meager sum, all my little living, against such an expensive undertaking? And yet I was willing to give it, and gave it gladly, for the benefit and uplift of my destitute race and for the spreading of Christ's kingdom.

I did not give the two hundred dollars, all my little living, from any selfish or vainglorious motive. It was not for praise, glory, or honor. From the time I received my diploma and went forth from the university halls into the battle of life, it had ever been my desire to serve the common, destitute people. I was always ready to serve under any and all conditions. My highest ambition is to serve, to be a faithful servant of God and my people. I would rather serve than be served. I have never desired a high position. I would rather do the humble work among the despised and outcast.

What, then, induced me to shoulder such great responsibility, to start out with no fund on which to draw, to face friend and foe and announce that I was going to build a school for the benefit of my race, the humble, the poor, the despised, the rejected, the downtrodden, the little outcast colored children in the dark sections of the rural districts throughout the Black Belt?

I will enumerate my reasons as follows:—

1. I saw the vile and grievous condition of my race, of my brothers and sisters. It was a pathetic sight. Ignorance and superstition in all matters prevailed beyond measure; indeed, the ignorance and superstition among the people were amazing.

2. Morals and manners were at a low ebb. It was a rare thing to see a man who did not have two or more wives or to see a woman who had only one husband. It was a common thing to see a young girl in her teens, approaching the age of twenty, who was a mother and was drifting about with no husband. It was a common sight to see young men and boys strolling along the highways with banjos strung from their necks and shoulders—both young and old had lost all regard for

the holy estate of matrimony. It was no longer considered a holy or divine ordinance. There were hundreds of people who had been married, but were separated. It was a common thing to see girls or women living by themselves in little huts dotted over the plantations. Young girls would often bundle their clothes, move out from their father's home, away from the care and protection of a loving mother, and start keeping house by themselves.

The reputation of some of these people was shameful. Their manners in all places, at home, in church, on the roadsides, in public places, such as stores and railroad stations, was rough, uncouth, boisterous. Even their word of honor was of no account.

Their manner of dressing was embarrassing to behold. Only a few grown-up people wore shoes. Most of them went barefoot. The men wore their trousers rolled half-way up their limbs or to their knees. The women wore their dresses tied half-way up their limbs, with a long string around their waists. They dressed their hair by wrapping it with white, red, or black strings.

3. The third reason why I desired to build a school was because of the condition of the homes. The homes in which these poor people lived were horrible. In every community there were two classes of people, the Big-dogs and the Little-dogs. Of course, in the homes of the so-called Big-dogs conditions were a little more decent. In the homes of the so-called Little-dogs, conditions, upon the whole, were indecent. There were no arrangements made for bathing or ventilation in the houses. In most of them there was too much ventilation. While sitting in the house behind closed doors, one could look up and see the sky, the moon, and the stars through the holes in the roof; one could look down and through the holes in the floor see the ground—chickens, hogs, little pigs, and dogs. One could seldom find a decent pair of steps at a door. The chimneys were made of sticks daubed with red mud and reached only half-way up the houses. On a cold day it might happen that the wind would blow down the chimney, and the smoke would prevent the family from having a fire.

In many cases the whole family, half-grown young men and women, smaller children, and father and mother, had to sleep and cook in the same room. The bed-clothing was filthy; almost all the members of the family would sleep in the clothes they had worn during the day. The dishes and cooking-utensils remained unwashed from meal to meal, day after day. The bed-clothes, dishes, and cooking-utensils were covered with swarms of flies. Scarcely any lamps could be found in the homes, and in most cases where there were lamps they had no chimneys.

There were no dinner-tables on which to serve when the dinner was prepared. The good old mother gave each member of the family his or her dinner on a plate, pan, bucket, or skillet. Some would sit in the doorway, some on the steps, others out in the yard, and the little children on the floor. All ate with their hands and fingers.

They used gourds for dippers, broom-sage and pine-tops for brooms. A few chairs, boxes, blocks, wagon-body seats, on the floor, were used for seats. The floors were seldom, if ever, scrubbed and not often swept. About the yard lay all kinds of filthy rags, inviting pestilence and disease.

4. The children, the dear little children of the rural districts, whom I love so well and in whom I am so interested, were in a sad condition. They were pitiful sights; some of them had to come to school partly dressed in adults' clothing. In the dead of winter some of them would have to come to my school with only one or two pieces of clothing on as a protection against the stings and howls of the winter winds, half hungry, half naked, barefooted, toes and heels cracked open from the rain, ice, and frost. Their little heads looked horrible. The little girls' hair was combed only once in a while. It was knotty, kinky, dirty, matted, and full of cockleburs. The boys, poor things, their hair was never combed. Once in a while some members of the family would take a pair of scissors and cut the boys' hair, which was so gummy and matted that the hair cut off would come off in a caplike form. In many cases there were hog-lice in the little boys' hair. On their hands, wrists, forearms, in the back of their necks, on their kneecaps, on the front part of their legs, on their ankles, heels, feet, and toes, grew banks of dirt until it formed a scaly crust, so thick that you could take a pin and stick deep or scrape hard, and the poor little things would not feel it. The finger- and toe-nails were long and dirty. They ate with their little hands all the time. Their teeth were yellow with stain. The best they knew to do was to steal, lie, curse, swear, and fight like cats and dogs.

5. The educational advantages offered these children by the State were entirely inadequate. The school-terms lasted only three or four months a year. Before the children could get a good start in school, the term would be over. During the long vacation of eight or nine months the children would forget most, if not all, of what they had learned during the previous term before the time came for the reopening of the school.

6. Among the poor little, destitute children of whom I write there were some bright boys and girls, filled with high ambitions, with the marks of leadership on their dusky brows, which shone like diamonds in

a coal-bed in the bright sun. Their poor parents were unable to send
them to school. They had nothing with which to pay their board; they
were just barely existing themselves.

However, most of the children were dull and backward. There were
large boys and girls said to be in the fifth, sixth, and seventh grades who
could not read a paragraph through correctly. If they were asked to spell
a simple word, for instance, the word "smooth," they would be liable
to begin to spell it with a p or a q. There were large children who could
not write the letters of the alphabet or do primary work in arithmetic.
They would not have the slightest idea of how to solve the simplest
problem. Some ten- and fifteen-year-old boys and girls could not read
the first lesson on the chart or in the primer.

7. As a general thing, there were no schoolhouses; for the most part
the public schools were taught in the churches. Most of the churches
were dilapidated and so exposed to the elements that one might as well
teach outdoors under an oak-tree. There were big holes in the roofs and
in the floors. Many a time during a heavy shower of rain the large children would have to hold an umbrella over me while I heard a class
recite.

In some of those churches there were small heaters, but no flues;
so we had to take out a window pane and run the stovepipe out through
the side of the wall. When the wind was high on a cold day, the smoke
would turn us all away from the fire. In churches where there were no
heaters we were obliged to build big fires outdoors. Then I would have
to watch the little fellows to prevent their clothes from catching fire, for
many of them were patched like little rag-men. All kinds of patches and
all kinds of thread were used on the same garment.

The blackboards were made of rough planks and dyed with ink.
Each child would bring an egg or a penny for a piece of crayon. Each
child had to go to the woods and bring armfuls of wood for the fire.
The children drank water out of their dinner buckets or the tops. We
used broom-sage straw and pine-tops for brooms to sweep the floors.

8. The poor people were lacking in leadership. It is one of the
great needs of the colored race even to this day to have sufficient and
efficient leaders. The number of able, prepared leaders is so small in
proportion to the vast number of worthless leaders that not much real
work can be done very rapidly.

The public-school teachers were inefficient. Not more than one-
third of them could pass a third-grade state examination fairly well.
Some of them did not have the least idea of how to grade a school.
They would permit children to enter the sixth and seventh grades that
should have been in the third. Discipline in the school was unknown.

Before one reached the school-building or church where the school was being held, one could hear the children giggling, murmuring, and shuffling their feet. There was a continual commotion during the school-hours. The teachers would ask the children questions about their lessons and have to look in the book to see if the child answered correctly.

These teachers would permit the children to sing all kinds of songs and give some of the most ridiculous recitations. The public-school teachers would sometimes have Christmas-trees and present Christmas programs. The following are some of the recitations the children would recite. A little ashy-faced country lad comes forward, so happy that he has a chance to speak that his face is wreathed in smiles. He recites as follows:—

> Black gum bits and bullet rains,
> White oak saddle and hickory horse,
> Um gwine to ride all up and down the line.

At this all the people would just whoop, hollo, and laugh. Then another child would come forward and give his Christmas selection:—

> Milk in the pitcher and butter in the bowl;
> I cannot get a sweetheart to save my soul.

Then another would step forward and recite:—

> With a jug of molasses and a pan of biscuits in my hand,
> I'll sop my way to the Promised Land.

Now, such recitations were given on the solemn occasion of the commemoration of the birth of Jesus, the Savior of the world. Gross darkness covered the people.

The so-called preachers, with a few exceptions, were worse than those to whom they preached. They were both ignorant and immoral. It seemed to be their ambition to destroy the morals of the very brightest women and girls in every community over which they presided. The better class of laymen could not trust them in their homes during their absence. These big so-called sectarian preachers have been the downfall of many poor, ignorant, young girls. They have destroyed the peace and harmony in many a humble country home.

The majority of those big so-called preachers were regular whisky heads. It was a common thing to see a big leader at one of those annual meetings just out of the pulpit staggering down some dark alley, drunk with wine, beer, "shinny," or whisky, heaving like a dog, while the other preachers looked upon it as a joke. Besides this, those preachers were greedy for money. They would rove the rural districts, holding out false inducements to the poor, ignorant people, enticing them to join all kinds of fraternal societies that lead hellward. They would offer the people sick-, accident-, and death-benefits, and every other kind of benefit, just to get their money. The poor, ignorant people could not resist the temptation. Those who had credit would go to their landlords and borrow the money to join. The other people would sell their corn, eggs, pigs, chickens, the very food out of the mouths of their little children, to obtain money with which to join these societies. After they had stripped the people of all the money they could get, these scoundrels would escape and no more would be heard from them, while the people were left in need as before.

They would impose heavy taxation, or assessment, upon the church people, and if those who were thus taxed, failed to pay, they were excommunicated, or their names were put on the dead list. A person whose name was on the dead list was not permitted to partake of the Lord's Supper. If he became sick, no pastor visited him, and if he died, no pastor would bury him or preach the funeral sermon. Some of these preachers would hire out to the people to preach so many sermons a year or month for so much money. Visiting the sick and burying the dead was not included. A baptism was performed for twenty-five cents and up per head. When a member died, the funeral was used as an occasion to draw a large crowd in order to get a lot of money.

These preachers would not humble themselves, or feel enough interest in the people, to live in the parsonages the people had provided for them. The homes these poor people had strained themselves to build for them they allowed to go to ruin and flocked to the cities, hanging around the streets in the towns during the week. On Saturdays they would go out to their country churches, do their kind of preaching, get all the money, chickens, eggs, etc., they could from the people and on Monday mornings board the train for the city with these gifts, joking about the people, calling them "niggers," and saying, "I told them niggers so and so." Instead of trying to enlighten the people, they were calling them fools.

9. I always believed in the education of the heart; for a bright head with a wicked heart stands for naught. It only tends to breed trouble. I knew something was wrong with the kind of religion my people had, but I did not know what was wrong about it. I desired a better Christian training for myself and my people, but I did not know where to find it. The religion of my people was a mere pretense, a kind of manufactured religion. Those who belonged to church were no better than those who did not. In most of the homes the so-called Christian families as well as the unbelievers lived in envy, strife, malice, prejudice, bitter hatred, yea,

hellish riot; in covetousness; in adultery and fornication; in theft and lying.

In hundreds of homes the Bible was never read, a prayer was never spoken, and a Christian hymn was never sung. The whole family lay down at night and rose the next morning, and each went out to do his work like the beast of the field, without saying a word of thanks to God. Sin was looked upon by most people as a small thing. They did not fear to sin; to them sin was nothing. They held divine services in their churches twelve times a year, on the average once a month. No one took the time to teach them Christian hymns; they sang old plantation songs during their services, such as the following:—

> Drinking the wine, O wine,
> Drinking the wine to heal my soul.
> Good Lord, I ought to been da ten thousand years
> Drinking the wine.

Another:—

> Heavy load, heavy load, heavy load, heavy load;
> Um gyng to lay down dis heavy load.
> The devil is a lie and a conjure, too,
> Um gyng to lay down dis heavy load;
> And if you don't mind, he will conjure you,
> Um gyng to lay down dis heavy load.
>
> My load so heavy I can't get along,
> Um gyng to lay down dis heavy load.
> The devil wear dem iron shoes,
> Um gyng to lay down dis heavy load.
> If you don't look out, he will slip dem on you,
> Um gyng to lay down my heavy load.

Now, if a Christian hymn was lined out, not ten in the whole congregation could sing the words. For instance, suppose the following hymn were lined out: "Alas! and did my Savior bleed," etc., all in the congregation would start singing at the top of their voices, just as loud as they could sing; but instead of singing the words of the hymn, the poor, ignorant people would be singing as follows: "Dey hey mey sey, ley hey dey sey, hey mey fey sey, hey hey." Their preachers never took the time to see if the people were singing the words given out to them or not.

Both men and women would get down on their knees and pray just as loud as they could hollo, using all kinds of profane language and blasphemy. They would call on God as if He were asleep or dead. The preachers would read a text and then branch off and preach all kinds of man-made doctrines, telling the people that these things are in the Bible. Many a time the name of Jesus was not mentioned during a whole sermon. The preachers would whoop, hollo, pat, and stamp, snort, and blow until the people were in an uproar, shouting and holloing, too. Then the preachers would just say anything. I once heard a preacher laughing and telling how he curses when he gets "niggers" to shouting and holloing.

The people were obliged to carry on most of the church-work without the preachers; they just came and preached. The people would have Sunday-school about three months out of the year, beginning a few Sundays before Easter each year and continuing until July or August.

The people had the wrong conception of Christmas altogether, considering it a time of great rejoicing; but they had the wrong kind of joy. They held frolics, dances, horse races, shooting-matches, with gambling, fighting, drinking, cursing, and swearing. There were rough times at Christmas. For meek people it was advisable to remain indoors, for it was dangerous even to walk out in one's yard for fear of being shot down by rough passers-by. At Christmas time all the little children were given whisky to drink; the old folks said it was to get their blood hot.

On Easter also the people held celebrations, but only a few knew why Easter is celebrated. They would use any kind of songs or recitations. Some of the Easter songs were: "Home, Sweet Home," "Ding Dong, Sweet Bell, Ding Dong," etc. The recitations were such as: "The Village Smith," "The Farmer Boy," etc. Many a time on Easter the name of Jesus was not mentioned.—Gross darkness had covered the people. Is. 60, 2.

10. The teaching of the Bible, of the Six Chief Parts of the Christian religion. But I cannot say that this was one of my reasons for wanting to build a school for my race, for in this respect I was in the dark myself. Sad! Sad! We were all blind and leaders of the blind. We did not know the Bible, neither did the preachers know it. We did not know what we must do to be saved, neither did the preachers. They were preaching false doctrine, and we did not know it. We did not know that Jesus has done all that is necessary for our salvation, and the preachers did not know it. We did not know what Jesus, the Savior, meant to us. We did not know that we were sinners. We wanted to go to heaven; but we did not know the way, and the preachers did not know it. We were trying to work our way to heaven, and the preachers were doing the same. We were not following our Bibles, neither were the preachers.

Now, what was to be done? Our white people had given us our schools and churches. We sent calls and had our leaders; and I presume the white people thought we were getting along fine.

The Lord, our Savior, who loved us saw all this and had compassion on us. He saw that the sad plight of our immortal souls was far worse than our physical condition. The Lord looked down from heaven upon us. He saw this hellward-leading teaching, this man-made doctrine of salvation by works. He saw darkness had covered our land. Our eyes were blind to the knowledge contained in His blessed Gospel. The Lord saw that we were all on the wrong road, regardless of how well we meant, and could never reach heaven that way.

God saw that I was concerned, that I was worried, about many things pertaining to the temporal welfare of my people. God saw my eager desires and longings to do something for Him and my race. I did not have the least idea of what was to be done. I could not preach, for women are not allowed to preach. But the Lord instilled in me the thought of building a school, gave me strength to begin this work, and sustained me. . . .

SUPPLEMENTARY READINGS

Dickinson, Richard C. *Roses and Thorns: The Centennial Edition of Black Lutheran Mission and Ministry in the Lutheran Church—Missouri Synod.* St. Louis: Concordia Publishing House, 1977.

Harlan, Louis R. *Booker T. Washington: The Making of a Black Leader 1865–1901.* New York: Oxford University Press, 1972.

Powdermaker, Hortense. *After Freedom: A Cultural Study in the Deep South.* New York: Viking Press, 1939, 1967.

Puckett, Newbell Niles. *Folk Beliefs of the Southern Negro.* Chapel Hill: University of North Carolina Press, 1926.

Sisk, Glenn N. "Churches in the Alabama Black Belt, 1875–1917." *Church History* 23, no. 2 (June 1954): 153–74.

36

CARTER G. WOODSON

"Things of the Spirit"

The decline of rural America troubled church leaders in the early 1900s. Emigration to the cities accelerated during and after World War I. The movement of blacks off the land and into the cities (both northern and southern), the mechanization of agriculture, and the breakup of a rural social structure that often revolved around family churches caused great concern. Most of the major white denominations established rural life commissions to study the effects of such rapid change on rural churches. Carter G. Woodson (1875–1950) founded The Association for the Study of Negro Life and History in 1915 as the "first systematic effort of the Negro to treat the records of the race scientifically and to publish their findings." Woodson published the first edition of his classic The History of the Negro Church *in 1921 and returned to examine "things of the spirit" in* The Rural Negro, *published in 1930. A historian trained in the new methods of social science and a firm believer in the efficacy of knowledge, Woodson sought scientific objectivity but conducted his research with passionate devotion to racial advancement. Thus, his portrait of the religious culture of the black "peasantry" of the rural South reveals as much about Woodson's notions of what black churches should be doing as about what they actually were. He concluded that the urban church had become "a sort of uplift agency," but that the rural church remained "a mystic shrine."*

IN THEIR SIMPLE WAY the rustic people of color contend for the principles originally enunciated by the Protestant Church fathers. Christ came into the world to reveal God to man. He gave His life to save evildoers, who must die in their sins and be brought to life in Jesus, if they hope to escape the fire and brimstone of hell; and even after being thus born again they must be careful, for the devil is always busily planning to swerve the faithful from the way to glory. Thousands of snares may hang the feet, but none should hold them fast. Do right at all times, do not become frivolous, and take life too leisurely. Do not in-

Source: The Rural Negro. Washington, D.C.: The Association for the Study of Negro Life and History, Inc., 1930. Pp. 154–65.

dulge in the modern dance, but keep up the buck and wing dance if in so performing you do not cross your feet. Quit playing cards, throw away your checker-board, give up croquet, shun baseball, or football, and never bet. If you do these things the devil will claim you finally as his own. You may take a little home-made wine, or persimmon beer; and you may occasionally take a mint-julep or a toddy on Sunday morning before you have family prayers, but you must be temperate. You must not become intoxicated. Furthermore, never swear. "Let your communication be yea, yea, and no, no, for whatsoever cometh of more than these cometh of evil."

The importance of such teaching is best appreciated in understanding that the Negro Church, whether rural or urban, is the only institution which the race controls. The whites being Occidental in contradistinction to the Negroes who are Oriental, do not understand this Oriental faith called Christianity and consequently fail to appreciate the Negroes' conception of it. White people, therefore, have urged a separation in church as in other things; and much more so in the case of this than in other institutions: for, while they separate the Negroes in education, recreation, and the like, the whites, nevertheless, keep control of these things. They make little effort, however, to influence the Negro church. This institution, then, has had the chance to develop in the way the Negroes would have it. In their church they have more freedom than in any other sphere, and the Negro preacher among his own is in a class by himself.

Who, then, is this high priest in the rural community? He is not the man required to direct the religious work of an urban center, but "an inspired man" whom the fates have superimposed. He had a vision and he heard a voice which called him to preach. He had "to answer this divine call lest God might strike him dead." Such an inspired creature may have the rudiments of education or he may be illiterate; for in spite of his lack of mental development he can find a following sufficient to maintain a church. The Methodist conferences have done much to eliminate such clergy, but the Baptist conventions, although making a similar effort, have not yet succeeded. The Baptists enjoy so much democracy that they have no power to coerce the local churches. No Baptist church is subject to any authority but God, and sometimes it will disregard Him and run its affairs to suit itself.

As a rule, however, the Negro rural preachers are morally clean, much more so than those who labor in cities. There are certain shortcomings in all groups, but investigation has shown that the Negro rural priestcraft bears a good name. Their gravest fault is that they do not often pay their debts promptly. It seems that, having become accus-

tomed to receiving things gratis, they cannot abandon the idea that in
some way they can escape meeting such obligations. As a rule they will
not lie or steal, and not many of them are found guilty of corrupting
men's wives and daughters. In some communities where ministers have
been found guilty of such things the whole class is given a very bad
name for the offenses of one or two who happen to be exceptionally
immoral. In this case all ministers are made responsible for the crimes
of one, very much as a white community denounces all the Negroes as
criminals when one of them happens to commit a dastardly crime. Of
the thousands of questionnaires received and studied by the author
only a few state that the reputation of the Negro rural preacher is bad,
whereas in the case of cities this was often the comment.

What, then, is the preparation of the Negro rural ministers? For
the special task in which they are engaged their formal preparation is
practically blank. They do well to be able to read and write intelligibly.
It may be that they have seen a few books on the rural church, but it
is doubtful that they have enough mental development to understand
them. Of late the white religious agencies are giving special training to·
ministers who will work among rural people. From summer to summer
now most of the sects hold special schools for Negro pastors for about
four or six weeks, and some good has thereby been accomplished.[1] Negro rural churches, however, cannot draw freely upon such well prepared
workers. At present there are only a few Negro youth aspiring to the
ministry, and those, who do, go into the best churches in the cities. Because this condition obtains the ministry of the rural Negro church must
be recruited from the mentally undeveloped members who have any
amount of spirit but little understanding.[2] The rural church must take
largely volunteer workers who cannot find opportunities elsewhere or
who have other interests in the rural districts. While it must be admitted that by experience some of these rural ministers are better prepared than town preachers with a little more book learning, there is
nothing in the average one of the group to indicate possibilities of leadership which the new program of the rural community requires.

The Negro rural church, therefore, has not made much progress
beyond its status of reconstruction or antebellum days. Some Negroes
in towns and cities enjoying contact with the outer world have remade
their religion according to Caucasian requirements. The backwoods

1   Dr. James H. Dillard, of the John F. Slater Fund, and Bishop R. A. Carter, of
the C.M.E. Church, have been very active in this work. Such conferences at Paine
College, Hampton, and Tuskegee have been well attended.
2   Immediately after the Civil War most educated Negroes went into the ministry.
Now they go into other professions.

Negroes, however, have not been similarly moved. They see no need for changes in religion. Inasmuch as God changes not, and is just the same to-day as yesterday, how can a minister of Jehovah advocate such innovations? "Give me, therefore, that old time religion," they say, "it's good enough for me." The rural Negro minister, then, will not proclaim a new thought. He will preach the same gospel in the same way. He has not changed and never intends to do so. "Others calling themselves ministers," he contends, "are bringing worldly things into the church; but as for me and my house we will serve the Lord."

What, then, is this institution which the Negro rural minister directs? This question is difficult to answer, for while the outward appearances of the Negro rural church may seem like the urban, the two are inherently different. The urban church has become a sort of uplift agency; the rural church has remained a mystic shrine. While the urban church is often trying to make this a better world in which to live, the rural church is engaged in immediate preparation for the "beautiful land of by and by." The rural church building may be used for social uplift purposes, but this is not the church thus in action. These things originate without the spiritual group. When the rural church assembles in the spirit it is more of a séance. Persons have come together to wait upon the Lord. He promised to meet them there. They have no time for the problems of this life except to extricate themselves from the difficulties which will ever beset them here until that final day.

The worship of such an assembly is simple. There must be merely a reading of the scripture, singing, preaching, and praying. Then one must wait until the spirit moves him. The preacher makes his emotional appeal and the seekers within the courts respond with manifestations of the spirit resembling paroxysms which could hardly be expected outside of an insane asylum. With the spirits of the people thus fired up they can retire to their homes sufficiently uplifted to face the toils of another week or month. On assembling for similar services again they will have their spiritual strength renewed. This is the church visible and invisible. As such it considers itself the church militant, which, according to their faith, will some day be triumphant and take heaven by storm. "Sinner, you had better join the army before it is too late. Now is the accepted time."

The occasions for large accessions to the church, however, are not the regular preaching days or prayer meetings, for these are mainly to edify the elect. "To bring a large number into the fold" the rural churches hold camp meetings or protracted efforts. In July and August or at some other time when the peasants have harvested their crops they hold these revival assemblies. Food and money are more abundant at that time and the people are at leisure. No two churches close together will have such a meeting at the same time. One takes up the first week of the month and another the second and so on to give the people of various communities the opportunity to follow these meetings from church to church. People from afar, who once came in carts and wagons, drawn by oxen and horses, may come to-day in automobiles. As the whole day for a week is taken up with services in the morning, afternoon, and evening, families must daily bring sufficient food for at least two meals. These feasts, then, are important functions of the assembly. The preachers must be fed, and sinners stricken with guilt must be cared for until "the Lord speaks peace to their souls."

There arrives, then, an abundance of nicely cooked vegetables, cakes, pastries, chickens, and watermelons galore. At noon everything is spread and made free. One may go from table to table and eat to his own satisfaction without price. Worldly people not the least interested in the religious effort often attend these meetings to feast and socialize with friends who are not otherwise brought together during the whole year. Men come to exchange news on the state of the community and to find out the prospects in various quarters. Girls expect to find there new fellows who may be attracted to them in gay summer attire. Young men similarly inclined come looking for new conquests. And with these are to be seen not a few widows and widowers bereft during the closing season but still believing that fortune may bring another companion with whom to continue on life's journey.

The seriousness of these people, however, does not permit the social to overshadow the spiritual. The minister and his visiting assistants are preaching three times a day on temperance, righteousness, and judgment to come. Prayers are offered hourly for those who are out of the "ark of safety." Repeatedly they sing such songs as

> "Where are you going, sinner?
> Where are you going, I say?
> Going down to the river of Jordan
> And you can't cross there.
>
> "Oh you must have that true religion!
> You must have your soul converted!
> You must have that true religion!
> Or you can't cross there."

The pleasure-seeking worldly persons, then, cannot long withstand this fervent appeal. Even the young ladies seeking beaux will refuse to socialize with sinners. "Before you talk love with me," one would say, "you must get your soul right with God."

Sinners, then, begin to weaken. They may stand up very well for the Sunday when the meeting opens and probably until Monday or Tuesday, but before the middle of the week you hear that some notorious person has been "convicted of his sins." This means that he has become thoroughly alarmed as to his lost condition and while in a state of prayer for deliverance from sin, he falls into a trance, prostrate like a man in dying condition. Friends come rushing up to minister unto his physical needs, trying to revive him. He gradually awakens from his stupor, praising God for pardoning him of his sins, usually saying with a peculiarly primitive intonation: "Thank God! Thank God! Thank God that I was born to die! He snatched me like a brand from eternal burning and saved me from hell's dark door. He said, 'O my little one, go in yonder world and tell both saints and sinners what a dear Savior you have found! I have plucked your feet out of the mire and the clay and placed them on the solid rock of ages where the wind may blow and the storm may rise but none shall frighten you from the shore!' "

This is what is considered a conversion. When noised abroad that a vile sinner has been thus saved his whole ilk and others of less crime become precipitously excited and readily answer the call to the anxious seat where they bow praying in the midst of sobs and tears, earnestly entreating the brethren "to take them to a throne of grace in their prayers." Friends, especially interested in these sinners at the anxious seat, bow with them and whisper in their ears how "to find the way," while the minister vociferously contrasts the joys of heaven with the tortures of hell. Numbers of other sinners, then, become more easily "convicted," and soon they declare themselves "converted" and fill the woods around with outbursts of praise to God for what He has done for their souls. Before the end of the week, therefore, practically all malefactors in the neighborhood, except those commonly referred to as being "hardened in their sins," will be converted. At the end of the week the convocation closes with a sort of love feast, friends of the redeemed proclaiming more forcefully than the converts themselves their praise to God for "killing these people dead in their sins and bringing them to life in Jesus."

A few weeks thereafter comes the meeting when those proposed for membership in Baptist churches must demonstrate that they are actually converted and qualified for full privileges of the body. In the case of Methodists they must pass through a probation period. This is always easy, however, for all the candidate needs to do is to convince the brethren that he had some such experience as they themselves had— that he saw a light, heard a voice, had a vision, outwitted the devil, or received a visit from Jesus. With such a straight story they find ready acceptance in the church.

Most of these people, however, are frantically excited or "hell-scared." Yet, they go into the church with the intention to lead a better life. Having never thought the matter out carefully, however, and having never learned to practice restraint, many of them within a few months, easily go back into the life they formerly led; and the minister at his next revival meeting has to do his work over again. In all of these communities, then, one finds a number of persons who must "get religion" every summer because they "throw it away" during the winter social season.

Losing one's religion, too, is an easy matter in this Puritanic atmosphere; for you cannot sing worldly songs, cross your feet in dancing, play games, or go afishing on Sunday. Christ has called his people out from among the worldly. Yet if one indulges in these things only occasionally he merely backslides, and from him the right hand of fellowship must be withheld until, as a result of his prayers, the Lord condescends to heal his backsliding. Such a person, however, is often regarded as worse than a confirmed sinner, for "he that putteth his hands to the plow and then turns back is not fit for the kingdom."

SUPPLEMENTARY READINGS

Brunner, Edmund deS. *Church Life in the Rural South*. New York: George H. Doran Co., 1923.

Felton, Ralph A. *These My Brethren*. Madison, N.J.: Department of the Rural Church, Drew Theological Seminary, 1950.

Johnson, Charles S. *Shadow of the Plantation*. Chicago: University of Chicago Press, 1934. Chap. 5.

Logan, Rayford W. "Carter G. Woodson: Mirror and Molder of His Time, 1875–1950." *The Journal of Negro History* 58, no. 1 (January 1973): 1–17.

Richardson, Harry V. *Dark Glory: A Picture of the Church among Negroes in the Rural South*. New York: Friendship Press, 1947.

37

BENJAMIN E. MAYS AND
JOSEPH W. NICHOLSON

"The Genius of the Negro Church"

In the summer of 1930 the Institute of Social and Religious Research—a Rockefeller-financed agency established in 1921 to apply scientific methods to the study of socio-religious phenomena—contacted Benjamin E. Mays (1894–1984). Then on the staff of the National Y.M.C.A., the thirty-five-year-old South Carolina native and Bates College graduate was asked to direct a study of black churches in the United States. He and Joseph W. Nicholson, a minister of the Colored Methodist Episcopal Church, spent fourteen months gathering data and ten months writing The Negro's Church. Based on information about 609 urban churches in twelve cities, both northern and southern, and 185 rural churches in four southern counties, this study, according to Mays, was the first of its kind and thoroughly represented the black church at the time. A pioneering attempt to apply social survey techniques to the study of Afro-American religious institutions, The Negro's Church unearthed much useful information. In his autobiography, Born to Rebel, Mays asserts: "Our study showed that the most distinctive thing about the Negro church is its origin." He refers to five factors that gave rise to black churches: growing racial consciousness, individual initiative, splits and withdrawals, migration, and missions of other churches. When he and Nicholson searched for the genius or "soul" of black churches, they pointed to the pride of ownership, democratic fellowship, and spirit of freedom that blacks could enjoy within them.

PERHAPS THE READER feels that the analysis of the Negro church so far presented, though encouraging here and there, gives a rather dark picture; and that it offers nothing exceptionally promising for the future church life of 12,000,000 people.

The analysis reveals that the status of the Negro church is in part the result of the failure of American Christianity in the realm of race-relations; that the church's program, except in rare instances, is static,

Source: *The Negro's Church*. New York: Institute of Social and Religious Research, 1933. Pp. 278–92.

non-progressive, and fails to challenge the loyalty of many of the most critically-minded Negroes; that the vast majority of its pastors are poorly trained academically, and more poorly trained theologically; that more than half of the sermons analyzed are abstract, other-worldly, and imbued with a magical conception of religion; that in the church school less than one-tenth of the teachers are college graduates; that there are too many Negro churches; that the percentage of Negro churches in debt is high; that for the most part the Negro church is little concerned with juvenile delinquency and other social problems in its environment; that less than half of the reported membership can be relied upon to finance the church regularly and consistently; and that the rural church suffers most because of the instability and poverty of the rural Negroes.

Yet the authors believe that there is in the genius or the "soul" of the Negro church something that gives it life and vitality, that makes it stand out significantly above its buildings, creeds, rituals and doctrines, something that makes it a unique institution. For this reason, the writers, in this chapter, lean more heavily than in previous chapters upon the observations and personal experiences gained during the two-year, intensive study of the Negro church; and these are supplemented here and there by the experiences of the race.

The Church is the Negro's Very Own

The church was the first community or public organization that the Negro actually owned and completely controlled. And it is possibly true to this day that the Negro church is the most thoroughly owned and controlled public institution of the race. Nothing can compare with this ownership and control except ownership of the home and possibly control of the Negro Lodge. It is to be doubted whether Negro control is as complete in any other area of Negro life, except these two, as it is in the church.

A statement of this character may sound paradoxical in the light of the facts discovered in the chapter on finance, which show that 71.3 per cent. of the churches of this study are in debt. But churches are unique institutions, for which reason they enjoy special privileges.

Churches, unlike houses and business enterprises, are not very valuable to their creditors. Residence property, if taken from the buyer, is usually very valuable, and may return a profit. This is not true with churches. A church taken over by creditors is generally of little value to them and usually cannot be used for any other purpose. Ordinarily the financiers want the money and not the church; and they are not concerned with either the ownership or the control of the church. Another reason is the good reputation enjoyed by churches for eventually paying off their debts. Thus, for both of these reasons, indebtedness on churches generally does not involve loss of control to the creditors.

Furthermore, a glance through the chapter on finance shows that the huge total indebtedness of the Negro churches is more striking because of the high percentage of churches in debt than because of the amount of the indebtedness per church. For example, 45.6 per cent. of the 386 churches in debt have an average indebtedness of less than $5,000; and only 15.0 per cent. of them have debts ranging between $25,000 and $160,000; with twenty-one owing $50,000 or more, and only three owing more than $100,000.

Even if indebtedness carried control, most of the churches would not be so heavily in debt as to warrant creditor-control. Therefore, whatever the Negro church is in the United States, it is largely the outcome of the Negro's own genius and his ability to organize. Like other institutions it has glaring defects; and improvements in many spheres are greatly needed.

It is equally true, however, that there are hundreds of Negro churches that operate sufficiently well to warrant the commendation of critical minds.

Not only is this institution controlled by Negroes, but nine-tenths of the local churches are self-supporting. A few Negro churches, organically connected with white churches, churches of Negro denominations, and several Baptist churches were helped in an organized way between 1927 and 1931; but during the same period, 88.3 per cent. of the churches of this study received no systematic organized support from outside sources. Certainly in the majority of cases the amounts received from outside sources were so negligible that the churches would continue to exist if the outside help were entirely cut off. Even in the cases of the 11.7 per cent. of churches that received some organized support due to denominational connections and otherwise, there was sufficient evidence to show that control of the church was primarily in the hands of the Negro congregations.

Through and through, with or without outside help, the Negro churches of this study are principally governed by Negroes. Many Negroes, though unable to own homes of their own, take a peculiar pride in their churches. It gives them a sense of ownership that can hardly exist with respect to any other institution in the community. Since thousands do not own their homes, they develop a loyalty and devotion to their churches that commands respect and admiration. It is characteristic of the Negro church that the Negro owns it and that it is largely the product of his hand and brain.

Ownership and Control Provide
Opportunity for the Common Man

With races and individuals, there must be an opportunity for the development of initiative and self-direction if real character is to be developed, and if hidden potentialities are to be brought to the fore. Certainly the Negro church has been the training school that has given the masses of the race opportunity to develop.

The opportunity found in the Negro church to be recognized, and to be "somebody," has stimulated the pride and preserved the self-respect of many Negroes who would have been entirely beaten by life, and possibly completely submerged. Everyone wants to receive recognition and feel that he is appreciated. The Negro church has supplied this need. A truck driver of average or more than ordinary qualities becomes the chairman of the Deacon Board. A hotel man of some ability is the superintendent of the Sunday church school of a rather important church. A woman who would be hardly noticed, socially or otherwise, becomes a leading woman in the missionary society. A girl of little training and less opportunity for training gets the chance to become the leading soprano in the choir of a great church. These people receive little or no recognition on their daily job. There is nothing to make them feel that they are "somebody." Frequently their souls are crushed and their personalities disregarded. Often they do not feel "at home" in the more sophisticated Negro group. But in the church on X Street, *she* is Mrs. Johnson, the Church Clerk; and *he* is Mr. Jones, the chairman of the Deacon Board.

It can be argued, and justly, that this untrained leadership is partly responsible for the fact that the Negro church has progressed so slowly. But still it is important that recognition and inspiriting opportunity have been given to people who would not have achieved the one or risen to the other elsewhere. Granted also that the same may be said of the churches of other racial groups, nevertheless it can hardly be denied that it is more accentuated among Negroes because they are more highly segregated and restricted in American life.

Freedom to Relax

The Negro church furnishes the masses, to a less extent now than formerly, an opportunity for self-expression that no other enterprise affords. Not expression in leadership as just described, but release from the restraint, strain and restriction of the daily grind. If in their church services Negroes show more emotion than members of some other racial groups, it can hardly be proved that they are by nature more expressive. The explanation lies in the environmental conditions under which they live. This is true because, as the Negro becomes more intellectual and less restricted in the American life, he becomes less expressive in emotion. A few churches in practically every large-sized American city show the truth of this. But the point urged here is, whatever one may think to the contrary and despite the advance made in the realm of improved race-relations, that as the Negro moves about in most areas of the American Commonwealth he is less free than other Americans. He not only feels, but he knows, that in many places he is not wanted. He knows that in most white churches of the United States he is not desired, even though a sign on the outside of the church may read "Welcome to All." He understands perfectly well that the welcome does not include him. He comprehends clearly that in many of them he would be ushered to the rear or to the gallery, or be refused admission altogether; and in some other instances he would be patronized and tolerated.

A sign on the outside of an important church in a metropolitan southern city reads thus: "We offer riches to the poorest, friendliness to the friendless, comfort to the sorrowing—a welcome to all, step in." But every Negro child in that city is aware of the fact that the invitation is not meant for him.

The Negro is conscious of the fact that in many courthouses, city halls, public parks, city auditoriums, institutions supported by the taxes of all the people, he is not a welcomed guest; and that special arrangements must be provided for him. He appreciates the fact that in privately owned stores in many sections, where the money of all groups is sought, places of comfort and relaxation are quite often not provided him; and, if they are, they are provided in such a way as to make him feel humiliated.

The Negro is not unmindful of the fact that as he elbows his way through the crowded thoroughfare, he must be just a little more careful than most people; and that if he were to do what others would be excused for doing, he would be condemned. He works on the job ever aware that to hold his position he must often go the second mile, do more and take more, and work for less money. He must be an epitome of politeness; must smile when ordinarily he would frown; must pretend that it is all right when the respect that is habitually given others is deliberately denied him.

In this tense situation, the Negro lives. In many instances he expresses himself in song, dance and laughter; but for thousands of Negroes this release from restraint, this complete freedom and relaxation for the sake of mere expression, if nothing more than a faint "Amen," a nodding of the head as the minister preaches, a feeling of oneness with the crowd in song and prayer, is to be found only in the Negro church. Here he gathers poise, courage and strength to make it through another week. Langston Hughes' "Negro Servant," though related to Harlem, is somewhat illustrative of what is portrayed here, and if the Negro church is kept in mind as well as Harlem, the idea expressed in this poem becomes more universal in its application.

> All day, subdued, polite,
> Kind, thoughtful to the faces that are white.
> O, Tribal dance!
> O, drum!
> O, Veldt at night!
> Forgotten watch-fires on a hill somewhere!
> At six o'clock, or seven, or eight,
> You're through.
> You've worked all day.
> Dark Harlem waits for you.
> The el, the sub.
> Pay-nights,
> A taxi through the park.
> O, drums of life in Harlem after dark!
> O, dreams!
> O, songs!
> O, saxophones at night!
> O, sweet relief from faces that are white!
>   —Quoted by permission of the publishers of *Opportunity*.

It might be urged that this kind of expression is not helpful; that it makes religion an escape from reality; that it serves as an opiate for the people. The possibilities are great that this is true, and that it does happen no one can deny. But whether it is true or not depends in a large measure upon what the minister provides and the kind of instruction he gives the people. If these expressions or outlets help the people to live, they can hardly be set aside as of no value.

Negro Church as Community Center

Three quotations are illustrative of the use of the Negro church as a social center. George E. Haynes writes:

The Negro as a worker makes contact with the white world when on his job, and receives information, instruction, and stimulus so far as his occupation influences his ways of life. All his leisure-time activities that condition intellectual development and emotional motivation under present conditions of segregated Negro life must find their channel mainly through the principal community agency the Negro has—his church.[1]

Forrester Washington states:

From the very beginning the Negro has had to make numerous approximations and substitutions to supply himself with decent recreational opportunities. In both city and country he has made of the Negro church a quasi community center.[2]

The Mayor's Interracial Committee of Detroit reports in its 1926 Survey:

The Negro has been humiliated in so many public and privately owned institutions and amusement places that he has resorted to the church as a place in which he can be sure of spending his leisure time peacefully. To a large extent it takes the place of the theatre, the dance hall, and similar amusement places, and fills the vacancy created by the failure of public and commercial places of recreation and amusement to give him a cordial welcome. Consequently, the average Negro church in Detroit keeps its doors open constantly for the use of the community. Numerous suppers, lectures, recitals, debates, plays, and the like are given by clubs and individuals from without and within the congregation.

The Church Has Encouraged Education and Nurtured Negro Business

Through the years, the Negro church through its ministry has encouraged Negroes to educate themselves. The rather naïve and blind faith that many Negro parents have had that education is a panacea for all ills came from the Negro pastors. Mostly illiterate, and greatly lacking in formal training himself, he has continually urged the parents of his congregation to sacrifice much in order that their children might enjoy a better day. Many a country boy or girl would never have had the chance to attend college if the pastor of his or her church had not urged it. Even in cases where Negro education was graciously supported by

1 Haynes, George E., "The Church and Negro Progress," *The Annals of the American Academy of Political and Social Science,* November, 1928.
2 Washington, Forrester B., "Recreational Facilities for the Negro," *The Annals of the American Academy of Political and Social Science,* November, 1928.

white people who were kindly and justly disposed toward the Negro, the Negro minister was often needed, and relied upon, to give sanction to and boost education. The parents did not always see the light; but the pastor insisted on it, and somehow the parents believed that the preacher knew. The existence of a large number of weak denominational schools as well as some strong ones is testimony to the fact that the Negro church has greatly encouraged education. Not only has the church urged Negroes to secure an education, but the church has nurtured and still nurtures Negro business. The great medium for the advertisement of Negro business is the church. Not only in sermons but in other ways, the authors were impressed with the way Negro pastors advise their people to help make strong Negro business such as insurance, banking, privately owned Negro enterprises and the like.

Democratic Fellowship

In the main, there are no social classes in the Negro church. In one or two city churches of the 609, there was evidence that some of the members were particular about the people who joined and wanted a "certain brand" for members. In a few cases there was a natural development whereby people of supposedly similar cultural levels assembled. But even in these churches, there are members who represent all grades of culture and varying occupational levels.

Bridging the Gap

In practically all of the 609 churches there exists a thorough democratic spirit. The church is the place where the Negro banker, lawyer, professor, social worker, physician, dentist, and public-school teacher meet the skilled and semi-skilled tradesmen, the maid, the cook, the hotel man, the butler, the chauffeur and the common laborer; and mingle with them. The Negro church still furnishes the best opportunity for Negroes of different social strata and various cultural groups to associate together in a thoroughgoing democratic way.

The Negro race is young in emancipation. It has not had sufficient time to build churches of the wealthy nor of the cultured. As the race gets older in freedom, the number of college-trained business and professional people will inevitably increase. There will be more grouping and mingling among people of similar interest, and the tendency will be in the direction of a more rigid separation between Negroes of different interests and achievements. Up to this time, the Negro church has been one of the most outstanding channels through which this gulf between the "high" and the "low," the "trained" and the "untrained" has been bridged. It will continue to be for years to come; because the vast majority of Negroes who reach the business and professional classes are the sons and daughters of parents whose opportunities for training have been meager and who for the most part have kept this Negro church in operation.

The tendency is, and may continue to be, for the intellectual Negroes to break away from many of our churches because they are not attracted by services that differ so widely from those of the college and university. On the other hand, a good many of these more highly privileged Negroes see great possibilities in Negro churches, and work in them weekly; a goodly number of the Negro students are closely connected with the church. Of 2,594 students, professional and lay people whose attitudes toward the church were ascertained, 67 per cent. attend church weekly and 56 per cent. have specific church duties, such as work in the Sunday church school, singing in the choir or some other activity of the church.

As the writers moved about in sixteen communities during the period of the field work of the study, one thing stood out conspicuously—there was a warmth, a spontaneity in worship, and welcome that one could actually feel on entering most Negro churches. In most of them, the atmosphere is congenial and a timid or tense person is set at ease immediately. Perfect relaxation is possible. Frequently it is a hearty handshake by a member of the church, or a cordial greeting by the usher who seems to sense that this man is a stranger, or some word from the pastor in his sermon or at the end of the services. At any rate, the atmosphere is conducive to a feeling of "at-home-ness." To the ultra-sophisticated, it may seem naïve and primitive, but there is a virtue in it which the truly wise will not scorn.

Transcending Racial Barriers

The democratic fellowship that exists within the race transcends racial barriers in the church. The Negro church generally preaches love and tolerance toward all races and abides by these ideals in its practice. Members of other racial groups are welcomed in Negro churches. Other races experience no rebuffs, no discrimination. Chinese, Japanese, and white people are never deliberately given the back seats in Negro churches. They are never ushered to the gallery for worship. They are never refused admission to Negro churches. If there is any discrimination, it is usually to the advantage of the members of other racial groups. Precaution is taken in Negro churches to see that white visitors are given, not gallery seats, but often the very best seats in the house. The members of churches occupying front seats frequently give their seats to the visitors of other races. They give the stranger and the chance guest of different color, not the worst, but the best.

Negro Ministers Welcome White Ministers

White ministers are not barred from Negro pulpits.

In the interviews, a few Negro ministers expressed the conviction that they would be perfectly willing to have white ministers preach to their people provided they could preach for the white ministers. But in the vast majority of instances the Negro pastors were willing to have white pastors preach to their people even though they knew that the white ministers would not, or could not, have them preach in their pulpits.

In securing the services of white ministers, most Negro preachers experience no difficulty from their board or congregation. It was the unanimous testimony of the 600 pastors and officials interviewed that their people did not object to visiting white ministers.

Not a single case was observed by the investigators, in interviews and worship, where Negroes did not cordially receive members of other racial groups in their worship. As one minister expressed it: "My church is always glad to have members of any racial group worship with us and I know of no case where our visitors have experienced embarrassments in our church."

Negro ministers who do not invite white pastors because the white ministers cannot invite them, nevertheless insist that in their services no lines shall be drawn against white worshippers.

A Potentially Free Ministry

It is the firm conviction of the writers that the Negro pastor is one of the freest, as well as most influential, men on the American platform today. This is due to various causes, but chief among them is the factor of the long-time prestige of the Negro minister, the respect for him and for religion; and the poverty and the financial freedom of the Negro church.

It is not the aim of the writers to extol poverty or economic insecurity as a virtue per se. This cannot be done any more than wealth can be set up as a virtue of itself. But there is some virtue in being identified with the under-privileged. It is usually more likely that the man farthest down will advocate complete justice for all than that the man farthest up will. It is hardly possible for the most privileged to be as sensitive to the injustices, the restrictions and the limitations imposed upon the weak as it is for the weak themselves; or for him to feel these wrongs with the same degree of intensity as they are felt by the under-privileged. They who sit in the seat of the mighty, or those who are racially identified with the ruling class, are more likely to feel that they have too much to lose if they begin to champion too ardently the cause of the man farthest down. It is more difficult for them even to see the wrong. The danger is that they view the evil from lofty heights, if at all. They fear economic insecurity and social ostracism, which may come to them if they identify themselves too openly with the oppressed group.

Perhaps the white minister was correct when he said in an interracial seminar that if he were to take an open and vigorous stand in opposing economic and interracial evils the Negroes would have to give him a pastoral charge. Possibly, too, there is much truth in some of the answers given by many white pastors in response to questionnaires on inter-racial church coöperation, that their congregations would not tolerate an exchange of pulpits between Negro and white ministers.

On the other hand, the suffering man feels the sting more keenly and is more likely to complain. Being the under dog, he has nothing to lose and all to gain when he goes forth in the name of God advocating a square deal for all men. It is not an accident that possibly the most outstanding prophets of religion such as Jesus, Moses, Jeremiah, Isaiah, Micah, Hosea, Amos, and Ezekiel were members of an under-privileged race. It is not argued for a moment that prophets of the ruling class have not and do not exist; but often they must break with the ruling majority and identify themselves with those who suffer. It is simply argued that, all things considered, it is easier for the man who is down to see wrongs and injustices and in many cases easier for him to become an apostle of righteousness.

Thus, one of the main theses of this chapter is that it is a part of the genius of the Negro church that it is owned by a poor race, supported by its members and, further, that this fact alone gives the Negro minister an opportunity and freedom in his church life that ministers of some racial groups might well covet. If the Negro pastor sees fit to condemn from his pulpit practices with respect to low wages, long hours, the working of children in industry, the unfair treatment of women in factories, the denying to the worker the right to organize, and the injustices of an economic system built on competition, self-interest, and profit—he is more likely not to be censured, and less likely to lose his position than his white brother who preaches in the same city. It is more than likely that no committee will wait on him advising him to go slow. No leading financier will walk out of the church threatening never to return. To the contrary, it is highly possible that the Negro minister would receive many congratulations and "Amens" from his congregation if he were to preach such a gospel.

When the Negro pastor feels the urge to preach a thoroughgoing gospel of brotherhood, applying it to the Negroes, whites, Japanese, Chinese, and other races, it is gladly received by Negro audiences. It is taken for granted that Negro ministers will courageously oppose lynching, Jim Crow law, and discrimination in the expenditure of tax money, especially as applied to schools, parks, playgrounds, hospitals, and the like.

This fellowship and freedom inherent in the Negro church should be conducive to spiritual growth of a unique kind. It furnishes the foundation for the Negro church and the Negro ministry to become truly Christian and prophetic in the truest sense. The Negro church has the potentialities to become possibly the greatest spiritual force in the United States. What the Negro church does and will do with these potentialities will depend in a large measure upon the leadership as expressed in the Negro pulpit.

SUPPLEMENTARY READINGS

Henri, Florette. *Black Migration: Movement North 1900–1920*. Garden City, N.Y.: Doubleday Anchor Books, 1976.

Mays, Benjamin E. *Born to Rebel: An Autobiography*. New York: Charles Scribner's Sons, 1971.

Mays, Benjamin E. *The Negro's God as Reflected in His Literature* [1938]. New York: Atheneum, 1968.

Ransom, Reverdy C., ed. *Year Book of Negro Churches*. Wilberforce, Ohio: Bishops of the A.M.E. Church, 1935–36.

Woodson, Carter G. *The History of the Negro Church*. Washington, D.C.: Associated Publishers, 1921, 1945, 1972. Chaps. 14–16.

38

ST. CLAIR DRAKE AND
HORACE R. CAYTON

"The Churches of Bronzeville"

The U.S. Census for 1940 reported that since 1910 there had been a net migration of blacks from the South of 1,750,000. Ninety percent of these had settled in urban areas such as the "Bronzeville" studied by St. Clair Drake and Horace Cayton. Their black metropolis was Chicago's South Side, which by the end of the Great Depression was a city unto itself. Their social survey began as a series of projects financed by the Works Progress Administration to investigate the conditions that gave rise to juvenile delinquency; it soon expanded to become a study of the culture and structure of the entire South Side. W. Lloyd Warner, a professor of sociology and anthropology at the University of Chicago, noted for his Middletown investigations, gave direction and counsel. St. Clair Drake did monographic research on churches and voluntary associations; others worked on different topics. The material was then condensed and rewritten as Black Metropolis, *which appeared in 1945. Richard Wright hailed it as "the definitive study of Negro urbanization" and felt that it corroborated the findings of the Swedish sociologist Gunnar Myrdal in* An American Dilemma, *published a year earlier.* Black Metropolis *has special sections on the religious life of the lower and middle classes in Bronzeville that are worth consulting. The following excerpt is a more general survey of the impact of the black church and black preacher.*

The Grip of the Negro Church

THE NEGRO NEWSPAPER is a business institution which Bronzeville expects to "serve The Race." The Negro church is ostensibly a "religious" organization, but Bronzeville expects it, too, to "advance The Race." There are nearly 500 churches in Black Metropolis, claiming at least 200,000 members and distributed among over thirty denominations. Almost half of the churches, and over two-thirds of the people who claim church membership, are affiliated with one of the two Negro National

Source: *Black Metropolis: A Study of Negro Life in a Northern City*. Introduction by Richard Wright. New York: Harcourt, Brace, 1945. Pp. 412–29.

Baptist Conventions. These congregations and their ministers have virtually no face-to-face relationships with any of their white co-religionists. The first Negro Baptist Convention arose as a split from white organizations primarily because colored preachers felt that they were being denied an opportunity to express their talents without discrimination. Negro Baptists think of their organization as a "Race church," and their leaders concern themselves with such matters as fighting the Job Ceiling and demanding equal economic opportunity as well as "serving the Lord." There are also three Negro Methodist denominations represented in Bronzeville, and the colored Holiness, Spiritualist, and Community churches. There are also a number of small denominations indigenous to Bronzeville and such all-Negro "cults" as the African Orthodox Church, the Christian Catholics, the Temple of Moorish Science, and numerous fly-by-night groups organized around enterprising but untrained preachers.

About ten per cent of the churches and less than ten per cent of the church-goers in Bronzeville are affiliated with predominantly white denominations, such as the Methodist Episcopal Church, the Episcopal, Presbyterian, Congregational, Roman Catholic, Lutheran, Christian Scientist, Seventh-Day Adventist, and Disciples of Christ. Though in the state and national organizations of these churches Negroes wield very little influence, a number of the churches have extensive educational and social welfare projects for Negroes throughout the United States. Some people in Bronzeville who would prefer to be identified with these relatively powerful white groups have found that individual white congregations in these sects do not welcome Negro members, even though the Negro church officials and the white church officials often have very close ties. On the whole, Bronzeville sticks to the "Race churches."[1]

---

1 During the last ten years an intensive drive by the Roman Catholic Church has met with considerable success in Bronzeville. There are three large Catholic Churches in the Black Belt, and the Masses are well attended. Interviews with Negro Catholics, and with non-Catholics whose children go to parochial schools, seem to indicate that one of the primary attractions of the Catholic Church is its educational institutions. With the public schools running on double shifts during those years, many parents felt that the parochial school offered a more thorough education in a quieter atmosphere with adequate discipline and personal attention for all students. The Catholic approach to the Negroes has been aided by the establishment of a small community house, by the extensive athletic program of the Catholic Youth Organization, and by the forthright stand against race prejudice taken by an auxiliary Bishop of the Chicago diocese. In 1944, the Catholics purchased the most imposing piece of church property in Bronzeville—Sinai Temple, a wealthy Jewish synagogue—and converted it into a school and community center.

As we have noted previously, Negroes purchased the white churches and synagogues in the Black Belt area as the white population moved out. These financial deals often embittered Negroes against their white brethren, whom they accused of unloading church property on them at exorbitant rates during the Fat Years. In 1933, Chicago Negro churches were carrying the second highest per capita indebtedness among all urban Negro churches in the country. Some of these were fine buildings in good repair. Others were deteriorating. Many had formerly been maintained by well-to-do white congregations, and the Negroes found difficulty in keeping the properties in good condition. Thus during the last twenty years all the larger Negro churches have been forced to spend a great deal of their income on paying off mortgages and maintaining church property. Some have also spent a great deal upon interior decoration. All this financial activity brings Negro church trustees into contact with white businessmen and sharpens somewhat the antagonisms between Negroes and whites in Midwest Metropolis.

There are five churches in Bronzeville seating over 2,000 persons and claiming more than 10,000 members, and some fifty church buildings seating between 500 and 2,000 persons. Seventy-five per cent of Bronzeville's churches are small "store-front" or house churches, with an average membership of fewer than twenty-five persons. Many of these represent survivals from the period of the Great Migration. Others are the result of leadership conflicts within the larger churches. The proselytizing drive in certain denominations has also helped to swell the number. Although there were "missions" in the Black Belt prior to the Great Migration, the prevalence of store-front churches seems to have resulted from the lack of available edifices during the first years of the influx. Church memberships skyrocketed during this period, and competition between congregations for the abandoned white churches and synagogues resulted, on the one hand, in the payment of exorbitant prices for church property, and, on the other, in the proliferation of makeshift churches. In many cases, pastor and congregation hoped some day either to build or to move into a larger edifice. Many of them did one or the other. In other cases the congregation remained where it was, or moved into another store. Several large congregations boast of their evolution from store-fronts, and in their anniversary souvenir programs proudly display "before and after" photographs. The enterprising pastor who leads his congregation from store-front to edifice is well on his way to success in the church world. If he ever pays off the mortgage, he is a hero.

"*Serving the Lord (and Man)*": While about a third of Bronzeville's churches have only worship as an activity, the majority of them also sponsor some associated activities, if no more than a Sunday School and an usher board or several money-raising clubs. The key activity for all is what the people call "Sunday service." An average Sunday morning probably finds at least 65,000 of Bronzeville's 300,000 persons in some church, and many persons who do not themselves attend church hustle their children off to Sunday School as a part of their "right raising."

Sunday morning in Bronzeville is a colorful occasion. At 9 o'clock, little knots of children and adolescents, in their Sunday best, begin to gather around the doors of the store-fronts in the poorer neighborhoods to joke and play before going inside for two hours of singing, studying the lesson, and lifting the collection—all amid a great deal of friendly banter. At the larger churches the picture is similar, except that once inside the building the various groups of pupils are more likely to study the lesson in separate classrooms with teachers who boast certificates from the Interdenominational Council of Religious Education, and the teachers are likely to stray from the Bible to discuss current events, the race problem, or questions of personal adjustment. It has been estimated that an average of 60,000 Negro children attend Sunday School each week. Sunday School out, most of the youngsters are ready to spend the rest of the day in play at some park or on the streets. Many of them, too, begin to queue up for the opening of the movies. A few may "stay for church," especially those who attend the one or two congregations that have a special "junior church."

"Eleven o'clock service" is the main event of the day, and some of the larger churches are filled by 10:45 A.M., when the older members start the pre-service prayer meeting. Jitneys, streetcars, and buses do a rushing business. Rows of automobiles, freshly polished, line the streets around all the larger churches and many of the smaller ones. "Church mothers," their little gray caps perched on their heads and secured by chin straps, mingle around the door with the younger folks clad in their stylish Sunday best. On special occasions such as Easter and Christmas it is impossible, at 10:45 A.M., to secure a seat in any of the five largest Protestant churches. (These churches each seat more than 2,500 persons.) A surprisingly large number of young people attend these morning services, and special usher boards and junior choirs provide them with specific functions.

Afternoon services, though not a definite part of most church programs, are by no means rare. These are usually "special services"—lodge turnouts, rallies, "Women's Day," "Children's Day," etc. Most churches also have a young people's society, which meets late in the afternoon, though it draws comparatively few youngsters.

Some of the higher-status churches have dispensed with night services entirely, especially in the summer months. Others, in order to meet the competition of Chicago's night life, have evolved the custom of giving "special programs" in addition to, or instead of, preaching. These take the form of dramas, musical extravaganzas, or occasional movies. These Sunday night services are usually entertaining enough to appeal to a circle far wider than the membership of the church. In fact, a great deal of interchurch visiting takes place without regard to denominational lines, and many persons will attend services of this type who make no claim to being religious. It is good entertainment with no cover charge and no compulsion even to drop a nickel in the "free-will offering."

Throughout the week, most churches are centers of activity—singing and praying in the smaller, lower-status churches, and club meetings, socials, plays, concerts, movies, and mass meetings in the larger ones. Community organizations may ordinarily have access to a church building, provided the church itself has nothing scheduled for the night. Bronzeville's churches are centers of free speech, and many a bulletin board is just as likely to list a meeting of a left-wing labor union, or even of a Communist organization, as a meeting of an American Legion post.

Church *attendance*, however, is not a reliable index to church membership in Bronzeville. A careful study of the four largest churches, each averaging over a thousand Sunday morning worshipers and claiming more than 5,000 members—indicates that the actual dues-paying membership may hardly exceed 1,500 persons. Church rolls are seldom pruned, and a boasted "10,000 members" may include the dead, "backsliders," and persons who have shifted to other churches. The largest proportion of people who maintain relationships with the church probably do so, except in very small congregations, through sub-organizations. In fact, many persons have their only relationship in this indirect manner. Such associated organizations range from purely social clubs to cooperative stores. Yet were it not for the primacy of the worship service, and for the hard labor of the "sustaining members" (predominantly women), the average church could not maintain itself. As it is, all the larger churches are saddled with heavy mortgages, and much of the money raised through frequent rallies must be applied to debts. Those interested in "serving the Lord" provide an institution for "serving man."

"*A Bone of Contention*": Forty years ago, church news was "big news" in Negro newspapers. Today, churches and preachers seldom make the front page unless some sensational incident is involved. In total bulk, too, church news falls far behind club news. The church is not the *center* of community life as it was in Midwest Metropolis before the

Great Migration or as it is today in the small towns of the South. Yet the church is the oldest and wealthiest institution in the community, and in competition with a wide range of secular organizations it has managed to remain an important element in the life of Bronzeville. The southern migrants brought to Chicago a tradition of church membership which has persisted in the metropolitan setting. The preachers have adjusted speedily to rapid changes in the urban community, and have thus been able to compete with the "worldly" organizations in an environment notorious for its secular emphasis.

For many people the church is still the center of attention. For an even larger number it is an interesting topic of conversation. Commanding the allegiance of so many people and handling such a large amount of Bronzeville's money, the church inevitably becomes a matter for public discussion. The Cayton-Warner Research staff collected thousands of random comments during the Depression years. The most striking thing about these comments was the prevalence of grumbling against preachers and the church—a habit found among members and non-members alike. The major criticisms ran somewhat as follows:

(1) Church is a "racket," (2) Too many churches, (3) Churches are too emotional, (4) There's no real religion among the members, (5) Churches are a waste of time and money, (6) Ministers don't practice what they preach, (7) Ministers don't preach against "sin," (8) Church places too much emphasis upon money, (9) Negroes are too religious.

During the Depression the charge that the church was a "racket" was encountered everywhere in Bronzeville. This typically Chicago reaction expressed a doubt of motives that did not necessarily mean refusal to co-operate with the church but did indicate disapproval of the emphasis placed upon money by the preachers. It also implied a suspicion that funds were being used dishonestly or unproductively; non-church members made the latter charge more frequently than did the "faithful." The proprietor of a gambling establishment, for instance, observed: "The church is getting to be too big a racket for me. I'd rather support my own racket." A flat-janitor who attended church infrequently confided to an interviewer, "You know churches are nothing but a racket." The proprietor of a small business said: "I just don't care anything about the churches because I think they are rackets." An optometrist was caustic in his comment: "I was baptized in a Baptist church but I don't go regularly. . . . It's just racketeering on people's emotions anyway." A young business woman used the same term: "I used to be a member of the Flaming Sword Baptist Church, but I've dropped my membership. One of my brothers is a deacon. My other brother, like myself, thinks the church is just a racket." A housewife in the lower income brackets states that her husband objects to her attendance at church. He calls the church "nothing but a racket" and insists that "nobody gets anything out of it but the preachers." His wife is inclined to agree.

Even when Bronzeville's people do not bluntly characterize churches as "rackets," they often make the charge by implication. Thus, a hotel maid states: "I just haven't made up my mind to join a church. Of course I was a Baptist at home in the South, but most of these churches are full of graft. You pay and pay money and the church is still in debt." A WPA worker stated that he didn't attend church because "they don't help anybody, and all they want is money to keep the big shots going."

Inevitably the criticisms focus on the preachers. "Blood-suckers!" snapped a skilled laborer; "they'll take the food out of your mouth and make you think they are doing you a favor."

"You take some of these preachers," observed a steel-mill worker; "they're living like kings—got great big Packard automobiles and ten or twelve suits and a bunch of sisters putting food in their pantry. Do you call that religion? Naw! It ain't nothing but a bunch of damn monkey foolishness."

Church members, too, while retaining their membership, are sometimes as caustic as the "unbelievers," making statements like the following:

"I'm a church member. I believe churches are still useful. But like everything else, there's a lot of racketeering going on in the church."

"The preachers want to line their pockets with gold. They are supposed to be the leaders of the people, but they are fake leaders."

"Ministers are not as conscientious as they used to be. They are money-mad nowadays. All they want is the almighty dollar and that is all they talk about."

"When you are making plenty of money and share it with them you are all right, you're a fine fellow. When the crash comes and you are not doing so well, they forget all about you."

Closely related to the charge that churches are a racket is the contention that there are too many churches. One businessman expresses a very general complaint when he says: "I am a churchman and I believe that the church occupies an important place in the life of any community. But I'm also positive that there are too many Negro churches in Chicago and too many false preachers."

Large numbers of people combine a belief in religion with a denunciation of the church, as in the case of the woman who said: "I thinks there's only one heaven where we all will go, but the biggest thieves are running the churches, so what can they do about saving us? Nothing!"

These criticisms express the annoyance and frustration of a group trying to survive on a subsistence level during a depression. The church, too, was trying to survive, and the ministers were forced to emphasize money-raising to keep their doors open and to gather sufficient funds to meet obligations incurred during the Fat Years.[2] Except for a dozen pastors of the largest churches, ministerial salaries averaged less than $2,000 a year, but most preachers, whether in charge of big churches or of small, were conspicuously better off than most of the laity, and hence served as convenient targets for attack. Few churches have adequate systems of accounting and it was virtually impossible to verify or disprove charges of stealing and misappropriation of funds. The truth of such charges is, however, largely irrelevant, since antagonism to the church seems to lie deeper than mere hostility toward preachers or concern over clerical probity.

Bronzeville's loyal church members, thrown on the defensive by these criticisms, usually defend the institution in conventional terms. A "racial angle" (note the italicized passages) is sometimes added. The following expressions are typical of the "defense":

> "I am a member of the Solid Rock A.M.E. Church. Churches are a necessity, for I believe that *it is through them that our people first got the idea that we must co-operate with each other.* Take the church away with its teachings and I'm afraid we would not be able to live because it is fear of the beyond that causes one to think of his fellow man and respect his feelings."

> "My opinion is that the church is a good influence on the community. People seem to have a certain amount of respect for the church that no other institutions can enjoy. People who are members of churches are the ones that you find trying to accomplish something worth while and are very seldom in the clutches of the law."

> "My wife and I are members of Pleasant Green Baptist Church and get a lot of pleasure out of attending services. I think the church is a great necessity, for the people get something from it that is resting and gives them a feeling of peace."

2 Frequent newspaper accounts of mortgage-burning ceremonies in the autumn and winter of 1943–44 indicated that churches in Bronzeville were taking advantage of the war boom to institute drives for clearing off their debts.

"My family and I are members of Zion's Star A.M.E. Church. I think the church is a good influence. The store-front churches are all right too, and I am sure they are able to interest some people that otherwise would not go to church at all."

"My whole family belongs to St. Simon's Baptist Church. I am of the opinion that the church fills a great need. It is hard to picture the amount of evil that would take hold of the world if the church were done away with. *I also believe that many of our folks have learned from the church that big things can be accomplished only by the joining of forces of a large group of people.*"

What the Church Has to Offer

"Why," it may be asked, "in the face of widespread criticisms and such apparent dissatisfaction, does the church still flourish?" Underlying the conventional reasons which the faithful give for supporting the church are more fundamental satisfactions that bind them to the institution. Churches offer a wide variety of activities, and a person may take his choice.

The collective ceremonies lend a certain rhythm to existence, and there is little emphasis upon theology. If a person has talent, is a Race Leader, or even a moderately successful business or professional man, he can believe anything he chooses, so long as he "supports the church." In the South, people are sometimes "churched" (i.e., accused publicly) when they have breached the moral code or the church rules, verbally or in their conduct. In Bronzeville this hardly ever happens. One critic commented cynically, "The only thing they might put you out of church for up here is not paying dues." One of the most striking aspects of Bronzeville's church life is a mutually shared core of religious custom that cuts across denominational lines. People "feel at home" in any of the major Protestant denominations, and interdenominational visiting and shifts in church membership are widespread. Bronzeville's churches provide a congenial environment for the thousands of people who were taught as children that they "ought to go to church."

Many people who attend church offer no "religious" reasons at all in explaining their behavior. They attend church, they say, because they "like good singing" and "good speaking," or because the services are "restful and beautiful." Bronzeville's churches are centers of entertainment as well as places of worship. Popular preachers and a wide variety of musical offerings draw large crowds both on Sundays and on week nights. It is not unusual to find a total of over 10,000 people attending Sunday evening musicales in the four largest churches, and an equal number distributed among the smaller churches. The most popular pastors in the Black Belt are excellent showmen. Their sermons are replete with humor and apt illustration, as well as pithy epigram, good jokes, and rousing flights of oratory. Preachers who can flay sin in an original manner, who can denounce iniquity with a "knowing" air and with some sexual innuendo, attract large crowds. In addition to this incidental entertainment, all of Bronzeville's churches are continually offering concerts, pageants, plays, suppers, and other similar activities. Many people without formal membership in any church might be attracted, for example, to the horse shows and fashion shows featuring Joe Louis's wife, Marva, which some Bronzeville churches have sponsored within the last few years.

It is probable, however, that the church's main attraction is the opportunity it gives for large masses of people to function in an organized group, to compete for prestige, to be elected to office, to exercise power and control, to win applause and acclaim. Even church fights, although dubbed "unchristian," are interesting.

The Church as a Race Institution: Much of the grumbling against the church is on the basis of "race loyalty." Both members and nonmembers expect the church to play a prominent part in "advancing The Race," and they often judge the institution from this angle alone. As we have mentioned, segregation of Negroes from whites at the congregational level is almost absolute. Negroes seldom see white people in their congregations. The great mass denominations—the Baptists and Negro Methodists—have separate state and national organizations. The relations between white and Negro ministers are rare and formalized. The larger white denominations have a tendency to look upon the Negro churches as a field for "home mission" work. Negroes, as a low-income group, are somewhat dependent upon these white groups for assistance in paying off mortgages, and whenever large community programs are contemplated, Negro churches must either approach these white boards for assistance or seek assistance from other white people.

In enlisting support for their special projects, Bronzeville's churches have had to develop a technique for extracting donations from "white friends." At one extreme is the attractive folder written by a sociologist to get money for a new church building and community center. The appeal is directed to high-status whites as

an opportunity to build a model, influential Negro church that can serve as an example and standard for institutions of similar kind throughout the country. The need of such a high example of intelligent ministry, rational religious services, adequate recreational and community social service, is imperative as the Negro gropes for an intelligent, sincere, and fearless religion.

At the other extreme is the almost illiterate plea of a Negro Pentecostal evangelist, soliciting funds and gifts over the radio each Sunday night: " 'Now you white folks in my radio audience mus' have some ol' pianos an' sewin' machines up in yo' attic that yuh kin sen' me. We need 'em. Our church kin use 'em.' "

In between is the pastor of one of Bronzeville's largest churches who has noticed some white people at the Sunday evening musical:

"Now, Mr. ———— of the ———— Steel Company is here tonight. I didn't know he an' his frien's were coming, but since they're here we're gonna make them pay for it. [Laughter.] Pass those baskets, ushers! We're tryin' to build up a church here that will make good citizens out of these Negroes on the South Side. I've got 15,000 members and they're all spillin' outa the place. We need a building on that lot we've bought over there, an' if you white folks will put up the building we can save the South Side.

"Now, Deacon ———— works for this steel company. Stand up over there, Deacon. He may have told these visitors to come. I didn't. But we're glad you're here. You know Negroes always did love white folks, anyhow—that is, we love the *men*. [Laughter from the audience at this daring play on a socially tabooed subject, the relations between Negro men and white women—a type of joke that could not have been used in addressing white visitors in the South.]"

Such "begging from white folks" is distasteful to many of Bronzeville's church people, but it is mixed with admiration for those preachers who can do it with finesse and without "Uncle Tomming" or sacrificing their dignity.[3] The following incident illustrates the mixed reactions of Negroes, dependent upon whites for financial support

3 One of the authors observed another case of flattering powerful white people. A large church was giving its annual music festival. The Chicago postmaster had been invited to attend, since many Negroes worked under his supervision, including the choir director. Near the end of the program, while the audience was expectantly awaiting the *Hallelujah Chorus*, all postmen in the audience were asked to stand. The postmaster proceeded to deliver a 45-minute harangue while the audience twisted, squirmed, and muttered in disapproval. After "honoring" the postmaster, the choir director announced that a prominent white banker was present. He explained that this man had flown to Chicago from New York especially to attend this service. Both the pastor and the choir director praised him fulsomely. The banker was the main mortgage-holder on the church property!

but desirous of preserving their independence of action. In this case the trustee board of a small school for training store-front preachers was in session. The funds for the experiment had been supplied by a white denominational board, and the Negroes were trying hard to meet a pledge they had made. They felt, however, that they would have more success if they had a concrete objective such as buying a building to house the school. They planned a large money-raising campaign around this financial project. The white co-sponsors felt that the purchase of a building was a too ambitious goal. After the enthusiastic speeches of Bronzeville's ministers had all been delivered, a young white minister representing the Home Mission Board of his denomination rose. He was very blunt.

"Before you brethren start discussing the purchase of a building, I think we should pay some attention to the fact that we are running a $300 deficit on this year's budget. I am sure Dr. ——— [the white president of the Home Mission Board] would want this wiped out before we make any further commitments."

The Negro ministers were incensed. It was a fact that they had fallen behind on their pledges for the year, but the white speaker had touched a raw spot: he had reminded them of their subordinate position. He had implied that they were putting nonessentials first. He had assumed the air of a missionary or a tutor lecturing his improvident wards. The chairman of the meeting, a well-educated Negro minister, rose to defend the honor of The Race.

"I think the time has come [he said] when Negroes ought to take up their own responsibilities and maintain their own organizations. There are 126 churches in our denomination on the South Side. I think we can support this institution by ourselves. White people have helped me. They gave me money to go to Harvard. They helped me pay the mortgage on my church. But I think the time has come when Negroes can handle their own affairs. Now, I feel we should pay these brethren [the whites] what we owe them, then buy our building, and run this institution by ourselves."

The atmosphere was tense. The three white board members were embarrassed and disconcerted, the Negro ministers uneasy. At this point a skillful and eloquent Bronzeville preacher took the floor and began to restore the atmosphere of "goodwill," using all the techniques of handling white folks which Negroes in the South have developed— humor, a little "stooping to conquer," playful denunciation of Negroes.

At the same time he threw in some concessions to race pride to appeal to the Negroes. His approach is a striking illustration of the technique of a Race Leader handling a mixed audience in a crisis situation:

> "Brother Chairman, you may be ready to cut loose from the white folks, but I'm not. I'm going to get all the money I can out of them. [Laughter from both Negroes and whites.] I'm going down *tomorrow* to see about getting some money for *my* church. You know it's the *duty* of white folks to help their colored brothers, and I'm not going to do anything to stand in the way of letting a man do his Christian duty.[4]
>
> "Negroes are poor. You know the white folks have all the money. Just because Negroes ride around in fine automobiles and wear good clothes doesn't mean that they've got any money. You said that we have 126 churches. Now, you know as well as I do that if we come right down to it, there are only about 26 real churches, and every one of them is so interested in taking care of his own corner that they can't get together.
>
> "Now, I'm tired of so much talk. Negroes can preach longer, pray louder, and make more noise than any folks on God's earth. [Both Negroes and whites laughed at this bit of racial depreciation.] I think we ought to pay that $300 deficit just to show the brethren that we are co-operating with them. I think we ought to put up or shut up. I have a check for $50 in my pocket that I was getting ready to use to pay another bill. I'm going to give that $50. Who'll match it?"

At this point the chairman was forced to pledge $25 in order to save face. Within ten minutes $125 had been pledged. The peacemaker assured the white members of the board that the Negroes would have the remainder by the next Sunday. He then turned to the subject of the building:

> "Now I think that if the colored brethren want a building they ought to have it. I think that the finance committee should look the site over and report back to us. We've got a great future and, Brother Chairman, I believe we can buy that building if we want to."

4 In 1939 only two or three Negro churches were receiving aid from white church boards in paying off mortgages, but the number has been much larger in the past. At a state convention of one large Negro denomination in 1939, the moderator was heard telling the delegates: "They [the whites] will help us if we help ourselves. The whites are looking at what we are doing. . . . If you need help go down and tell them. Some arrangement will be made."

Despite the dependence of Negro congregations upon the occasional friendly aid of white co-religionists, the Negro church is largely free of white control. Negro preachers have the greatest "freedom" of any Race Leaders. Politicians must fit themselves into machine politics. Most "civic" leaders are dependent upon white philanthropy. Most of Bronzeville's preachers are answerable to no one except their congregations. They can say what they please about current affairs and race relations; there are no church superiors to discipline them and no white people to take economic reprisals. Because they are so largely free of the political and economic controls of the white community, Bronzeville expects them to be *real* Race Men. Preachers are subjected to continuous community criticism, and to retain the allegiance of their followers they are forced to concern themselves with a wide range of secular activities—political action, protest against discrimination, advice on securing jobs and legal aid, and the encouragement of Negro business enterprises.

Yet, when a preacher responds to these demands, he immediately risks being accused of "racketeering."[5] For instance, most of the larger churches advertise Negro-owned businesses on the theory that successful colored businessmen are "advancing The Race." They try to throw business toward certain Negro undertakers, physicians, and retail stores. Church newspapers carry ads of colored enterprises in Bronzeville and of white stores that employ Negroes. Sometimes a pastor will appoint special agents or representatives within his church to plug specific stores or products.[6] Naturally, the community assumes that the ministers get "kickbacks" and special considerations from these businessmen.

5 This charge is very frequently made with respect to political campaigns. The ministers are accused of promising to "deliver the vote" for a sizable financial reward or for the promise of some position. The ministers, on the other hand, are likely to insist that they accept donations for the church but no personal gifts from politicians. There have been ministers in Bronzeville who were actively engaged in politics. One of them, Bishop Archibald J. Carey, held several high appointive positions under Mayor Thompson and finally secured a post on the state Civil Service Commission. He was accused of accepting bribes, although there was widespread belief that he had been "framed." Any minister who does business with the political machines lays himself open to criticism. Yet many people in Bronzeville feel that their preachers should go into politics. The popularity of clerico-politicians in Negro communities is illustrated by the elections of 1944 in which a Negro preacher was elected from New York's Harlem to represent the area in Congress, another was made Recorder of Deeds in Washington shortly before the election, and still another was elected to the state legislature in Ohio.

6 The following ads have been selected as typical of hundreds appearing in church newspapers of Bronzeville's largest churches:

—ELECTRIC SERVICE COMPANY—Inquire about our special plan to the members of —— Baptist Church. Miss ——, Representative. At your own authorized dealer.

Bronzeville is very critical of its preachers when accusing them of tying up too much money in church property or in other "noneconomic" uses. Ordinarily these sentiments are expressed in rather vague and general terms, such as one man's comment:

"I used to be active in the church; I thought we could work out our salvation that way. But I found out better. These Negro preachers are not bothered about The Race—about all they think of is themselves."

The ministers counter with the argument that the church is not *primarily* a business or political institution, and insist that if they weren't meeting the people's "needs" they couldn't survive. Often the criticisms are by no means vague—they are an insistent demand that the Negro churches should encourage the support of Negro businessmen who "make jobs for The Race."

SUPPLEMENTARY READINGS

Daniel, Vattel Elbert. "Ritual and Stratification in Chicago Negro Churches." *American Sociological Review* 7 (June 1942): 353–58.

MuKenge, Ida Rousseau. *The Black Church in Urban America: A Case Study in Political Economy*. Lanham, Md.: University Press of America, 1983.

Myrdal, Gunnar. *An American Dilemma*. New York: Harper & Row, 1944, 1962. Vol. 2, chap. 40.

Scheiner, Seth M. "The Negro Church and the Northern City, 1890–1930." In *Seven on Black*, edited by William G. Shade and Roy C. Herrenkohl. Philadelphia: Lippincott, 1969. Pp. 91–117.

Spear, Allan H. *Black Chicago: The Making of a Ghetto, 1890–1920*. Chicago: University of Chicago Press, 1967.

—SHOE AND DRY GOODS STORE—Headquarters for Florsheim Shoes. Men's, Ladies', Children's Ready to Wear. We Employ Colored Salesmen.

WHEN IN NEED OF FURNITURE SEE REV. WM. P. ——, Representative of the —— FURNITURE COMPANY.

39

E. FRANKLIN FRAZIER

"The Negro Church and Assimilation"

E. Franklin Frazier (1894–1962) achieved international recognition as a sociologist. The Negro Church in America, published posthumously, began as the Frazier Lecture in Social Anthropology at the University of Liverpool in 1953. Frazier was then chief of the division of the Applied Social Sciences in the Department of Social Sciences of UNESCO in Paris. In succeeding years he expanded on his views concerning Afro-American religion, taking a position against those, such as the anthropologist Melville J. Herskovitts, who argued for African retentions. Frazier believed strongly in the ideals and practical benefits of racial integration. His critics complained that he defined integration too much in terms of assimilation, as if Afro-Americans could solve their problems simply by joining the white mainstream. Since the black church represented the largest racially distinct organization, Frazier felt it would remain a barrier "as the walls of segregation tumble[d] down." When Afro-Americans advanced in economic and social status, and the secularism of the middle class took its toll, the traditional black churches, Frazier believed, would be left behind. The social turmoil of the 1960s, however, renewed black pride in black cultural institutions and raised questions about Frazier's definition of cultural assimilation as a one-way street. In 1969 C. Eric Lincoln wrote in The Black Church Since Frazier, "The 'Negro Church' that Frazier wrote about no longer exists."

The Walls Came Tumbling Down

IN THE LAST CHAPTER we have studied the transformations which have occurred in the Negro church and in the religion of Negroes as the result of urbanization. We have seen how the migrations of Negroes to cities have tended to uproot the traditional organization of the Negro community and changed the outlook of Negroes. As the result of the social disorganization of Negro life there has been a reorganization of

Source: *The Negro Church in America.* New York: Schocken Books, 1964. Pp. 68–81.

life on a different basis in order to meet the demands of the city. Life in the cities of the North has brought a larger measure of freedom from racial prejudice and discriminations which had characterized race relations in the South. This new freedom has enabled Negroes to enter more into the mainstream of American life. Since this new freedom has been due partly to broad changes in the economic and social organization of American life, the Negro in the South benefited from these changes. The success which Negroes have achieved in breaking down racial barriers has been due partly to their own efforts. They have carried on a constant struggle in the courts and they have influenced to some extent public opinion. As the midcentury drew to a close a distinguished white woman, who had been associated with their struggle, could look back at the success which Negroes had made in breaking through racial barriers and say in the words of the well-known Negro spiritual, 'the walls came tumbling down.'[1]

However, as the racial barriers are broken down and Negroes increasingly enter into the mainstream of American life, the traditional organization of Negro life is constantly being undermined. The so-called process of integration, which is only an initial stage in the assimilation of Negroes into American society, does not have the same effect on all parts of the social structure of the Negro community. The extent and the nature of the participation of Negroes in the wider American community is determined first by their class position. Negroes in the Black Belt or rural counties in the South where they constitute 50 per cent or more of the population are still almost completely isolated from the main currents of American culture. Although lower-class Negroes in cities, who include those engaged in domestic and personal services and those employed as unskilled labourers, have more contacts with American life, they are still more or less confined to the Negro community. As Negro workers acquire skills and become members of labour unions, they begin to enter into the mainstream of American life. This is, of course, more characteristic of Negro workers in the North than of those in the South. Many Negroes in the North who are employed as white-collar workers and in technical and professional occupations enter even more fully into the main currents of American society. Not only does their work enable them to share more fully in American culture but they

1 Joshua fit de battle of Jericho,
   Jericho, Jericho,
   Joshua fit de battle of Jericho,
   And de walls came tumbling down.
   Mary White Ovington, *The Walls Came Tumbling Down* (New York, 1947).

associate more freely with their white fellow workers than any other section of the Negro population.

The second factor and a factor of equal importance, which determines the nature and extent of the participation of Negroes in the wider American community, is their own institutional life. The system of racial segregation in the United States has resulted in an almost complete duplication of the institutions of the American community within the Negro community.[2] We shall begin by considering those institutions which embody the secular interests of Negroes. As Negroes have moved from the world of the folk, they have established insurance companies and banks which have a purely secular end. These institutions are becoming a part of the different associations of insurance companies and banks and they are subject to state supervision. Then there are many other kinds of business enterprises, many of which cater especially to the personal and other needs of Negroes, and thus supply services often refused by white establishments. Negroes are expected to patronize these various so-called 'Negro' businesses because of 'racial loyalty.' There is a National Negro Business League and numerous Negro chambers of commerce. Among the more successful Negro businesses should be included the Negro weekly newspapers which have circulations running into the hundreds of thousands.

Then there are certain cultural institutions among which are included the various secret fraternal organizations such as the Masons, Odd Fellows, and the Elks. In this group we would also include the various college Greek letter societies for men and women. Although they would not qualify as institutions, there are numerous social clubs which may be considered along with the cultural institutions. The most important cultural institution is, of course, the Negro church. It embodies, as we have seen, the cultural traditions of Negroes to a far greater extent than any other institution.

As 'the walls of segregation tumble down,' it is the institutions which embody the secular interests of Negroes which are being undermined more rapidly than those representing their cultural interests. As white establishments cater to the personal needs of Negroes there is less need for what is known as 'Negro' businesses to supply such services. Moreover, as the large corporations and other so-called white business enterprises employ Negroes in all capacities, there is less need for an association of people engaged in 'Negro' businesses. Likewise, as

2   See Frazier, *The Negro in the United States*, Part 3, "The Negro Community and Its Institutions."

white newspapers carry more news concerning Negroes and employ Negro journalists, the Negro newspapers decline in circulation as the foreign language newspapers have done. Although schools are cultural institutions, the segregated Negro public schools and state colleges will become less important.

The situation is different in regard to the cultural institutions within the Negro community. There are some privately supported Negro educational institutions with deeply rooted traditions in Negro life that resist the trend towards the integration of the Negro. On the other hand, as Negro professors are increasingly taken on the faculties of so-called white colleges and universities and Negro students are admitted to such institutions, Negroes are joining the mainstream of American life. When one comes to the Negro church which is the most important cultural institution created by Negroes, one encounters the most important institutional barrier to integration and the assimilation of Negroes. White churches may open their doors to Negroes and a few Negro ministers may be invited to become pastors of white churches; the masses of Negroes continue, nevertheless, to attend the Negro churches and the Negro church as an institution continues to function as an important element in the organized social life of Negroes.

The Church Is No Longer a Refuge

The strength of the Negro church as a barrier to the integration of Negroes into the main currents of American life should not be overestimated, especially since the process of integration has not progressed very far. Moreover, it is necessary to differentiate the situation in the North from that in the South. In the South the Negro has scarcely begun his struggle to participate in the secular and public institutions of the American community. On the other hand, in the border states and in the North there is much larger participation of Negroes in the secular and public institutions of the American community. In the South the lives of Negroes still revolve about the activities of the Negro community. Even where they gain entrance into labour unions, they are excluded from the 'social' activities of these organizations. In the North Negroes are included increasingly in the 'social' activities of the various labour unions. Nevertheless, in the North the proliferation of organizations which provide for the 'social' needs of Negroes indicate the extent to which Negroes are still outsiders, so to speak. Moreover, the ecological or spatial segregation of Negroes, which is often the result of impersonal economic and social forces rather than prejudice and discrim-

ination, tends to maintain the separate institutions of the Negro community. The church is the most important of these institutions in which
the masses of Negroes find a refuge within white society which treats
them with condescension if not contempt.

But the Negro church can no longer serve as a refuge as it did in
the past when the majority of Negroes lived in the South under a system of racial segregation and the majority of the Negroes in the South
lived in rural areas. Willy-nilly Negroes are drawn into the complex
social organization of the American community. This is necessary for
mere survival. Recognizing the need for a more complex social organization to serve the needs of urbanized Negroes and at the same time taking cognizance of the fact that Negroes were still excluded from labour
unions, a Negro sociologist proposed that the Negro church, being the
largest organized unit of Negro life, incorporate some of the functions
of the new forms of organized social life which are required in the city.[3]
It is apparent, however, that this proposal was impractical since the
Negro church could not perform the functions of the new types of associations necessary to life in the city.

It was inevitable that the Negro should be drawn into the organized forms of social life in the urban environment. As a consequence,
the Negro church has lost much of its influence as an agency of social
control. Its supervision over the marital and family life of Negroes has
declined. The church has ceased to be the chief means of economic co-
operation. New avenues have been opened to all kinds of business ven-
tures in which secular ends and values are dominant. The church is no
longer the main arena for political activities which was the case when
Negroes were disfranchised in the South. Negro political leaders have
to compete with the white political leaders in the 'machine' politics of
the cities. In a word, the Negroes have been forced into competition
with whites in most areas of social life and their church can no longer
serve as a refuge within the American community.

We have seen how Negroes in the established denominational
churches developed secular interests in order to deal with race prejudice
and discriminations to which they are exposed when the 'walls of segregation come tumbling down.' We have seen how lower-class Negroes
have reacted to the cold impersonal environment of the city and of the
large denominational churches by joining the 'storefront' churches and
the various cults. These all represented their reaction to the crumbling
traditional organization of Negro life as Negroes are increasingly cast
afloat in the main stream of American life where they are still outsiders.

3 See the proposal of Dr. George E. Haynes of the Federal Council of Churches,
quoted in Drake and Cayton, *Black Metropolis*, p. 683.

The Gospel Singers

Although the lower strata in the Negro community do not participate to the same extent as the upper strata in the main currents of American life, they are nevertheless increasingly assimilating the manners and customs of American society. There is thus achieved a certain external conformity to the patterns of American culture.[4] They continue to be influenced in their thinking and especially in their feelings and sentiments by the social heritage of the Negro which is represented by the Spirituals and religious orientation towards the world contained in the Spirituals. The masses of Negroes may increasingly criticize the church and their ministers, but they cannot escape from their heritage. They may develop a more secular outlook on life and complain that the church and the ministers are not sufficiently concerned with the problems of the Negro race,[5] yet they find in their religious heritage an opportunity to satisfy their deepest emotional yearnings.

Out of the revolt of the lower strata against the church and the growing secularization of Negro religion there has come an accommodation between traditional Negro religion and the new outlook of Negroes in the new American environment. This accommodation is symbolized by the Gospel Singers. The songs which the Gospel Singers sing have been described as a compound of 'elements found in the old tabernacle songs, the Negro Spirituals and the blues.'[6] Since the Negro has become urbanized, there has been an amazing rise and spread of 'gospel singing.' This has been attributed, and correctly so, to the fact that, 'As Negro churches have become more European in decorum and programme, the great mass of less Europeanized Negroes began to look elsewhere for full vented religious expressions in music and preaching.'[7] The important fact is that although the Gospel Singers have gone outside the church for a congenial form of religious expression, they nevertheless remain in the church and are a part of the church. Recently when a Gospel Singer died and her funeral was held in a large Baptist church in the Nation's Capital, it was reported that 13,000 persons viewed her remains, a thousand persons jammed the church, and another thousand lined the sidewalks outside the church. Dozens of gospel-

4   Cf. "Racial Assimilation in Secondary Groups," in Robert E. Park, *Race and Culture* (Glencoe, Ill., 1950), Chapter 16.
5   See Drake and Cayton, pp. 650–4, concerning the rebellion of the lower classes against the church.
6   Arna Bontemps, "Rock, Church, Rock," in Sylvester C. Watkins (ed.), *Anthology of American Negro Literature* (New York, 1944), p. 431.
7   Willis Laurence James, "The Romance of the Negro Folk Cry in America," *Phylon*, Vol. XVI (1955), p. 23.

singing groups came from neighbouring areas and as far away as Pennsylvania and Illinois. The white owner of a broadcasting company flew from Ohio to attend the funeral. Between 150 and 200 cars accompanied the body to the cemetery.[8]

More important still for us here is the fact that the Gospel Singers symbolize something that is characteristic of Negro religion from the standpoint of assimilation. Some of the so-called advanced Negro churches resented these gospel singers and refused to permit them to sing within their churches. They have gradually become more tolerant and let down the bars as the Gospel Singers have acquired status and acceptance within the white world. Such well-known gospel singers as Mahalia Jackson, Rosetta Thorpe, and the Ward Sisters have been accepted as 'artists.' The Gospel Singer not only sings to the Negro world but sings to the white world. One of the famous Ward Sisters stated that the gospel singing is popular because '. . . it fills a vacuum in people's lives. For people who work hard and make little money it offers a promise that things will be better in the life to come.'[9] She was thinking, of course, of Negroes but the Gospel Singers sing to white America as well. This is indicated by their hold on the record industry and their popularity on radio and television programmes.

Gospel singing has, of course, become commercialized and that is another indication of the relation of Negro religious life to assimilation. It indicates in a sense the terms on which the Negro is being assimilated. Moreover, white men in the South are beginning to imitate the Negro Gospel Singers. And Negro gospel singing is often featured as a part of the programmes on television. Thus, the religious folk-songs of the Negro are becoming secularized despite the fact that the singing of them in secular entertainment is a concession to the so-called religious revival in the United States. The Gospel Singers, then, unlike the cults, do not represent a complete break with the religious traditions of the Negro. They represent or symbolize the attempt of the Negro to utilize his religious heritage in order to come to terms with changes in his own institutions as well as the problems of the world of which he is a part.

In a sense, therefore, the attempts of the Negro to resist segregation in the sit-down strikes in the South represent the same falling back upon

8 See *Washington Afro-American*, 5 April, 1960, for featured article on front page concerning death and funeral of Thelma Greene, at which a member of the Robert Martin Singers of Chicago sang a solo, "God Specializes," causing a number of persons to faint and to be carried out by nurses.
9 Interview with Clara Mae Ward in Winston-Salem, who claims she is the only gospel singer ever to have visited the Holy Land. "Singing for Sinners," *News Week*, Vol. 50 (2 September 1957), p. 86.

his religious heritage in time of crisis. This movement on the part of Negro students in the South is supposed to be based upon the non-violent resistance movement of Gandhi.[10] Some of its intellectual leaders like the Reverend Martin Luther King may use Gandhi's non-violent resistance as an ideological justification of the movement, but Gandhism as a philosophy and a way of life is completely alien to the Negro and has nothing in common with the social heritage of the Negro. As Negro students go forth singing the Spirituals or the Gospel hymns when they engage in sit-down strikes or sing their Gospel songs in response to violence, they are behaving in accordance with the religious heritage of the Negro.

Then there is another aspect of this movement which needs to be considered in relation to the changes in the religion of the Negro. Because of the improvement in their economic conditions, an increasing number of Negro students are able to attend the colleges for Negroes in the South. They are being drawn from those strata in the Negro population closest to the rural background and who, therefore, are closest to the folk heritage of the Negro. Education, or more specially the opportunity to attend college, is the most important factor enabling Negroes to achieve middle-class status. Moreover, the leaders of this movement have seen something of the world because of their army or other experiences, or their parents have had similar experiences. In their revolt against the racial discrimination they must fall back upon the only vital social heritage that has meaning for them and that social heritage is the religious heritage represented by the Spirituals which are becoming secularized.

The Religion of the New Middle Class

We have already seen in the last chapter how the Negro church and Negro religion have been affected by the new class structure which is emerging among Negroes in cities, especially in the North. Here we are interested in the religious outlook of the new Negro middle class which has become important among Negroes during the past twenty years or so. It is this class whose outward appearance and standards of behaviour approximate most nearly the norms of the white American society. Moreover, Negroes who have achieved middle-class status participate more largely than any other element in American life. It is for this reason that we shall focus attention upon the new middle class in studying the changes in the religious life of Negroes as they are related to the assimilation of Negroes into American society.

10   See "The Revolt of Negro Youth," *Ebony* (May, 1960).

The growing importance of the new middle class in the Negro community is due to the continual differentiation of the population along occupational lines. Therefore, the new middle class is composed almost entirely of those persons who derive their incomes from services rendered as white-collar workers and as professional men and women. Despite the dreams of Negro leaders, fostered by the National Negro Business League at the turn of the century, that Negroes would organize big industries and large financial undertakings, Negroes have not become captains of industry nor even managers of large corporations. So-called 'Negro' business continues to consist mainly of small retail stores catering to the personal needs of Negroes. There are a small number of insurance companies, small banks, and newspapers which constitute their larger business enterprises. The owners and managers of these enterprises constitute the upper layer of the middle class while the increasing number of Negroes in skilled occupations constitute its lowest stratum. For reasons which have been indicated, in the North and West about 25 percent of the Negro population is able to maintain middle-class standards while in the South only about 12 per cent are in this position.

The new Negro middle class is a new phenomenon in the Negro community because it has a different economic base and a different social heritage from the relatively small middle class which had become differentiated from the masses of Negroes by the first decade of this century.[11] This older middle class was an 'aristocratic' élite in a sense because its social status and preeminence were based upon white ancestry and family and its behaviour was modelled after the genteel tradition of the Old South. The upper layer derived their incomes from land but the majority of the members of the 'élite' were employed in a large variety of occupations including positions as trusted retainers in white families. The new middle class has a different occupational basis and occupation is one of the important factors in determining status.

Since the opening of the century there had been a faith among middle-class Negroes in 'Negro' business as a means of solving their social as well as economic problems. This faith was somewhat as follows: as Negroes became businessmen they would accumulate capital and give employment to Negroes and once Negroes possessed wealth, white men would respect them and accord them equality. The new middle class has accepted without the critical attitude which experience should have given them, the faith in 'Negro' business as a way to social and economic salvation.

11   E. Franklin Frazier, "The Negro Middle Class and Desegregation," *Social Problems*, Vol. IV (April 1957), pp. 291–301.

Since the emergence of the new middle class involves the rise of the more ambitious and energetic elements among the masses of Negroes to middle-class status, this new class does not possess the genteel tradition of the older middle class. This new class is largely without social roots except the traditions of the Negro folk represented in the Spirituals. But as these Negroes rise to middle-class status they reject the folk heritage and seek to slough off any reminders of their folk inheritance. However, since their rise to the middle-class status has enabled them to marry into families with the genteel tradition of the old middle class, there is often a confusion of 'aristocratic' and folk values. It is for this reason that many middle-class Negroes exhibit in their manners and behaviour the characteristics of both a peasant and a gentleman. Among this new class there is much confusion as to standards of behaviour and beliefs. There is a constant striving to acquire money in order to engage in conspicuous consumption which provides the outward signs of status and conformity to white American standards. They all possess the same goal, which is acceptance into the white community and they all profess, at least, a desire to be integrated into the white community.

Integration for the majority of middle-class Negroes means the loss of racial identity or an escape from the lowly status of Negroes and the contempt of whites. With integration they began to remove as much as possible from the names of their various organizations anything that would identify them as Negroes. This even extended to their church organizations. The Colored Methodist Episcopal Church became the 'Christian' Methodist Episcopal Church. It is significant, however, that when the middle-class leaders in the African Methodist Episcopal Church attempted to take 'African' out of the name and substitute the word 'American,' there was a revolt on the part of the masses who demanded that 'African' be retained. This incident is indicative of the general attitude of the middle class towards the African background of the Negro. While there is some outward profession of pride in African independence and identification with Africa, the middle class rejects identification with Africa and wants above all to be accepted as 'just Americans.' It was the new middle class which was rising to importance in the 1920s that was most bitterly opposed to the Garvey Movement which had as its goal the identification of Negroes with Africa and African interests.[12] Middle-class Negroes seize upon identification with Africa only as a means of compensating for their feeling of inferiority and improving their status in the eyes of American whites.

12   See Frazier, *The Negro in the United States*, pp. 528–31.

Despite the fact that middle-class Negroes conform to the standards of whites and accept without question the values of American society, they are still rejected by the white world. They feel this rejection more keenly than lower-class Negroes who participate less in the white man's world and conform to the standards of their own separate world. Moreover, because of their position, middle-class Negroes have an ambivalent attitude towards their identification as Negroes. On the one hand, they resent the slightest aspersion upon Negroes. When placed in competition with whites they have feelings of inadequacy and when they find themselves in close association with whites they have feelings of insecurity though they may clamour for integration into the white world.[13] They are status seekers in a double sense; they strive to keep up with the expectations of their class in the Negro community and they seek or hope to gain status in the white world. In order to maintain high standards of consumption often both husband and wife work but they constantly complain of the 'rat race' to maintain life as they would live it. They live frustrated lives despite their efforts to compensate for their feelings of inferiority and insecurity. They have little time for leisure and the enjoyment of what they call the 'cultural' things of life. As a matter of fact, they have little appreciation of music or art and they read very little since reading has not become a tradition in the new middle class.

Their ambiguous position in American society together with their recent rise to middle-class status are reflected in the religious behaviour and attitudes of middle-class Negroes. There is first a tendency for middle-class Negroes to sever their affiliation with the Baptist and Methodist churches and join the Presbyterian, Congregational, and Episcopal churches. The middle-class Negroes who continue their affiliation with the Baptist and Methodist churches choose those churches with intelligent ministers and a relatively large middle-class membership. As a consequence there is a solid core of the Negro middle class that continues to be affiliated with the Negro church. However, middle-class Negroes continue their affiliation with the Negro church for a number of reasons. Their families may have been associated with the churches and the churches which they have known since childhood provide a satisfying form of religious worship. Although many middle-class Negroes continue to be affiliated with the church, the church is no longer the centre of social life for them as for the lower class. They are members of professional and business associations and Greek letter fraternal organizations, though 'social' clubs constitute the vast majority of these

13   E. Franklin Frazier, *Black Bourgeoisie* (Glencoe, Ill., 1957), pp. 216 ff.

other forms of organized social activities. Some are thus able to satisfy their striving for status outside the church. But for others it is necessary to leave the Baptist and Methodist churches and join the Presbyterian, Congregational, and Episcopal churches in order to satisfy the desire for status.

The striving for status and the searching for a means to escape from a frustrated existence is especially marked among the middle-class Negroes who cannot find a satisfactory life within the regular Negro church organization. This probably accounts for the fact that during the past two decades middle-class Negroes have been joining the Catholic church.[14] Sometimes they send their children to Catholic schools where they will receive a discipline not provided in the public schools for Negroes. Very often after joining the Catholic church with the expectation that they will escape from their status as Negroes, they find that they are still defined as Negroes by whites. Some middle-class Negroes in their seeking to find escape from the Negro identification have gone from the Catholic church to the Christian Science church and then to the Bahaist church. Moreover, there is a tendency among middle-class Negroes to be attracted to Moral Re-armament, hoping that they would find a group in which they could lose completely their identification as Negroes and escape from their feelings of inferiority and insecurity. A small intellectual fringe among middle-class Negroes have affiliated with the Unitarian church. But some of them may still attend more or less surreptitiously the Methodist and Baptist churches on Friday nights.

This type of dual church affiliation is more characteristic of Negro professional men who affiliate with churches mainly for social and professional reasons. Some professional Negroes affiliate with a church which their friends or middle-class Negroes attend, and at the same time affiliate with churches attended by the lower class who are their clients. They are representative of the growing number of middle-class Negroes who have a purely secular outlook on the world. Some of them express contempt for religion and do not attend church though they may pretend to have some church affiliation. Since they have neither an intellectual heritage nor a social philosophy except a crude opportunism which enables them to get by in the white man's world, they may turn to all forms of superstition. This is because they are still haunted by the fears and beliefs which are a part of their folk heritage. They are often

14 The recent increase during the past twenty years in the number, which remains relatively small, of lower-class Negroes in the Catholic church has been due to aid provided them during the *Depression years* and the better educational facilities, as compared with the public schools, provided them by the Catholic church.

interested in 'spiritual' and 'psychic' phenomena. Very often the real religious feelings and faith of middle-class Negroes are expressed in their obsession with poker and other forms of gambling.[15]

The religious behaviour and outlook of the middle-class Negroes is a reflection of their ambiguous position as Negroes rise to middle-class status and become increasingly integrated into the American community. To the extent that they are becoming really assimilated into American society, they are being beset by the religious dilemmas and doubts of the white middle-class Americans. On the other hand, for the masses of Negroes, the Negro church continues to be a refuge, though increasingly less of a refuge, in a hostile white world.

SUPPLEMENTARY READINGS

Edwards, G. Franklin, ed. E. Franklin Frazier on Race Relations: Selected Writings. Chicago: University of Chicago Press, 1969.

Frazier, E. Franklin. Black Bourgeoisie. Glencoe, Ill.: The Free Press, 1957.

Frazier, E. Franklin. The Negro Church in America. C. Eric Lincoln. The Black Church Since Frazier. Two vols. in one. New York: Schocken Books, 1974.

Gordon, Milton. Assimilation in American Life: The Role of Race, Religion, and National Origins. New York: Oxford University Press, 1964.

Washington, Joseph. Black Religion. Boston: Beacon Press, 1966.

15   See Black Bourgeoisie, pp. 209 ff.

SIX

Twentieth-Century
Religious Alternatives

Garvey Tells His Own Story

Marcus Garvey's Universal Negro Improvement Association (U.N.I.A.) is usually not thought of as a religious organization. Garvey (1887–1940) was baptized Roman Catholic, and George Alexander McGuire linked his African Orthodox Church to the U.N.I.A. Yet the religious nature of the movement was Garveyism itself, that blend of black nationalism, charismatic messianism, and emotional commitment to the vision of returning to Africa that attracted hundreds of thousands in post-World War I urban black America.

Garvey came to the United States from Jamaica in 1916, a year after the death of Booker T. Washington. W. E. B. Du Bois and others in the N.A.A.C.P. who subscribed to the notion of "the talented tenth" had not inspired the black masses. Garvey did. His "Back to Africa" movement included the Black Star Line, steamships intended to make triangular voyages between New York City, the West Indies, and Africa. But this scheme failed, and Garvey was arrested in 1923 on charges of mail fraud. He had many critics, some of whom imputed to him the aim of creating a black Ku Klux Klan. Others accused him of being a supreme egotist, while Du Bois and the N.A.A.C.P. warred with his separatist philosophy. Convicted in 1925, Garvey remained in prison until President Coolidge commuted his sentence in 1927 and had him deported to Jamaica. He died in 1940 in London, largely forgotten until the revival of interest in black nationalism during the 1960s.

I WAS BORN in the Island of Jamaica, British West Indies, on August 17, 1887. My parents were black Negroes. My father was a man of brilliant intellect and dashing courage. He was unafraid of consequences. He took human chances in the course of life, as most bold men do, and he failed at the close of his career. He once had a fortune; he died poor. My mother was a sober and conscientious Christian, too soft and good

Source: *Philosophy and Opinions of Marcus Garvey.* Edited by Amy Jacques-Garvey. New York: Atheneum, 1969. Vol. II, pp. 124–34. Copyright 1923, 1925 by Amy Jacques-Garvey.

for the time in which she lived. She was the direct opposite of my father. He was severe, firm, determined, bold and strong, refusing to yield even to superior forces if he believed he was right. My mother, on the other hand, was always willing to return a smile for a blow, and ever ready to bestow charity upon her enemy. Of this strange combination I was born thirty-six years ago, and ushered into a world of sin, the flesh and the devil.

I grew up with other black and white boys. I was never whipped by any, but made them all respect the strength of my arms. I got my education from many sources—through private tutors, two public schools, two grammar or high schools and two colleges. My teachers were men and women of varied experiences and abilities; four of them were eminent preachers. They studied me and I studied them. With some I became friendly in after years; others and I drifted apart, because as a boy they wanted to whip me, and I simply refused to be whipped. I was not made to be whipped. It annoys me to be defeated; hence to me, to be once defeated is to find cause for an everlasting struggle to reach the top.

I became a printer's apprentice at an early age, while still attending school. My apprentice master was a highly educated and alert man. In the affairs of business and the world he had no peer. He taught me many things before I reached twelve, and at fourteen I had enough intelligence and experience to manage men. I was strong and manly, and I made them respect me. I developed a strong and forceful character, and have maintained it still.

To me, at home in my early days, there was no difference between white and black. One of my father's properties, the place where I lived most of the time, was adjoining that of a white man. He had three girls and two boys; the Wesleyan minister, another white man, whose church my parents attended, also had property adjoining ours. He had three girls and one boy. All of us were playmates. We romped and were happy children, playmates together. The little white girl whom I liked most knew no better than I did myself. We were two innocent fools who never dreamed of a race feeling and problem. As a child, I went to school with white boys and girls, like all other Negroes. We were not called Negroes then. I never heard the term Negro used once until I was about fourteen.

At fourteen my little white playmate and I parted. Her parents thought the time had come to separate us and draw the color line. They sent her and another sister to Edinburgh, Scotland, and told her that she was never to write or try to get in touch with me, for I was a "nigger." It was then that I found for the first time that there was some difference in humanity, and that there were different races, each having its own separate and distinct social life. I did not care about the separation after I was told about it, because I never thought all during our childhood association that the girl and the rest of the children of her race were better than I was; in fact, they used to look up to me. So I simply had no regrets.

After my first lesson in race distinction, I never thought of playing with white girls any more, even if they might be next-door neighbors. At home my sisters' company was good enough for me, and at school I made friends with the colored girls next to me. White boys and I used to frolic together. We played cricket and baseball, ran races and rode bicycles together, took each other to the river and to the sea beach to learn to swim, and made boyish efforts while out in deep water to drown each other, making a sprint for shore crying out "Shark, shark, shark!" In all our experiences, however, only one black boy was drowned. He went under on a Friday afternoon after school hours, and his parents found him afloat, half eaten by sharks, on the following Sunday afternoon. Since then we boys never went sea bathing.

"You Are Black"

At maturity the black and white boys separated, and took different courses in life. I grew then to see the difference between the races more and more. My schoolmates as young men did not know or remember me any more. Then I realized that I had to make a fight for a place in the world, that it was not so easy to pass on to office and position. Personally, however, I had not much difficulty in finding and holding a place for myself, for I was aggressive. At eighteen I had an excellent position as manager of a large printing establishment, having under my control several men old enough to be my grandfathers. But I got mixed up with public life. I started to take an interest in the politics of my country, and then I saw the injustice done to my race because it was black, and I became dissatisfied on that account. I went traveling to South and Central America and parts of the West Indies to find out if it was so elsewhere, and I found the same situation. I set sail for Europe to find out if it was different there, and again I found the stumbling block—"You are black." I read of the conditions in America. I read "Up from Slavery," by Booker T. Washington, and then my doom—if I may so call it—of being a race leader dawned upon me in London after I had traveled through almost half of Europe.

I asked: "Where is the black man's Government?" "Where is his King and his kingdom?" "Where is his President, his country, and his

ambassador, his army, his navy, his men of big affairs?" I could not find
them, and then I declared, "I will help to make them."

Becoming naturally restless for the opportunity of doing something
for the advancement of my race, I was determined that the black man
would not continue to be kicked about by all the other races and nations of the world, as I saw it in the West Indies, South and Central
America and Europe, and as I read of it in America. My young and
ambitious mind led me into flights of great imagination. I saw before
me then, even as I do now, a new world of black men, not peons, serfs,
dogs and slaves, but a nation of sturdy men making their impress upon
civilization and causing a new light to dawn upon the human race. I
could not remain in London any more. My brain was afire. There was a
world of thought to conquer. I had to start ere it became too late and
the work be not done. Immediately I boarded a ship at Southampton for
Jamaica, where I arrived on July 15, 1914. The Universal Negro Improvement Association and African Communities (Imperial) League
was founded and organized five days after my arrival, with the program
of uniting all the Negro peoples of the world into one great body to
establish a country and Government absolutely their own.

Where did the name of the organization come from? It was while
speaking to a West Indian Negro who was a passenger on the ship with
me from Southampton, who was returning home to the West Indies
from Basutoland with his Basuto wife, that I further learned of the
horrors of native life in Africa. He related to me such horrible and piti-
able tales that my heart bled within me. Retiring to my cabin, all day
and the following night I pondered over the subject matter of that
conversation, and at midnight, lying flat on my back, the vision and
thought came to me that I should name the organization the Universal
Negro Improvement Association and African Communities (Imperial)
League. Such a name I thought would embrace the purpose of all black
humanity. Thus to the world a name was born, a movement created,
and a man became known.

I really never knew there was so much color prejudice in Jamaica,
my own native home, until I started the work of the Universal Negro
Improvement Association. We started immediately before the war. I
had just returned from a successful trip to Europe, which was an exceptional achievement for a black man. The daily papers wrote me up with
big headlines and told of my movement. But nobody wanted to be a
Negro. "Garvey is crazy; he has lost his head." "Is that the use he is
going to make of his experience and intelligence?"—such were the criticisms passed upon me. Men and women as black as I, and even more
so, had believed themselves white under the West Indian order of so-

ciety. I was simply an impossible man to use openly the term "Negro"; yet every one beneath his breath was calling the black man a nigger.

I had to decide whether to please my friends and be one of the "black-whites" of Jamaica, and be reasonably prosperous, or come out openly, and defend and help improve and protect the integrity of the black millions, and suffer. I decided to do the latter, hence my offense against "colored-black-white" society in the colonies and America. I was openly hated and persecuted by some of these colored men of the island who did not want to be classified as Negroes, but as white. They hated me worse than poison. They opposed me at every step, but I had a large number of white friends, who encouraged and helped me. Notable among them were the then Governor of the Colony, the Colonial Secretary and several other prominent men. But they were afraid of offending the "colored gentry" that passed for white. Hence my fight had to be made alone. I spent hundreds of pounds (sterling) helping the organization to gain a footing. I also gave up all my time to the promulgation of its ideals. I became a marked man, but I was determined that the work should be done.

The war helped a great deal in arousing the consciousness of the colored people to the reasonableness of our program, especially after the British at home had rejected a large number of West Indian colored men who wanted to be officers in the British army. When they were told that Negroes could not be officers in the British army they started their own propaganda, which supplemented the program of the Universal Negro Improvement Association. With this and other contributing agencies a few of the stiff-necked colored people began to see the reasonableness of my program, but they were firm in refusing to be known as Negroes. Furthermore, I was a black man and therefore had absolutely no right to lead; in the opinion of the "colored" element, leadership should have been in the hands of a yellow or a very light man. On such flimsy prejudices our race has been retarded. There is more bitterness among us Negroes because of the caste of color than there is between any other peoples, not excluding the people of India.

I succeeded to a great extent in establishing the Association in Jamaica with the assistance of a Catholic Bishop, the Governor, Sir John Pringle, the Rev. William Graham, a Scottish clergyman and several other white friends. I got in touch with Booker Washington and told him what I wanted to do. He invited me to America and promised to speak with me in the Southern and other States to help my work. Although he died in the Fall of 1915, I made my arrangements and arrived in the United States on March 23, 1916.

Here I found a new and different problem. I immediately visited some of the then so-called Negro leaders, only to discover, after a close study of them, that they had no program, but were mere opportunists who were living off their so-called leadership while the poor people were groping in the dark. I traveled through thirty-eight States and everywhere found the same condition. I visited Tuskegee and paid my respects to the dead hero, Booker Washington, and then returned to New York, where I organized the New York division of the Universal Negro Improvement Association. After instructing the people in the aims and objects of the Association, I intended returning to Jamaica to perfect the Jamaica organization, but when we had enrolled about 800 or 1,000 members in the Harlem district and had elected the officers, a few Negro politicians tried to turn the movement into a political club.

Political Faction Fight

Seeing that these politicians were about to destroy my ideals, I had to fight to get them out of the organization. Then it was that I made my first political enemies in Harlem. They fought me until they smashed the first organization and reduced its membership to about fifty. I started again, and in two months built up a new organization of about 1,500 members. Again the politicians came and divided us into two factions. They took away all the books of the organization, its treasury and all its belongings. At that time I was only an organizer, for it was not then my intention to remain in America, but to return to Jamaica. The organization had its proper officers elected, and I was not an officer of the New York division, but President of the Jamaica branch.

On the second split in Harlem thirteen of the members conferred with me and requested me to become President for a time of the New York organization so as to save them from the politicians. I consented and was elected President. There then sprang up two factions, one led by the politicians with the books and the money, and the other led by me. My faction had no money. I placed at their disposal what money I had, opened an office for them, rented a meeting place, employed two women secretaries, went on the street of Harlem at night to speak for the movement. In three weeks more than 2,000 new members joined. By this time I had the Association incorporated so as to prevent the other faction using the name, but in two weeks the politicians had stolen all the people's money and had smashed up their faction.

The organization under my Presidency grew by leaps and bounds. I started The Negro World. Being a journalist, I edited this paper free of cost for the Association, and worked for them without pay until November, 1920. I traveled all over the country for the Association at my own expense and established branches until in 1919 we had about thirty branches in different cities. By my writings and speeches we were able to build up a large organization of over 2,000,000 by June, 1919, at which time we launched the program of the Black Star Line.

To have built up a new organization, which was not purely political, among Negroes in America was a wonderful feat, for the Negro politician does not allow any other kind of organization within his race to thrive. We succeeded, however, in making the Universal Negro Improvement Association so formidable in 1919 that we encountered more trouble from our political brethren. They sought the influence of the District Attorney's office of the County of New York to put us out of business. Edwin P. Kilroe, at that time an Assistant District Attorney, on the complaint of the Negro politicians, started to investigate us and the association. Mr. Kilroe would constantly and continuously call me to his office for investigation on extraneous matters without coming to the point. The result was that after the eighth or ninth time I wrote an article in our newspaper, The Negro World, against him. This was interpreted as a criminal libel, for which I was indicted and arrested, but subsequently dismissed on retracting what I had written.

During my many tilts with Mr. Kilroe, the question of the Black Star Line was discussed. He did not want us to have a line of ships. I told him that even as there was a White Star Line, we would have, irrespective of his wishes, a Black Star Line. On June 27, 1919, we incorporated the Black Star Line of Delaware, and in September we obtained a ship.

The following month (October) a man by the name of Tyler came to my office at 56 West 135th Street, New York City, and told me that Mr. Kilroe had sent him to "get me," and at once fired four shots at me from a .38-calibre revolver. He wounded me in the right leg and the right side of my scalp. I was taken to the Harlem Hospital, and he was arrested. The next day it was reported that he committed suicide in jail just before he was to be taken before a City Magistrate.

Record-Breaking Convention

The first year of our activities for the Black Star Line added prestige to the Universal Negro Improvement Association. Several hundred thousand dollars worth of shares were sold. Our first ship, the steamship Yarmouth, had made three voyages to the West Indies and Central America. The white press had flashed the news all over the world. I, a young Negro, as President of the corporation, had become famous. My name was discussed on five continents. The Universal Negro Improvement Association gained millions of followers all over the world. By

August, 1920, over 4,000,000 persons had joined the movement. A convention of all the Negro peoples of the world was called to meet in New York that month. Delegates came from all parts of the known world. Over 25,000 persons packed the Madison Square Garden on August 1 to hear me speak to the first International Convention of Negroes. It was a record-breaking meeting, the first and the biggest of its kind. The name of Garvey had become known as a leader of his race.

Such fame among Negroes was too much for other race leaders and politicians to tolerate. My downfall was planned by my enemies. They laid all kinds of traps for me. They scattered their spies among the employes of the Black Star Line and the Universal Negro Improvement Association. Our office records were stolen. Employes started to be openly dishonest; we could get no convictions against them; even if on complaint they were held by a Magistrate, they were dismissed by the Grand Jury. The ships' officers started to pile up thousands of dollars of debts against the company without the knowledge of the officers of the corporation. Our ships were damaged at sea, and there was a general riot of wreck and ruin. Officers of the Universal Negro Improvement Association also began to steal and be openly dishonest. I had to dismiss them. They joined my enemies, and thus I had an endless fight on my hands to save the ideals of the Association and carry out our program for the race. My Negro enemies, finding that they alone could not destroy me, resorted to misrepresenting me to the leaders of the white race, several of whom, without proper investigation, also opposed me.

With robberies from within and from without, the Black Star Line was forced to suspend active business in December, 1921. While I was on a business trip to the West Indies in the Spring of 1921, the Black Star Line received the blow from which it was unable to recover. A sum of $25,000 was paid by one of the officers of the corporation to a man to purchase a ship, but the ship was never obtained and the money was never returned. The company was defrauded of a further sum of $11,000. Through such actions on the part of dishonest men in the shipping business, the Black Star Line received its first setback. This resulted in my being indicted for using the United States mails to defraud investors in the company. I was subsequently convicted and sentenced to five years in a Federal penitentiary. My trial is a matter of history. I know I was not given a square deal, because my indictment was the result of a "frame-up" among my political and business enemies. I had to conduct my own case in court because of the peculiar position in which I found myself. I had millions of friends and a large number of enemies. I wanted a colored attorney to handle my case, but there was none I could trust. I feel that I have been denied justice because of prejudice.

Yet I have an abundance of faith in the courts of America, and I hope yet to obtain justice on my appeal.

Association's 6,000,000 Membership

The temporary ruin of the Black Star Line has in no way affected the larger work of the Universal Negro Improvement Association, which now has 900 branches with an approximate membership of 6,000,000. This organization has succeeded in organizing the Negroes all over the world, and we now look forward to a renaissance that will create a new people and bring about the restoration of Ethiopia's ancient glory.

Being black, I have committed an unpardonable offense against the very light-colored Negroes in America and the West Indies by making myself famous as a Negro leader of millions. In their view, no black man must rise above them, but I still forge ahead determined to give to the world the truth about the new Negro who is determined to make and hold for himself a place in the affairs of men. The Universal Negro Improvement Association has been misrepresented by my enemies. They have tried to make it appear that we are hostile to other races. This is absolutely false. We love all humanity. We are working for the peace of the world, which we believe can only come about when all races are given their due.

We feel that there is absolutely no reason why there should be any differences between the black and white races, if each stop to adjust and steady itself. We believe in the purity of both races. We do not believe the black man should be encouraged in the idea that his highest purpose in life is to marry a white woman, and we do believe that the white man should be taught to respect the black woman in the same way as he wants the black man to respect the white woman. It is a vicious and dangerous doctrine of social equality to urge, as certain colored leaders do, that black and white should get together, for that would destroy the racial purity of both.

We believe that the black people should have a country of their own, where they should be given the fullest opportunity to develop politically, socially and industrially. The black people should not be encouraged to remain in white people's countries and expect to be Presidents, Governors, Mayors, Senators, Congressmen, Judges and social and industrial leaders. We believe that with the rising ambition of the Negro, if a country is not provided for him in another 50 or 100 years, there will be a terrible clash that will end disastrously to him and disgrace our civilization. We desire to prevent such a clash by pointing the Negro to a home of his own. We feel that all well-disposed and broad-minded

white men will aid in this direction. It is because of this belief no doubt
that my Negro enemies, so as to prejudice me further in the opinion of
the public, wickedly state that I am a member of the Ku Klux Klan,
even though I am a black man.

I have been deprived of the opportunity of properly explaining my
work to the white people of America, through the prejudice worked up
against me by jealous and wicked members of my own race. My success
as an organizer was much more than rival Negro leaders could tolerate.
They, regardless of consequences, either to me or to the race, had to
destroy me by fair means or foul. The thousands of anonymous and
other hostile letters written to the editors and publishers of the white
press by Negro rivals to prejudice me in the eyes of public opinion are
sufficient evidence of the wicked and vicious opposition I have had to
meet from among my own people, especially among the very light colored. But they went further than the press in their attempts to discredit
me. They organized clubs all over the United States and the West
Indies, and wrote both open and anonymous letters to city, State and
Federal officials of this and other Governments to induce them to use
their influence to hamper and destroy me. No wonder, therefore, that
several Judges, District Attorneys and other high officials have been
opposing me without knowing me. No wonder, therefore, that the great
white population of this country and of the world has a wrong impression of the aims and objects of the Universal Negro Improvement Association and of the work of Marcus Garvey.

The Struggle of the Future

Having had the wrong education as a start in his racial career, the Negro
has become his greatest enemy. Most of the troubles I have had in advancing the cause of the race have come from Negroes. Booker Washington aptly described the race in one of his lectures by stating that we
were like crabs in a barrel, that none would allow the other to climb
over, but on any such attempt all would combine to pull back into the
barrel the one crab that would make the effort to climb out. Yet, those
of us with vision cannot desert the race, leaving it to suffer and die.

Looking forward a century or two, we can see an economic and political death struggle for the survival of the different race groups. Many of
our present-day national centres will have become overcrowded with
vast surplus populations. The fight for bread and position will be keen
and severe. The weaker and unprepared group is bound to go under. That
is why, visionaries as we are in the Universal Negro Improvement Association, we are fighting for the founding of a Negro nation in Africa, so

that there will be no clash between black and white and that each race will have a separate existence and civilization all its own without courting suspicion and hatred or eyeing each other with jealousy and rivalry within the borders of the same country.

White men who have struggled for and built up their countries and their own civilizations are not disposed to hand them over to the Negro, or any other race, without let or hindrance. It would be unreasonable to expect this. Hence any vain assumption on the part of the Negro to imagine that he will one day become President of the Nation, Governor of the State, or Mayor of the City in the countries of white men, is like waiting on the devil and his angels to take up their residence in the Realm on high and direct there the affairs of Paradise.

SUPPLEMENTARY READINGS

Burkett, Randall K., ed. *Black Redemption: Churchmen Speak for the Garvey Movement.* Philadelphia: Temple University Press, 1978.

Burkett, Randall K. *Garveyism as a Religious Movement.* Metuchen, N.J.: Scarecrow Press, 1978.

Cronon, E. David. *Black Moses: The Story of Marcus Garvey and the Universal Negro Improvement Association.* Second edition. Madison: University of Wisconsin Press, 1969.

Jacques-Garvey, Amy. *Garvey and Garveyism.* New York: Collier Books, 1970.

Hill, Robert A., ed. *The Marcus Garvey and Universal Negro Improvement Association Papers.* Berkeley: University of California Press, 1983.

41

MILES MARK FISCHER

"Organized Religion and the Cults"

The demise of Garvey's movement along with the failure of the established black denominations to reach out to the urban masses left a religious vacuum that was filled by numerous cults and sects. Miles Mark Fischer (1899–1970) was professor of church history at Shaw University, Raleigh, North Carolina, and pastor of the White Rock Baptist Church in Durham. An acute observer of the changing Afro-American religious scene, he took note of the amazing proliferation of alternative religious groups, some of them distinctly non-Christian. Bishop Grace, Elder Michaux, and Father Divine caught the eye of the public press, but there were many more whom Fischer felt should be included in any religious census. He was struck by several features of these black-led cults and sects. They frequently had racially mixed followings; women had leadership roles they did not hold in the historic black denominations; the cults and sects provided social services not available elsewhere. Many of the groups that Fischer described for The Crisis in 1935 disappeared after the loss or death of a particular leader. Others evolved into established sects, gradually taking on more of the institutional characteristics of the mainstream black churches.

I NOMINATE the religious movements which are led by Bishop Grace, Elder Michaux, Father Divine et al. for inclusion in the *Census of Religious Bodies: 1936*. Kindred holiness and pentecostal groups with 1248 churches and a membership of 70,500 persons are included in the 1926 Religious Census. These represent 8 of the 54 denominations which enroll Negroes—the Church of the Living God, Christian Workers for Fellowship, organized in 1889; the Church of Christ (Holiness) U.S.A., 1894; the Church of God in Christ, 1895; the Church of God and Saints of Christ, 1896; the Pentecostal Assemblies of the World, 1908; the Churches of God, Holiness, 1914; the Apostolic Overcoming Holy Church of God, 1916, and the Church of the Living God, "The Pillar and Ground of Truth," 1925.

Source: *The Crisis* 44, no. 1 (January 1937): 8–10 and 29–30.

Of the 54 denominations 24 "were exclusively Negro," and there were "30 which were primarily white." Yet denominations like the Church of God and Saints of Christ and the Pentecostal Assemblies of the World belong neither to the "exclusively Negro" nor to the "primarily white" religious bodies. The Census itself states that the Church of God and Saints of Christ was begun by "William S. Crowdy, a Negro man," its first bishop, and that "one white man who was associated with him was subsequently raised to the same office." In 1933 the Pentecostal Assemblies of the World had 7 bishops of whom 4 were black and 3 were white. These churches enroll white members. It would seem, therefore, that some holiness and pentecostal churches have protested against the "exclusively Negro" and the "primarily white" denominations and have organized, shall I say, "Christian churches"?

The Religious Census of the United States could not possibly mention individuals like Elder James Morris Webb, who helped to revive racialism within the Negro churches when he published *The Black Man The Father of Civilization Proven by Biblical History*, Seattle, Washington, 1910. This booklet contained a letter from Bishop H. M. Turner who commended Webb "to the ministry and churches of our race of every denomination." Elder Webb's *Lecture: Jesus Was Born Out of the Black Tribe*, which was published in Chicago, was widely received because Negro churches delighted to hear "that the blood of the Negro coursed through the veins of Jesus and Solomon."

The "exclusively Negro" churches have been multiplying. The United Holy Church of America, founded at Durham, North Carolina, in 1894, must be added to the number. This church has reached points as far removed as the Bermuda Islands and California. Then there are the House of Jacob, Holiness and Sanctified Church which was founded by the late Supreme Chief and Bishop, G. W. Israel, and Bishop W. D. Barbour's Triumph Church of the New Age at Pittsburgh. The Free Will Holiness Association has existed in North Carolina since 1914. In September, 1923, the respectable Council of Community Churches originated in Chicago primarily because of alleged irregularities in the African Methodist Episcopal Church. The Kodesh Church of Philadelphia had no such historic model. Elder F. R. Killingsworth began this church in 1927 and in 1934 had 11 branches. Elder Holland Goff, an evangelist from Milwaukee, went to Fayetteville, North Carolina, in August, 1928, and within a month had established the Saints of the Solid Rock of Holiness. Goff founded "Zora," a sort of industrial community for the Saints about three miles from Fayetteville. The division of the Church of God in Christ became the Church of God in Christ (Pentecostal) in 1931.

Non-Christian Churches

As in former years the 1936 Religious Census will undoubtedly include all known types of religious bodies. It will indeed be of value to know those religious organizations which undertake to win the allegiance of Negroes by other than recognized Christian propaganda. Islam is spreading in the United States from its Chicago headquarters. Both the beliefs of Mohammed and of Jesus were drawn upon by Timothy Drew who founded the religious, race-conscious, philanthropic Moorish Science Temple at Chicago in 1925. The Moors, as the disciples of this cult are called, are still prominent in Chicago and Baltimore. The similar "University of Islam" is at Detroit, while Sufi Abdul Hamid, a purported Hitler aid, has his Industrial Clerical Alliance in New York City. No Census has taken notice of communism or has attempted to measure the extent of primitivism.

The following spiritualist churches, which consider themselves distinctly "Christian," could be mentioned in a religious census—the Anthony Spiritual Temple of America, founded by the "diamond tooth evangelist," Anthony George of Philadelphia, and the Christian Spiritual Union of the late Archbishop M. N. Henry, a native woman of Benares, India, also with headquarters in Philadelphia. The Negro National Spiritualist Association with headquarters in Detroit was founded in 1925, and the Orthodox Spiritualist Church of America with headquarters in New York City, in 1932. The Interdenominational Ministers' Council and United Churches of Christ Institutional (1933) works from Baltimore but is considering New York headquarters. When the Independent Universal Spiritualist Churches were last heard of (1934), their founder, Bishop Simon D. Brooks, was serving a 1 to 5 year term in Waupun Penitentiary in Wisconsin.

Almost in every center, particularly urban, is some unorthodox religious group which makes a definite appeal to Negroes. In Washington, D.C., about three doors from the Mt. Carmel (Institutional) Baptist Church, is a meeting place of the unnoticed international cult of Jehovah's Witnesses. Jehovah's Witnesses, which was founded by "Pastor" Russell and popularized by Judge Rutherford, and other "primarily white" adventist and holiness bodies shows that white people have religious organizations which are in direct opposition to the churches. This movement runs immediately back to the "restless" last quarter of the nineteenth century and has been intensified by the Spanish American War, the World War and the Fundamentalist stir.

Rise of the Cults

The 1936 Religious Census should also show the Negro's attack upon organized Christianity. The small but numerous faith healing groups like the Church of One Faith in New York City and the Miracle Temple of Christ in Richmond, Virginia, should not be omitted. Individual "prophets" like Thompson of Chicago, Darnley of Atlanta, Moses of Pleasantville, New Jersey, Martin and Joseph of Washington, D.C., and Jones of Brooklyn might escape the census, but not Prophet Kiwah Costonie. He and his Church of the Almighty God in Brooklyn are too important. Bishop Charles Manuel Grace has founded fully 50 branches of the United House of Prayer from New York to Florida. He claims 200,000 members since 1921. Elder Lightfoot Solomon Michaux established his Church of God in Washington in 1928 and since then has become internationally known as "radio's *Happy Am I* evangelist." In about seven years Father Divine can claim an international organization that has grown from "Kingdoms" in New York City. There are other kindred groups, but they are not as well-known. For example, Elder Lucy Smith's Langley Avenue All Nations Pentecostal Church was begun in Chicago before the World War. Branches are now established in the West and in the South. Bishop R. C. Lawson has his Refuge Church of Christ not only in New York City but also in fourteen states, the Virgin Islands and Panama. Mother Rosa Horne's Mt. Calvary Assembly Hall of the Pentecostal Faith of All Nations has spread to several places outside of New York City.

My observation is that the 1936 religious census can show considerable denominational losses during the last ten years. The "cults" have made it difficult to say who is a church member. It might not be without significance that one of my earliest Sunday school teachers was indeed a cult member but was buried as an outstanding member, the superintendent of the primary department of the Sunday school of a Chicago church. I remember her demise several years ago and how the "saints" virtually took charge of her body. A pastor in a cult center facetiously remarked to me: "If you want to see my folks on a Sunday night, go to Elder Lucy Smith's." It is not accidental that church attendance, particularly on Sunday nights, has decreased while cult attendance has increased, that cult meetings become crowded on Sundays after the churches have about dismissed and that the cults hold meetings during the week at times when the churches have no worship services. As a matter of fact, the holiness and pentecostal groups are modeled after the Baptist and Methodist churches, are often led by ex-Baptists and ex-Methodists and enroll many members who formerly belonged to the popular denominations.

Of course the churches of the last ten years have gone through a depression, but many of them are practically bankrupt not only because of the economic crisis but also because they did not compete successfully with the cults which generally thrived all during the period. Church members have been known to withhold their financial support from the already debt-ridden historical churches and then to give offerings to the cults. Cult literature has been and is sold in abundance to church members. Witness the widespread dissemination of the Watch Tower publications of Jehovah's Witnesses. There is probably an astounding number of Negro church members who subscribe to *Unity* magazine. The average Negro church member cannot buy cult literature and at the same time give full allegiance to his church. Matthew 6:21 is still true, "For where your treasure is, there will your heart be also."

Cults Point the Way

A glance beyond the excesses of the holiness and pentecostal movement will reveal an abiding way of life. Beyond the strong individual cult denials of a unity of ideals are similar aims and purposes. The cults and not the denominations point out directions for organized religion to take.

The cults have said distinctly that *the future Negro churches shall neither be "exclusively Negro" nor "primarily white" but "Christian."* The cults mean that it shall no longer be a badge of honor and an occasion for the widest possible Negro publicity when a black man preaches to whites. Says Bishop R. C. Lawson in the Preface of his booklet, *The Anthropology of Jesus Christ Our Kinsman:* "I have pastored a mixed congregation of white and black folk ever since I have been pastoring." Crowdy, Haygood, Horne, Smith, Costonie, Grace, Michaux, Divine, and others are cult leaders who are not excited because they preach to and are the pastors "of white and black folk." Whites and blacks are just people. The continued success of this experiment outside of the historical churches has profound significance for the churches and for the bi-racial United States. Already, the Young People's Interracial Fellowship Church has been organized in Philadelphia and has held monthly meetings for one year. It has entered upon its second year of interracial worship services with alternating black and white speakers.

Simplicity distinguishes the cults and might as well characterize the churches. Cult leaders are not degreed clergymen but are former cooks, like Crowdy and Grace, and an ex-dressmaker, like Horne, and an exfish peddler, like Michaux, and an ex-barber (?) like Divine, all of whom would hardly be licensed to preach by any of the popular denominations. Occasionally, there is an "Archbishop" and a "D.D." among them, but more often their lack of a title is in striking contrast to the church leaders. Holiness and pentecostal leaders are as elaborate as Negro preachers only perhaps in their creature comforts. Unlike the worship places of many of the local churches, the cult places of meeting are tents or "store-fronts" or other plain audience rooms. The Church of God and Saints of Christ has gone so far as to have no instrumental accompaniments to its music, although "saints" generally employ a variety of musical instruments.

The cults are most prosperous where intelligence abounds, establishing their headquarters in our cultural and educational centers like New York City, Chicago, Philadelphia, Washington and Memphis, primarily because the evangelical denominations appeal less and less to the untrained masses. In proportion as the churches are becoming unemotional—fine, fashionable and formal,—their programs become less intelligible to the common man. Unsophisticated churchmen and the "forgotten" masses, therefore, furnish the great majority of the cult members who are held by the weirdest type of abandon and emotionalism. It is to be hoped that the churches are not destroying the very foundation of their superstructure by neglecting the common man, for it is no secret that the cults are attracting respectable attention. Elder Michaux went to Philadelphia in the late spring of 1934. According to the *Afro-American*, June 9, 1934, "a feature of his appearance here (in Philadelphia) was the organization of a citizens' committee to serve as host to the Michaux organization. This committee is headed by Major R. R. Wright and one of its members is serving each night to introduce the elder." The Norfolk *Journal and Guide*, May 25, 1935, heads almost a half column thus: "BISHOP HOWARD PLUMMER HEARD BY MASS. NAACP; Belleville Leader Shares Program with Elite." Bishop Howard Z. Plummer, one knows, was the "leader of the Church of God and Saints of Christ." When Elder Lucy Smith observed her sixty-second birthday at the All Nations Church on the fourteenth of January, 1936, the Chicago *Defender* of January 18 carried her cut and the statement that "among the distinguished guests were: Alderman William Dawson, Attorney and Mrs. A. M. Burroughs, Attorney and Mrs. George C. Adams . . . W. T. Brown, Jr. (a leading undertaker), the mayor of Bronzeville. . . ."

Equality for Women

In no one of the popular denominations is full standing given to women. Regardless of a Constitutional amendment and of the fact that the larger percentage of church members are women, women are not leaders of the historical churches. Here and there a woman is on a Baptist church board of trustees and is sometimes licensed and ordained to preach by the Baptists. Among the Methodists she is usually an evangelist. Only among the cults has a woman the highest offices of leadership, being sometimes an "Archbishop" or a "Bishop" or an "Elder." Miss Laura L. R. Perry left the St. Mark's Community Church in Norfolk, Virginia, in 1934, to become the "Bishop" of the Perry Community Holiness Church. Lucy Smith went to Chicago from the Baptist stronghold in Atlanta and organized her All Nations Pentecostal Church, becoming its Elder. Elder Rosa Artimus Horne of the Methodist faith finally got to New York City from her native Sumter, South Carolina, with a new-found pentecostal fire and organized the Mt. Calvary Assembly Hall. The well-to-do holiness Bishop Ida Robinson is in Philadelphia. Father Divine associates "Faithful Mary" with himself.

"Faithful Mary!" Her real name is Viola Wilson, "a former notorious police character in the Third Ward of Newark," but reformation under Father Divine brought her the "new name." Here Father Divine follows Revelation 2:17 and 3:12 and in the New York Supreme Court won the right for the Divinites to register their new kingdom names for voting purposes. This is an illustration of the extreme Biblical position of the cults. Historical criticism, however, has made the churches less sure that they have a supreme biblical warrant. Expository preaching and doctrinal sermons, particularly about sanctification, have about ceased in the churches. Time was when popular preachers would have their pictures taken with the open Bible in one hand, but that pose is now out of date except for cult leaders, like Michaux and Perry. The cults depend upon the Bible for their authority. The names of their leaders, "Bishop," "Elder," "Father," and "Mother," and of their churches, "Kodesh (Hebrew for Holy!)," "Church of God," "House of Prayer for All People," and "Kingdoms," and of their customs, a common meal, washing "the saints' feet," the "holy kiss," and gifts of the "Holy Ghost," "tongues," and "of healing," are all in the Bible. Cult preaching is largely of the proof-text variety.

Cult Leaders Are Prophets

Churches have much to learn from the cult leaders of religion who are our ethical prophets, though truly "crazy." Crowdy "was arrested 22 times, six times for insanity." "Father" Chester Talliafero, the founder of the Saints' Rest in Philadelphia, was charged with gross misconduct in 1928, 1933 and 1935 only to be detained in an asylum from which he was released. It is exceptional when a cult leader is adjudged guilty of anything other than insanity. Cult leaders have the courage to denounce this world. "Belleville (Virginia)" of the Church of God and Saints of Christ, the Kingdoms of Father Divine and "Zora (North Carolina)" of the Saints of the Solid Rock of Holiness are more or less communistic headquarters of these groups. All popular amusements are taboo. Nowhere at a local or a sectional or a national meeting of the United Holy Church will a saint be found using tobacco. Saints are just not supposed to use it. The cults are such vehement advocates of temperance that bodies like the Church of God and Saints of Christ and the Churches of the Living God, Christian Workers for Fellowship substitute water for the wine which is ordinarily used in the Lord's supper. All know that the Divinites, whose slogan is "Peace! It is wonderful," are probably the first pacifist religious group among Negroes, even though Bishop Grace rejoins: "I am the only man in the world preaching peace." Moreover, the cults attack present social and economic practices by fostering businesses that are not run primarily for profit.

The churches used to lead in social work. Trained Negro clergymen now content themselves with the current philosophy that churches are to furnish the inspiration for social work rather than to do it. The cults, however, operate social agencies even though their plants are often dilapidated and unsanitary. The Divinites in particular conduct fuel, food, clothes and kindred businesses. *Happy News*, the official organ of Elder Michaux, advertises 5 "Happy Are We" 5 and 10 cents meat markets in Washington. The Elder operates settlement houses also. There are numerous farms which are under cult control. Cult relief work and orphanages, old folks' homes, schools, newspapers and hotels are not of extraordinary social significance. It is important that social pronouncements have but recently come from the historical denominations.

Mark you, Christianity itself and all evangelical denominations were once cults. I nominate the religious movements which are led by Bishop Grace, Elder Michaux, Father Divine, et al., for inclusion in the *Census of Religious Bodies: 1936*.

SUPPLEMENTARY READINGS

Fauset, Arthur H. *Black Gods of the Metropolis*. Philadelphia: University of Pennsylvania Press, 1971.

Reid, Ira De A. "Let Us Prey!" *Opportunity* 4, no. 45 (September 1926): 274–78.

Washington, Joseph R., Jr. *Black Sects and Cults*. Garden City, N.Y.: Doubleday/ Anchor Books, 1972.

Webb, Lilian A. *About My Father's Business: The Life of Elder Michaux*. Westport, Conn.: Greenwood Press, 1981.

Whiting, Albert N. "From Saint to Shuttler—An Analysis of Sectarian Types." *Quarterly Review of Higher Education Among Negroes* 13, no. 4 (October 1955): 133–40.

42

Black Judaism in Harlem

In "New World A-Coming" Roi Ottly gave a portrait of Harlem's Rabbi Matthew, as he appeared in 1942—a "grave, intelligent black man who appears to be about fifty years of age with the vigor of a man of thirty. He dresses in severe black—definitely unusual in Harlem—and wears the traditional yarmulke, or skullcap. He looks like one of the Negro figures in Rubens' Bacchanale." Matthew led a group of black Jews, more accurately known as the Commandment Keepers. Born in Lagos, West Africa, in 1892, he came to New York via the West Indies and established his version of orthodox Judaism for blacks in 1919. Many of the Commandment Keepers were former Garveyites, and a significant percentage were West Indian immigrants. Rabbi Matthew instructed his members in Yiddish and kosher dietary regulations. He taught a variant of Ethiopianism and tried to make connections with the Falashas of Ethiopia. Eventually this led to the idea that white Jews were spurious and that the black Jews were the chosen people of God.

Matthew rejected Christianity and attacked, because of what he termed "niggeritions," the enthusiastic pentecostal style of worship southern blacks brought to Harlem. He designed a rather rigorous curriculum for his Ethiopian Hebrew Rabbinical College and in 1935 announced a plan for converting "two-thirds of the colored population of America to the Orthodox Hebrew faith." The Amsterdam News reported in 1954 that Matthew's nationwide following amounted to eight thousand.

IN ORDER TO SPEED along to a quick understanding, I must treat briefly the history of the sons of men, from Adam, of whom it is only necessary to say that when God decided on the necessity of man's existence, He did not choose to make a black man, or a white man: He simply decided to make man—not white nor black—from the dust of the earth, in whom He encased the reproductive power of all colors, all species, all shades of all races and eventual nationalities. From Adam to Noah,

Source: Howard Brotz, *The Black Jews of Harlem*. New York: Schocken Books, 1970. Pp. 19–22 passim.

there were only two classes of men, known as the sons of God and the sons of men: a Godly and an ungodly group. In other words, a carnal and a spiritual-minded race of the sons of men, both from Adam.

The two classes eventually met in Noah and his wife: Noah was a son of the Godly (a son of God), he chose a wife from the daughters of men (the carnal-minded), and to the time of the flood he had three sons: Shem, Ham, and Japheth. After the flood Ham took the lead. Nimrod, one of his descendants, created the idea of a tower as the landmark of their capital, that if they became lost upon the face of the earth they might have something to look for as a guide, and also as a security against future floods. They called the name of their tower, or city, Babel. Some have said that Babel means confusion, but this is not so; the word means "Coming to God."

As Cush rose in power, Africa, the entire continent, including Egypt, became the center of the world's cultural and religious education, and thus Ham secured for himself and his posterity for all time, a name—Pioneers of the World's Civilization.

After the fall of Cush came Egypt, under Mizri the second son of Ham, into power. He and Shem amalgamated by intermarriage and the Mesopotamians were produced, an interrace between Shem and Ham. After this came Abraham, the son of Tera; he married his sister Sarah, who was the daughter of his father but not of his mother. She was barren to him, but after many years she conceived by aid of a Hamitic god (Priest) and brought forth Isaac who, in turn, married Rebecca, his uncle's daughter. When she also, after many years, conceived, she brought forth twins, one red and hairy all over like a hairy garment, while the other was plain and smooth, as the black man invariably is. The first, the red and hairy one was called Esau; the plain and smooth brother was called Jacob. This same Jacob, by four wives, begot twelve sons. After twenty years his name was changed from Jacob to Israel, and automatically his sons became the sons of Israel.

They went into Egypt and abode there four hundred and thirty years. They mingled greatly with the Egyptians by intermarriage, and thus Shem and Ham were merged into one great people. Of those who left Egypt, there were six hundred thousand footmen, twice as many women, three or four times as many of the half-breed and a host of children. All those who had reached maturity before leaving Egypt died in the wilderness except Joshua and Calen; even Moses, the greatest of all legislators, died there. But before coming out of Egypt Moses had fled to Median in Ethiopia, only to become servant to the Ethiopian Priest whose daughter he eventually married and begot two sons.

Those two boys were as much Ethiopians as it was possible to be because they were created out of the soil and born in the land, as they were Israelites of the Tribe of Levi, the Priest, because Moses their father was of the tribe of Levi and of the household of Israel. They of necessity had to be black because their father was black, and so was their mother. They were the first Ethiopian Hebrews of the Tribe of Levi. They were half Hamitic and half Semitic. I could go on endlessly to prove the direct connection all along the ages of the two greatest peoples that ever lived in the earth, but I must hasten along.

This great admixture of two great people left Egypt, tarried in the wilderness forty years, and finally came into the land of Canaan. Eventually David, son of Jesse of the Tribe of Judah, came to the throne of Israel, and in time his son Solomon succeeded him.

When Solomon came to the throne, his fame spread the world over, and to the Queen of Sheba, whose name was Candace Queen of the South, she being also of the children of Rachel, one of the wives of Jacob. She also came to pay her respects and to make her portion of the kingdom subject to King Solomon. Eventually she became the wife of Solomon, the son that was born to them was Menelik the 1st. The line of the Falashas are counted from Menelik 1st to Menelik the great, who was the uncle of his Imperial Majesty, Haile Selassie, the 1st, the Lion of the Tribe of Judah. It is roughly calculated that before the war there were about a million Falasha Jews in Ethiopia (about a tenth of the population of 13 million); however, since the war they have been greatly reduced, and fear is entertained for their continued existence. In Harlem, N.Y., there are about three thousand adherents to the faith and who, with pride, lay claim to this glorious heritage. At the central Congregation, 1 West 123rd Street, N.Y.C., there are about eight hundred registered. At 434 Franklin Ave., Brooklyn are also a goodly number. In Philadelphia, Media, Pittsburgh and Sharon, Pa., are goodly groups, also at Youngstown and Ferrell, Ohio, Chicago, Ill., Cullen, Va., St. Thomas, V.I., and Jamaica, W.I.

It is claimed by these that they are among the oldest families of the Jewish or Hebraic race upon the face of the earth, and that they are the only ones to retain their king to sit upon the Throne of David and, outside of Palestine, to retain the six point star on their money. Our manner and customs are strictly orthodox; we are strictly Koshered. Our children are taught to speak the Hebrew language and to live in keeping with all the commandments of the Almighty.

I am the only rabbi with credentials from Ethiopia, sanctioned by both the Chief Rabbi of the Falashas and the National Coptic Church of St. Michael. The National Church must sanction the existence of all other religious bodies in Ethiopia, but none are ever barred or hindered.

Religious practices are as free in Ethiopia as in the U.S.A. Thus it is time for the two great people to come together and stand for the true doctrine of the oneness of God.

My prayer is that peace may soon come to the earth, and good will to all men, and an eternal victory for Israel, the elect of the Eternal. . . .

Curriculum

Curriculum of the Ethiopian Hebrew Rabbinical College of the Royal Order of Ethiopian Hebrews and the Commandment Keepers Congregation of the Living God, Inc.

First-year Course for all Field Workers, including Revivalists, Daughters of Israel, Prophets and Exhorters:

1. The twelve principles of the doctrines of the cultural house of Israel.
2. Elementary Hebrew.
3. Bible poetry (The Psalms).
4. Prophecies and their allusion to the kingdom to come.
5. Harmony of the Prophecies of the four great prophets: namely, Isaiah, Jeremiah, Ezekiel, and Daniel.
6. Ministerial decorum.
7. Cultural and domestic aid—Grammar.

THE ADVANCED COURSE

1. Study of the chomesh (The five books of Moses).
2. Lyrics.
3. Advanced decorum and manner of speech in mixed congregations.
4. Ethical presentation of Jewish history.
5. Geography and topography of the holy land.
6. Chronology of sacred writings.
7. The names and characteristics of the congregations of God.
8. Etiquette.
9. Theocracy.
10. Natural history of sacred writings.

This is divided into four terms, comprising two years.

SPECIAL SHEPHERD AND TEACHER'S COURSE

1. The study of the Mishnah.
2. The apocrypha.
3. Jewish ancient history.
4. Hebraic ancient history.

5. The entire works of Josephus.
6. The Israelites and their related people.
7. Israelitish ancient and medieval history.
8. Topography of the countries connected with sacred writings.

FINAL TERM

1. Jewish months and their scriptural proofs.
2. Talmudic Legalism.
3. Clerical Legalism.
4. Etiquette in general principles.
5. Parliamentary rules.
6. Levitical Priesthood and Temple worship.
7. Special Talmud Torah information.
8. Elementary Greek, Latin, French, Advanced Hebrew, and Sociology.
9. Certificates are given to those who complete the course.

An efficient and able staff of teachers is maintained at all times to accommodate all students.

SUPPLEMENTARY READINGS

Brotz, Howard. *The Black Jews of Harlem*. New York: The Free Press of Glencoe, 1964.

Ehrman, Albert. "The Commandment Keepers: A Negro 'Jewish' Cult in America Today." *Judaism* 8 (1959): 266–72.

Gerber, Israel J. *The Heritage Seekers: Black Jews in Search of Identity*. Middle Village, N.Y.: Jonathan David Publishers, 1977.

Landers, Ruth. "Negro Jews in Harlem." *Jewish Journal of Sociology* 9 (December 1967): 175–90.

Shapiro, Deanee. "Factors in the Development of Black Judaism." In *The Black Experience in Religion*, edited by C. Eric Lincoln. Garden City, N.Y.: Doubleday/Anchor Books, 1974. Pp. 253–72.

"The Realness of God, to you-wards . . ."

The Harlem renaissance poet Claude McKay said of Major Jealous Divine, better known as Father Divine, that he was the originator of religion "on the chain-store plan." Divine certainly emerged from the ashes of the Great Depression with an extensive following. Some of his followers were former Garveyites; some were poor blacks and whites who flocked to his Sayville, Long Island, retreat to participate in sumptuous meals; some were middle-class whites who believed that Divine had risen above the problem of race; and countless others were people drawn to the extensive system of communal security provided by the Peace Mission Movement.

The press viewed Divine as a black messiah. His followers believed him to be God incarnate in a human body, who never taught or represented a single race but was the father of one worldwide family. Major Divine's control of cosmic forces was first confirmed for true believers by an incident on June 7, 1932, when a judge who sentenced him for disturbing the peace in Sayville died unexpectedly of a heart attack. Father Divine subsequently expanded on his "God in me, God in you" metaphysics by stressing powers of omnipresence, victory over death and sickness, and the virtues of the celibate life. Though Father Divine relinquished mortal existence on September 10, 1965, the faithful believe he will return in bodily form. Mother Divine, the former Edna Rose Ritchings, a Canadian disciple whom Father Divine married in 1946, presides over the movement's estate called Woodmount in a suburb of Philadelphia. Father Divine's banquet messages are still reprinted in the New Day, as they were originally transcribed.

Father Divine's Message at the Banquet Table
152–160 West 126th Street, New York City, N.Y.
Sunday, June 14, 1936 A.D.F.D. Time: 11:35 P.M.

AT THE RECENT court proceedings in which the state of New York tried unsuccessfully to compel Peace Mission Extensions and industries to

Source: "As A Man Thinketh In His Heart So Is He And as You Visualize and Act From That Angle So Will It be just As You Think Vividly Enough." *The New Day.*

carry Workmen's Compensation Insurance, reporters from most of New York City's daily papers gathered eagerly around the press table. They expected to get inside information on the mystery of how the greatest Movement of all time is conducted.

This they received in abundance as evidence was introduced that caused even the Judges to marvel. There were other features, however, that kept their pencils busy and their eyes and ears alert, such as the prosperous and happy appearance of the Followers who filled the court room and their unanimous enthusiastic declaration, "FATHER DIVINE is GOD ALMIGHTY," when the Judge asked a witness the question, "Who is FATHER DIVINE?"

Following this demonstration, one of the reporters asked the question, "How do they know FATHER DIVINE is GOD? The answer was given, "The same as converted Christians know that JESUS is CHRIST." The reporter's response was, "Well I never did believe much in that, but I can see where it would be easy to believe FATHER DIVINE is GOD because of what HE is doing, and because one can actually see HIM." Subsequently in The New York Sun appeared the statement referring to this demonstration, "Such a display of faith probably has not been seen since Constantine's time."

This incident was recalled when thousands filled the 126th Street of the Kingdom, Sunday evening, June 14th in the Presence of the beloved Body of GOD. As they rejoiced in the realness and the genuineness of HIM Who said in the Body called Jesus, "All who ever came before ME are thieves and robbers," they sang with radicalness and enthusiasm as follows:

> "HE's Real, HE's Real,
> FATHER DIVINE is Real.
> Oh, sweet FATHER, gave me the Victory.
> I can't live without HIM,
> I should die if I doubt HIM,
> FATHER DIVINE, I know HIM,
> HE'S REAL, REAL, REAL!"

Then speaking Words of Spirit and of Life, unfolding the science of salvation in psychological truths hid from the sages but condescending to speak in the language of men, FATHER arose speaking Personally as follows:

June 25, 1936, 3–5. "We Shall Have a Righteous Government." *The New Day.* July 9, 1936, 16.

PEACE EVERYONE!

Here we are again, and there I sit in the midst of the children of men. I AM there as though I AM here, and here as I AM there, though you may not understand. That little song, it has been stressed vividly, but whether you believe it or believe it not, it is a fact. The realness of GOD is not confined nor bound to one place geographically, neither is it confined nor bound to one apparent Personality; nevertheless the words that you have spoken in that composition, they are facts and figures too stout to be denied.

The realness of GOD to you-wards, it has been stressed since you believed. Because you realized or visualized the realness of GOD and concentrated in the positive direction with harmonious thoughts toward your Maker, harmonious conditions have resulted. Therefore you said in the composition, "I would die if I doubt HIM." You said firstly, you could not live without HIM. The realness of GOD is as any other expression, it is as real as you will receive it, and as real as you will let it be.

Realness of God Hid in Your Untruthfulness

GOD said, "Let there be light and there was light." If you refuse to let GOD be real to you, to you the realness of GOD may not be discerned, but to those whom the realness of GOD is revealed, to them it is real. But if you close the way up—in other words close the way behind you and before you as you go, by your selfish ideas and opinions, by trying to measure GOD with the measure of a man, it will be a matter of impossibility for GOD to you to express HIS realness. But as you visualize GOD from the positive angle of expression and visualize the realness of GOD according to your profession, by such a visualization as you vividly visualize the Perfect Picture, you will tend to materialize it and to you, you will make it "real-er."

It is not because it is not real. If the realness of GOD is not discerned by you nor manifested in you as real, it is because of the lack of the realness of your thoughts to GOD, and the lack of the realness of yourselves in your hearts, your minds and your souls. Oh it is something to consider! You can create for yourselves desirable conditions if you will but dial in on the positive and in the positive direction direct your thoughts. But if you desire to dial in on the negative, and direct your thoughts in the negative direction, the negative conditions will result, according to the negative thoughts you have been thinking. But it is a privilege to realize, as real as you observe GOD to be, even so real will GOD be to thee.

The realness of GOD is made real in your realness, and the realness of

GOD is hid from you in your untruthfulness and in your unrealness. But if you are sincere in all of your endeavors, persistent in your ambition and will think in the positive direction and walk in the same direction whatever may oppose, it matters not what opposes I might say, the same of that which you have visualized will be materialized, and you will realize that which you have visualized, though you had not seen it in reality in the beginning. That which is hid in the invisible will come forth into expression by your realness and by your sincerity. By you being real in your endeavors even as you expect GOD to be, so real will GOD be to thee, according to your faith in HIM. But when you refuse to continue to believe in the realness of GOD in a Body, GOD will cease to make HIMSELF real to you as a person.

You may observe GOD merely as spirit and as mind from the spiritual and from the mental realms, and you will only receive the blessings according to same, from the mental and spiritual planes. But when you turn to realize the realness of GOD as made Perfect, in other words, the Perfection as manifested in that which is termed mortality, realize GOD as HE is in reality from every angle of expression, you can, by your conscious conviction of the realness of GOD, bring into outer expression the real and the desirable condition.

Reaching the Hearts and Minds

For this cause we are rejoicing, to observe the unfoldment of it daily. This is not something merely to be surmised; this is not merely something to be considered as an expression to be brought into the outer in the future, but we are observing it here and now today. As said the Scripture, "Today is the day of salvation, today is the day of grace."

Now at this juncture I will extend MYSELF again. Oh it is indeed Wonderful! I AM going from shore to shore and from land to land. I AM going from heart to heart, and from mind to mind. I shall reach the hearts and the minds of men that have not yet believed. Even though they may have lived in sin, I will reach the hearts and the minds of them. Oh it is a privilege to realize GOD as Omnipotent, to realize GOD as Omniscient; GOD having all power, all dominion and all authority; GOD having all wisdom, all understanding and all knowledge—able to reach your condition wheresoever you are and lift you from sinking sand. Oh it is a privilege to realize it.

I mention this because as mortality in its egotistic ways of expression rises and manifests itself in the mortal minded people as critics, there and then is the time I shall rise on the hearts and minds of men as I have never done. Oh it is indeed Wonderful! I shall bring them from every so-called tribe, from every so-called nation, from every so-called language and every so-called people. I shall bring them to the recognition of GOD in a Body, and they as well as you shall recognize their FATHER. Oh it is something to consider. Every individual under the sound of MY voice and not only so but wheresoever man is found, if he or she will make that mental and spiritual contact tonight, from their undesirable conditions where they have been bound, I will set them free.

Contact Made by Relaxing Conscious Mentality

Make your mental and your spiritual contact. I have long since said, you make your mental and your spiritual contact by the relaxation of your conscious mentality, by relaxing your preconceived ideas and opinions, and renouncing your former ways once and forever. By this you will contact ME and will receive the results speedily, yea, spontaneously the results will be exhibited and you will fully receive it.

Oh while thinking along this line, I thought of the mission of hundreds of people coming from far and near, merely to see ME Personally. As I said this afternoon, if you could but make your mental and spiritual contact even though you have come from afar, some have followed ME up continually from a Personal point of view, having not had a chance to contact ME Personally as they desire to do. But if you will but make your mental and your spiritual contact, your prayers will be heard and answered.

As I said, it is immaterial to ME what may come or rise or go, the Spirit of MY Presence will do exactly what I came to do. All earth may rise in opposition, but it is a matter of impossibility to prohibit ME, for this is not matter, personality nor individuality; it is an Impersonal Presence working for the common good of humanity. When you realize GOD is not confined nor bound to observation, or visible expressions whichever, then and there you can trust HIM wholeheartedly. But until you realize GOD as Infinite, Omnipotent, Omnipresent and yet Ever Present, you cannot gain the Victory over your thoughts of limitation and over your thoughts of what mankind may do to you or some other individual. But when you deny yourselves wholeheartedly and present your bodies as living sacrifices Holy, you can relax your conscious mentality and GOD will work more effectively for you.

When you relax your conscious mentality and cease to struggle, still yourselves as individuals, then and there GOD HIMSELF will work for you. But so long as you are struggling and worrying, contending and trying to prevent certain conditions, it is an open expression by your open attention that it is not faith in the fulness, developed in you. When your faith shall have been developed in you completely once and forever, you can and will relax your conscious mentality in the act of contention and in the act of trying to prevent, as an expression for prevention, for preventions cannot act saving by the Infinite. Oh it is something to consider!

God Will take Care of You

When GOD's Body, in which I AM now living, went through thirty-two lynch mobs without a thought of prevention and without a thought of prohibitation, refusing to allow MYSELF to place MYSELF in a way where there would be a visible prohibitation and possible prevention, but that the prevention would come from within ME, as the Master of Omnipotency and the Controller of your destiny—when you can stand before bayonets and guns, when you can stand before everything that may come, and praise GOD wholeheartedly and refuse to fret or murmur, refuse to tremble, but stand in the liberty upon the promises I have given, you can relax your conscious mentality then and there, and know GOD will take care of you.

When you sang the song, "GOD will take care of you," this is not a supposition, this is not an imagination, this is not merely to be sung for to be reiterated, and to be repeated and spoken as a melody, but it is a song sung. When it is reiterated spontaneously by the true and the faithful, if you say it sincerely and mean it sincerely, the very reaction of your conscious conviction according to your sincerity will respond within you. Oh it is something to consider! That is why the vibrations are so high here; it is because the believers are sincere. It is because they will not say it unless they mean it! If they happen to start to say it and do not mean it, I will change the version instantaneously and cause the reincarnation of sincerity, and quicken the Spirit of the meaning and cause them to mean it and sing it sincerely. Oh it is indeed Wonderful!

When you live in this recognition and dial in on it continually, in other words, keep your dials on this number, you will not have to dial in on it continually for the dials being on this number, when the Message is broadcast, the Message will come forth through the station, therefore you will receive it.

Realness of God

There are many things I could say, but I feel if I refrain from speaking Personally you may relax yourselves individually a little more that MY Spirit might tell you. If you relax your conscious thinking and allow MY

Spirit to tell you, then and there the Scripture is fulfilled within you, "It is better revealed than told." GOD in the midst of you, I say, is mighty to save—to bring about the conditions you have been seeking, and to adjust matters satisfactorily. When you realize it, you can be still; you can still yourselves personally and know GOD is real.

I heard you say, "FATHER is real." As real as you see ME to be, even so real will I be to thee. The realness is created between you and the object you visualize to be real or unreal, but especially of GOD. As you visualize HIM to be, so will it be with thee. Now isn't that Wonderful! There are those who have not seen ME Personally, but merely thought on ME vividly. Through vividly thinking on ME harmoniously, harmonious conditions resulted in the place of inharmony, sickness, diseases and corruption. That is the mystery! With harmonious thoughts in the positive direction, by concentrating on the Perfect Person, the reaction of your concentration was the result. That result was the desirable condition. By the desirable you had visualized vividly, the reaction of the nature and the characteristics of such an expression was reincarnated in you through transmission, by concentrating on ME as an Individual.

Try Me Now

I believe I have said enough to stir up your pure minds, but I desire to see others in this land of Perfection, even as those of you MY Followers concentrated on this light of understanding and concentrating on it harmoniously, the reaction of your concentration will bring an harmonious and a desirable result, and you will be abundantly blessed. Oh it is something to consider! I stress it vividly, because if you will only try ME without coming near ME Personally—TRY ME NOW! I heard one say by composition, "I tried everything but it failed." Now TRY ME! It is indeed Wonderful! You need not come near ME Personally to concentrate on the Impersonal Presence, and yet PERSONIFIED as I AM expressing it. The contact through your concentration will bring harmonious conditions immediately. Tell all of your friends, whether they be in trouble through sickness, afflictions, diseases or disappointments and failures, whatsoever may be the cause, if you concentrate on ME harmoniously I will answer your heart's faintest cry. . . .

"We Shall Have a Righteous Government"

RIGHTEOUSNESS, JUSTICE AND TRUTH
Shall have access in the land;
These together with MERCY shall govern every man;

EQUITY and FAIR DEALING exercised on every hand,
For GOD is REIGNING now!

Chorus
Now we have a righteous Government,
Now we have a righteous Government,
Now we have a righteous Government,
For GOD is reigning now.

Verses

(2)
Crime, vice and corruption shall never more have sway,
In these transformed Temples from which sin is washed away;
GOD is dwelling in them and forever HE shall stay,
For GOD is reigning now.

(3)
Every unjust official shall be moved off of the bench;
No more political corruption, no more judicial stench,
No more fraud and gambling shall be practiced in our defense,
For GOD is reigning now.

(4)
The Kingdom it has come and the Will is being done;
All men have been brought together and unified in ONE:
No more separation, for GOD HIMSELF has come,
And HE is reigning now!

(5)
No races, creeds nor colors shall be known here in this land;
We all shall be UNITED in just one big Holy Band.
GOD HIMSELF is ruling, for the time is out for man,
Since GOD is reigning now.

(6)
GOD's condescension to us to bring Heaven to the earth,
Was to bring about Salvation of mankind's mortal birth,
And thus fulfil the Scriptures that "the last shall be the first,"
For GOD is reigning now.

(7)
This happy day has dawned for all since FATHER DIVINE is here,
For in HIS precious BODY HE has made HIS meaning clear:
That the Righteous, Just and True Ones now have nothing more
    to fear,

For GOD is reigning now.
(Presented—January 10, 11, 12, 1936 A.D.F.D.)

SUPPLEMENTARY READINGS

Burnham, Kenneth E. *God Comes to America: Father Divine and the Peace Mission Movement.* Boston: Lambeth Press, 1978.

Divine, Mrs. M. J. [Mother Divine]. *The Peace Mission Movement Founded by Reverend M. J. Divine Better Known as Father Divine.* Philadelphia: Imperial Press, 1982.

Harris, Sarah. *Father Divine: Holy Husband.* New York: Collier Books, 1971.

Parker, Robert Allerton. *The Incredible Messiah: The Deification of Father Divine.* Boston: Little, Brown, 1937.

Weisbrot, Robert. *Father Divine and the Struggle for Racial Equality.* Urbana: University of Illinois Press, 1983.

44

WALLACE D. MUHAMMAD

"Self-Government in the New World"

The Lost-Found Nation of Islam was established by Master Wali Fard Muhammad, otherwise known as Wallace Fard, in Detroit in 1930. The Honorable Elijah Muhammad, who as Elijah Poole (b. 1897) migrated to Detroit in the 1920s, assumed the title "Prophet" and identified Fard with Allah after Fard's mysterious disappearance in 1934. Muhammad moved to Chicago and promoted a black separatist movement that underwent its greatest growth from the middle 1950s through the middle 1960s. Orthodox Muslim groups shunned Muhammad because of his racial heresies, and black civil rights organizations opposed his separatist philosophy. Malcolm X broke with Elijah Muhammad after visiting Mecca and experiencing the interracial brotherhood of fellow pilgrims. Wallace Muhammad, the fifth of Elijah's sons, assumed leadership of the Nation of Islam upon his father's death in 1975 and attempted to steer it into doctrinal conformity with orthodox Islam. The Yakub story Elijah Muhammad told of a mad black scientist who experimented with hybrids of the original black race and accidentally produced a white "devil" race was demythologized and a second "resurrection of the mind" promoted. Whites could now join.

Wallace abandoned separatism for patriotism, and disaffected members left in response to the call by Louis Farrakhan, former national spokesman for Elijah Muhammad, for a return to the old Nation of Islam. In 1976 Wallace Muhammad announced that henceforth all Afro-Americans were to refer to themselves as Bilalians, after Bilal, said to be an African follower of the prophet Muhammad, who called the ancient community to prayer.

THE HONORABLE MASTER Fard Muhammad has been called by names. He was called Professor Fard Muhammad, Prophet Fard Muhammad, W. F. (Wali Fard) Muhammad, Wallace D. Fard Muhammad, and many other names. This should tell us something about this great personality. Obviously he was not known by the people to whom he was introducing himself. We have said here in the Lost-Found Nation of Islam that the only one who knew him was the one that he taught and

Source: *Bilalian News* 1, no. 19 (March 19, 1976), 23–26.

prepared to do the job of resurrecting the black community—the Honorable Master Elijah Muhammad (peace be upon him).

The Honorable Master Elijah Muhammad taught very vaguely about the Honorable Master Fard Muhammad as a person. He said that he was a "saviour," he said that he was "God," and he said that he was "God in the person of Master Fard Muhammad." He also said that Master Fard told him that he would have to go away and that he (the Honorable Elijah Muhammad) would have to do the job. This did not please the Honorable Master Elijah Muhammad because he had become very much attached to Master Fard Muhammad, as were the other followers in the early days of the mission of the founding of the Nation of Islam. He said that he told Master Fard that he wanted to be with him. Master Fard told him that he would be with him, but that he should do the job because he did not need him anymore. Almighty God would never tell any creature that it did not need Him anymore. We always need Almighty God. But, Master Fard told the Honorable Elijah Muhammad, "You don't need me anymore." He also told the believers, "Accept Elijah, follow Elijah, you don't need me anymore."

Master Fard Muhammad was a "shrewd" planner. He had observed the situation here in America and he knew the conditions that kept us down as a people. He, himself, was a Muslim who believed in the scripture called the Holy Quran. Master Fard let us know that by having his picture taken with the Holy Quran in his hands. In fact, the only picture that we have of him is a picture of him holding the Holy Quran in his hand, in a very pious, sincere and reverent manner.

If "God" cherished the Holy Quran, that should also suggest something to our mind. He was saying something very important to us, but he had to say it in such a way as to get us to come where he wanted us to come, without us discovering his shrewd plan. If we had discovered his plan, we would have walked away before we arrived at the goal that he wanted to bring us to.

Master Fard saw that the church was a failure in the Bilalian (black) community. In the early 1930's, the Bilalian church community was mostly a community of dead, so-called Negroes. Most of the church people were hating their own identity, and they didn't even know it. They hated their black skin, and they hated any connection or association with so-called Africa. They hated their so-called "Negroid" features. This is the condition in which Master Fard Muhammad found us in the early 1930's when he came to America. He observed that the so-called Orthodox Muslims had come here and tried to reach us, but they had failed. They invited us to Islam, to Allah, and to the Holy

Quran. They told us that Islam was a better religion, but only a very few of us listened to them. Master Fard discovered the real problem, and then he designed a skillful plan to bring home the prize. Master Fard Muhammad is not dead, brothers and sisters, he is physically alive and I talk to him whenever I get ready. I don't talk to him in any spooky way, I go to the telephone and dial his number.

When he saw that our problem was that we were already too spiritual (too wrapped up in the Bible), he devised a plan. He knew he could not get us if he came at us with the Holy scripture. Whatever anyone had come at us with, it would not have been any stronger than what we already had in the way of spiritual force. Who was more spiritual in America or in the world than the Bilalian community in America? Our churches were filled with more spirit than anybody else's churches. No one could come to us telling us that we needed spirit. Anyone who would have come to us would have had less spirit than we had, and we would not have paid any attention to them.

Master Fard Muhammad discovered that what was absent in the dead Bilalian community was material—we were totally ignorant to material worth. So he began to study scripture, and he designed his plan step by step after the plan of Almighty God.

People had come to us with God and religion and they have approached us with the spirit, talking to us about holiness, righteousness, divinity, God and the saints. Master Fard discovered that that is not the way Almighty God develops the community of His people. When you study the Holy Quran and the Bible, you will see that that is not the way that God does it. The Bible says that God made His man out of the physical earth. The first thing that He made was a physical man and the next thing that He did was to give that physical man a physical world and a physical mate. After He gave the man a physical body and a physical world, then God told him that there were two kinds of knowledge in the world. One knowledge is pure divine knowledge that is from God, and the other kind of knowledge is mixed up with falsehood. God warned the man not to eat of the tree of corrupt knowledge. But, God did not give him that kind of instruction until he had already made him physically and given him an opportunity to live with other people. In Genesis, if you follow that story in the later chapters, you will see that God did not make just one Adam. The Bible says that God made the man and made for him a mate, but He made a society when He did that.

It says that God made male and female and that He named them "Adam." God made a society of physical people, He introduced them to a physical world, and He let their minds grow to become aware of the physical environment and to grow in the physical environment first. The physical world is not in existence for no reason.

The birth of the human being into the world is not a spiritual birth first. No baby comes from the womb as a spirit. The first body that comes out of the womb of the mother is a flesh body, and the first thing that the baby wants is some physical milk. Master Fard discovered this secret of the high knowledge that is in the scripture that people had overlooked. When you find a people completely dead, you do not come to them with the spirit. You can come to a society that is alive socially and economically by teaching them the spirit (the "heaven"), but you cannot teach the "heavens" to a society that has not yet been formed in the earth. You have to teach them the earth, first. That was the wisdom (the key) that Master Fard Muhammad discovered. He said, "The way to get these people, Elijah, is to hold out to them the bait that represents to them the things that they need and want right now. Tell them, Elijah, that if they follow you to me, they will get good homes, money, and friendship in all walks of life. Tell them that the streets of the holy land where their ancestors came from are paved with solid gold." That kind of description made us want to go there. He did not say that the streets were filled with spirits playing on invisible harps, walking around with golden slippers that did not really exist. He said to tell us that there was real gold over there. This bait of a well-to-do society was the right bait to attract our people. He said that we would get money, good homes, and friendship. He included friendship because the Bilalian people in America were friendless. We knew that we did not have any friends. We could not even trust each other as friends.

Master Fard offered friendship because he knew that the only friend we identified with was the friend "Jesus." We identified with that friend because our suffering resembled his suffering. Master Fard began to take our minds off that Jesus because he realized that until we could see our own suffering, we would never be able to be serious about doing something to remove that suffering—so he began to tell us about our own suffering. The church had made the mistake of telling us about the suffering of the Hebrew boys in the fiery furnace and the suffering of the Jews under Pharaoh. They made the mistake of telling us about what was happening "over yonder across Jordan" instead of bringing our minds home to see what was happening to us right here in America.

Master Fard Muhammad sneaked into America and used a name that made it hard for them to identify him. Because he did not wear a turban, he looked like an American. He called himself "Wallace Fard." He was wise because he knew how to hide his identity, to do his job, and sneak out. Master Fard Muhammad worked for almost three years in Detroit and Chicago to bring the dead Bilalian community to life so that they could grow into the religion of Islam. What was his objective? What did he want for us?

He wanted us to be free when the new world came. He was wise and he had vision and foresight. He knew that the America of the 1930's was a dying America and that the hand of God was against it. It would only be so long before it would be killed, or die outright. He did not want to see the Bilalian people of America come to life in that new world under somebody else's leadership. If it was not for him, we would have come to life under somebody else's leadership. We would have come to life because everything was moving us in this direction. The reality of the many African nations that had come into independence would have affected our minds over here and forced us to get together and come into some kind of idea of self-government or leadership in the society. If Master Fard had never brought Islam to us, the natural development would have eventually brought us together as a family. I do not mean that it would have "integrated" us. Integration with the society is something that you do after you have integrated with yourself. How can you integrate before you put yourself together? We would have as a family if we had not received Islam and we would have had a voice as a family, but that voice would have been under somebody else's voice. We would have come under the socialist voice, the capitalist voice, or some other established voice. Anything other than what Master Fard Muhammad brought was not designed to bring about the total birth of the total person. It was designed to only take care of part of your human needs.

The Bilalian people of America were a different people in the world. You can go to poor people on any continent and you can teach them civilization if they do not have it; you can teach them science and industry if they do not have it; you can teach them religion if they do not have it; but you do not have to teach them everything because they have not lost everything. You can deal with the people, teach them, build them up, and bring them into a self-government, pride and dignity without going about a thorough restoration of the human form. But, over here it was different with us. We had nothing at all but the false picture of ourselves that was given to us by a people who were intent upon keeping us empty-headed slaves for all of our lives.

How do you bring that kind of man back to existence? Can you teach him economics and bring him back to existence? No, the man is not even alive as a human being. You have to teach him what it means to be human. You have to teach him that a human being is a natural creation. You have to first put the life that belongs to the empty vessel back into the vessel. This world was putting foreign life into the empty vessel, and the foreign life could not grow in a vessel that was foreign to it. They wanted to make us anything but ourselves. So the Honorable Master Elijah Muhammad said that we should know ourself. For the first time, thanks to Master W. F. Muhammad, Bilalian people in America began to act naturally. The Muslims who followed the teachings of Master W. F. Muhammad and the Honorable Master Elijah Muhammad, were singled out in the community as "foreign people" or "crazy people." Those people who were pointing at us were unnatural people themselves, so they saw us as being unnatural.

Master Fard Muhammad's masterful plan was to do first things, first, and keep last things out of sight until we could first get the people established in first things. His first aim was to get us firmly grounded in reality, as we were capable of knowing reality. The community of poor, robbed, deprived, dejected, so-called Negroes was not capable of knowing a spiritual reality since they were not yet alive in a social reality or a physical reality. He first had to establish us in a physical reality, doing it as Almighty God did it according to the Holy Quran and the Bible Genesis. He formed us physically and then put desire in us. When he brought our attention to our physical needs and showed us that we were obligated to do something about fulfilling those physical needs, the desire in us for physical pleasures and physical wealth increased. We had been satisfied with a little of nothing, but the more Master Fard's teachings went into our ears, the more our appetite for physical things expanded. Pretty soon we were not satisfied to have a little apartment and a few shabby pieces of furniture in the house. We wanted our own house and our own automobile. Before, we had no incentive or desire in us for these things. Our only desire was to be accepted by Caucasian people because that is the way this world had fashioned our minds. We were an artificial society, it took this real teaching to make us real. Master Fard told the Honorable Elijah Muhammad to get the people to come into the temple at any cost. Once they were gotten into the temple, they would gradually come into the knowledge of themselves and their own. When they woke up, they were then able to value and to appreciate Islam. He did not worry about teaching them Islam then, he wanted to teach them to know self, to do for self, and to separate from the destructive relationship that they had with the Caucasian people. That is what Master Fard did, and he was successful.

He told the Honorable Elijah Muhammad that he could not attract the "fish" to come into this ideal society (the Lost-Found Nation of Islam) with knowledge alone because the fish had been mentally, spiritually and morally killed. He was not able to see the value that was in this heavenly order. He had to hold out to him the things that he knew in his life, and attract him with the bait of meat that satisfied only the stomach—money, food, good homes, and good clothes. He said, "Put that bait on the hook, Elijah, and bring him into your self. One day you will be able to put that fish into the waters of the new world, but it will take time." When we examine the works of the Honorable Master Fard Muhammad and the works of the Honorable Master Elijah Muhammad, we can see the terminology in the real substance, the real sense. We now see that what was said also had another meaning.

When we examine these great lessons, we get a message out of them that is tied in with the Bible scripture and even with the Holy Quran. Master Fard's first lesson asked the question, "Who is the original man?" We know now that "original man" did not mean original flesh man, but it meant the original form that man takes. Man is first a physical person before he becomes a moral person and a spiritual person. When the Honorable Master Fard Muhammad found us, we were the original man. The Caucasian man was not the first man. The first man was a man of the earth that knew nothing of moral values or spiritual values, he was just a earthly man. Adam was a man formed of the earth and then God breathed into him His spirit. If you go to primitive societies, you will find that human beings come up first like animals, desiring physical food and things to take care of their pressing needs. As they progress, they grow up the rungs of civilization in the ladder of society to a level where they desire moral and spiritual excellence.

Master Fard called us the original man in such a way as to make us think that we were the best man, and in a sense we were the best man. We were more natural and more human in our feelings, and our conscience was more human than the conscience of white America at that time. We were also the original man in that sense. He was referring to the fact that man takes steps or stages in his growth, and his first step in flesh. He discovered us to be nothing but a fleshly community, only begging for food, sex, and some good entertainment. The original man (the flesh man) progresses and evolves from the flesh man to the moral conscious man. After he becomes morally conscious, he rises up to still another stage of development, which is a spiritual conscious man. These are the natural steps of human development.

First (original) things are not always superior. When we look at the growth of nature we find that first things are always inferior, but they grow to be superior. If you study the germ of life in any family or species, you will see that the first form is inferior or weak. Then it grows to reach its strength or superior form.

The work of Master Fard Muhammad was the work of change or revolution. Revolution is not the final object or the final aim of his great work, revolution is a means for reaching the final object.

If you design a revolution to bring people out of their condition into another condition, you cannot continue to always put emphasis on revolution. The emphasis has to be taken off of revolution and put on objectives or aims one day. Master Fard Muhammad had a design to bring about changes that would bring us into a new world, a new life, and a new mind. The steps of the change cannot be looked at today as part of our world structure, but they are steps towards the structure. Now, we are at the structure. The emphasis should be taken off of change and revolution and be put on building and construction. We want to save our people who are in the hands of strong people. We know that we cannot just go and ask for them—we have to take them. So the first thing that we had to do was to design a plan to get our people. Once we get our people, we cannot continue to preach to them the philosophy of attack and capture. We have to teach to them the philosophy of construction because, if we take them out of one world, we are going to have to build another world for them to live in.

Master Fard Muhammad taught us the plan (the philosophy) of reaching our goal and the Honorable Master Elijah Muhammad began to gradually take the emphasis off of battle strategy and put it on building.

Today we have arrived at our goal and the trip was successful. The great plan achieved what it was designed to achieve. If we get busy right now and build the new world, I assure you that we will not be ruled by any other government in the new world but our own self-government.

Your brother,
W. D. Muhammad

SUPPLEMENTARY READINGS

Essien-Udom, E. U. *Black Nationalism: A Search for an Identity in America*. Chicago: University of Chicago Press, 1963.

Lincoln, C. Eric. *The Black Muslims in America*. Rev. ed. Boston: Beacon Press, 1973.

Malcolm X and Alex Haley. *The Autobiography of Malcolm X*. New York: Grove Press, 1965.

Parenti, Michael. "The Black Muslims: From Revolution to Institution." *Social Research* 31 (1964): 175–94.

Whitehurst, James Emerson. "The Mainstreaming of the Black Muslims: Healing the Hate." *The Christian Century* 97, no. 7 (February 27, 1980): 225–29.

SEVEN

Civil Rights, Black Theology, and Beyond

45

JOSEPH H. JACKSON

"National Baptist Philosophy of Civil Rights"

Joseph H. Jackson served as president of the National Baptist Convention, Inc., for nearly three decades—from 1953 to 1982. Born at Rudyard, Mississippi, in 1900, he pastored churches in Mississippi, Nebraska, and Pennsylvania before coming to historic Olivet Baptist Church in Chicago in 1941. As convention president, Jackson inaugurated a program of developing land in Liberia to finance Baptist missions in Africa and stressed the need for Afro-Americans to move from protest to production. His generally conservative political and social views, which emphasized the spiritual mission of the church more than civil rights activism, precipitated a schism in 1961, when Martin Luther King, Jr., and other insurgents led approximately a half-million members out of the organization to form the Progressive National Baptist Convention. Jackson viewed the controversy with the activists as a disagreement over means rather than ends. He broke company, however, with those who promoted black nationalism or who sought to articulate a distinctive "black theology."

The Reverend Theodore Judson Jemison succeeded Jackson in 1983 and appears to be moving the National Baptist Convention into a more activist stance. The organization is the nation's third largest Protestant denomination and claims more than 6.8 million members and 26 thousand local congregations. In The Story of Christian Activism, *Joseph Jackson reflects on the civil rights philosophy of the National Baptist Convention as a testament to his presidency.*

As a member of the American community the National Baptist Convention has for almost one hundred years been concerned about the welfare of our race as well as that of our nation. There are, to be sure, many schools of thought within this vast organization and many different opinions regarding what a religious body should be or do in the context of civil rights. There are many ideas and doctrines of our racial struggle

Source: Joseph Harrison Jackson. A *Story of Christian Activism*. Nashville: Townsend Press, 1980. Pp. 270–76.

among us. There are different emphases on what we should do and how it ought to be done. In our National Baptist Convention there are also many points of view, many different ideas as to methodology. But for the majority of the members of the National Baptist Convention the key idea is that we must have protest, but the methods used must somehow be suggested or dictated by the objectives and the goals desired. Without attempting to force any ideas upon others, we have advanced a philosophy of civil rights that was recommended to our National Baptist Convention. That philosophy has been adopted by the Convention as its official position, but this act does not in any way restrict or hinder the thinking of any individuals or groups within the Convention. Our philosophy of civil rights has been for us a cry in the face of changing circumstances. It has been a rallying point. It has been a guiding star amidst conflicting notions and ideas. It has tended to save us from drifting with the tide or from being satisfied to imitate what others say and do. We realize that as a religious body we must at all times maintain a position that is in harmony with and that can be supported by our faith, our doctrine of life, and our social ethic.

In the *Annual Address* of 1962 (delivered on September 6th in the Coliseum at Chicago, Illinois) the following statement was made which illustrates the key philosophy on our racial struggle:

The American Negro today faces the greatest crisis of his history since the days of reconstruction. And his future as a man and as an American citizen and as a citizen of the world depends on how well he faces the test of this hour and how constructively he uses the opportunities at hand.

With the progressive defeat of segregation in this country, not only are the walls of separation falling from around the Negro community, allowing them the opportunity for larger and unrestricted participation in the nation's life, but the primary force (namely segregation), which has pressed the Negro into a community has been greatly weakened and the Negro community is sure to fall apart or to disintegrate unless some positive force is found as a sure and unfailing bond of racial togetherness.

But because in the past our racial togetherness has been ascribed to segregation, many of us shy away from racial togetherness for fear of being accused of the practice of segregation, and those who would work for racial togetherness in the positive are frequently called 'Uncle Toms.'

Some of our young people tend to look down upon and to discredit many of those past achievements of the race that came (as they could only come in the past), in the pattern and framework of American racial segregation. Hence along with the curse of segregation they tend to discredit, and in some cases, actually spurn the achievement of their fathers. They would in the language of an old proverb, 'throw out the baby with the bath.' But if life is to continue and the evolution and progress of the race be maintained, we must learn to draw a line between the soiled waters of the past and the living and growing infant of the present. We must throw out the waters of segregation along with all other social and moral evils, but make sure we keep the baby in our hands; that is, we must keep racial appreciation, racial aspirations, and a firm patriotic spirit as we move out into a wider circle of participation in the nation's life.

The revolt of the young against their elders and present leaders is wholesome when that revolt is against the shortcomings, the imperfections, and the failures of the older generation. But when such a revolt is due to the negative reactions of the young against the values of the past because those values are realized and achieved under the hated system of segregation, then they are associating value with disvalue and are losing the former because of the latter. In this context the creative days of the past are cursed and the generation labors to destroy the righteous with the wicked, the good with the bad, and the savory with the sordid. While we appreciate all the fine things that this present student generation is doing for civil rights and for racial improvement, but if they be the first to possess a true love of liberty among their people and must serve as both pioneer and producer, foundation and super structure, then I say the upward journey of racial development is much longer than we once expected, and the task more difficult than we had ever dreamed. For this generation then would be called upon to make brick without straw and to build a durable structure in the present for the present and the future without an adequate supply of material from the generation of the past.

We also face the further danger of mistaking means for ends, acquired opportunities for achieved objective realities. Any defeat of segregation by the forces of integration is at most, the creation of another opportunity for further growth and development. If the opportunity is not used and the values at hand not invested, then the potential fruits of the privileged will fade and die in the bud of promise and the second state will be worse than the first.

The next forward step in racial development and progress will not be made by our white friends for their Negro neighbors, but will be made by Negroes for themselves. And this step depends not on what Negroes can force others to give or do for them, but what Negroes in the light of new opportunities will do for themselves and for the social order in which they live. We then must possess a new courage to face frankly the failures and shortcomings in our local community and address ourselves with boldness to the correction of the same. For it takes far more courage to face the personal problems in our own lives and those in our immediate families and communities than it does to analyze the shortcomings of those who oppose our growth and development. We must go from protest to production.

From Protest To Production

My economic philosophy as it relates to our racial struggle has been stated more than once, so by this time many of you should be able to state it as clearly as I can. But because of the nature of our struggle, and because of different views regarding it, I think it wise to state again my economic philosophy with some further amplification.

Protest has its place in our racial struggle. It is a vocal and dramatic expression of our resentment and reaction against all forms of segregation and discrimination. Protest is an attempt to impress, convince, and persuade the segregationist and all who practice discrimination with him, of the tragic and ill-effects of the sins of exploitation and discrimination against any personality, and it also reveals how cruel and damnable it is to steal from any people their God-given rights and to snatch from them the equal opportunities to earn a decent living and to make a good life in every area of human existence. Protest ideally aims at showing to our social order that sin against any segment of human society damages and endangers the whole of it. Protest reveals in practice what it is clearly known in theory that the oppression of the many by the few will soon place upon the spirits of the few the same type of malcontent, and will ultimately involve the rich in the same type of insecurity with which the poor have been damned and doomed.

Protest has its place in the economic, political and social struggle of mankind, and by it much good has been achieved. But I repeat, protest is not enough. We must go from protest to production. That is, we must seize every opportunity new and old, in order to become creators as well as consumers of goods. We must become inventors as well as the users of the tools of production and also the investors of capital as well as the spenders of it. Our strategy in this struggle must not be based on an assumption that the relationship of manager and laborer, owner and user of capital, will or should always characterize the relationship between our white opponents and the Negro race. Any Negro leader who shapes his philosophy, his theory, and his practice as if the end of our economic struggle has been attained when we win the right to be hired in a factory owned by another, is a traitor to the highest potentials of his race and a dangerous enemy to social progress, and a stumbling block to mankind. While we know employment is an economic necessity, earning and spending is not enough for a progressive people. After we have earned our money there is no economic necessity laid upon us to spend it all within twenty-four hours for things that are not economically essential or morally sound. It is not wise to talk big and to spend big and then to save and invest little. We must learn how to organize our capital, harness our earnings, and set them to work for us so that we may produce more and finally, develop independent factories and companies of our own. Remember my friends, that no people have ever been given their independence simply on petition, and no race has come to its deserved heights of equality by resolutions adopted by powerful assemblies, and no people have ever been fully emancipated by the mere writing of new laws or the amendments of old ones. Neither have any struggling people been moved to the unquestioned heights of freedom by the verdicts of courts or the rulings of judges however lofty and far-reaching the verdicts might be. Freed men are not really free until they learn to exercise their new acquired opportunities to gain for themselves the economic, intellectual, political, moral and spiritual independence and self-reliance. For hands freed of manacles, and feet liberated from chains will atrophy and will grow weaker still, unless employed immediately and constantly in the pursuit of freedom and in the task of human betterment, moral and spiritual uplift. Freed men who beg will become beggars, and the liberated who seek to ride another's train without paying the just fare will become hobos and tramps. For hobos and tramps seek more for themselves than they are willing to pay for, and ask for more than they hope to give in return. They would gather where they have not strewn, reap where they have not sown, and borrow with no intention of ever paying it back. Some persons fitting this description may have college and university degrees. They may dress in Hickey-Freeman suits, wear fifty dollar hats and drive Cadillac cars too big for the land they own and too long for their short pocketbooks, and occupy high offices in school, church, and state. But they are as truly hobos and tramps as are the ragged, unkempt and hungry beggar who has just arrived in the city on the last freight train. Remember the wisdom of the words of the ancient Hebrew leader who once said to his people, "If ye be a great people go up to the wood country and cut down for yourselves." Great people do not run after and cry for the finished product owned and possessed by others. But they with courage, determination, and faith, will go to the place of natural resources, to the land of potentialities—the wood country if you please, and there cut down the trees, prepare the timber, and build a place for themselves and for others.

As if by consensus, the above statement seemed to capture the sentiment and the thinking of many of our people; hence, our official position might well be summarized in the widely-adopted brief statement: "Protest has its place in our racial struggle, but we must go from protest to production." This general idea is set forth in many addresses delivered to the Convention and in other sections of the country. I have espoused this philosophy in conferences, workshops, in lectures before many groups in America and in plans that have been advanced in concrete situations with peoples of all walks of life. This philosophy is evidenced in proposals for the education of the young and in suggestions that the philosophy of education must somehow emphasize more than theories. Education must deal with practical things which will aid young people in the skilled use of the tools of production and in the art of saving, investing, and the wise use of money. This same philosophy is dramatized in some of the practical ways by which Negroes today as well as other minority groups can meet the challenge which they face and solve the problems that confront them.

When discussing the missionary program of the Convention, we also maintained the importance of production. Generally this means that a person is not really educated unless he knows something about the economic tools of production or how to take part in the sciences and arts of production. A person who thinks is a person who knows how to meet existing conditions and how to turn the raw materials of a foul or negative circumstance into something creative, productive, and beautiful. In Home Missions this philosophy has directed people to use the soil as a veritable gold mine for the precious values which it holds. Clearly not only professional people and businessmen have a place in this philosophy but also the farmer must be as creative as the scientist in his laboratory or the philosopher in his academy of thought.

So impressive was this idea of production when presented to the president of the Republic of Liberia that he granted 100,000 acres of the rich soil of Liberia to the Convention. (There is a more detailed story of this grant in the section on Foreign Missions.) Not all of the constituents in the mission field, however, have completely grasped the idea of production from this point of view. It may be some time yet before it becomes a strong and impelling force in the lives of those who work on foreign fields. But this doctrine of production has made its imprint upon the missionary enterprise of the National Baptist Convention, U.S.A., Inc. We firmly believe that preaching the gospel involves more than the printed text, the written, or the spoken phrase. There is a gospel of the soil; there is a gospel of economic know-how; there is a gospel of creative production.

The National Baptist Convention is by origin, structure, and mission, a strictly religious body; but it is a religious body with concerns that relate it to human suffering, human needs, and human aspirations. Therefore, it is by nature related to the civil rights struggle. It has never insisted that other organizations devoted to civil rights accept its philosophy and work according to its policies and programs. It has shown its civil rights concern by working with other civil rights organizations and by taking responsibilities in the same field peculiar to its nature and its mission. It is therefore a helper of other organizations whose purposes include an unselfish service to mankind. The National Baptist Convention has supported the local branches of the NAACP as well as the national office. This support has continued and, in many ways, is on the increase. However, there are three civil rights organizations with which our member churches and pastors have been vitally related. In addition to the National Association For The Advancement Of Colored People, National Baptists have played important roles in The Montgomery Improvement Association and The Southern Christian Leadership Conference.

SUPPLEMENTARY READINGS

Jackson, Joseph H. *A Story of Christian Activism: The History of the National Baptist Convention, U.S.A., Inc.* Nashville: Townsend Press, 1980. Chaps. 5–10.

Jackson, Joseph H. *Unholy Shadows and Freedom's Holy Light.* Nashville: Townsend Press, 1967.

Kluger, Richard. *Simple Justice: The History of Brown v. Board of Education and Black America's Struggle for Equality.* New York: Vintage Books, 1977.

Paris, Peter J. *Black Leaders in Conflict: Joseph H. Jackson, Martin Luther King, Jr., Malcolm X, and Adam Clayton Powell, Jr.* New York: Pilgrim Press, 1978.

Pelt, Owen D., and Ralph Lee Smith. *The Story of the National Baptists.* New York: Vantage Press, 1960.

46

MARTIN LUTHER KING, JR.

"Letter from Birmingham Jail— April 16, 1963"

Martin Luther King, Jr.'s "Letter from Birmingham Jail" is now a classic in protest literature. It eloquently expresses the goals and philosophy of the nonviolent civil rights movement. King (1929–68) was arrested on Good Friday, 1963, in Birmingham, Alabama, for participating in a civil rights march, and was held in jail for eight days. While imprisoned he felt obliged to respond to a public letter that eight white Alabama religious leaders had drafted urging Birmingham blacks to withdraw support from King and the civil rights activists. King addressed his letter (begun on the margins of the copy of the Birmingham News in which the published criticism of him appeared) primarily to moderate Christians of both races throughout the nation who had yet to give wholehearted support to the drive to eliminate segregation and achieve justice for all.

One by one King here takes up the charges against the nonviolent movement and offers ethical and philosophical refutation. He directs readers to the best in the American dream and to the most sacred values in the nation's Judaeo-Christian heritage, and argues that all great political questions are fundamentally moral questions to which the churches must speak. King's marshaling of southern black churches in the cause of justice, his reaching out to men and women of goodwill in the white churches and synagogues, made the civil rights movement a religious crusade as much as a social or political campaign.

April 16, 1963

MY DEAR FELLOW CLERGYMEN:[1]

While confined here in the Birmingham city jail, I came across your recent statement calling my present activities "unwise and un-

1 Author's Note: This response to a published statement by eight fellow clergymen from Alabama (Bishop C. C. J. Carpenter, Bishop Joseph A. Durick, Rabbi Hilton L. Grafman, Bishop Paul Hardin, Bishop Holan B. Harmon, the Reverend George M. Murray, the Reverend Edward V. Ramage and the Reverend Earl Stallings) was composed under somewhat constricting circumstances. Begun on the margins of the newspaper in which the statement appeared while I was in jail, the letter was con-

timely." Seldom do I pause to answer criticism of my work and ideas. If I sought to answer all the criticisms that cross my desk, my secretaries would have little time for anything other than such correspondence in the course of the day, and I would have no time for constructive work. But since I feel that you are men of genuine good will and that your criticisms are sincerely set forth, I want to try to answer your statement in what I hope will be patient and reasonable terms.

I think I should indicate why I am here in Birmingham, since you have been influenced by the view which argues against "outsiders coming in." I have the honor of serving as president of the Southern Christian Leadership Conference, an organization operating in every southern state, with headquarters in Atlanta, Georgia. We have some eighty-five affiliated organizations across the South, and one of them is the Alabama Christian Movement for Human Rights. Frequently we share staff, educational and financial resources with our affiliates. Several months ago the affiliate here in Birmingham asked us to be on call to engage in a nonviolent direct-action program if such were deemed necessary. We readily consented, and when the hour came we lived up to our promise. So I, along with several members of my staff, am here because I was invited here. I am here because I have organizational ties here.

But more basically, I am in Birmingham because injustice is here. Just as the prophets of the eighth century B.C. left their villages and carried their "thus saith the Lord" far beyond the boundaries of their home towns, and just as the Apostle Paul left his village of Tarsus and carried the gospel of Jesus Christ to the far corners of the Greco-Roman world, so am I compelled to carry the gospel of freedom beyond my own home town. Like Paul, I must constantly respond to the Macedonian call for aid.

Moreover, I am cognizant of the interrelatedness of all communities and states. I cannot sit idly by in Atlanta and not be concerned about what happens in Birmingham. Injustice anywhere is a threat to justice everywhere. We are caught in an inescapable network of mutuality, tied in a single garment of destiny. Whatever affects one directly, affects all indirectly. Never again can we afford to live with the narrow, provincial "outside agitator" idea. Anyone who lives inside the United States can never be considered an outsider anywhere within its bounds.

---

tinued on scraps of writing paper supplied by a friendly Negro trusty, and concluded on a pad my attorneys were eventually permitted to leave me. Although the text remains in substance unaltered, I have indulged in the author's prerogative of polishing it for publication.

Source: *Why We Can't Wait.* New York: Harper & Row, 1963. Pp. 77–100.

You deplore the demonstrations taking place in Birmingham. But your statement, I am sorry to say, fails to express a similar concern for the conditions that brought about the demonstrations. I am sure that none of you would want to rest content with the superficial kind of social analysis that deals merely with effects and does not grapple with underlying causes. It is unfortunate that demonstrations are taking place in Birmingham, but it is even more unfortunate that the city's white power structure left the Negro community with no alternative.

In any nonviolent campaign there are four basic steps: collection of the facts to determine whether injustices exist; negotiation; self-purification; and direct action. We have gone through all these steps in Birmingham. There can be no gainsaying the fact that racial injustice engulfs this community. Birmingham is probably the most thoroughly segregated city in the United States. Its ugly record of brutality is widely known. Negroes have experienced grossly unjust treatment in the courts. There have been more unsolved bombings of Negro homes and churches in Birmingham than in any other city in the nation. These are the hard, brutal facts of the case. On the basis of these conditions, Negro leaders sought to negotiate with the city fathers. But the latter consistently refused to engage in good-faith negotiation.

Then, last September, came the opportunity to talk with leaders of Birmingham's economic community. In the course of the negotiations, certain promises were made by the merchants—for example, to remove the stores' humiliating racial signs. On the basis of these promises, the Reverend Fred Shuttlesworth and the leaders of the Alabama Christian Movement for Human Rights agreed to a moratorium on all demonstrations. As the weeks and months went by, we realized that we were the victims of a broken promise. A few signs, briefly removed, returned; the others remained.

As in so many past experiences, our hopes had been blasted, and the shadow of deep disappointment settled upon us. We had no alternative except to prepare for direct action, whereby we would present our very bodies as a means of laying our case before the conscience of the local and the national community. Mindful of the difficulties involved, we decided to undertake a process of self-purification. We began a series of workshops on nonviolence, and we repeatedly asked ourselves: "Are you able to accept blows without retaliating?" "Are you able to endure the ordeal of jail?" We decided to schedule our direct-action program for the Easter season, realizing that except for Christmas, this is the main shopping period of the year. Knowing that a strong economic-withdrawal program would be the by-product of direct action, we felt that this would be the best time to bring pressure to bear on the merchants for the needed change.

Then it occurred to us that Birmingham's mayoral election was coming up in March, and we speedily decided to postpone action until after election day. When we discovered that the Commissioner of Public Safety, Eugene "Bull" Connor, had piled up enough votes to be in the run-off, we decided again to postpone action until the day after the run-off so that the demonstrations could not be used to cloud the issues. Like many others, we waited to see Mr. Connor defeated, and to this end we endured postponement after postponement. Having aided in this community need, we felt that our direct-action program could be delayed no longer.

You may well ask: "Why direct action? Why sit-ins, marches and so forth? Isn't negotiation a better path?" You are quite right in calling for negotiation. Indeed, this is the very purpose of direct action. Nonviolent direct action seeks to create such a crisis and foster such a tension that a community which has constantly refused to negotiate is forced to confront the issue. It seeks so to dramatize the issue that it can no longer be ignored. My citing the creation of tension as part of the work of the nonviolent-resister may sound rather shocking. But I must confess that I am not afraid of the word "tension." I have earnestly opposed violent tension, but there is a type of constructive, nonviolent tension which is necessary for growth. Just as Socrates felt that it was necessary to create a tension in the mind so that individuals could rise from the bondage of myths and half-truths to the unfettered realm of creative analysis and objective appraisal, so must we see the need for nonviolent gadflies to create the kind of tension in society that will help men rise from the dark depths of prejudice and racism to the majestic heights of understanding and brotherhood.

The purpose of our direct-action program is to create a situation so crisis-packed that it will inevitably open the door to negotiation. I therefore concur with you in your call for negotiation. Too long has our beloved Southland been bogged down in a tragic effort to live in monologue rather than dialogue.

One of the basic points in your statement is that the action that I and my associates have taken in Birmingham is untimely. Some have asked: "Why didn't you give the new city administration time to act?" The only answer that I can give to this query is that the new Birmingham administration must be prodded about as much as the outgoing one, before it will act. We are sadly mistaken if we feel that the election of Albert Boutwell as mayor will bring the millennium to Birmingham.

While Mr. Boutwell is a much more gentle person than Mr. Connor, they are both segregationists, dedicated to maintenance of the status quo. I have hope that Mr. Boutwell will be reasonable enough to see the futility of massive resistance to desegregation. But he will not see this without pressure from devotees of civil rights. My friends, I must say to you that we have not made a single gain in civil rights without determined legal and nonviolent pressure. Lamentably, it is an historical fact that privileged groups seldom give up their privileges voluntarily. Individuals may see the moral light and voluntarily give up their unjust posture; but, as Reinhold Niebuhr has reminded us, groups tend to be more immoral than individuals.

We know through painful experience that freedom is never voluntarily given by the oppressor; it must be demanded by the oppressed. Frankly, I have yet to engage in a direct-action campaign that was "well timed" in the view of those who have not suffered unduly from the disease of segregation. For years now I have heard the word "Wait!" It rings in the ear of every Negro with piercing familiarity. This "Wait" has almost always meant "Never." We must come to see, with one of our distinguished jurists, that "justice too long delayed is justice denied."

We have waited for more than 340 years for our constitutional and God-given rights. The nations of Asia and Africa are moving with jetlike speed toward gaining political independence, but we still creep at horse-and-buggy pace toward gaining a cup of coffee at a lunch counter. Perhaps it is easy for those who have never felt the stinging darts of segregation to say, "Wait." But when you have seen vicious mobs lynch your mothers and fathers at will and drown your sisters and brothers at whim; when you have seen hate-filled policemen curse, kick and even kill your black brothers and sisters; when you see the vast majority of your twenty million Negro brothers smothering in an airtight cage of poverty in the midst of an affluent society; when you suddenly find your tongue twisted and your speech stammering as you seek to explain to your six-year-old daughter why she can't go to the public amusement park that has just been advertised on television, and see tears welling up in her eyes when she is told that Funtown is closed to colored children, and see ominous clouds of inferiority beginning to form in her little mental sky, and see her beginning to distort her personality by developing an unconscious bitterness toward white people; when you have to concoct an answer for a five-year-old son who is asking: "Daddy, why do white people treat colored people so mean?"; when you take a cross-country drive and find it necessary to sleep night after night in the uncomfortable corners of your automobile because no motel will accept you; when you are humiliated day in and day out by nagging signs reading "white" and "colored"; when your first name becomes "nigger," your middle name becomes "boy" (however old you are) and your last name becomes "John," and your wife and mother are never given the respected title "Mrs."; when you are harried by day and haunted by night by the fact that you are a Negro, living constantly at tiptoe stance, never quite knowing what to expect next, and are plagued with inner fears and outer resentments; when you are forever fighting a degenerating sense of "nobodiness"—then you will understand why we find it difficult to wait. There comes a time when the cup of endurance runs over, and men are no longer willing to be plunged into the abyss of despair. I hope, sirs, you can understand our legitimate and unavoidable impatience.

You express a great deal of anxiety over our willingness to break laws. This is certainly a legitimate concern. Since we so diligently urge people to obey the Supreme Court's decision of 1954 outlawing segregation in the public schools, at first glance it may seem rather paradoxical for us consciously to break laws. One may well ask: "How can you advocate breaking some laws and obeying others?" The answer lies in the fact that there are two types of laws: just and unjust. I would be the first to advocate obeying just laws. One has not only a legal but a moral responsibility to obey just laws. Conversely, one has a moral responsibility to disobey unjust laws. I would agree with St. Augustine that "an unjust law is no law at all."

Now, what is the difference between the two? How does one determine whether a law is just or unjust? A just law is a man-made code that squares with the moral law or the law of God. An unjust law is a code that is out of harmony with the moral law. To put it in the terms of St. Thomas Aquinas: An unjust law is a human law that is not rooted in eternal law and natural law. Any law that uplifts human personality is just. Any law that degrades human personality is unjust. All segregation statutes are unjust because segregation distorts the soul and damages the personality. It gives the segregator a false sense of superiority and the segregated a false sense of inferiority. Segregation, to use the terminology of the Jewish philosopher Martin Buber, substitutes an "I-it" relationship for an "I-thou" relationship and ends up relegating persons to the status of things. Hence segregation is not only politically, economically and sociologically unsound, it is morally wrong and sinful. Paul Tillich has said that sin is separation. Is not segregation an existential expression of man's tragic separation, his awful estrangement, his terrible sinfulness? Thus it is that I can urge men to obey the 1954 decision of the Supreme Court, for it is morally right; and I can urge them to disobey segregation ordinances, for they are morally wrong.

Let us consider a more concrete example of just and unjust laws. An unjust law is a code that a numerical or power majority group compels a minority group to obey but does not make binding on itself. This is *difference* made legal. By the same token, a just law is a code that a majority compels a minority to follow and that it is willing to follow itself. This is *sameness* made legal.

Let me give another explanation. A law is unjust if it is inflicted on a minority that, as a result of being denied the right to vote, had no part in enacting or devising the law. Who can say that the legislature of Alabama which set up that state's segregation laws was democratically elected? Throughout Alabama all sorts of devious methods are used to prevent Negroes from becoming registered voters, and there are some counties in which, even though Negroes constitute a majority of the population, not a single Negro is registered. Can any law enacted under such circumstances be considered democratically structured?

Sometimes a law is just on its face and unjust in its application. For instance, I have been arrested on a charge of parading without a permit. Now, there is nothing wrong in having an ordinance which requires a permit for a parade. But such an ordinance becomes unjust when it is used to maintain segregation and to deny citizens the First-Amendment privilege of peaceful assembly and protest.

I hope you are able to see the distinction I am trying to point out. In no sense do I advocate evading or defying the law, as would the rabid segregationist. That would lead to anarchy. One who breaks an unjust law must do so openly, lovingly, and with a willingness to accept the penalty. I submit that an individual who breaks a law that conscience tells him is unjust, and who willingly accepts the penalty of imprisonment in order to arouse the conscience of the community over its injustice, is in reality expressing the highest respect for law.

Of course, there is nothing new about this kind of civil disobedience. It was evidenced sublimely in the refusal of Shadrach, Meshach and Abednego to obey the laws of Nebuchadnezzar, on the ground that a higher moral law was at stake. It was practiced superbly by the early Christians, who were willing to face hungry lions and the excruciating pain of chopping blocks rather than submit to certain unjust laws of the Roman Empire. To a degree, academic freedom is a reality today because Socrates practiced civil disobedience. In our own nation, the Boston Tea Party represented a massive act of civil disobedience.

We should never forget that everything Adolf Hitler did in Germany was "legal" and everything the Hungarian freedom fighters did in Hungary was "illegal." It was "illegal" to aid and comfort a Jew in Hitler's Germany. Even so, I am sure that, had I lived in Germany at the time, I would have aided and comforted my Jewish brothers. If to-day I lived in a Communist country where certain principles dear to the Christian faith are suppressed, I would openly advocate disobeying that country's antireligious laws.

I must make two honest confessions to you, my Christian and Jewish brothers. First, I must confess that over the past few years I have been gravely disappointed with the white moderate. I have almost reached the regrettable conclusion that the Negro's great stumbling block in his stride toward freedom is not the White Citizen's Counciler or the Ku Klux Klanner, but the white moderate, who is more devoted to "order" than to justice; who prefers a negative peace which is the absence of tension to a positive peace which is the presence of justice; who constantly says: "I agree with you in the goal you seek, but I can-not agree with your methods of direct action"; who paternalistically be-lieves he can set the timetable for another man's freedom; who lives by a mythical concept of time and who constantly advises the Negro to wait for a "more convenient season." Shallow understanding from peo-ple of good will is more frustrating than absolute misunderstanding from people of ill will. Lukewarm acceptance is much more bewildering than outright rejection.

I had hoped that the white moderate would understand that law and order exist for the purpose of establishing justice and that when they fail in this purpose they become the dangerously structured dams that block the flow of social progress. I had hoped that the white mod-erate would understand that the present tension in the South is a neces-sary phase of the transition from an obnoxious negative peace, in which the Negro passively accepted his unjust plight, to a substantive and posi-tive peace, in which all men will respect the dignity and worth of human personality. Actually, we who engage in nonviolent direct action are not the creators of tension. We merely bring to the surface the hidden ten-sion that is already alive. We bring it out in the open, where it can be seen and dealt with. Like a boil that can never be cured so long as it is covered up but must be opened with all its ugliness to the natural medi-cines of air and light, injustice must be exposed, with all the tension its exposure creates, to the light of human conscience and the air of na-tional opinion before it can be cured.

In your statement you assert that our actions, even though peaceful, must be condemned because they precipitate violence. But is this a logi-cal assertion? Isn't this like condemning a robbed man because his possession of money precipitated the evil act of robbery? Isn't this like condemning Socrates because his unswerving commitment to truth and his philosophical inquiries precipitated the act by the misguided popu-

lace in which they made him drink hemlock? Isn't this like condemning
Jesus because his unique God-consciousness and never-ceasing devotion
to God's will precipitated the evil act of crucifixion? We must come to
see that, as the federal courts have consistently affirmed, it is wrong to
urge an individual to cease his efforts to gain his basic constitutional
rights because the quest may precipitate violence. Society must protect
the robbed and punish the robber.

I had also hoped that the white moderate would reject the myth
concerning time in relation to the struggle for freedom. I have just received a letter from a white brother in Texas. He writes: "All Christians
know that the colored people will receive equal rights eventually, but it
is possible that you are in too great a religious hurry. It has taken Christianity almost two thousand years to accomplish what it has. The teachings of Christ take time to come to earth." Such an attitude stems from
a tragic misconception of time, from the strangely irrational notion that
there is something in the very flow of time that will inevitably cure all
ills. Actually, time itself is neutral; it can be used either destructively or
constructively. More and more I feel that the people of ill will have used
time much more effectively than have the people of good will. We will
have to repent in this generation not merely for the hateful words and
actions of the bad people but for the appalling silence of the good people. Human progress never rolls in on wheels of inevitability; it comes
through the tireless efforts of men willing to be co-workers with God,
and without this hard work, time itself becomes an ally of the forces of
social stagnation. We must use time creatively, in the knowledge that
the time is always ripe to do right. Now is the time to make real the
promise of democracy and transform our pending national elegy into a
creative psalm of brotherhood. Now is the time to lift our national policy from the quicksand of racial injustice to the solid rock of human
dignity.

You speak of our activity in Birmingham as extreme. At first I was
rather disappointed that fellow clergymen would see my nonviolent
efforts as those of an extremist. I began thinking about the fact that I
stand in the middle of two opposing forces in the Negro community.
One is a force of complacency, made up in part of Negroes who, as a
result of long years of oppression, are so drained of self-respect and a
sense of "somebodiness" that they have adjusted to segregation; and in
part of a few middle-class Negroes who, because of a degree of academic
and economic security and because in some ways they profit by segregation, have become insensitive to the problems of the masses. The other
force is one of bitterness and hatred, and it comes perilously close to
advocating violence. It is expressed in the various black nationalist

groups that are springing up across the nation, the largest and best-known being Elijah Muhammad's Muslim movement. Nourished by the Negro's frustration over the continued existence of racial discrimination, this movement is made up of people who have lost faith in America, who have absolutely repudiated Christianity, and who have concluded that the white man is an incorrigible "devil."

I have tried to stand between these two forces, saying that we need emulate neither the "do-nothingism" of the complacent nor the hatred and despair of the black nationalist. For there is the more excellent way of love and nonviolent protest. I am grateful to God that, through the influence of the Negro church, the way of nonviolence became an integral part of our struggle.

If this philosophy had not emerged, by now many streets of the South would, I am convinced, be flowing with blood. And I am further convinced that if our white brothers dismiss as "rabble-rousers" and "outside agitators" those of us who employ nonviolent direct action, and if they refuse to support our nonviolent efforts, millions of Negroes will, out of frustration and despair, seek solace and security in black-nationalist ideologies—a development that would inevitably lead to a frightening racial nightmare.

Oppressed people cannot remain oppressed forever. The yearning for freedom eventually manifests itself, and that is what has happened to the American Negro. Something within has reminded him of his birthright of freedom, and something without has reminded him that it can be gained. Consciously or unconsciously, he has been caught up by the *Zeitgeist*, and with his black brothers of Africa and his brown and yellow brothers of Asia, South America and the Caribbean, the United States Negro is moving with a sense of great urgency toward the promised land of racial justice. If one recognizes this vital urge that has engulfed the Negro community, one should readily understand why public demonstrations are taking place. The Negro has many pent-up resentments and latent frustrations, and he must release them. So let him march; let him make prayer pilgrimages to the city hall; let him go on freedom rides—and try to understand why he must do so. If his repressed emotions are not released in nonviolent ways, they will seek expression through violence; this is not a threat but a fact of history. So I have not said to my people: "Get rid of your discontent." Rather, I have tried to say that this normal and healthy discontent can be channeled into the creative outlet of nonviolent direct action. And now this approach is being termed extremist.

But though I was initially disappointed at being categorized as an extremist, as I continued to think about the matter I gradually gained a measure of satisfaction from the label. Was not Jesus an extremist for love: "Love your enemies, bless them that curse you, do good to them that hate you, and pray for them which despitefully use you, and persecute you." Was not Amos an extremist for justice: "Let justice roll down like waters and righteousness like an ever-flowing stream." Was not Paul an extremist for the Christian gospel: "I bear in my body the marks of the Lord Jesus." Was not Martin Luther an extremist: "Here I stand; I cannot do otherwise, so help me God." And John Bunyan: "I will stay in jail to the end of my days before I make a butchery of my conscience." And Abraham Lincoln: "This nation cannot survive half slave and half free." And Thomas Jefferson: "We hold these truths to be self-evident, that all men are created equal . . ." So the question is not whether we will be extremists, but what kind of extremists we will be. Will we be extremists for hate or for love? Will we be extremists for the preservation of injustice or for the extension of justice? In that dramatic scene on Calvary's hill three men were crucified. We must never forget that all three were crucified for the same crime—the crime of extremism. Two were extremists for immorality, and thus fell below their environment. The other, Jesus Christ, was an extremist for love, truth and goodness, and thereby rose above his environment. Perhaps the South, the nation and the world are in dire need of creative extremists.

I had hoped that the white moderate would see this need. Perhaps I was too optimistic; perhaps I expected too much. I suppose I should have realized that few members of the oppressor race can understand the deep groans and passionate yearnings of the oppressed race, and still fewer have the vision to see that injustice must be rooted out by strong, persistent and determined action. I am thankful, however, that some of our white brothers in the South have grasped the meaning of this social revolution and committed themselves to it. They are still all too few in quantity, but they are big in quality. Some—such as Ralph McGill, Lillian Smith, Harry Golden, James McBride Dabbs, Ann Braden and Sarah Patton Boyle—have written about our struggle in eloquent and prophetic terms. Others have marched with us down nameless streets of the South. They have languished in filthy, roach-infested jails, suffering the abuse and brutality of policemen who view them as "dirty nigger-lovers." Unlike so many of their moderate brothers and sisters, they have recognized the urgency of the moment and sensed the need for powerful "action" antidotes to combat the disease of segregation.

Let me take note of my other major disappointment. I have been so greatly disappointed with the white church and its leadership. Of course, there are some notable exceptions. I am not unmindful of the fact that each of you has taken some significant stands on this issue. I commend you, Reverend Stallings, for your Christian stand on this past Sunday, in welcoming Negroes to your worship service on a nonsegregated basis. I commend the Catholic leaders of this state for integrating Spring Hill College several years ago.

But despite these notable exceptions, I must honestly reiterate that I have been disappointed with the church. I do not say this as one of those negative critics who can always find something wrong with the church. I say this as a minister of the gospel, who loves the church; who was nurtured in its bosom; who has been sustained by its spiritual blessings and who will remain true to it as long as the cord of life shall lengthen.

When I was suddenly catapulted into the leadership of the bus protest in Montgomery, Alabama, a few years ago, I felt we would be supported by the white church. I felt that the white ministers, priests and rabbis of the South would be among our strongest allies. Instead, some have been outright opponents, refusing to understand the freedom movement and misrepresenting its leaders; all too many others have been more cautious than courageous and have remained silent behind the anesthetizing security of stained-glass windows.

In spite of my shattered dreams, I came to Birmingham with the hope that the white religious leadership of this community would see the justice of our cause and, with deep moral concern, would serve as the channel through which our just grievances could reach the power structure. I had hoped that each of you would understand. But again I have been disappointed.

I have heard numerous southern religious leaders admonish their worshipers to comply with a desegregation decision because it is the law, but I have longed to hear white ministers declare: "Follow this decree because integration is morally right and because the Negro is your brother." In the midst of blatant injustices inflicted upon the Negro, I have watched white churchmen stand on the sideline and mouth pious irrelevancies and sanctimonious trivialities. In the midst of a mighty struggle to rid our nation of racial and economic injustice, I have heard many ministers say: "Those are social issues, with which the gospel has no real concern." And I have watched many churches commit themselves to a completely otherworldly religion which makes a strange, un-Biblical distinction between body and soul, between the sacred and the secular.

I have traveled the length and breadth of Alabama, Mississippi and all the other southern states. On sweltering summer days and crisp autumn mornings I have looked at the South's beautiful churches with their lofty spires pointing heavenward. I have beheld the impressive outlines of her massive religious-education buildings. Over and over I have found myself asking: "What kind of people worship here? Who is their God? Where were their voices when the lips of Governor Barnett dripped with words of interposition and nullification? Where were they when Governor Wallace gave a clarion call for defiance and hatred? Where were their voices of support when bruised and weary Negro men and women decided to rise from the dark dungeons of complacency to the bright hills of creative protest?"

Yes, these questions are still in my mind. In deep disappointment I have wept over the laxity of the church. But be assured that my tears have been tears of love. There can be no deep disappointment where there is not deep love. Yes, I love the church. How could I do otherwise? I am in the rather unique position of being the son, the grandson and the great-grandson of preachers. Yes, I see the church as the body of Christ. But, oh! How we have blemished and scarred that body through social neglect and through fear of being nonconformists.

There was a time when the church was very powerful—in the time when the early Christians rejoiced at being deemed worthy to suffer for what they believed. In those days the church was not merely a thermometer that recorded the ideas and principles of popular opinion; it was a thermostat that transformed the mores of society. Whenever the early Christians entered a town, the people in power became disturbed and immediately sought to convict the Christians for being "disturbers of the peace" and "outside agitators." But the Christians pressed on, in the conviction that they were "a colony of heaven," called to obey God rather than man. Small in number, they were big in commitment. They were too God-intoxicated to be "astronomically intimidated." By their effort and example they brought an end to such ancient evils as infanticide and gladiatorial contests.

Things are different now. So often the contemporary church is a weak, ineffectual voice with an uncertain sound. So often it is an arch-defender of the status quo. Far from being disturbed by the presence of the church, the power structure of the average community is consoled by the church's silent—and often even vocal—sanction of things as they are.

But the judgment of God is upon the church as never before. If today's church does not recapture the sacrificial spirit of the early church, it will lose its authenticity, forfeit the loyalty of millions, and be dismissed as an irrelevant social club with no meaning for the twentieth century. Every day I meet young people whose disappointment with the church has turned into outright disgust.

Perhaps I have once again been too optimistic. Is organized religion too inextricably bound to the status quo to save our nation and the world? Perhaps I must turn my faith to the inner spiritual church, the church within the church, as the true *ekklesia* and the hope of the world. But again I am thankful to God that some noble souls from the ranks of organized religion have broken loose from the paralyzing chains of conformity and joined us as active partners in the struggle for freedom. They have left their secure congregations and walked the streets of Albany, Georgia, with us. They have gone down the highways of the South on tortuous rides for freedom. Yes, they have gone to jail with us. Some have been dismissed from their churches, have lost the support of their bishops and fellow ministers. But they have acted in the faith that right defeated is stronger than evil triumphant. Their witness has been the spiritual salt that has preserved the true meaning of the gospel in these troubled times. They have carved a tunnel of hope through the dark mountain of disappointment.

I hope the church as a whole will meet the challenge of this decisive hour. But even if the church does not come to the aid of justice, I have no despair about the future. I have no fear about the outcome of our struggle in Birmingham, even if our motives are at present misunderstood. We will reach the goal of freedom in Birmingham and all over the nation, because the goal of America is freedom. Abused and scorned though we may be, our destiny is tied up with America's destiny. Before the pilgrims landed at Plymouth, we were here. Before the pen of Jefferson etched the majestic words of the Declaration of Independence across the pages of history, we were here. For more than two centuries our forebears labored in this country without wages; they made cotton king; they built the homes of their masters while suffering gross injustice and shameful humiliation—and yet out of a bottomless vitality they continued to thrive and develop. If the inexpressible cruelties of slavery could not stop us, the opposition we now face will surely fail. We will win our freedom because the sacred heritage of our nation and the eternal will of God are embodied in our echoing demands.

Before closing I feel impelled to mention one other point in your statement that has troubled me profoundly. You warmly commended the Birmingham police force for keeping "order" and "preventing violence." I doubt that you would have so warmly commended the police force if you had seen its dogs sinking their teeth into unarmed, nonviolent Negroes. I doubt that you would so quickly commend the policemen if you were to observe their ugly and inhumane treatment of Negroes here in the city jail; if you were to watch them push and curse old Negro women and young Negro girls; if you were to see them slap and kick old Negro men and young boys; if you were to observe them, as they did on two occasions, refuse to give us food because we wanted to sing our grace together. I cannot join you in your praise of the Birmingham police department.

It is true that the police have exercised a degree of discipline in handling the demonstrators. In this sense they have conducted themselves rather "nonviolently" in public. But for what purpose? To preserve the evil system of segregation. Over the past few years I have consistently preached that nonviolence demands that the means we use must be as pure as the ends we seek. I have tried to make clear that it is wrong to use immoral means to attain moral ends. But now I must affirm that it is just as wrong, or perhaps even more so, to use moral means to preserve immoral ends. Perhaps Mr. Connor and his policemen have been rather nonviolent in public, as was Chief Pritchett in Albany, Georgia, but they have used the moral means of nonviolence to maintain the immoral end of racial injustice. As T. S. Eliot has said: "The last temptation is the greatest treason: To do the right deed for the wrong reason."

I wish you had commended the Negro sit-inners and demonstrators of Birmingham for their sublime courage, their willingness to suffer and their amazing discipline in the midst of great provocation. One day the South will recognize its real heroes. They will be the James Merediths, with the noble sense of purpose that enables them to face jeering and hostile mobs, and with the agonizing loneliness that characterizes the life of the pioneer. They will be old, oppressed, battered Negro women, symbolized in a seventy-two-year-old woman in Montgomery, Alabama, who rose up with a sense of dignity and with her people decided not to ride segregated buses, and who responded with ungrammatical profundity to one who inquired about her weariness: "My feets is tired, but my soul is at rest." They will be the young high school and college students, the young ministers of the gospel and a host of their elders, courageously and nonviolently sitting in at lunch counters and willingly going to jail for conscience' sake. One day the South will know that when these disinherited children of God sat down at lunch counters, they were in reality standing up for what is best in the American dream and for the most sacred values in our Judaeo-Christian heritage, thereby bringing our nation back to those great wells of democracy which were dug deep by the founding fathers in their formulation of the Constitution and the Declaration of Independence.

Never before have I written so long a letter. I'm afraid it is much too long to take your precious time. I can assure you that it would have been much shorter if I had been writing from a comfortable desk, but what else can one do when he is alone in a narrow jail cell, other than write long letters, think long thoughts and pray long prayers?

If I have said anything in this letter that overstates the truth and indicates an unreasonable impatience, I beg you to forgive me. If I have said anything that understates the truth and indicates my having a patience that allows me to settle for anything less than brotherhood, I beg God to forgive me.

I hope this letter finds you strong in the faith. I also hope that circumstances will soon make it possible for me to meet each of you, not as an integrationist or a civil-rights leader but as a fellow clergyman and a Christian brother. Let us all hope that the dark clouds of racial prejudice will soon pass away and the deep fog of misunderstanding will be lifted from our fear-drenched communities, and in some not too distant tomorrow the radiant stars of love and brotherhood will shine over our great nation with all their scintillating beauty.

> Yours for the cause of Peace and Brotherhood,
> Martin Luther King, Jr.

SUPPLEMENTARY READINGS

King, David L. *King: A Critical Biography*. Baltimore: Penguin Books, 1970.

King, Martin Luther, Jr. *Stride Toward Freedom*. New York: Harper and Brothers, 1958.

Oates, Stephen B. *Let the Trumpet Sound: The Life of Martin Luther King, Jr.* New York: Harper & Row, 1982.

Smith, Kenneth L., and Ira G. Zepp, Jr. *Search for the Beloved Community: The Thinking of Martin Luther King, Jr.* Valley Forge, Pa.: Judson Press, 1974.

Walton, Haynes, Jr. *The Political Philosophy of Martin Luther King, Jr.* Westport, Conn.: Greenwood Press, 1971.

47

MAHALIA JACKSON

Singing of Good Tidings and Freedom

Clara Ward, Aretha Franklin, Marion Williams, James Cleveland, the Dixie Hummingbirds, the Five Blind Boys of Alabama, the Staple Singers, and Shirley Ceaser—these are only a few of the names in the litany of great gospel singing. Perhaps no single individual embodied the gospel sound more than Mahalia Jackson (1911–72). Daughter of a Baptist minister, she grew up in New Orleans absorbing the musical styles of Baptist hymns, the Holiness or Sanctified churches, jazz, and the blues. Bessie Smith and Thomas Dorsey contributed influences that melded into the gospel blues. After leaving New Orleans in 1937 for Chicago, where she worked as a maid and a laundress, Jackson sang leads in the choir of Greater Salem Baptist Church. She cut her first record with Decca in 1937. It included an adaptation of a New Orleans funeral wake, a Baptist hymn, and the gospel classic, "God Shall Wipe All Tears Away."

Mahalia Jackson developed a distinctive "stretch-out" style and became noted for her "going to heaven tunes." Her gospel songs were songs of hope, rooted in the music southern blacks sang to "keep on keeping on." She collaborated with Dorsey in the 1940s and signed with Apollo Records in 1946. "Move On Up a Little Higher," her third Apollo recording, brought her a national audience and the title of "the Gospel Queen." Whether in the churches, on stage, touring Europe, or on her own radio and television programs, Mahalia Jackson sang as the spirit moved her. Success brought tremendous adulation but also personal problems. She died in 1972 and was buried in New Orleans.

I say this out of my heart—a song must do something for me as well as for the people that hear it. I can't sing a song that doesn't have a message. If it doesn't have the strength it can't lift you. I just can't seem to get the sense of it.

It's been that way ever since I started singing and I guess I was singing almost as soon as I was walking and talking. I always had a big

Source: Mahalia Jackson with Evan McLeod Wylie. *Movin' on Up*. New York: Hawthorn Books, 1966. Pp. 29–33, 56–59, 62–66, 180–85, and 196–99.

voice, even as a small child, and I was raised with music all around me.

New Orleans was full of music when I was born and all the time I was growing up there. It was the time when they had all the brass bands. There was still music on the showboats on the Mississippi River and there were all the cabarets and cafes where musicians like Jelly Roll Morton and King Oliver were playing. Ragtime music and jazz and the blues were being played all over.

Everybody was buying phonographs—the kind you wound up on the side by hand—just the way people have television sets today—and everybody had records of all the Negro blues singers—Bessie Smith . . . Ma Rainey . . . Mamie Smith . . . all the rest.

The famous white singers like Caruso—you might hear them when you went by a white folks' house, but in a colored house you heard blues. You couldn't help but hear blues—all through the thin partitions of the houses—through the open windows—up and down the street in the colored neighborhoods—everybody played it real loud.

I saw lots of the famous New Orleans brass bands when I was growing up. They advertised the fish fries and the house-rent parties and played for the secret order lodge dances and funerals. When there was going to be a big fish fry or lodge dance they would fill a wagon up with a load of hay or they'd put some chairs in it. The brass band—some of them were five pieces—would climb up in that wagon and they would drive around town, stopping and playing at every street corner to drum up a crowd.

Everybody who possibly could would go that night to the fry or the lodge party. They would put sawdust down in the yard and string up lots of those pretty-colored Japanese lanterns and have eats on the inside and dancing on the outside. Those parties were the only social diversion Negroes had except for the church. No decent Negro—no church-going Negro, at least—would be caught dead down in Storyville where all the saloons and sportin' houses used to be.

They had the brass bands for the funerals—when a very popular man or a secret lodge man or a sportin' man died. They never had a band behind a minister or an unimportant man.

But people today are mixed up about the brass bands. They didn't play jazz at the funerals. The band would play as solemn as a choir or a big pipe organ—right out in front of the church where the funeral service was being held. Then they would march behind the hearse—all the way to the cemetery. They didn't play jazz on the way either—that's the bunk. After the family had left and the man was buried, then on the way back they would jazz it up. The musicians had been paid so they would play coming back from the cemetery, full of spirit—blow it out free of charge—and the folks along the way would have a good time. That's the way a funeral band really was.

I liked it and approved it. The Scripture says: "Rejoice at the out-going." So why not have bands for funerals?

The only day I hated to hear the bands in New Orleans was Carnival Day during Mardi Gras when they had the Zulu Parade down St. Charles Avenue. To me Carnival Day was the devil's day, and it's one holiday in New Orleans I will never go back to see. There was too much killing. It was a day of revenge and you'd read the next day in the papers about the deaths.

All week downtown during Mardi Gras the whites had their parades with floats down Canal Street and fireworks and costume balls. Then on Carnival Day, both white and black people put on the masks. Enemies would meet and knife each other. Colored members of Indian clubs like the Blackhawks, the Yellow Pocahontas and the Red, White and Blue Tribe used to "Wa-Wa" against each other, stabbing and slashing. They made the whole city a battleground. One day I was caught between two tribes who were raiding a grocery store with a billiard parlor in the back. I had to crawl on my hands and knees through the yelling, fighting, drunken men and it gave me a horror that has stayed with me to this day.

A day I did like was All Saints' Day. Thousands of New Orleans people went to the cemeteries to put flowers on the graves of loved ones who had passed on, and spend the day singing songs and picnicking on the grass.

Aunt Duke stood for so little play at home that I used to spend all my spare time at the Baptist church. If you helped scrub it out, they might let you help ring the big bell for the early-morning service. On Saturday nights they showed silent movies in the church community hall. There were services there every evening and in those days people thought as much of the evening prayer service as they did of the Sunday service so there was always lots going on for children to watch. Sinners who sat in the back would come forward to be prayed over by the preacher and be saved. On Baptism Sundays the women, all dressed in white, would lead the way out the door and across the street to the levee singing "Let's Go Down to the River Jordan," and the preacher would hold the services right down in the Mississippi, blessing the water and baptizing the congregation.

In those days, once you were baptized, you were looked after properly by the church. You were under the eye of the missionaries of the church, who kept track of whether you attended church and prayer meeting and led a Christian life. The churches of today have gotten away from this. They accept you on your word that you believe in the Lord and they don't see you again until the next Sunday. Today they are not doing the job they should to help people keep the faith. There's bad in all of us and most of us can't save ourselves without help.

I loved best to sing in the congregation of our church—the Mount Moriah Baptist Church. All around me I could hear the foot-tapping and hand-clapping. That gave me bounce. I liked it much better than being up in the choir singing the anthem. I liked to sing the songs which testify to the glory of the Lord—those anthems are too dead and cold for me. As David said in the Bible—"Make a joyous noise unto the Lord!"—that's me.

I know now that a great influence in my life was the Sanctified or Holiness Churches we had in the South. I was always a Baptist, but there was a Sanctified Church right next door to our house in New Orleans.

Those people had no choir and no organ. They used the drum, the cymbal, the tambourine, and the steel triangle. Everybody in there sang and they clapped and stomped their feet and sang with their whole bodies. They had a beat, a powerful beat, a rhythm we held on to from slavery days, and their music was so strong and expressive it used to bring the tears to my eyes.

I believe the blues and jazz and even the rock and roll stuff got their beat from the Sanctified Church. We Baptists sang sweet, and we had the long and short meter on beautiful songs like "Amazing Grace, How Sweet It Sounds," but when those Holiness people tore into "I'm So Glad Jesus Lifted Me Up!" they came out with real jubilation.

First you've got to get the rhythm until, through the music, you have the freedom to interpret it. Perhaps that's why white folks just never do clap in time with my music the right way. I tell them, "Honey, I know you're enjoying yourself but please don't clap along with me." . . .

Many of the young colored people lost their way during Depression times in Chicago. The times were so hard that it broke their spirits. And although I didn't realize it at the time, I know now that the Lord must have had his arms around me in those days and he protected me. God moves in mysterious ways—and in a mysterious way, the Depression became responsible for my whole career in gospel singing.

It came about because at the Greater Salem Baptist Church the Johnson boys had formed a little singing and entertainment group. There were the three brothers, Prince, Robert and Wilbur, a girl named Louise Barry, and myself.

Robert Johnson was only eighteen years old, but he was a spirited young man. He was like Sammy Davis, Jr.—just full of pep and energy all the time. He loved to sing and act. He was good at writing skits and directing them, and he had what they needed. They would collect a little admission money to pay for the coal and mortgage and give us the rest. Sometimes we got as much as $1.50 each a night.

We sang all over the South Side and then began to get invitations outside the city to colored churches in downstate Illinois and in Indiana. We sang at the Baptist Conventions in St. Louis and Cleveland and got more invitations still. So, as strange as it seems, deep in the Depression and only twenty years old, I had a dollar or two in my pocketbook at the end of the week after I'd given Aunt Alice and Aunt Hannah my share of the food and rent money.

People who heard me sing were always complimenting me on my voice and telling me I should be taking lessons. One night in 1932 when we each had made four dollars singing at a church, my girl friend and I took our money and went around to see Professor DuBois about some singing lessons. Professor DuBois was a great Negro tenor who had a music salon on the South Side. He was a tall, light-skinned Negro who had a very grand way about him. He was very proud of his career as a concert and operatic singer and it didn't take me long to find out that he didn't think much of my way of singing a song.

First off, he had me sing the spiritual "Standing in the Need of Prayer." I had such a rhythm inside of me that I kept picking up the beat and out of the corner of my eye I could see the Professor frowning. He held up his hand. "That's no way to sing that song," he said. "Slow down. Sing it like this."

He clasped his hands together and sang in a real sad and solemn kind of way. I tried again, but his way was too slow and mournful for me. I got going again with my rhythm, but the Professor shrugged his shoulders and broke me off in the middle.

"You try it," he told the girl who had come with me.

My friend had a nice voice and she sang the song sweet and slow just the way the Professor wanted it.

"Now that's singing!" he exclaimed. "You've got a fine voice and great possibilities."

Turning to me, he said, "And you've got to learn to stop hollering. It will take time to build up your voice. The way you sing is not a credit to the Negro race. You've got to learn to sing songs so that white people can understand them."

I felt all mixed up. How could I sing songs for white people to understand when I was colored myself? It didn't seem to make any sense. It was a battle within me to sing a song in a formal way. I felt it was too polished and I didn't feel good about it. I handed over my four dollars to the Professor and left.

"Wasn't he wonderful?" exclaimed my friend as we went down the stairs. "I'm going to take some more lessons as soon as I can."

The numbness in me was wearing off and I felt hurt and angry. "Not me," I snapped back. "I don't want to sing none of his high-class music!"

It was a long time before I had another extra four dollars, but even when I did, I never went back to Professor DuBois's music salon. It turned out to be my one and only singing lesson. I haven't had one since. . . .

I had met Professor A. Dorsey, the great writer of gospel songs—he is to gospel music what W. C. Handy is to the blues—and we used to travel together to the same church meetings and conventions.

A lot of folks don't know that gospel songs have not been handed down like spirituals. Most gospel songs have been composed and written by Negro musicians like Professor Dorsey.

Before he got saved by the Lord and went into the church, Professor Dorsey was a piano player for Ma Rainey, one of the first of the blues singers. His nickname in those days was "Georgia Tom" and everybody who went to the tent shows used to know him for the rocking, syncopated beat he had on his piano.

When he began to write gospel music he still had a happy beat in his songs. They're sung by thousands of people like myself who believe religion is a joy.

There are still some Negro churches that don't have gospel singers or choirs and only sing the old hymns and anthems, but among Baptists and the Methodists and the Sanctified church people you will always hear gospel music.

Professor Dorsey would have copies of his wonderful songs like "Precious Lord" and "Peace in the Valley" along with him when we traveled together and he would sell these for ten cents a piece to the folks who wanted to own them. Sometimes he would sell five thousand copies a day. But I was still what you call a "fish and bread" singer in those days. I was still singing for my supper as well as for the Lord.

The more gospel singing took hold in Chicago and around the country, the more some of the colored ministers objected to it. They were cold to it. They didn't like the hand-clapping and the stomping and they said we were bringing jazz into the church and it wasn't dignified. Once at church one of the preachers got up in the pulpit and spoke out against me.

I got right up, too. I told him I was born to sing gospel music. Nobody had to teach me. I was serving God. I told him I had been reading the Bible every day most of my life and there was a Psalm that said: "Oh, clap your hands, all ye people! Shout unto the Lord with the voice of a trumpet!" If it was undignified, it was what the Bible told me to do.

The European hymns they wanted me to sing are beautiful songs, but they're not Negro music. I believe most Negroes—unless they are trained concert artists or so educated they're self-conscious—don't feel at home singing them. Like me, they like to use their hands and their feet. How can you sing of Amazing Grace? How can you sing prayerfully of heaven and earth and all God's wonders without using your hands?

I want my hands . . . my feet . . . my whole body to say all that is in me. I say, "Don't let the devil steal the beat from the Lord! The Lord doesn't like us to act dead. If you feel it, tap your feet a little— dance to the glory of the Lord!"

When I'm singing at concerts, sometimes I whisper . . . sometimes I exclaim and drive the rhythm real hard and sometimes I get right down off the stage on my knees and sing with the folks and keep right on singing afterward in my dressing room before I've said all that I feel inside of me.

Most of the criticism of my songs in the early days came from the high-up society Negroes. There were many who were wealthy, but they did nothing to help me. The first big Negro in Chicago to help me was an undertaker and a politician. His name was Bob Miller. He was the first to present me in a concert in a high school and to raise my admission price from a dime to forty cents. He didn't criticize my simple songs or laugh because I nailed up my own cardboard signs on fences and telephone posts and got in my car and drove around town asking storekeepers to put them in their windows.

In those days the big colored churches didn't want me and they didn't let me in. I had to make it my business to pack the little basement-hall congregations and store-front churches and get their respect that way. When they began to see the crowds I drew, the big churches began to sit up and take notice because even inside the church there are people who are greedy for money. . . .

The Negroes' new fight for rights had come to a new focus down in the heart of the "Black Belt" in Albany, Georgia, where the colored people have never been granted their rights, including the right to vote. Two weeks before Christmas, 737 colored people led by Dr. W. G. Anderson, a Negro doctor from Albany, and the Reverend King, marched together in downtown Albany. They held a meeting and prayed for the white people to please see the light and let them have their rights.

In that great Christmas congregation there were young people, old women in their seventies, working men, doctors, lawyers and housekeepers. They were all arrested and put in jail.

Martin Luther King, Jr., and Ralph Abernathy were convicted of leading the demonstration and went to jail. Later, Reverend King and nine other Negroes were jailed again when they prayed on the steps of the City Hall, but the Albany Movement only grew stronger.

The Negroes began letting the white people know their feelings by not going into the city's downtown stores, and the boycott emptied the streets of shoppers.

Once again it was in the churches that the colored people rallied for their cause. The white people oppressed them and threatened them, but the Negroes would swing into hymns like "We Are Climbing Jacob's Ladder" and "Pass Me Not, O Gentle Saviour" and the song that got famous during the student sit-ins—"We Shall Overcome."

It has meant so much to me that a great part of the brave fight for freedom down South now is coming from inside the church and from the hymns and gospel songs the people are singing.

The "Freedom Songs" began back during the Montgomery boycott when the Negroes began singing in the churches to keep up their courage. When the students began to go to jail during the sit-ins they began to make up new words to the spirituals and hymns and old gospel melodies that the Negroes had been singing in their churches for generations. Some got printed, some got put on records and some just got passed around.

Using songs as a way of expressing protest and gaining strength and hope runs way back deep in the American Negro's past. When the colored slaves on the plantations sang, "Steal away to Jesus, I ain't got long to stay here," they weren't talking just about Heaven; they were expressing their secret hope that they, too, would have their chance to escape up North to freedom.

The soul of the Negro just naturally has so much rhythm and music in it that "testifying" to music in church and "getting happy" with singing has always been a way in which the Negro has sought to renew his strength.

Now all through the South the Negroes are singing. They sang while they were put in jail by the hundreds and sometimes the power of their music was so great that the white guards began singing right along with them.

They sing in churches and in mass meetings while deputies and sheriffs go around taking names and white gangs burn up their cars.

The big song of the movement that is now sung in the South by thousands of Negroes almost every night is "We Shall Overcome," which says—

> We shall overcome, we shall overcome,
> We shall overcome some day.
> Deep in my heart I do believe
> We shall overcome some day.

The "Freedom Songs" have caught on because music speaks a language to individual souls that cannot always be expressed by the spoken word. There's something about music that is so penetrating that your soul gets the message. No matter what trouble comes to a person, music can help him face it. Some who didn't believe in God have found him through music.

Many colored people in the South have been kept down so hard that they have had little schooling. They can't handle a lot of reading, but as one preacher said, "The singing has drawn them together. Through the songs they have expressed years of suppressed hopes, suffering and even joy and love."

One young Negro leader said, "Without music there could have been no Albany Movement."

And Martin Luther King, Jr., said, "The Freedom Songs are giving people new courage, a radiant hope in the future in our most trying hours."

The white folks got so confused by the way the Negroes kept gaining strength that gangs of men began prowling the countryside around Albany at night burning Negro churches. And it is to the everlasting shame of the white Baptist preachers in the South that they have not spoken out loud against these cowardly attacks on a sanctified place.

In fact, when a group of ministers and rabbis from the northern states came down to Albany to let the colored people know they had plenty of support, the white preachers of Albany ran out of town and hid somewhere. And when the ministers from the North were arrested and thrown into the Albany jails for holding a prayer meeting, the white churches of Albany kept silent. It still beats me how a man can go around preaching about the love of God, whom he has never seen, and scorn his brothers, whom he meets every day on the face of the earth! . . .

All morning, as the charter buses and special trains kept pouring into town, the crowds grew larger and larger. When they added it up later it was found that two hundred thousand Americans, white and colored—the largest protest crowd that had ever come to Washington— had joined in the great march.

Soon the singing began and all through the throngs of people you could hear the stirring melodies of old spirituals and church hymns and the new Freedom Songs. People gathered in groups to sing "We Shall Overcome," and "We Shall Not Be Moved," and "Before I'll Be a Slave I'll Be Buried in My Grave and Go Home to My Lord and Be Free," and "Blowin' in the Wind."

Just before noon when it came time for the last stage of the march, there was a great surge toward the Lincoln Memorial. People streamed into the two great avenues bordering the beautiful reflecting pool that runs between the Washington Monument and the Memorial.

It was a parade that you see only once in a lifetime. Thousands were walking twenty abreast singing hymns and songs, waving American flags and banners and signs about the Civil Rights Bill, flowing like two great rivers toward the Memorial. There were old folks in wheelchairs and men and women on crutches. I saw a white man help a colored woman who was marching alone with four children. He picked up one child and they all walked along together.

To me it was like marching with a mighty host that had come for deliverance. I kept thinking of the words of the Bible—"And nations shall rise up . . ."

And it seemed to me that here was a nation of people marching together. It was like the vision of Moses that the children of Israel would march over into Canaan.

After we got to the Lincoln Memorial I climbed the marble steps to where the great statue of Abraham Lincoln sits looking out over Washington and took my seat in a wooden chair to listen to the speakers introduced by Philip Randolph and await my turn to sing for the marchers.

The summer sun was beating down on us but I never gave it a thought as I sat looking out at the great sea of people and banners, spread out as far as I could see. I couldn't look hard enough or long enough. The beautiful day and the great multitude gathered there had such a special meaning for me that I felt as if I were hypnotized. I was living and breathing history.

I myself was the granddaughter of Negro slaves who had labored on a Louisiana plantation. All around me were the great Negro leaders of my own generation—men like Philip Randolph and Roy C. Wilkins—and the new young leaders like Martin Luther King and Whitney Young and John Lewis who with the help of the young Negroes were bringing about another revolution in American history. Sitting and standing side by side with us were white people—Catholic, Jewish and Protestant clergymen and union men like Walter Reuther.

Near me sat Dr. Ralph Bunche, who had raised the American Negro to a new eminence in the United Nations, and Thurgood Marshall, now a federal judge, who, as an NAACP lawyer, had waged the case against segregated schools until he won the famous Supreme Court decision in 1954.

Here on these same marble steps Marian Anderson had sung in 1939 after being rebuked and barred from Constitution Hall by the white members of the Daughters of the American Revolution.

I thought back on how in the fifty years since I was a child on the Mississippi levee I had seen my people and my country move forward in so many ways until now we were at the threshold of salvation.

It seemed to me that despite the hatred and fears Negroes still had to face, the American people were beginning to fall into step with us and the hopes for days to come seemed as bright as the sunshine that sparkled over the Potomac River and shone on the tall Washington Monument.

With a truly exalted feeling I rose to sing. I'd thought long and hard about what was the right song for me to sing that day. It had been Martin Luther King who gave me the answer. When he heard me talking about it, he had said, "Mahalia, why don't you sing 'I Been 'Buked and I Been Scorned' for us?"

There's probably only a few white people who ever heard of that song, but it's an old spiritual that is known to colored people up and down the land. It was exactly the right choice for the day because its words reflected the depth of feeling of all the colored people who had come to Washington and it would reach out to all the millions who might be watching and listening to us on radio and on TV.

At first I sang the words softly . . .

> I been 'buked and I been scorned.
> I'm gonna tell my Lord
>   When I get home.
> Just how *long* you've been treating me wrong.

As I sang the words I heard a great murmur come rolling back to me from the multitude below and I sensed I had reached out and touched a chord.

All day long I had been going back and forth between tears and laughter. Now I wanted to let the joy that was inside me about this day come pouring out. I was moved to shout for joy. I lifted up the beat of the rhythm to a gospel beat.

I found myself clapping my hands and swaying and the great crowd joined in with me with a great wave of singing and clapping.

I had my new hat pinned tight on my head so I could let myself go. I could sway and bounce as much as I wanted and Mildred Falls at the piano went right along with me.

People were joining in to sing with me. All through the great crowd I could see their hands clapping and people who had been dipping their tired feet in the long reflection pool began to splash and rock to the rhythm.

Flags were waving and people shouting. It looked as if we had the whole city rocking. I hadn't planned to start a revival meeting but for the moment the joy overflowed throughout the great rally.

They said later my singing seemed to bounce off the golden dome of the Capitol far down the Mall and I've always hoped it reached inside to where some of those Congressmen were sitting!

I had scarcely sat down and caught my breath when Martin Luther King was on his feet delivering a speech that was to make him famous. . . .

SUPPLEMENTARY READINGS

Boyer, Horace C. "Thomas A. Dorsey, 'Father of Gospel Music.'" *Black World* 23, no. 9 (July 1974): 20–32.

Floyd, Samuel A., Jr., and Marsha J. Reisser. *Black Music in the United States: An Annotated Bibliography of Selected Reference and Research Materials*. Milwood, N.Y.: Kraus International Publications, 1983.

Goreau, Laurraine. *Just Mahalia, Baby*. Waco, Texas: Word Book Publisher, 1975.

Heilbut, Tony. *The Gospel Sound*. Garden City, N.Y.: Doubleday/Anchor Books, 1975.

Marks, Morton. " 'You Can't Sing Unless You're Saved': Reliving the Call in Gospel Music." In *African Religious Groups and Beliefs: Papers in Honor of William R. Bascom*, edited by Simon Ottenberg. Sadar, India: Published by Archana Publications for the Folklore Institute, 1982. Pp. 305–31.

48

HOWARD THURMAN

"The Anatomy of Segregation and Ground of Hope"

Howard Thurman was dean of Marsh Chapel at Boston University when The Luminous Darkness *was published in 1965. He had already distinguished himself as a minister, philosopher, and educator. Born in 1900, Thurman grew up in Florida in a segregated town. He enrolled at Morehouse College in 1919 and majored in economics. In 1923 he entered Rochester Theological Seminary, where he took refuge from a totally white world in the library. In 1926 he accepted a call to Mount Zion Baptist Church in Oberlin, Ohio. He soon came under the influence of Rufus Jones, the Quaker mystic and philosopher, and was drawn to Haverford College. Thurman taught at Morehouse and Spelman Colleges (1928–31) and served as dean of Rankin Chapel at Howard University (1932–44). In 1944 Thurman went to San Francisco where he co-founded the famous Interdenominational Fellowship Church, an interracial and intercultural congregation. Nine years later he moved to Boston.*

Thurman's editor at Harper & Row asked him to make available his reflections on the meaning of segregation in American life as a contribution to the literature of the civil rights struggle in the 1960s. Having rejected all forms of segregation as fundamentally at war with Christianity, and personally aware of the damage segregation did to black and white alike, Thurman wrote The Luminous Darkness *to express his concern and his hope for a world free of racial strife.*

THE CRISIS set in motion by the Supreme Court Decision of 1954 introduced a radically new situation. To dishonor segregation has been preempted by Negroes as a right, not as a whim or a private prerogative. This decision, more than any other which the Court has rendered in the area of Civil Rights, created an entirely new issue for the South particularly. Why? Because it declared segregation itself to be unconstitutional.

Source: *The Luminous Darkness*. New York: Harper & Row, 1965. Pp. 12–14, 21–24, and 110–13.

It made its declaration concerning the most critical seedbed for the perpetuation of the Southern pattern: the tax-supported public schools. It dealt with the fundamental responsibility of a society to educate the young, who in turn would become the responsible adults of the future. This is the taproot of the society and here it was declared that all children must be free to learn to live together with easy access to one another while the mind is developing and the heritage of the culture is being transmitted. The instinct to reject the decision sprang out of the profound awareness that it sounded the death gong for the pattern of segregation in all of its far-flung and complex dimensions.

The decision created a particularly traumatic experience for the man of good will in the white South. I mean the man who had a basic humanitarianism and who wanted the Negro to get the maximum fulfillment he could within the structure of the pattern. Such a person would be in favor of, and often would work for, improvement of the schools, decent buildings, and adequate salaries for Negro teachers. He would give of his time and money in working to improve race relations. The period following hard upon the close of World War I marked the heyday of his activity. The work of the Southern Interracial Commission under the leadership of Dr. Will Alexander is a case in point. Here were men and women of definite good will and, for the period, of enlightened social concern. They took strong and often courageous positions against police brutality and the vastly inhuman treatment of helpless Negroes on the chain gangs in the South. Often in their private relations they associated with Negroes, not only because the experience was in itself satisfying but also because they were bearing witness to a real social concern. Included among these were certain groups within the churches of the South and particularly the Methodist Church, South, through its region-wide influential women's society.

But it must be kept in mind that all this activity took place within a framework which accepted and did not challenge the pattern. Even this behavior required a certain kind of courage which when looked at in the light of the present may not seem particularly significant. Always care was taken to get as much done as possible without challenging the pattern of segregation itself.

During the years when I was a teacher in Atlanta, I was invited to attend one of the meetings of the Interracial Commission. At the end of the morning session, I was beside myself with disgust. It seemed to me to be a waste of time and I could not accept the honesty and integrity of the Southern white people at the meeting. I was walking out of the door when one of the Negro college presidents stopped me to ask for my reaction. When I finished he said, "I understand how you feel,

Thurman, but the thing that I keep saying to myself is that if we do not work with these people, there are no others in the South with whom we can work."

Later at one of the meetings I listened to one of the great liberal Southern Presbyterian preachers of Atlanta talk about the growth of the commission in its breadth of view. He told of the long and heated discussion concerning a question that had arisen when a world-famous Negro singer was coming to Atlanta for a concert in the city auditorium. Since the artist was Negro, it seemed too bad (and this was some growth) for the Negroes to be segregated in the customary balcony. The question was, "What shall we do with the Negroes if we permit them out of the balcony?" The predominant opinion was to have the Negroes sit in the very rear of the auditorium. The clergyman opposed that, and with tears running down his cheeks, he shared with the group a feeling of triumph when they divided the house perpendicularly rather than horizontally. Above all else the pattern must not be changed in any manner that is basic; it may be juggled, rearranged, but not changed.

But the fateful decision of the Court challenged the very foundations of the pattern. One of the inevitable heartbreaking effects is that the spirits and the souls of the children of the South are caught up in the struggle which really belongs to the adult world. Now for the first time in the South, white as well as Negro children are grappling with their environment as if they are adults. It is impossible even to imagine the kind of harvest that such a planting will bring forth. And yet the children left to themselves may not be so deeply scarred as one would think. . . .

It is a great irony that the Negro church has figured so largely as a rallying center for the civil rights movement in the South primarily because of its strategic position as an institution in Negro life; it has not become a civil rights rallying center because of its religious ethical teaching as such. But the logic of the impact of the religious experience in the Negro church made it inevitable that it would become such a center. For a long time the Negro church was the one place in the life of the people which was comparatively free from interference by the white community. A man may be buffeted about by his environment, or may be regarded as a nobody in the general community; a woman may be a nurse in a white family in which the three-year-old child in her care calls her by her first name, thus showing quite unconsciously the contempt in which she is held by his parents. When this Negro man and this Negro woman come to their church, however, for one terribly fulfilling moment they are somebody.

Perhaps this immunity from interference and violence which the

Negro church enjoyed until recent times was owing not to reverence or respect for the religious institution as such but perhaps to superstition. One day a friend of mine, who was a clergyman, and I were driving in the downtown section of a Southern city. We were so engrossed in conversation that my friend, who was driving the car, drove through a red light without seeing it. The white policeman on the corner blew his whistle and ran up behind us, ordering my friend to pull over. He came around to the driver's seat, swearing violently, pulled out his billy and reached into the open window of the car to grab my friend by the neck to make his head available for cracking. My friend looked him in the eye and said very quietly, "You would not hit a man of God, would you, officer?" The policeman froze, muttered something, and ended up telling him to drive on. It may be that here was at work an ancient taboo which gave to the religious immunity from interference so as not to offend the gods.

When I was a student in Atlanta, a blind Negro was killed by a policeman. Feeling ran high all through the Negro community. When his funeral was held, officers of the law, fearing that it would be an occasion for some kind of uprising, came to the service but remained outside the church. In his sermon, the minister had only words of consolation to give to the family. In his prayer to God, he expressed his anger and hostility toward the white community. He could do this in a prayer without exposing the Negro community to retaliation.

This whole picture has changed almost overnight since the Negro church became the overt center for rallying the spirit of Negroes. Thus churches are bombed, burned, and generally are under constant attack and pressure.

It is a curious phenomenon that the personality who has played a major part in the inspiration for nonviolent action is not Thoreau, or Whittier, or even Tolstoi, but a man from an entirely different culture and an entirely different faith: Mahatma Gandhi. One wonders deeply about the meaning of this fact. However, the image of the citizen who is acting as one who maintains in himself a sense of responsibility for the fate of his country is a compelling one and one capable of making the large and imperative demand. Men have always been able to rally when the very life of the nation is at stake. It can be argued that the enthusiasm engendered, the call to sacrifice, the sense of participation in a collective destiny that involves the total nation—all these have a religious dimension, but it is outside of the religious institution. And that is my point.

The thing that made the deepest impression on me at the ceremonies at the base of the Lincoln Monument on the day of the March

on Washington in 1963, was not the vast throng, as thrilling as it was
to be a part of such a tremendous movement of peoples on the march;
it was not the inspired oratory of all the participating speakers, including the dazzling magic of the music and utter vitality springing from
the throat of Martin Luther King; it was not the repeated refrain of
Eugene Blake, saying on behalf of the church, we are late but we are
here—no, it was none of these things. What impressed me most was a
small group of young people representing student nonviolent groups,
fresh from the jails and violences of the South, who time and time
again caught the spiritual overtones of the speakers and led the critical
applause which moved like a tidal wave over the vast audience. I do not
know but this observation may be an embarrassment to them, but this
is how it seemed to me. These young people were tuned to the spiritual
dimension of what they were about even as what they were about was
the exercising of their civic rights inherent in their citizenship. . . .

Perhaps there is something inherent in the religious experience that
always pulls back toward the personal center out of which the individual operates and the religious context that gives existential meaning to
the experience itself. It is this latter frame of reference that creates the
categories out of which the dogma of a particular faith comes. In this
sense it may seem an unrealistic demand that religious experience be
universal. If this is a true picture, then such notions or concepts as
brotherhood, reverence for life, respect for personality, do not rightfully
belong to the behavior pattern of the religious devotee. Such ideas
would then invade the religious man's life from the wider context of
his living, the areas of his life that are beyond and outside of the parochial and the sectarian character of his religious faith. I have often pondered the fact that men of different faiths may share common experiences which are outside of their specifically religious fellowship, and
that on behalf of such demands they may make tremendous sacrifices,
without feeling under any necessity to share the intimacy of their experience of God.

Or it may be in order to raise a question about the universality of
an ethic which grows out of a sectarian or parochial religious experience.
Could it be that we are face to face with an inherent weakness in religious experience, as such, that it is private, personal, and binding upon
the individual only to the extent that he identifies himself with another
and thereby becoming one with him at all the levels and all the ways
that are significant? Here may be a clue, for wherever the Christian
religious experience has made a difference in the one-to-one relationship
of the believer, one sees this kind of private, personal identification at
work. When I identify with a man, I become one with him and in him

I see myself. I remember a quotation out of the past—the statement "know thyself" has been taken more mystically from the statement "thou hast seen thy brother, thou hast seen thy God." This is the true meaning of the reference earlier about listening for the sound of the genuine in another. Such an experience cannot become a dogma—it has to remain experiential all the way. It is a probing process trying to find the opening into another. And it requires exposure, sustained exposure. One of the great obstacles to such exposure is the fact of segregation.

The religious experience as I have known it seems to swing wide the door, not merely into Life but into lives. I am confident that my own call to the religious vocation cannot be separated from the slowly emerging disclosure that my religious experience makes it possible for me to experience myself as a human being and thus keep a very real psychological distance between myself and the hostilities of my environment. Through the years it has driven me more and more to seek to make as a normal part of my relations with men the experiencing of them as human beings. When this happens love has essential materials with which to work. And contrary to the general religious teaching, men would not need to stretch themselves out of shape in order to love. On the contrary, a man comes into possession of himself more completely when he is *free* to love another.

I have dwelt at length upon the necessity that is laid upon the church and the Christian because the Christian Church is still one of the major centers of influence in the American community. Too, the Christian Church claims to be under the judgment of God as it fulfills itself in human history. But it must be remembered that what is true in any religion is to be found in that religion because it is true, it is not true because it is found in that religion. The ethical insight which makes for the most healthy and creative human relations is not the unique possession of any religion, however inspired it may be. It does not belong exclusively to any people or to any age. It has an ancient history, and it has been at work informing the quality of life and human relations longer than the records and the memories of man. Just as scattered through the earliest accounts of man's journey on this planet are flashes and shafts of light illuminating the meaning of man and his fellows, so in our times we find the widest variety of experiments pointing in the same direction and making manifest the same goals. Men are made for one another. In this grand discovery there is a disclosure of another dimension: this experience of one another is not enough. There is a meaning in life greater than, but informing, all the immediate meanings—and the name given to this meaning is religion, because it embodies, however faintly, a sense of the ultimate and the divine.

There is a spirit abroad in life of which the Judaeo-Christian ethic is but one expression. It is a spirit that makes for wholeness and for community; it finds its way into the quiet solitude of a Supreme Court justice when he ponders the constitutionality of an act of Congress which guarantees civil rights to all its citizens; it settles in the pools of light in the face of a little girl as with her frailty she challenges the hard frightened heart of a police chief; it walks along the lonely road with the solitary protest marcher and settles over him with a benediction as he falls by the assassin's bullet fired from ambush; it kindles the fires of unity in the heart of Jewish Rabbi, Catholic Priest, and Protestant Minister as they join arms together, giving witness to their God on behalf of a brotherhood that transcends creed, race, sex, and religion; it makes a path to Walden Pond and ignites the flame of nonviolence in the mind of a Thoreau and burns through his liquid words from the Atlantic to the Pacific; it broods over the demonstrators for justice and brings comfort to the desolate and forgotten who have no memory of what it is to feel the rhythm of belonging to the race of men; it knows no country and its allies are to be found wherever the heart is kind and the collective will and the private endeavor seek to make justice where injustice abounds, to make peace where chaos is rampant, and to make the voice heard on behalf of the helpless and the weak. It is the voice of God and the voice of man; it is the meaning of all the strivings of the whole human race toward a world of friendly men underneath a friendly sky.

SUPPLEMENTARY READINGS

Kelsey, George D. *Racism and the Christian Understanding of Man.* New York: Charles Scribner's Sons, 1965.

Smith, Luther E., Jr. *Howard Thurman: The Mystic as Prophet.* Lanham, Md.: University Press of America, 1982.

Thurman, Howard. *Deep is the Hunger.* New York: Harper & Row, 1951.

Thurman, Howard. *With Head and Heart: The Autobiography of Howard Thurman.* New York: Harcourt Brace Jovanovich, 1979.

Young, Henry J., ed. *God and Human Freedom: A Festschrift in Honor of Howard Thurman.* Richmond, Ind.: Friends United Press, 1983.

49

NATIONAL CONFERENCE OF
BLACK CHURCHMEN

"Black Power" Statement, July 31, 1966
"Black Theology" Statement, June 13, 1969

Dr. Benjamin A. Payton, the executive of the Commission on Religion and Race of the National Council of Churches, called a meeting in July 1966 to discuss, as participant Gayraud Wilmore remembers, "the hysterical reaction of some white ministers to black power, the way the slogan was being distorted by whites and bandied about thoughtlessly by blacks, and the obvious inability of King's SCLC to respond to the new situation." In the wake of urban riots and a shift toward a more race-conscious and ideological posture by many black groups, these black religious leaders, many of whom worked within predominantly white ecclesiastical structures, decided to address the white establishments that molded public opinion. The resulting statement on black power, with additional signatories, first appeared in the July 31, 1966, edition of the New *York Times. Dr. Wilmore, now dean of New York Theological Seminary, recalls that the historic black Methodist denominations and three major black Baptist conventions took no official notice of the statement or the National Committee of Negro Churchmen. In 1969, following James Forman's "Black Manifesto" demanding reparations from the white churches, and the publication of James H. Cone's first book,* Black Theology and Black Power, *the National Committee of Black Churchmen (a designation adopted in 1967) met in Atlanta and produced a statement on black theology that heralded a radical rethinking of the theological demands of the black experience.*

Statement by the National Committee
of Negro Churchmen, July 31, 1966

WE, an informal group of Negro churchmen in America, are deeply disturbed about the crisis brought upon our country by historic distortions

Source: *Black Theology: A Documentary History, 1966–1979.* Edited by Gayraud S. Wilmore and James H. Cone. Maryknoll, N.Y.: Orbis Books, 1979. Pp. 23–30 and 100–102.

of important human realities in the controversy about "black power." What we see shining through the variety of rhetoric is not anything new but the same old problem of power and race which has faced our beloved country since 1619.

We realize that neither the term "power" nor the term "Christian conscience" is an easy matter to talk about, especially in the context of race relations in America. The fundamental distortion facing us in the controversy about "black power" is rooted in a gross imbalance of power and conscience between Negroes and white Americans. It is this distortion, mainly, which is responsible for the widespread, though often inarticulate, assumption that white people are justified in getting what they want through the use of power, but that Negro Americans must, either by nature or by circumstance, make their appeal only through conscience. As a result, the power of white men and the conscience of black men have both been corrupted. The power of white men is corrupted because it meets little meaningful resistance from Negroes to temper it and keep white men from aping God. The conscience of black men is corrupted because, having no power to implement the demands of conscience, the concern for justice is transmuted into a distorted form of love, which, in the absence of justice, becomes chaotic self-surrender. Powerlessness breeds a race of beggars. We are faced now with a situation where conscienceless power meets powerless conscience, threatening the very foundations of our nation.

Therefore, we are impelled by conscience to address at least four groups of people in areas where clarification of the controversy is of the most urgent necessity. We do not claim to present the final word. It is our hope, however, to communicate meanings from our experience regarding power and certain elements of conscience to help interpret more adequately the dilemma in which we are all involved.

I. To the Leaders of America: Power and Freedom

It is of critical importance that the leaders of this nation listen also to a voice which says that the principal source of the threat to our nation comes neither from the riots erupting in our big cities, nor from the disagreements among the leaders of the civil rights movement, nor even from mere raising of the cry for "black power." These events, we believe, are but the expression of the judgment of God upon our nation for its failure to use its abundant resources to serve the real well-being of people, at home and abroad.

We give our full support to all civil rights leaders as they seek for basically American goals, for we are not convinced that their mutual reinforcement of one another in the past is bound to end in the future. We would hope that the public power of our nation will be used to strengthen the civil rights movement and not to manipulate or further fracture it.

We deplore the overt violence of riots, but we believe it is more important to focus on the real sources of the eruptions. These sources may be abetted inside the ghetto, but their basic causes lie in the silent and covert violence which white middle-class America inflicts upon the victims of the inner city. The hidden, smooth and often smiling decisions of American leaders which tie a white noose of suburbia around their necks, and which pin the backs of the masses of Negroes against the steaming ghetto walls—without jobs in a booming economy; with dilapidated and segregated educational systems in the full view of un-enforced laws against it; in short: the failure of American leaders to use American power to create equal opportunity *in life* as well as *in law*—this is the real problem and not the anguished cry for "black power."

From the point of view of the Christian faith, there is nothing necessarily wrong with concern for power. At the heart of the Protestant reformation is the belief that ultimate power belongs to God alone and that men become most inhuman when concentrations of power lead to the conviction—overt or covert—that any nation, race or organization can rival God in this regard. At issue in the relations between whites and Negroes in America is the problem of inequality of power. Out of this imbalance grows the disrespect of white men for the Negro personality and community, and the disrespect of Negroes for themselves. This is a fundamental root of human injustice in America. In one sense, the concept of "black power" reminds us of the need for and the possibility of authentic democracy in America.

We do *not* agree with those who say that we must cease expressing concern for the acquisition of power lest we endanger the "gains" already made by the civil rights movement. The fact of the matter is, there have been few substantive gains since about 1950 in this area. The gap has constantly widened between the incomes of non-whites relative to the whites. Since the Supreme Court decision of 1954, de facto segregation in every major city in our land has increased rather than decreased. Since the middle of the 1950s unemployment among Negroes has gone up rather than down while unemployment has decreased in the white community.

While there has been some progress in some areas for equality for Negroes, this progress has been limited mainly to middle-class Negroes who represent only a small minority of the larger Negro community.

These are the hard facts that we must all face together. Therefore we must not take the position that we can continue in the same old paths.

When American leaders decide to serve the real welfare of people instead of war and destruction; when American leaders are forced to make the rebuilding of our cities first priority on the nation's agenda; when American leaders are forced by the American people to quit misusing and abusing American power; then will the cry for "black power" become inaudible, for the framework in which all power in America operates would include the power and experience of black men as well as those of white men. In that way, the fear of the power of each group would be removed. America is our beloved homeland. But, America is not God. Only God can do everything. America and the other nations of the world must decide which among a number of alternatives they will choose.

II. To White Churchmen: Power and Love

As black men who were long ago forced out of the white church to create and to wield "black power," we fail to understand the emotional quality of the outcry of some clergy against the use of the term today. It is not enough to answer that "integration" is the solution. For it is precisely the nature of the operation of power under some forms of integration which is being challenged. The Negro Church was created as a result of the refusal to submit to the indignities of a false kind of "integration" in which all power was in the hands of white people. A more equal sharing of power is precisely what is required as the precondition of authentic human interaction. We understand the growing demand of Negro and white youth for a more honest kind of integration; one which increases rather than decreases the capacity of the disinherited to participate with power in all of the structures of our common life. Without this capacity to *participate with power*—i.e., to have some organized political and economic strength to really influence people with whom one interacts—integration is not meaningful. For the issue is not one of racial balance but of honest interracial interaction.

For this kind of interaction to take place, all people need power, whether black or white. We regard as sheer hypocrisy or as a blind and dangerous illusion the view that opposes love to power. Love should be a controlling element in power, not power itself. So long as white churchmen continue to moralize and misinterpret Christian love, so long will justice continue to be subverted in this land.

III. To Negro Citizens: Power and Justice

Both the anguished cry for "black power" and the confused emotional response to it can be understood if the whole controversy is put in the context of American history. Especially must we understand the irony involved in the pride of Americans regarding their ability to act as individuals on the one hand, and their tendency to act as members of ethnic groups on the other hand. In the tensions of this part of our history is revealed both the tragedy and the hope of human redemption in America.

America has asked its Negro citizens to fight for opportunity *as individuals* whereas at certain points in our history what we have needed most has been opportunity for the whole group, not just for selected and approved Negroes. Thus in 1863, the slaves were made legally free, as individuals, but the real question regarding personal and group power to maintain that freedom was pushed aside. Power at that time for a mainly rural people meant land and tools to work the land. In the words of Thaddeus Stevens, power meant "40 acres and a mule." But this power was not made available to the slaves and we see the results today in the pushing of a landless peasantry off the farms into big cities where they come in search mainly of the power to be free. What they find are only the formalities of unenforced legal freedom. So we must ask, "What is the nature of the power which we seek and need today?" Power today is essentially organizational power. It is not a thing lying about in the streets to be fought over. It is a thing which, in some measure, already belongs to Negroes and which must be developed by Negroes in relationship with the great resources of this nation.

Getting power necessarily involves reconciliation. We must first be reconciled to ourselves lest we fail to recognize the resources we already have and upon which we can build. We must be reconciled to ourselves as persons and to ourselves as an historical group. This means we must find our way to a new self-image in which we can feel a normal sense of pride in self, including our variety of skin color and the manifold textures of our hair. As long as we are filled with hatred for ourselves we will be unable to respect others.

At the same time, if we are seriously concerned about power then we must build upon that which we already have. "Black power" is already present to some extent in the Negro church, in Negro fraternities and sororities, in our professional associations, and in the opportunities afforded to Negroes who make decisions in some of the integrated organizations of our society.

We understand the reasons by which these limited forms of "black power" have been rejected by some of our people. Too often the Negro church has stirred its members away from the reign of God in *this world* to a distorted and complacent view of *an otherworldly* conception of God's power. We commit ourselves as churchmen to make more meaningful in the life of our institution our conviction that Jesus Christ reigns in the "here" and "now" as well as in the future he brings in upon us. We shall, therefore, use more of the resources of our churches in working for human justice in the places of social change and upheaval where our Master is already at work.

At the same time, we would urge that Negro social and professional organizations develop new roles for engaging the problem of equal opportunity and put less time into the frivolity of idle chatter and social waste.

We must not apologize for the existence of this form of group power, for we have been oppressed as a group, not as individuals. We will not find our way out of that oppression until both we and America accept the need for Negro Americans as well as for Jews, Italians, Poles and white Anglo-Saxon Protestants, among others, to have and to wield group power.

However, if power is sought merely as an end in itself, it tends to turn upon those who seek it. Negroes need power in order to participate more effectively at all levels of the life of our nation. We are glad that none of those civil rights leaders who have asked for "black power" have suggested that it means a new form of isolationism or a foolish effort at domination. But we must be clear about why we need to be reconciled with the white majority. It is *not* because we are only one-tenth of the population in America; for we do not need to be reminded of the awesome power wielded by the 90% majority. We see and feel that power every day in the destruction heaped upon our families and upon the nation's cities. We do not need to be threatened by such cold and heartless statements. For we are men, not children, and we are growing out of our fear of that power, which can hardly hurt us any more in the future than it does in the present or has in the past. Moreover, those bare figures conceal the potential political strength which is ours if we organize properly in the big cities and establish effective alliances.

Neither must we rest our concern for reconciliation with our white brothers on the fear that failure to do so would damage gains already made by the civil rights movement. If those gains are in fact real, they will withstand the claims of our people for power and justice, not just for a few select Negroes here and there, but for the masses of our citizens. We must rather rest our concern for reconciliation on the firm ground that we and all other Americans *are* one. Our history and destiny are indissolubly linked. If the future is to belong to any of us, it must be prepared for all of us whatever our racial or religious background. For in the final analysis, we are *persons* and the power of all groups must be wielded to make visible our common humanity.

The future of America will belong to neither white nor black unless all Americans work together at the task of rebuilding our cities. We must organize not only among ourselves but with other groups in order that we can, together, gain power sufficient to change this nation's sense of what is *now* important and what must be done *now*. We must work with the remainder of the nation to organize whole cities for the task of making the rebuilding of our cities first priority in the use of our resources. This is more important than who gets to the moon first or the war in Vietnam.

To accomplish this task we cannot expend our energies in spastic or ill-tempered explosions without meaningful goals. We must move from the politics of philanthropy to the politics of metropolitan development for equal opportunity. We must relate all groups of the city together in new ways in order that the truth of our cities might be laid bare and in order that, together, we can lay claim to the great resources of our nation to make truth more human.

IV. To the Mass Media: Power and Truth

The ability or inability of all people in America to understand the upheavals of our day depends greatly on the way power and truth operate in the mass media. During the Southern demonstrations for civil rights, you men of the communications industry performed an invaluable service for the entire country by revealing plainly to all ears and eyes, the ugly truth of a brutalizing system of overt discrimination and segregation. Many of you were mauled and injured, and it took courage for you to stick with the task. You were instruments of change and not merely purveyors of unrelated facts. You were able to do this by dint of personal courage and by reason of the power of national news agencies which supported you.

Today, however, your task and ours is more difficult. The truth that needs revealing today is not so clear-cut in its outlines, nor is there a national consensus to help you form relevant points of view. Therefore, nothing is now more important than that you look for a variety of sources of truth in order that the limited perspectives of all of us might be corrected. Just as you related to a broad spectrum of people in Mississippi instead of relying only on police records and establishment figures, so must you operate in New York City, Chicago and Cleveland.

The power to support you in this endeavor *is present* in our country. It must be searched out. We desire to use our limited influence to help relate you to the variety of experience in the Negro community so that limited controversies are not blown up into the final truth about us. The fate of this country is, to no small extent, dependent upon how you interpret the crises upon us, so that human truth is disclosed and human needs are met.

SIGNATORIES

Bishop John D. Bright, Sr., A.M.E. Church, First Episcopal District, Philadelphia, Pennsylvania

The Rev. John Bryant, Connecticut Council of Churches, Hartford, Connecticut

Suffragan Bishop John M. Burgess, The Episcopal Church, Boston, Massachusetts

The Rev. W. Sterling Cary, Grace Congregational Church, New York, New York

The Rev. Charles E. Cobb, St. John Church (UCC), Springfield, Massachusetts

The Rev. Caesar D. Coleman, Christian Methodist Episcopal Church, Memphis, Tennessee

The Rev. Joseph C. Coles, Williams Institutional CME Church, New York, New York

The Rev. George A. Crawley, Jr., St. Paul Baptist Church, Baltimore, Maryland

The Rev. O. Herbert Edwards, Trinity Baptist Church, Baltimore, Maryland

The Rev. Bryant George, United Presbyterian Church in the U.S.A., New York, New York

Bishop Charles F. Golden, The Methodist Church, Nashville, Tennessee

The Rev. Quinland R. Gordon, The Episcopal Church, New York, New York

The Rev. James Hargett, Church of Christian Fellowship, U.C.C., Los Angeles, California

The Rev. Edler Hawkins, St. Augustine Presbyterian Church, New York, New York

The Rev. Reginald Hawkins, United Presbyterian Church, Charlotte, North Carolina

Dr. Anna Arnold Hedgeman, Commission on Religion and Race, National Council of Churches, New York, New York

The Rev. R. E. Hodd, Gary, Indiana

The Rev. H. R. Hughes, Bethel A.M.E. Church, New York, New York

The Rev. Kenneth Hughes, St. Bartholomew's Episcopal Church, Cambridge, Massachusetts

The Rev. Donald G. Jacobs, St. James A.M.E. Church, Cleveland, Ohio

The Rev. J. L. Joiner, Emanuel A.M.E. Church, New York, New York

The Rev. Arthur A. Jones, Metropolitan A.M.E. Church, Philadelphia, Pennsylvania

The Rev. Stanley King, Sabathini Baptist Church, Minneapolis, Minnesota

The Rev. Earl Wesley Lawson, Emanuel Baptist Church, Malden, Massachusetts

The Rev. David Licorish, Abyssinian Baptist Church, New York, New York

The Rev. Arthur B. Mack, St. Thomas A.M.E.Z. Church, Haverstraw, New York

The Rev. James W. Mack, South United Church of Christ, Chicago, Illinois

The Rev. O. Clay Maxwell, Jr., Baptist Ministers Conference of New York City and Vicinity, New York, New York

The Rev. Leon Modeste, The Episcopal Church, New York, New York

Bishop Noah W. Moore, Jr., The Methodist Church, Southwestern Area, Houston, Texas

The Rev. David Nickerson, Episcopal Society for Cultural and Racial Unity, Atlanta, Georgia

The Rev. LeRoy Patrick, Bethesda United Presbyterian Church, Pittsburgh, Pennsylvania

The Rev. Benjamin F. Payton, Commission on Religion and Race, National Council of Churches, New York, New York

The Rev. Isaiah P. Pogue, St. Mark's Presbyterian Church, Cleveland, Ohio

The Rev. Sandy F. Ray, Empire Baptist State Convention, Brooklyn, New York

Bishop Herbert B. Shaw, Presiding Bishop, Third Episcopal District, A.M.E.Z. Church, Wilmington, North Carolina

The Rev. Stephen P. Spottswood, Commission on Race and Cultural Relations, Detroit Council of Churches, Detroit, Michigan

The Rev. Henri A. Stines, Church of the Atonement, Washington, D.C.

Bishop James S. Thomas, Resident Bishop, Iowa Area, The Methodist Church, Des Moines, Iowa

The Rev. V. Simpson Turner, Mt. Carmel Baptist Church, Brooklyn, New York

The Rev. Edgar Ward, Grace Presbyterian Church, Chicago, Illinois
The Rev. Paul M. Washington, Church of the Advocate,
Philadelphia, Pennsylvania
The Rev. Frank L. Williams, Methodist Church, Baltimore, Maryland
The Rev. John W. Williams, St. Stephen's Baptist Church, Kansas
City, Missouri
The Rev. Gayraud Wilmore, United Presbyterian Church U.S.A.,
New York, New York
The Rev. M. L. Wilson, Covenant Baptist Church, New York,
New York
The Rev. Robert H. Wilson, Corresponding Secretary, National Baptist
Convention of America, Dallas, Texas
The Rev. Nathan Wright, Episcopal Diocese of Newark, Newark,
New Jersey

Statement by the National Committee
of Black Churchmen, June 13, 1969

Why Black Theology?

Black people affirm their being. This affirmation is made in the whole experience of being black in the hostile American society. Black Theology is not a gift of the Christian gospel dispensed to slaves; rather it is an *appropriation* which black slaves made of the gospel given by their white oppressors. Black Theology has been nurtured, sustained and passed on in the black churches in their various ways of expression. Black Theology has dealt with all the ultimate and violent issues of life and death for a people despised and degraded.

The black church has not only nurtured black people but enabled them to survive brutalities that ought not to have been inflicted on any community of men. Black Theology is the product of black Christian experience and reflection. It comes out of the past. It is strong in the present. And we believe it is redemptive for the future.

This indigenous theological formation of faith emerged from the stark need of the fragmented black community to affirm itself as a part of the Kingdom of God. White theology sustained the American slave system and negated the humanity of blacks. This indigenous Black Theology, based on the imaginative black experience, was the best hope for the survival of black people. This is a way of saying that Black Theology was already present in the spirituals and slave songs and exhortations of slave preachers and their descendants.

All theologies arise out of communal experience with God. At this moment in time, the black community seeks to express its theology in language that speaks to the contemporary mood of black people.

What Is Black Theology?

Black Theology is a theology of black liberation. It seeks to plumb the black condition in the light of God's revelation in Jesus Christ, so that the black community can see that the gospel is commensurate with the achievement of black humanity. Black Theology is a theology of "blackness." It is the affirmation of black humanity that emancipates black people from white racism, thus providing authentic freedom for both white and black people. It affirms the humanity of white people in that it says No to the encroachment of white oppression.

The message of liberation is the revelation of God as revealed in the incarnation of Jesus Christ. Freedom IS the gospel. Jesus is the Liberator! "He . . . hath sent me to preach deliverance to the captives" (Luke 4:18). Thus the black patriarchs and we ourselves know this reality despite all attempts of the white church to obscure it and to utilize Christianity as a means of enslaving blacks. The demand that Christ the Liberator imposes on all men *requires* all blacks to affirm their full dignity as persons and all whites to surrender their presumptions of superiority and abuses of power.

What Does This Mean?

It means that Black Theology must confront the issues which are a part of the reality of black oppression. We cannot ignore the powerlessness of the black community. Despite the *repeated requests* for significant programs of social change, the American people have refused to appropriate adequate sums of money for social reconstruction. White church bodies have often made promises only to follow with default. We must, therefore, once again call the attention of the nation and the church to the need for providing adequate resources of power (reparation).

Reparation is a part of the Gospel message. Zaccheus knew well the necessity for repayment as an essential ingredient in repentance. "If I have taken anything from any man by false accusation, I restore him fourfold" (Luke 19:8). The church which calls itself the servant church must, like its Lord, be willing to strip itself of possessions in order to build and restore that which has been destroyed by the compromising bureaucrats and conscienceless rich. While reparation cannot remove the guilt created by the despicable deed of slavery, it is, nonetheless, a positive response to the need for power in the black community. This nation, and, a people who have always related the value of the person to his possession of property, must recognize the necessity of restoring property in order to reconstitute personhood.

What Is The Cost?

Living is risk. We take it in confidence. The black community has been brutalized and victimized over the centuries. The recognition that comes from seeing Jesus as Liberator and the Gospel as freedom empowers black men to risk themselves for freedom and for faith. This faith we affirm in the midst of a hostile, disbelieving society. We intend to exist by this faith at all times and in all places.

In spite of brutal deprivation and denial the black community has appropriated the spurious form of Christianity imposed upon it and made it into an instrument for resisting the extreme demands of oppression. It has enabled the black community to live through unfulfilled promises, unnecessary risks, and inhuman relationships.

As black theologians address themselves to the issues of the black revolution, it is incumbent upon them to say that the black community will not be turned from its course, but will seek complete fulfillment of the promises of the Gospel. Black people have survived the terror. We now commit ourselves to the risks of affirming the dignity of black personhood. We do this as men and as black Christians. This is the message of Black Theology. In the words of Eldridge Cleaver:

We shall have our manhood.
We shall have it or the earth will be leveled by our efforts to gain it.

SUPPLEMENTARY READINGS

Brown, Clifton F. "Black Religion—1968." From In Black America, 1968: The Year of Awakening, edited by Patricia H. Romero. Washington, D.C.: United Publishing Corporation for the Association for the Study of Negro Life and History, 1969. Pp. 345–53.

Carmichael, Stokely, and Charles V. Hamilton. Black Power: The Politics of Liberation in America. New York: Alfred A. Knopf, 1967.

Harding, Vincent. "The Religion of Black Power." In The Religious Situation: 1968, edited by Donald R. Cutler. Boston: Beacon Press, 1968. Pp. 3–38.

Nelsen, Hart M., and Anne Kusener Nelsen. Black Church in the Sixties. Lexington: University Press of Kentucky, 1975.

Watts, Leon. "The National Committee of Black Churchmen." Christianity and Crisis 30, no. 18 (November 1970): 237–43.

50

JAMES H. CONE

"Black Theology and the Black Church: Where Do We Go From Here?"

Born in 1938 at Fordyce, Arkansas, and raised within the A.M.E. Church, James H. Cone obtained a divinity degree from Garrett Theological Seminary and a doctorate from Northwestern University. He taught at Philander Smith College and Adrian College before going in 1969 to Union Theological Seminary, New York City, where he is now Charles A. Briggs Professor of Systematic Theology. Cone has been one of the most prolific and widely read proponents of black theology. The following essay first appeared as a presentation before the Black Theology Project of the Theology in the Americas Conference held in Atlanta in 1977. Cone's articulation of black theology, beginning with his watershed publication, Black Theology and Black Power *in 1969, drew criticism from a variety of points of view. Some saw his version of black theology as an uncritical allegiance to the political-secular philosophy of black power; others felt he was too dependent upon European theological categories. Not a few asserted that Cone had departed from the ideal of Christian universalism. Several critics, such as Cone's brother, Cecil Wayne Cone, an A.M.E. pastor and dean of Turner Theological Seminary, pointed to an identity crisis in the writings of James Cone, maintaining that he had failed to draw from black folk religious experience as the essential core of black theology. It is these issues, among others, that Professor Cone addresses in the Atlanta lecture.*

SINCE THE APPEARANCE of black theology in the late 1960's, much has been written and said about the political involvement of the black church in black people's historical struggle for justice in North America. Black theologians and preachers have rejected the white church's attempt to separate love from justice and religion from politics because we are proud descendents of a black religious tradition that has always interpreted its confession of faith according to the people's commitment to the struggle for earthly freedom. Instead of turning to Reinhold

Source: *Cross Currents* 27, no. 2 (Summer 1977): 147–56.

Niebuhr and John Bennett for ethical guidance in those troubled times, we searched our past for insight, strength and the courage to speak and do the truth in an extreme situation of oppression. Richard Allen, James Varick, Harriet Tubman, Sojourner Truth, Henry McNeal Turner and Martin Luther King, Jr. became household names as we attempted to create new theological categories that would express our historical fight for justice.

It was in this context that the "Black Power" statement was written in July 1966 by an ad hoc National Committee of Negro Churchmen.[1] The cry of Black Power by Willie Ricks and its political and intellectual development by Stokely Carmichael and others challenged the black church to move beyond the models of love defined in the context of white religion and theology. The black church was thus faced with a theological dilemma: either reject Black Power as a contradiction of Christian love (and thereby join the white church in its condemnation of Black Power advocates as un-American and unchristian), or accept Black Power as a sociopolitical expression of the truth of the gospel. These two possibilities were the only genuine alternatives before us, and we had to decide on whose side we would take our stand.

We knew that to define Black Power as the opposite of the Christian faith was to reject the central role that the black church has played in black people's historical struggle for freedom. Rejecting Black Power also meant that the black church would ignore its political responsibility to empower black people in their present struggle to make our children's future more humane than intended by the rulers in this society. Faced with these unavoidable consequences, it was not possible for any self-respecting church-person to desecrate the memories of our mothers and fathers in the faith by siding with white people who murdered and imprisoned black people simply because of our persistent audacity to assert our freedom. To side with white theologians and preachers who questioned the theological legitimacy of Black Power would have been similar to siding with St. George Methodist Church against Richard Allen and the Bethelites in their struggle for independence during the late 18th and early 19th centuries. We knew that we could not do that, and no amount of white theological reasoning would be allowed to blur our vision of the truth.

But to accept the second alternative and thereby locate Black Power in the Christian context was not easy. First, the acceptance of Black

1 This statement first appeared in the *New York Times*, July 31, 1966 and is reprinted in Warner Traynham's *Christian Faith in Black and White* (Wakefield, Mass.: Parameter, 1973).

Power would appear to separate us from Martin Luther King, Jr., and we did not want to do that. King was our model, having creatively combined religion and politics, and black preachers and theologians respected his courage to concretize the political consequences of his confession of faith. Thus we hesitated to endorse the "Black Power" movement, since it was created in the context of the James Meredith March by Carmichael and others in order to express their dissatisfaction with King's continued emphasis on non-violence and Christian love.[2] As a result of this sharp confrontation between Carmichael and King, black theologians and preachers felt themselves caught in a terrible predicament of wanting to express their continued respect for and solidarity with King, but disagreeing with this rejection of Black Power.

Secondly, the concept of Black Power presented a problem for black theologians and preachers not only because of our loyalty to Martin Luther King, but also because many of us had been trained in white seminaries and had internalized much of white people's definition of Christianity. While the rise and growth of independent black churches suggested that black people had a different perception of the gospel than whites, yet there was no formal theological tradition to which we could turn in order to justify our definition of Black Power as an expression of the Christian gospel. Our intellectual ideas of God, Jesus, and the Church were derived from white European theologians and their textbooks. When we speak of Christianity in theological categories, using such terms as revelation, incarnation and reconciliation, we naturally turn to people like Barth, Tillich and Bultmann for guidance and direction. But these Europeans did not shape their ideas in the social context of white racism and thus could not help us out of our dilemma. But if we intended to fight on a theological and intellectual level as a way of empowering our historical and political struggle for justice, we had to create a new theological movement, one that was derived from and thus accountable to our people's fight for justice. To accept Black Power as Christian required that we thrust ourselves into our history in order to search for new ways to think and be black in this world. We felt the need to explain ourselves and to be understood from our own vantage point and not from the perspective and experiences of whites. When white liberals questioned this approach to theology, our response was very similar to the bluesman in Mississippi when told he was not

2 For an account of the rise of the concept of Black Power in the Civil Rights Movement, see Stokely Carmichael and Charles Hamilton, *Black Power: The Politics of Black Liberation* (New York: Random House). For Martin King's viewpoint, see his *Where Do We Go From Here: Chaos or Community?*

singing his song correctly: "Look-a-heah, man, dis yere *mah song,* en I'll sing it howsoevah I pleases."[3]

Thus we sang our Black Power songs, knowing that the white church establishment would not smile upon our endeavors to define Christianity independently of their own definitions of the gospel. For the power of definition is a prerogative that oppressors never want to give up. Furthermore, to *say* that love is compatible with Black Power is one thing, but to demonstrate this compatibility in theology and the praxis of life is another. If the reality of a thing was no more than its verbalization in a written document, the black church since 1966 would be a model of the creative integration of theology and life, faith and the struggle for justice. But we know that the meaning of reality is found *only* in its historical embodiment in people as structured in societal arrangements. Love's meaning is not found in sermons or theological textbooks but rather in the creation of social structures that are not dehumanizing and oppressive. This insight impressed itself on our religious consciousness, and we were deeply troubled by the inadequacy of our historical obedience when measured by our faith claims. From 1966 to the present, black theologians and preachers, both in the church and on the streets, have been searching for new ways to confess and to live our faith in God so that the black church would not make religion the opiate of our people.

The term "Black Theology" was created in this social and religious context. It was initially understood as the theological arm of Black Power, and it enabled us to express our theological imagination in the struggle of freedom independently of white theologians. It was the one term that white ministers and theologians did not like, because, like Black Power in politics, black theology located the theological starting point in the black experience and not the particularity of the western theological tradition. We did not feel ourselves accountable to Aquinas, Luther or Calvin but to David Walker, Daniel Payne and W. E. B. DuBois. The depth and passion in which we express our solidarity with the black experience over against the western tradition led some black scholars in religion to reject theology itself as alien to the black culture.[4] Others, while not rejecting theology entirely, contended that black theo-

3   Cited in Lawrence W. Levine, *Black Culture and Black Consciousness* (New York: Oxford University Press, 1977), p. 207.
4   This is especially true of Charles Long who has been a provocative discussant about black theology. Unfortunately, he has not written much about this viewpoint. The only article I know on this subject is his "Perspectives for a Study of Afro-American Religion in the United States," *History of Religions,* Vol. 11, no. 1, August 1971.

logians should turn primarily to African religion and philosophy in order to develop a black theology consistent with and accountable to our historical roots.[5] But all of us agreed that we were living at the beginning of a new historical moment, and this required the development of a *black* frame of reference that many called "black theology."

The consequence of our affirmation of a black theology led to the creation of black caucuses in white churches, a permanent ecumenical church body under the title of the National Conference of Black Churchmen, and the endorsement of James Forman's "Black Manifesto." In June 1969 at the Interdenominational Theological Center in Atlanta and under the aegis of NCBC's Theological Commission, a group of black theologians met to write a policy statement on black theology. This statement, influenced by my book, *Black Theology and Black Power*, which had appeared two months earlier, defined black theology as a "theology of black liberation."[6]

Black theology, then, was not created in a vacuum and neither was it simply the intellectual enterprise of black professional theologians. Like our sermons and songs, black theology was born in the context of the black community as black people were attempting to make sense out of their struggle for freedom. In one sense, black theology is as old as when the first African refused to accept slavery as consistent with religion and as recent as when a black person intuitively recognizes that the confession of the Christian faith receives its meaning only in relation to political justice. Although black theology may be considered to have formally appeared only when the first book was published on it in 1969, informally, the reality that made the book possible was already present in the black experience and was found in our songs, prayers, and sermons. In these outpourings are expressed the black visions of truth, pre-eminently the certainty that we were created not for slavery but for freedom. Without this dream of freedom, so vividly expressed in the life, teachings, and death of Jesus, Malcolm, and Martin, there would be no black theology, and we would have no reason to be assembled in this place. We have come here today to plan our future and to map our strategy because we have a dream that has not been realized.

To be sure, we have talked and written about this dream. Indeed, every Sunday morning black people gather in our churches, to find out where we are in relation to the actualization of our dream. The black

5 The representatives of this perspective include Gayraud S. Wilmore, *Black Religion and Black Radicalism* (New York: Doubleday, 1972), and my brother, Cecil W. Cone, *Identity Crisis in Black Theology* (Nashville: AMEC, 1976).
6 This statement was issued on June 13, 1969 and is also reprinted in Warner Traynham, op. cit.

church community really believes that where there is no vision the people perish. If people have no dreams they will accept the world as it is and will not seek to change it. To dream is to know what is ain't suppose to be. No one in our time expressed this eschatological note more clearly than Martin Luther King, Jr. In his "March on Washington" address in 1963 he said: "I have a dream that one day my four children will live in a nation where they will not be judged by the color of their skin but by the content of their character." And the night before his death in 1968, he reiterated his eschatological vision: "I may not get there with you, but I want you to know tonight that we as a people will get to the promised land."

What visions do we have for the people in 1977? Do we still believe with Martin King that "we as a people will get to the promised land"? If so, how will we get there? Will we get there simply by preaching sermons and singing songs about it? What is the black church doing in order to actualize the dreams that it talks about? These are hard questions, and they are not intended as a put-down of the black church. I was born in the black church in Bearden, Arkansas, and began my ministry in that church at the early age of sixteen. Everything I am as well as what I know that I ought to be was shaped in the context of the black church. Indeed, it is because I love the church that I am required, as one of its theologians and preachers, to ask: When does the black church's actions deny its faith? What are the activities in our churches that should not only be rejected as unchristian but also exposed as demonic? What are the evils in our church and community that we should commit ourselves to destroy? Bishops, pastors, and church executives do not like to disclose the wrong-doings of their respective denominations. They are like doctors, lawyers, and other professionals who seem bound to keep silent, because to speak the truth is to guarantee one's exclusion from the inner dynamics of power in the profession. But I contend that the *faith* of the black church lays a claim upon all church people that transcends the social mores of a given profession. Therefore, to cover-up and to minimize the sins of the church is to guarantee its destruction as a community of faith, committed to the liberation of the oppressed. If we want the black church to live beyond our brief histories and thus to serve as the "Old Ship of Zion" that will carry the people home to freedom, then we had better examine the direction in which the ship is going. Who is the Captain of the Ship, and what are his economic and political interests? This question should not only be applied to bishops, but to pastors and theologians, deacons and stewards. Unless we are willing to apply the most severe scientific analysis to our church communities in terms of economics and politics and are willing to confess and repent of our sins in the struggle for liberation, then the black church, as we talk about it, will remain a relic of history and nothing more. God will have to raise up new instruments of freedom so that his faithfulness to liberate the poor and weak can be realized in history. We must not forget that God's Spirit will use us as her instrument only insofar as we remain agents of liberation by using our resources for the empowerment of the poor and weak. But if we, like Israel in the Old Testament, forget about our Exodus experience and the political responsibility it lays upon us to be the historical embodiment of freedom, then, again like Israel, we will become objects of God's judgment. It is very easy for us to expose the demonic and oppressive character of the white church, and I have done my share of that. But such exposures of the sins of the white church, without applying the same criticism to ourselves, is hypocritical and serves as a camouflage of our own shortcomings and sins. Either we mean what we say about liberation or we do not. If we mean it, the time has come for an inventory in terms of the authenticity of our faith as defined by the historical commitment of the black denominational churches toward liberation.

I have lectured and preached about the black church's involvement in our liberation struggle all over North America. I have told the stories of Richard Allen and James Varick, Adam Clayton Powell and Martin Luther King. I have talked about the double-meaning in the Spirituals, the passion of the sermon and prayer, the ecstasy of the shout and conversion experience in terms of an eschatological happening in the lives of people, empowering them to fight for earthly freedom. Black theology, I have contended, is a theology of liberation, because it has emerged out of and is accountable to a black church that has always been involved in our historical fight for justice. When black preachers and laypeople hear this message, they respond enthusiastically and with a sense of pride that they belong to a radical and creative tradition. But when I speak to young blacks in colleges and universities, most are surprised that such a radical black church tradition really exists. After hearing about David Walker's "Appeal" in 1829, Henry H. Garnet's "Address to the Slaves" in 1843, and Henry M. Turner's affirmation that "God is a Negro" in 1898, these young blacks are shocked. Invariably they ask, "Whatever happened to the black churches of today?" "Why don't we have the same radical spirit in our preachers and churches?" Young blacks contend that the black churches of today, with very few exceptions, are not involved in liberation but primarily concerned about how much money they raise for a new church building or the preacher's anniversary.

This critique of the black church is not limited to the young college students. Many black people view the church as a hindrance to black liberation, because black preachers and church members appear to be more concerned about their own institutional survival than the freedom of poor people in their communities. "Historically," many radical blacks say, "the black church was involved in the struggle but today it is not." They often turn the question back upon me, saying: "All right, granted what you say about the historical black church, but *where* is an institutional black church denomination that still embodies the vision that brought it into existence? Are you saying that the present day AME Church or AME Zion Church has the same historical commitment for justice that it had under the leadership of Allen and Payne or Rush and Varick?" Sensing that they have a point difficult to refute, these radicals then say that it is not only impossible to find a black church denomination committed to black liberation but also difficult to find a local congregation that defines its ministry in terms of the needs of the oppressed and their liberation.

Whatever we might think about the unfairness of this severe indictment, we would be foolish to ignore it. For connected with this black critique is our international image. In the African context, not to mention Asia and Latin America, the black church experiences a similar credibility problem. There is little in our theological expressions and church practice that rejects American capitalism or recognizes its oppressive character in Third World countries. The time has come for us to move beyond institutional survival in a capitalistic and racist society and begin to take more seriously our dreams about a new heaven and a new earth. Does this dream include capitalism or is it a radically new way of life more consistent with African socialism as expressed in the *Arusha Declaration* in Tanzania?[7]

Black theologians and church people must now move beyond a mere reaction to white racism in America and begin to extend our vision of a new socially constructed humanity for the whole inhabited world. We must be concerned with the quality of human life not only in the ghettoes of American cities but also in Africa, Asia and Latin America. Since humanity is one, and cannot be isolated into racial and national groups, there will be no freedom for anyone until there is freedom for all. This means that we must enlarge our vision by connecting it with that of other oppressed peoples so that together all the victims of the world might take charge of their history for the creation of a new humanity. As Franz Fanon taught us: if we wish to live up to our peo-

7   See Julius Nyerere, *Ujamaa: Essays on Socialism* (Dar es Salaam: Oxford University Press, 1968).

ple's expectations, we must look beyond European and American capitalism. Indeed, "we must invent and we must make discoveries. . . . For Europe, for ourselves and for humanity, we must turn over a new leaf, we must work out new concepts, and try to set afoot a new [humanity]."[8]

New times require new concepts and methods. To dream is not enough. We must come down from the mountain top and experience the hurts and pain of the people in the valley. Our dreams need to be socially analyzed, for without scientific analysis they will vanish into the night. Furthermore, social analysis will test the nature of our commitment to the dreams we preach and sing about. This is one of the important principles we learned from Martin King and many black preachers who worked with him. Real substantial change in societal structures requires scientific analysis. King's commitment to social analysis not only characterized his involvement in the civil rights movement but also led him to take a radical stand against the war in Viet Nam. Through scientific analysis, King saw the connection between the oppression of blacks in the U.S.A. and America's involvement in Viet Nam. It is to his credit that he never allowed a pietistic faith in the other world to become a substitute for good judgment in this. He not only preached sermons about the promised land but concretized his vision with a political attempt to actualize his hope.

I realize, with Merleau-Ponty, that "one does not become a revolutionary through science but through indignation."[9] Every revolution needs its Rosa Parks. This point has often been overlooked by Marxists and other sociologists who seem to think that all answers are found in scientific analysis. Mao Tse-tung responded to such an attitude with this comment: "There are people who think that Marxism is a kind of magic truth with which one can cure any disease. We should tell them that dogmas are more useless than cow dung. Dung can be used as fertilizer."[10]

But these comments do not disprove the truth of the Marxists' social analysis which focuses on economics and class and is intended as empowerment for the oppressed to radically change human social arrangements. Such an analysis will help us to understand the relation between economics and oppression not only in North America but

8 Franz Fanon, *The Wretched of the Earth* (New York: Grove Press, 1966), p. 255.
9 Cited in Jose Miguez Bonino, *Christians and Marxists* (Grand Rapids, Michigan: Eerdmans, 1976), p. 76.
10 Cited in George Padmore, *Pan-Africanism or Communism* (New York: Anchor Books, 1972), p. 323.

throughout the world. Liberation is not a process limited to black-white relations in the United States; it is also something to be applied to the relations between rich and poor nations. If we are an African people, as some of the names of our churches suggest, in what way are we to understand the political meaning of that identity? In what way does the economic investment of our church resources reflect our commitment to Africa and other oppressed people in the world? For if an economic analysis of our material resources does not reveal our commitment to the process of liberation, how can we claim that the black church and its theology are concerned about the freedom of oppressed peoples? As an Argentine peasant poet said:

> They say that God cares for the poor
> Well this may be true or not
> But I know for a fact
> That he dines with the mine-owner.[11]

Because the Christian church has supported the capitalists, many Marxists contend that "all revolutions have clashed with Christianity because *historically* Christianity has been structurally counter-revolutionary."[12] We may rightly question this assertion and appeal to the revolutionary expressions of Christianity in the black religious tradition, from Nat Turner to Martin Luther King. My concern, however, is not to debate the fine points of what constitutes revolution, but to open up the reality of the black church experience and its revolutionary potential to a world context. This means that we can learn from people in Africa, Asia and Latin America, and they can learn from us. Learning from others involves listening to creative criticism; to exclude such criticism is to isolate ourselves from world politics, and this exclusion makes our faith nothing but a reflection of our economic interests. If Jesus Christ is more than a religious expression of our economic and sexist interests, then there is no reason to resist the truth of the Marxist and feminist analyses.

I contend that black theology is not afraid of truth from any quarter. We simply reject the attempt of others to tell us what truth is without our participation in its definition. That is why dogmatic Marxists seldom succeed in the black community, especially when the dogma is filtered through a brand of white racism not unlike that of the capital-

11 Cited in Bonino, *Christians and Marxists* (Grand Rapids, Michigan: Eerdmans, 1976), p. 71.
12 A quotation from Giulio Girardi, cited in Bonino, *Christians and Marxists* (Grand Rapids, Michigan: Eerdmans, 1976), p. 71.

ists. If our long history of struggle has taught us anything, it is that if we are to be free, we black people will have to do it. Freedom is not a gift but is a risk that must be taken. No one can tell us what liberation is and how we ought to struggle for it, as if liberation can be found in words. Liberation is a process to be located and understood only in an oppressed community struggling for freedom. If there are people in and outside our community who want to talk to us about this liberation process in global terms and from Marxist and other perspectives, we should be ready to talk. But *only* if they are prepared to listen to us and we to them will genuine dialogue take place. For I will not listen to anybody who refuses to take racism seriously, especially when they themselves have not been victims of it. And they should listen to us *only* if we are prepared to listen to them in terms of the particularity of oppression in their historical context.

Therefore, I reject dogmatic Marxism that reduces every contradiction to class analysis and thus ignores racism as a legitimate point of departure in the process of liberation. There are racist Marxists as there are racist capitalists, and we must struggle against both. But we must be careful not to reject the Marxist's social analysis simply because we do not like the vessels that the message comes in. If we do that, then it is hard to explain how we can remain Christians in view of the white vessels in which the gospel was first introduced to black people.

The world is small. Both politically and economically, our freedom is connected with the struggles of oppressed peoples throughout the world. This is the truth of Pan-Africanism as represented in the life and thought of W. E. B. DuBois, George Padmore, and C. L. R. James. Liberation knows no color bar; the very nature of the gospel is universalism, i.e., a liberation that embraces the whole of humanity.

The need for a global perspective, which takes seriously the struggles of oppressed peoples in other parts of the world, has already been recognized in black theology, and small beginnings have been made with conferences on African and black theologies in Tanzania, New York, and Ghana. Another example of the recognition of this need is reflected in the dialogue between black theology in South Africa and North America. From the very beginning black theology has been influenced by a world perspective as defined by Henry M. Turner, Marcus Garvey, and the Pan-Africanism inaugurated in the life and work of W. E. B. DuBois. The importance of this Pan-African perspective in black religion and theology has been cogently defended in Gayraud Wilmore's *Black Religion and Black Radicalism*. Our active involvement in the "Theology in the Americas," under whose aegis this conference is held, is an attempt to enlarge our perspective in relation to Africa, Asia, and Latin America as well as to express our solidarity with other oppressed minorities in the U.S.

This global perspective in black theology enlarges our vision regarding the process of liberation. What does black theology have to say about the fact that two-thirds of humanity is poor and that this poverty arises from the exploitation of the poor nations by rich nations? The people of the U.S.A. compose 6% of the world's population, but we consume 40% of the world resources. What, then, is the implication of the black demand for justice in the U.S. when related to justice for all the world's victims? Of the dependent status we experience in relation to white people, and the experience of Third World countries in relation to the U.S.? Thus, in our attempt to liberate ourselves from white America in the U.S., it is important to be sensitive to the complexity of the world situation and the oppressive role of the U.S. in it. African, Latin American, and Asian theologians, sociologists and political scientists can aid us in the analysis of this complexity. In this analysis, our starting point in terms of racism is not negated but enhanced when connected with imperialism and sexism.

We must create a global vision of human liberation and include in it the distinctive contribution of the black experience. We have been struggling for nearly 400 years! What has that experience taught us that would be useful in the creation of a new historical future for all oppressed peoples? And what can others teach us from their historical experience in the struggle for justice? This is the issue that black theology needs to address. "Theology in the Americas" provides a framework in which to address it. I hope that we will not back off from this important task but face it with courage, knowing that the future of humanity is in the hands of oppressed peoples, because God has said: "Those that hope in me shall not be put to shame" (Is. 49:23).

SUPPLEMENTARY READINGS

Cone, Cecil Wayne. *The Identity Crisis in Black Theology*. Nashville: A.M.E. Church, 1975.

Jones, Major J. *Christian Ethics for Black Theology*. Nashville: Abingdon Press, 1974.

Roberts, J. Deotis. *Liberation and Reconciliation: A Black Theology*. Philadelphia: Westminster Press, 1971.

Wilmore, Gayraud S. *Black Religion and Black Radicalism*. Rev. ed. Maryknoll, N.Y.: Orbis Books, 1983. Chap. 8.

Wilmore, Gayraud S., and James H. Cone, eds. *Black Theology: A Documentary History, 1966–1979*. Maryknoll, N.Y.: Orbis Books, 1979.

51

LAWRENCE N. JONES

"The Black Churches: A New Agenda"

In this contribution to "The Churches Where from Here?" series for The Christian Century, Lawrence N. Jones *(b. 1921) discusses a new agenda for the black churches for the 1980s and beyond. An ordained minister of the United Church of Christ, Jones served as dean of the chapel at Fisk University. In 1970 he became the first holder of the chair in Afro-American church history at Union Theological Seminary, New York City. Currently he is dean of Howard University's school of religion.*

As Bishop John Hurst Adams of the African Methodist Episcopal Church observed recently, black churches are operating essentially on the agenda given to them by their founders. The first agenda of early black American congregations and then of emergent denominations included (1) the proclamation of the gospel, (2) benevolences, (3) education and, by the mid-19th century, (4) foreign missions. (Of course, in the antebellum period a concern for the eradication of slavery was also central.) That these items continue to dominate the churches' mission priorities and stewardship planning may be attributed in part to the continuing marginality and relative powerlessness of blacks in American society. It is due also in part to the fact that religious institutions in black communities have not been sufficiently cognizant of the radical implications which the changing political, economic and social realities have for their life. Bishop Adams's antidote for this institutional inertia is "zero-based" mission planning—an imaginative and valid suggestion.

I

Some early black congregations began as benevolent societies, and all of them were concerned for the welfare of the sick, the widowed and the orphaned. Most congregations continue to maintain benevolent funds, but they are no longer accorded high priority. It is obvious in the light of

Source: *The Christian Century* 96, no. 14 (April 18, 1979): 434–38.

massive need that the churches' impact in this area can be only palliative. The social welfare programs sponsored by the government and by community and private agencies are far better resourced and programmatically more comprehensive than those that individual churches can sustain. The churches' task in the area of benevolence has become that of ensuring that persons gain access to the benefits for which they are eligible.

The churches' historic concern for education initially focused on efforts to compensate for the exclusion of blacks from access to elementary education. After emancipation, the most pressing concern became that of establishing and supporting secondary schools and colleges. By 1900 the churches had compiled an impressive record: black Baptist associations were supporting some 80 elementary schools and 18 academies and colleges; the African Methodist Episcopal churches were underwriting 32 secondary and collegiate institutions; and the smaller AME Zion denomination was supporting eight. The denomination now named the Christian Methodist Episcopal Church, only 30 years old in 1900, had established five schools. Blacks now have broad access to public secondary and higher education, and the need for church-related institutions to fill an educational vacuum has lessened considerably. The question as to whether there is a qualitative difference in the education being offered in church-sponsored colleges as over against state-supported institutions is a matter that has to be debated in the zero-based mission planning that Bishop Adams suggests.

Blacks have traditionally directed their modest foreign mission efforts to the Caribbean islands and to Africa. The institutional forms of these missions have not differed significantly from those of the majority churches; they have focused on church development, health-care institutions and education. (It may be observed that black churches have established hospitals in Africa but none in America.) The need for such missionary services is diminishing and will doubtless decline more rapidly as independent African and Caribbean nations preempt these areas of responsibility for the state.

If the traditional concerns for education, benevolences and foreign missions need to be carefully scrutinized and their priority status evaluated, the first priority in the life of the churches does not require such rethinking. The *raison d'être* of black churches has not differed from that of churches in any age. They have been the bearers of the good news that God cares about, affirms, forgives and redeems human beings to whom he has given life, and that he acts in their history. This message of divine concern has enabled black believers to survive humanely in inhumane circumstances. The communities of faith have been the social matrixes within which individual significance and worth have been given concrete embodiment and a sense of belonging has been conferred. The form in which this message is conveyed may change, but its essential content will remain the same.

Though not a part of the formal agenda of the churches, church buildings have been crucial community assets. From the earliest times they were the only assembly halls to which the black community had access. They housed schools, dramatic productions, cultural events, social welfare programs, rallies and benefits of all sorts, and civil and human rights activities. The requirements in these areas are less critical today. But if the need for meeting space has declined, the claims placed on church members by movements for social, political and economic justice have not diminished. W. E. B. DuBois once remarked that the NAACP could not have survived without the support of black churches and their members. This is still the case. Though many social organizations and unions give support to such movements, church members form an indispensable segment of their constituencies, as the recent financial crisis involving the NAACP in Mississippi made clear. The churches continue to have access to the largest audience that can be gathered in black communities.

II

It is important to perceive clearly that there is no "black church" in the conventional understanding of that term. There are denominations, composed of congregations of black persons and under their control, and there are countless free-standing congregations, but there is no one entity that can be called the black church. There are also numerous black congregations in predominantly white denominations; though these are properly covered by the rubric "black churches," it is not with such congregations that this article is concerned.

Several caveats should be entered. It is virtually impossible to make generalizations to which significant exceptions cannot be cited. Yet there is a sense in which all black congregations and denominations respond to identical external circumstances and share common internal strengths, pressures and tensions.

Unlike their white counterparts, black churches have not developed effective centralized bureaucracies. This lack may be counted as an advantage by some, but historically it has had a negative effect. For example, it is impossible to obtain accurate statistical data on such matters as membership, budgets, numbers of pastors, value of church assets, and the level of training achieved by the clergy. Not only do black churches lack fully developed administrative structures; mission structures within a given denomination often do not engage in joint strategy and program planning designed to ensure maximum effective use of all available resources. Church unity is expressed primarily in annual or quadrennial meetings rather than in integrated mission planning and cooperation.

Failure to develop strong centralized structures can be attributed to polity (particularly among the Baptists), accidents of history, patterns of church growth, migration to the cities by rural blacks and, most critically, lack of money. Religious bodies among Afro-Americans have not devised the means for generating financial surpluses sufficient to enable them to maintain national headquarters staffs. As a consequence, the mission activity of the churches is, with limited exceptions, carried out by regional or local judicatories. Denominational loyalty has rarely been fervent among black Christians. Except among black Methodists in earlier times, churches owe their origins not to the initiative of home missions boards but to concerned laypersons or clergy who undertook "to raise the flag of Zion." In recent years the national bodies of predominantly white denominations have been experiencing diminishing support from congregations and regional judicatories. Among blacks, local support for denominational programs has rarely been directed to concerns other than foreign missions, theological education, and a college here and there. Local or regional proprietorship and support of church institutions has been the rule.

In addition to inhibiting the growth of national church structures, the generalized economic deprivation of blacks in America has contributed to the continued fragmentation of the Afro-American religious community. It has meant that irrespective of polity, each congregation, with few exceptions, is a "tub resting on its own bottom." No black denomination has significant building or salary-support funds. Similarly, there are no means other than denominational journals, most of which have limited distribution, through which a consensus may be developed with respect to important moral, religious, social, political and economic questions.

The absence of a "sense of the church" deprives many congregations and their leaders of the information and guidance that are foundational to effective Christian witness. This need is critical in a religious community where an estimated 70 per cent of the clergy lack formal theological education. Black church people receive limited guidance from their national judicatories on such issues as abortion, homosexuality, capital punishment, women's rights and the like. The AME Church has recently drafted "working papers" on some of these subjects. The absence of consensus on important public issues means that the power of the churches to influence public policy tends to be proportional to the charisma and prestige of individual church leaders.

The underdevelopment of church structures and limited financial resources have also inhibited the growth of clergy retirement funds. Several denominations have made modest beginnings with pension programs, but most black pastors cannot afford to retire. Consequently, pastorates tend to be marked by long tenure, and access is restricted for younger men and women. The difficulty in finding good placements has diminished the attractiveness of the ministry as a vocation for many promising young persons.

III

Counterbalancing these observations about the weaknesses of the churches corporately is the fact that many local congregations are vibrantly involved in mission in their communities and are growing in membership as a result. Church-sponsored housing projects, some of them congregationally funded, are commonplace in major urban centers. Church buildings house Head Start schools, day-care facilities, senior citizens' centers, tutorial programs, "Meals on Wheels," and similar publicly funded projects. Funds are raised to amortize building mortgages—a common obligation of most black churches. Mission funds are sent to national headquarters or conventions, and church member assessments are paid. Members continue to participate in the quest for social justice through community organizations and form these groups' stable center.

The net growth of black churches has not exceeded the rate of growth in the general population. In general, long-established congregations appear to hold their own or to slip a little in terms of total membership, while Pentecostal and charismatic churches seem to have an increasing appeal, particularly for youth. Young people appear to be attracted to churches in which worship is free-form and spontaneous, and in which gospel music has supplanted the hymns of Watts and Wesley.

Like their white counterparts, black churches are commuter churches. They tend to be homogeneous with respect to social class— except for Pentecostal or charismatic churches, which are no longer the exclusive havens of the disinherited.

As has been suggested above, no one knows the exact membership of the black churches. It is estimated that the total numbers of black Baptists are in excess of 8 million, with the National Baptist Convention, Inc., having approximately 6.3 million members; the Progressive

National Baptist Convention, 750,000; and the National Baptist Convention, Unincorporated, 1 million. The total membership of black Methodist bodies is around 2.8 million. The largest Pentecostal body, the Church of God in Christ, estimates its total membership at 3 million, and there are uncounted numbers of persons affiliated with less well-known church groupings and thousands of free-standing congregations. According to the conventional wisdom, approximately 61 per cent of blacks are members of Christian churches, Catholic and Protestant. By this standard, a total of 13.4 million Afro-Americans are carried on church rosters, though the active membership must be well below this figure. But if these figures are reasonably accurate, they are an index to the potential of the churches to influence public policy if their strengths can be marshaled.

IV

As we look toward the future, the agenda for black churches is a complex one. The existence of the churches is not in jeopardy; they are and will continue to be for large numbers of persons the only accessible institutions that will meet their need to be affirmed in their identity and sense of belonging in both a human and a divine dimension. What is in jeopardy is the capacity of the churches to attract urban dwellers in large numbers while church programs are geared to a 19th century rural ethos.

The most significant phenomenon to impact black churches in this century has been migration to the cities. Urban churches grew and prospered as a result of that population movement, but the rural ethos continued to be reflected in worship, organization and mission priorities. There are now persons in the pews who were born in the city, who are secular in their outlook, who are keenly aware of the ways in which their lives are shaped by structures which they do not control, and who are concerned that their religious institutions should be active agents of social change. This new constituency requires programs of Christian nurture that address the consciousness, realities and urgencies of contemporary urban life. In this connection the church must become bilingual: it must understand the language of the world and translate the gospel into the idioms and symbols of that language. Christian nurture must also be bifocal. It must keep its eye on heaven, but it must not fail to see the world at hand and seek to enable persons to wrest meaning and significance from their lives in it.

Perhaps the central agenda of the black churches in the years ahead is accurately to assess their corporate potential for impacting the quality of life available to their constituencies. This task will require, as a matter of first priority, careful determination of mission priorities and the mobilization of resources for their implementation. These activities must be carried out in recognition of the fact that many of the problems affecting the lives of individuals in negative ways are systemic, and can be dealt with only at that level. This effort will inevitably involve individual congregations in difficult decisions concerning the allocation of resources formerly committed to the traditional mission agenda. Local autonomy will have to yield to functional ecumenism for the sake of faithfulness in pursuing God's will and purpose that justice and peace shall prevail among human beings.

Historically, black churches have been clergy-dominated. This situation must change if religious institutions are to continue to attract gifted persons to their company. It is imperative that the talents of church members be increasingly utilized on behalf of the mission of the church. An important byproduct of the involvement of laity in mission is that better-trained lay and clergy leadership will be required. Warm evangelicalism will not compensate for naïve understanding of the powers and principalities of the world.

It has frequently been observed that the quality of life in inner-city communities is deteriorating at alarming rates, and that part of this deterioration is attributable to the erosion of moral and humane values. Churches must not ignore these phenomena. They must be concerned that large numbers of young people never come within the sphere of their teaching or influence. While it is widely agreed that the causes for the morbidity of communities in urban centers are traceable to diverse factors, churches cannot be quiescent in the face of them. Family structures must be reinforced, and churches must be active agents and participants in organizations seeking to help communities improve themselves.

Missionary conventions and church boards face an important period of self-examination. They must ask themselves what the increasing sense of self-identity in the Third World has to say to missionary structures. What does the indigenization of churches mean for black missionaries in black countries? Black church missions early reflected the "redemption of Africa" theme. What does that term connote at a time when cultural Christianity is undergoing rigorous scrutiny? What does it mean to affirm indigenous religion while proclaiming the gospel of Jesus Christ? In the light of Third World realities, have the terms "missions" and "missionary" become anachronistic?

Another entry that must be prominent on the agenda of black churches is the nature of worship. Is the "old-time religion" good enough for contemporary urbanites? How can churches respond to the desire of individuals for spontaneity in worship so that form is not mistaken for substance? Can churches devise means for accommodating a genuine desire to abandon outmoded forms without derogating from the claims of the gospel and the truth that worship is the service of God? The ability to sing a gospel song with feeling is not to be equated with transformation of one's life nor with continued commitment to the One who is Lord.

Black churches must begin to examine the economic realities of their existence, not in the light of their individual or denominational budgets alone, but in view of their tremendous possibilities to effect social change by utilizing the considerable resources that pass through their hands. In a city with 300 churches, it is fair to assume conservatively that the average Sunday offering would amount to $300 per church or nearly $100,000 for all churches. If this sum were put in a single bank, considerable leverage would be generated to influence that bank's loan policy in regard to urban neighborhoods. Churches need to consider what cooperative buying of goods and services might mean in savings, influence on the employment practices of vendors, and overall economic impact.

It will be noted that an agenda has been suggested for black churches irrespective of their denominational affiliation. I offer no apology for this lack of differentiation since the situation of one black church is, in large measure, the situation of all black churches. All are addressing themselves to the needs of an oppressed people. One might even suggest that the agenda is appropriate for all churches that wish to take seriously the ministry of Christ in the world.

V

While the challenges facing black churches are difficult ones, there are important harbingers that bode well for the future. Modestly increasing numbers of bright young people from all denominations are seeking theological training. They are exerting increasing pressure on educational institutions to equip them to be resources to the communities in which they will serve, as well as competent leaders of religious institutions. There are also evidences that the denominational leadership of the church is becoming more aware of the changed context within which mission must be implemented. Another important sign is that church membership has been holding steady and that middle-class defections have not been as numerous as some had predicted.

At the local level laypersons are increasingly asserting their right to participate in the governance of the churches. Clergy serving churches with congregational polity are finding themselves to be governed by constitutions and by-laws in direct contrast to the monarchical clergy styles of a passing generation. Laypeople are also exerting pressure on their churches to demonstrate an authentic sense of social responsibility.

Another favorable index is the broadening effort to provide basic training for church leaders who are not formally qualified to pursue graduate theological education. This theological training which is both theoretical and practical will have a significant impact on the churches and their ministries.

But the most significant development in recent years has been an increasing awareness among blacks not affiliated with the churches that religious institutions are as critical to the survival of Afro-Americans in the present as they have been in the past. Thus there is pressure from all quarters for the churches to actualize their potential as agents of social change without derogation of their traditional role as communities of faith. Black churches need not abandon their historic mission agendas but rather should consider them in the light of new realities in the world where [their] mission must be implemented.

SUPPLEMENTARY READINGS

Childs, John Brown. *The Political Black Minister: A Study in Afro-American Politics and Religion.* Boston: G. K. Hall, 1980.

Oliver, John A. *Eldridge Cleaver: Reborn.* Plainfield, N.J.: Logos International, 1977.

Roberts, J. Deotis. *Roots of a Black Future: Family and Church.* Philadelphia: Westminster Press, 1980.

West, Cornell. *Prophesy Deliverance! An Afro-American Revolutionary Christianity.* Philadelphia: Westminster Press, 1982.

Wilmore, Gayraud S. "The New Need for Intergroup Coalition." *The Christian Century* 99, no. 5 (February 17, 1982): 170–73.

Index

Permission to reprint selections from the following sources is gratefully acknowledged:

3 *Francis Le Jau:* From *The Carolina Chronicle of Dr. Francis Le Jau, 1706–1717*, ed. Frank W. Klingberg (Berkeley: University of California Press, 1956), pp. 60–61, 69–70, 76–77, 124–25, 128–30, and 136–37.

8 *Sister Kelly:* From *Unwritten History of Slavery: Autobiographical Accounts of Negro Ex-slaves* (Nashville: Fisk University, 1945; reprinted, Washington, D.C.: Microcard Editions, 1968), pp. 81–84.

14 *Richard Allen:* From *The Life Experience and Gospel Labors of the Rt. Rev. Richard Allen*, introd. George A. Singleton (Nashville, Tenn.: Abingdon Press, 1960), pp. 15–36.

29 *Henry McNeal Turner:* From *Respect Black: The Writings and Speeches of Henry McNeal Turner*, comp. and ed. Edwin S. Redkey (New York: Arno Press and *The New York Times*, 1971), pp. 52–57.

32 *Elsie W. Mason:* From *The Man, Charles Harrison Mason (1866–1961)* (Memphis, Tenn.: Church of God in Christ, 1979), pp. 10–20.

33 *Reverdy C. Ransom:* From *The Spirit of Freedom and Justice* (Nashville, Tenn.: A.M.E. Sunday School Union, 1926), pp. 128–37.

34 *W. E. B. Du Bois:* From *The Souls of Black Folk*, ed. Herbert Aptheker (Milwood, N.Y.: Kraus-Thomson Organization Ltd., 1973), pp. 189–206.

35 *Rosa Young:* From *Light in the Dark Belt* (St. Louis: Concordia Publishing House, 1951), pp. 46–58.

36 *Carter G. Woodson:* From *The Rural Negro* (Washington, D.C.: The Association for the Study of Negro Life and History, Inc., 1930), pp. 154–65.

37 *Benjamin E. Mays and Joseph W. Nicholson:* From *The Negro's Church* (New York: Institute of Social and Religious Research, 1933), pp. 278–92.

38 *St. Clair Drake and Horace R. Cayton:* From *Black Metropolis*, pp. 412–29. Copyright 1945 by St. Clair Drake and Horace R. Cayton; renewed 1973 by St. Clair Drake and Susan C. Woodson. Reprinted by permission of Harcourt Brace Jovanovich, Inc.

39 *E. Franklin Frazier:* From *The Negro Church in America*, by E. Franklin Frazier (New York: Schocken Books, 1964), pp. 68–81. Copyright © 1964 by Schocken Books, Inc. Reprinted by permission of Schocken Books, Inc.

40 *Marcus Garvey:* From *Philosophy and Opinions of Marcus Garvey*, ed. Amy Jacques-Garvey (New York: Atheneum, 1969), vol. 2, pp. 124–34. Copyright 1923, 1925 by Amy Jacques-Garvey.

41 *Miles Mark Fischer:* "Organized Religion and the Cults," from *The Crisis* 44, no. 1 (January 1937): 8–10 and 29–30. Reprinted with permission of the Crisis Publishing Company.

42 *Rabbi Matthew:* From Howard Brotz, *The Black Jews of Harlem* (New York: Schocken Books, 1970), pp. 19–22, 29–31.

43 *Father Divine:* From "As a Man Thinketh in His Heart So Is He and as You Visualize and Act from That Angle So Will It Be Just as You Think Vividly Enough," *The New Day* (25 June 1936): 3–5; "We Shall Have a Righteous Government," *The New Day* (9 July 1936): 16.

44 *Wallace D. Muhammad:* From *Bilalian* News 1, no. 19 (19 March 1976): 23–26.

45 *Joseph H. Jackson:* From *A Story of Christian Activism* (Nashville, Tenn.: Townsend Press, 1980), pp. 270–76.

46 *Martin Luther King, Jr.:* "Letter from Birmingham Jail, April 16, 1963," from *Why We Can't Wait*, by Martin Luther King, Jr. (New York: Harper & Row, 1963), pp. 77–100. Copyright © 1963, 1964 by Martin Luther King, Jr. Reprinted by permission of Joan Daves and Harper & Row, Publishers, Inc.

47 *Mahalia Jackson:* Excerpted from *Movin' On Up*, by Mahalia Jackson with Evan McLeod Wylie (New York: Hawthorn Books, 1966), pp. 29–33, 56–59, 62–66, 180–85, and 196–99. Copyright © 1966 by Mahalia Jackson and Evan McLeod Wylie.

48 *Howard Thurman:* From *The Luminous Darkness: A Personal Interpretation of the Anatomy of Segregation and the Ground of Hope*, by Howard Thurman (New York: Harper & Row, 1965), pp. 12–14, 21–24, 110–13. Copyright © 1965 by Howard Thurman. Reprinted by permission of Harper & Row, Publishers, Inc.

49 *National Conference of Black Churchmen:* "Black Power" and "Black Theology," from *Black Theology: A Documentary History, 1966–1979*, ed. Gayraud S. Wilmore and James H. Cone (Maryknoll, N.Y.: Orbis Books, 1979), pp. 23–30 and 100–102.

50 *James H. Cone:* "Black Theology and the Black Church: Where Do We Go from Here?" from *Cross Currents* 27, no. 2 (Summer 1977): 147–56.

51 *Lawrence N. Jones:* "The Black Churches: A New Agenda?" from *The Christian Century* 96, no. 14 (18 April 1979): 434–38. Copyright 1979 Christian Century Foundation. Reprinted by permission from the April 18, 1979 issue of *The Christian Century*.